NORTH SEA

POLAND

OF

GERMANY

Ha...

Bremen

Weser

Hanover

Osnabruck

Salzgitter

Oder

Neisse

IJmuiden

Amsterdam

NETHERLANDS

Rotterdam

Ems

Dortmund

Duisburg

Siegen

WEST

CZECHO-
SLOVAKIA

...nkirk

Antwerp

...sbergues

Brussels

Maastricht

Aachen

Liège

BELGIUM

Namur

Andernach

Koblenz

Frankfurt

GERMANY

Sulzbach-
Rosenberg

Valenciennes

Charleroi

Rhine

LUXEMBOURG

Luxembourg

Mannheim

Longwy

Thionville

SAAR

Oise

Paris

Moselle

Nancy

Strasbourg

Munich

Seine

FRANCE

Basel

AUSTRIA

SWITZERLAND

Gueugnon

Commentry

Aosta

Milan

Verona

Venice

St.-Etienne

Allevard

Turin

Rhône

Genoa

ITALY

Marseilles

MEDITERRANEAN SEA

Piombino

Elba

Corsica

Rome

EUROPE'S COAL AND STEEL COMMUNITY

EUROPE'S COAL AND STEEL COMMUNITY

AN EXPERIMENT IN ECONOMIC UNION

BY LOUIS LISTER

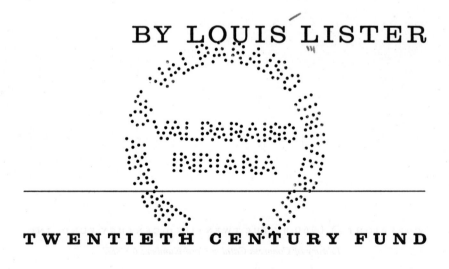

TWENTIETH CENTURY FUND

NEW YORK • 1960

FOREWORD

The shaping of new institutions cutting across national boundaries has been one of the major challenges to the post-war generation; it will undoubtedly continue to be so through the remaining decades of the twentieth century. The emergence of a new world order, following the breakdown of the Western imperialisms and the rise of hitherto underdeveloped areas, is not likely to take place within time-worn channels and old forms. Nationalism remains powerful as an aspiration; but the nation-state as an institution obviously fails to meet many of the needs of the modern world.

Wide diversity marks the ways by which the forces of internationalism, regionalism and economic integration are finding expression. It is well that there should be experimentation at different levels and in different parts of the world. In the European experience nothing is more striking than the functional organizations which have grown up in the past decade. These old nations may be said to have sliced off a part of themselves—at least in the areas of coal and steel and of atomic power—giving portions of their life to a regional authority while maintaining intact the traditional forms of national sovereignty. It is an inventive approach, and its results can be watched with profit.

The most firmly established of these functional institutions, the European Coal and Steel Community, forms the substance of this study. Not quite a decade old, the Community has amassed a considerable body of experience. In 1955 Mr. Lister, an economist with wide experience as a representative of the United States government in international organizations, including the European Coal and Steel Community, undertook at the Fund's request a careful economic survey of the Community's background, methods and results. Whatever may be done by way of institution-building in the next decades must take account of the ECSC; Mr. Lister's study will surely provide one of the significant documents in the appraisal.

The Fund is grateful to Mr. Lister for carrying through so judicious an analysis in an area vital with implications for the future.

AUGUST HECKSCHER
Director, The Twentieth Century Fund

41 East 70th Street, New York
January 1960

PREFACE

This study deals from the economic standpoint with the European Coal and Steel Community as a part of the movement for European integration. For over a decade the idea of European federation has carried the hope for a better future in Western Europe; it is perhaps the only large idea to have stirred Western Europe in the postwar era. Encompassing in its broadest sense political and military as well as economic institutions, the idea counts its adherents in nearly every country in Western Europe and has found staunch support in the United States as well.

Whatever their views on ultimate political and military unification, the proponents of European federation have concentrated on economic unification since the French Assembly rejected the idea of military unification in 1954. The European Coal and Steel Community, established in 1952, the European Economic Community and the European Atomic Energy Community, organized in 1958, are the expression of the economic aspect of the federal movement. Though the European Coal and Steel Community constitutes only a part of European economic integration, a study treating of the first of the experiments in this field carries general significance for the European federation movement as a whole. Including thus far Belgium, France, Italy, Germany, Luxembourg and the Netherlands, the Communities represent an important part of Western Europe but exclude the United Kingdom, Switzerland, Austria, Spain, Portugal and Scandinavia. This study nevertheless draws the British and American coal and steel industries into the discussion at many points, for they are within the same web of problems.

Terminating early in 1959, this study covers the essential economic developments of the first six years of the Community's life, a period sufficient to uncover the major trends and problems. It does not attempt to give a comprehensive, much less a day-to-day, account of all the events or aspects of the Community, but focuses on the major points of significance—how efficiency can be increased through greater international specialization, how new institutions can bend, or be bent by, well-established ways of conduct—by relating developments to the specific economic goals of the Community and to the broader aspects of the economic life of the member States.

Preface

A critical analysis in depth revealing so many complex problems may appear to take the bloom off the simple and inspired ideal of European federation, but this study is presented with the hope that an understanding of the difficulties will strengthen sympathy for the ideal and will help promote more effective methods for its realization.

My acknowledgments go first of all to the Trustees of the Twentieth Century Fund for their interest and generous support and to its Director, Mr. August Heckscher, as well as to Mr. J. Frederic Dewhurst, former Director, for their continuous encouragement. The staff members of the Fund extended their help unfailingly and graciously. Editing a manuscript can be a chore but turned out to be a pleasure, thanks to Mrs. Frances Klafter of the Fund, who took the manuscript under her wing and improved it vastly. I am equally grateful to Mrs. Elizabeth Blackert, in charge of editorial planning at the Fund, and to Mrs. Ruth Rocker for the skill and competence with which they saw the manuscript through to publication.

I thank Mr. John Hackett for preparing some of the data for Chapters 3 and 4, as well as for reading the manuscript and offering many valuable suggestions. I also thank the several secretaries who assisted me at different times, in particular Mrs. Gloria King, and Mr. F. Frederiksen for statistical assistance.

I was fortunate to have advice and comment from M. Roger Hutter, the distinguished authority on European transport problems, who read Chapter 12. M. Julien Laveugle as well as Mr. Philip Mullenbach kindly read and criticized Chapters 9 and 10. Mr. George Simpson was of invaluable assistance in criticizing an early version of the first few chapters from the point of view of presentation. I wish also to thank Messrs. Konrad Ebert and William N. Parker.

Mr. William Diebold, who reviewed the whole manuscript in its penultimate stage, offered a number of suggestions that led to its improvement.

Mr. Samuel Lipkowitz read the manuscript in galley proofs; I am deeply indebted to him for several critical suggestions and for a number of improvements in diction. Mr. Aaron Noland, to whom I am much indebted, gave me the benefit of his comments on the manuscript in galley proofs.

The various organs of the European Coal and Steel Community, in particular the High Authority, kindly supplied all the published information I requested. Mr. Derek Prag of the Information Division was particularly helpful. Though I was once a member of the United States Delegation to the European Coal and Steel Community at Luxembourg, the data used in this study are drawn entirely from published information. The study was carried out and written in Europe, with headquarters in Paris.

Preface

I thank Jeanne, my wife, for coming to my rescue at several critical points, but most of all for enduring with sympathy the unremittent claim the study made upon my time.

LOUIS LISTER

Appendix A contains a list of abbreviations for some of the publications by the Community as well as by the other organizations and individuals that are cited in this study. It also contains some general notes to the study.

CONTENTS

APPENDICES

TABLES

Tables

Tables

Tables

APPENDIX TABLES

Appendix Tables

FIGURES

EUROPE'S COAL AND STEEL COMMUNITY

CHAPTER 1

BACKGROUND AND

OBJECTIVES OF THE

COMMUNITY

The European Coal and Steel Community (ECSC), known in French as the Communauté Européenne du Charbon et de l'Acier (CECA), was established in 1952 with headquarters in Luxembourg. It comprises the European territory of six States: Belgium, France, Germany,[1] Italy, Luxembourg and the Netherlands; these are frequently called the Six or Little Europe. In January 1957 the Saar, theretofore in the French customs area, became part of Germany.

In May 1950 Robert Schuman, French Foreign Minister, proposed the plan that colloquially bears his name. The plan presaged the beginning of European unification by federative measures; it consequently provided a psychological shock and aroused more political than economic interest. The treaty for the ECSC was drafted and signed within a year of Schuman's proposal. Another year was required for parliamentary ratification.

All customs barriers against the trade of coal and steel between the six States were abolished; the ECSC is consequently a free trade area, among other things. Its aim is to promote greater average productivity or efficiency in the coal and steel industries—or to reduce costs—by means of greater regional specialization in the most advantageous producing districts. The treaty expresses this goal by referring to the "most rational distribution of production at the highest possible level of productivity" (Article 2).

Unions that bring together highly developed industrial countries producing the same products in previously protected national markets are rare in history. All the member countries produce steel and all but two produce substantial

---

[1] References to Germany after the second world war are to West Germany throughout this study, unless otherwise indicated.

quantities of coal—and these products enjoyed substantial preference in their respective national markets.

Though a free trade area has an economic basis, it inevitably has a political background. Without a political ideal, the members of the ECSC would not have incurred the risks and pains involved in the potential economic transformations. Some leaders in all the six countries that sponsored the ECSC believe the countries share a common destiny which can best be controlled to their greatest advantage only through common action. They believe this road also holds the promise of cooperation between France and Germany. Considering intergovernmental cooperation to be insufficient, they have, not without misgivings, chosen the way that might lead to ultimate federation, though all the six countries are not fully committed to this choice. The ECSC is thus the expression of one proposal among others directed toward European unification. Some of these proposals were abortive (the proposals for a European Defense Community and for a European Political Community) but others were successful (the European Economic Community and the European Atomic Energy Community which began to operate in 1958). It should be noted that these developments rest on the thesis that economic unification can precede political federation and that various economic sectors can be organized under individual institutions and treaties.

HISTORICAL BACKGROUND

Interwar Period

The unification of Europe, based on the idea of common traditions and beliefs, has had a strong appeal through the ages. Some States, hoping to exercise hegemony, have tried to promote unity by means of war. Culturally, the idea of European unification stems from cosmopolitan sentiment antedating the age of nationalism; politically, it represents a belief that the national State in Europe is no longer equal to the problems of the day.[2]

While proposed forms of European unification have changed with circumstances and varied with the interests involved, recent proposals for unification have tried to arrest the economic decline of Europe relative to the rest of the world. European proposals for an economic union as early as the mid-1800s were directed against American competition, and during the 1920s were inspired by the desire to strengthen Europe against American and Soviet growth.[3]

[2] This notion was well expressed by José Ortega y Gasset, *Revolt of the Masses*, Allen and Unwin, London, 1932, p. 162.

[3] Jacob Viner, *The Customs Union Issue*, Carnegie Endowment for International Peace, New York, 1952, pp. 57–58.

The anti-American motives have since diminished on the ground that America and Europe now have a common interest in strengthening the Western alliance.

The third decade of this century saw a great deal of activity in Europe in behalf of European unification, but it was not well organized or clear cut. The proposal for a "pan-Europe" sponsored by Coudenhove-Kalergi in the 1920s was prophetic of more recent organized efforts. He appealed to the democratic center parties, holding the communist and monarchist extremes to be outside the possible field of coalition, and he held that unification would enable Europe to keep pace with American, British and Russian industry. He called for a customs union to combine German coal with French ore and to develop "a pan-European mining industry" in which France and Germany could work together in order to forestall a potential rapprochement between Russia and Germany. Coudenhove-Kalergi believed that Russia, whether White or Red, would ultimately dominate a Europe disunited.[4]

During the 1920s proposals were formulated for unification or cooperation of specific industries. The notion of unification by sectors began to take shape. This movement may have been influenced by syndicalist and guild socialist doctrines, according to which political and economic power should be dispersed among the constituent associations of society.[5]

The continental steel cartel, officially L'Entente International de l'Acier (EIA), organized in 1926, was in some circles hailed as a model for international cooperation for the protection of European interests, especially against American competition, and as a foundation for peace. Using oversimplified notions of economic determinism, some groups that were not even sympathetic to Marxism believed that cooperation among steel producers would eliminate the economic rivalry that leads to war.[6]

The French government, in the late 1920s and early 1930s, advanced a proposal for an economic union that would reduce tariffs within a network of cartels. This idea of cooperation through international industrial agreements was also sponsored by various committees of the League of Nations and by the International Chamber of Commerce. The French Minister of Commerce, Louis Loucheur, was the leading spokesman for this idea in the Geneva Economic Conference of 1927. Aristide Briand issued his famous memorandum

---

[4] Richard N. Coudenhove-Kalergi, *Pan-Europe*, Knopf, New York, 1926, pp. 17, 127–128, 141–143, 177, and Chap. 4.

[5] The functional "parliaments" in fascist Italy represented a parallel development but the Fascists also believed in centralized political power.

[6] For a more detailed description of the hopes stimulated by the first EIA, see Chapter 6. For the alleged anti-American bias of the EIA, see Ervin Hexner, *The International Steel Cartel*, University of North Carolina Press, Chapel Hill, 1943, pp. 224–226.

on the "Organization of a Régime of European Federal Union" in May 1930, and in 1931 the French government, at the League Commission of Enquiry for European Union, recommended that cartels should control imports within an economic union, and that the import duty on cartel products be refunded.[7] Edouard Herriot, in his book *The United States of Europe*, reflected the proposals that were in the air at the time.[8] He extolled the advantages of international industrial agreements in stabilizing production and employment, rationalizing the organization of production and lowering costs and prices. Herriot, holding that customs barriers are a consequence rather than a cause of economic instability, recommended that producers stabilize production as a condition for tariff reform. He pointed out that customs duties play an important role in international control schemes by giving the partners something to bargain with and the means to enforce the provisions of the cartel. Showing impatience with "politicians," Herriot believed that European unity should follow the example of the United States where, he thought, the business community had promoted federation in order to create more stable and uniform business conditions, which had been hindered by local tradition and regulation. But Herriot believed that cartel agreements should also protect the consumer and should therefore be published and include representatives from government, consumers or workers.[9]

The committees of the League of Nations made similar proposals for safeguarding the public. Their long and unsuccessful efforts, as well as those of the International Labor Office, to grapple with the European "coal problem" were based on the device of tripartite international agreements in the public interest.[10]

It would be a mistake to see these interwar efforts as an attack on, or an effort to limit, the principle of national sovereignty. Both Coudenhove-Kalergi and Herriot, for example, approached this aspect of the problem very circumspectly. The League of Nations itself was based on the notion of cooperation among sovereign States, not on the subordination of sovereignty. The interwar proposals were more concerned with cooperation, agreements and larger areas of contact. But some observers also felt that complete national sovereignty was incompatible with substantial progress in international cooperation.

[7] Edouard Herriot (R. J. Dingle, tr.), *The United States of Europe*, Viking, New York, 1930, p. 73; Viner, *op, cit.*, pp. 75–78.

[8] François Perroux, *L'Europe sans rivages*, Presses Universitaires de France, Paris, 1954, p. 75, suggests that Herriot was a spokesman for the French *patronat*.

[9] Herriot, *op. cit.*, pp. 109, 116, 120, 126, 273–274.

[10] ILO, *The World Coal Mining Industry*, Geneva, 1938, Vol. I, Introduction, especially pp. 11–14. For a general description of League of Nations efforts to stabilize production in the public interest, see *Raw Material Problems and Policies*, League of Nations, Geneva, 1946.

Postwar Years

The idea of European unity was kept alive in France during the Resistance, when some groups advanced the notion of transferring some national sovereignty to an international body.[11] These programs, more cosmopolitan than European, envisaged a democratic and popular world order that would actively suppress any attempt to revive fascism, would democratize Germany and control its heavy industry.[12] Other proposals, growing out of wartime planning experience, called for a European planning and allocating body for basic commodities.

While some form of political union might have had a much greater chance of success immediately after the second world war than later when national sovereignty, traditional beliefs and habits had had a chance to reassert themselves, the immediate problems of reconstruction rather than unification received first attention. The schism between East and West and the large electoral following attracted by the Communists in France and Italy introduced a period of uncertainty until the West reacted positively with a program of its own, beginning with the Marshall Plan or European Recovery Program (ERP) launched by the United States in 1947. In the Organization for European Economic Cooperation (OEEC), established in 1948, the recipients of United States aid agreed to coordinate their economic policies.[13] The following year saw the establishment of the Council of Europe, a consultative body, which had developed indirectly out of a speech by Winston Churchill at Zurich in 1946 calling for "a kind of United States of Europe."[14] In the summer of 1950 at the Council of Europe Churchill suggested the creation of a European army. A year later, Churchill, who had meanwhile become Prime Minister, indicated that the United Kingdom could not join a European federation, but the six countries that today comprise the ECSC decided to go ahead with a European Defense Community anyway. Thereafter, the Six rather than the Council of Europe carried the hopes for European unification.[15]

Broached in May 1950, the Schuman Plan preceded Churchill's call for a European army. The United States, in the meantime, had encouraged European unity by granting ERP aid on the condition that Europe would take steps to aid itself through freer trade.[16] The United States later pinned its

[11] Henri Michel, *Les Idées politiques et sociales de la résistance*, Presses Universitaires de France, Paris, 1954, pp. 398 ff. Each political and regional group within the Resistance tended to have its own program, so that it would be a mistake to think of a unified program.

[12] Program of the French socialist party, in *Le Populaire*, July 1, 1943, cited in *ibid.*, pp. 389–391; Barbara Ward, *The West at Bay*, Allen and Unwin, London, 1948, pp. 193–194.

[13] The North Atlantic Treaty Organization, primarily military and political in function, was established by 1949.

[14] *Britain in Western Europe*, Royal Institute of International Affairs, London, 1956, p. 12.

[15] *Ibid.*, pp. 1–16, gives a concise summary of the early postwar efforts for a united Europe.

[16] Viner, *op. cit.*, pp. 129–133.

hopes on the Six, who were willing to surrender some national sovereignty, but did not cease to encourage the more traditional efforts at cooperation through the OEEC and the General Agreement on Tariffs and Trade (GATT).[17]

It had become clear by 1950 that the French government's desire for international control of the Ruhr was not consistent with the conception of a role for West Germany in a common allied defense.[18] This inconsistency disturbed allied relations and German sentiment. By inviting Germany into the ECSC pool as an equal partner, the Schuman Plan killed two birds with one stone.

Within a month of Schuman's announcement, the British government declined to transfer any sovereignty over coal and steel but wished the plan success. The British Labor and Conservative parties were both opposed to full British membership; the former, in fact, issued a pamphlet that warned against a revival of the prewar steel cartel.[19]

On the Continent negotiations proceeded amidst some opposition. Had the governments accepted the views of the management of the coal and steel industries, which were against "bureaucratic" control, they probably would have concluded a much different treaty, if any. German industry, however, finally came around by accepting the plan as a sacrifice to German equality. The German trade unions also accepted the plan, but the German socialist party opposed it.[20] The communist parties in all the countries opposed the plan as a plot against peace and the working class. The Belgian coal industry and the Italian steel producers fought the plan stubbornly; many concessions were consequently made, as discussed in subsequent chapters, to protect the last two from the effects of the common market during the five-year transitional period. The French Right, including de Gaulle's supporters, were also hostile.[21]

In the eyes of those who promoted European federalism, the ECSC was part of a comprehensive strategy to "unify" or "integrate" the national States under supranational authority. The Draft Treaty for a European Defense Community followed close upon the ECSC. It was ratified by all

[17] For the benefits and shortcomings of GATT and OEEC in freeing trade and payments and the belief that these forms of cooperation had reached, by the early 1950s, the limit of achievement, see ECE, *Economic Survey of Europe in 1956*, Geneva, 1957, Chap. 4.

[18] See Chapter 5 for further details on the evolution of allied policy after the war and of the position of the Ruhr in the occupation of Germany.

[19] For a short history of the British reaction, see *Britain in Western Europe*, pp. 19–21.

[20] Six years later, however, the German socialist party accepted the European Economic Community and Euratom.

[21] For an interesting description and history of the negotiations and parliamentary debates, see William Diebold, Jr., *The Schuman Plan: A Study in Economic Cooperation, 1950–1959*, Praeger, New York, 1959; Georges Goriely, *Naissance de la Communauté Européenne du Charbon et de l'Acier*, HA, Luxembourg, Doc. No. 7889/56f (mimeo.).

parliaments but the French, which rejected the treaty late in the summer of 1954. The proponents of European integration revived the federal movement with an appeal in 1955 for economic union and an atomic agency cutting across national boundaries. Within two years the six governments involved in the ECSC drafted and ratified a treaty for a European Economic Community (EEC) and another for a European Atomic Energy Community (Euratom), both of which began operations in 1958. Embodying some of the experience gained during the ECSC's early operation, these new institutions will have much influence on the ECSC. The creation of an economic union among some of the most industrialized continental countries stimulated Great Britain, and through her nearly every other Western European country, to start negotiations to make the economic union of the Six part of a larger free trade area. This proposal encountered difficulties; a larger free trade area would have had much influence on the ECSC.

There had been a difference of opinion in Europe as to whether unification should take a political or economic form,[22] but the latter view prevailed. Those who favored the economic approach, however, had by 1955 backed away from their belief in integration by sectors and had begun to favor more comprehensive forms of economic unification as represented by the EEC treaty. Although Euratom, formulated at the same time as the EEC, still reflected the sector approach, it deals with a very specialized field. Several years' experience with the ECSC had revealed that integration by sectors created new problems of distortion.[23]

The ECSC is more than a free trade area. The member States gave up to federal institutions some of their formal powers over the industries in question. The attainment of common measures and policies depends on mutual agreement between the States and the federal institutions with regard to certain other powers retained by the States.

THE INSTITUTIONS OF THE COMMUNITY[24]

The individual ECSC States still enjoy veto power over some subjects. A complete economic community—which would be impossible without federal political institutions—would encompass the free movement of capital and labor, common standards for social and fiscal legislation, common commercial

[22] See André Philip, *L'Europe unie et sa place dans l'économie internationale*, Presses Universitaires de France, Paris, 1953, p. 180. The "constitutionalists" recommended complete unification while the "functionalists" suggested progressive economic unification, sector by sector; the two differed on strategy, not on ultimate goals.

[23] *The Economist*, August 11, 1956, p. 500.

[24] For a detailed analysis of the institutions of the ECSC, as well as of the other provisions of the treaty, see the excellent study by Paul Reuter, *La Communauté Européenne du Charbon et de l'Acier*, Librairie Générale de Droit et de Jurisprudence, Paris, 1953.

policies vis-à-vis the rest of the world and common standards for transport rates. These subjects are still controlled by the individual States. The States by and large gave up their powers over prices and trade. These limitations on their powers represent the supranational aspect of the ECSC.

The High Authority and the Council of Ministers

The High Authority, the executive and lawmaking body, acts by majority vote. It consists of nine independent members each representing the Community as a whole rather than his individual country. The High Authority shares many of its powers with the Council of Ministers. The latter represents the interests of the member governments individually and collectively; in effect, it curbs the federative principle. In some cases the Council of Ministers can act by qualified majority, but in others unanimous decisions are required. Where the treaty requires the High Authority to obtain concurrence by the Council of Ministers, the latter may approve by qualified majority, provided the majority includes a State that produces at least 20 per cent of the total value of the coal and steel. If the High Authority resubmits a proposal after a tie, it can be approved by two States that each control 20 per cent of the value of the production. France and Germany each controlled 20 per cent as long as the Saar was in France. Though France controls about 16 per cent without the Saar it still exercises equal weight in the Council. The Council has initiatory as well as concurrent powers.

The Council has become very powerful in practice, but the attempt to limit the veto power of the individual State by making decisions of the High Authority and of the Court of Justice (described later) binding upon the enterprises conferred a "supranational" character on the ECSC. The Council's importance was adumbrated when the treaty was still in the drafting stage when the "intergovernmental" thesis (supported by the Dutch delegation) made headway against the "supranational" one (supported by the French delegation) on the ground that it would be impractical to deprive the governments of sovereignty over affairs that were by nature indivisible.[25]

The High Authority is assisted by a large professional staff, organized by divisions covering economics, law, statistics, concentrations and agreements, production, investments, transport, marketing and finance. It also collects taxes from the enterprises. The resulting revenue is used for administrative expenses, for "nonrepayable assistance" to workers and enterprises, for guaranteeing loans contracted by enterprises and loans contracted by the High Authority itself on behalf of the Community.

[25] HA, *Chronologie des travaux préparatoires du Plan Schuman*, n.d., *passim*, particularly pp. 21, 32.

Consultative Committee

The Consultative Committee consists of fifty-one members appointed by the Council of Ministers in equal numbers from producers', workers' and consumers' (including dealers') organizations. This body serves the High Authority in an advisory capacity.

Court of Justice

The treaty provides for a Court of Justice, "to ensure the rule of law in the interpretation and application of the present Treaty" (Article 31). It is modeled on the United States Supreme Court. It consists of seven judges appointed for six years "by agreement" among the governments of the member States (Article 32). All parties—enterprises, associations, member States and the Council of Ministers—that are affected by the decisions of the High Authority may appeal to the Court on questions of law, of procedure, of legal competence, of abuse of power, or of failure to act. The decisions of the Court are final and binding. The ECSC, the European Economic Community and Euratom now have a common Court of Justice.

Common Assembly

The Common Assembly consists of members appointed each year by, and from among, the parliaments of the member States. The treaty also authorizes the States to provide for their election by "direct universal suffrage" (Article 21) but the States have not yet put this provision into effect. The treaty requires the Common Assembly to meet once a year. Upon its own initiative or upon that of the Council or High Authority, it can also meet in extraordinary session and has frequently done so. It is not a law- or constitution-making body. Its formal power is limited; if two thirds of the constituent membership give a vote of no confidence to the annual general report submitted by the High Authority, the latter must resign (Article 24). The Assembly may also give its "opinion" (Article 23) on questions put to it by the Council, but it has no power over the Council. In practice the Assembly has acquired more power than the treaty provides. Through specialized committees that meet regularly with the High Authority, it exercises continuous influence on the executive and has often urged it on to bolder action.

Since 1958 the ECSC, the European Economic Community and Euratom have had a Common Assembly consisting of 142 members under the name of Assemblée Parlementaire Européenne.[26] Though the Assembly has different

---

[26] See *Convention Relative à Certaines Institutions Communes aux Communautés Européennes.* This convention adopted by the six governments annuls Articles 21 and 32 of the ECSC treaty dealing, respectively, with the membership of the Assembly and of the Court.

prerogatives and powers in each of these three Communities, it remains to be seen whether the Assembly's role will vary much from one Community to the other.[27]

MAJOR TREATY OBJECTIVES[28]

The treaty came into force July 25, 1952, for fifty years (Articles 97 and 99). Membership is open to other States (Article 98). After a six-month "preparatory period" during which the administrative machinery was set up, the five-year transitional period began in February 1953 with the establishment of the common market for coal, iron ore and scrap; the common market for ordinary steel began two months later, in April 1953. Alloy steels were incorporated into the common market in August 1954. The five-year transitional period ended in February 1958.

Table 1

OUTPUT AND EMPLOYMENT IN ECSC INDUSTRIES
AS PER CENT OF GROSS NATIONAL PRODUCT AND TOTAL EMPLOYMENT,
BY COUNTRY, 1955

Country	ECSC Products as Per Cent of GNP[a]	Employment in ECSC Industries as Per Cent of Total Employment
Germany	10	2.7
France-Saar	6	2.3
Belgium-Luxembourg	16	5.7
Italy	4	0.3
Netherlands	4	1.5
ECSC	8	2.0

Sources: GNP and total employment: OEEC, *General Statistics.* Employment in the coal, steel and iron ore industries: HA, *Bulletin statistique.* Value of coal and steel for Germany from Statistisches Bundesamt, Düsseldorf.

[a] Figures based on a valuation of $130 per metric ton of finished steel and $12 per metric ton of coal for Germany; for other countries an average value of $125 per metric ton of steel has been assumed and the following values per metric ton of coal: France-Saar, $15; Belgium, $17; Netherlands, $13; Italy, $10. Coal consumed in steel production deducted.

The member nations of the ECSC—Germany, France, Belgium, Luxembourg, Italy and the Netherlands—have a total population of about 160 million people and a gross national product of about $140 billion (in 1955). With a slightly lower population than the United States, their GNP was only

[27] For comparison of the Assembly's powers in each Community, see Pierre Wigny (member of the Assembly), *L'Assemblée parlementaire dans l'Europe des Six*, ECSC, Luxembourg, 1958, especially pp. 59–72.

[28] All references to the Treaty of the European Coal and Steel Community, the official text of which is in French, are to the English version, published by the High Authority of the Community.

37 per cent as great. The coal and steel industries in these countries, employing nearly 1.5 million workers, account for only 2 per cent of the six countries' combined employment of 72 million. The output of these industries accounts for about 8 per cent of the combined GNP of the member countries. (Table 1 shows the percentage for each country.) The coal and steel industries are more important, both by value and employment, in Belgium-Luxembourg, Germany and France-Saar[29] than in Italy and the Netherlands, but account for only a small portion of GNP everywhere but Luxembourg.

The coal and steel industries are more important as integral parts of the economy, as a source of raw and semifinished products for further production, as a basis of industrial concentration or as a source of foreign exchange than indicated by their share of GNP or total employment.

In the course of a year's bargaining in the drafting period, the treaty became a complex document, reflecting a complicated adjustment between federal and national responsibility, between "normal" and "abnormal" phases of the business cycle. For preliminary purposes, the major objectives are described below; subsequent chapters will give further attention to detailed aspects of the treaty.

(1) Provisions vary with the business cycle; those for normal business conditions represent the long-term ideal and are considered more representative of the spirit of the union. Deviations from the ideal are permitted when supplies are surplus or are scarce according to criteria which cannot be closely defined in advance. Deviations were also permitted during the five-year transitional period in order to give labor, management and the national governments an opportunity to adjust to new conditions.

(2) The fundamental aim is expressed in the following terms:

> The Community must progressively establish conditions which will in themselves assure the most rational distribution of production at the highest possible level of productivity, while safeguarding the continuity of employment and avoiding the creation of fundamental and persistent disturbances in the economies of the member States (Article 2).

The safeguards mentioned in the quotation need to be emphasized; it is characteristic of the treaty to thus qualify its objectives. These safeguards apply at all times, even during the so-called normal periods.

(3) Coal, steel and the raw materials for steel production (iron ore, coke and scrap) are treated as common resources to which all members have equal access on equal terms (Article 3).

[29] See p. 43 for the history of the changes in jurisdiction over the Saar between France and Germany.

(4) The treaty requires the elimination of tariffs, quotas and public subsidies because they protect high-cost producers, reduce trade and interfere with the most rational distribution of production (Article 4).

(5) Competition under the price system is the treaty's objective in normal periods.

(a) Producers must sell at equal prices for comparable sales; opposition to price discrimination is one of the strictest features of the treaty and is, of course, the keystone of free access (Article 60).

(b) An equally strict feature of the treaty prohibits agreements in restraint of trade (Article 65).

(c) Excessive concentrations are also incompatible with competition and are subject to controls of a less inflexible nature (Article 66).

(6) Since Article 2 (already quoted) refers to "conditions which will in themselves assure the most rational distribution of production," it follows that the treaty encourages private decisions under the price mechanism, in preference to public influence, with respect to production, distribution and investments.

(7) Factor movements, or the right of capital and labor to circulate freely, are not assured except under special circumstances mentioned in (8) below.

(8) The States retain their competence over taxation, social security schemes, transportation, third-country commercial policy, labor and capital mobility (Articles 67 to 75 inclusive), even though all of these elements influence costs, prices, trade and the use of resources. Had the States tried to equalize or modify these conditions, they would in effect have had to create an economic union for the whole economy because taxation, social legislation, commercial policy and the other elements still under the control of the individual States are indivisible. The Six therefore accepted the principle that retention by the States of control over these elements of public policy was not incompatible with a common market. (This principle has since been used for the European Economic Community as well.) Nevertheless, the States agreed in the treaty to take some steps to "harmonize" conditions, notably in the field of transport, commercial policy and labor mobility.

(9) The ECSC has an expansionist philosophy with respect to investments and production:

> The mission of the European Coal and Steel Community is to contribute to the expansion of the economy, the development of employment and the improvement of the standard of living in the participating countries through the creation . . . of a common market (Article 2).

A high level of business activity and an expanding economy are necessary conditions for the attainment of the goals of the Community even though they are beyond its competence. Within its own field, the Community has some powers to promote investments at efficient producing units and to provide for the necessary expansion and renewal of plant (Article 54). The investment aspect is important, for, if the Community is effective, resources will be withdrawn from some regions and introduced in others, with a shift in the direction of investments and a possible shift in their total volume.

(10) In dealing with the valleys and peaks of the business cycle, the treaty provides other methods than those described above. Production quotas and minimum prices may be applied during an oversupply "crisis" and distribution quotas and maximum price controls may be applied during a period of scarcity (Articles 58, 59 and 61). During slack periods production quotas are to be "equitable" and plants that exceed the quota may have to pay a levy to support those that fall below it. Supplies when scarce are to be controlled as between exports and internal consumption. Prices also may be controlled for a number of purposes independent of the business cycle, notably to prevent them from rising to the cost of the marginal producer (Article 62).

(11) These powers, together with those in relation to investments, give the Community latitude in the choice of economic policy. The choice of policy depends on the climate of opinion, on the policies of the governments and the groups in control, and on business conditions. This flexibility is described by Pierre Uri, a French expert who participated in the treaty negotiations:

[The treaty] was conceived with flexibility to enable it to adapt itself to different systems of property, economics and economic policies. The economic climate, rather than the personal opinions of the members of the High Authority, will determine whether the Community has a liberal or dirigistic orientation. The High Authority evidently will not be liberal at any cost if the surrounding world is intervening and planning in a permanent fashion. By the same token, the High Authority could not conceivably submit coal and steel to rigorous planning in a world inclined to liberalism.[30]

(12) During the transitional period, which ended February 1958, the treaty authorized temporary subsidies, duties and equalization payments in specific instances and under specific conditions to help high-cost producers, mainly Belgian coal and Italian steel and coke producers, get ready for competition, and to give workers and producers generally the time to make the necessary adjustments. It also defined the sequence and timing of various measures, contacts with third countries and other organizations, the establishment of common tariffs and waiver of the most-favored-nation clause.

---

[30] The statement, made to the French Conseil Economique, is cited in *Communauté Européenne du Charbon et de l'Acier*, Conseil Economique, Etudes et Travaux No. 2, Presses Universitaires de France, Paris, n.d., p. 116.

THE GENERAL EFFECTS OF
ECONOMIC UNION

purp

An economic union should promote two types of benefits; these are, to use James E. Meade's terms, "optimization of trade" and "maximization of production."[31] If consumers in one country place a different relative value on the same products than consumers in another country, an economic union will optimize trade between the two countries because all consumers will give up goods on which they place a lower value in return for goods of a higher value. If, to take an improbable example, Frenchmen placed a higher value on coal than steel, and if the opposite were true in Germany, then France might give up some of its steel in exchange for more coal. Trade would be "optimized." All consumers will consequently obtain a higher average satisfaction, even if total production does not shift or increase. This result can occur only if the market prices to consumers in each member country correspond to the importance which the consumer places on various products.

If one country can produce additional goods with less additional effort than another, an economic union will maximize production because each country will tend to concentrate its resources on the goods that it can produce with the least additional effort and import from the other country goods that require the greater effort. If Italy, for example, found that it had to make a greater effort to produce steel than Belgium or France, it might give up some of its facilities in order to obtain cheaper steel from other parts of the economic union. Production would be "maximized" by means of specialization and the average output per unit of capital and labor would rise, provided the price reflected the producer's marginal cost.

Of the two potential benefits, the second, with its implications for the direction and volume of investments, is the more important. The over-all benefits of a partial economic union—as in the ECSC—cannot, however, be inferred from those of a complete union and cannot therefore be taken for granted. The labor withdrawn from the coal industry in a partial union may be re-employed in the same country by an industry even less efficient than the coal industry. The country as a whole would consequently lose rather than gain in average efficiency.[32]

Anything—such as monopolies, cartels or government influences—that interferes with setting a price at which marginal costs to society and marginal value to consumers are balanced, will interfere with the potential benefits of an

[31] *Problems of Economic Union*, University of Chicago Press, Chicago, 1953, pp. 9 ff, on which the subsequent definitions are based.

[32] Tibor Scitovsky, *Economic Theory and Western European Integration*, Allen and Unwin, London, 1958, pp. 140 ff, calls attention to the limitations of partial union.

economic union, because it prevents resources from flowing to the most efficient areas of production. But the long-term beneficial effects of an economic union do not depend entirely on price competition based on the free price mechanism. An economic union may enhance the fear of competition and may therefore still cause the firms to make investments in order to enlarge their share of the market; such investments may raise average efficiency by promoting economies of scale.[33]

An economic union would not raise average efficiency unless the same product were produced in two countries with a great difference in average efficiency. If two areas combine, they must not have equal potentials in the same fields; i.e., there must be room for specialization in the use of resources in alternative fields of production. Most economic unions in recent history have not satisfied this condition. About a dozen economic unions were in existence in the early 1950s, but only Benelux included more than one industrialized country, while the remainder were unions of similar agricultural economies.[34] One of the problems dealt with in this book is whether or not the ECSC countries—Little Europe—include areas of sufficient diversity in comparative advantage to lay the basis for potential specialization in coal and steel production.

There are differences of opinion as to the proper range of integration. Many critics believe that Little Europe is not viable politically or economically. This idea was evident even during the French Resistance when some groups opposed the idea of European unification because they preferred a world order in which the United States and Britain would guarantee Europe against the revival of German aggression.[35] This idea of the role of the greater Atlantic community in keeping the political or economic balance is still common in Europe.

Of more immediate concern, however, is the question whether an economic union interferes with the efficient use of world resources by giving preference to internal producers whose costs may be higher than those of producers outside the union. Owing to this danger some writers are unhappy with the idea of customs unions and prefer more universal arrangements to promote trade.[36] Most writers agree, however, that the problem must be settled empirically rather than abstractly. This question is discussed further in later chapters.

[33] See Scitovsky, *op. cit.*, Chap. 3, especially pp. 133 ff.

[34] Viner, *op. cit.*, p. 129. Several current proposals for economic union in Latin America and of Japan with southeast Asia present some interesting problems for analysis.

[35] Michel, *op. cit.*, pp. 391–394.

[36] E.g., Viner, *op. cit.*, pp. 53 and 139, refers to the ultimate end of a customs union as a "mirage" and adds that it is "unlikely to prove a practicable and suitable remedy for today's economic ills, and it will almost inevitably operate as a psychological barrier to the realization of the more desirable but less desired objectives of the Havana Charter—the balanced multilateral reduction of trade barriers on a nondiscriminatory basis."

The next chapter describes the anatomy of the common market as well as the trade currents between areas. Subsequent chapters examine matters within the ECSC to see what influence it has had on some of the broader issues already raised. Costs and investments, corporate concentrations, restrictive agreements and price behavior in each of the two industries are therefore discussed in sequence. While each of these topics constitutes a single chapter and each chapter is complete in itself, the findings in the earlier chapters converge in Chapter 7, dealing with steel, and in Chapters 9 and 10, dealing with coal and energy, which relate the market organization of each industry to the all-important question of improving average efficiency. Chapters 11, 12 and 13, devoted to commercial policy, transport rates and social policies, respectively, deal with the fields in which the individual States are still sovereign and the efforts to reconcile the objectives of economic union with national sovereignty.

CHAPTER 2

PRODUCTION AND

MARKETS

PRODUCTS INCLUDED IN THE ECSC[1]

Nearly all the solid fuels—bituminous coal and anthracite, coke and brown coal briquettes—are included in the ECSC. In European terminology, the term "hard coal" refers to bituminous coal as well as anthracite, as distinguished from lignite and brown coal, whereas in the United States hard coal refers only to anthracite. The term is used in this study in its European sense. The term "solid fuels" refers to all types of coal and their solid derivatives, mostly coke and briquettes. Most of the brown coal in the ECSC is produced near Cologne, south of the Ruhr, where it is either processed into briquettes or consumed at the mines for the production of electricity. The industry is monopolized and employs relatively few workers. Though brown coal is a fairly important source of energy in Germany, it is not of central importance for the ECSC. Only the briquettes are under its jurisdiction.

The coal industry provides coking coal for the steel industry, and in many districts is technically as well as financially integrated with it. In some cases the coal industry produces coke for sale to the steel industry. In other cases the steel industry produces its own coke. Independent cokeries are rare.

Liquid fuels, natural gas and other products also produce heat and power but are excluded. The by-products from coal processing, such as gas and chemicals, and the electricity produced for sale by mine power plants are not included in the ECSC. Surplus gas and electricity produced for sale by the steel industry are also excluded. But if the facilities which produce these surplus products and by-products are an integral part of a coal mine or steel plant, they are eligible for financial assistance from the ECSC.

The steel industry under the ECSC encompasses raw materials (iron ore, scrap and coke), pig iron, crude steel, whether carbon or alloy grades, semi-

1 The products included are enumerated in Annex I of the treaty.

finished and finished products, but does not encompass liquid steel for castings produced in small and independent plants, steel tubes, wire products and iron castings.

Appendix B gives a brief description of steel producing processes and the uses of different types of coal.

AREAS AND MARKETS WITHIN THE ECSC

The ECSC is a congeries of producing areas each of which disposes as much as possible of its output in the nearest markets. The freight costs for bulky low-value products force the producer to locate near the raw materials and the customer to purchase from the nearest source. The national, as distinct from regional, characteristics of the common market are important, too, because the individual governments still influence the firms and because producers and customers are still under the spell of national habits of action. Since an economic union influences specialization and trade, the common market should be understood in terms of the underlying national and regional characteristics. These characteristics are discussed in this chapter as background to the rest of this study.

Most of the coal, iron ore and steel in the ECSC are produced in a relatively small area, consisting of a sort of inverted triangle, over 200 miles on all sides, the apex at the Saar, the eastern side running up to the Ruhr and the western side running along the Franco-Belgian border, as shown by the endpaper map. Italy is outside the triangle; the coal mines and steel plants in the center and western part of France and the iron ore, steel and coal production centers near Sulzbach-Rosenberg (Bavaria) and Hanover (Lower Saxony) are also outside the triangle.

Minable coal deposits occur on a line stretching across northern Europe from Pas-de-Calais near Dunkerque to Silesia. West of the Iron Curtain, there are essentially three groups of mines in this line. One group runs from Dunkerque along the northern border of France and the southern border of Belgium. Another group, called the Limburg mines, runs from the Campine in eastern Belgium across the southerly portion of Holland and on to the Aachen area of Germany west of the Rhine. The Ruhr mines occur on the other side of the Rhine, on the right bank. Farther south, where the French-German border runs parallel to the Saar River, occurs another mining area, from which coal is mined in both Saar and Lorraine. These coal mining areas, all within the triangle, account for 93 per cent of the coal production in the ECSC, as Table 2 shows.

The most important iron ore field, accounting for 76 per cent of the ECSC's ore output, extends southward from southern Luxembourg along the eastern part of France to Nancy but is not mined throughout its way. There are four steel producing areas located along it: one in southern Luxembourg and three in France, at Longwy, Thionville and Nancy.[2] The rest of the iron ore produc-

Table 2
PERCENTAGE DISTRIBUTION OF COAL PRODUCED BY
MAJOR COAL FIELDS IN THE ECSC, 1955

Coal Field	Percentage Distribution
Ruhr, Aachen, Limburg, Campine	60.7
Nord and Pas-de-Calais, south Belgium	19.8
Saar, Lorraine	12.4
Other fields	7.1
Total	100.0

Source: HA, *Bulletin statistique.*

tion in the ECSC occurs in the Salzgitter (Lower Saxony) and Rhineland areas (near Siegen) of Germany (but not in the Ruhr) and in scattered fashion in parts of France—Normandy, Brittany and the Pyrenees area. The northwestern Alpine region of Italy (at Aosta) and the Island of Elba also produce some ore.

Iron ore and coal rarely occur anywhere together in sufficient quantity of the desired quality, Birmingham, Alabama, being one of the rare cases. Some steel plants are located near iron ore, drawing coal from other areas, and conversely. The location of a steel plant therefore generally represents an attempt to balance advantages and disadvantages relative to assembly of materials and outbound freight costs. Although location near ore reduces inbound freight because a ton of steel requires more ore than coal, location near coal usually offers other advantages, for coal mining regions, usually more industrialized, provide nearby customers and an adjacent source of capital scrap. Most of the coal-based steel producing areas in the ECSC have a large local market but not all of the coal producing areas in the ECSC have attracted steel plants. Most ore-based steel producing areas in the ECSC do not enjoy a local market. As imported iron ore and coal have been getting cheaper relative to the domestic product, plants are being increasingly located at tidewater, so as to call on overseas supplies, or else at great industrial cities to obtain scrap. Moreover, areas of abundant electric power attract electric-furnace plants.

[2] For the economic characteristics of these areas in France, which are by no means homogeneous although based on the same ore, see J. E. Martin, "Location Factors in the Lorraine Iron and Steel Industry," in *The Institute of British Geographers, Transactions and Proceedings*, Publication No. 23, 1959.

More than 55 per cent of the steel production in the ECSC is located near coal and more than 27 per cent near iron ore. (See Table 3.) All together, the

Table 3

PERCENTAGE DISTRIBUTION OF ECSC CRUDE
STEEL PRODUCTION, BY MAJOR COAL AND IRON ORE DISTRICT, 1955

District	Percentage Distribution
Near coal deposits:	
North Rhine–Westphalia	33.4
South Belgium	11.0
Nord and Pas-de-Calais	5.3
Saar	6.1
Total	55.8
Near iron ore deposits:	
Salzgitter	4.0
Lorraine	15.8
Luxembourg	6.1
Other	1.5
Total	27.4
Other	16.8
TOTAL	100.0

Sources: Chambre Syndicale de la Sidérurgie Française; ECE, *Quarterly Bulletin of Steel Statistics* and *Quarterly Bulletin of Coal Statistics;* Statistisches Bundesamt, Düsseldorf; HA, *Bulletin statistique; Jahrbuch.*

location of 83 per cent of the ECSC steel production is based on one or the other raw material. The remaining 17 per cent is at tidewater, near abundant electric power, or in or near a great city like Milan. The steel plants near coal, and often those near tidewater and abundant power, are in industrialized areas; those near iron ore are not.[3]

The distribution of the production of coal, steel and iron ore by regions in 1955 is shown in Fig. 1 (based on Table 2-1 in Appendix E). The Ruhr, in North Rhine–Westphalia, produces nearly half the coal and one third of the steel in the ECSC, about 92 per cent of German coal and 83 per cent of German steel (excluding the Saar). The Aachen area, on the left bank of the Rhine and southwest of the Ruhr, produces coal but no steel, and Lower Saxony, northeast of the Ruhr, produces coal, iron ore and steel.

Nord and Pas-de-Calais, in northern France, is the largest coal producing area in France and the second largest in the ECSC. It produces a little more than 20 per cent of French and 5 per cent of ECSC steel but no iron ore. Lorraine, in eastern France, is the largest steel producing area in France and

[3] "L'Industrie du charbon et l'industrie de l'acier en Europe occidentale," ECE, *Bulletin économique pour l'Europe*, Vol. II, No. 2, Geneva, 1950, pp. 18–59, contains a concise description of the two industries in Western Europe as a whole.

the second largest in the ECSC; it is also the largest iron ore producing center in the ECSC but is one of the smaller coal producing areas. Coal, steel and iron ore production also are additionally dispersed over a wide area of France, largely south of the Loire River, an area called the Centre-Midi.

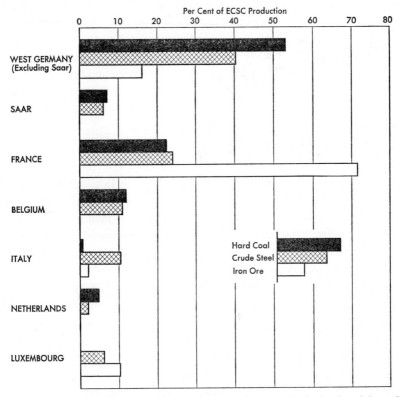

Fig. 1. Percentage Distribution of Coal, Crude Steel and Iron Ore Production, ECSC, by Country, 1955

Source: Table 2-1, Appendix E.

Belgium produces coal in the Campine, an agricultural area in the south-eastern part of the country, but there are no steel plants in the Campine. Belgium also produces coal in the south, along the French border, near Liége, Namur and Charleroi. The south is the larger of the two Belgian coal mining districts and serves as a base for its steel industry. Southern Belgium is the third largest coal and steel producing district in the ECSC.

Luxembourg and the Saar produce about the same amount of steel. But in Luxembourg it is iron ore that has attracted steel production whereas in the

Saar it is coal. In the Netherlands steel and coal are produced in different parts of the country. The Dutch tidewater steel plants work with imported iron ore and some imported coal.

With practically no coal and only a small output of iron ore, Italy neverthe-less has a relatively large steel industry constituting 10 per cent of ECSC pro-duction. Owing to the Italian deficiency in coal and iron ore, some of the steel plants are located at tidewater and the inland plants are located where hydro-electric power is abundant.

The Ruhr, northern France, southern Belgium and the Saar are deficient in iron ore but plentiful in coal and steel, whereas Lorraine has plenty of iron ore and steel but is deficient in coking coal. But the deficit and surplus areas are not necessarily complementary; in many cases they are even competitive.

GERMANY AND THE RUHR

The Ruhr[4] is by far the most industrialized region in continental Europe. With the loss of Silesian coal after the second world war, the Ruhr's position in Germany increased in relative importance. Rather small in area—it is but thirty-three miles from Duisburg in the west to Dortmund in the east, and fifteen miles from the northern edge to the Ruhr Valley in the south, an area of two hundred square miles in all—with a population of about five million (10 per cent of the population of West Germany), the Ruhr is served by a dense and elaborate network of railroad and water transportation, connecting not only every important point within the area but also the area as a whole with the rest of Germany, with the sea and with the neighboring countries. On the west the Ruhr area has access to the North Sea through the Rhine and the Low Country ports of Rotterdam and Amsterdam. The Rhine also con-nects the Ruhr with southern Germany and Switzerland. From the Rhine the Ruhr is penetrated by several east-west canals which traverse the area to the east-ern limit at Dortmund and which provide another outlet to the North Sea at Bremen and Hamburg via the Dortmund-Ems Canal. Water transport enables the Ruhr at low cost to import iron ore, to export steel, and to exchange ma-terials within the area. One third of the Ruhr solid fuels that are distributed to the rest of Germany and one half of those exported are carried by water.[5] Solid fuels from the Ruhr are carried up and down the Rhine as far south as

---

[4] The Ruhr is an economic and geographic rather than an administrative area; it is part of the province of North Rhine–Westphalia, one of the states of the Federal Republic of Germany. For descriptions of the importance of the Ruhr, see the study by the Institut National de la Statistique et des Etudes Economiques, *L'Economie de la Ruhr*, Presses Universitaires de France, Paris, 1947; and Norman J. G. Pounds, *The Ruhr*, Indiana University Press, Bloomington, 1952.

[5] *Jahrbuch*, 1956, p. 693.

Basle in Switzerland and north to the Low Country ports, westward by rail to Lorraine and Luxembourg and eastward by canal to steel plants in Lower Saxony.

There is a very close and elaborate vertical integration in the Ruhr: between the coal and steel industries; between the coal and coal consuming industries such as coke works, chemicals, gas and electric power plants; between steel producing and steel transforming and engineering industries. A large proportion of the solid fuels and steel produced in the Ruhr is consequently consumed in the area and stays within the vertically integrated orbit, whether the integration is physical, corporate or financial.

Markets for German Coal

The Ruhr accounts not only for one half of the coal produced in the ECSC as a whole, but also for nearly three fourths of the coking coal, as indicated by Table 4. The large amount of coking coal produced in the Ruhr—nearly 70 per cent of the coal produced in the Ruhr is of that grade—offers enormous

Table 4

PRODUCTION OF COKING COAL IN THE ECSC, BY DISTRICT, 1955[a]

Country and District	Amount (*Millions of Metric Tons*)	As Per Cent of:	
		All Coal Produced in Respective District	All Coking Coal Produced in the ECSC
Germany			
North Rhine–Westphalia	83.5	69	73
Aachen	1.1	15	1
Other	0.8	31	1
Total	85.4	65	75
Belgium			
Campine	4.1	41	4
South	2.7	14	2
Total	6.8	23	6
France			
Nord and Pas-de-Calais	11.5	39	10
Lorraine	—	—	—
Centre-Midi	4.5	35	4
Total	16.0	29	14
Saar	—	—	—
Netherlands	6.3	53	5
TOTAL	114.5	46[b]	100

Source: HA, *Bulletin statistique.*

[a] The definition of coking coal varies somewhat from district to district, as the source shows. Some Saar and Lorraine coal is used for coking but is not strictly speaking classified as such.

[b] All coking coal as per cent of total coal production in the ECSC.

possibilities there for the production of coke and by-product gas and chemicals. The large volume and high quality of its coking coal support the high degree of vertical integration and provide the basis for processing a high proportion of the primary coal into secondary energy and end products—gas, electric power and coke. In 1955, 60 per cent of all the energy provided by coal in Germany, and 44 per cent of all the energy combined, was furnished in the form of secondary products. (See Table 5.) Primary coal and secondary prod-

Table 5

GERMANY: PERCENTAGE DISTRIBUTION OF TOTAL ENERGY
CONSUMED AND OF ENERGY FROM HARD COAL, BY FORM OF ENERGY,
1936, 1950, 1955[a]

	Per Cent of:					
	Total Energy to Final Consumers			Energy from Hard Coal		
Form of Energy	1936	1950	1955	1936	1950	1955
Hard coal consumed:						
Raw	42.15	37.74	29.31	52.85	49.42	40.06
Secondary	37.61	38.62	43.87	47.15	50.58	59.94
Briquettes	4.25	4.62	5.43	5.33	6.06	7.42
Coke	22.62	22.13	24.89	28.36	28.98	34.00
Gas	8.75	8.76	9.72	10.97	11.46	13.29
Electricity	1.30	2.53	2.99	1.63	3.32	4.08
Liquid fuel	0.69	0.58	0.84	0.86	0.76	1.15
Total hard coal	79.76	76.36	73.18	100.00	100.00	100.00
Other forms	20.24	23.64	26.82			
TOTAL	100.00	100.00	100.00			

Source: Derived from Konrad Ebert, "Die Energiebilanz des Bundesgebietes," in *Glückauf*, June 23, 1956, p. 754.

[a] Exclusive of energy consumed for conversion and of interchange among integrated energy works. Data for 1936 refer to postwar territory.

ucts derived from it supplied together 73 per cent of the total energy.[6] The proportion of coal processed into gas, electricity and coke has increased considerably since 1936. There are advantages to selling secondary products instead of primary coal because the returns per unit of labor rise as the industry becomes more capital intensive. The demand for the secondary products—gas, electricity and coke for space heating—is, furthermore, more stable than for primary coal.

A high rate of conversion from primary to secondary forms of coal, geographical and vertical concentration of consumption, and centralized sales agencies help to protect the coal industry in the Ruhr from competition in that area.

[6] Table 2-4 in Appendix E, showing 70 per cent, is on a somewhat different basis.

The Ruhr mining companies consumed about 55 per cent of the coal produced there in 1955.[7] Three fourths of the coal retained by the mining companies, which produce 90 per cent of the metallurgical coke output in Germany, was used for the production of coke. The mining companies used the rest of the coal they retained in integrated electricity and briquetting works and for distribution to mine employees. The public gas system in North Rhine–Westphalia is largely dependent on the mines.[8] Thus the Ruhr production of coke is tied in closely with the market for gas.

The mine power plants generated about one fourth of the power produced in North Rhine–Westphalia in 1955, and sold 45 per cent of their net availability to the public power system as compared with 20 per cent in 1936.[9] The electric power plants provide a market for the growing volume of high ash, fine coal created by increasing underground mechanization. The brown coal mines near Cologne also provide a large amount of power to the public power system.

About 8 per cent of the Ruhr coal is shipped to southern Germany, which is penetrated by coal from Aachen, the Saar and Lorraine, and an equal part to northern Germany, penetrated by American, British and Polish coal arriving by sea.[10] American coal has at times also penetrated southern Germany by way of the Rhine. In neither of these two markets is there any important local coal production.[11] All suppliers in these two markets must deliver over relatively long distances. These two markets are "contested markets," to use the terms employed by the prewar Ruhr coal cartel.

About 10 per cent of the primary coal produced by the Ruhr is exported to other parts of the ECSC and to third-party countries.[12] Since Lorraine coal until recent years could be used for coking only to a limited extent, the steel plants in this area have been mainly dependent on solid fuels from the Ruhr. The Saar, Belgium and the Netherlands also need Ruhr coal to blend with their own coal for coke production, while Italy is, of course, entirely dependent on imported coal. Scandinavia, Austria and Switzerland are the main customers outside the ECSC for primary coal from the Ruhr.

Though Germany is a large exporter, it also imports large quantities, mainly for use in the coastal and southern provinces. In 1957 it imported 50 per cent

[7] Calculated from ECE, *Quarterly Bulletin of Coal Statistics; Jahrbuch.*

[8] In 1955 the mine cokeries accounted for 80 per cent of Germany's total production of manufactured gas. *Jahrbuch*, 1956, p. 672.

[9] *Jahrbuch*, 1956, p. 673.

[10] HA, *Transports des produits du traité*, September 1958. Another 3 per cent of the Ruhr coal is shipped to the center of Germany.

[11] Preussag, the government-owned mining company in Lower Saxony, produces about 2.5 million tons of noncoking coal.

[12] *Glückauf*, May 11, 1957, p. 594.

more coal than it exported in primary form. The United States is now the major source of the coal imported by Germany. American and Ruhr coal are rivals not only in Germany but also in other ECSC markets.

Markets for German Coke

The German steelworks—for the most part vertically integrated with the coke producers, whether mines or otherwise—have in recent years taken about 40 per cent of the metallurgical coke produced in Germany, produced for the most part in the Ruhr, with secondary areas of production in Aachen and Lower Saxony. Nearly 30 per cent has been exported, three fifths of which has gone to the other ECSC countries. Steel firms in Lorraine and Luxembourg that are financially integrated with German coke producers take most of the Ruhr coke that moves to the rest of the ECSC. The Scandinavian countries take most of the remaining two fifths of the coke exported by Germany and use it either for steel production (Sweden) or heating (the small sizes of coke taken by Denmark). The remaining 30 per cent of the coke that remains in Germany—most of which consists of the smaller sizes not suitable for use in the blast furnace—is distributed mainly in the northern and southern provinces for space heating in competition with briquettes and liquid fuels.[13] The Ruhr enjoys a near monopoly of the metallurgical coke required by steel producing districts outside Germany that need additional quantities to supplement their own.

Markets for German Steel

Open-hearth and electric-furnace steel account for 58 per cent of the total steel produced in Germany. Thomas steel is based on low-grade domestic ores, while the open-hearth steel is based on imported high-grade ores. The open-hearth plants also use local scrap since the Ruhr is a highly developed steel transforming center for engineering, heavy equipment and other investment goods. Producing five sixths of the steel in Germany, North Rhine–Westphalia in 1952 consumed nearly 60 per cent of its own steel production, shipped 28 per cent to the rest of Germany, and exported 12 per cent. It supplied more than 85 per cent of its own consumption and obtained a small quantity from the rest of Germany and from abroad.[14]

---

[13] HA, *Sixième rapport général*, Vol. II, pp. 351 ff; HA, *Transports des produits du traité*, Part III, Table 3; ECE, *Quarterly Bulletin of Coal Statistics* and *Quarterly Bulletin of Steel Statistics*.

[14] Harald Jörgensen, *Die westeuropäische Montanindustrie und ihr gemeinsamer Markt*, Vandenhoeck, Göttingen, 1955, p. 160 and Appendix Table 22. Data include tubes but exclude special quality steel, semifinished steel and forgings. Cf. Hanns-Jürgen Kunze, *Die Lagerungsordnung des westeuropäischen Eisen- und Stahlindustrie im Lichte ihrer Kostenstruktur*, Kieler Studien, Kiel, 1954.

Germany favors the "indirect" export of steel in the form of manufactured and durable goods, on which the returns are higher than on steel itself. It therefore imports as well as exports steel. This structure of production also promotes the accumulation of scrap and improves the terms of trade by enabling the Ruhr to exchange capital-intensive goods for imports of labor-intensive products like iron ore, other raw materials and foodstuffs. Manufacturing and mining are responsible for a much higher proportion of national product in Germany than in the other ECSC countries or the United Kingdom. Percentages for 1955 were:[15]

	Per Cent of Net Domestic Product from Mining and Manufacturing
Germany	59
France	40*
Belgium	36
Luxembourg	41
Italy	33
Netherlands	44
United Kingdom	41

* The figure for France refers to 1950, the last year for which data were available.

Coal and steel in the Ruhr thus show similar structural characteristics in geographical concentration of production and consumption, vertical integration between producing and processing industries, transformation of raw and semifinished products into finished goods and exporting of transformed rather than raw products.

OTHER GERMAN AREAS

The coal mines near Aachen on the left bank of the Rhine are in the same administrative district, North Rhine–Westphalia, as the Ruhr; but by location, ownership (they are largely owned by non-German steel companies) and type (only 15 per cent, strictly speaking, is coking coal though a larger proportion is put to that use) are not tied to the Ruhr complex. They provide solid fuels for foreign steel groups and also ship coal to the rest of Germany, particularly southern Germany, to which they are nearer than is the Ruhr. Transportwise, the Aachen mines can ship northward through the Dutch canals, at Maastricht, and southward through the Rhine, or by rail and river. Rail connections from Aachen to the Ruhr ports add to freight costs, however, and tend to offset the freight advantage in some parts of southern Germany.

[15] UN, *Monthly Bulletin of Statistics*, March 1957.

The rest of Germany, apart from North Rhine–Westphalia and the Saar, produces only 17 per cent of the steel, only 3 per cent of the hard coal, but nearly all the iron ore. The Lower Saxony is the most important of the other areas, producing over 10 per cent of the steel and nearly three fifths of Germany's iron ore. The steel plants there, aside from the one at Bremen, are based on local ore but draw on the Ruhr for solid fuels. The growth of the Salzgitter as a steel producing center was made feasible by this turnabout traffic. The Salzgitter ore in Lower Saxony averages 30 to 32 per cent iron but is low in phosphorus; two thirds of the production is shipped to the Ruhr. Some of these plants were established in the late 1930s, when they were known as the Hermann Göring works.

Not in an industrialized steel consuming area and having lost their prewar markets in eastern Germany, the Salzgitter steel plants for the most part must sell in other industrial centers against competition from local steel producers there. In 1952 they sold about 40 per cent of their steel along the north German coast, 20 per cent in North Rhine–Westphalia, 15 per cent to export and the remainder in other parts of Germany.[16] In their most important market, along the coastline, the steel plants in Lower Saxony are now challenged by the new steelworks of the Klöckner Company at Bremen. Operating with foreign ore and United States coal, this Bremen plant started production in 1957 with an initial capacity of 350,000 tons of open-hearth steel, rolled largely into flat products for shipbuilding and export. The plant is similar in conception to the Ijmuiden plant in the Netherlands, discussed later in this chapter.

Outside North Rhine–Westphalia, the Saar and Lower Saxony, German production of the ECSC products is negligible and of purely local significance.

MARKETS IN FRANCE

The markets for French steel and solid fuels, shown in Tables 6 and 7, respectively, are widely scattered and not as geographically concentrated as in Germany. Paris, the largest consuming area, is outside the steel producing districts. The French steel industry, moreover, exports about one third of its production. Only northern France consumes a large portion of its own steel and coal output. Lorraine steel and a large portion of Lorraine coal have to be marketed elsewhere. The coal produced in Centre-Midi is also marketed over a large area. Coal consumption is much less concentrated geographically, and imports of solid fuels are much more important, than in Germany. Gross imports of solid fuels have provided about 20 per cent of total consumption since the second world war (as against 35 per cent in 1929); they provided 10 per

[16] Jörgensen, *op. cit.*, p. 160 and Appendix Table 22.

Table 6

FRANCE: PERCENTAGE DISTRIBUTION OF STEEL CONSUMPTION, BY AREA, 1950–1951

Area	Per Cent
Paris region	30.8
Nord and Pas-de-Calais	21.4
Nancy and Alsace	11.8
Lyons	9.8
Reims	6.1
Rouen	4.4
Nantes	4.2
Dijon	2.8
Marseilles	2.6
Other[a]	5.1
Total	100.0

Source: Avis, Conseil de la République, No. 64, 1952, p. 29, Note 2. For data on geographic distribution of principal shapes, see *ibid.,* pp. 29–34. For slightly different percentages, see *Inventaire,* p. 134.

[a] Includes Bordeaux, Montpellier, Toulouse, Limoges and Clermont-Ferrand.

cent of German coal consumption in 1955–1956. France is not a large coal exporter. Many of the areas, including Paris and Lorraine, use a larger proportion of imported solid fuels than the nation as a whole. Imported coal is used for coking purposes, for space heating and for the production of briquettes, the producers of which are located along the Atlantic coast.

Table 7

FRANCE: PERCENTAGE DISTRIBUTION OF CONSUMPTION OF SOLID FUELS OF FRENCH ORIGIN AND OF ALL SOLID FUELS, BY AREA, 1929[a]

Area	French Origin	Total	French Solid Fuels as Per Cent of Total
Paris region	13.0	14.5	55
Nord	37.0	26.1	88
Est	14.0	24.4	36
Lyons and Centre	16.8	11.7	88
Champagne	3.2	3.0	64
Rouen	1.7	3.5	30
West Coast	1.0	6.3	10
Mediterranean	7.1	5.7	77
Other[b]	6.2	4.8	73
Total	100.0	100.0	(65)

Source: Robert Lafitte-Laplace, *L'Economie charbonnière de la France,* Marcel Giard, Paris, 1933, pp. 505–507.

[a] Coal equivalent of solid fuels, exclusive of consumption by railroads and internal navigation.
[b] Includes the Loire area and Toulouse.

LORRAINE

Lorraine is divided into two French departments, Meurthe-et-Moselle, which comprises the western portion of Lorraine, and the Moselle along the river of the same name. The steel plants are in both departments but most of the iron ore and all the coal are in the Moselle. The Germans acquired the present Moselle area in 1871 by the Treaty of Frankfurt but they were then unaware of the importance of the iron ore deposit, which is high in phosphorus. It had little commercial value before the Thomas converter for removing phosphorus from steel was invented in 1879. Afterward the Germans built several large steelworks in the Moselle area. These plants, being only partially integrated, supplied pig iron and raw steel to the Ruhr for further processing, as well as to their own limited rolling facilities. The Germans were not interested in developing the area as a rival to the Ruhr. The French in the late nineteenth century also developed several steel plants in Meurthe-et-Moselle.

The French regained the Moselle in 1918 by the Treaty of Versailles and the French government took over the German facilities for the French steel industry but did not further industrialize the area because of its exposed strategic position. Nor did the French promote the canalization of the trinational (France, Germany, Luxembourg) Moselle River for fear of having Lorraine fall under the domination of the German economy and the Ruhr.[17]

Despite its large steel production Lorraine has remained basically agricultural and it produces steel products for consumption elsewhere. Lorraine has therefore been compared to a colonial area,[18] though the French government reversed its policy on Lorraine after the second world war.

Lorraine Coal

Only about 13 per cent of Lorraine coal was used for metallurgical purposes in 1955, partly at mine, partly at steel, coke works (compared with nearly 45 per cent metallurgical use for Ruhr coal). Only in a blend with Ruhr and Saar coal could Lorraine coal be used in the coke oven. But recent experiments have indicated that larger quantities of Lorraine coal can be used metallurgically (up to 85 per cent of the coke-oven charge).[19]

[17] The Metz-Thionville Canal to Strasbourg, opened in 1932, and giving the Lorraine steel industry access to the upper Rhine and to Paris by the Rhine-Marne Canal, was of secondary importance. Frederic Benham, *The Iron and Steel Industry of Germany, France, Belgium, Luxembourg and the Saar*, London and Cambridge Economic Service, London, October 1934, p. 6.

[18] Emile Rideau, *Essor et problèmes d'une région française*, Les Editions Ouvrières, Paris, 1956, p. 230.

[19] On the metallurgical input of Lorraine coal, see Charbonnages de France, *Rapport de gestion*, 1955, p. 55; Chambre Syndicale de la Sidérurgie Française (série rose), *France*, 1954. The Lorraine steel plants operate their own adjacent coke ovens using mainly coal from other areas. They sell surplus gas and electricity to the public power system. *Avis*, Conseil de la République, No. 64, 1952, p. 22, note 1, foresees the Lorraine coal mines supplying 100 per cent of the coal for coking by 1961, an estimate that may be overoptimistic; other reports indicate that Lorraine mines will furnish up to 85 per cent.

Only 35 per cent of the coal produced in Lorraine in 1955 was consumed by the mines and other consumers in the area; most of the coal not consumed in Lorraine itself is shipped to widely scattered parts of France, including the Paris area.[20]

Lorraine Steel

Lorraine iron ore is more easily mined than Lorraine coal. Since the seams are thick, flat and shallow, the Lorraine iron mines compare favorably with American bituminous coal mines in efficiency and mechanization. Though low in iron content, the Lorraine ore is partly self-fluxing. The availability of ore but dearth of capital scrap have caused Lorraine to concentrate on Thomas steel, which accounts for 75 per cent of its production.[21] Being landlocked as well as nonindustrialized, Lorraine does not have the opportunity to draw on overseas supplies of coal, high-grade iron ore or scrap to increase its open-hearth production. Though the proportion of open-hearth to total steel production is low, Lorraine is also the largest open-hearth steel producing area in France with a capacity largely geared to absorb its circulating scrap. Some of the scrap consumed in Lorraine is, however, purchased. All together Lorraine produces nearly 70 per cent of French steel and 78 per cent of French pig iron.

Owing to the dearth of local supplies of coking coal in Lorraine, 90 per cent of the combined coal and coke consumed by its steel plants in 1954 originated outside the area, though this ratio may be reduced by the recent experiments in the use of Lorraine coal. Lorraine obtains solid fuels from the north of France, the Ruhr, Belgium, the Netherlands and the Saar. Nearly 75 per cent originated outside of France entirely (Saar considered outside). About one third of the coal and 90 per cent of the coke France imported that year were consigned to the French steel industry, largely to the steelworks in Lorraine,[22] as shown in Table 8.

[20] Charbonnages de France, *Rapport de gestion*, 1953; Rideau, *op. cit.*, p. 76; HA, *Transports des produits du traité*, Part III, Table 1. The mining industry in 1955 accounted for over 35 per cent of the thermal power produced in France. The power stations operated by the Lorraine coal mines accounted for one fourth the power produced by the mining industry as a whole. Lorraine accounted for only 17 per cent of the gas and coke produced by the French mining industry though it produces one fourth the coal in France.

[21] The high proportion of Thomas steel aggravates the local scarcity of coking coal since the Thomas process requires a high ratio of pig iron to steel. Furthermore, since Lorraine iron ore is low in iron, more coke per ton of pig iron is consumed in Lorraine than in most other areas. In 1955, for example, 1.021 tons of coke were consumed per ton of pig iron in France (with Lorraine predominant) as compared with Germany, 0.933; Saar, 1.011; Belgium, 0.883; Italy, 0.928; but Luxembourg, which uses a lower grade of ore, 1.101. Table 14, showing input of raw materials per ton of steel for France as a whole, clearly indicates how the input of coal increases with the input of iron ore.

[22] In 1954 the French steel industry as a whole obtained 77 per cent of its coking smalls outside the country (with 40 per cent from Germany and 23 per cent from the Saar) and 64 per cent of its coke from abroad (35 per cent from Germany). HA, "Bilan de deux ans de fonctionnement du marché commun pour la sidérurgie française," Luxembourg, June 4, 1955 (unpublished memorandum), Appendix Table 2.

The Lorraine steel industry is vertically integrated both as to production and ownership with Lorraine iron ore and with foreign coal. But it is not integrated with nationalized French coal at all. The Lorraine steel firms, however, control a large amount of foreign coking coal and coke. (See Chapter 5.) Such control provides a part but not all of its input.

The Lorraine steel industry—indeed, the French steel industry almost as a whole—is much less integrated with metal consuming plants than the German. As a result of this lesser integration and lack of local metal transforming plants, Lorraine steel seeks its markets far from the point of production.

Table 8

FRANCE: PER CENT OF SOLID FUEL IMPORTS CONSIGNED
TO THE STEEL INDUSTRY, BY ORIGIN, 1954[a]

Origin	Coal	Coke	Total
Germany	41	92	61
Saar[b]	26	66	31
Belgium	32	91	47
Netherlands	49	100	81
Total ECSC	33	89	50
United Kingdom	27	—	27
United States	50	—	50
TOTAL	33	89	48

Sources: ECE, *Quarterly Bulletin of Coal Statistics* for total imports; Chambre Syndicale de la Sidérurgie Française (série rose), *France*, 1954, for consignments to steel industry.

[a] Coal and coke are ton for ton. A small quantity of coal consigned to the steel industry for fuel is excluded.

[b] Exclusive of Saar coal consigned to the Lorraine coke works of Charbonnages de France.

Only about 13 per cent of Lorraine steel stays in the region.[23] About 54 per cent is delivered to the rest of France excluding the Lorraine area. About 13 per cent is exported to the rest of the ECSC (Saar included) and about 20 per cent to third countries. One third of the Lorraine steel is thus exported. The Moselle contributes much more to export than Meurthe-et-Moselle because the latter, being closer to French consuming areas, supplies a larger portion of its output to the internal market.[24]

Most of the outbound steel and inbound fuel is shipped by rail. The Ruhr steel industry, on the other hand, receives its iron ore by water transport and markets most of its steel in the area. Lorraine steel's advantage in being lo-

[23] Lorraine takes about one half million tons of finished steel, in addition, from the Saar and northern France. HA, *Transports des produits du traité*, Part III, Table 9.

[24] These estimates covering 1957 and finished products only (excluding semifinished steel) are from *ibid.*, and from HA, *Bulletin statistique*. Cf. Kunze, *op. cit.*, pp. 79–80, for the distribution of Lorraine steel in 1936–1937.

cated near a cheap source of iron ore is thus offset by its distance from markets and the lack of satisfactory connections for water transport.

NORD AND PAS-DE-CALAIS

Northern France is more balanced and self-contained than Lorraine. It is a small-scale Ruhr. Perhaps the most industrialized part of France, it is the largest coal producing and the second largest steel producing area in that country. A large proportion of its steel and coal is marketed within the area. It has access to the sea at Dunkerque, to which it is linked by a none-too-modern canal, and at Antwerp. The area, as the combined name indicates, comprises two departments. Pas-de-Calais, west of the Nord, is predominantly a coal producing and agricultural region; the Nord contains a complex of coal, steel and metal transforming industries. The area also encompasses a large number of nonintegrated rolling mills in the valley of the Sambre that obtain metal from the larger works and fabricate a variety of specialized products. The integrated steelworks are at Valenciennes, Denain, Anzin, Hautmont, Louvroil and at Isbergues, close to the port of Dunkerque.

Although the mines in northern France and southern Belgium are on the same coal deposit and steel plants are located on both sides of the frontier, each area is oriented by economic and historic ties and by transport routes to its own national economy.

The Northern Area and Its Steel Market

The north as a whole accounts for 22 per cent of French crude steel output. More than half the steel in the north is open hearth (39 per cent of the total French production of that type); 38 per cent is Thomas (14 per cent of total French Thomas production). The ratio of pig iron to steel is lower, and the ratio of scrap to steel higher, than in Lorraine or the country as a whole because of the capital scrap generated by local transforming industries.

The availability of scrap and coking coal and the propinquity to Dunkerque give the steel plants of the north definite advantages in themselves and these advantages also serve to compensate for the high cost of assembling low-grade ore from Lorraine by railroad. The north has reduced the need for ore per ton of steel by relying on a high scrap ratio and by using rich iron ore from Normandy and overseas ore brought in at Dunkerque. A lower ore ratio per ton of pig iron also reduces the need for coke, although the area has a surplus of coke.[25]

[25] Chambre Syndicale de la Sidérurgie Française (série rose), *France,* 1954.

The northern area has turned increasingly to the production of specialized steel products such as tubes, flat products and cold-rolled sheet. These specializations reduce its vulnerability to competition and increase its returns per unit of sale. Lorraine, on the other hand, produces a wide range of the more competitive, low-profit products.

The sales pattern of the steel produced in the north differs markedly from that of Lorraine. Whereas Lorraine exports over one third of its steel, the steel plants in the north export only 14 per cent;[26] the plants in Lorraine sell 13 per cent of their steel output locally, those in the north sell 41 per cent locally (Nord and Pas-de-Calais) and distribute another 20 per cent in the adjacent area between the north and greater Paris. Only 25 per cent of the steel produced in the north goes farther than Paris.[27] But while Nord and Pas-de-Calais consume more of their own production than Lorraine, they do not provide as great a local market as the Ruhr.

The North and Its Coal Market

Nord and Pas-de-Calais is the only French coal producing area in which coking coal is produced where required. (Although the Centre-Midi also produces coking coal, it does not produce much pig iron.) Thirty-nine per cent of the coal produced there is of coking quality. (See Table 4.) The area accounts for 75 per cent of the coke produced by Charbonnages de France and for about 40 per cent of all French coke production.[28] The north supplies nearly all the coke required by local blast furnaces and has a surplus for shipment to Lorraine. About 45 per cent of the coal produced in Nord and Pas-de-Calais is consequently used for coke production, processed into secondary products —electricity and briquettes—and distributed to miners. Compared with Lorraine, the area also enjoys the advantage of producing a wider variety of coals.[29] The proportion of high-flame coal, which tends to be marginal, is small in Nord and Pas-de-Calais but high in the Lorraine mines.

As in the Ruhr, the coke works in the north are operated by the mines rather than by the steel plants. But unlike the Ruhr mines, the northern mines are nationalized rather than financially integrated with the steel industry. Since the steel firms of the north do not own the cokeries, they do not have an integrated fuel economy; they purchase not only their coke but also much of

[26] *Inventaire*, p. 125; the figures for the north refer to 1949–1953, for Lorraine to 1957.

[27] *Ibid.*, pp. 125–134.

[28] Data are for 1955 and are drawn from Charbonnages de France, *Rapport de gestion*, 1955, p. 55; ECE, *Quarterly Bulletin of Coal Statistics;* Chambre Syndicale de la Sidérurgie Française (série rose), *France*, 1954.

[29] See HA, *Bulletin statistique*, for coal production by type.

their gas and electricity from Charbonnages de France or the public power system.[30]

About a third of the total solid fuel production (coal, coke and briquettes) is marketed locally, 37 per cent in Paris and the intervening area (water transport being used rather extensively for the shorter hauls) and another 20 per cent in Normandy and Lorraine. Exports are not significant.[31] The market is characterized by a relatively short radius, by customers who have no alternative supplies, the larger ones buying directly from the producers. The mines in Nord and Pas-de-Calais are therefore in a relatively "protected" position, although they sometimes complain in business recessions of competition from Belgian anthracite shipped to Paris and from Ruhr coke delivered in Lorraine.

OTHER FRENCH AREAS

Other smaller areas of French production of ECSC products are in the Centre-Midi, the southeast (Alps region), the west and the southwest. These areas produce 13 per cent of the steel in France. Three fifths of electric steel production, which accounts for about 8 per cent of the total French output of steel, is concentrated in the Centre-Midi and southeast (Alps). The steel produced in the southwest is primarily of open-hearth grade.

The Centre-Midi covers a wide area; St.-Etienne is the most important steel producing center in the area. Until the development of Lorraine, the Centre-Midi was the major pig iron producing area in France. Its steel plants are still located near sources of coal but coal is no longer very important there since electric and open-hearth steel are based largely on scrap. The steel plants in the Centre-Midi serve a special market consisting of producers of ordnance, machine tools and engineering goods. These customers, such as Schneider et Cie., are located near the steel plants and are for the most part financially integrated with them.

The western steel plants (at Caen and Rouen) and the southwestern steel plants (at St.-Nazaire and Bordeaux) are at tidewater. They use imported coal largely and obtain iron ore from scattered local deposits. These mainly open-hearth plants serve specialized end uses, such as shipbuilding steel and tinplate for the canning industry or export.

The widely dispersed mines in the Centre-Midi account for about 23 per cent of the French coal output; the principal producing areas are at Commentry, St.-Etienne and Le Creusot. Some of the mines are very high cost,

---

[30] In 1953 the steel plants of the north purchased one third of their gas and 60 per cent of their electricity requirements. *Inventaire*, pp. 83–89. The steel plant at Isbergues, near Dunkerque, is the only one that operates its own cokery, and it uses imported coal.

[31] *Ibid.*, p. 77; Charbonnages de France, *Rapport de gestion*, 1953, p. 22.

especially the Loire mines, which are, however, practically the only source of coking coal in the Centre-Midi; others, such as those at Blanzy, are efficient. The production of coke, gas and thermal power by the mines is not highly developed. Lacking a strong local market, located in an agricultural area and burdened with high costs, some of the mines in Centre-Midi are the coal "problem" of France. But the distance of the mines from other producers plus their dispersion protect them from outside competition though not from rivalry of liquid fuels and natural gas, the latter produced in the southwest at Lacq.

TRANSPORT IN FRANCE

Though the markets in France are dispersed, the movement of materials between regions within France and between France and other countries— either for the assembly of raw materials for steel production or for the outbound movement of coal and finished steel—occurs mainly by rail rather than water. Water transport is more economic than rail transport for bulky goods of low value, but Lorraine and Nord and Pas-de-Calais are not well served by adequate waterways though a cursory inspection of a waterways route map might indicate the contrary. Nearly all the coal that leaves Lorraine and 85 per cent of the solid fuels inbound are moved by rail. At least 90 per cent of the outbound steel also is shipped by rail, a good deal to Antwerp or Dunkerque. Present connections from Lorraine eastward to the Ruhr (except for the unsatisfactory water route through Strasbourg), northwestward to the north of France, and northward to the Low Country ports (the overseas export channel) are primarily by rail. The Moselle Canal project, when finished, will provide water connections to the Ruhr and Low Country ports via the Rhine. (See Chapter 12.) Although Saar coal can be transported to Lorraine by water and iron ore can be transported by water in the reverse direction, the route is slow, long and inadequate. The bulk of this traffic is therefore carried by the shorter rail route.

Water transport is but slightly better for Nord and Pas-de-Calais. Outward bound, 10 per cent of the steel and 58 per cent of the solid fuels are carried by water but only 10 per cent of the inbound iron ore, that coming via Dunkerque, is carried by water.[32] The canal-river systems in the northern part of the country were constructed during the First Empire or earlier and have been poorly maintained since. They are now inadequate for the size, speed and

[32] These data, from HA, *Transports des produits du traité, passim,* refer to 1957 and cover coal, coke, finished and semifinished steel products. They refer to shipments within the ECSC; the data on the mode of transport between these regions and third-party countries would not materially affect the distribution of traffic.

capacity of modern barges and river boats and lack the connections and carrying capacity of the waterways systems in Belgium, the Netherlands and
Germany. On the northern French waterways the carriers can travel at an
average speed of only 4 kilometers per hour as against 15 kilometers for carriers in Germany. Small locks and inadequate depth limit the French barges to
500 tons capacity. By contrast, German barges have a length of 85 meters and
a capacity of 1,500 tons.[33] Only the Seine River system between Paris and Le
Havre and the Rhone River system with an outlet at Marseilles have been
adequately developed, though the latter system, running through a less industrialized part of France, does not carry as much traffic as it is capable of. The
Rhine River system between Strasbourg and Switzerland (Basle) has also been
highly developed, but water connections between Strasbourg and Lorraine
are not satisfactory.

PROBLEMS OF
RUHR-LORRAINE INTEGRATION

Can Lorraine and the Ruhr form an integrated complex within the ECSC?

Their separation after 1919 has often been deplored on economic grounds
by writers who thought they were complementary.[34] The ECSC was in part
promoted to rebind Lorraine and the Ruhr.

When leaders in the German steel industry—Thyssen, Klöckner and
Deutsch-Luxemburgische—built and controlled the Moselle plants before
1918 they brought to the Ruhr pig iron and crude steel produced in Lorraine.
Since it requires three tons of Lorraine ore to produce one ton of metal, the
Germans preferred to transport metal. Even when Germany controlled the
Moselle, Lorraine ore provided only 25 per cent of the Ruhr's total consump-
tion of ore. The Ruhr, on the other hand, provided Lorraine with surplus coke
for smelting the ore where it was mined.

However complementary the two areas were under common German financial control, there was nothing "natural" about it. And after 1918 quite a
different structure was created which made Lorraine and the Ruhr rivals. In
the 1920s the Lorraine steel firms, under French ownership, built additional
rolling mills in Lorraine and the German steel firms additional metal producing facilities in the Ruhr. The steel plants in each area became more integrated
locally. By 1929 the Ruhr had reduced its input of Lorraine ore to 14 per cent

---

[33] *Le Monde*, February 14, 1957, p. 10, contains an excellent analysis of the waterways in
northern France.

[34] J. M. Keynes, *Economic Consequences of the Peace*, Harcourt, Brace and Howe, New York,
1920, pp. 99–100; Guy Greer, *The Ruhr-Lorraine Industrial Problem*, Macmillan, New York, 1925.

of Ruhr ore consumption,[35] and by 1937 to nearly zero. Lorraine supplied about 3 per cent of the ore used in the Ruhr in 1957. In cutting its links to Lorraine ore, the Ruhr increased its open-hearth steel output, its import of high-grade ores, and the production and input of high-cost domestic low-grade iron ore in order to become more self-sufficient in ore. It is hardly likely that the Ruhr would change its policy of importing high-grade ore for the sake of taking Lorraine ore, or that the Ruhr would displace German ore with Lorraine ore because home-produced ore will become scarcer in the ECSC relative to total needs. The opening of the Moselle Canal in the late 1960s might encourage the Ruhr to take more Lorraine ore but not enough of it to change the basic relationships between the two areas. The investment involved on both sides is now too great to return to the relationship antedating the first world war. In fact, the Lorraine steel plants look to the Moselle Canal as a means of transport for import into Lorraine of some high-grade foreign ores and for export of finished steel. The relationship between the two is therefore likely to remain one-sided with respect to raw materials and competitive with respect to steel.[36]

LUXEMBOURG

The steel plants in Luxembourg use low-grade ore from within the country and also import a slightly higher grade from Lorraine. Practically all the steel produced in Luxembourg is thus of Thomas quality. Blast furnace coke comes entirely by rail from the Ruhr and Aachen. Scrap requirements are negligible. Thus Luxembourg, of all the steel producing countries, has the highest ore ratio, one of the highest coal ratios, and the lowest scrap ratio per ton of steel. (See Table 14 in Chapter 3.) The Luxembourg steelworks generate most of the electricity and gas required by the country. But their heat production is not integrated at the coking stage because coke must come from outside. Integration of heat production in Luxembourg would not be advantageous, anyhow, because of the limited market for surplus gas and electricity in this small country.

Luxembourg is mainly an exporter of steel. An extension geographically of the Lorraine steel industry, it is organizationally within the orbit of the Belgium-Luxembourg economic union. With a population of only 300,000, in 1957 it retained less than 100,000 tons of its steel, which is only about 4 per

---

[35] Benham, *op. cit.*, p. 20.

[36] For a discussion of the Moselle Canal and its consequences, see Chapter 12.

The annual report for 1957 of the Groupement de l'Industrie Sidérurgique expressed the intention of the French steel industry to import larger quantities of rich ore in order to offset the declining reserves of lean ore in Lorraine; report summarized in *Handelsblatt*, August 8–9, 1958, p. 6.

cent of production. Landlocked, Luxembourg's steel is shipped entirely by rail. One third of it went to Belgium in 1957, and 40 per cent to Antwerp for export by maritime transport. Fifteen per cent went to Germany, largely to southern Germany, the rest to France and the Saar. It contributed over one third of the steel exported by the Belgium-Luxembourg customs union. Rail haulage to Antwerp is less of a disadvantage to Luxembourg than to Lorraine, the distance to this port being shorter from Luxembourg.[37]

BELGIUM

The Belgian steel industry is organizationally within the orbit of the Belgium-Luxembourg economic union. But geographically the main portion of it is closer to the French steelworks in the north, both essentially located on the same coal field. (See Table 3.) The Belgium-Luxembourg economic union produces steel mainly for export. Northern France, on the other hand, though contiguous to the Belgian works, produces steel largely for French customers.

There are two coal fields in Belgium—one in the south and another in the east, called the Campine, in a deposit which crosses the southern part of the Netherlands and extends to the left bank of the Rhine. The southern field extends, with breaks, from Liége to Charleroi and then into the area of France called Nord and Pas-de-Calais. The mines in the Campine as well as their counterparts in Holland are relatively new, intensive exploitation having started shortly after the first world war. These new mines are much better laid out and larger than the mines in southern Belgium. The Campine also yields a higher proportion of coking coal than the southern mines (Table 4), though no coke is produced there.

The coal mines in southern Belgium rank with some of the British mines as the oldest in Europe. These Belgian mines are also the deepest, their seams thin and heavily faulted. They have the highest production costs in Europe but have been kept in production by subsidies. The coal problem of southern Belgium is examined in Chapters 4 and 9.

The Belgian steel plants are concentrated at Charleroi and Liége, near the southern coal field and at Athus, which is in the southeastern corner of the country near that part of the Lorraine-Luxembourg iron ore field on which the steel plants in Luxembourg and northern Lorraine (the Longwy district) are also located. Largely dependent on Lorraine ore, the Thomas process accounts for 90 per cent of Belgian steel. Ore requirements and coking coal requirements are lower than in Lorraine or Luxembourg because the Belgian steel plants

[37] The data on the movement of finished steel products in 1957 are from HA, *Transports des produits du traité*, Part III, Table 9.

can more economically draw on imported high-grade ore (through Antwerp) and because the area is more industrialized than Lorraine or Luxembourg, thus enabling the steel plants to obtain a large amount of capital scrap for blast furnace pig iron production. The domestic supply of coking coal is inadequate and not up to the quality of Ruhr coal. The Belgian coke ovens import over 20 per cent of their requirements; these imports account for about 60 per cent of the total coal imported by Belgium.

The high cost of coke in Belgium, owing to high production costs of coal, has encouraged the steel industry there to reduce the input of coke through a high scrap charge at the blast furnace stage. This charge is the highest on the Continent. To further reduce coke requirements the Belgian steel industry has replaced some Lorraine ore with high-grade Swedish ore. In 1955, 2.5 million tons of Swedish ore were imported compared with 0.3 million tons in 1937.

The Belgian steel industry is highly integrated. Since it produces about 75 per cent of its coke requirements, it derives the benefits of an integrated heat economy, for one thing. The steel industry is substantially under the same financial control as the large metal transforming plants and the shipyards; it is thus financially integrated with its end-product customers. It is, furthermore, close to them geographically; the Sambre-Meuse river valley, in which steel, coal and other industries are located, is the most industrialized part of the country. Finally, the same financial groups that control the steel industry also control a considerable part of the coal industry.

Exporting is the dominant marketing feature of Belgian steel. Belgium by itself supplies about two thirds of the steel exported by the Belgium-Luxembourg union, which in turn is the largest exporter of steel in the world.[38]

Access to the sea at Antwerp, which is linked to the industrial hinterland of Belgium by a dense and highly developed system of canals, has been a vital factor in the Belgian export trade. That trade is in turn the dominant feature of the country's economy. Belgium also has the densest railway system in the world. Even so, the highly organized river canal system, traversing the main cities and connecting Ostende and Zeebrugge as well as Antwerp to the hinterland, is the core of its transportation network. Through the mining and steel producing area in the south run the Sambre and Meuse rivers, which are canalized from Charleroi to Liége; at Liége the Albert Canal begins and runs north through the Campine to Antwerp. A canal is now being built to connect Charleroi directly with Antwerp by water, thus bypassing the Albert Canal. The Belgian waterways system also connects with the other Low Country areas and with the Ruhr.

[38] See Carlo Hemmer, *L'Economie du Grand-Duché de Luxembourg*, 2ème Partie, Joseph Beffort, Luxembourg, 1953, pp. 150–156; Kunze, *op. cit.*, p. 81.

THE SAAR

As small in area as Luxembourg[39] but with almost one million inhabitants (thrice the density of Luxembourg), the Saar has been politically afloat since World War I. By the Treaty of Versailles the Saar was in the French customs union but was controlled by a League of Nations commission until 1935 when the inhabitants chose to return to Germany in a referendum provided for by the treaty. In October 1947 the Saar, again by popular referendum, rejoined the French economic union. In 1956 the populace voted for reincorporation into Germany and this became politically effective January 1, 1957. Exit from the French customs union was completed gradually by the end of 1959. In spite of these changing political fortunes, production and trade in Saar coal and steel have been remarkably stable, though exports from, and imports into, France or Germany fluctuate statistically with the Saar's inclusion in one or the other.[40]

The Saar coal mines, which are public property, changed ownership with each change in political orientation. Some of the Saar steelworks, all of which are under private control, were transferred from German to French ownership after the first world war, but from the 1920s to date their ownership has been more stable.

With a small population and a relatively large output of coal and steel, the Saar produces mainly for export. Essentially landlocked and east of Lorraine, it trades chiefly with southern Germany and with France. France and Germany in 1955 absorbed 90 per cent of the steel exported by the Saar (or 60 per cent of its production) and about 85 per cent of the solid fuels exported (about one third the coal produced). It does not import coal or steel in large quantities,[41] but for its iron ore it depends almost entirely on Lorraine. It therefore produces mainly Thomas steel, 76 per cent Thomas and 23 per cent open hearth, or about the same proportions as Lorraine. The Saar's supply of Lorraine ore is either captive or purchased on long-term contract.

A river system partly canalized by the Saar and the Rhine canals between the Saar and Lorraine is not now heavily used, for it is winding and slow. Nearly all the bulky products move in and out of the Saar by rail. The Saar takes about four tons of ore from Lorraine for every ton of solid fuels it ships to that area.

[39] Both are less than 1,000 square miles in area.

[40] Trade between the Saar and other regions is shown separately in this study wherever necessary, provided separate data are available.

[41] Imports of coal from the Ruhr and of semifinished steel from Lorraine are almost entirely for the steel industry for further processing.

With local coal supplying about 85 per cent of the coking requirements, the Saar steel plants enjoy the advantage of an integrated heat economy. Eighty per cent of the Saar coke is produced by the steel industry. Mined from the same geological deposit as Lorraine coal, Saar coal nevertheless includes a type called Gras A as distinguished from Lorraine's higher-volatile Gras B. Gras A is adaptable for coke production when blended with Ruhr coal. The Lorraine steel industry thus imports Gras A and coke from the Saar in relatively important quantities.

The Saar produces two fifths as much steel as Lorraine and about the same volume of steel as Luxembourg but markets more of its steel locally, a fact which distinguishes it from both Luxembourg and Lorraine. In 1957 the Saarland consumed about one quarter of its output of finished steel for metal transformation.[42] Compared with 1926–1934 when the Saarland retained an average of 11 per cent of its own steel, industrialization has increased considerably. The Saar produces rolling stock, iron wares, machinery and construction equipment. The scrap supply is thus also proportionately higher than in Luxembourg or Lorraine.

The Saar, Lorraine and the Ruhr are rivals in the south German steel and coal markets. The Saar and Lorraine also are rivals in the French steel market. That part of the solid fuels exported by the Saar that is not consigned to French metallurgical needs also competes with Lorraine coal in French markets.

THE NETHERLANDS

The Netherlands produces several varieties of coal. In the Netherlands, as in the Ruhr, the conversion of coal to coke increases the returns on this labor-intensive raw material. One third of indigenous Netherlands coal production is consumed in the Limburg cokeries. The Juliana Canal, passable by vessels of 2,000-ton capacity, connects the Limburg area to the Low Country ports. The Netherlands exported 29 per cent of its coal—stated in coal equivalents— in 1955 and imported eight million tons, a figure equal to two thirds of its own coal output.

The Dutch steel plant at Ijmuiden, situated on the North Sea coast west of Amsterdam and north of the entrance to the harbor of Rotterdam, assembles its iron ore by sea. Largely geared to export and to the needs of the Dutch shipyards, the Ijmuiden works produce open-hearth steel of high unit value, mainly flat-rolled products. About two thirds of its finished steel is exported;

---

[42] *Handelsblatt*, October 26, 1956; and HA, *Transports des produits du traité*, Part III, Table 9. Kunze, *op. cit.*, pp. 78–79, says the Saarland consumed 31.8 per cent of its own steel production in 1951–1952. See also Benham, *op. cit.*, p. 46.

Germany is the largest single customer but non-ECSC countries as a whole take most of its exported steel. The Netherlands also exports semifinished steel, largely to Germany, and substantial quantities of foundry pig iron. The Netherlands imports and exports a relatively large quantity of steel as well as coal. It is potentially one of the most competitive import markets in the ECSC for coal and steel.

ITALY

Italy lacks coal and has a limited supply of iron ore. But a relatively large steel industry has been created in Italy in spite of these deficiencies. Imported raw materials furnish a large percentage of all materials used in the steel industry as shown below:[43]

	Per Cent
Iron ore	60
Scrap	52
Coal for coke production	100

No other country in the ECSC is so dependent on imports for all steel-making materials. Owing to these deficiencies, nearly a third of the steel industry is located at tidewater where it has access to imported materials; most of the remainder, producing a relatively large amount of electric-furnace steel, is

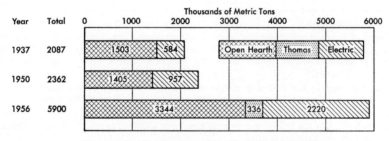

FIG. 2. Italy: Production of Crude Steel, by Grade[a]

Source: British Iron and Steel Federation, *Yearbooks.*

[a] A small quantity of Bessemer steel is included in the open-hearth figures for 1937.

located in the north, where Alpine water power is abundant and local scrap is furnished by the industrial centers of Milan, Genoa and Turin.[44]

The Italian steel industry almost trebled its output between 1937 and 1956 (Table 2-2 in Appendix E). The production of electric steel nearly quad-

[43] ECE, *Quarterly Bulletin of Coal Statistics;* Statistisches Bundesamt, Düsseldorf; and Table 11.

[44] The plant at Aosta, in the northwest corner, is based on a local iron ore deposit.

rupled; the production of Thomas steel was a postwar development. Open-hearth production only doubled. The growth of crude steel production, by grade, is given in Fig. 2.

Prior to its postwar expansion Italian steel production had been confined to small open-hearth and electric-furnace plants treating scrap and to non-integrated rolling mills. Many of these prewar plants still survive and are the problem children of the Italian steel industry; the ECSC treaty consequently allowed Italy to maintain a tariff on imports (though progressively diminishing) until the end of the transitional period of the ECSC in February 1958.

Table 9

ITALY: PIG IRON AND CRUDE STEEL PRODUCTION,
BY REGION AND PROCESS, 1953[a]

(*Thousands of Metric Tons*)

Product and Process	Tidewater[b]	Inland[c]	Total
Pig iron:			
Blast furnace	676.5	262.7	939.2
Electric furnace	—	283.1	283.1
Total	676.5	545.8	1,222.3
Crude steel:			
Open hearth	648.8	1,084.2	1,733.0
Thomas	258.1	—	258.1
Electric	187.3	1,321.4	1,508.7
Total	1,094.2	2,405.6	3,499.8

Source: British Iron and Steel Federation, *Yearbook, 1953*, Part II.

[a] Some of the production classified in the source as coming from "other districts" had to be assigned arbitrarily. "Other" pig iron has been classified as inland since it must have originated in Umbria or Veneto-Trentino. "Other" steel must have originated in Venezia Giulia and is thus assigned to tidewater.

[b] Plants located in the following provinces have been classified as tidewater: Campagna (Naples), Liguria (Genoa), Tuscany (Piombino), Venezia Giulia. Some of the plants in Tuscany and Venezia Giulia are not directly at tidewater but nevertheless enjoy favorable access to the sea.

[c] Plants located in the following provinces have been classified as inland: Aosta, Lombardy, Piedmont, Umbria, Veneto-Trentino.

The Italian steel industry has adapted to its peculiar conditions by: (1) a very large use, as in Sweden, of hydroelectric power for electric steel production; (2) a large use of scrap, enabling the industry to minimize the need for coking coal in which Italy is wholly deficient; (3) a limited but intensive use of local iron ore; (4) the concentration of specialized capacity near transforming industries; and (5) tidewater steel plants based on imported materials. These adaptations have given the industry a structure that is brought out by Table 9.

The Italian tidewater plants, being more accessible than the inland plants to imported supplies of iron ore and coal (even the Italian ore moves by sea—

within Italian waters from Elba) produce only open-hearth and Thomas steel except for some electric steel production in Genoa based on hydropower. These tidewater plants, relying largely on pig iron, have a rather low scrap ratio for Italy.

The plants inland, on the contrary, produce close to 90 per cent of Italian electric-furnace steel. Such steel accounts for about 45 per cent of total steel production, a very unusual ratio. The inland plants also produce more than 60 per cent of the open-hearth steel on an extremely high scrap ratio, estimated at close to 80 per cent of the charge. The inland plants produce less than 30 per cent of the pig iron of blast-furnace grade. (All figures are for 1953.)

Italy consumes about four tons of scrap to every five tons of crude steel. Half of this scrap was imported in 1955; half of the imports came from areas outside the ECSC, mostly from the United States. The Italian steel industry is therefore at the mercy of the market for scrap, the price of which is extremely unstable. This circumstance provides the ECSC with one of its main chronic problems, examined in more detail in Chapter 3.

Italian steel expansion is fraught with problems. Any further increase in open-hearth or electric steel capacity will aggravate the problem of scrap supply. Seaboard location is one future way to reduce the scrap problem but an increase in pig iron capacity at tideland will aggravate the problem of iron ore supply and especially of coal supply.

Italian steel expansion has been geared to the home rather than the export market, though Italy exports a small quantity of specialty products, including steel pipe for the petroleum industry, largely to countries outside of the ECSC. Italy imports from the ECSC, Austria and the United States a large quantity of pig iron and of semifinished steel, mainly for use by the small nonintegrated steel plants.

Italy produces one million tons of coal in Sardinia. This coal is very high in sulphur and ash and includes an exceedingly high ratio of coal dust. The Sardinian output is therefore of dubious value, and Italy depends almost entirely on imported coal. But coal provided only 23 per cent of total energy in 1955 (Table 2-4 in Appendix E). The Ruhr and the United States then provided Italy with nearly all its imported coal. Two thirds of the Ruhr coal comes by rail through the Alpine route, the rest by sea.

STEEL AT TIDEWATER AND OTHER AREAS

Tidewater sites for steel have been growing in importance for the ECSC steel industry (and for the United States and United Kingdom industries, too). Steel production outside the older main inland areas increased threefold compared with a twofold increase in the main areas. (See Fig. 3, and Table 2-5 in Appendix E.) The newer plants, most of which are at tidewater, today represent 22 per cent of total production in the ECSC as against 16 per cent in 1913.[45] Since the second world war, integrated steelworks on new or "greenfield" sites have been developed only at tidewater. Tidewater plants are therefore among the newest in the industry. The new, rebuilt or modernized tide-

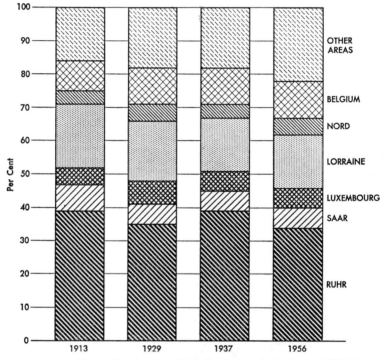

FIG. 3. Production of Crude Steel and Castings, ECSC, Percentage Distribution by Region, Selected Years, 1913–1956

Source: Derived from Table 2-5, Appendix E.

water plants are at Ijmuiden, Genoa, Piombino, Naples, Bremen and Mondeville (near Caen, France). In addition, there are the tidewater plants at Basse-Indre and Hennebont, in western France, and at Les Dunes and Isbergues near Dunkerque. All of these tidewater units except those at Hennebont, Basse-Indre and Les Dunes are integrated.

Seven entirely new projects were in prospect in mid-1958; a new plant at Savona in Italy and another at Dunkerque were definite; five additional

[45] Some inland locations, such as Salzgitter and northern Italy, are also included in these figures.

plants were considered—another plant near Ijmuiden in the Netherlands, another on the north German coast where the Bremen plant is also located, a plant at Marseilles on the southern French coast, and two plants, at Taranto and La Spezia, in Italy.[46]

Tidewater development increases the potential rivalry for world steel markets and also for supplies of scrap, iron ore and coal. As the supply of local coal and iron ore declines relative to requirements, the trend to tidewater is bound to continue.

A NOTE ON BRITISH STEEL AND COAL

Sixty per cent of the British steel industry is at tidewater.[47] The industry as a whole enjoys a number of outstanding advantages even by comparison with the Ruhr:

(1) British coking coal is good though not abundant.

(2) British steel plants are well located. Tidewater plants have advantages both for export and for the assembly of foreign materials; inland sites have the advantage of local ore. In both types of locations home-produced coal is available within a very short radius. Some of the locations, such as those in Wales, Scotland and on the northeast coast, combine coal and tidewater sites. Several British iron deposits are near the coast and some of them are quite near the coal mines also.[48] Owing to the availability of scrap and the low phosphorus content of home iron ores, 85 per cent of British crude steel output is open hearth but the Bessemer process, using oxygen, is growing.

(3) The British steel plants are rarely far from internal markets. Outbound freight costs are therefore low and capital scrap supplies are readily available.

(4) Metal transforming industries are well developed and expanding, enabling the United Kingdom, like Germany, to concentrate on "indirect" exports of steel.

Before the second world war, British coal was predominant in the world coal trade. The United Kingdom exported an average of 72 million tons of solid fuels per year in 1927–1928, nearly as much as the volume exported from

[46] "Coastal Steel Works: A New Development on the Continent," *Steel Review*, January 1957, pp. 53–55. Portugal has also decided to build its first steel plant at tidewater to produce 250,000 tons of crude steel per year. *Handelsblatt*, January 20, 1958, p. 1.

[47] A booklet called "The British Steel Industry, 1958," special issue of *Steel Review*, 1959, pp. 38–40, contains an excellent summary of the location of British steel. D. L. Burn, *The Economic History of Steel Making, 1867–1939*, Cambridge University Press, Cambridge, 1940, believes that United Kingdom steel is overconcentrated at tidewater and that the subsidized importation of scrap and iron ore aggravates this trend. P. W. S. Andrews and Elizabeth Brunner, *Capital Development in Steel*, Basil Blackwell, Oxford, 1952, contains a valuable analysis of the structure of the British steel industry.

[48] See British Iron and Steel Federation, *Yearbook, 1955*, Part I, map, pp. 1–2.

the ECSC countries and the United States combined. But in 1957 it exported only 11 million tons, equal to less than 10 per cent of the volume exported from the other two areas. (See Table 2-6 in Appendix E.) Though British coal production declined from 260 million tons in 1929 to 225 million tons in 1955, British home consumption increased from 180 million tons to 214 million tons in that period. (See Tables 2-4 and 2-7 in Appendix E.) British coal markets thus are now predominantly internal. The poor physical condition of the mines—a good number of them are among the oldest in Europe—the loss of markets in the interwar period, and the lack of manpower since the second world war are mainly responsible for the long-term decline in output.

THE ECSC AND OTHER MARKETS

The ECSC is not a closed system because it sells a large proportion of its steel in the world market in competition with steel from the United Kingdom, the United States and other areas and because it draws a large proportion of its iron ore, scrap, coal and other forms of energy from other parts of the world. These ties to the world markets set the background for many aspects of internal market organization as well as for the problems of commercial policy treated in later chapters. The main problems concern the relation of steel exports to domestic markets in the ECSC and the relation of world prices for petroleum and for American coal to the price of coal produced in the ECSC.

THE ECSC AND WORLD PRODUCTION

The ECSC accounts for 20 per cent of the steel, 15 per cent of the coal and 19 per cent of the iron ore production of the world, as shown in Table 10. It produces more coal and steel than any country in the West except the United States. The United Kingdom produces 40 per cent as much steel and nearly one fourth as much iron ore but about the same amount of coal as the ECSC. The United States, on the other hand, produces nearly twice as much steel and coal and 50 per cent more iron ore. Japan is a small producer by comparison with the ECSC, producing slightly more coal than Belgium and about as much steel as Belgium-Luxembourg combined; Japan's output of iron ore is negligible. But Japan is an aggressive competitor in world steel markets.

The "West" as a whole, in which from the trading point of view the so-called "neutral" countries are included, accounts for over 70 per cent of world production in these three industries. The ECSC accounts for roughly one fourth of Western production of these products, the United States for half the steel and 40 per cent of the coal and iron ore. The United Kingdom, the United

States and the ECSC combined account for over 80 per cent of the steel and coal in the West and for over 70 per cent of the iron ore. Whether measured in relation to total world or total "Western" production, steel and coal are thus highly concentrated in these three areas. Iron ore production is somewhat more dispersed, a large portion of it being produced in nonindustrialized areas

Table 10

PERCENTAGE DISTRIBUTION OF WORLD STEEL, COAL AND IRON ORE
PRODUCED BY SELECTED COUNTRIES AND AREAS, 1955

Country or Area	Steel[a]		Coal		Iron Ore[b]	
	Of World	Of "West"[c]	Of World	Of "West"[c]	Of World	Of "West"[c]
Germany	8.0	10.4	8.3	11.9	3.0	4.2
Saar	1.2	1.6	1.1	1.6	—	—
France	4.7	6.2	3.5	5.0	13.4	18.5
Belgium	2.2	2.9	1.9	2.7	0.0	0.0
Luxembourg	1.2	1.6	—	—	1.9	2.6
Italy	2.0	2.6	0.1	0.1	0.4	0.5
Netherlands	0.4	0.5	0.7	1.1	—	—
Total ECSC	19.7	25.7	15.5	22.3	18.8	25.8
United Kingdom	7.6	9.9	14.1	20.3	4.4	6.1
United States	39.7	52.1	28.1	40.6	28.4	39.2
Japan	3.6	4.6	2.6	3.8	0.4	0.5
Rest of "West"	5.8	7.7	9.0	13.0	20.6	28.4
Total "West"[c]	76.4	100.0	69.3	100.0	72.6	100.0
USSR	16.8		17.3		19.2	
USSR satellites	6.8		13.4		9.2	
TOTAL WORLD	100.0		100.0		100.0	

Sources: ECE, *Quarterly Bulletin of Coal Statistics* and *Quarterly Bulletin of Steel Statistics;* HA, *Bulletin statistique;* UN, *Monthly Bulletin of Statistics;* Statistisches Bundesamt, Düsseldorf.
[a] Ingots and castings.   [b] Merchantable quantities.
[c] Includes the countries outside the Soviet bloc, because even the so-called neutral countries are within or partly within the Western trading system.

like South America. The USSR and satellites account for 24 per cent of the world steel, 30 per cent of the coal and 28 per cent of the iron ore. The ECSC and the United Kingdom are the largest producers in Europe, excluding the USSR. As of 1955 the USSR by itself was about equal in size to the ECSC as a producer of the three products.

TRADE IN STEEL

The ECSC imports very little steel from the rest of the world. But it is the most important steel exporter in the world, measuring exports either as a percentage of home production or of world trade, as indicated by Fig. 4. The ECSC exported 22 per cent of its steel production to the rest of the world in

1955 and the individual members of the ECSC exported an additional 12 per cent of their output to each other. One third of the production is, therefore, sold outside the country of origin, third-party countries taking nearly twice as great a tonnage as the other members of the union. Except for Germany and Italy, the steel producers in the ECSC countries send one third or more of their output outside the national market and (the Saar excepted) more to third than to partner countries. The Saar is the only steel producing entity in the ECSC whose market is mainly within the rest of the union. Belgium-Luxembourg, the third largest producer in the ECSC, is the largest exporter in the world.

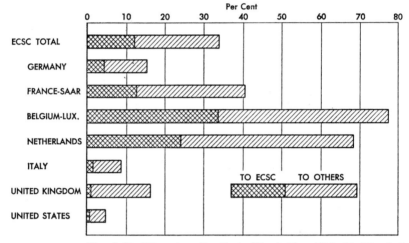

FIG. 4. Steel Exports as Per Cent of Production, Main Steel Producing Countries, 1955

Sources: Tables 2-2 and 2-3, Appendix E (the latter raised to crude steel equivalents).

France with the Saar is not far behind Belgium-Luxembourg as an exporter; France alone is also a major factor in the world steel market; exporting about one third of its steel output, it ranked third in 1955, not far behind the United States but ahead of Germany and the United Kingdom. Although Germany is the largest steel producer in Western Europe, it exported only 15 per cent of its output of steel in 1955. Italy is the smallest exporter in the ECSC. Though the Netherlands produces only a sixth as much steel as Italy, it exports more steel than that country.

The United Kingdom exports about as much steel as Germany by volume and as a percentage of production. The United States exports only about 5 per cent of its output but its volume of exports in 1955 was exceeded only by

Belgium-Luxembourg. The United States exports 50 per cent more steel than either Germany or the United Kingdom but, along with these two countries, produces largely for home consumption. (See Fig. 4.)

To which world markets do each of the three major exporting areas supply steel? Which markets do they share? Which do they dominate?

The ECSC, the United Kingdom and the United States exported 14 million tons of steel in 1955, excluding the trade between the members of the ECSC. (See Table 2-8 in Appendix E and Fig. 5. The table does not show the steel

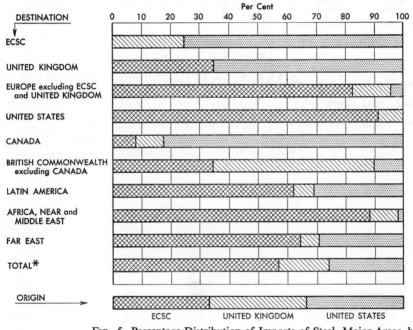

Fig. 5. Percentage Distribution of Imports of Steel, Major Areas, by Origin, 1955[a]

Source: Table 2-8, Appendix E.

[a] Total exports by the ECSC, the United Kingdom and the United States are equal to 100 per cent; about 85 per cent of world exports are covered.
* Includes exports to the USSR and undistributed exports.

exported by the smaller non-Soviet producing areas of the world—Japan, Austria, Sweden and a few other areas—but covers at least 85 per cent of world trade.)

If exports from the three major areas are taken as 100 per cent of total deliveries to the several importing areas shown in Table 2-8, Appendix E, then the ECSC is the dominant supplier in all the major steel importing areas except

Canada, the United Kingdom and other British Commonwealth countries. It also supplies one third of the steel exported to the United Kingdom and other Commonwealth countries exclusive of Canada.

In contrast to the ECSC, which supplies comparatively large quantities to nearly all markets, the United Kingdom has a dominant position only in the Commonwealth exclusive of Canada; the Commonwealth took more than half the steel exported by the United Kingdom and Canada was its largest single customer in 1955. But the United States is the largest supplier to the Canadian steel market, the only market in which it has a dominant position. The United States enjoys additionally a strong but not dominant position in Latin America and the Far East.

IRON ORE TRADE

The iron ore in the ECSC is too low in iron content to be exported long distances to third-party countries. But France does export a large amount to

Table 11

IRON ORE IMPORTS FROM THIRD AREAS BY ECSC COUNTRIES
AND THE UNITED KINGDOM, 1955[a]

(*Millions of Metric Tons*)

| Destination | Origin | | | | Imports as Per Cent of Blast Furnace Charge[b] |
	Sweden	Western Hemisphere	Other	Total	
Germany	6.3	2.0	5.2	13.5	70
France	0.2	0.0	0.3	0.5	2
Belgium	2.6	—	0.1	2.7	35
Netherlands	0.2	0.1	0.6	0.9	90
Italy	0.2	0.1	0.6	0.9	60
Total ECSC	9.5	2.2	6.8	18.5	29[c]
United Kingdom	4.1	2.0	7.0[d]	13.1	32
TOTAL	13.6	4.2	13.8	31.6	30[c]

Source: Table 2-9, Appendix E.

[a] Tonnages refer to salable iron ore before adjustment for iron content; manganese ore and iron pyrites are excluded. Data for France and Belgium are partly estimated. The Saar and Luxembourg do not import much ore from third countries.

[b] Iron content of ore from third countries as per cent of iron content of total ore charged, exclusive of manganese ore and pyrites. Figures are approximations because the charge of ore from third countries is inferred from imports without adjustment for stock changes.

[c] Includes Saar and Luxembourg.   [d] Includes 700,000 tons from the ECSC.

nearby ECSC partners. In 1955 France exported about 20 million tons, or over one third of its production, mainly to the Saar, Belgium and Luxembourg, as Table 2-9 in Appendix E shows. Within the ECSC, French exports constitute the only substantial movement of ore across frontiers. No member of the ECSC—not even France—produces enough ore of desirable quality to satisfy every need. All members—except France—therefore import relatively large quantities of high-grade ore from third-party countries to supplement their own output and the ore imported from France. Overseas ore furnishes a large part of the blast furnace charge in all countries but France. (See Table 11.)

World rivalry for limited supplies of high-grade ore is therefore keen. But the rivalry expresses itself through search for concessions and long-term contracts rather than through an open world market and price mechanism. The main sources of ore supply are Sweden, Spain, Canada, Latin America and North Africa.

SCRAP TRADE

The ECSC is a large importer of scrap from third-party countries, especially the United States, when steel production is high. (See Table 12.) Italy accounts for half the scrap imported by the ECSC at such times and obtains more than

Table 12

IMPORTS OF SCRAP FROM THIRD COUNTRIES BY ECSC COUNTRIES AND
THE UNITED KINGDOM, 1955

(Thousands of Metric Tons)

Destination	Origin			Imports as Per Cent of Total Charge[a]
	United States	Other	Total	
Germany	729	114	843	8.3
France-Saar	236	25	261	4.0
Belgium-Luxembourg	147	27	174	6.5
Netherlands	43	16	59	8.1
Italy	822	319	1,141	26.8
Total ECSC	1,977	501	2,478	10.2
United Kingdom	927	523[b]	1,450	12.0
TOTAL	2,904	1,024	3,928	10.8

Sources: ECE, *Quarterly Bulletin of Steel Statistics;* HA, *Bulletin statistique;* and Statistisches Bundesamt, Düsseldorf.

[a] Blast and steel furnace charge. Figures are approximations since the consumption of imported scrap is inferred from imports without adjustment for stock changes.
[b] Includes 44,000 tons from the ECSC.

one fourth the scrap it requires from third-party countries. Since world scrap prices are very unstable, imports of scrap have been subsidized both in the ECSC and the United Kingdom in order to stabilize domestic prices.

TRADE IN COAL AND COKE

Only about 7 per cent of ECSC coal production is now exported to third-party countries. More than twice that much moves across frontiers within the ECSC. Most ECSC countries have a local surplus of some types and sizes of solid fuels and a deficit of others; this fact explains the active trade in solid fuels within the ECSC. Germany, which controls about 50 per cent of the coal

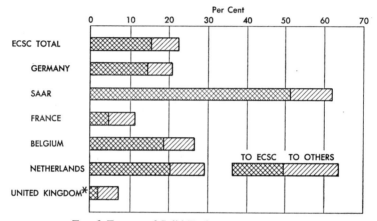

FIG. 6. Exports of Solid Fuels as Per Cent of Coal Production, ECSC Countries and United Kingdom, 1955[a]

Sources: Tables 2-6 and 2-7, Appendix E.

[a] Exports include coal and the coal equivalent of coke.

* Includes foreign bunkers and exports to Ireland.

production in the ECSC, accounts for an equal share of the coal and coke exported by all ECSC countries to each other and to the rest of the world. In steel there is no such massive concentration. The Saar is the only area that exports most of its coal output, 62 per cent in 1955. At the other extreme, France normally exports only 5 per cent of its output though it exported more in 1955 when producers' stocks were high. (See Fig. 6.) Scandinavia, Austria, Switzerland, East Germany and (occasionally) the United Kingdom take most of the coal exported by the ECSC countries.

The ECSC is now a net importer of coal, as shown by Table 13, and a large importer of petroleum, which competes with coal in some parts of the energy market. Third-party sources furnish a particularly high proportion of coal consumption in Italy and the Netherlands. With a decline of United Kingdom and Polish exports, the United States is now the main source of coal imported by the ECSC from third-party countries. The ECSC countries in 1957 im-

Table 13

COAL IMPORTS BY ECSC COUNTRIES FROM THIRD COUNTRIES,
ANNUAL AVERAGE, 1955–1956

(Millions of Metric Tons)

	Origin					Imports as Per Cent of Apparent Coal Consumption
Destination	United States	United Kingdom	Poland	Other	Total	
Germany	9.3	1.3	0.8	0.3	11.7	9.1
France	3.4	0.9	0.8	0.7	5.8	8.0
Belgium	1.4	0.6	0.0	0.2	2.2	6.6
Netherlands	2.7	0.8	0.0	0.2	3.7	20.8
Italy	6.1	0.6	0.1	0.3	7.1	60.9
Total[a]	22.9	4.2	1.7	1.7	30.5	11.8

Sources: ECE, *Quarterly Bulletin of Coal Statistics;* OEEC, *General Statistics;* and Tables 2-4 and 2-6, Appendix E.

[a] Excludes Saar and Luxembourg, which obtain their solid fuels from within the ECSC.

ported twice as much coal from the United States as the coal equivalent of the coal and coke supplied by Germany to the rest of the ECSC. Only the Saar and Luxembourg do not import from third-party areas. (See Fig. 7.)

The need for supplies from the United States is of much economic significance to the ECSC and the United States. In past years the tonnage of United

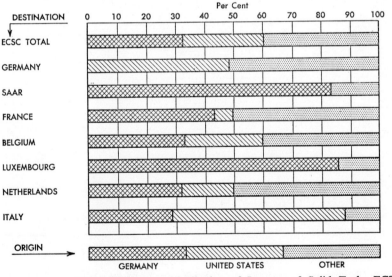

FIG. 7. Percentage Distribution of Imports of Solid Fuels, ECSC Countries, by Origin, 1955

Source: Table 2-6, Appendix E.

States coal imported by the ECSC countries has fluctuated violently with the business cycle; imports dropped to zero in some postwar years and rose to 38 million tons in 1957, a year of strong business activity. Imported petroleum and coal, with flexible prices relative to the price of coal produced in the ECSC, have created pressure for protection in the ECSC. European import policies also create a problem for the United States coal industry. Most of the United States bituminous coal imported by the ECSC comes from West Virginia through the port of Hampton Roads, Virginia. Imported anthracite comes from Pennsylvania through the port of Philadelphia. The ECSC takes only 3 to 6 per cent of total United States coal production but 10 to 20 per cent of the coal produced in West Virginia. West Virginia furnishes up to another 10 per cent of its total output to the rest of Europe. European outlets are therefore important to some parts of the American coal industry.

Thus, although the ECSC encompasses the coal and steel industries of the most important industrialized areas of the European continent, it is not a closed system. The economic union therefore influences, and is influenced by, the use of resources in the rest of the world. The extent of these influences is examined in later chapters.

CHAPTER 3

STEEL: COSTS OF

PRODUCTION AND

INVESTMENTS

An economic union should promote specialization on the basis of comparative advantage. How do the producing areas compare in this respect?

COST OF RAW MATERIALS

Raw materials and fuels—coal, coke, and other fuels, iron ore and purchased scrap—account for about 50 per cent of the sales value of production in the European steel industry (including depreciation, interest and profit before income taxes). They account for about 45 per cent of sales value in the United States steel industry.[1] The input of raw materials per ton of finished steel produced in 1956 by the main producing countries is shown in Table 14. The weight of raw materials assembled varies considerably from country to country. It is highest in those countries that produce a high proportion of Thomas steel—the Saar, France, Belgium and Luxembourg—because that grade of steel is generally based on a low-grade high-phosphorus ore and a high proportion of pig iron rather than scrap; it consequently also requires a higher intake of energy. The producers of open-hearth steel—Germany, where 55 per cent of the output is open hearth, the United Kingdom and the United States, where virtually all the output is open hearth—use a smaller amount of materials. But the input of materials in the United Kingdom is

---

[1] In 1956 the figure was 46 per cent for the United States including freight; 51 per cent for Germany and 50 per cent for the United Kingdom excluding freight. American Iron and Steel Institute, *Charting Steel's Progress*, 1957, p. 60; United Kingdom, Iron and Steel Board, *Annual Report for 1957*, p. 25; German data covering the business year 1955–1956 are from *Handelsblatt*, April 26–27, p. 6, August 16–17, p. 8, 1957. Cf. *Britain and Europe*, The Economist Intelligence Unit Limited, London, 1957, pp. 67 ff.

higher than that in the other open-hearth producing countries because the United Kingdom uses a high proportion of low-grade domestic ore that is nevertheless low in phosphorus. The input of materials is lowest in Italy because electric-furnace steel, based mainly on scrap rather than pig iron, accounts for a high proportion of the output there.

The cost of materials per ton of finished steel does not necessarily follow the weight of materials. Costs are determined by the unit value of the materials

Table 14

ESTIMATED INPUT OF RAW MATERIALS PER TON OF FINISHED STEEL, MAIN STEEL PRODUCING COUNTRIES, 1956[a]

(Metric Tons)

Material	Germany	Saar	France	Belgium	Luxembourg	Italy	United Kingdom	United States
Fuel and power:[b]								
Coal	1.367	1.884	1.793 ⎫	1.750[c]	1.703	0.467	1.581	1.092
Other fuels	0.298	...	0.373 ⎭		0.007	0.858	0.382	0.359
Iron ore	1.571	3.070	3.541	2.329	4.037	0.727	1.862	1.497
Purchased scrap	0.307	0.105	0.300	0.231	0.009	0.623	0.356	0.308
Limestone	0.344	0.154	0.202	...	0.161	...	0.309	0.389
Total	3.887	5.213	6.209	4.310	5.917	2.675	4.490	3.645

Sources: Data on input and production are from ECE, *Quarterly Bulletin of Steel Statistics;* HA, *Bulletin statistique;* United Kingdom, Iron and Steel Board, *Annual Report for 1956;* American Iron and Steel Institute, *Annual Reports;* and British Iron and Steel Federation, *Yearbooks.*

[a] The total input of materials was divided by the quantity of hot-rolled steel produced, including castings and semis for sale.

Materials used for the total production of pig iron were included even though some pig iron goes to merchant channels, exports and iron castings. Semifinished steel and pig iron acquired by purchase from other countries were not included.

Iron ore, on a raw basis, comprises the input for pig iron, ferroalloys and sinter production.

The Netherlands was omitted because a large portion of the pig iron is produced for export and a large portion of the finished steel is based on imported semis.

[b] In hard coal equivalents. The following conversion ratios were used: coke, the respective country ratios or the ratio for the country from which it was imported; fuel oil, 1 to 1.5; electricity, 1 billion kilowatt-hours to 0.6 million tons of coal; natural gas, 1 billion cubic meters to 1.33 million tons of coal. In all cases but the United States total electricity was included because purchased electricity was not shown separately.

[c] Coal and other fuels combined; calculated from data in Comité Mixte report, p. 48.

at the point of consumption. A high intake of materials may be offset by low unit prices or a low intake by high prices. The delivered value is influenced by the distance of the steel plant from the source of the material and by the mode of carriage, for water transport gives a steel plant a longer economic reach than railroad transport. National policies with respect to freight rates and discriminatory freight rates can thus have an important influence on differences in the cost of producing steel. The provisions of the ECSC treaty with respect to the elimination of discriminatory freight rates have consequently tended to equalize competitive conditions among the different steel producing sites. Equal producers' prices for all consumers in the ECSC—another requirement of the treaty—have also contributed to this end.

The difference in the approximate total cost of raw materials (before adjust-

Table 15

ESTIMATED COST OF MATERIALS PER METRIC TON OF FINISHED STEEL,
MAIN STEEL PRODUCING COUNTRIES, 1956

Material	Ger-many	Saar	France	Bel-gium	Luxem-bourg	Italy	United Kingdom	United States
Coal and fuel	$20.85	$27.70	$35.55	$26.85	$31.65	$24.40	$25.10	$14.55
Iron ore	21.95	19.00	13.25	23.70	18.15	7.20	20.00	20.65
Purchased scrap	16.95	5.75	13.15	13.70	9.55	38.60	13.50	16.45
Total	59.75	52.45	61.40	64.25	59.35	70.20	58.60	51.65
Other metallics (+ or −)	+1.60	+7.00	−1.00	+9.25[a]	...	+8.80	+4.40	...
TOTAL	61.35	59.45	60.40	73.50	59.35	79.00	63.00	51.65

Sources: Using Table 14, input costs were derived from market values. This is consistent with the business accounts of the steel industry, for even captive raw materials are generally produced by separately incorporated daughter companies. Turnover taxes are excluded.

The values for coal were taken from Table 47, adjusted for freight if obtained from another area and weighted according to the supply from different areas.

Iron ore prices were taken from Statistisches Bundesamt, Düsseldorf and Wiesbaden. The value of imported ores was also checked with the data in UN, *Commodity Trade Statistics*, from which the delivered value of imported ore can be derived. The value of iron ore was weighted according to source and price. The price of British domestic iron ore was inferred from data in United Kingdom, Iron and Steel Board, *Annual Report for 1956*, p. 22, which gives the value of total materials, from which the value of domestic ore was derived by subtracting the estimated cost of other materials and imported ore.

The composite prices of purchased scrap for ECSC countries are from HA, *Cinquième rapport général*, p. 104; though referring to January 31, 1957, they are not very far above the average, and reflect the same country variations as those, for 1956. The price of United Kingdom scrap represents the weighted average price of domestic and imported scrap, from United Kingdom, Iron and Steel Board, *op. cit.*, pp. 15–16, and Statistisches Bundesamt, Düsseldorf. The price for United States scrap, from Statistisches Bundesamt, Wiesbaden, is for the heavy melting grade at Pittsburgh. The charge (or credit) for equalizing imported and domestic scrap prices is included for the United Kingdom and the ECSC.

The debits and credits for other metallics reflect the net value of exported and imported pig iron and the value of imported semis. Semis produced for sale are treated as finished steel and therefore need not be included in the credits. Data on these items are from ECE, *Quarterly Bulletin of Steel Statistics*, and Statistisches Bundesamt, Düsseldorf.

The results for France reflect the (then) prospective 20 per cent devaluation of August 1957; this reduced the cost of domestic but increased the value of imported materials. The estimates for the United Kingdom agree with data given by United Kingdom, Iron and Steel Board, *op. cit.*, p. 22, according to which materials cost represents 30 per cent, and fuels cost 20 per cent, of total turnover, including the cost of nearly one million tons of imported pig iron and semis. These exceptional imports added about $4.40 to the ton of finished steel. British costs, therefore, are normally more favorable. The use of large quantities of imported semimanufactured metallics is also abnormal in Italy and Belgium and occurs only in a bull market when the rolling mills can take more metal than local metal producing facilities can furnish.

[a] The upward adjustment is high owing to the importation of metallics by nonintegrated plants. The costs at integrated Belgian plants were consequently much lower than the national average shown here.

Note: The figures in this table are approximate, at best; for further remarks and qualifications, see the text as well as the notes to Table 14, which explain the omission of the Netherlands.

ment for metallics) is much smaller between countries than the difference in the cost of the constituent materials, as Table 15 shows.[2] The total cost of raw materials (before adjustment for metallics) varies from $59 to $64 per ton of finished steel in the main European producing countries, the Saar and Italy excepted.[3] The Saar, with lower costs, draws a large amount of semifinished steel from Lorraine; its costs after adjustment for this factor are closer to those in the other countries. Italy, with higher costs, produces a larger proportion of electric-furnace steel than any other country included in Table 15. With a production cost estimated at $70 per ton before, and $79 per ton after, adjustment for metallics, Italy is a high-cost producer because the electric-furnace steel produced there serves many purposes for which ordinary carbon steel can be substituted.

A country's comparative status is affected by a combination of factors. Though steel plants located at coal producing sites do not as a class enjoy lower costs, most of them are in more industrialized areas and consequently enjoy nearby markets. They also enjoy greater by-product revenue, especially from the sale of coke-oven gas. The Belgian steel industry, for example, is located near coal but the coal is high cost. It produces Thomas steel mainly, but because it is farther from the iron ore its costs are higher than those of steel producers in Lorraine and Luxembourg who produce steel of the same grade. On the other hand, it is closer to its market in Belgium and to Antwerp for export than are the other two producing areas to their markets. These considerations illustrate a very important factor bearing on the relation of outbound freight to the cost of production. Steel products from different sources compete on the basis of delivered price. A plant with a low cost of materials but far from the steel market may thus be no better off than a rival with higher costs.

The higher the input of purchased scrap, which is collected in great industrial centers, the closer a steel plant needs to be to such centers and therefore to its market. The closer a steel plant is to such a center, the lower the amount of outbound freight and the lower the transport cost for assembling scrap.[4] The steel plants in Italy thus need to be closer to the market than those in other countries. The producers in the Saar, Belgium and Luxembourg are

[2] Costs per ton of finished steel in the Netherlands were not included because a large part of the pig iron produced by that country is exported and a large part of the finished steel is produced from imported semifinished steel.

[3] For a study of the comparative cost of producing a ton of pig iron in 1950 see "L'Industrie du charbon et l'industrie de l'acier en Europe occidentale," in ECE, *Bulletin économique pour l'Europe*, Geneva, October 1950, pp. 18 ff. This study does not, however, discuss the influence of outbound freight on competitive ability.

[4] See Harold Wien, "Iron and Steel," in Sam H. Schurr and Jacob Marschak, *Economic Aspects of Atomic Power*, Princeton University Press, Princeton, 1950, p. 160, for the concept of the "weight of the market."

least tied to the market from the point of view of the assembly of scrap.[5] In these countries, as well as in Lorraine, the market has a small relative weight because the steel plants there maximize the advantage of low-grade ore. But though Lorraine has a low assembly cost owing to its propinquity to low-grade, but low-cost, ore, this advantage tends to be offset by its distance from markets and dependence on railroad haulage.

Though the data on approximate costs in Table 15 reveal no major differences between the countries in Western Europe—except for Italy—they should be interpreted in relation to the following considerations:

(1) The European steel industry operated at capacity in 1956 and incurred costs justified by a sellers' market only. Germany, Belgium, Italy and the United Kingdom had a deficit for import of pig iron and semifinished steel in order to keep steel furnaces and rolling mills going at capacity, whereas France had a net surplus of pig iron for export. The exceptional movement of unfinished products accounts for the debits and credits for metallics shown at the bottom of Table 15. Though comparative costs in Belgium and Italy appear exceptionally high, the steel industry in Belgium and Italy was still able to sell at a profit. In less buoyant times the steel industry in Belgium, for one, would be more competitive with respect to cost because it would be able to operate without using costly semifinished products or large amounts of high-cost scrap. The data on the cost of raw materials as shown in Table 15 therefore reflect costs in prosperity rather than recession, as will be further indicated by the discussion below of scrap prices.

(2) Average costs of production for each country as a whole conceal the variations between different areas in the same country. Steel production is especially dispersed in France, Italy, the United Kingdom and the United States; it is more geographically concentrated in Germany, the Saar, Belgium and Luxembourg. Costs of production in the central part of France are probably above the average for France shown in Table 15. Those in Milan, where most of the small nonintegrated mills are located, are probably above the average for Italy.

(3) Receipts from joint products, notably from the sale of energy, small-sized coke, fertilizers and building materials, are large at the sites based on local coal or ore. Integrated coke batteries thus provide a great advantage. Plants preponderantly based on scrap, as in Italy, or imported coke, as in Luxembourg and partly in Lorraine, do not enjoy this advantage.

---

[5] An elaborate comparative study of each of the main steel producing sites in Western Europe, giving the inbound ton-miles for each raw material from each source, the aggregate ton-miles of material per ton of steel and the weight of the market, has been made by Dr. Hanns-Jürgen Kunze, *Die Lagerungsordnung der westeuropäischen Eisen- und Stahlindustrie im Lichte ihrer Kostenstruktur*, Kieler Studien, Kiel, 1954, particularly Tables I and II, pp. 90–99.

(4) Costs and sales value are influenced by the grade and type of steel. Electric-furnace alloy steels are costly but command a high price. Open-hearth steel also commands a high price on the Continent. There also are variations between countries in the pattern of products produced. European and American patterns differ considerably; 50 per cent of American, but less of European, production is flat rolled. Flat-rolled products in Europe command a much higher price than other products. But there are differences between European countries in this respect, too. The ratio of flat-rolled products in 1956 to the total output of hot-rolled products including semifinished steel for sale was as follows:[6]

Germany	38	Luxembourg	26
Saar	30	Italy	33
France	37	United Kingdom	44
Belgium	39		

Flat-rolled products are costlier to produce because they yield a lower recovery per ton of crude steel and because they require more finishing and labor. The two areas—the Saar and Luxembourg—with the lowest cost of materials per ton of finished steel, after adjustment for metallics, as shown in Table 15, also produce the lowest percentage of flat-rolled products.

(5) The price of raw materials is not always a "free" price. The price of coal is held down by most governments. (See Chapter 9.) So is the price of scrap.

The Scrap Subsidy

The price equalization schemes for scrap in the ECSC as well as in the United Kingdom have held the price of scrap down when it was scarce. The producers of Thomas steel were favored in 1956 (Table 15) because the large scrap consuming countries—Italy, Germany, the United Kingdom and the United States—were using a material that was nevertheless costly. Scrap markets were organized on a countrywide basis before the ECSC was established. The High Authority in February 1953 ordered each of the national scrap organizations then in existence to dissolve but it authorized the steel producers in the ECSC to establish a common scrap purchasing agency. The following year it authorized the producers to establish a common financial agency to tax scrap consumers and to use the proceeds to subsidize scrap imported from outside the ECSC.[7]

In 1956 the steel industry in the ECSC consumed about 27 million tons of scrap, half of which was purchased or capital scrap. Twenty-five per cent of

[6] Calculated from data in ECE, *Quarterly Bulletin of Steel Statistics.*
[7] HA, *Sixième rapport général*, Vol. II, p. 90.

the purchased scrap was imported from third-party countries.[8] Nearly three fifths of the gross amount of scrap imported by Italy, 10 per cent of Germany's imported scrap, 14 per cent of France-Saar's, 44 per cent of Belgium-Luxembourg's and 12 per cent of Holland's came from outside the ECSC that year. World prices were considerably higher than domestic prices; the delivered price of scrap obtained outside the ECSC must have been $73 per ton in 1956.[9] This price was from $20 to $30 per ton above domestic scrap prices in the ECSC countries. Though the ECSC countries are not equally dependent on imported scrap, they are entitled by the terms of the treaty to bid on equal terms for the scrap collected within the ECSC as a whole. The disparity between requirements and home supplies is greatest in Italy. Only Luxembourg had a net export surplus. If each country had to bid freely for the internal supply, internal prices would rise to the world price. To avoid this development, the High Authority compensated the have-nots for the sake of allowing the other countries to hold on to most of their domestic supplies. Italy and Belgium were the only countries to receive credits from the scrap pool; the others were debited.[10] The difference between the price of scrap purchased in domestic and in world markets was spread over all purchased scrap. The High Authority pointed out that this system did not yield an artificially low average price since the composite price to each producer—domestic price plus the tax on scrap—was equal to the average cost of imported and domestic scrap. But it did tend to equalize the cost of scrap among all consumers. A marginal cost or free price, it pointed out, would have disturbed the cost relationships between the producers of Thomas and open-hearth steel and hence the relationships between countries that specialize in Thomas steel—which uses less scrap—and those that produce a large proportion of open-hearth steel. A free scrap price, the High Authority further pointed out, would have fluctuated sharply with maritime freight rates for scrap purchased on world markets.[11]

Equalization of scrap prices may be antieconomic insofar as it encourages high-cost producers.[12]

The system of scrap equalization payments authorized by the High Author-

[8] *Ibid.*, p. 146.

[9] The United Kingdom paid $72.80 per ton for imported scrap; the domestic price was $29.00. United Kingdom, Iron and Steel Board, *Annual Report, 1956*, pp. 15–16. Domestic scrap prices in the ECSC countries were higher than in the United Kingdom. For domestic scrap prices in the latter countries in 1956–57, see HA, *Cinquième rapport général*, p. 101.

[10] See *Handelsblatt*, July 11–12, 1958, p. 2.

[11] These observations by the High Authority are from its *Sixième rapport général*, Vol. I, pp. 28–31, and Vol. II, pp. 69 ff.

[12] D. L. Burn, *The Economic History of Steel Making, 1867–1939*, Cambridge University Press, Cambridge, 1940, cited by P. W. S. Andrews and Elizabeth Brunner, *Capital Development in Steel*, Basil Blackwell, Oxford, 1952, pp. 76–99, argues that scrap and ore subsidies encourage the British steel industry to locate at tidewater and neglect local ore sites that are more economic.

ity started in March 1954; it encouraged the importation and use of scrap, whereas the reverse was wanted. The High Authority in March 1955 consequently required the financial agency to pay a premium to those plants that reduced the use of scrap by using pig iron. In February 1957 the use and importation of scrap were further discouraged by taxing consumers who increased their scrap consumption over a base tonnage and by paying a premium to those who consumed less than the base tonnage.[13] The High Authority also encouraged the steel industry to build more blast furnaces and to increase the use of pig iron relative to the production of steel. It consequently disapproved projects that did not meet this goal and extended loans to those that did.

The scrap subsidy did not equalize prices completely. Reflecting the weight of imported scrap, the price varied with use. The scrap equalization scheme was furthermore adjusted for transport costs in the Community; the price of scrap was consequently higher in Italy than in other parts of the union.

Among the main steel producing areas, only the United States had a free scrap price, but the United States, as the High Authority observed, does not import scrap and has a more homogeneous industry, for all its steel production is of open-hearth and electric-furnace grades. The British steel industry also controlled imported scrap and equalized its cost; though it too produces open-hearth and electric-furnace grades of steel mainly, it is dependent on imported scrap.

A high scrap ratio is not entirely disadvantageous. The price of scrap is much more elastic than the price of pig iron or coal. When the price of scrap is high, steel prices are also high and the steel producer can pass along the higher price of scrap. In a buyers' steel market, the scrap price falls more rapidly than the price of other raw materials. The steel producer who uses a large amount of scrap is at such times also less burdened with idle capital-intensive facilities for pig iron production. When the demand for steel contracts, Italian steel producers, along with the other producers who have a high scrap ratio, are therefore in a more favorable position than the data for 1956, as shown by Table 15, indicate.

In the 1958 recession world and domestic prices for scrap approached equality. Domestic prices for pig iron, less flexible than world scrap prices, were then higher than scrap prices, discouraging the use and expansion of blast furnace capacity all over again. The British ceased equalizing the price for imported scrap. The High Authority in November 1958 introduced a proposal in the Council of Ministers to compensate the steel producers during a period limited to twenty-seven months for using more pig iron during a recession when

---

[13] Article 53 (a) is the legal basis for equalizing the cost of imported scrap. For details, see HA, *Sixième rapport général*, Vol. II, pp. 68 ff, and pp. 146 ff, and citations given therein.

pig iron prices are above scrap prices, and to compensate producers for using scrap when the price relationships are reverse. This proposal would have helped equalize competitive conditions in all phases of the business cycle. Italy disagreed with the first part of the proposal, while Germany refused to accept the second part unless the first was included. For lack of agreement, the scrap equalization fund was discontinued as of early 1959, and the scrap market in the ECSC countries was freed for the first time since World War II.[14]

Though the High Authority has attempted to discourage the development of plants based on scrap, the question remains whether or not the use of a subsidy to spread the cost of imported scrap during periods of peak demand retards the long-run locational adjustments that a free scrap market might have induced and prolongs the operation of high-cost plants, especially in Italy. The High Authority has declared that scrap equalization schemes should not become permanent[15] but it remains to be seen whether or not it would withstand the pressure for such a subsidy during a business boom if the United Kingdom were to reinstate its subsidy.

LABOR COSTS

Labor is another major element in the total cost of production. Data on labor costs are presented in Table 16, which shows hourly payroll costs, man-hours per ton of finished steel produced and labor costs per ton. These data are simply approximate.

The difference between hourly payroll costs in the United States and Europe is striking; costs in the United States were 3.2 times those in Germany and 3.8 times those in the United Kingdom in 1956. But productivity in the United States is much higher, 2.3 times that in Germany and the United Kingdom.[16] The American advantage in productivity does not, however, completely offset its disadvantage in payroll costs. Approximate labor costs per ton are therefore still 1.3 times those in Germany and 1.7 times those in the United Kingdom. But the American advantage in the cost of raw materials (Table 15) offsets its disadvantage in labor costs. The sum of labor costs and material costs in the United States and in the major European producers consequently is approximately equal, but comparisons are misleading unless they are based on the same products, for the major share of payroll costs occurs in the rolling mill. Though the European steel industry is far less efficient than the American

---

[14] HA, *Bulletin mensuel d'information*, October-November 1958, p. 11; *Handelsblatt*, November 28, 1958, p. 13.

[15] HA, *Journal officiel*, February 9, 1959, pp. 182 ff.

[16] See British Productivity Council, *Iron and Steel*, London, 1956, p. 18.

in the use of manpower, it is, along with the Japanese, nevertheless competitive because of lower wage scales. If wages were equalized, the European steel industry would have to become equally capital intensive in order to remain competitive. Low wages and an aggressive export policy have enabled the

Table 16

ESTIMATED LABOR COSTS IN THE STEEL INDUSTRY,
SELECTED COUNTRIES, 1956

Country	Hourly Payroll Costs[a]	Man-Hours per Metric Ton of Finished Steel (Approximate)[b]	Approximate Labor Cost per Ton[c]
	(1)	(2)	(3)
Germany	$.90	30.5	$27.5
Saar[d]	.82	25.0	20.5
France[d]	.80	30.5	24.4
Belgium	.98	23.5	23.0
Luxembourg	1.15	18.5	21.3
Italy	.79	27.0	21.3
United Kingdom	.78[e]	28.5	22.2
United States	2.95	12.5	36.9

Sources: American Iron and Steel Institute, *Annual Report for 1956;* United Kingdom, Iron and Steel Board, *Annual Report for 1956,* p. 23. Data on payroll costs in continental steel from HA, *Les Salaires et les charges sociales dans les industries de la Communauté,* 1956, p. 28. The latter gave data for 1954. These were adjusted for 1956 from the index of payroll cost changes given in HA, *Sixième rapport général,* Vol. II, p. 225.

[a] The data give payroll costs, not earnings, and therefore include the cost of pensions and payroll taxes.

[b] HA, *Bulletin statistique;* Statistisches Bundesamt, Düsseldorf. Finished steel limited to hot-rolled products and semifinished steel for sale. Wage workers limited to processing and maintenance men in blast furnace, steel smelting and rolling mill operations, but the data are far from comparable as between countries. Those countries, moreover, that imported much steel for further processing in 1956—the Saar, Italy, Belgium and the United Kingdom—show a deceptively high productivity. The results, influenced also by product mix, are therefore simply suggestive.

[c] Col. 1 multiplied by col. 2.

[d] 420 francs to the dollar.

[e] Data on average weekly earnings adjusted for 48-hour week and raised by 2 per cent to reflect payroll tax.

European steel producers, especially those in Belgium and Luxembourg, to supply a large share of the American market for wire products and concrete reinforcing bars, which are consumed by a large number of small consumers without further processing. But imports by the United States accounted for only 4 per cent of total consumption even in the first half of 1959 when they rose to unprecedented heights.[17]

[17] *New York Times* (domestic edition), September 5, 1959, p. 19.

Within Europe itself the productivity of labor varies with the grade of steel and the distribution of products produced. But there are probably no major variations in productivity or labor costs among integrated European steel producers using comparable processes and producing comparable products. Producers of Thomas steel—Luxembourg, Belgium, Saar and France—require less labor per unit of output because this process of crude steel production requires less control than open-hearth steel. Though the Italian steel industry is less integrated and includes a large number of small plants, the industry produces relatively little coke and pig iron and consequently employs proportionately fewer workers engaged directly in production. And the variations between European countries with respect to labor costs per ton are even smaller than those with respect to productivity.

THE ROLE OF INVESTMENTS

If the rate of capital expenditure is high, plants will be modern and more homogeneous with respect to operating costs and average efficiency will be maximized. High rates of expenditure occur when business is expanding. Stagnation, neglect of plant, protection of obsolete facilities and market control schemes tend to go together. An expanding economy therefore facilitates the purposes of economic union and a stagnant one could interfere with them.

Investments in the steel industry are more easily adjusted to short-term changes in business activity than those in the coal industry. A completely new steel plant on a new site can be completed in four years and a developed site can be enlarged in an even shorter period. Investments therefore do not have to begin long in advance. However, the development of an underground coal mine must start eight or more years (in some cases twelve to fifteen years) before the mine can be brought to full production. Long-term forecasts of demand for steel are thus of little significance because funds do not have to be tied up that long in advance, but they cast a much longer shadow in the European coal industry. The relatively short investment cycle in the steel industry enables the firms to adjust investment programs quickly to the business cycle, to push ahead during boom periods and to curtail investments during a recession.

The treaty does not leave investments entirely to private decisions and the price mechanism. The High Authority has three broad classes of power in the field of investment: (a) it can review, and in some cases veto, the investment projects of individual firms; (b) it can make loans and guarantees; and (c) it can issue long-term market forecasts which may affect future expectations of the industry or its customers.

Review of Investment Projects

Articles 54, 46 and 47 define the powers of the High Authority in reviewing investments. The treaty requires individual coal and steel firms to submit their programs to the High Authority in advance and authorizes the latter to issue an opinion or a decision (Article 54). Opinions are not binding. If the High Authority finds that the plant would not be competitive, it may issue an adverse decision which is binding. The firm is prohibited from seeking outside funds in that case though it may still use its own capital.[18] The firm may, however, hesitate to use its own capital because an adverse decision evidently has a strong moral influence. If a firm disobeys a decision the High Authority may fine it an amount equal to the value of the illegal investment.

The High Authority began to exercise its powers over investments in October 1953. In July 1955 it notified the coal and steel firms to submit investment programs three months in advance of placing contracts for capital goods if the program involved investment in a new facility exceeding $500,000 or investment in an existing facility exceeding one million dollars. In July 1956, the High Authority furthermore notified the steel firms that if steel melting facilities are involved, they must submit the program for approval regardless of value; the High Authority took this step in order to limit the expansion of scrap-using processes, scrap being scarce.[19]

The High Authority examined a large number of projects from September 1955, when the obligation to give prior notice came into force, to the end of 1957.[20]

Loans and Guarantees

The treaty authorizes the High Authority to make loans and guarantees to the firms. Article 50 allows the High Authority to collect revenue for administrative expenses, nonrepayable assistance, research and a guarantee fund. It can borrow money for the purpose of granting loans to help the coal and steel firms finance their investment programs. The High Authority cannot use its tax proceeds to make loans but can use them to guarantee its obligations. The High Authority can also guarantee loans granted to enterprises by third parties. (Article 51.)

The treaty (Article 50) authorizes the High Authority to tax the coal and steel producers up to one per cent per year on the average value of their output. The High Authority had set a limit of $100 million for its guarantee fund

---

[18] An uneconomic firm would probably not have much internal reserve for self-financing.

[19] These High Authority decisions are: No. 38–53, *Journal officiel*, July 21, 1953; No. 27–55, *Journal officiel*, July 26, 1955; No. 26–56, *Journal officiel*, July 19, 1956.

[20] From September 1, 1955 to December 31, 1957 the High Authority examined 264 declarations involving 392 individual investment projects; HA, *Sixième rapport général*, Vol. II, April 1958, pp. 305–306.

and it reduced the tax as the limit was approached. The rate, set at 0.9 per cent in February 1953, was reduced to 0.7 per cent on July 1, 1955, to 0.45 per cent on January 1, 1956 and to 0.35 per cent on July 1, 1957. At the last rate the Community's revenue amounted to $29 million annually.[21] Current expenses then amounted to about 50 per cent of proceeds; the remainder of the income went to various funds—for relocation of workers, research, pensions and other purposes. The High Authority had thus by 1958 reduced the Community's revenue pretty close to a minimum.[22]

The coal and steel producers favored the progressive reduction in tax rates. They were afraid that the High Authority might otherwise try to influence their decisions by means of a large loan program coupled with a strict scrutiny of individual investment projects under Article 54. They expressed their distaste for such an eventuality by attacking "dirigisme and bureaucracy."

The High Authority put these fears to rest when it published a statement in 1954 on the principles and procedures it would use in granting loans from the $100 million it had borrowed from the United States government.[23] Programs for investment and borrowing, the High Authority indicated, were to come from the bottom up rather than from the top down. The High Authority would only supplement the funds borrowed by the firms from other sources and would grant loans only where other lenders would also put up funds. These principles served to allay the fear that the High Authority might try to displace conventional lenders or the initiative of the individual firm.

By June 1958 the High Authority had borrowed $216 million, $185 million of which was from the United States. The loans from the United States consisted of a long-term loan of $100 million from the United States government and of $85 million from two public bond issues. The equivalent of $31 million was borrowed in other countries ($12 million in Switzerland, an equal amount in Germany and about $7.3 million in the Saar, Belgium and Luxembourg).[24] The High Authority's guarantee fund as of 1958 was at the ratio of $1 to every $2 borrowed. The $100 million guarantee fund could support an obligation of at least $500 million, for a ratio of 1 to 5 is probably adequate.[25]

[21] HA, *Quatrième rapport général*, April 1956, pp. 249 ff, and *Sixième rapport général*, Vol. II, pp. 339 ff. The Community's potential revenue at the one per cent tax rate would have been $85 million a year.

[22] From February 1953 to mid-1958 the High Authority had collected $204 million in tax proceeds and $17 million in interest and fines, or $221 million. Nearly 50 per cent of the proceeds was used for the guarantee fund, 25 per cent for other funds, 20 per cent for administration and 5 per cent for research and readaptation.

[23] See "Guide pour l'établissement des demandes de prêt à la Haute Autorité" and "Principes de l'action de la Haute Autorité dans le domaine de financement des investissements," in *Journal officiel*, July 31, 1954.

[24] HA, *Cinquième rapport général*, Annexe, April 1957, p. 13; *Sixième rapport général*, Vol. II, pp. 312, 344–346; *Bulletin mensuel d'information*, July 1958, pp. 16 ff.

[25] Assemblée Parlementaire Européenne, Doc. No. 22, 1958, p. 34.

The coal and steel industries spent an aggregate of about $1 billion annually on capital investments from the beginning of 1953 to the end of 1957, or $5.2 billion in all. In the corresponding period the High Authority made loans to the two industries of nearly $150 million, two thirds of which were for the coal industry. The loans made by the High Authority therefore represented 3 per cent of total capital expenditures in the five-year period 1953–1957 but they covered 20 per cent of the cost of the projects aided.[26] The High Authority had not as of December 1957 guaranteed any third-party loans made to the coal and steel industries. Thanks to the $100 million guarantee fund, the High Authority was able to borrow at interest rates of from 3.5 to 5 per cent and to lend the money to the firms at the same rate plus a small charge for service. These interest rates were lower than those then prevailing in most European countries.

The High Authority had as of April 1958 advanced $46 million in loans for 30,000 lodgings, built at a total cost of $155 million,[27] and $12 million in loans or nonrepayable grants to help workers and firms weather the changes created by the common market. The grants helped 19,000 workers, 70 per cent of whom were Italian.[28]

Long-Term Supply Requirements Estimates

The High Authority made great use of its power (Article 46) to draw up long-term market forecasts as a means of guiding investments. The first report, made in July 1955,[29] indicated that general supply and production objectives would be issued from time to time to help the firms to orient their investment programs and the High Authority to review their applications.

The expansionist views of Jean Monnet, President of the High Authority from 1952 to 1955, influenced the views of that body.[30] He believed that enough steel and coal should be available to support and stimulate a reasonable rate of economic expansion.

In addition to the formal methods at its disposal, the High Authority influences investment programs by means of informal contacts with the governments and producers.[31]

---

[26] HA, *Sixième rapport général*, Vol. II, p. 346; *Bulletin mensuel d'information*, October-November 1958, p. 21.

[27] HA, *Sixième rapport général*, Vol. II, pp. 266 ff.

[28] *Ibid.*, p. 203.

[29] *Journal officiel*, July 19, 1955.

[30] Monnet, theretofore head of the French Commissariat du Plan, was also responsible for the postwar reconstruction program for heavy industry in France (the so-called "Monnet Plans"). These plans laid the groundwork for French industrial expansion after the second world war.

[31] Assemblée Parlementaire Européenne, Doc. No. 22, 1958, p. 27.

A NOTE ON THE UNITED KINGDOM

The British government also has the power to influence the rate of expansion and individual capital projects in the steel industry. The location of new plants, investment projects exceeding £100,000, and the over-all expansion rate in the industry are subject to examination and approval by the Iron and Steel Board. The British Iron and Steel Federation coordinates investments for the industry as a whole. The Iron and Steel Board also establishes maximum steel prices that provide a margin for depreciation at historical cost and for internal financing of new projects at current capital costs. The British coal industry has also been under centralized control ever since its nationalization.

GROWTH TRENDS

The steel industry has experienced three phases. The period 1880 to 1913, and that after the second world war, were expansive; the 1930s were stagnant, following a decade of plant reconstruction and expansion induced by national boundary changes following the first world war.

INTERWAR PERIOD

World steel markets were sluggish throughout the interwar years owing to depression and because the importing countries developed local plants. Though steel consumption in Europe in the period 1913–1937 expanded more than total steel production, as shown by Fig. 8, renewal and upkeep of plant

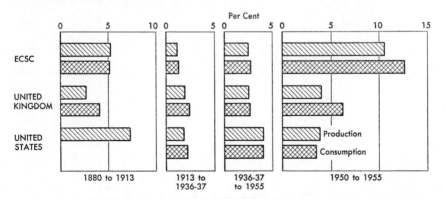

FIG. 8. Average Annual Growth Rates in Consumption and Production of Crude Steel, Main Steel Producing Areas, Selected Periods, 1880–1955

Sources: Ingvar Svennilson, *Growth and Stagnation in the European Economy*, ECE, Geneva, 1954, pp. 261, 274; Tables 2-2 and 7-3, Appendix E. (United States consumption in period 1880 to 1913 not available.)

Table 17

OPERATING RATES OF PIG IRON AND CRUDE STEEL PRODUCERS,
MAIN STEEL PRODUCING COUNTRIES, SELECTED INTERWAR YEARS[a]

(Per Cent)

A: Pig Iron   B: Crude Steel and Castings

Country	1927		1929		1932		1934		1937		1938		Average, 1932–1938[b]	
	A	B	A	B	A	B	A	B	A	B	A	B	A	B
Germany	86.2	94.2	86.8	93.6	25.7	33.5	57.2	59.5	90.1	87.5	102.6	100.5	66.9	67.1
France	83.0	83.8	92.9	98.0	49.1	56.6	55.4	63.3	70.5	80.6	54.5	63.3	56.1	66.3
Saar	90.0	82.6	105.0	95.7	65.0	65.2	78.3	76.0	95.7	92.0	104.3	104.0	84.3	82.4
Luxembourg	93.1	89.3	100.0	96.4	69.0	71.4	69.0	67.9	86.2	89.3	55.2	50.0	67.6	68.9
Belgium	97.4	92.5	105.3	102.5	71.1	70.0	76.9	70.7	97.4	95.1	61.5	56.1	76.3	72.5
ECSC	87.2	90.1	92.9	96.1	43.9	48.8	61.1	63.3	84.8	87.0	79.2	83.2	65.7	68.6
United Kingdom	60.7	75.4	63.1	80.3	29.5	43.4	49.6	70.3	69.9	103.1	56.1	82.8	50.8	75.0
Main European	80.3	86.4	85.2	92.2	40.2	47.4	58.2	65.0	81.0	90.9	73.2	83.1	61.9	70.2
United States	69.9	74.7	81.4	93.9	16.5	22.8	32.3	37.4	74.4	72.4	38.5	40.6	42.1	45.8

Sources: Calculated from Tables 2-2 and 5-8, Appendix E.

[a] Operating rates for 1927, 1929 and 1932 based on 1927 capacity; for subsequent years based on 1936 capacity.

[b] Based on 1936 capacity.

74

were discouraged by low operating rates in 1932–1938; steel producing facilities then operated at 69 per cent of capacity in the ECSC, at 75 per cent of capacity in the United Kingdom and at 46 per cent of capacity in the United States. (See Table 17.) The introduction of the continuous strip mill, the major technical development of the interwar period, helped modernize the American steel industry in the 1930s—and partly explains its growth in that period—but hardly affected Europe. The British steel producers, however, overcame the stagnation that affected the industry in other parts of Europe during the 1930s and embarked, with encouragement from the government, on a long overdue program of planned renewal after the tariff was introduced in 1932. Italian steel production also expanded in the late 1930s, with the help of public funds. German expansion in the late 1930s was largely confined to Lower Saxony and served a military purpose.

POST–WORLD WAR II

The Western European steel industry emerged from the war with a high proportion of obsolescent plant, a huge volume of unsatisfied demand and the temporary loss of a major part of Ruhr capacity.

Steel production grew at a faster rate in 1950–1955 than in the very expansive period 1880–1913. (See Fig. 8.) The postwar expansion of steel capacity did not fail to arouse fear of overexpansion. A report in 1949 by the United Nations Economic Commission for Europe (ECE) sharply brought this apprehension into view by questioning the exuberance of the expansion program.[32] But the market for steel was seriously underestimated by the report of the ECE, for the steel industry in Western Europe operated close to 100 per cent of capacity much of the time from 1950 to the end of 1957.

FORECASTS TO 1975

Over-All Economic Expansion

The High Authority published in May 1957 a forecast of economic growth called "Objectifs généraux" covering 1955–1975.[33]

In 1950–1955 gross national product increased at a rate of 5.6 per cent a year in the ECSC countries combined and industrial production by 9.2 per

---

[32] *European Steel Trends in the Setting of the World Market*, Geneva, 1949.

[33] The report is in *Journal officiel*, May 20, 1957. It was also published in the *Cinquième rapport général* but citations herein are to the former source. The forecasts are also discussed in *Etude sur la structure et les tendances de l'économie énergetique dans les pays de la Communauté*, Comité Mixte, Luxembourg, 1957, and in Louis Armand, *et al.*, *Un objectif pour Euratom*, Paris, 1957. The last two reports deal specifically with energy; only the "Objectifs généraux" contains forecasts on steel.

cent. The forecast assumed a lively but slower rate of economic expansion in 1955–1975 than in 1950–1955. The employed population was expected to grow from 69 million in 1955 to 76 million by 1975, an increase of 10 per cent. Though working time was expected to decline by 3 per cent, productivity per hour was expected to increase at a rate of 3 per cent a year,[34] compared with 4.3 per cent in 1950–1955. GNP was expected to rise by 3.5 per cent annually for the two decades compared with 5.6 per cent in 1950–1955. (See Table 18.)

Table 18

RATES OF ECONOMIC GROWTH AND PERCENTAGE INCREASE
IN CONSUMPTION OF PRIMARY ENERGY AND CRUDE STEEL, ECSC, 1950–1955
AND FORECASTS, 1955–1975

| Years | Productivity | GNP | Industrial Production | Consumption | |
				Energy	Crude Steel
1950–1955	4.3	5.6	9.2	5.8	12.6
1955–1965	3.5	4.1	4.9	3.5	4.8[a]
1965–1975	2.6	3.0	3.3	2.7	3.3[a]
1955–1975	3.0	3.5	4.1	3.1	4.0[a]

Sources: Comité Mixte report; HA, "Objectifs généraux," *Journal officiel*, May 20, 1957.

[a] This represents an "intermediate" rather than a maximum rate of growth; see Comité Mixte report, p. 109. The maximum rate for 1955–1965 is forecast at 5.6 per cent.

The forecasts assumed that industrial production would increase by 124 per cent in 1955–1975, rising more rapidly than GNP owing to the growth of capital-intensive and consumers' durable goods industries.[35] (See Table 19.)

The forecasts of industrial production are particularly pertinent. Though future demand for steel and energy can be estimated in relation to the requirements of specific industries, the High Authority based its forecasts on the growth in over-all production and GNP. It did not claim the predictions to be more than suggestive.

The Investments Committee of the Common Assembly, criticizing the High Authority's forecasts from the public welfare point of view, said that the forecasts should have been based on desirable rather than probable goals and that the High Authority should have requested the governments to define their goals of economic progress. The committee pointed out that the High Author-

[34] The OEEC anticipated a 2.8 per cent rate of growth for its seventeen member countries; *Europe's Growing Needs of Energy, How Can They Be Met?*, p. 66.

[35] Industrial production in 1950–1955 increased about 1.7 times faster than GNP; it was expected to increase about 1.17 times faster than GNP in 1955–1975. The period 1950–1955 encompassed a number of nonrepetitive phenomena—the absorption of a large number of unemployed; the phenomenal recovery in Germany; reconstruction to eradicate the effects of the war years and of the Great Depression; and the Korean War boom.

ity, for example, should have indicated whether or not a 3 per cent decline in working time is compatible with a desirable rate of progress. The governments and industries should be obligated, the report went on, to help achieve the goals considered desirable. The "Objectifs Généraux" would then have been

Table 19

PRODUCTION AND CONSUMPTION OF PRIMARY ENERGY AND CRUDE STEEL,
ECSC, 1955 AND FORECASTS, 1965 AND 1975

	1955	1965	1975	Index (1955 = 100) 1965	1975
	(Millions)				
Labor force	69	73	76	106	110
Gross national product				152	206
Industrial production				162	224
Primary energy (hard coal equivalent):	*(Millions of Metric Tons)*				
Consumption	400	565	730	141	183
Production:					
Hard coal	246	264	285	107	116
Other classical energy[a]	72	119	156	165	217
Total	318	383	441	120	139
Net imports before nuclear contribution	84	182	289	217	344
Crude steel:					
Consumption	44[b]	70[c]	96[d]	159	218
Production	52	79[c]	105[d]	152	202

Sources: HA, "Objectifs généraux," *Journal officiel*, May 20, 1957, and Comité Mixte report for forecasts of over-all economic activity and steel. Louis Armand *et al.*, *Un objectif pour Euratom*, Paris, May 1957, is the main source for the energy projections, with modifications by the author of this study, principally regarding coal production and the probable nuclear contribution. Estimates of residual imports, showing coal and other classical energy separately, are the author's.

[a] The "probable" estimate in *Un objectif pour Euratom*, p. 58. Lignite is included.

[b] Table 7-3, Appendix E, shows a slightly lower consumption of 43 million tons.

[c] "Intermediate" rather than maximum forecasts, which are 76 million tons of consumption and 86 million tons of production.

[d] "Intermediate" forecast.

a statement of policy rather than of information.[36] This reproach suggests an alternative which, whatever its merits, should have been addressed to the member governments rather than to the High Authority. The alternative called for a type of planning to which none of the governments was committed and implied a coordination of national fiscal, monetary and employment

[36] Commission des Investissements, Assemblée Commune, *Rapport sur les objectifs généraux*, Exercice 1956–1957, 2ème session extraordinaire, February 1957, pp. 11–15.

policies that might be more appropriate to the European Economic Community than to a Community that encompasses two industries only.

Crude Steel Forecasts

Steel production is expected to increase at a rate of 3.5 per cent a year in 1955–1975; though this rate is a third of that for 1950–1955 and two thirds of that for 1880–1913, it is still a lively rate of expansion, implying a doubling of production in twenty years. (See Fig. 8.) Like industrial production, steel consumption is expected to more than double in twenty years. Steel production will increase more slowly than consumption because the High Authority estimates assumed that world steel markets had reached the saturation point in 1955 and that steel exports from the ECSC to third-party areas would remain fairly constant—at 8 to 9 million tons a year (in crude steel equivalents) from 1955 to 1975. The whole increase in production will therefore be absorbed by domestic consumption.

Though steel production in the ECSC is expected to rise more slowly than home consumption, the reverse is expected in Britain; their forecasts, covering 1954–1962, assume that British home production will suffice to eliminate imports of steel, which amounted to nearly 2 million tons in 1955 (in crude steel equivalents) and which have been high during peak consumption periods.[37]

In 1955 Britain consumed 801 pounds of crude steel per capita; Germany-Saar, 939 pounds; France, 511 pounds; Belgium-Luxembourg, 604 pounds; Netherlands, 537 pounds; Italy, 259 pounds; and the United States 1,360 pounds.[38] The ECSC as a whole consumed 594 pounds per capita in 1955. Per capita consumption in the ECSC was thus 44 per cent of that in the United States and 74 per cent of that in the United Kingdom. The prospective rates of growth will help close, but not eliminate, these differences.

A Note on Iron Ore Forecasts[39]

Western Europe will have to draw on imports for most of its additional needs for iron ore. Western Europe rather than the ECSC is the proper focus of attention because both of the main producers, the United Kingdom and the ECSC, face a common problem and, except for France and Luxembourg, draw on the same sources of world supply.

[37] United Kingdom, Iron and Steel Board, *Development in the Iron and Steel Industry*, HMSO, London, 1957. The data on Britain in this subheading are in long tons.

[38] *Ibid.*, p. 13.

[39] The High Authority deals with the supply and demand for iron ore up to 1960 in "Objectifs généraux," pp. 216–218. Commission des Investissements, Assemblée Commune, *op. cit.*, pp. 20–23, supplied data up to 1975 and called on the High Authority to have another report prepared on the problems. This section is based mainly on the article, covering 1955–1965, by Eugen Plotki, "Stand und voraussichtliche Entwicklung der Eisenerzversorgung," in *Stahl und Eisen*, December 27, 1956, pp. 1728–1734.

In 1955 Western Europe produced 75 million tons of crude steel and consumed 46 million tons of iron ore (in iron content), of which 28 million tons
were home produced and 18 million imported. On the assumption that Western Europe will produce 100 million tons of crude steel in 1965, and that scrap
will remain scarce, iron ore requirements (in iron content) were estimated
as follows:

	1955	*1965*	
	(Millions of Metric Tons)		*Change (Per Cent)*
Crude steel output	75	100	33
Requirements for iron from ore (iron content)	46	65	41
Home production	28	35	25
Imports*	18	30	67

* Assumes iron ore of 55 per cent iron content.

Imports thus will rise by about 65 per cent between 1955–1965 but home
production will rise by only 25 per cent.[40] Home production will reach its
peak about 1960. Imported ore will have to meet an increasing deficit after
that date and may triple by 1975 as compared with 1955. Most of the additional
home production will come from Lorraine. But France, which contributed
about 50 per cent of the aggregate iron ore charge in the ECSC in 1955 (in
iron content), will account for a diminishing proportion in the future as imports rise. Most of the Lorraine ore will continue to be consumed in France,
Belgium and Luxembourg.

Western Europe must count on new world sources for imported ore because
the traditional ones, including Swedish ore, can meet only a fraction of growing requirements. Latin America, Africa and Canada are the sources of prospective supply. Besides the need to develop new iron ore reserves and new
mines abroad, Western Europe is also confronted with the rather staggering
problem of developing new shipping, harbor and stocking facilities and with
locating new steel plants at favorable locations for imported iron ore.

CAPITAL EXPENDITURES

The steel producers in the ECSC spent an average of $527 million a year on
gross capital formation in 1952–1956. (See Table 20 and Fig. 9.)

The capital cost of a completely new steel plant in Europe, from coke to
rolling mills and finishing facilities, averaged about $225 to $250 per metric

[40] HA, *Informations statistiques*, October 1958, pp. 345–359, gives data on the limited life of
the iron ore reserves in the ECSC.

ton of crude steel at 1956 prices. It was about $320 per metric ton in the United States, where the industry is more capital intensive per ton of capacity. Capital costs vary with the complexity of the plant; they were $160 per ton of crude steel capacity in the United Kingdom for a plant producing a simple product

Table 20

CAPITAL EXPENDITURES FOR EXPANSION AND RENEWAL,
MAIN STEEL PRODUCING COUNTRIES, 1952–1956[a]

Country	1952	1953	1954	1955	1956	Annual Average, 1952–1956	
						Total (*Millions*)	Per Ton Produced
			(*Millions*)				
Germany	$163	$196	$210	$289	$247	$221	$11.90
Saar	20	20	16	19	35	22	7.30
France	188	188	126	108	150	152	13.20
Belgium	29	37	33	33	45	35	6.50
Luxembourg	20	24	25	22	19	22	7.30
Italy	105	69	36	36	51	59	13.10
Netherlands	21	8	8	16	26	16	17.75
Total	545	542	453	524	572	527	11.25
United Kingdom	126	138	146	162	210	156	8.25
United States	1,298	988	609	714	1,299	982	10.30

Sources: 1952–1956: ECSC from HA, *Les Investissements dans les industries du charbon et de l'acier de la Communauté*, Luxembourg, September 1957, Annex Table 13; United Kingdom from Iron and Steel Board, *Development in the Iron and Steel Industry*, HMSO, London, July 1957, p. 72; United States from American Iron and Steel Institute, *Charting Steel's Progress*, 1957, p. 64.

[a] Investments not corrected for price changes. Actual capital expenditures in the ECSC refer only to gross outlays for fixed assets that are activated in the enterprises' financial reports and therefore exclude the value of stocks and working capital. Those for the United Kingdom and the United States also refer only to gross fixed investment. The ECSC excludes projects under $500,000 for new plant and $1 million for replacement; the British Iron and Steel Board cuts off at $280,000. Investments cover total plant, from coking and iron ore preparation to rolling mills, including gas and power production and distribution. Investment data for the ECSC include only the "treaty products," but those for the United Kingdom and the United States also include tubes and wire products.

to $320 per ton for a tin plate producing plant. Since a completely new plant in Europe on a new site with an annual crude steel output of 1 million tons costs an average of about $225 to $250 million at 1956 prices, the investment is large indeed, equivalent to two to two and one half times the annual sales turnover. It is therefore less costly and quicker to enlarge an existing plant than to build a new one. It is very difficult to separate net investment—that for enlargement or expansion—from gross investment; the attempt if made is sure to be arbitrary. An existing plant can be enlarged and modernized for about

70 per cent of the expenditure required for a new one—$160 to $175 per metric ton.[41]

The average steel plant has to be modernized or rebuilt about every twenty years; the theoretical rate of capital formation in the European steel industry at 1956 prices should thus run about $8 to $9 a year per ton of crude steel

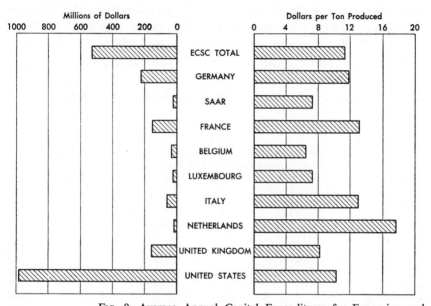

Fig. 9. Average Annual Capital Expenditures for Expansion and Renewal, Main Steel Producing Countries, 1952–1956

Source: Table 20.

produced—if the plants are operating at capacity, as they were during much of the period 1952–1956—for modernization and enlargement of existing plants, and about $11 to $12 per ton for completely new plants, though completely new steel plants on new sites are rarely built. Capital formation for modernization and enlargement should therefore be somewhere between $8 and $12 per ton of production, depending on the type of expansion involved.[42]

[41] United Kingdom Iron and Steel Board, *Development in the Iron and Steel Industry*, p. 71; *Steel Review*, October 1956, p. 7; Ernest Weir, chairman of the board of the National Steel Corporation, cited in *New York Times*, March 23, 1956. The president of Usinor (France) gave the cost of a new steel plant at $235 per ton of crude steel at 1957 prices, in *Le Monde*, December 6–7, 1957, p. 15.

[42] An estimate in *Steel Review*, January 1957, p. 23, cautiously put the proportion of replacement to gross investment in the British steel industry in 1946–1956 at 30 per cent, expansion taking 70 per cent of the gross figure. The British steel industry believed that expansion would absorb two thirds of gross capital formation between 1954–1962. "The British Steel Industry, 1958," special issue of *Steel Review*, 1959, p. 45.

The steel industry in the ECSC invested from 1952 to 1956 an average of $11.25 a year per ton of steel produced, as Table 20 shows.[43] This high rate of investment, at the upper part of the theoretical range, permitted the industry to expand considerably in those years.

The rate of investment in France—$13.20 per ton—was extremely high even if the overvaluation of the franc is taken into consideration. A large part of the French industry was reorganized in this period and new facilities were placed in operation. But French crude steel output increased by only 20 per cent in 1952–1956, compared with 35 per cent in the ECSC as a whole, because rolling mills and power, rather than crude steel production, were emphasized. Nearly one fourth the total investment made by the French steel industry was devoted to gas and power producing facilities, as Table 21 shows.

Table 21

PERCENTAGE DISTRIBUTION OF TOTAL INVESTMENT IN THE STEEL INDUSTRY, ECSC, BY COUNTRY AND TYPE OF FACILITY, 1954–1956[a]

Country	Blast Furnaces, Preparation Plants and Cokeries	Steel Melting	Rolling Mills	Gas and Power Distribution Facilities	Total
Germany	14	15	58	13	100
Saar	24	10	51	15	100
France	22	10	45	23	100
Belgium	31	12	41	16	100
Luxembourg	38	15	33	14	100
Italy	6	13	65	16	100
Netherlands	30	19	30	21	100
Total	18	13	52	16	100

Source: Calculated from data in HA, *Investissements dans les industries du charbon et de l'acier de la Communauté*, September 1957, Appendix Tables 14 to 17, inclusive.

[a] Only gross capital expenditures added to fixed assets in company balance sheets are included.

Investments per ton were also high in Italy and the Netherlands; crude steel output increased by 70 per cent in the former and by 50 per cent in the latter in 1952–1956. Though the German steel industry had gotten off to a late start in making postwar investments, its rate of investment climbed to nearly $12 a ton in 1952–1956, and investments in some years in that period were at a much higher rate. Crude steel production increased by 50 per cent, partly owing to the revival of idle capacity.

[43] Cf. HA, *Sixième rapport général*, Vol. II, pp. 414 ff, where the data cover 1953–1956 and exclude investments in iron ore, coke and power plants, which are included in the figures in Table 20.

Investments in the Saar, Luxembourg and Belgium—at about $7 per ton— were below the average for the ECSC. Production increased in these three areas also, but at a lower rate than in the ECSC as a whole.

Capital expenditures in the British steel industry averaged $8.25 a ton in 1952–1956 and were higher toward the end of the period. Crude steel production increased by 25 per cent during the period. Expenditures in the American steel industry averaged $10.30 a ton. Since capital costs in the United States are higher, the theoretical annual rate of capital formation on a twenty-year life of plant is $11 (compared with $8 to $9 in Europe) for renewing and enlarging developed sites and $16 (compared with $11 to $12 in Europe) for a new plant and new site. The rate of investment in the American steel industry in 1952–1956 was therefore lower than that in the ECSC partly because its period of intense development came earlier.

Owing to the high rate of investment and growth since World War II, steel plant facilities in Western Europe and the United States are fairly new and efficient. The average annual output of pig iron per blast furnace—a good indicator of efficiency—has increased steadily since the second world war, as Table 22 shows.

Table 22

AVERAGE ANNUAL OUTPUT OF PIG IRON PER BLAST FURNACE, MAIN STEEL PRODUCING COUNTRIES, SELECTED YEARS, 1913–1955[a]

(*Thousands of Metric Tons*)

Year	Germany	Saar	France	Belgium	Luxem-bourg	United Kingdom	United States
1913[b]	59	53	47	46	59	31	104[c]
1937	147	97	78	82	103	70	217[d]
1950	132	102	83	94	110	98	261
1955	159	111	94	106	112	128	311

Sources: Ingvar Svennilson, *Growth and Stagnation in the European Economy*, ECE, Geneva, 1954, p. 265; HA, *Bulletin statistique;* Statistisches Bundesamt, Düsseldorf; American Iron and Steel Institute, *Annual Statistical Report*, 1956, and *Charting Steel's Progress*, 1957; *Metal Statistics*, American Metal Market, N. Y.

[a] Calculated by dividing annual production by number of blast furnaces in operation or existence, depending on availability of data. Italy excluded owing to erratic variations from year to year and inadequate data.

[b] Postwar territory.   [c] 1917.   [d] 1939.

The United States has the largest average output per blast furnace; Germany has the largest in Europe. Great Britain is rapidly catching up with the rest of Europe after having had the smallest in Europe between the two wars. Average output per blast furnace increased in all countries. The growth in average size is as significant as relative size because it indicates that a high proportion of facilities are new and efficient. Differences in operating costs tend to diminish as an increasing number of plants are modernized.

FINANCING OF INVESTMENTS

The investment in a new plant represents two to two and one half times the value of a unit of output in the steel and coal industries, compared with one to one and one half times the value in industry as a whole.[44]

Government Policy

The requirements for capital were so large and private capital was so limited after the second world war that the governments came to the rescue of the steel industry. The French steel industry relied on a large amount of government credits including Marshall Plan aid and bankers' short-term loans. It organized the Groupement de l'Industrie Sidérurgique (GIS) to help obtain funds on the capital market. GIS centralizes the flotation of long-term bonds and distributes the proceeds to the member firms. The German steel industry was in an extremely abnormal situation under the occupation and the deconcentration program. It was not until 1951 that the status of the industry and of particular firms was sufficiently clarified to encourage the German steel industry to begin investments on a large scale. The German government allowed internal steel prices to rise sharply in the middle of 1952 in order to provide a margin for self-financing and the German parliament passed an act providing for rapid amortization in the coal and steel industries. Nationalized in 1949 and denationalized in 1952, conditions were not quite normal for the British steel industry either.

To what extent do tax policies influence internal financing? In all the countries in Western Europe except Belgium depreciation rates are based on original capital cost adjusted for currency changes; in Belgium they are based on value when operations begin. The writeoff period is determined by negotiation everywhere but Italy and the United Kingdom, where the authorities determine the writeoff period for each class of asset according to fixed rates. All the countries have some form of accelerated depreciation. In France the first year's writeoff may be doubled if the life of the asset exceeds five years and the steel and coal industries may amortize at a value equivalent to 2.5 to 15 per cent of annual turnover (excluding turnover tax); the difference between the

---

[44] Cf. ECE, *Economic Survey of Europe for 1952*, p. 210, and also the statement by the president of Usinor in *Le Monde*, December 6–7, 1957, p. 15.

Investments in the coal and steel industries accounted in 1953–1955 for nearly 5 to 6 per cent of gross capital formation in Germany, France-Saar and Belgium, for 30 per cent in Luxembourg, about 2 per cent in the Netherlands, 0.5 per cent in Italy and 3.7 per cent in the United Kingdom. Calculated from data in OEEC, *General Statistics*, and Tables 20 and 28.

normal and the accelerated allowance may be carried forward if not claimed. In Belgium accelerated depreciation may be allowed by negotiation to meet particular situations. In the Netherlands there is an initial allowance of one third the capital cost, spread over ten years. In Italy new plants receive a 40 per cent allowance spread over four years. In the United Kingdom the authorities may grant accelerated writeoff in particular cases. In Germany the Investment Aid Act, valid from 1952 to 1955, allowed the coal and steel industries to write off 50 per cent of movable, and 30 per cent of fixed, assets in three years.[45] On the expiration of the Investment Aid Act, a new act, described in Chapter 4, was passed to help the coal industry. The American steel industry, among others, received the benefit of accelerated amortization under special tax certificates for defense expansion under an act effective in 1951; steel projects were declared ineligible for such certificates in 1956.[46]

Source of Capital Funds

Data on financing by the steel industry in Germany, France, Britain and the United States in 1953–1956 are shown in Table 23.[47] The German steel industry covered more than 70 per cent of total investments from retained earnings, no new equity capital having been obtained in 1953–1955. Accelerated amortization under the Investment Aid Act of 1952–1955 provided a substantial proportion of total funds appropriated to amortization:[48]

	Accelerated Amortization as Per Cent of Total Amortization
1953	41
1954	36
1955	46
1956	34

The proportion of internal financing—and the ratio of total investments to turnover as well—declined in 1956 as the Investment Aid Act expired.

The French steel industry went through an abnormal period from 1948 to 1955. As already mentioned, investments per ton of steel were very high. The ratio of investments to turnover was unusually high, nearly one quarter in 1953, and declined to more normal levels, 13 per cent, in 1956. It did not exceed 13 per cent in Germany at any time in 1953–1956. Pressed for funds, the

[45] The data for this rapid summary are from a report by the Federation of British Industries, *Taxation in the Proposed European Free Trade Area*, London, October 1957.

[46] *New York Times*, December 27, 1956, p. 1.

[47] See the notes thereto on the limitations of the data.

[48] Institut für Bilanzenanalysen, *Die eisenschaffende Industrie*, 1957, p. 12; also *Stahl und Eisen*, December 20, 1956, p. 1778.

French steel industry covered a very high proportion of investments from medium- and short-term loans; internal financing covered only one fourth of

Table 23

FINANCING OF INVESTMENTS IN THE STEEL INDUSTRY,
SELECTED STEEL PRODUCING COUNTRIES, 1953–1956[a]

Country and Year	Investments as Per Cent of Turnover	Self-Financing as Per Cent of:	
		Investments	Turnover
	(1)	(2)	(3)
Germany			
1953	13	73	9.5
1954	13	75	9.8
1955	12	76	9.1
1956	11	71	7.8
France			
1953	23	24[b]	5.5
1954	16	37[c]	5.9
1955	18	48[c]	8.6
1956	13	59[c]	7.7
United Kingdom			
1946–1955	[d]	81	(7.0–8.0)
United States[e]			
1953	9	42	3.4
1954	5	48	2.4
1955	6	93	7.3
1956	11	43	4.7

Sources: Germany: Institut für Bilanzenanalysen, *Die Eisenschaffende Industrie,* 1957, covering 91 per cent of German crude steel. France: *Annual Reports* of the Groupement de l'Industrie Sidérurgique, covering virtually all French crude steel. United Kingdom: "Finance and Investment," in *Steel Review,* January 1957; "Financing Steel Production," *Steel Review,* October 1956; virtually all British steel is covered. United States: American Iron and Steel Institute, *Charting Steel's Progress* and *Annual Statistical Reports;* these cover 95 per cent of American steel.

[a] Investments (col. 1) in Germany refer to gross capital expenditures on fixed assets; those in France, the United States and the United Kingdom include also net changes in working capital. The investment data in this table are therefore not comparable with those in Table 20, which are confined to investments inscribed in the balance sheets to fixed assets. Investments cover all facilities from coke to rolling mills. Turnover taxes excluded.

Self-financing (col. 2) refers to fiscal allowance and reserves, excluding funds from equity issues, which were small in the United Kingdom and Germany, on gross fixed investment and net changes in working capital. The French data in col. 2 refer to self-financing on debt repayment, as well as on capital outlays for fixed assets and working capital. The French steel industry made large debt repayments during these years on an extremely high ratio of short-term debt to total debt.

Col. 3 = Col. 1 x Col. 2

[b] Includes a small amount of equity capital.

[c] The French steel industry obtained equity funds equivalent to 5 per cent of investments in 1954–1955 and 8 per cent in 1956; these are not included in col. 2.

[d] According to data furnished by the Iron and Steel Board in *Development in Steel* and in the *Annual Reports,* investment on turnover in 1954–1956 was 9 to 10 per cent; this excludes changes in working capital, which would add about another 1.5 per cent.

[e] The American steel industry, in addition, obtained a large amount of equity capital not shown in col. 2.

investments in 1953 and 37 per cent in 1954. Not until 1955 did the ratio of self-financing rise to more normal levels as the ratio of investments to turnover declined. The financial costs therefore represented a high charge on the trading profit. Though the ratio of internal financing to total investment was low in France, it was still substantial in absolute figures because investments were high. France's rate of self-financing to turnover compared more favorably with Germany's than its rate of self-financing to investments. Self-financing on turnover in 1956 was as high in the French as the German steel industry— nearly 8 per cent—though it accounted for a smaller percentage of total investment in the former than in the latter. The Third Modernization Program for 1957–1961 drawn up by the steel industry and the Commissariat Général du Plan indicated that self-financing would be more normal, covering 65 per cent of total capital requirements in 1957–1961—closer to the results obtained in 1956.[49]

Self-financing covered 81 per cent of total investments in the British steel industry in 1946–1955. This high rate was expected to decline—to 65 per cent in 1954–1962—as total investments rose.[50] The high rate of self-financing in the United Kingdom was achieved at the expense of a lower rate of total investment per ton of steel produced than in most of the other major steel producing countries (Table 20). Though self-financing covered 81 per cent of investment it was only 7 to 8 per cent of turnover. Self-financing in the German steel industry covered a smaller portion of investments but accounted for a higher proportion of turnover. The United Kingdom Iron and Steel Board fixes prices to provide a margin for expansion. These margins take account of new plant expansion at current capital cost as well as of depreciation at historical cost.[51]

Financial results in the United States steel industry in 1953–1956 varied with business conditions. Investments as per cent of turnover were somewhat lower than in Germany or France but the industry had already gone through its major postwar expansion. The ratio of retained profit to investments was 93 per cent in 1955 but less than 45 per cent in 1953, 1954 and 1956. At 93 per cent on capital expenditures it was only 7 per cent on turnover, lower than in Germany.

Prices and Internal Financing

An expansion price is one that permits the average firm in an industry to earn enough to cover a large part of its capital expenditures for expansion

[49] *Le Monde*, September 21, 1957, p. 13; October 20–21, 1957, p. 7.

[50] *Steel Review*, January 1957, pp. 32 ff.

[51] The *Annual Reports* of the Iron and Steel Board for 1954 and 1955 describe the price-fixing principles.

from earnings after paying taxes and dividends, in comparison with a price that merely yields a fixed return on invested capital, as in regulated public utilities, which cover their capital expenditures by borrowing. Since the capital cost of a new steel plant in Europe is between $225 and $250 per ton of ingot capacity, and the annual turnover is between 40 and 50 per cent of the capital cost, an expansion price would yield a margin of about 10 to 13 per cent of turnover for investment in new plant and about 7 to 9 per cent for investment in developed plants.[52]

The ratio of self-financing to turnover in the European steel industry in 1953–1956 was within the range required for expansion of developed plants (col. 3, Table 23). Prices were consequently moderately expansionist, though the governments restrained home prices from rising freely—especially in France—thanks in part to higher proceeds from export sales.

INFLUENCE OF THE ECSC ON INVESTMENTS

The influence of the ECSC on investments in the steel industry is discussed from four aspects: the volume of investments; the distribution of investments by type of facility; the location of production; and the influence of individual governments.

VOLUME OF INVESTMENTS

If an economic union encourages producers to look to their costs of production—instead of to protection—for the sake of maintaining or enlarging their share of the market, it will stimulate investments, whether price competition occurs or not. Investments by the steel industry in the ECSC were high during the first five years of the common market. But it is difficult to separate the influence of the economic boom from that of the economic union by itself, though the latter might have helped push investments up, too, for the same reason that it stimulated concentrations. (See Chapter 5.) Faced with a new situation, not knowing which way rivals would jump, each steel producer in the common market had to strengthen his position. Concentrations, as well as improvements in efficiency, followed. The economic boom of 1954–1957 must also have stimulated the volume of investments, as witnessed by the fact that expansion programs for 1960 slipped in the ECSC and the United Kingdom in the recession beginning in 1958.[53] Loans by the High Authority made only

---

[52] Cf. the statement by the president of Usinor to the effect that depreciation on a new plant at 1956 prices would represent 13 per cent of turnover, annual turnover equaling 40 per cent of original capital cost; *Le Monde*, December 6–7, 1957, p. 15.

[53] *Observer*, October 5, 1958, p. 2, and October 12, 1958, p. 2.

a small contribution to the volume of investments in the steel industry—$50 million on a volume of about $3 billion in the five-year period 1953–1957,[54] or 1.7 per cent.

INVESTMENTS BY TYPE OF FACILITY

The High Authority wished to stimulate investments in pig iron producing facilities in order to reduce dependence on imported scrap. The trend away from pig iron started after the first world war, as Table 24 shows. The ratio of

Table 24

PIG IRON PRODUCTION AS PER CENT OF CRUDE STEEL PRODUCTION,
MAIN STEEL PRODUCING COUNTRIES, SELECTED YEARS, 1909–1956[a]

Country	1909–1913	1926–1930	1934–1938	1952–1956
Germany	97	86	77	76
Saar	[b]	95	94	90
France	115[c]	111	96	86
Belgium	96	100	101	92
Luxembourg	229	110	102	99
Italy	42	32	37	32
Total ECSC	103	94	83	79
United Kingdom	145	79	66	64
United States	104	77	66	67

Sources: Tables 2-2 and 3-1, Appendix E.

[a] Production of pig iron and ferroalloys divided by production of crude steel and castings, expressed as a percentage.

[b] Saar included in Germany.   [c] Pre–World War I territory.

pig iron to crude steel production in the ECSC declined from 103 to 79 per cent between 1909 and 1956, from 145 to 64 per cent in the United Kingdom and from 104 to 67 per cent in the United States. The production of open-hearth and electric steel in the ECSC increased 45 per cent from 1952 to 1956, that of Thomas steel—which consumes pig iron mainly—only 28 per cent. The preference for open-hearth steel is, apart from other factors, no longer justified for reasons of quality because Thomas steel of equal quality can be produced with the oxygen process.

The High Authority in 1952 informed the steel industry that the ratio of pig iron to steel production should be raised.[55] It influenced the ratio in the desirable direction by loans and by decisions discouraging projects that would have raised the scrap ratio.[56] The effort to increase blast capacity should fall largely

[54] HA, *Bulletin mensuel d'information*, October-November 1958, p. 21.

[55] *Ibid.*, July 1957, pp. 16–18.

[56] *Ibid.*; HA, *Cinquième rapport général*, p. 325. The High Authority called attention to the need for more investment in blast furnace capacity in *Journal officiel*, July 19, 1956, p. 209, and believed it should account for one third of total investments in 1957–1960, compared with 18 per cent in 1954–1956.

on those countries that have the lowest ratio of pig iron to steel, especially Italy and Germany. These countries were already making an effort in this direction.[57] While increased pig iron capacity will reduce scrap requirements relative to steel, it will, on the other hand, raise requirements for coking coal and iron ore. The shift from imported scrap to imported coal and iron ore may be a dubious advantage to Italian steel producers. Though scrap prices rise more rapidly than coal and ore prices, they can be passed along to the consumer during an economic boom but they fall much more than coal and iron ore prices during a recession. The plants that have a high scrap ratio are not burdened at such times with fixed charges on idle blast furnace capacity. But what is of advantage to the Italian steel producer is not necessarily to the advantage of the Italian economy if the steel fabricator is hampered by high costs in the export market.

There was a deficiency of crude steel as well as of pig iron during the boom of 1954–1957. Postwar investments favored rolling mill facilities, which accounted for more than half the total investments made by the ECSC steel firms in 1954–1956, as Table 21 shows. The wide-strip mill, continuous and semicontinuous facilities for flat products—facilities in which Europe had been deficient—were introduced on a large scale.[58] The steel firms in the ECSC will consequently also devote a larger proportion of investments to crude steel facilities.

LOCATION OF PRODUCTION

Will the common market stimulate a shift in the location of production in accordance with comparative advantage?[59] This question is fraught with difficulties. Seen from the interregional rather than interfirm point of view, the producing areas within the ECSC appear to be on fairly equal terms, except for the Italian steel industry, when assembly costs are balanced against outward freight costs in relation to markets. But taken as a whole, the European steel industry still has a long way to go to catch up with American efficiency in the use of labor—the latter being two to two and one half times as efficient —though present wage differentials enable the former to compete on equal terms. There do not seem to be any differences of equal magnitude in efficiency within Europe, except for the Italian steel industry.

[57] See *Financial Times*, August 26, 1957, p. 1, on the German effort, and *Le Monde*, October 20–21, 1957, p. 7, for the French effort within the Third Modernization Plan. The United Kingdom hopes to raise the production of Thomas steel from 6 per cent of total output in 1957 to 11 per cent in 1962. The Italian effort involves the construction of more facilities at tidewater.

[58] Ingvar Svennilson, *Growth and Stagnation in the European Economy*, ECE, Geneva, 1954, pp. 131–133.

[59] Norman J. G. Pounds and William N. Parker, *Coal and Steel in Western Europe*, Faber and Faber, London, 1957, discussing this matter in Chapters 10 and 11, indicated they did not expect much of a change.

There were no startling shifts among the six main and well-established steel producing areas in the ECSC between 1913–1956, as Table 2–5 in Appendix E shows.

Rather striking is the fact that the six main producing areas as a whole have lost ground to the newer producing areas in the ECSC; the main areas' aggregate share of total ECSC output dropped from 84 per cent in 1913 to 78 per cent in 1956. The newer steel producing sites—in Italy, Holland and the Salzgitter region in Germany—some of which are at tidewater, accounted for 22 per cent of the output in 1956. Production at these sites doubled between 1937 and 1956, compared with an increase of 56 per cent in total production; it accounted for 30 per cent of the total increase. The shift toward tidewater sites is, however, a logical development in view of the growing imports of raw materials. But the shift is not entirely attributable to comparative advantage. The Italian steel industry and the steel industry in the Salzgitter area owe their growth to the autarkic policies of the late 1930s. The costs at Salzgitter are not uneconomic but the steel plants there are rather far from markets, especially since the division of Germany.

Steel production in Italy occurs at both inland and tidewater sites, as indicated in Chapter 2. The average size of plant in an industry where economies of size are so important is much smaller in Italy than elsewhere. Even the two modern tidewater plants are relatively small, under a half million tons of crude steel per year each. The two "large" private firms—Falck (Milan) and Fiat (Turin)—are no larger. Only one of the eight state-controlled firms—Ilva—produced over one million tons of crude steel in 1956; but Ilva itself encompassed about eight crude steel producing plants scattered throughout Italy, only one of which—Bagnoli near Naples—produced over 300,000 tons of crude steel. Even the most modern portion of the Italian steel industry thus loses out when it comes to economies of size, for many of the efficient steel plants in other parts of the Community produce over one million tons each.

Besides the sharp difference between the most efficient plants Italy has to offer and the average modern plant in the rest of the Community, there is also a large variation in size of plant within Italy itself. At least 65 small firms—grouped largely around Milan, with secondary clusters in other parts of the country—produced a total of one million tons of crude steel in 1954, or 25 per cent of the Italian output. Seventy per cent of these small firms employed under 1,000 men each. Average costs in Italy are high (Table 15) but costs at the smaller plants are probably even higher. Though the smaller plants no doubt survive on the basis of a low capitalization and the fact that the price of scrap declines more than proportionately to that of steel during a recession, they are no doubt squeezed when home steel prices fall.

Italian steel lived with the protection of a tariff wall, which was eliminated in February 1958, vis-à-vis the producers in other parts of the ECSC. The Italian steel industry enjoys some geographical protection; when business is good rival producers will not wish to absorb freight. But will a contraction in demand precipitate intense rivalry between Italian producers, divided into integrated and nonintegrated plants, as well as between them and foreign sources of supply? (See Chapter 7.)

Locational shifts in production should be measured over long periods. The ECSC was still too young in 1958 to indicate whether it had had any influence on the locational pattern of production. The European Economic Community might, furthermore, have an important influence on steel markets and steel sites. As tariff walls fall, metal consuming plants and steel plants may begin to attract each other. The former may gravitate toward steel producing centers to reduce freight costs; the latter may be attracted to consuming centers in order to avoid freight absorption.

GOVERNMENT INFLUENCE

Comparative advantage in a common market is not the only influence working on the steel industry. The member governments still influence expansion and investments in the industry—particularly in France, Germany and Italy. National tax policies influence the all-important matter of self-financing for expansion. A high rate of expansion supported by self-financing also requires an expansionist price. Business has been lively enough during much of the time since the second world war to support such a price. But most governments in Western Europe have restrained steel prices—by price ceilings until 1952–1953 and by informal influence since the common market—though prices were nevertheless moderately expansionist especially in world export markets. Expansion, investments and prices are three facets of a problem that come up for negotiation between the governments and their respective steel producers. The French government, in addition, guides the expansion of the steel industry through the Commissariat Général du Plan, which collaborates with the producers. Government influence on steel prices and the national character of price decisions are discussed further in Chapter 7. Government influence therefore can thwart the potential growth of regional specialization by means of freer trade.

CHAPTER 4

COAL: COSTS OF

PRODUCTION AND

INVESTMENTS

Costs are greatly influenced by natural conditions, which can be only partly offset by mechanization. The depth of the coal seam and its other characteristics determine the mining methods and the capital and operating costs.

MINING CONDITIONS

The differences in natural conditions from country to country are broadly described in Table 25. Bituminous coal is closer to the surface in America than in Europe.[1] In America it frequently outcrops on the hillside and is mined from slopes or drifts. European coal occurs in less hilly country and is now mined from vertical shafts, the outcrops having been exhausted long ago. Average depth of mining in the United States is 400 feet; in Europe it is 1,200 to 2,600 feet; some mines are close to the limit, presently considered to be 4,000 feet. The mines in southern Belgium, the Ruhr and Nord and Pas-de-Calais are the deepest in Europe; those in the United Kingdom, Netherlands and Centre-Midi are the shallowest.

Capital costs of coal mining are consequently much higher in Europe than in America. The capital cost at 1956 prices of a new coal mine in Europe was

[1] American anthracite mines enjoy much less favorable conditions than American bituminous mines and account for only 5 per cent of American coal output. Mining conditions in Europe are most favorable in the Silesian coal fields, now under Polish control. For sources and further data on natural conditions, see Paul Wiel, *Untersuchungen zu den Kosten- und Marktproblemen der westeuropäischen Kohlenwirtschaft*, Rheinische-Westfälisches Institut für Wirtschaftsforschung, Essen, June 1953, pp. 37–40; Reid Report, *passim;* Erich W. Zimmerman, *World Resources and Industries*, Harper, New York, 1951 (rev. ed.), pp. 479–481; Norman J. G. Pounds and William N. Parker, *Coal and Steel in Western Europe*, Faber and Faber, London, 1957, Parts I and II, *passim;* ILO, *Productivity in Coal Mines*, Geneva, 1951, p. 34. The problems in American anthracite are sketched in F. Leichter, "Pennsylvänischer Anthrazit, seine Entwicklung und seine Probleme," in *Glückauf*, December 22, 1956, pp. 1567–1569.

about \$35 to \$40 per ton of new capacity compared with about \$8 for an underground bituminous coal mine in America.[2]

Thicker coal seams are easier to mine up to a point and more adaptable to mechanization. Difficulties increase rapidly as seams fall below four to five feet in thickness. Most bituminous coal seams in the United States are thicker than this, most of those in Europe are thinner, as Table 25 shows.

Table 25

TYPICAL MINING CONDITIONS IN SELECTED COAL PRODUCING COUNTRIES[a]

Country	Depth (Feet)	Seam Thickness (Feet)	Gradient	Faulting	Roof and Floor	Friability
Ruhr	2,480	4^1/$_3$	Steep	Much	Moderate	Rather hard
Saar	1,700–2,100	3¾	...	...	...	Soft
France[b]	1,465	4⅝	50% under 20° 37% 20°–45°	Much	Moderate	Soft
Belgium[c]	2,625	2^2/$_3$	Steep	Much	Moderate	Soft
Netherlands	1,300–1,800	3½	Moderate	Moderate	Poor roof, moderate floor	...
United Kingdom	1,180	3^5/$_6$	80% flat	Moderate	Moderate floor, poor roof	Rather hard
United States (bituminous)	400	31%, 4 / 37%, 4–6 / 32%, over 6	Flat, Average of 2°	Negligible	Good	Mostly hard

Source: ILO, *Productivity in Coal Mines*, Geneva, 1953, Appendix V and VI, and pp. 7, 13.

[a] Data refer to late 1940s and early 1950s.

[b] Lorraine has roughly the same conditions as the Saar—gassy, wet and faulted.

[c] In southern Belgium the seams are thin, the mines gassy and wet, the roof weak and the floor heaving; average depth in the Campine is 2,739 feet.

The seams in Europe are moderately to steeply inclined, except in the United Kingdom, where they are rather flat; American seams are exceptionally flat. Floor and roof conditions in Europe are much more unfavorable than in the United States. European mines are wetter and gassier and European seams are more faulted.

All mining in Europe, except for the German brown coal deposits and about 5 per cent of the British production, is by underground methods. As much as 25 per cent of American coal is now won by open-pit or strip mining, where the daily output per man (surface and underground workers combined) in

[2] Institut für Bilanzenanalysen, *Der Ruhrbergbau*, 1957, p. 9; HA, *Sixième rapport général*, Vol. II, p. 296. A new 5 million ton mine in the Ruhr would cost \$36 per ton and a new one million ton mine \$47 per ton, according to Fritz Lange, "Wirtschaftlichkeit des Bergbaus in grossen Teufen," *Glückauf*, January 4, 1958, pp. 12–14.

1953 was two and one half times greater than in American underground mines.[3]

The room-and-pillar system, originally developed in the early English coal mines, is nearly universal in America, whereas long-wall mining predominates in Europe, including the United Kingdom. Thick seams, strong roof conditions and a relatively flat coal bed favor the use of room-and-pillar mining. The room-and-pillar system was abandoned in England as the mines deepened

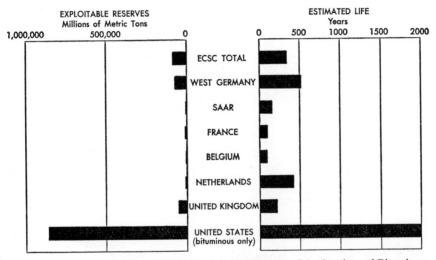

FIG. 10. Estimated Exploitable Reserves of Anthracite and Bituminous Coal, Selected Countries

Sources: OEEC, *Europe's Growing Needs of Energy, How Can They Be Met?* Paris, May 1956, p. 103; National Coal Association, *Bituminous Coal Trends, 1956*, Washington, p. 142.

and the seams narrowed. Long-wall mining permits fully productive operations to begin after comparatively little development.

The American mining system "saves labor but not coal; the European system saves coal but not labor."[4] Like many a generalization, this needs qualification. The European system requires more labor per ton of coal because natural conditions are more difficult, but mine operators in Europe have also tried to rationalize production and economize on labor, especially since the 1920s when excessive capacity created cutthroat competition. Mechanization in Europe has been further intensified by the scarcity of labor since the second world war. The statement that the ". . . United States is long on coal

[3] National Coal Association, *Bituminous Coal Trends*, 1956, pp. 72–73.
[4] Zimmerman, *op. cit.*, p. 481.

but short on labor; the reverse is true in many parts of Europe"[5] is no longer true of the European labor supply either.

The last quotation is much more accurate with respect to relative coal reserves. Probable aggregate reserves in America are ten times those in the ECSC, eighteen times those in the United Kingdom, and nearly seven times those in the two areas combined. (See Fig. 10.) At present rates of extraction, reserves in the United Kingdom have a life of 215 years and those in the ECSC 340 years, compared with 2,000 years in the United States.

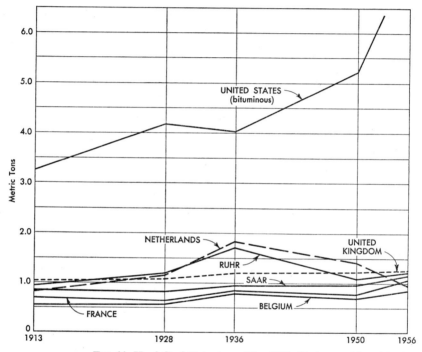

Fig. 11. Hard Coal Output per Man-Shift, Underground and Surface Workers Combined, Selected Countries and Years, 1913–1956

Source: Table 4-1, Appendix E.

Since the long-wall system of mining yields a higher extraction, its use in Europe is more consistent with the shorter life of its reserves. It also retards the increase in depth. The greater supply of reserves in the United States encourages the industry there to mine extensively, and to open a new mine when existing workings exceed a depth considered uneconomic by American standards. This alternative is not available in Europe, where the choice often is

[5] *Ibid.*

between deepening an existing mine and opening a new one that is even deeper; in the Ruhr, for example, the virgin areas to the north are under a greater overburden than are the mines in the rest of the Ruhr.

The difference in natural conditions also has an important bearing on production policy. The shallowness, dryness and flatness of American coal seams enable the American coal industry to reduce output by closing mines without necessarily running the risk of losing reserves. American mines can be reopened more easily than European mines or can be maintained in standby condition at lower cost. Mines in Europe cannot be closed without the risk of losing scarce reserves. The European coal industry thus has much less flexibility to adjust to the business cycle.

More favorable mining conditions in America and the room-and-pillar system of mining used there have given the American coal industry an enormous advantage in productivity. The output per man-shift (underground and surface workers combined) in American underground bituminous coal mines in the early 1950s was more than eight times greater than that in the Belgian coal mines, the lowest in Western Europe, and more than five times greater than in the United Kingdom, the highest in Western Europe. (See Fig. 11, based on Table 4-1, Appendix E.)

LABOR COSTS

Coal mining is a labor-intensive industry. Labor costs account as a rule for about 55 to 65 per cent of the sales value of the coal produced.[6]

Estimated average labor costs per ton of coal produced in Western Europe in 1956 varied from $6.20 in Lorraine, the lowest-cost area, to $9.60 in southern Belgium, the highest-cost area, a difference of 50 per cent, as Table 26 shows. Labor costs in the Ruhr, the Campine and the Saar, as well as in the United Kingdom, were close to those in Lorraine. But average labor costs in the Centre-Midi, in the Netherlands and in Aachen were from 15 to 25 per cent higher; those in the Nord and Pas-de-Calais were above those in Lorraine by one third.

Payroll costs per man-shift in 1956 did not differ markedly between mining regions except in Lorraine (col. 4 of Table 26) and consequently did not have a marked influence on variations in labor costs per ton. Though Lorraine had the highest payroll costs, $9 per man-shift, it had the lowest labor cost per

---

[6] Interest, taxes and amortization vary considerably from area to area. For an estimate of labor and other costs in the interwar period and in 1949–1950, when wage differentials and rates of production were different from what they are now, see Wiel, *op. cit.*, pp. 91, 95–96, 100, 107. See also ECE, *Economic Survey of Europe Since the War*, Geneva, 1953, p. 228. ECE, "L'Industrie du charbon et l'industrie de l'acier en Europe occidentale," in *Bulletin économique pour l'Europe*, Geneva, October 1950, pp. 28–33.

Table 26

AVERAGE AGE, SIZE OF MINE, PRODUCTIVITY AND PRODUCTION COSTS,
SELECTED COAL MINING AREAS, 1956

Area, by Age Group	Percentage Change in Output, 1913–1956[a]	Average Annual Output per Mine (*Thousands of Metric Tons*)	Output per Man-Shift, Underground and Surface Workers Combined (*Tons*)	Estimated Labor Cost per Man-Shift	Estimated Labor Cost per Ton
	(1)	(2)	(3)	(4)	(5)
Newest:					
Campine	b	1,500	(1.076)	$7.20	$6.70
Netherlands	640	983	0.963	7.30	7.60
Lorraine	350	1,209	1.458	9.00	6.20
Aachen	221	800	(0.954)	7.35	7.70
Intermediate:					
Saar	130	1,000	1.158	8.10	7.00
Ruhr	109	903	(1.203)	7.80	6.50
Oldest:					
Nord and Pas-de-Calais	104	440	0.977	7.90	8.10
Centre-Midi[c]	96	379	1.098	7.80	7.20
South Belgium	84	169	(0.774)	7.45	9.60
United Kingdom[d]	74	164	1.250	7.78	6.25

Sources:

Col. 1: Calculated from Table 27 and HA, *Bulletin statistique.*

Col. 2: Data on the number of mines, from HA, *Momento de statistiques,* are for 1957. Average output per mine calculated on the basis of production in 1956, from Table 2-7, Appendix E, from Charbonnages de France, *Rapport de gestion, 1956,* p. 38, and from HA, *Bulletin statistique.*

Col. 3: Data in parentheses estimated by applying the same percentage change as for underground output per man-shift between 1954 and 1956; over-all output per man-shift in 1954 from *Kohlenwirtschaft.*

Col. 4: Data on 1954 hourly payroll costs per man (including direct and indirect payments) for operating wage workers only (excluding auxiliary operations and salaried workers) are from HA, *Les Salaires et les charges sociales dans les industries de la Communauté,* 1956, pp. 16–17, 83–90. These were adjusted for 1956 by the index in HA, *Cinquième rapport général,* p. 200. Resulting hourly costs for 1956 were multiplied by the hours per shift shown in the notes to Table 4-2, Appendix E.

The British data are from Ministry of Fuel and Power, *Statistical Digest;* National Coal Board, *Quarterly Statistical Reports.*

Col. 5: The figures in col. 4 were divided by over-all output per man-shift in col. 3, and converted to dollars by the Federal Reserve Board exchange rates; but French costs were converted at 420 francs to the dollar (devaluation of August 1957), the French franc having been seriously overvalued in 1956.

Other data on labor costs are also available, notably from composite financial reports, but such reports are not available for all districts (Belgium, for example) and, in any case, are quite incomparable because they include the labor cost for auxiliary operations and salaried workers, not to speak of differences in accounting. The area divisions of Charbonnages de France give data on the *prix de revient professionel à la tonne marchande* but these are not comparable with reports for other districts.

[a] Provides an "objective" measure of the relative "age" of the several coal fields and, reading upward, roughly expresses the historical sequence in which the fields were developed.

[b] The Campine started producing after 1913.   [c] Comprises six divisions.

[d] Data represent a composite of all districts (twenty-five in all), but refer to deep-mined production only.

Note: The data shown in cols. 4 and 5 are probably subject to an error of roughly 5 per cent.

ton. Average payroll costs in the other mining regions varied from $7.20 to $8.10 per man-shift, a variation of less than 15 per cent.

SIZE OF MINE AND AVERAGE PRODUCTIVITY

Differences in yield per unit of labor and capital are determined partly by natural conditions in extractive, as well as in agricultural, industries. But size of mine, other conditions being equal, has a great influence on output per man-shift, as cols. 2 and 3 of Table 26 show. Size of mine would, however, be a misleading criterion of efficiency if applied to widely different natural conditions. The average American mine produced less than 70,000 tons in 1953. The average mine in the ECSC produced 600,000 tons in 1956. Seventy-five per cent of the coal produced in the ECSC in 1956 came from districts that had an average mine size of 900,000 tons or more. American mines that produced over a half million tons in 1953 also had an average output of 900,000 tons but accounted for less than half the aggregate American output.[7]

Since American mines are shallower, have thicker and flatter seams, and are cooler and dryer than European mines, they are more productive even when smaller than European mines. Since European mines require more capitalization and overhead, they have to resort to greater economies of scale to achieve a given degree of efficiency.

Average output per man-shift (all workers combined) was one of the major variables (col. 3 of Table 26). In 1956 the highest output per man-shift (in Lorraine) was twice that of the lowest (in southern Belgium). The areas with the lowest productivity had the highest labor costs per ton. Differences in sales price do not, however, coincide with differences in productivity; to take a flagrant example, the price of Ruhr coal in 1956 was only twice as great as the price of American coal though the average output per man (all workers combined) was one sixth of that in the United States. Owing to analogous discrepancies in the ECSC, especially between France and the rest of the Community, French costs in Table 26 are estimated on the basis of the French franc as devalued in August 1957 (420 francs to the dollar).

Differences in natural conditions partly explain the differences in yield per man and labor costs per ton. The seams in Lorraine, the Saar, the United Kingdom and the Ruhr are thicker than in southern Belgium or in Nord and Pas-de-Calais; those in the Netherlands, the Campine and Aachen are of intermediate thickness. The coal seams in the Campine are less faulted than those

[7] Calculated from data in U. S. Department of Interior, *Minerals Yearbook*, Washington, 1953, Vol. II, pp. 47–48. The figures include open-pit production, which accounts for nearly one fourth the total output.

in southern Belgium; they are also wider and flatter. The same type of difference permits the British mines to compare favorably with larger continental mines, as Table 26 shows.

Though economies of scale are important under European conditions, the mine with an annual capacity of 2 million tons is rare; a one million ton mine is considered large. Many mines are much smaller; some mining districts are made up of small mines and small firms only—southern Belgium, for example.

The newer mining districts on the Continent have the larger average size of mine and, as a rule, the higher productivity and lower labor costs, as Table 26 shows.[8] Since the mining districts have an overlapping history of operations, age is expressed in col. 1 of Table 26, according to whether the districts produced more or less coal in 1956 than in 1913, in order to measure "age" in relation to a fixed historical point. The method gives a fairly good correlation between average size of mine and age of mining district. The Campine, the newest district, in 1956 had the largest mines (averaging 1.5 million tons each). Those in southern Belgium, the oldest district, had the smallest mines in the ECSC (averaging 169,000 tons each).

The newest mining districts, where present production is considerably above that in 1913, are the Campine, Limburg, Aachen and Lorraine; all but the last are on the same coal deposit and were opened or greatly expanded after the 1920s. The intermediate districts—the Ruhr and the Saar—were opened for intensive production in the three or four decades preceding the first world war and are still expanding moderately. The oldest districts—southern Belgium, Centre-Midi, Nord and Pas-de-Calais—were in production well before the turn of the century and have passed their peaks. The newest areas in 1956 accounted for 17 per cent of the coal output in the ECSC, the intermediate for 58 per cent and the oldest for 25 per cent. (See Table 27.)

Two of the mining districts in the newest group—Lorraine and the Campine—have not yet reached their potential peak production; they have the highest average size of mine—1.2 million tons in Lorraine and 1.5 million tons in the Campine in 1956. Labor costs in both areas were under $7 per ton in 1956. Productivity in the Campine, though high, is no higher than that in the Ruhr, the Saar or Centre-Midi, which are older areas. Lorraine has the highest productivity and the lowest labor cost, though the coal is by no means easily won, the seams being rather "dirty" and faulted. Coal production in Lorraine doubled between 1938 and 1956; no other field grew so rapidly in recent years. The Netherlands mines (in Limburg), also among the newest districts, have a low productivity and a high labor cost for their average size. Though the

---

[8] The history of the mining fields is sketched in Pounds and Parker, *op. cit., passim,* including the tables on p. 277.

State-owned mines in Limburg, with an average annual output of nearly 2 million tons, are among the largest and most efficient in Western Europe, Mauritz, the largest mine in Limburg, is nearing exhaustion at present depth; its productivity has therefore been declining. A new State-owned mine, Beatrix, is being sunk to maintain output. Aachen is the oldest district among the newest areas; the mines there produced an average of only 800,000 tons in

Table 27

PRODUCTION OF COAL IN THE PRINCIPAL EUROPEAN COAL MINING AREAS, SELECTED YEARS, 1900–1955 AND FORECAST FOR 1975

(Amounts in Millions of Metric Tons)

Area	1900	1913	1929	1938	1955	1975
Oldest areas:						
South Belgium	23.5	22.8	23.7	23.0	19.8	17.5
Nord and Pas-de-Calais	20.3	27.4	34.9	28.2	29.1	29.5
Centre-Midi	13.1	13.5	14.0	11.2	12.7	12.5[a]
Total	56.9	63.7	72.6	62.4	61.6	59.5
Per cent	44	32	31	26	25	21
Intermediate areas:						
Saar	9.6	13.2	13.6	14.4	17.3	19.0
Ruhr	60.1	114.2	123.6	127.3	121.1[b]	150.0
Total	69.7	127.4	137.2	141.7	138.4	169.0
Per cent	53	64	58	59	56	59
Newest areas:						
Netherlands	0.3	1.9	11.6	13.5	11.9	12.0
Campine	0.0	0.0	3.2	6.5	10.1	14.0
Aachen	1.8	3.3	6.0	7.8	7.0	8.5
Lorraine	1.1	3.8	6.1	6.7	13.2	17.0
Total	3.2	9.0	26.9	34.5	42.2	51.5
Per cent	3	4	11	14	17	18
Other[c]	...	...	0.3	3.8	4.2	4.5
Per cent	...	...	0.1	2	2	2
TOTAL ECSC[d]	129.8	200.1	237.0	242.4	246.4[b]	284.5
Per cent	100	100	100	100	100	100
United Kingdom	228.8	292.0	262.0	230.6	225.1	250.0

Sources: Data for 1955 are from HA, *Bulletin statistique*. All data for prior years are from *Kohlenwirtschaft* and *Statistisches Übersicht*, except that the data on the French districts through 1929 are from Robert Lafitte-Laplace, *L'Economie charbonnière de la France*, Marcel Giard, Paris, 1933, p. 185. HA, *Momento de statistiques*, 1956, was also helpful.

The ECSC forecasts for 1975 are, with small modifications, from Louis Armand, *et al.*, *Un objectif pour Euratom*, Paris, May 1957, pp. 68–69; this gives total output by country; the distribution by districts is estimated by the author with the help of HA, "Objectifs généraux," *Journal officiel*, May 20, 1927.

The United Kingdom forecast is from National Coal Board, *Investing in Coal*, London, April 1956, and OEEC, *Europe's Growing Needs of Energy, How Can They Be Met?* Paris, May 1956.

[a] The French are sinking new pits in the Jura area included here.

[b] "Small mines" excluded.   [c] Comprises Sardinia, Lower Saxony and Bavaria.

[d] The figures for the ECSC up to and including 1929 are larger in Table 2-7, Appendix E, because they include production in territories now outside the ECSC.

1956. One of the mines, Emil Mayrisch, was still being developed. Both the Limburg and Aachen fields are probably at peak production.

The Ruhr, always in a class by itself, still has extensive virgin reserves in the northern part of the area though it is by no means a new area. It reached its peak output between the wars but still has a potential for a larger output and will no doubt surpass its interwar peak. The Ruhr has a better performance with respect to productivity and labor costs—$6.50 per ton in 1956—than any of the new areas except Lorraine. Intensively exploited since the 1890s, the mines in the Ruhr were vigorously reorganized and physically concentrated in the middle 1920s. This program is to be distinguished from corporate concentration; twenty companies already controlled 90 per cent of the coal production in 1926.[9] The number of mines was reduced from 237 in 1926 to 161 in 1936. Average annual output was raised from 466,000 tons per mine to 778,000 tons per mine in the corresponding period.[10] (Average output per mine reached 900,000 tons in 1956.) There were 23,178 working places in 1926 each producing an average of 4,760 tons annually; in 1936 there were 3,749 working places with an average output of 32,270 tons each.[11] Output rose from 1.386 tons per man-shift underground in 1927 to 2.199 tons in 1936, an increase of nearly 60 per cent in ten years. (See Table 4-2, Appendix E.) Physical concentration and rationalization can therefore help overcome some of the natural difficulties in European coal mining.[12]

The Saarbergwerke, with six operating divisions, had eighteen mines in 1955; those that produced over 800,000 tons accounted for 84 per cent of the total output.[13] Productivity in the Saar thus compares favorably with that in the Ruhr, though labor costs per ton are slightly higher owing to higher payroll costs per man-shift.

The Centre-Midi encompasses six coal divisions, some old, some new, among which are some very poor areas like the Loire and some very good areas like Blanzy. Productivity is high and labor costs low ($7.20 per ton in 1956) for the small average size of mine (380,000 tons in 1956) owing to the influence of the more efficient mining divisions within the area as a whole. Nord and Pas-de-Calais has a small average size of mine (440,000 tons in 1956) and a low productivity; efficiency has, however, risen sharply in recent years as a result of a thoroughgoing physical concentration that is still in

[9] Reid Report, p. 16.

[10] *Ibid.*

[11] *Ibid.*

[12] The influence of size of mine on efficiency has been well brought out by Lange, *op. cit.*, pp. 1–17.

[13] *Jahrbuch*, 1956 edition, pp. 769–770; data are for 1955. HA, *Momento de statistiques*, reported seventeen mines for 1957. The latter figure was used to compute average output per mine in 1956 as shown in Table 26.

process. A similar program could lead to higher efficiency in the mines in southern Belgium, too.

Should prices in the common market reflect average cost or the cost of the less efficient operating units or firms? Since costs differ widely between mines or firms in the same district as well as between districts, this question is of considerable significance for the policies of the ECSC. This pricing problem is discussed in Chapters 9 and 10, which bring together the findings of Chapter 5 with respect to concentrations and nationalization and the findings of Chapter 8 with respect to concerted practices.

INVESTMENTS

Have investments been sufficient? How have they been distributed as between mining, coking and electric power producing facilities and as between producing districts? Has the economic union influenced these matters? The function of investments in an economic union and the role of the High Authority have already been discussed in Chapter 3.

CAPITAL EXPENDITURES

A one million ton mine in Europe requires a capital outlay of $35 to $40 million at 1956 prices. A mine usually encompasses a coke plant and a power plant; these, like many other industrial facilities, have a useful life of about twenty years. Theoretical obsolescence is therefore 5 per cent a year for the power and coking divisions. Replacement cost of the coking and power divisions, which represent an investment of $10 to $15 per ton of capacity (of the mine), and which have a twenty-year life, is thus $0.50 to $0.75 per ton of coal produced.

The mining division of a European mine is usually planned to last fifty years; the fifty-year life refers to the reserves and the major fixed assets, such as shafts and galleries, but not to the machinery, which has a shorter life. Even the shafts and galleries are renewed in less than fifty years in mines that maintain efficiency. Theoretical obsolescence or wastage in the mining division is thus at a minimum of 2 per cent per year. This theoretical rate is close to actual recent wastage in the British mines (4 million tons a year on 215 million tons of underground production) but greater than that in the Ruhr mines, which recently have been wasting at a rate of less than 0.5 per cent a year (or 500,000 tons a year on 125 million tons of output).[14] Actual wastage rates in the short

[14] *Glückauf*, December 21, 1957, p. 1600. The wastage rate for the United Kingdom is from *The Economist*, April 28, 1956, pp. 395 ff. An additional one million tons per year are lost in the United Kingdom owing to the rising proportion of rejects.

run thus deviate from hypothetical rates in accordance with the age of the mine and the amount of upkeep. The mining and preparation division, which has the longer life, accounts for roughly two thirds the total capital cost of a mining venture, or about $25 of a total of $35 to $40 per ton of capacity. The annual theoretical replacement cost of the mining division at 1956 prices is

Table 28

AVERAGE ANNUAL CAPITAL EXPENDITURES, TOTAL AND PER TON OF COAL
PRODUCED, SELECTED COAL PRODUCING AREAS, 1952–1956[a]

Country and Area	All Divisions		Mining Division	
	Total (*Millions*)	Per Ton	Total (*Millions*)	Per Ton
Germany				
Ruhr	$159	$1.34	$ 82	$0.69
Aachen	10	1.47	8	1.15
Lower Saxony	7	2.75	3	1.25
Saar	20	1.20	13	0.80
France				
Nord and Pas-de-Calais	65	2.26	41	1.44
Lorraine	53	4.21	29	2.27
Centre-Midi	32	2.48	17	1.33
Belgium				
South	(35)	(1.72)	25	1.23
Campine	18	1.83	14	1.48
Netherlands	(21)	(1.70)	13	1.08
ECSC[b]	427	1.76	250	1.03
United Kingdom[c]	165	0.78	134	0.63

Sources: HA, *Les Investissements dans les industries du charbon et de l'acier de la Communauté*, September 1957; production from HA, *Bulletin statistique*. United Kingdom from National Coal Board, *Investing in Coal*, 1956, Appendix.

[a] Average annual gross capital expenditure, excluding working capital. Independent cokeries are excluded; the mining division includes preparation plants. Belgian and Dutch expenditures on cokeries, given without breakdown, were estimated.

[b] Italy included.   [c] 1950–1955.

thus at least $0.50 per ton of production (at capacity operation). The theoretical rate of replacement at current costs for the mine as a whole is thus between $1.00 and $1.25 a year per ton of coal produced. Since the coal produced in the ECSC in 1956 had an average value of about $15 per ton, theoretical replacement at current cost was equivalent to about 7 to 8 per cent of turnover.[15]

Average annual gross capital expenditures, in the aggregate and per ton produced, by the European coal industry in 1952–1956 are shown in Table

[15] Replacement at historical value may be calculated at half of current capital cost and would thus be 4 per cent of annual turnover, or $0.65 per ton produced. See Institut für Bilanzenanalysen, "Erträge und Bilanzen des Ruhrbergbaus," in *Wochendienst*, December 16, 1955, p. 1.

28.[16] The mines in the ECSC as a whole spent an average of $427 million per year and $1.76 per ton produced for all divisions combined. They spent $250 million, or $1.03 per ton produced, on the mining division; this division accounted for 60 per cent of total expenditures. The British mines (1950–1955) spent $0.78 per ton produced, 80 per cent of which, or $0.63 per ton, was devoted to the mining division. Capital expenditures in that division of the British mines were 40 per cent below those in the ECSC.

Gross investments per ton in the ECSC were well above the theoretical total annual replacement cost of $1.25 per ton and of $0.50 per ton in the mining division, though they varied considerably from district to district.

FINANCING OF INVESTMENTS

Data on the sources of the funds appropriated to investment in the coal industry in the Community in 1953–1956 are available only for Germany, France and the Saar, covering 80 per cent of production in the ECSC. (See Fig. 12, based on Table 4-3, Appendix E.)[17]

Germany

Self-financing covered up to 80 per cent and more of total investments in 1954–1956, thanks to accelerated amortization provisions. Accelerated amortization represented more than 40 per cent of the total allowances for amortization in the Ruhr mining firms in 1953–1955:[18]

	Accelerated Amortization as Per Cent of Total Amortization
1953	41
1954	45
1955	38

The Investment Aid Act, which ran from 1952 to the end of 1955, made the high rate of self-financing possible in the coal as well as in the steel industry. Tax allowances thus financed a large part of the cost of expansion. Self-financing represented 11 to 13 per cent of turnover in the German coal industry in 1954–1956, a higher rate than in France or the Saar. The rapid amortization policy was prolonged by a law passed in the summer of 1957, retroactive to

---

[16] Data on investments in earlier years may be found in ECE, *Economic Survey of Europe Since the War*, Geneva, 1953, p. 203. Data on investments in 1953–1956 in the mining division only may be found in HA, *Sixième rapport général*, Vol. II, pp. 408–409.

[17] Particular attention is called to the notes in Table 4–3, Appendix E, explaining the limitations of the data.

[18] Institut für Bilanzenanalysen, *Der Ruhrbergbau*, 1957, pp. 24–25, and "Erträge und Bilanzen des Ruhrbergbaus," *Wochendienst*, December 16, 1955, p. 4.

January 1, 1956, applicable to coal and iron ore mining but not to the steel industry.[19] While the Investment Aid Act provided rapid writeoff for all capital outlays, the new act is limited to expansion projects rather than to short-

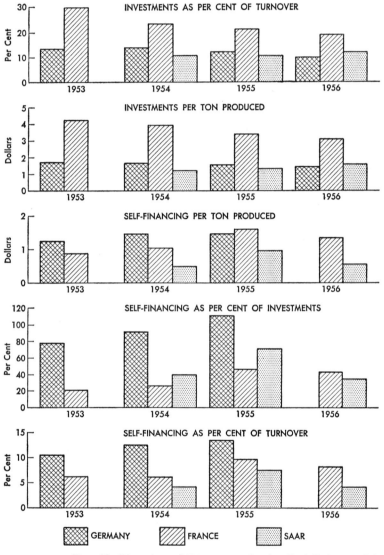

FIG. 12. Financing of Investments in the Coal Industry, Selected Countries and Years, 1953–1956

Source: Table 4-3, Appendix E.

[19] The new act is summarized in *Glückauf,* August 17, 1957, pp. 1044–1048. The rhythm of investments in coal declined in 1955–1956 as the first act ran out.

term investments; it covers new shaft sinking, concentration of mines and virgin field development. Ancillary facilities (coke, patent fuel and power plants) are excluded. Thirty per cent of the value of fixed assets and 50 per cent of the value of movable equipment (machinery, etc.) may be written off in four years, in addition to normal depreciation; movable equipment is covered only if it increases capacity. These provisions apply to equipment ordered before the end of 1960, to new shaft development in old mines to the end of 1965 and to virgin field development to the end of 1970. Amortization will thus continue to support a high rate of self-financing if prices yield a sufficient margin.

The firms drew on reserves as well as on current earnings in order to make the high rate of self-financing possible. Shareholders' equity fell from 57 per cent of the total assets in 1953 to 49 per cent in 1955, though hardly any new ordinary shares had been issued, as capital reserves per ton produced declined and reserves for pensions rose.[20]

Borrowed capital provided the remainder of the funds appropriated to investment—or roughly 20 per cent of the total from currency reform in mid-1950 to 1956.[21]

France and the Saar

Only one quarter of the funds appropriated to capital investments in the French coal mines in 1953–1954, and about 45 per cent in 1955–1956, was covered by self-financing. Only about a third of capital investments was so covered in the Saar mines in 1954 and 1956; in 1955, an exceptional year, 71 per cent of them was covered. Since self-financing supplied only a small part of the high volume of investment, the French mines were forced to rely mainly on borrowed funds and to incur high fixed charges. Government loans made by the Modernization and Equipment Fund or the public treasury (with the help of counterpart funds from the Marshall Plan) were the major source of borrowed capital. Contributions from the Modernization and Equipment Fund supplied 87 per cent of total financing in 1949; this contribution fell to 32 per cent in 1951 but was still 29 per cent in 1956. As the contributions from the public treasury declined, Charbonnages de France increasingly appealed to the long-term capital market by floating bonds whose value was indexed to the price of coal. The annual contribution from these bonds varied from 27 to 50 per cent of total investments in 1953–1956.[22]

---

[20] Institut für Bilanzenanalysen, *Der Ruhrbergbau*, 1957, p. 8. The Ruhr mines as a whole paid a 5 per cent dividend in 1955 compared with 7.1 per cent for all German industry. *Ibid.*, pp. 10–11.

[21] Werner Moritz, *Der Steinkohlenbergbau der Bundesrepublik als Investor*, Vierteljahresheft zur Wirtschaftsforschung, 1957, Drittesheft, pp. 319 ff; H. Hembeck, "Problèmes des charbonnages de la Ruhr," *Revue française de l'énergie*, January 1958, pp. 139–147. Some of the data refer to all German mines and some to Ruhr mines only, but since the latter account for 92 per cent of the output, the discrepancies are small.

[22] Data are from annual reports of the Charbonnages de France.

Charbonnages de France will in the future probably cover a larger portion of capital investments from self-financing as the rate of investment declines, provided the government allows prices to provide a larger margin.[23] The proportion of self-financing had already begun to rise in 1955–1956 as the volume of investments dropped.

Though the ratio of self-financing to investment in the French mines was low, the amount of self-financing was high in absolute figures—a phenomenon witnessed in the French steel industry also. Investments per ton of coal produced in 1953–1956 were more than twice as great in France as in Germany. They represented 20 to 30 per cent of turnover in France and half as much in Germany.[24] Self-financing per ton of coal produced was consequently nearly as great in France in 1954–1956 as in Germany. (See Table 4-3, Appendix E.) Self-financing as a percentage of turnover was nevertheless lower in France than in Germany (6 to 10 per cent in the former, 11 to 13 per cent in the latter, in 1953–1955). This difference indicates that margins are lower in France although prices support the cost of expansion in both cases, with a difference in degree.

The mines in the Saar had a good postwar record from the point of view of production and productivity; the concentration of output in relatively few pits and the large average output per mine were no doubt responsible for the good record. But investments per ton in the mining division were lower than in any other basin but the Ruhr. (See Table 28.) Self-financing available from earnings was also lower—in 1954 and 1956 about a third as great per ton of coal produced as in Germany and France. Since investments and self-financing were both lower per ton of coal produced, the ratio of self-financing to turnover was only 4 per cent in 1954 and 1956 and 7.5 per cent in 1955—much lower than in France or Germany. Prices in the Saar mines were consequently less expansionist than in the other two areas. But the ratio of investments to turnover (col. 1 of Table 4-3, Appendix E) in France, Germany and the Saar was above the theoretical replacement rate of 7 to 8 per cent, indicating that investments contributed to expansion in all three areas.

The coal mining industry in the ECSC spent a total of $2.2 billion on investments in the five-year period 1953–1957.[25] Loans made by the High Authority contributed $100 million, or 4.5 per cent of the total, as compared with 1.7 per cent of total investments in the steel industry.

[23] For a criticism of French price policy in relation to the financial position of the coal industry, see Commission de Vérification des Comptes des Enterprises Publiques, *Cinquième rapport d'ensemble*, Paris, 1957, pp. 203, 205.

[24] Investments vary in concept in France and Germany; see the notes to Table 4-3, Appendix E. This difference was not eliminated from the financial reports of the companies but was eliminated from the investment reports collected by the High Authority.

[25] HA, *Bulletin mensuel d'information*, October-November 1958, p. 21.

Trend in Capital Expenditures

Though the common market stimulated capital formation in the steel industry, it did not affect the coal industry similarly; investments in the coal industry in the ECSC as a whole declined from $505 million in 1952 to $484 million in 1957, while they rose from $545 million to $711 million in the steel industry.[26] The decline in investments by the coal industry in the ECSC is mainly attributable to a reduction in investments in France and Belgium; investments in Germany remained fairly constant, with a change in emphasis toward the mining rather than coking or power division.

A Note on the British Mines

Depreciation allowances in the United Kingdom in 1950–1955 were based on historical cost plus a small margin for replacement at current cost. The National Coal Board covered about 45 per cent of capital expenditures from depreciation allowances (in 1950–1955). It borrowed the remainder directly from the Treasury. Although the other nationalized industries in the United Kingdom go to the capital market with a Treasury guarantee, earnings in the coal industry were too low to permit the National Coal Board to do likewise. The British government would have had to authorize a higher price level for coal to have enabled the coal board to borrow directly or to cover a higher proportion of investments. Self-financing was expected to cover about 45 per cent of the capital investments scheduled for 1956–1960 and total capital outlays thereafter.[27] If a higher rate of self-financing is achieved, coal prices will be more expansionist, implying a departure from past policy. A more expansionist coal price may not materialize, however, in view of the structural failure in demand following the 1958 recession and may, in any case, be rejected in view of the pressure from oil.

Although both the French and British governments required their nationalized mines to keep coal prices down, prices in France sustained a more liberal rate of investment because self-financing per ton of coal produced was about three and a half times greater in the French than the British mines in the early 1950s.

TRENDS IN PRODUCTIVITY
AND PRODUCTION

In spite of the large investment made in 1952–1956, results were not brilliant. With few exceptions capital outlays were devoted to renewing, concentrating

[26] *Ibid.*, pp. 21–23.
[27] National Coal Board, *Investing in Coal*, 1956.

and modernizing existing mines in order to raise output in the short run and restore the efficiency lost after the war; the development of new mines received less attention.

PRODUCTIVITY TRENDS

Output per man underground in the ECSC as a whole increased at a rate of 2.20 per cent a year in 1951–1956 compared with 8.45 per cent during a similar period of large capital investment in 1925–1929. At that time new areas came into production and the mines in the Ruhr were thoroughly reorganized. Output per man exceeded all previous peaks in the 1930s because surplus capacity enabled the mines to concentrate production on the best seams and the newly modernized operations.[28]

The yield from investments made after the second world war was limited by the difficulty of improving efficiency with old shafts, galleries and underground roadways.[29] In the Ruhr, where most efforts between 1950–1955 were focused on modernizing old mines rather than opening new ones, output per man-shift underground increased only 10 per cent, though the amount of coal mined on a continuous operating cycle at working faces where pit props were not required doubled, accounting for nearly one third of total output in 1956.[30]

Most of the present coal production in Europe comes from mines developed before the first world war and rationalized in the 1920s, when, in addition, new mines were developed in the Campine, Limburg and Lorraine. Very few new mines have been put into production since then.

Output per man-shift underground in 1956 was still below that of the inter-war period in all the European mining districts except the French and the Saar, as Table 29 shows. It reached its peak in the United Kingdom in 1951 and declined from 1952 to 1956.

Owing to the fact that large investments in old mines have not yielded brilliant results, the High Authority recommended that new mines be developed where virgin resources are available, mainly in the northern part of the Ruhr and in the Campine, and that permanently high-cost mines be closed.[31] The development of new mines is not, however, an alternative to modernizing old ones, for the latter must maintain their output in any case.

---

[28] For the productivity trend from 1881, see "l'Industrie du charbon et l'industrie de l'acier en Europe occidentale," in ECE, *Bulletin économique pour l'Europe*, Geneva, October 1950, p. 32.

[29] "Die Wirtschaftlichkeit der Mechanizierung und Elektrifizierung in französischen Steinkohlenbergbau," in *Glückauf*, November 10, 1956, pp. 1352 ff, contains a valuable bibliography on the economics of underground electrification and mechanization.

[30] Calculated from data in *Jahrbuch;* HA, *Bulletin Statistique;* and *Kohlenwirtschaft*. For a discussion of the meager results from increasing mechanization of old mines in the United Kingdom, see the Reid Report, p. 29, and *The Economist*, April 28, 1956, pp. 395 ff.

[31] "Objectifs généraux," *Journal officiel*, May 20, 1957, pp. 205–206.

The High Authority thus also recommended that small mines be physically concentrated and that the production of secondary products be intensified.[32]

On the hypothesis that the length of the shift would not decline, the High Authority estimated in 1957 that output per man-shift underground in the ECSC as a whole would reach 2 tons in 1975 as compared with 1.529 tons in 1956, an increase of 30 per cent. The annual rate of growth will be 1.40 per cent as compared with 2.20 per cent in 1951–1956. A continuation of the 2.20 per cent rate of growth would yield an output of 2.4 tons per man underground

Table 29

OUTPUT PER MAN-SHIFT UNDERGROUND, SELECTED COAL MINING AREAS,
SELECTED YEARS AS PER CENT OF PEAK YEAR

Area	Peak Year	Tons in Peak Year	Per Cent of Peak Year				
			1925	1929	1937	1951	1956
Newest:							
Netherlands	1936	2.670	44	64	95	65	56
Lorraine	1956	2.275	37	49	...	87	100
Aachen	1933	1.535	59	75	95	78	83
Intermediate:							
Saar	1956	1.819	...	...	79	89	100
Ruhr	1936	2.199	49	71	93	67	72
Oldest:							
Nord and Pas-de-Calais	1956	1.484	53	65	...	79	100
Centre-Midi	1956	1.590	50	59	...	77	100
Belgium[a]	1936	1.173	60	71	97	90	99
United Kingdom	1951	1.632	...	85	94	100	98

Source: Table 4-2, Appendix E.

[a] Interwar figures not available separately for the Campine, one of the newest areas, and south Belgium, one of the oldest.

in 1975. That high a rate of increase is improbable as the returns from rationalizing old mines will decrease and as completely new mines—which may produce as much as 3 tons per man underground—will produce no more than 30 to 40 million tons a year by 1975.[33]

Future improvements in productivity will be hard won because depth is increasing—in the Ruhr and in Nord and Pas-de-Calais, for example, at about twenty feet annually.[34] The volume of coal rejected also is increasing with greater mechanization; in the Ruhr, for example, rejects increased from 14

[32] HA, *Cinquième rapport général*, p. 325.

[33] The High Authority's estimate of productivity in 1975 is to be found in "Objectifs généraux," pp. 207, 211.

[34] Wiel, *op. cit.*, p. 75; Charbonnages de France, *Rapport de gestion*, 1954, pp. 33–34. ILO, *Productivity in Coal Mines*, Geneva, 1953, pp. 11–12, gives increasing depth to the year 2000. For the difficulties in producing more coal in the Ruhr at increasing depth, see the article by Fritz Lange, *Handelsblatt*, November 8, 1957, Beilage, p. 1.

per cent of the material hoisted to the surface in 1936 to 28 per cent in 1956.[35] The number of productive workers underground also is declining—in the Ruhr, for example, from 28 per cent of the total labor force underground in 1938 to 22 per cent in 1956.[36] The number of productive hours also is declining as the mines get deeper and the working faces get farther from the shafts.[37]

PRODUCTION TRENDS

The High Authority estimated in 1956 that coal production in the ECSC would rise to 320 million tons in 1975.[38] This estimate represents the upper limit of expansion. Terming the 320 million ton estimate "optimistic," *Un objectif pour Euratom* advanced a "prudent" estimate of 277 million tons and a "probable" one of 293 million tons.[39] The probable estimate, with some modifications, is used here and included in Table 27, where production is forecast at 285 million tons in 1975—16 per cent above that of 246 million tons in 1955—and where output is distributed by mining districts.[40]

Reserves, even "virgin" reserves, are sufficient in the Ruhr and other areas to open substantial amounts of additional capacity were labor available. The limiting factors are labor supply and the availability at lower cost of other types of energy—petroleum and nuclear power—as well as of American coal. The forecast of coal production does not imply that 285 million tons of European coal would be produced at competitive prices; it assumes that the European governments might wish to produce that much coal for the sake of security. If so, coal output in the ECSC, which had in 1955 barely regained the volume reached in 1938, will have by 1975 exceeded production in 1913 by 42 per cent and that in 1938 by 16 per cent. Output in the United Kingdom, estimated at 250 million tons in 1975, will have declined by 15 per cent from 1913. (See Table 27.)

PRODUCTION BY REGIONS

Though the ECSC is still too young to provide any conclusive evidence as to whether or not it has caused production to shift to the right locations,[41] it is

[35] Moritz, *op. cit.*, p. 313.

[36] *Handelsblatt*, November 11, 1957, p. 11.

[37] Wiel, *op. cit.*, p. 63, gives the percentage of working time on total time in 1951 in various coal fields.

[38] Louis Armand *et al.*, *Un objectif pour Euratom*, Paris, May 1957, p. 56.

[39] *Ibid.*, pp. 57–58.

[40] See "Objectifs généraux," p. 206, for a rather different estimate of the volume of expansion by districts but similar forecast of which districts will expand and which remain stationary.

[41] The number of mines in the Ruhr, Nord and Pas-de-Calais, Centre-Midi and southern Belgium was reduced in 1952–1957, though many more in southern Belgium still needed to be concentrated. Average output per mine consequently increased in most areas according to data in HA, *Momento de statistiques*, and HA, *Recueil statistique*, June 1953, p. 47.

nevertheless more feasible to foresee the location pattern in coal than in steel because investments have to be started long before a new mine is completed. Predictions with respect to regional changes in production should, however, be revised from time to time.

Production in the older mining areas as a whole might remain stationary at 60 million tons, though it will decline in southern Belgium (Table 27). Production in the new areas might rise by 25 per cent—from 42 million tons in 1955 to 52 million tons in 1975. Most of the increase will occur in the Campine and Lorraine. Output in the Ruhr might rise from 121 million tons in 1955 to 150 million tons by 1975,[42] but might be hindered by considerable retirement of high-cost mines owing to the effects of the 1958 recession.

A slight shift in the right direction might therefore occur. Production in the older, and therefore higher-cost, areas may fall from 25 per cent of total output in 1955 to 21 per cent in 1975. The newer areas, which contributed 17 per cent in 1955, might increase their share slightly. The Ruhr, an exceedingly efficient area, might, together with the Saar, increase its share of the output in the ECSC from 56 per cent in 1955 to 59 per cent in 1975. (See Table 27.) Inasmuch as the Ruhr is the major low-cost area with the most desired assortment of grades, this increase would be highly desirable. Average efficiency in coal production in the ECSC may therefore rise.

The Ruhr

Large but deep reserves in the northern part of the Ruhr were until recently undeveloped though they have been under concession to mining firms operating in other parts of the Ruhr. The concessionaires in recent years traded and regrouped concessions and began to develop several mines in the middle 1950s. Nearly a third of the mines operating in the Ruhr in 1955 date from before 1860, 60 per cent date from before 1880, more than 80 per cent from before 1913; less than 10 per cent of the mines operating in 1955 were put into production between 1924–1954.[43]

Of the 50 million tons of gross capacity that the Ruhr operators hoped to put into operation by 1975, 20 million tons were to come from new mines in the virgin areas and 30 million tons from rationalization and mechanization of old mines.[44]

---

[42] The Unternehmensverband Ruhrbergbau mentioned a goal of 50 million tons above 1956 capacity less 10 million to be retired, a net increase of 40 million tons over 1956, which would bring production in 1975 to 165 million tons; see *Glückauf*, December 21, 1957, p. 1600.

[43] Institut für Bilanzenanalysen, *Der Ruhrbergbau*, 1957, p. 9; H. Hembeck, "Problèmes actuels des charbonnages de la Ruhr," in *Revue française de l'énergie*, January 1958, pp. 139–147.

See the charge by Sidney Willner in W. Friedmann, *Anti-Trust Laws, A Comparative Symposium*, Stevens and Sons, London, 1956, pp. 184–185, that the Ruhr coal industry deliberately neglected the development of these virgin areas in order to keep coal scarce. Though the deconcentration program delayed any plans to open the northern part of the Ruhr until about 1951, the Ruhr coal industry was several years late getting started thereafter.

[44] For the German program, see *Glückauf*, December 21, 1957, p. 1600.

France

Most of the postwar efforts of Charbonnages de France were also devoted to the consolidation and mechanization of existing mines, at an extremely high rate of capital investment but with good operating results. Charbonnages de France, which inherited many old and small mines, repeated the experience, with thirty years' delay, on which the operators in the Ruhr embarked after the first world war. Of the 250 pits in operation in France in 1946, 40 per cent were over fifty years old.[45] The older mines were in all the districts but Lorraine. The problem in France was to concentrate production and raise productivity in Nord and Pas-de-Calais, and to increase efficiency in the older mines in the Centre-Midi.

The early Monnet plan was ambitious with respect to output; it called for 60 million tons of coal by 1952 compared with 47 million tons in 1946.[46] The matter was restudied at the end of 1951 in relation to the implications of the ECSC. When the demand for coal declined in the 1953 recession, the French government decided to focus on efficiency instead of volume. French coal production hence leveled off at 55 to 57 million tons a year. The expansion of coal production under the second modernization plan was thenceforth adjusted to the rhythm at which the cokeries and other producers of secondary energy could absorb additional coal; i.e., the volume of coal available in primary form was not to be increased.[47]

The second modernization plan sought to make coal from the Nord and Pas-de-Calais district competitive with Ruhr coal in the Paris market. This goal required the output per man-shift underground in Nord and Pas-de-Calais to be brought to within at least a half ton of that in the Ruhr—a half ton per man-shift representing the margin of geographical protection.[48] The gap was greater than a half ton before the second world war; it was reduced to one third of a ton in 1952 and to one tenth of a ton in 1956 (Table 4-2, Appendix E). The goal was surpassed largely because one third of the pits in Nord and Pas-de-Calais were closed, the number of pits having been reduced from 109 in 1945 to 70 in 1956.[49]

The goals for the mines in the Centre-Midi—whose markets are limited by competition from the natural gas produced at Lacq in southwestern France— having been achieved by the early 1950s, the second modernization plan did

[45] Charbonnages de France, *Rapport de gestion, 1956*, p. 74, compares the goals with the achievements of the modernization plans.

[46] *Ibid., 1953*, pp. 63–65.

[47] *Ibid.*, p. 23. See M. Lorimy, "Les Investissements des charbonnages français dans le cadre du Plan Schuman," in *Revue française de l'énergie*, February 1952, pp. 142–147.

[48] M. Cadel, "L'Industrie houillère française et le Plan Schuman," in *Revue française de l'énergie*, February 1952, pp. 138–141.

[49] Houillères du Bassin du Nord and Pas-de-Calais, *Rapport de gestion, 1956*, p. 15.

not include any important new investments for that area but continued to rely on additional output from Lorraine.[50]

France paid a great deal in capital expenditure to obtain a modest increase in production and a large increase in efficiency. France is the only country in Western Europe where output per man-shift underground was considerably higher (30 per cent) in 1956 than in 1937. Productivity in the other countries

Table 30

DISTRIBUTION OF AVERAGE ANNUAL CAPITAL EXPENDITURES IN THE COAL INDUSTRY, SELECTED COAL PRODUCING AREAS, BY DIVISION, 1952–1956[a]

Country and Area	Amount (*Millions*)	Per Cent				
		Mining	Coke	Briquettes	Power	Total
Germany						
Ruhr	$159	52	19	1	28	100
Aachen	10	80	6	0	14	100
Lower Saxony	7	43	2	0	55	100
Saar	20	65	11	—	24	100
France						
Nord and Pas-de-Calais	65	63	16	2	19	100
Lorraine	53	55	20	0	25	100
Centre-Midi	32	53	6	3	38	100
Belgium[b]						
South	(35)	(71)	(11)	(2)	(16)	100
Campine	(18)	(78)	(3)	(—)	(19)	100
Netherlands[b]	(21)	(62)	(19)	(1)	(18)	100
ECSC[c]	427	59	15	1	25	100
United Kingdom[d]	165	81	19			100

Sources: Calculated from data in HA, *Investissements dans les industries du charbon et de l'acier de la Communauté*, September 1957, Appendix Tables 14 to 17, inclusive. United Kingdom from National Coal Board, *Investing in Coal*, 1956, Appendix.

[a] Gross capital expenditures, without changes in working capital. Independent cokeries excluded.

[b] Since a total figure was given on expenditures for cokeries by Belgium and the Netherlands combined, the breakdown shown is estimated.

[c] Italy included.   [d] Deep-mined coal only; 1950–1955.

in 1956 was still below or barely equal to that of 1937 though it was higher than productivity in France to begin with. Capital expenditures in the mining division per ton of coal produced in Nord and Pas-de-Calais and Centre-Midi in 1952–1956 were about 40 per cent above the average for the ECSC as a whole; in Lorraine they were more than twice the average for the ECSC and thrice that of the Ruhr. (See Table 28.) Facilities for the production of secondary products also absorbed a very high proportion of total investments in the French mines. (See Table 30.)

[50] Charbonnages de France, *Rapport de gestion, 1953*, pp. 63–65.

The third modernization plan, covering the years 1957–1961, and containing some longer forecasts, foresaw 65 million tons of production in 1975—an increase of 10 million tons over 1955. Seventy per cent of the increase was expected to come from the mines in Lorraine.[51] But capacity will probably be raised by less than half this goal; production in France in 1975 is not likely to exceed 59 million tons, and perhaps less in view of the large oil discoveries in the Sahara. Lorraine will carry the total net expansion. Since the Warndt mines will have been transferred to the Saar, gross output in the remaining Lorraine mines will have to be increased by 50 per cent for a net increase of 25 per cent—from 13 million tons in 1955 to 17 million tons by 1975.

THE BELGIAN INDUSTRY

The mines in southern Belgium still could not stand on their own feet in the common market at the end of the transitional period; their situation had if anything deteriorated.

Some forty-eight firms operate about 113 mines in southern Belgium with an average annual output of less than 400,000 tons per firm and 170,000 tons per mine. These units are the smallest in the Community, in spite of the fact that four groups control 58 per cent of the production. In the Campine, by contrast, seven firms with one mine each produce an average of nearly 1.5 million tons a year (data as of 1957).

What explains the lack of physical and corporate, as distinct from financial, concentration in the southern field?[52]

First, the more profitable firms do not wish to absorb the poorer ones.

Second, the poorer and older mines are able to survive because of subsidies and because the major capital costs have been written off.

Third, the antiquated structure has been preserved by, and the operators are evidently gambling on a continuation of, the postwar scarcity of coal.

Fourth, although Belgian coal prices seem to reflect less than average cost in the southern field, they are nevertheless high enough to give the mines in the Campine, which have usually sold at the same prices as the southern mines, a comparatively large economic rent, as indicated by the financial results shown below:[53]

---

[51] Commissariat Général du Plan, *Rapport général de la Commission de l'Energie*, March 1957, pp. 28–32.

[52] The southern field consists of four districts or basins, Centre, Charleroi, Liége, Borinage; the highest-cost mines tend to be in the Liége and Borinage districts.

[53] Calculated from data in R. Fritz, "Der belgische Bergbau im gemeinsamen Markt der Montanunion," in *Glückauf*, September 15, 1956, p. 1117. The data, drawn from company accounts, are after interest and depreciation allowance but before subsidy payments. The Campine mines in 1957 began to quote somewhat lower prices on some grades of coal than the southern mines.

	Profit or Loss Per Ton Produced	
	Campine	South
1952	$1.58	$−1.23
1953	1.20	−0.98
1954	0.92	−0.88
1955	2.42	−0.46

Fifth, the country is badly divided on the question of nationalization. The socialists and free trade unions, relying on the example provided by the British and French mines, believe that nationalization is the proper road to concentration. The confessional unions, strong in the Campine, and the conservative and liberal parties prefer a solution that would safeguard private ownership. In 1946 a socialist compromise proposal to regroup the mines into five large enterprises, one for each major district, was defeated in Parliament. Other proposals called for the formation of a public council, with representation from the government, consumers, unions and industry, to guide the industry. Whatever the proposal ultimately adopted, government influence is bound to grow. Unable to reach a compromise, a long-term solution was in the meantime discouraged by uncertainty.

The development of new mines in the Campine has consequently been delayed. No new mines have been opened there since the 1920s though there are large reserves, which the government has not conceded for development. In 1953 the socialist members of Parliament defeated a bill to concede additional reserves in the Campine in the hope of having them nationalized at a later date. In June 1957 the Belgian government, consisting of a coalition of socialists and liberals, submitted a bill to Parliament to grant additional concessions in the Campine.[54]

The Convention for the Transitional Provisions (CTP) granted the Belgian mines a special position for five years, terminating February 1958, in order to give them time to integrate into the common market.[55] It placed a limit on the amount of Belgian coal producing capacity that could be retired each year and hence limited the potential penetration of the Belgian market by coal from other areas, mainly the Ruhr. This provision was not used, because coal was scarce until mid-1957 and Belgian coal was not displaced. It provided for two

[54] *Bulletin d'information et de documentation*, Banque Nationale de Belgique, October 1957, p. 295. The High Authority in 1956 had asked the Belgian government to take action on these unconceded reserves; HA, *Bulletin mensuel d'information*, June 1956, p. 15. See also Fritz, *op. cit.*, p. 1118; ECSC Common Assembly, *Informations mensuelles*, September 1957, p. 35; *Le Monde*, December 7, 1956. Paul Finet, member of the High Authority and its president in 1957–1959, formerly in the Belgian trade union movement, personally favors nationalization if the private owners fail to concentrate the mines in the south, according to *Steel Review*, April 1958, p. 28.

[55] Paragraphs 25 and 26 of the CTP.

types of subsidies which were to taper off during the five-year transitional period: (a) A subsidy amounting to the difference between the selling prices approved by the High Authority and the price scale which would provide the mines with the income they were receiving when the common market opened in 1953. This provision thus placed selling prices under the control of the High Authority for five years. (b) A subsidy on 80 per cent of the difference between the price of Belgian coal in other parts of the ECSC and the price of coal from other districts. This second subsidy was discontinued in April 1955.

The funds for the subsidies were raised by a tax on the coal produced in the Ruhr and the Netherlands; the low-cost producers thus came to the aid of the high-cost firms, though the former added the tax to the sales price. The Belgian government was to match, and in fact exceeded, the subsidy from the Community. The tax, established below the limit set by the treaty, amounted initially to about 12 cents per ton of solid fuels produced by the mines in the Ruhr and the Netherlands and was reduced progressively.[56]

The Convention for the Transitional Provisions contained no explicit policy regarding the use to which the subsidy was to be put, although it was understood that the operators would do whatever was necessary to put the mines on their feet by February 1958. From the opening of the common market to June 1955, a period of nearly two and a half years, subsidies were advanced without conditions; the low-cost mines in the Campine also received subsidy payments. The High Authority in consultation with the Belgian government and coal operators introduced a more selective policy as of June 1955, amended December 1956.[57] The new policy embraced the following measures:

(1) Some grades of high quality coal were no longer subsidized.

(2) The subsidy to firms in good economic shape, mostly in the Campine, was reduced. The firms in this group (Group 1) received no subsidies after January 1, 1957, one year before the subsidies expired altogether.

(3) The resultant saving in subsidies was used to give contractual aid to some very high-cost firms in the Borinage. The four firms in this group (Group 3) were judged to be unable to become competitive and ceased receiving the normal subsidy as of February 1957. But they still received the contractual subsidy.[58] Some of these pits were to be closed.

(4) An intermediate group of firms (Group 2), considered to be in temporary difficulty, received subsidies until the transitional period ended.

[56] HA, *Bulletin mensuel d'information*, March 1956, p. 8.

[57] HA, *Sixième rapport général*, Vol. II, pp. 29–49, contains an excellent account of the Belgian coal problem, as well as the necessary documentation; data on investments are in *ibid.*, pp. 424–425.

[58] *Journal officiel*, February 22, 1956, pp. 20 ff, and *Bulletin d'information et de documentation*, May 1956, p. 350.

(5) Part of the subsidy was set aside to permit the mines to reduce prices on some grades of industrial coal.

(6) The Belgian government undertook some supplementary obligations to help the mines to become assimilated in the common market; it was to grant loans at reduced interest; to extend funds for the stockpiling of coal and the construction of power stations; it was to withdraw subsidies from uncooperative firms.

(7) The High Authority retained the right to oversee the execution of these measures and to intervene further if necessary.

The Belgian coal industry asked the Court of Justice to annul those measures that reduced the subsidy to the low-cost firms on the ground that they were discriminatory. The Court sustained the High Authority, ruling that selective subsidies adjusted to financial ability are not discriminatory.[59]

What was accomplished in the Belgian mines in the five years from the beginning of the common market to February 1958, when normal subsidies and price control ended?[60]

Investments

From 1952 to 1956 the Belgian coal mining firms invested an average of $53 million a year (Table 28), of which $39 million, or 75 per cent, was invested in the mining division. The latter amounted to $1.23 per ton of coal produced in the southern mines, and to $1.48 in the Campine. Investments in the mining division were higher than the average for the ECSC as a whole, $1.03 per ton, and higher than that in the other districts of the Community except Lorraine and Nord and Pas-de-Calais. (See Table 28.)

Subsidy payments from the High Authority and the Belgian government from 1953 through 1956, by which time the major part of the subsidy had been paid, represented about 58 per cent of the funds appropriated to investments for all divisions.[61] The funds furnished by the Community (apart from the Belgian government) represented 24 per cent of total investments by the Belgian coal mines in 1953–1956.

The Belgian mine owners had already received more than half the subsidy before it was ruled that they must use the subsidy for capital expenditures.

---

[59] See the summary in HA, *Bulletin mensuel d'information*, December 1956, pp. 30–31.

[60] These measures were brought to an end by Decision No. 23–57, *Journal officiel*, December 7, 1957, p. 569; Decision 2–58, *Journal officiel*, February 8, 1958, p. 67.

[61] In 1953–1956, $150 million was appropriated to the mining divisions and $200 million to all divisions. Subsidy payments from 1953 through 1957 amounted to $117 million, of which $49 million was from the Community. The percentages above are calculated on the postulate that the bulk of the subsidy payments, which tapered off, had been made by the end of 1956. The German coal mines furnished 90 per cent of the $49 million from the Community, and the Dutch coal mines 10 per cent. Fritz, *op. cit.*, p. 1115.

Part of it had been used to cover business losses or had been appropriated to purposes other than capital expenditure. The subsidy nevertheless made the high rate of investment possible whatever the use to which it was put on the books.

The production of secondary products is less advanced in Belgium— another weakness of that coal industry—than in other districts in the ECSC, where a greater proportion of investments is devoted to electric power and coking plants (Table 30).

Productivity

Though investments were comparatively high and the number of mines in southern Belgium was reduced from 136 in 1952 to 113 in 1957, output per man-shift underground in southern Belgium deteriorated or remained station-ary relative to that of its main rivals in the ECSC, as the following indexes show:[62]

	1952	1956
Ruhr	100	100
Nord and Pas-de-Calais	82	93
Campine	86	94
Southern Belgium	64	65
ECSC	92	96

Productivity in the mines in southern Belgium in 1956 was still one third below that in the other major fields and in the Community as a whole.

Conclusions

The measures to make the southern mines viable were taken too late and applied without sufficient vigor; the results were therefore disappointing. Costs of production were still too high, and the typical firm was still too small to put up or to obtain the funds required for reorganization. Though the sub-sidy might have been used to help the firms to compete in the common market, it encouraged them, with the help of the business boom, to avoid the problem instead. The High Authority put the matter in the following words as the five-year transitional period came to an end: "The problem of integrating Belgian coal is therefore unresolved. Many questions remain to be solved, with respect to which the High Authority has some grave concern."[63]

[62] Calculated from data in HA, *Sixième rapport général*, Vol. II, p. 351.

[63] HA, *Sixième rapport général*, Vol. II, p. 47. A Common Assembly report severely criticized the lack of results: see Assemblée Parlementaire Européenne, Commission du Marché Intérieur, Doc. No. 12, 1958, pp. 5–9. The Ruhr coal industry is reported to believe that the tax on its coal and its deliberate decision to avoid penetrating the Belgian market further came to nought; see *Handelsblatt*, February 3, 1958, p. 9.

The mines in southern Belgium encountered the same problems in 1958, when the ending of the transitional period coincided with a business recession, as in 1953, another year of recession, as though nothing had been done to change their situation: stocks of coal at the mines grew and prices were too high. A serious strike broke out in the Borinage early in 1959 when the operators announced that several mines would be closed. As a result of the strike the government requested permission from the High Authority to pay a further subsidy. The life of the high-cost mines was prolonged for a short period and the High Authority agreed to extend readaptation payments to the miners but made any further subsidies conditional on the preparation by the government and operators of a long-term reorganization and modernization plan.[64]

The mines in southern Belgium face a severe social problem of relocation. Since a large percentage of the miners are foreigners, the problem is partially transferable to other countries, notably Italy. As a coal importing country, it is hardly to Italy's advantage to encourage high-cost coal production.

SUMMARY

What influence had the High Authority and the common market had on investments in the coal industry as a whole as of 1958?

Investments were not substantially influenced by loans from the High Authority but the High Authority by informal discussion with governments and producers probably encouraged greater physical consolidation, the development of new mines and a shift of output to the lower-cost districts.

But the coal industry in southern Belgium—the problem child of the continental coal industry—had not yet solved (or even made a beginning of solving) its difficulties.

Government policies with respect to amortization allowances and prices (see Chapter 9) still determined the rate of capital formation and self-financing. The High Authority did not displace the governments in this field nor did the governments coordinate their policies.

[64] *Le Monde*, February 15–16, 1959, p. 3, February 18, 1959, p. 1, February 19, 1959, p. 14. A program to reduce Belgian coal production to 23.4 million tons annually by 1962 was adopted late in 1959; see International Monetary Fund, *International Financial News Survey*, November 27, 1959.

CHAPTER 5

CONCENTRATIONS

Concentrations in the steel and coal industries are examined country by country to determine their influence in regional markets and the effect of the ECSC on the concentration movement. Their influence on market organization and price behavior is examined in subsequent chapters.

The ECSC began to influence the concentration movement toward the end of 1950, when it became obvious that a treaty would be adopted. The treaty itself takes the date of signature (April 1951) rather than the effective date (July 1952) as the pertinent date. In the following discussion the effect of the ECSC is measured from April 1951 or even earlier if there is evidence that the then prospective economic union influenced an enterprise to combine.

PROVISIONS OF THE TREATY

The treaty gives the High Authority much power to prohibit new concentrations that would undermine competition. The principal provisions are in Article 66 of the treaty and in Section 13 of the Convention for the Transitional Provisions.

Procedures

The enterprises are required under paragraph 1 of Article 66 to notify the High Authority of a prospective concentration; all but small enterprises are subject to this rule.[1] If only one enterprise in a prospective concentration is subject to the jurisdiction of the ECSC, that one is still obliged to notify.[2]

The transaction to be notified may involve "a person or an enterprise, or a group of persons or enterprises, whether it concerns a single product or different products, whether it is effected by merger, acquisition of shares or

[1] The High Authority, under Article 66, paragraph 3, defined the exemptions for small enterprises in *Journal officiel*, May 11, 1954.

[2] Article 66 presumably also applies to foreign enterprises that control production within the ECSC, but it probably does not apply to domestic enterprises that combine with foreign ones if the object is to control assets and trade outside the jurisdiction of the ECSC. See Paul Reuter, *La Communauté Européenne du Charbon et de l'Acier*, Librairie Générale de Droit et de Jurisprudence, Paris, 1953, pp. 216–217.

assets, loan, contract, or any other means of control." The High Authority has issued a regulation defining "control of an enterprise" and a regulation defining the nature of the transactions to be notified and the kind of information that may be required.[3] Such information is treated as a professional secret under Article 47. The High Authority consequently may not reveal the evidence on which it decides whether a concentration is permissible or not.

If an enterprise fails to notify the High Authority of a concentration, the High Authority may take the following measures (Article 66, paragraph 5):

(a) If the substance of the transaction is itself legal, the High Authority nevertheless shall make approval subject to the payment of a penalty; if the penalty is not paid, it shall take appropriate action as indicated below.

(b) If the substance of the transaction is itself illegal, the High Authority shall denounce it as such "in a reasoned decision" and, after having heard the interested parties, shall order a separation "as well as any other action which it considers appropriate to reestablish the independent operation of the enterprises or assets in question and to restore normal conditions of competition." If an enterprise appeals to the Court against the High Authority, the decision is suspended, but the High Authority may take temporary measures, unless the Court rules otherwise, to protect other enterprises in the meantime. If an enterprise does not comply after having exhausted its rights of appeal, the High Authority may impose a daily penalty up to one tenth of one per cent of the value of the assets in question. It may also suspend the rights to use assets illegally acquired, apply to judicial authorities for a receivership administration of the assets, organize a forced sale, or annul the acts and decisions of bodies which have illegally acquired such assets. The High Authority may, further, address a recommendation to the interested member State to obtain its help in executing these measures.

Illegal Concentrations

Concentrations are not illegal in themselves. Prior notification gives the High Authority the opportunity to authorize a concentration if it is not illegal or to disapprove it if it is illegal. It is to be approved by the High Authority provided the persons or enterprises involved do not thereby acquire the economic power

. . . to determine prices, to control or restrict production or distribution, or to prevent the maintenance of effective competition in a substantial part of the market . . . [or] . . . to evade the rules of competition as they result from the execution of this Treaty, in particular by establishing an artificially privileged position involving a substantial advantage in access to supplies or markets. (Article 66, paragraph 2.)

[3] These regulations are to be found in *Journal officiel*, May 11, 1954.

Horizontal and vertical concentrations are equally affected.

The provisions of Article 66 are *not retroactive* and do *not* empower the High Authority to dissolve a concentration that occurred before the ECSC was established.[4] But the High Authority may apply the provisions to any concentration completed after the treaty was signed (that is, after April 18, 1951) if it can prove that it was conceived to evade Article 66 (Section 13 of the Convention for the Transitional Provisions). The treaty thus mainly prohibits illegal *new* concentrations.

In deciding whether a proposed concentration is illegal or not, "the High Authority shall take account of the size of enterprises of the same kind existing in the Community, as far as it finds this justified to avoid or correct the disadvantages resulting from an inequality in the conditions of competition" (Article 66, paragraph 2). Concentrations in existence before the ECSC was created thus provide a standard by which prospective concentrations are to be judged.

Although the High Authority has no powers to dissolve concentrations that antecede the ECSC or concentrations that are below the norm, it may nevertheless control or supervise them in the public interest (Article 66, paragraph 7). If a public or private enterprise has "a dominant position which protects [it] from effective competition in a substantial part of the common market" the High Authority may address a "recommendation" to it in order to prevent it from using that position for purposes contrary to the treaty.[5] If these recommendations are not carried out, the High Authority, after consulting the interested governments, "will . . . fix the prices and conditions of sale to be applied by the enterprise in question, or draw up production or delivery programmes which it must fulfill" (Article 66, paragraph 7).

It is apparent from the size of the penalties provided for (Article 66, paragraph 6) that the antitrust provisions of the treaty were meant to have teeth. The penalties, calculated on the value of the assets affected and varying with the nature of the infraction, are as follows: (a) 3 per cent for not providing the necessary information under paragraph 4; (b) 10 per cent for failure to solicit prior authorization; (c) 10 per cent for supplying false information in order to obtain an authorization; (d) 15 per cent on enterprises "which have participated in or lent themselves to the carrying out of operations in violation of the provisions of" Article 66. An enterprise may appeal to the Court against a penalty imposed by the High Authority.

[4] See Reuter, *op. cit.*, p. 217.

[5] The treaty distinguishes three kinds of actions the High Authority may take (Article 14): (a) "decisions" which are binding "in every respect"; (b) "recommendations" which are binding with respect to "objectives" but which allow the persons affected to choose the "means"; (c) "opinions" which are "binding" with respect neither to objectives nor means.

Nationalization and Concentration

Is an act of nationalization subject to the rule of prior authorization and could it be ruled illegal? Article 66 ignores this question but Article 83 stipulates that the ECSC "does not in any way prejudice the system of ownership. . . ." The treaty thus permits a State to acquire the assets of one or more enterprises without the need for prior authorization on the ground that nationalization, being a political act within the competence of the State, is not subject to the treaty.[6] But the treaty's standards of economic conduct do apply to the management of public as well as private enterprises. The pricing and sales policies of a public enterprise are therefore subject to the treaty. Though the High Authority has no power to prevent an act of nationalization, it can nevertheless also control or supervise a public enterprise under paragraph 7 of Article 66 by fixing prices and conditions of sale and by drawing up obligatory production or delivery programs for it.

Acts of nationalization generally apply to whole industries but a State can also acquire all or part of the assets of a particular firm within an industry. There has as yet been no test case to indicate whether or not a State is subject to Article 66 (paragraph 1) when it or its agent sells or buys capital assets or engages in any other transaction affecting a particular firm.

COMPETITION AND ANTITRUST REGULATIONS IN EUROPE

Whereas restrictive agreements are inherently illegal in the United States, they are not flatly prohibited in European countries, which are concerned only with the identification and elimination of the flagrant abuses that may be engendered by such practices. The idea of competition as an end in itself provides a stronger basis for control legislation in the United States than in European countries. Whereas concentrations and market-dominating firms, as well as restrictive agreements, are singled out for control in American antitrust legislation, concentrations cannot be dissolved in any member country of the Community under present legislation, although some of the abuses created by such firms are subject to some control in Germany, Belgium and the Netherlands.

Europe therefore has a climate of opinion different from that of the United States with respect to bigness and concerted action. A good part of the popula-

---

[6] See Reuter, *op. cit.*, p. 217, for a discussion of the problem of nationalization and concentration; also *Probleme des Schuman-Plans*, Kieler Vorträge, Kiel, 1951, p. 33, where Walter Hallstein, chief of the delegation that represented Germany at the negotiations for the ECSC treaty, affirms the State's right to nationalize under the treaty.

tion in many European countries, believing public ownership to be a practical alternative to private ownership, as witnessed by the development of public ownership in many of them, are not unfriendly to bigness. Nor have the proponents in Europe of private ownership been any friendlier to antitrust as a means of preserving private enterprise through competition.

The cartel rather than the monopoly is the main problem in France, where the typical firm is apt to be small in any case. Under a French decree of August 1953 on restrictive practices, fixing prices is legal if prices and profits are not excessive.[7]

Cartels developed rapidly in the Netherlands during the Great Depression, when the government encouraged their formation as part of a general program to stabilize business.[8] An act of 1956 is designed to avoid excessive restriction as well as excessive freedom. Public officials may approve or nullify an agreement, or any part of an agreement, among firms. They may extend the agreement to nonmembers if they believe the general interest would be served. Concentrations in the Netherlands cannot be dissolved, but public officials may interdict undesirable consequences.

The Italian government encouraged concerted business activities during the fascist era between the wars and used them as instruments of public policy. Restraints on competition are still accepted if they are carried out in the general interest.[9] In Italy the price mechanism has never been considered the touchstone, nor competition the ideal, of business activity.

In Germany the cartel and the large concern appeared late in the nineteenth century; their importance increased in the 1920s when production was rationalized, and expanded after the inflation and the entry of foreign capital.[10] It has been suggested that, whether they favor private property or not, most Germans believe that competition leads inevitably to concentration and that the latter is the superior form of economic organization because it eliminates waste and promotes stability. The Germans are especially partial to vertical

---

[7] J. G. Castel's chapter on "France" in W. Friedmann, ed., *Anti-Trust Laws, A Comparative Summary*, Stevens and Sons, London, 1956, especially pp. 92–93 and 134, contains a full description of the 1953 decree and the historical background. See also the chapter on France by R. Goetz-Girey in Edward H. Chamberlin, ed., *Monopoly and Competition and Their Regulation*, Macmillan, London, 1954, hereafter referred to as *Monopoly*. Cf. Hans B. Thorelli, "Antitrust in Europe: National Policies after 1945," in the *University of Chicago Law Review*, Winter 1959, pp. 222–236, and "European Antitrust Policy" in the *Law School Record*, University of Chicago, Vol. 8, No. 2; he believes that competitive practices have begun to enjoy more favor in Europe in recent years but predicts that the European Economic Community might have a greater influence than antitrust legislation on the growth of competition.

[8] See the chapter on the Netherlands by P. Verloren Van Themaat, in Friedmann, *op. cit.*, especially pp. 258–260, from which these remarks on that country are drawn.

[9] See the chapter on Italy by F. Vito in Chamberlin, *Monopoly*.

[10] Franz Neumann, *Behemoth*, Oxford, New York, 1942, p. 15.

concentration on the ground that it stabilizes the supply of raw materials, provides by-product revenue and leads to tax reductions.[11]

There were no laws or decrees with respect to cartels and concentrations until 1923, the German courts having ruled that freedom of contract gave the firm the right to enter a cartel or to combine, provided it behaved according to the prevailing standards of business conduct. A decree of 1923, issued in response to public pressure, did not challenge the legality of cartels but did empower the State to curb those practices that caused excessive injury to freedom of contract, to third parties and consumers. No practices were ever interdicted under this decree.[12] The Nazis used the cartels as instruments of policy after 1933.[13]

After the World War II occupation authorities had terminated their program of deconcentration and decartelization, which had applied largely to the coal, steel and chemicals industries, the German government assumed the obligation to enact a law dealing with cartels and concentrations. After a difficult parliamentary history, a bill was passed in 1957, effective January 1, 1958. Distinguishing the useful from the harmful cartel, the law tries to make price fixing illegal but nevertheless authorizes specified types of cartels.[14]

Some types of agreements can become effective without the consent of the Cartel Authority, though the latter has three months in which to express an objection; other types of agreements are not valid without prior authorization. Agreements must be disclosed to the administration either for information or authorization; some of them must be published.[15]

The law of 1957 deals with concentrations under the heading of "market dominating enterprises." Any enterprise meets the definition if it is in a market without "material" or "essential" competition. The Cartel Authority may prohibit the enterprises in such markets from engaging in "abusive practices" or from entering into agreements. But it has no power to dissolve existing concentrations or to prohibit the formation of new ones. A new merger must, however, be reported to the Cartel Authority—presumably for future surveillance since approval is not required—if it controls more than 20 per cent of the market. A merger is defined as a transaction in which one proprietary in-

---

[11] See F. Boehm's chapter on Germany in Chamberlin, *Monopoly*, pp. 152 ff.

[12] Neumann, *op. cit.*, pp. 16, 264.

[13] See the chapter on Germany by H. K. Bock and H. Korsch in Friedmann, *op. cit.*, especially pp. 142–146; and the chapter on Germany by F. Boehm in Chamberlin, *Monopoly*. The relevant portions of Neumann's book, *op. cit.*, are extremely interesting; on p. 291, citing the conclusions of the Institut für Konjunkturforschung, Neumann indicates that in 1936 all raw and semifinished goods and half of all finished goods in Germany were bound by concentrations or cartels.

[14] A copy of the law, in English, was reprinted in *Wirtschaft und Wettbewerb*, January 1958.

[15] *The Economist*, July 20, 1957, p. 227, holds the law to be "richly hung with lawyers' fees and civil servants' salaries" owing to the escape clauses and the complicated administrative provisions.

terest or enterprise acquires 25 per cent of the voting capital in another enterprise.

With respect to antitrust philosophy, the ECSC treaty is thus closer to American conceptions than to the conceptions prevalent in the member States. Competition is regarded as an end in itself under the ECSC treaty. Agreements are forbidden if they run counter to that objective by price fixing, restricting production, allocating markets, supplies or customers. If a concentration possesses too much power in the market, it is illegal under Article 66 whether that power has actually been abused or not. New concentrations can be prohibited in the ECSC, as they can in the United States, though the High Authority cannot dissolve those that antedated the ECSC.[16]

New concentrations are not subject to prior authorization under the later treaty for the European Economic Community (EEC). The EEC thus has no authority to prohibit new concentrations or to dissolve old ones. The High Authority's power to prevent new concentrations in the ECSC is therefore still exceptional in European practice. But Article 86 of the EEC treaty, dealing with single or associated enterprises that have a "dominant position" in the common market, prohibits price fixing, production and sales restrictions and discrimination, and relies on the doctrine of prohibiting "abusive practices." The Council of Ministers is required under Article 87 of the EEC treaty to promulgate by 1960 the necessary federal rules and directives to make the principles of Article 86 effective. It decided early in 1959 that Article 86 of the EEC treaty has the force of law in the member States in the meantime insofar as interstate commerce is affected, entrusting the individual States with the enforcement of this interim measure.

THE FIRM AND THE GROUP

Many firms control more than one plant or mine. But a firm may be allied to other firms without losing its corporate identity. Such alliances may be horizontal, with firms producing similar products; or they may be vertical, with firms producing raw materials or final products.

One firm may own equity capital in another firm, or two or more firms may be controlled by a third firm—a holding company—or by a common owner.

[16] Friedmann, *op. cit.*, p. 512, says: "Articles 65 and 66 of the Treaty are strongly inspired by the United States' conception of restrictive trade practices." American conceptions, common also to Canada, were brought into Japan and Germany via the occupation after World War II but have been gradually attenuated under local sovereignty. American conceptions influenced the ECSC treaty via the deconcentration and decartelization program for the German coal and steel industries; see *ibid.*, pp. 525 ff. For good treatments of American antitrust practices see Temporary National Economic Committee (TNEC), *Competition and Monopoly in American Industry*, Monograph No. 21, Washington, 1940; Simon N. Whitney, *Antitrust Policies: American Experience in Twenty Industries*, Twentieth Century Fund, New York, 1958, especially Chaps. 1, 22 and 23.

Firms may also be allied by long-term contracts to buy from or sell to each other. These devices are not necessarily mutually exclusive.

The term *group* will be used to refer to allied firms having common interests in coal and steel enterprises. F. Vito has defined the term as follows:[17]

> . . . the expression "group" . . . refers to an aggregate of firms belonging to the same and/or different branches of production, distribution, transport, or banking, etc., i.e., an aggregate of vertically or/and horizontally concentrated firms, aiming at such large-scale economies as the single firm acting separately would never be able to attain. These economies may derive from a better exploitation of redundant capacity, a common buying organization, common research laboratories, a more appropriate transport organization, a fuller utilization of by-products, etc. The component firms remain legally independent but the coordination of their activities is obtained through a variety of devices, among which the most frequent are the following: (a) interpersonal connection (personal interlocking); (b) the holding of a majority of stocks or voting power; (c) long-term contracts. The primary aim of a group is reduction of costs; but the unified policy resulting from the co-ordination of their activities leads inevitably to a limitation, if not to the elimination, of competition among the firms concerned. Moreover, the strength acquired by the aggregate of firms on the market gives it a leading, if not a monopolistic, position in relation to competitors outside the group.
>
> The scientific concept of "group" was elaborated by myself some years ago (1930) and was accepted as a useful tool for studying a very complex matter by scholars outside of Italy. It is closely related to the German notion "Konzern." I would not say it corresponds to the American "trust" because of the different implications from the legal point of view. Neither does it correspond to "merger," since in the latter case the various firms lose completely their legal and economic independence; in fact, they lose their very individuality. In spite of the terminological affinity, the group should not be taken as an equivalent to what Americans define as "group monopoly." This last expression has been used to mean a situation where there are several large enterprises each of which may be convinced that price-cutting will involve retaliation, so that the result will be lower profits for all; consequently their individual price policies may establish rigid prices at a high level.

Control

Control may be exercised with less than majority stock ownership, especially if the rest of the owners are dispersed. A "predominant minority" controls from 30 to 50 per cent of the stock; a "substantial minority" from 10 to 30 per cent; a "small minority" less than 10 per cent.[18] A minority interest may even exercise some control when another minority interest, or even when a majority interest, is present. Control should therefore be understood in a qualitative rather than a strictly quantitative sense. The allied deconcentration

---

[17] In Chamberlin, *Monopoly*, pp. 48–49. Reduction of cost need not always be the primary aim or the result of the formation of groups.

[18] William Fellner, *Competition Among the Few*, Knopf, New York, 1949, pp. 169–171.

authorities in Germany considered anyone who had more than 15 per cent control a "large shareholder."[19] The German cartel law of 1957 considers acquisition of 25 per cent control sufficient for the definition of concentration or merger.[20] The High Authority has placed the figure at 10 per cent under paragraph 1 of Article 66.[21]

Two firms which produce similar products but own or control a third firm producing other products shall herein nevertheless be considered independent with respect to the first products unless there is other evidence to the contrary.

THE FRENCH STEEL INDUSTRY

HORIZONTAL CONCENTRATIONS

The group rather than the firm is the core of concentration in the French steel industry. The groups themselves are extremely interlocked.

The changes created by the Treaty of Versailles laid the groundwork for the pattern of concentration in Lorraine and also for French penetration of the steel industry in the Saar and Luxembourg. France produced 4.7 million tons of crude steel in 1913; the Germans produced another 2.3 million tons in their part of Lorraine.[22] The German assets in the Moselle were transferred to the French government as payment of indemnity. The French government transferred the German assets to the larger French steel groups—Schneider, Pont-à-Mousson, De Wendel. Each of these acquired a major interest in a separate plant formerly under German control. Since the steel industry required a large amount of capital (a) to balance the facilities in the Moselle where the steel plants had more pig iron capacity than they needed and more crude steel capacity than the rolling mills could absorb and (b) to rebuild the northern steel plants damaged by the war, two or more groups in some cases acquired a joint interest in a plant in order to broaden the financial basis for capital investment in it.[23] Though France acquired additional steel facilities and enlarged those it acquired for the sake of integrating them vertically, it did not

[19] K. H. Herchenröder, *Die Nachfolger der Ruhr Konzerne*, Econ-Verlag, Düsseldorf, 1953, p. 190.

[20] Article 23 of the Kartellgesetz in *Wirtschaft und Wettbewerb*, January 1958, p. 39. See Mary Jean Bowman and George L. Bach, *Economic Analysis and Public Policy*, Prentice-Hall, New York, 2nd edition, 1949, pp. 65–67, for a discussion of the methods by which corporations are controlled.

[21] Decision No. 26–54, in *Journal officiel*, May 11, 1954, pp. 350 ff.

[22] Benham, *op. cit.*, p. 28.

[23] The Schneider group acquired the German plants at Mondéville (near Caen) and at Knutange in the Moselle. De Wendel and Pont-à-Mousson each also acquired a substantial interest in Knutange. Pont-à-Mousson acquired control of the facilities now known as Hadir in Luxembourg, of the Dillinger works and of Halbergerhütte in the Saar, and of the Rombas plant in the Moselle. A large German plant at Hagondange was transferred to a newly organized firm called UCPMI, which was controlled by several large steel consumers and one of the large steel firms.

acquire any industrialized regions to consume the additional steel and thus became oriented to exports.

Combinations After World War II

Except for some coastal plants, the French steel industry emerged undamaged from the second world war. But it was fairly obsolete because investments had been neglected during the Great Depression, about one third of crude steel capacity having been idle during the early 1930s. (See Table 17.) Under the spur of Jean Monnet's postwar modernization plans large capital expenditures were made, largely with government credit, and many of the plants and firms were regrouped. Six major regroupings occurred between the end of the war and 1956. These combinations are described in Appendix C.

All the major French steel groups, involving about 75 per cent of French steel capacity, were reorganized between 1948 and 1956. Three of these reorganizations, involving the creation of Usinor, Sollac and Sidelor, occurred before the ECSC,[24] though the formation of the last might have been influenced by it. (See Appendix C.) The reorganizations that occurred after the ECSC (the legal date of April 1951) affected nearly 40 per cent of French steel capacity. If the reorganization of Sidelor is included (it occurred while the treaty was still under negotiation), about 50 per cent of French steel capacity was affected by reorganization from the end of 1950 to 1956—about one third of the capacity in the north of France, about 45 per cent of that in Lorraine and nearly all the capacity in the Centre-Midi.[25]

Degree of Concentration

Six French groups controlled about 76 per cent of French steel production as of 1958. (See Fig. 13, based on Table 5-1, Appendix E, which refers to output in 1954 but to control as of 1958.) A Belgian group, consisting of Société Générale and Launoit (Cofinindus and Brufina), controlled another 10 per cent. Several smaller firms and groups divided the remaining 14 per cent of the output among themselves.

The degree of concentration is much greater by geographical areas. Denain-Anzin, accounting for 14 per cent of total French steel production, controls two thirds of the production in the north. Two groups, Denain-Anzin and Longwy-Raty, control nearly 90 per cent of the northern steel output, which is specialized in open-hearth and flat-rolled products.

[24] See HA, *Sixième rapport général*, Vol. II, pp. 107–110, for a list of the transactions post-dating the ECSC.

[25] Most of the data on French mergers and concentrations are drawn from *La Concentration financière dans la sidérurgie française*, Etudes et Documents, Paris, April 1956; this study does not include the foreign assets of the French steel industry. It is the best of the studies on a tangled business. For additional references see Appendix C.

The Pont-à-Mousson group and the Schneider group control nearly 100 per cent of the Centre-Midi, specializing in special and electric steel. The Pont-à-Mousson group and the De Wendel group are the leading producers in the Alpine area, which specializes in alloy steel. The Schneider group, with 11 per cent of total French production, is the dominant producer in the west (Mondéville near Caen).

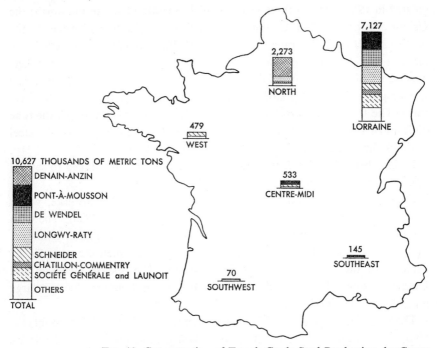

FIG. 13. Concentration of French Crude Steel Production, by Group and Region, 1958[a]

Source: Table 5-1; Appendix E.

[a] Concentrations as of 1958; production as of 1954.

Pont-à-Mousson, De Wendel, Longwy-Raty and Schneider control 65 per cent of the production in Lorraine. Chatillon-Commentry and the Belgian group control another 20 per cent of Lorraine steel. Six groups thus control 85 per cent of Lorraine crude steel. (See Table 5-1, Appendix E.)

Inbreeding Between the Groups

The groups are inbred rather than independent. (See Appendix C for the details.) The major links are between the De Wendel and the Longwy-Raty groups; between the Usinor group and the Longwy-Raty group; between the Pont-à-Mousson and De Wendel groups through Sollac; between Chatillon-

Commentry and Forges et Aciéries de la Marine et de Saint-Etienne (hence Pont-à-Mousson) through Ateliers et Forges de la Loire; between the Schneider, the Usinor and the De Wendel groups, because the last two own 16 per cent and 21 per cent, respectively, of the share capital of the Schneider group's steel plant at Knutange in Lorraine—the largest crude steel producing unit that the Schneider group controls in France. An important new link was created in 1956 between three groups which operate plants in the north: the Usinor group; Chatillon-Commentry (which has a plant at Isbergues in the north as well as in Lorraine and Centre-Midi), and Firminy (which has a plant at Les Dunes). These three organized a new company, Société Dunkerqueoise de Sidérurgie, to build an integrated steel plant at Dunkerque. The Usinor group is majority stockholder and presides over the board of directors.[26] The Usinor and Longwy-Raty groups are also linked through the tube division of the steel industry, an important and profitable part of the steel business that is outside the jurisdiction of the ECSC.[27]

Besides being interbred, the French steel groups are also linked to several non-French steel groups.

Outside France. Pont-à-Mousson controls Dillinger Hüttenwerke, which accounts for 21 per cent of the crude steel production in the Saar. The Otto Wolff and Stumm groups in Germany have a minority interest in Dillinger. Pont-à-Mousson is the largest stockholder in Hadir, which accounts for 27 per cent of the steel produced in Luxembourg. The Société Générale and Launoit groups that control Cockerill-Ougrée, in Belgium, have a large minority interest in Hadir.

The Schneider group has a 25 per cent interest in Arbed, which accounts for 60 per cent of the steel produced in Luxembourg and 23 per cent of the Saar's production. The groups that control Cockerill-Ougrée also have a substantial interest in Arbed.

The groups in control of Cockerill-Ougrée are the dominant steel producers in Belgium. They account for 15 per cent of the steel output in Lorraine—through two firms, Providence and Hauts Fourneaux de la Chiers. They are linked to the Schneider and Pont-à-Mousson groups and, through common interests in the tube division of the steel industry, to the Longwy-Raty and Usinor groups.

A study confined to the steel industry in France only has drawn the following conclusion:[28] ". . . no group is revealed to be totally independent. The

---

[26] Details on the new venture may be found in *Le Monde*, June 27, July 28 and 29, 1956; *Handelsblatt*, June 15, 1956; *Usine nouvelle*, January 24, 1957, p. 105.

[27] *La Concentration financière dans la sidérurgie française; Handelsblatt*, March 22–23, 1957, p. 18, and October 4–5, 1957, p. 10.

[28] *La Concentration financière dans la sidérurgie française*, pp. 30–31.

most powerful have interests in neighboring enterprises. . . . To battle against a competitor under these conditions would often be detrimental to one's own interests." This interbred situation does not, however, completely preclude some types of rivalry between groups.

VERTICAL CONCENTRATION IN FRENCH STEEL

The French steel industry has not controlled any coal mines in France since the nationalization of 1946.[29] But it controls a large amount of coal in the Ruhr, Aachen, Campine and Limburg, as shown in Table 31. The French steel industry controls non-French coal mines that produced over 16 million tons

Table 31

FOREIGN COAL PRODUCTION CONTROLLED BY FRENCH STEEL GROUPS, 1955[a]

(*Millions of Metric Tons*)

Area	De Wendel	Pont-à-Mousson	Sidéchar[b]	Total
Ruhr	3.7	—	6.5	10.2
Aachen	—	0.6	—	0.6
Campine	—	3.5[c]	—	3.5
Limburg	2.3[d]	—	—	2.3
Total	6.0	4.1	6.5	16.6

Sources: Annual financial reports of De Wendel et Cie., Sidelor, Harpener Bergbau; *Jahrbuch;* Wolf-Rodé, *Handbuch.* See also notes below.

[a] In most cases this represents control as of mid-1958, but see footnote *c* below. Production is for 1955.

[b] This French holding company owns 75 per cent of Harpener Bergbau. Schneider, Longwy-Raty and the Cockerill-Ougrée groups own about 20 per cent of Sidéchar; Pont-à-Mousson about 15 per cent; Usinor and Chatillon-Commentry about 10 per cent each. See *Handelsblatt*, December 23, 1957, p. 8.

[c] Included are Charbonnages de Limburg-Meuse (in which Pont-à-Mousson may or may not be majority stockholder) and Beeringen. See Wolf-Rodé, *Handbuch*, p. 176. The Launoit group also has an interest in Limburg-Meuse. See *Handelsblatt*, January 12, 1959, "Wer sind die Eigentümer?"

[d] Oranje-Nassau mine, H. Aszkenazy, "Le fonctionnement du marché charbonnier en Belgique et en Hollande," *Annales des mines*, May 1957, p. 319.

of coal in 1955. Most of this coal is of coking quality. The tonnage controlled is nearly twice the volume of primary coal exclusive of coke imported by France in 1955. Yet less than half the coal produced at these non-French coal mines is consigned to the French steel industry; consumers in the country of origin would otherwise be seriously harmed. In the circumstances, the mines can hardly be considered fully captive.

[29] It had theretofore controlled a large amount of coal; see Robert Lafitte-Laplace, *L'Economie charbonnière de la France*, Marcel Giard, Paris, 1933, p. 640. The nationalized mines are discussed below in the section on "State Ownership in the European Coal Industry," pp. 165 ff.

The French steel industry also obtains coke, in addition to coal, from its mines in the Ruhr and Limburg. Lorraine-Escaut (Longwy-Raty group), located in the northern part of Lorraine and therefore close to Belgium and Holland, controls coke plants at Sluiskil (Netherlands) and Zeebrugge (Belgium).[30]

The French steel industry is vertically integrated with French iron ore. Except for the Schneider group in the Centre-Midi and also UCPMI, in the latter of which several steel consumers, notably Renault (automobiles), have joint interests, the French steel industry is not vertically integrated with steel transforming industries.[31]

THE STEEL INDUSTRY IN BELGIUM-LUXEMBOURG

Two groups and their respective holding companies with important interests in all important aspects of Belgian financial and industrial life dominate the Belgian coal and steel industries. These are Société Générale and the Launoit groups.[32] In 1955 the two groups pooled their main interests in the Belgian steel industry.

Horizontal Concentration

Société Générale de Belgique (a holding company not to be confused with the group's Banque de la Société Générale de Belgique) prior to 1955 controlled the steel firm of John Cockerill (about one million tons of crude steel capacity in 1955) with 20 per cent of the share capital. Through John Cockerill or directly, Société Générale had an interest in a number of other steel firms: it directly owned 30 per cent of Forges de la Providence, a large firm astride the Franco-Belgian border with a crude steel capacity in 1955 of about 1.2 million tons equally divided between the two countries. It also directly owned 20 per cent of Société Métallurgique de Sambre et Moselle with a capacity of about 500,000 tons of crude steel in 1955. It directly owned 16 per cent of Arbed in Luxembourg. It owned directly and through John Cockerill 20 per cent in Hadir, also in Luxembourg. But the Schneider group has a large interest in Arbed and Pont-à-Mousson a larger interest in Hadir.[33]

[30] J. E. Martin, "Location Factors in the Lorraine Iron and Steel Industry," *The Institute of British Geographers, Transactions and Proceedings*, 1957, Publication No. 23, pp. 205–206.

[31] The Longwy-Raty and the De Wendel groups, producing tubes and tin containers, respectively, manufacture highly finished steel products but have not ventured far beyond the steel industry itself.

[32] For the origin of Société Générale, see J. H. Clapham, *The Economic Development of France and Germany, 1815–1914*, Cambridge University Press, Cambridge, 4th edition, 1951, pp. 127, 131. A royal decree of 1934 required banking and holding operations to separate.

[33] *Handelsblatt*, July 22, 1955, p. 14, and November 26, 1956, p. 6.

Société Générale consequently was the largest single stockholder in a number of firms with a combined crude steel capacity of 2.7 million tons in 1955; 2.1 million tons of the total were in Belgium and accounted for 36 per cent of total Belgian capacity. Société Générale also was a stockholder—but not the largest—in Luxembourg steel firms with a production of 2.8 million tons, representing 87 per cent of Luxembourg's steel output in 1955, and through Arbed of 740,000 tons in the Saar, accounting for 23 per cent of the Saar's steel output in 1955. Société Générale thus was secondary stockholder in firms that produced 3.6 million tons and had an interest in 6.3 million tons of steel all together.

Launoit, the other group (sometimes called Cofinindus-Brufina), comprises a number of interrelated holding companies: The Compagnie Financière et Industrielle (Cofinindus); the Banque de Bruxelles, which, with Cofinindus, controls the Société de Bruxelles pour la Finance et l'Industrie (Brufina). The Launoit group acquired control of an important segment of the steel industry in 1929 when it took over S. A. d'Ougrée-Marihaye and the Banque de Bruxelles; Ougrée-Marihaye was then a steel operating, a banking and a holding company. The steel division consisted of several plants in Belgium and a plant in Luxembourg. Following a royal decree of 1934, the steel plants in Ougrée-Marihaye were incorporated as separate operating companies. Cofinindus was founded to hold their stock. A new S. A. d'Ougrée-Marihaye was established to operate the steel plants in the area of Liége. Aciéries et Minières de la Sambre was created to operate the steelworks at Monceau-sur-Sambre in Belgium and a coal mine in Hainaut (Belgium) called Fontaine-l'Evêque. A separate company called Rodange was created to operate the steel plant in Luxembourg. Thy-le-Château et Marcinelle, another major steel firm in the Launoit group, was controlled through Brufina. The new Ougrée-Marihaye company and Cofinindus-Brufina each held stock in and controlled a steel firm in France called S. A. des Hauts-Fourneaux de la Chiers at Longwy. The new Ougrée-Marihaye firm also held stock in all the other of the Launoit group's steel firms but Thy-le-Château.[34]

Prior to 1955 Launoit controlled about 1.7 million tons of steel output in Belgium, 20 per cent of the total; it also controlled 400,000 tons in Luxembourg and 650,000 tons in France. It thus controlled 2.8 million tons of steel in all.

Société Générale, controlling 2.7 million and having a secondary interest in an additional 3.6 million tons, was thus larger than the Launoit group.[35]

[34] *Ibid.*, July 22, 1955, p. 14.

[35] See Albert Wehrer, "Les Fusions et concentrations d'entreprises dans les pays de la Communauté Européenne du Charbon et de l'Acier," HA, Luxembourg, November 1955, p. 10.

Table 32
SOCIÉTÉ GÉNÉRALE AND LAUNOIT GROUPS OF BELGIUM:
INTERESTS IN CRUDE STEEL PRODUCTION IN BELGIUM, FRANCE,
LUXEMBOURG AND THE SAAR, 1956[a]

Area and Group	Firm	Per Cent of Crude Steel Production of Respective Area
Belgium		
Société Générale and Launoit	Cockerill–Ougrée	34
Société Générale and Launoit	Aciéries and Minières de la Sambre	5
Launoit	Thy-le-Château et Marcinelle	6
Société Générale	Forges de la Providence	11
Société Générale	Hainaut–Sambre	18
Belgium total		74
France		
Société Générale	French Division of Providence	4
Société Générale and Launoit	S.A. des Hauts-Fourneaux de la Chiers	6
France total		10
Luxembourg		
Société Générale and Launoit	Arbed	60
Société Générale and Launoit	Rodange	13
Société Générale and Launoit	Hadir	27
Luxembourg total		100
Saar		
Société Générale and Launoit	Saar Division of Arbed	23
ECSC		
Société Générale and Launoit	All interests	18
	All interests except Hadir	16
	All interests except Arbed and Hadir	11
	All interests except Arbed, Hadir and Hainaut-Sambre	9

Source: Table 5-2, Appendix E.

[a] The two groups jointly control Cockerill–Ougrée, which owns stock in several other steel firms. Each group also owns stock directly in the same firms. Société Générale but not Launoit owns stock in Providence and possibly in Hainaut-Sambre; Launoit but not Société Générale owns stock in Thy-le-Château. Both groups otherwise have a joint interest in all the other firms shown. The notes to Table 5-2, Appendix E, provide additional qualifications.

In 1955 John Cockerill and Ougrée-Marihaye, the main firms in each group, merged to create Cockerill-Ougrée, with a capacity of 2.0 million tons of crude steel.[36] The degree of concentration created by this merger is shown in Table 32.

The High Authority authorized the merger on condition that Cockerill-Ougrée maintain the two sales agencies, Ucometal and Siderur, which had previously represented John Cockerill and Ougrée-Marihaye, respectively.[37]

[36] Cockerill-Ougrée also absorbed Ferblatil, in which John Cockerill had had the majority control. The merger really brought together 2.3 million tons but 300,000 tons were scrapped to make way for new facilities.

[37] The High Authority had authorized Ucometal to sell for John Cockerill, Providence, and Société Métallurgique de Sambre et Moselle, in Decision No. 42–54, *Journal officiel*, January 11, 1955. It had authorized Siderur to sell for Ougrée-Marihaye, Aciéries et Minières de la Sambre, and Rodange (Luxembourg) in Decision No. 40–54, *Journal officiel*, August 1, 1954.

Through Cockerill-Ougrée, the Launoit group and Société Générale pooled their interests in four other firms: Chiers, Aciéries et Minières de la Sambre, Rodange and Hadir. The Launoit group, through Cofinindus-Brufina, also owns stock in all these firms but Hadir, in addition to the stock that it owns in them through Cockerill-Ougrée. As a result of the merger of John Cockerill and Ougrée-Marihaye, Société Générale penetrated nearly all of Launoit's steel interests, except for Thy-le-Château, because Ougrée-Marihaye had held stock in all the other steel firms in the Launoit group except Thy-le-Château. The Launoit group, on the other hand, penetrated Hadir but not Arbed, Providence or Hainaut-Sambre, though it had already had a small participation in Arbed. Hainaut-Sambre represents a 1955 merger of Sambre et Moselle, in which Société Générale had had a 20 per cent interest, and of Usines Métallurgiques du Hainaut.[38]

It remains to be seen if the two major groups have joined in Cockerill-Ougrée in order to coordinate all their other interests or to create a rivalry between that new company and the firms which the two groups have not inter-penetrated, namely Providence and possibly Hainaut-Sambre in the Société Générale group and Thy-le-Château in the Launoit group. Launoit and Société Générale have in any case maintained their identity as groups even though the merger of Cockerill-Ougrée has brought them close together.

The two groups combined now control almost three quarters of Belgian crude steel, 10 per cent of French, and, exclusive of Société Générale's secondary interests, 13 per cent of Luxembourg's steel, a total of nearly 6.0 million tons or 11 per cent of ECSC production in 1955.[39] Although the two Belgian groups control only 13 per cent of the steel in Luxembourg, they also have substantial interests along with other groups in 100 per cent of the Luxembourg steel and 44 per cent of the Saar steel. Their interest in the Saar is through Arbed and indirectly in Dillinger, controlled by the Pont-à-Mousson group, which also controls Hadir, in which Cockerill-Ougrée and Société Générale have a large minority interest. The Société Générale and Launoit groups thus have interests in 9.5 million tons of crude steel in all, or 18 per cent of the ECSC's output in 1955.

Twenty-six per cent of the Belgian steel is not under the control of the two main groups. Small and nonintegrated plants have historically played a relatively important role in Belgian production of finished steel products, as

---

[38] It is not clear if Société Générale is still the most important single interest in the merged firm of Hainaut-Sambre. See footnote *e* to Table 5-2, Appendix E. This merger is not listed in the HA's list of mergers in *Sixième rapport général*, Vol. II, pp. 107–111.

[39] "Control" is here not measured in terms of majority stock ownership, for, in addition to the usual devices by which a group may control with less than a majority interest, a 20 per cent interest by a group like Société Générale or Launoit is sufficient in the absence of a rival group of equal importance. Furthermore, joint stock participation in the same firm by more than one group often represents an accommodation to potential rivalry.

shown in Chapter 6. These plants are dependent on merchant pig iron and semifinished steel from the two main steel groups or from foreign sources.[40]

Luxembourg, part of the German customs union before the first world war, had been penetrated by non-German, as well as German, capital shortly after the turn of the century. The Société Générale and Schneider groups had gained entrance into the German customs union by stock ownership in Arbed, the result of a merger in 1911 which included a plant at Burbach in the Saar.[41] The Ougrée-Marihaye group had penetrated the German customs union through the Rodange plant. The Belgian groups remained relatively stable in Luxembourg after the first world war except that Société Générale acquired a minority interest in Hadir, in which Pont-à-Mousson acquired 48 per cent control after German capital retired.

Three firms produce all the crude steel in Luxembourg. (See Table 5-2, Appendix E.) Arbed with 60 per cent, Hadir with 27 per cent and Rodange with 13 per cent of the production, are linked through a proprietary interest, Société Générale and Cockerill-Ougrée, that is common to all three of them. The Schneider group, Société Générale and the Barbanson family dominate Arbed; Pont-à-Mousson dominates Hadir and the Launoit group dominates Rodange. The Luxembourg steel industry is therefore controlled from elsewhere. Arbed controls 23 per cent of the crude steel output in the Saar, coal mines in Germany, iron ore mines in France and metal transforming plants in Belgium and Germany, to speak only of its European investments.[42] Arbed has its own sales organization called Columeta. Rodange sells through Siderur, which also sells for Cockerill-Ougrée and for Aciéries et Minières de la Sambre. Hadir sells through Davum Exportation, which exports for the firms belonging to the Pont-à-Mousson group.[43]

Vertical Concentration

Société Générale and Cockerill-Ougrée have extensive interests in steel fabricating works producing tubes and wire products. Société Générale controls a locomotive works and the only shipyard in Belgium, at Hoboken near Antwerp. The groups that produce steel in Belgium thus account through steel transforming firms under the same control for a large part of the small volume of steel consumed in Belgium.

[40] For the importance of the so-called Belgian "re-rollers" in the interwar steel cartel, see Benham, *op. cit.*, pp. 38–39.

[41] *Ibid.*, p. 46; Carlo Hemmer, *L'Economie du Grand-Duché de Luxembourg*, deuxième partie, *La Production secondaire: l'industrie sidérurgique*, Editions Joseph Beffort, Luxembourg, 1953, p. 107.

[42] See the sections in this chapter on the Ruhr coal industry and Tables 5-6 and 5-7, Appendix E, for Arbed's coal interests.

[43] Wolf-Rodé, *Handbuch*, p. 294; also the *Metal Bulletin*, November 1954, p. 25.

The Launoit and Société Générale groups control sufficient iron ore deposits in Luxembourg and France to cover their requirements for that type of ore. They have in recent years supplemented Lorraine ore with large quantities of Swedish ore in order to save coke, which is relatively expensive in Belgium owing to high costs of production in the coal mines in southern Belgium.

THE BELGIAN COAL INDUSTRY

The degree of corporate concentration in the Belgian coal industry is presented in Table 33. Société Générale controls 30 per cent of Belgian coal pro-

Table 33

CONCENTRATION OF CONTROL IN BELGIAN COAL PRODUCTION, 1955

(*Amount in Thousands of Metric Tons*)

Group	Campine		South		Total	
	Amount	Per Cent	Amount	Per Cent	Amount	Per Cent
Société Générale	3,802	37	5,354	27	9,156	30
Launoit	1,601[a]	16	4,513	23	6,114	20
Coppée	1,262	12	994	5	2,256	8
Sofina	—	—	572	3	572	2
French steel interests	3,540	35	—	—	3,540	12
Independents	—	—	8,385	42	8,385	28
Total	10,205	100	19,818	100	30,023	100

Sources: Holdings et Démocratie, Fédération Générale du Travail de Belgique, Liége, 1956, pp. 105–106, 118–121, 123, 139, 145, 181–184. 1955 financial reports of Hainaut–Sambre, Providence, Chiers, and Rodange and Arbed. Production data from *Jahrbuch*, 1956.

[a] Arbed's interest in Charbonnages de Helchteren et Zolder (1.6 million tons in 1955) is assumed to be a minority one, the major interest being in the hands of the Launoit group.

duction and the Launoit group 20 per cent. The two groups combined control 15 million tons of coal out of a total of 30 million tons. Only about a third of the 15 million tons is used for coking purposes. The Launoit and Société Générale groups therefore control more coal than they require for vertical integration. The Coppée group and the Sofina group, also important in Belgian financial and industrial activities, control 8 and 2 per cent, respectively, of Belgian coal production. Several French steel groups control 12 per cent. These five groups, counting the French as one group, thus control 72 per cent of Belgian coal.[44]

[44] Pont-à-Mousson has an interest in Charbonnages Limburg-Meuse and in Charbonnages Beeringen, in which De Wendel also has an interest; both mines are in the Campine. The steel plants operated in France by Providence and Chiers probably receive some of their metallurgical fuel from the Belgian mines under common proprietary control. Arbed has an interest in one Campine mine, Helchteren et Zolder, in which Launoit is assumed to have the majority. Arbed, *Rapport de gestion*, 1955.

Corporate concentration is much greater in the Campine than in southern Belgium. One hundred per cent of the coal production in the Campine is controlled by four groups—counting the French as one. Four groups control 58 per cent of the coal production in southern Belgium. Forty-two per cent of the production there is independent.

The southern mines, the oldest on the Continent, are quite small. The Campine mines, developed in the 1920s, are quite large, averaging close to 1.5 million tons of annual output each. The four main groups combined— Launoit, Société Générale, Coppée and Sofina—control a greater number of mines, but produce no more coal, in the south than in the Campine. Present conditions in southern Belgium resemble those in Great Britain between the wars insofar as most of the firms in southern Belgium are small and lack the capital resources necessary for large-scale modernization.

Belgium is the only country in the ECSC where all the coal mines are privately owned, but nationalization has been a political issue since the end of the war. Apart from the matter of ownership, many contiguous mines are ripe for physical concentration. Article 66 of the ECSC treaty is not responsible for the lack of concentration because the High Authority has recommended that the mines in southern Belgium be concentrated. This matter is discussed in Chapter 4.

The Belgian steel groups have no ownership interest in foreign coal production except for Société Générale's interest in Maatschappij tot Exploitatie van Steenkolenmijnen Laura in Limburg (Netherlands).[45]

THE SAAR STEEL INDUSTRY

There are four integrated plants in the Saar. (See Table 34.) Dillinger accounts for 21 per cent of the crude steel. The Arbed plant at Burbach, established before the first world war, accounts for 23 per cent; the Neunkircher firm, owned by the Stumm and the Otto Wolff groups, which also have interests in other parts of Germany, accounts for 26 per cent, and Völklingen, owned by the Röchling family, for 30 per cent.[46]

As German capital receded from the Saar after the first world war, the Pont-à-Mousson group increased its interest from 40 to 60 per cent in the Dillinger Hüttenwerke in the Saar. Dillinger, like Hadir, sells on world mar-

[45] H. Aszkenazy, "Le Fonctionnement du marché charbonnier en Belgique et en Hollande," *Annales des mines*, May 1957, p. 326, and *Handelsblatt*, October 5, 1956. This Limburg mine produces about 1.2 million tons annually.

[46] Herbert Steiner, *Grossenordnung und horizontale Verflechtung in der Eisen- und Stahlindustrie der Vereinigten Staaten, Grossbritanniens, Frankreichs, Belgiens, Luxemburgs und Deutschlands,* Kieler Studien, Kiel, 1952, pp. 58, 107; Wolf-Rodé, *Handbuch,* p. 294; Hemmer, *op. cit.,* pp. 111–117.

kets through Davum Exportation, which handles exports for all the firms in the Pont-à-Mousson group.[47] The plant at Burbach belonged to Arbed before the first world war. Neunkircher, controlled by the Wolff and Stumm groups, in 1956 acquired a direct 40 per cent interest in Dillinger.[48] There are therefore

Table 34

THE SAAR: MAJOR STOCKHOLDERS IN, AND PRODUCTION BY,
INTEGRATED STEELWORKS, 1956[a]

Firm	Location	Per Cent of Stock Owned by Major Stockholders		Crude Steel Output (1955)	
				Amount (*Thousands of Metric Tons*)	Per Cent
Arbed plant	Burbach	Arbed	100	739.7	23
Dillinger Hüttenwerke	Dillinger	Pont-à-Mousson group	60[b]	662.0[c]	21
		Neunkircher	40		
Neunkircher	Neunkirchen	Otto Wolff	50	814.9	26
		Stumm	50		
Völklingen	Völklingen	Röchling family[d]		(960.0)	30
Total				3,176.6	100

Sources: Arbed, *Rapport de gestion*, 1955; Dillinger and Neunkircher, financial reports, 1955; *Neue Zürcher Zeitung*, July 19, 1956; *Handelsblatt*, July 4, 6 and 13, 1956; Völklingen: see note *d* below.

[a] Ownership as of the end of 1956; production for 1955.

[b] The interests of the Pont-à-Mousson group are exercised through Hadir, Compagnie de Pont-à-Mousson, Mines et Usines de Redange-Dilling, and Sidelor, all of which are under common control. Neunkircher acquired its 40 per cent interest in 1956 by buying the Stumm interest in Dillinger; Stumm also owns 50 per cent of Neunkircher so that the purchase really represented a consolidation of control by the Otto Wolff interests, which not only control 50 per cent of Neunkircher but also own over 10 per cent of the capital stock of Gebrüder Stumm.

[c] Includes some raw metal from Sollac in Lorraine.

[d] Placed under sequestration by French military government after World War II because the family had been judged war criminals, the firm was resold to Röchling in 1956 as part of the series of events accompanying the Saar's return to Germany. The French and German governments theretofore had each agreed to purchase 50 per cent of the assets and to try to resell to respective private interests. For the postwar history of Völklingen, from the French point of view, see *Le Monde*, November 29, 1956; from the German point of view, *Handelsblatt*, April 27, 30, May 7, July 4, 1956.

no more than three independent groups in the Saar. Dillinger and Neunkircher, which produce a complementary line of products, control 47 per cent of Saar steel, Arbed 23 per cent and Völklingen 30 per cent. Non-German interests have majority control of 44 per cent of Saar crude steel and are

[47] Dillinger's steel is marketed in France by another Pont-à-Mousson firm, Société des Mines et Usines de Redange-Dilling, S. A., which holds 40 per cent of Dillinger's stock and which also operates an iron ore mine in Lorraine. Dillinger has an interest in Sollac, from which it receives coils. Wolf-Rodé, *Handbuch*, pp. 305, 380.

[48] The Stumm group had previously held the 40 per cent interest in Dillinger and sold it to Neunkircher. *Handelsblatt*, October 29, 1956.

linked to 70 per cent of it by virtue of the relationship between Neunkircher and Dillinger.

Some of the Saar steel firms are vertically integrated with the steel transforming industry. Dillinger controls the Waggonfabrik Fuchs, Heidelberg. In 1956 Völklingen bought the German government's 51.8 per cent interest in Rheinmetall (formerly Rheinmetall-Borsig), producer of machinery and tubes.[49]

The Saar steel firms do not themselves possess iron ore properties, but Dillinger and Arbed are nevertheless financially related to groups with extensive iron ore interests in Luxembourg and Lorraine. Völklingen and Neunkircher obtain iron ore from Lorraine on long-term contract.[50]

There are three nonintegrated steel plants in the Saar. Société des Usines à Tubes de la Sarre, specializing in tubes, is jointly owned by the Longwy-Raty group, the principal French tube manufacturers, by the Cockerill-Ougrée group and by Mannesmann.[51] Halbergerhütte produces pig iron and foundry products and Hadir operates a rolling mill at St.-Ingbert. The last two are controlled by Pont-à-Mousson.

The Saar coal industry is discussed later in this chapter.[52]

THE ITALIAN STEEL INDUSTRY

The Italian State controls 55 per cent of crude steel production in Italy. Two private firms, Falck and Fiat, control 10 per cent each. A large number of very small firms account for 25 per cent of Italian steel production.

The Italian State is the largest factor in the steel industry through the medium of Finsider, a holding company whose capital stock is 100 per cent State-owned by the Istituto per la Ricostruzione Industriale (IRI).[53] IRI has a direct interest in some steel firms also. Finsider and IRI combined own over 50 per cent of the stock in each of eight operating firms which had a combined output of 2.3 million tons of crude steel in 1954.

IRI is also important in other industries; in petroleum through Ente Nazionale Idrocarburi (ENI); in 1955 it controlled 80 per cent of shipbuilding

---

[49] Wolf-Rodé, *Handbuch*, pp. 305–311; *Handelsblatt*, July 4, 1956; Dillingerhütte, *Jahresbericht*, 1955.

[50] Neunkircher, *Jahresbericht*, 1955.

[51] Wolf-Rodé, *Handbuch*, pp. 75, 311.

[52] See the section "State Ownership in the European Coal Industry," pp. 165 ff.

[53] The Italian government created IRI in 1931 in order to supply financial assistance to firms in financial difficulty during the depression. IRI ultimately acquired large industrial assets. Hans-Joachim Otto, *Strukturwandlungen und Nachkriegsprobleme der Wirtschaft italiens*, Kieler Studien, Kiel, 1951, pp. 38–39. Finsider's interests are described in *Handelsblatt*, November 15–16, 1957, p. 11.

capacity, 18 per cent of shipping capacity, and 24 per cent of the national power production through Finelettrica, in which IRI has 80 per cent of the share capital and Finsider the remainder. The State also controls 90 per cent of the bituminous coal, 85 per cent of the anthracite, 80 per cent of the pig iron, 60 per cent of the iron ore, and about one third of the metallurgical coke.[54] The State-controlled share of metallurgical coke and pig iron is produced by the State-owned steel firms. But the State-owned iron ore is produced by Ferromin, a separate but 100 per cent State-owned enterprise;[55] the bituminous coal in Sardinia, which is not used in the steel industry, is controlled by Carbosarda, also a State-owned enterprise.

The State-owned complex in effect constitutes a large vertical concentration from raw materials to final products. The State, for example, produces four fifths of Italy's output of steel tubes through a firm called Dalmine. The natural gas and petroleum industries, also State-controlled in large part, are the main consumers of tubes and pipes.[56] ENI is an extremely important factor in energy; it monopolizes the production and distribution of natural gas, so important in northern Italy; has exclusive prospecting rights for petroleum in the Po Valley; and controls a large share of the refining and distribution of petroleum.[57]

The relation of IRI to public and private interests, and the degree to which it should be integrated with public economic policy, are still matters of public debate in Italy. Whether IRI is autonomous or not, a large number of firms fall under its control.[58]

The tidewater steel plants in Italy are sharply differentiated from the inland plants with respect to the input of raw materials and the resulting process of production. (See Table 9.) The degree of corporate concentration also varies with location, as Fig. 14, based on Table 5-3, Appendix E, shows.

The State controls 94 per cent of the production on tidewater sites and only 33 per cent of the production inland. In the tidewater category, the State controls all the Thomas steel, 96 per cent of the open-hearth (Siemens-Martin) steel and 78 per cent of the electric steel. Since the tidewater plants produce mainly open-hearth and Thomas steel (the only Thomas steel plant in Italy is at Naples), the State-controlled firms account for all the Thomas steel and 57 per cent of the open-hearth steel produced in Italy as a whole. But they account for only 45 per cent of the electric-furnace steel in Italy.

---

[54] *Neue Zürcher Zeitung*, April 24, November 9, December 25, 1956; Chamberlin, *Monopoly*, p. 59. Finelettrica also has a direct interest in several steel operating firms.

[55] *Neue Zürcher Zeitung*, April 17, 1956.

[56] *Financial Times*, January 24, 1956.

[57] See *Wirtschaft und Wettbewerb*, January 1958, pp. 29–30.

[58] For a description of some of the issues see *Neue Zürcher Zeitung*, April 24, 1956, and, with special reference to the oil industry, *The Economist*, April 20, 1957, pp. 234 ff.

Production inland is concentrated near Milan, Turin and also in Umbria, where the Terni electric steel plant is located. Two large private firms, Fiat and Falck, each control 16 per cent of inland production. Fiat is at Turin, Falck at Milan, where the State also controls some steel production. Both Fiat and Falck are vertically integrated, the former consuming its own steel for the automobile division,[59] the latter being an important factor in electrical equipment. It was reported in 1957 that both were considering the construction of a jointly owned steel plant at Vado-Ligure on the Italian Riviera.[60] If so, the State monopoly of tidewater steel would end.

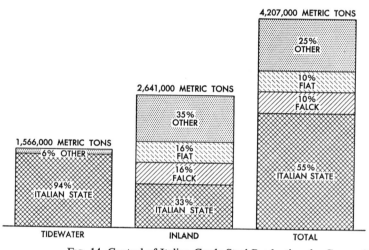

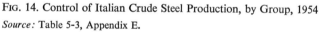

FIG. 14. Control of Italian Crude Steel Production, by Group, 1954

Source: Table 5-3, Appendix E.

The small firms, most of which are in the Milan area, account for 35 per cent of the inland production. In Italy as a whole there were over 65 small steel firms in the middle 1950s; 70 per cent of them employed under 1,000 men each.[61] These firms produced over one million tons of crude steel in 1954, equally divided between open-hearth and electric-furnace processes. Operating with a relatively small investment, using furnaces of exceedingly small capacity, these small firms operate on scrap supplemented with purchased pig iron. They chiefly fill small tonnage orders for a custom trade.

The Italian steel situation is full of questions. There are two sharply differentiated classes of steel firms. One class is highly concentrated, mostly under

[59] Wolf-Rodé, *Handbuch*, p. 262.
[60] *Le Monde*, December 5, 1957, p. 3.
[61] Based on a census of the firms listed in Wolf-Rodé, *Handbuch*, pp. 249–284.

State control, highly integrated, highly expansive, essentially modern, and at tidewater. The other consists of small, archaic, nonintegrated, but largely amortized plants located near consuming centers. The question whether the State-owned enterprises will drive the small plants out of existence and take the political consequences is discussed in Chapters 3 and 7.

STEEL IN THE NETHERLANDS[62]

Koninklijke Nederlandsche Hoogovens en Staalfabrieken, at Ijmuiden, produces three quarters of the crude steel in the Netherlands, and owns and manages an adjacent firm that produces flat products. The two firms purchase a considerable amount of raw metal and consequently account for nearly 100 per cent of the finished steel produced in the country.

The State owns one third and the city of Amsterdam 10 per cent of the share capital of the parent company.[63] Hoogovens controls Dortmund-Hörder, one of the largest steel producers in Germany, discussed later in this chapter.

THE ALLIED DECONCENTRATION PROGRAM IN GERMANY

The present state of concentrations in Germany cannot be understood without referring to allied policy after the second world war.

The allied powers tried to eliminate the concentration of economic power after the second world war, but did not always agree among themselves.[64] Objectives changed as over-all allied policies altered. Coal and steel in the Ruhr occupied the principal place in allied deconcentration policy.

The historic points of allied policy were Potsdam in July 1945 and the initialing of the ECSC treaty six years later. Early postwar notions as reflected in the Potsdam agreement were dominated by the idea of denazification, democratization and pacification. These objectives were to be attained in part by limiting industrial production to the peaceful needs of the German people, by decentralizing political authority to the benefit of the provincial governments, and by reducing the concentration of economic power.

[62] The Netherlands coal industry is discussed later in this chapter in the section "State Ownership in the European Coal Industry."

[63] Wolf-Rodé, *Handbuch*, pp. 299–302; Wehrer, *op, cit.*, pp. 8–9; Hoogovens financial report for 1955.

[64] The terms deconcentration and decartelization refer to two separate programs: deconcentration to the effort to reduce corporate size or control; decartelization to the effort to eliminate agreements or restrictive practices between corporations otherwise independent. See *L'Economie de la Ruhr*, Institut National de la Statistique et des Etudes Economiques (INSEE), Presses Universitaires de France, Paris, 1947, for a study of the Ruhr before the second world war.

But the policy of limiting Germany's industrial potential did not long survive. As West Germany became a positive element in the Atlantic alliance, it became necessary to increase Germany's economic potential for the sake of providing the German people with a higher standard of living and of helping Germany to contribute to economic recovery in the rest of Europe. To the United States, which was covering Europe's as well as Germany's external deficit, these goals seemed especially desirable. The change in policy was completed by the end of 1947, but several years were required to develop the actual measures to carry out the new policy.

Two successive statements to the British House of Commons by Ernest Bevin, Foreign Secretary, one in 1946 and another in 1948, bear witness to the change in policy. In October 1946 Bevin said:[65]

. . . we have also to consider the ownership of the basic German industries. These industries were previously in the hands of magnates who were closely allied to the German military machine, who financed Hitler, and who in two wars, were part and parcel of Germany's aggressive policy. We have no desire to see those gentlemen or their like return to a position which they have abused with such tragic results. As an interim measure, we have taken over the possession and control of the coal and steel industries . . . we shall shortly take similar action in the case of the heavy chemical industry and the mechanical engineering industry. Our intention is that these industries should be owned and controlled in the future by the public. The exact form of this public ownership and control is now being worked out. They should be owned and worked by the German people, but subject to such international control that they cannot again be a threat to their neighbors.

In June 1948, nearly two years later, Bevin stated:[66]

We have no desire to create a Germany which can ever be aggressive, but Germany cannot be allowed to remain a slum in the centre of Europe. On the contrary, our policy is that she must contribute to her own recovery and keep herself, and give her share to European recovery. . . . I have already dealt with our attitude to the Ruhr. The main principle is that there is to be no political separation. That was a very great difficulty in the early days of the discussion of this problem. There is also to be no international ownership or non-German management. The Germans have been given the greatest possible freedom consistent with security for Western Europe. Here let me say that we think it better to proceed with these great Ruhr industries in this way. Under the European Recovery Program and with the integration and planned development of Western Europe, we can fit it in better in this way than by any other means. We are convinced that international control is essential for security reasons and in order to see that the output is so allocated that it makes its common contribution to European rehabilitation as a whole.

[65] B. Ruhm von Oppen, *Documents on Germany Under Occupation*, Oxford, London, 1955, p. 184.

[66] *Ibid.*, p. 308.

The major issues of allied policy that the ECSC put to rest were: first, capacity and operating rates for the steel industry, as well as the question of dismantling for reparations; second, internationalization of the Ruhr; and third, deconcentration.

The ECSC treaty marked a turning point with respect to each of these matters, as explained below, because it conferred on Germany an equality toward which it had been moving for several years.

(1) German steel production was subject to severe tonnage limitations after the war but coal production was encouraged because coal was scarce and Germany was an important exporter to the rest of Europe. In 1946 coal production in the main European countries was 75 per cent, and in the Ruhr 40 per cent, of 1938.

The allies placed a limit on German steel capacity and marked the residual capacity for dismantling; the dismantled facilities were to be used for reparations or to be confiscated for security reasons, the division between the two objectives never being clearly marked. The limits on steel production and on capacity were raised three times in the course of four years as allied policy evolved. But the limits were always higher than and never interfered with actual output, which, prior to currency reform in June 1950, was hindered by economic disorder and a dearth of foreign exchange and raw materials.[67]

The policy of limiting German steel capacity and production was abandoned within the context of the negotiations for the ECSC which started in the middle of 1950.

(2) What to do with the Ruhr after the war was one of the most difficult questions affecting the economic potential and the territorial and administrative structure of Germany. The allies did not see eye to eye, not even in the early days of Potsdam. The French, who had not been invited to Potsdam, had joined the Allied Control Commission with the proviso that Germany be decentralized and that the Saar, Rhineland and Ruhr be detached.[68] The French hoped that the Ruhr would be placed under permanent international control. The British, as indicated by Bevin in the statement of October 1946 already quoted, also favored some form of international control but relied mainly on public ownership of Ruhr coal and steel as the method for eliminat-

---

[67] For the documentation on steel capacity, see *ibid.*, pp. 114, 242; "Report on Plants Scheduled for Removal as Reparations from the Three Western Zones of Germany," Economic Cooperation Administration, Industrial Advisory Committee, Washington, January 10, 1949 (Wolf Report), pp. 7, 25, 76–77; Martin Hillenbrand, "The Ruhr in the Post-War World," Foreign Institute Monograph, U.S. Department of State, Washington, May 1950, pp. 7–8, 17–18, 25. For a comprehensive survey of the allied program up to the end of 1948, see *Report of the Committee Appointed to Review the Decartelization Program in Germany to the Honorable Secretary of the Army*, Department of Defense, Washington, 1949; Garland S. Ferguson, Jr., member of the Federal Trade Commission, was chairman of the committee.

[68] Alfred Grosser (R. Rees, tr.), *Western Germany*, Allen and Unwin, London, 1955, p. 33.

ing excessive economic power. Russia opposed decentralization. The United States at first favored decentralization but stopped short of advocating a permanent international control of the Rhineland, the Ruhr and the Saar.[69]

The United Kingdom and the United States by 1948 opposed internationalizing the Ruhr, but accepted some form of international control over the distribution of coal and over the production of armaments. The allusion to "international control" in Bevin's statement of June 1948, already quoted, referred to the International Authority for the Ruhr (IAR). The idea of the IAR was announced in June 1948 but the terms of reference were not agreed until April 1949.[70] The IAR consisted of the Benelux countries, France, the United Kingdom, the United States and representatives of the German government. A qualified majority was sufficient for decisions. The IAR was responsible for determining the amount of Ruhr solid fuels which should be exported, for preventing discriminatory price and trade practices and for overseeing the measures against German rearmament.[71]

The export of Ruhr solid fuels had theretofore been determined by a formula of the Western occupying powers called the "Moscow Sliding Scale," which regulated the volume of solid fuels exported in relation to the production of Ruhr coal. The Economic Commission for Europe (ECE), a United Nations organization at Geneva, divided among claimant countries the solid fuels exported by the Ruhr, as well as by other countries. The ECE continued to distribute the quantities put aside for export by the IAR, after the latter replaced the Moscow Sliding Scale.

Though the IAR was not very effective, the Germans flayed it mercilessly and publicly on the ground that it was inconsistent with Germany's equality in the European recovery effort.[72] The establishment of the ECSC involved the abolition of the IAR,[73] and with it the forced export of coal, as well as the end of the limitation on steel production.[74]

(3) The ECSC also marked the dividing line with respect to deconcentration

[69] *Ibid.*, p. 27.

[70] Communiqué of the London Six Power Conference, June 7, 1948, in von Oppen, *op. cit.*, pp. 286 ff.

[71] The terms of reference for the IAR are to be found in *ibid.*, pp. 446–459.

[72] See, for example, a typical attack by K. H. Herchenröder, *Die Nachfolger der Ruhrkonzerne*, Econ-Verlag, Düsseldorf, 1953, pp. 40–41.

[73] The IAR's rearmament control functions were abolished because Germany foreswore the right to manufacture certain military items when it obtained full sovereignty from the Western allies. See the Paris Agreements of October 1954 and von Oppen, *op. cit.*, pp. 641 ff.

[74] The first Bundestag debate on the ratification of the ECSC treaty held in July 1951 having shown that the vote might be close unless Germany obtained specific assurances, France, the United Kingdom and the United States agreed in London, October 19, 1951, to terminate international control of the Ruhr, to dissolve the allied coal and steel agencies of the Ruhr, and to release Germany from the steel production limits. See Georges Goriely, *Naissance de la Communauté Européenne du Charbon et de l'Acier*, HA Luxembourg, No. 7889/56 f (mimeo.), pp. 54–55.

and reorganization of the old coal and steel firms. The final measures of de-concentration and reorganization were not worked out until 1951 because the problems were extremely complex.

The loss of the Saar, Moselle and Luxembourg after the first world war had encouraged the German steel producers to increase the degree of concentration in order to enable them as a group to stand up to rivalry from the steel firms in these lost territories. Many Ruhr steel firms merged, many small firms

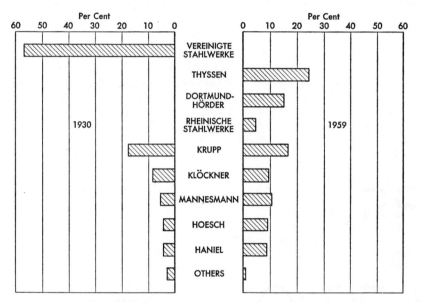

FIG. 15. Concentration of Control in the Ruhr Steel Industry Before and After Deconcentration[a]

Source: Table 35.

[a] Control as of 1959, but production as of 1954–1955.

were absorbed and their plants scrapped. Vereinigte Stahlwerke was organized in 1926—a merger of several firms including those that had lost their assets in the Saar, Luxembourg and the Moselle—the same year the first Entente International de l'Acier was formed.[75] Realizing that there would be a surplus of

[75] Four steel groups, with the help of the German government, merged to create the Vereinigte Stahlwerke; Rheinelbe-Union (comprising Gelsenkirchener, Deutsche Luxembourg and Bochumer Verein, the last two having lost large assets in the Saar, Luxembourg and Moselle); Thyssen; Phoenix; and Rheinstahl. For a description of the merged facilities and firms, see Herchenröder, *op. cit.*, pp. 57–118. The merger made Vereinigte the second largest steel firm in the world after the United States Steel Corporation. Vereinigte Stahlwerke subsequently eliminated competitors by purchasing a number of other steel companies at inflated values, a fact which contributed considerably to its overcapitalization and financial embarrassment early in the Great Depression. Gelsenkirchener provided Vereinigte Stahlwerke with an integrated supply of solid fuels.

steel capacity in Europe because the French also were expanding and the British had expanded during the first world war, the German steel industry had also created an internal cartel and in 1924–1926 had taken the lead in promoting the first over-all European steel cartel.

The coal mines in the Ruhr were also reorganized in the early 1920s by reducing the number of mines and firms, as discussed in Chapter 4.

In the 1930s Vereinigte Stahlwerke controlled nearly three fifths of Ruhr steel; two groups, Vereinigte Stahlwerke and Krupp, controlled nearly three

Table 35

CONCENTRATION OF CONTROL IN THE RUHR STEEL INDUSTRY,
BEFORE AND AFTER DECONCENTRATION[a]

(*Amount in Thousands of Metric Tons of Crude Steel Capacity*)

Group	1930		1954–1955	
	Amount	Per Cent	Amount	Per Cent
Vereinigte Stahlwerke	9,304[b]	56.7	—	—
Thyssen group			4,085	24.4
Dortmund-Hörder			2,529[c]	15.1
Rheinische Stahlwerke			801	4.8
Krupp	2,874	17.5	2,801	16.7
Klöckner	1,350	8.2	1,610	9.6
Mannesmann	894	5.4	1,768	10.5
Hoesch	751	4.6	1,512	9.0
Haniel	750	4.6	1,484	8.8
Others	(500)	3.0	(180)[d]	1.1
Total	16,423	100.0	16,770	100.0

Sources: 1930, Frederic Benham, *The Iron and Steel Industry of Germany, France, Belgium, Luxembourg and the Saar*, London and Cambridge Economic Service, London, October 1934, p. 25, where several obvious typographical errors have been corrected; 1954–1955, Tables 5-4 and 5-5, Appendix E.

[a] The post-deconcentration data refer to proprietary control as of early 1959 but to production for the business year ending September 1955, when the industry was operating at practical capacity. The 1930 data also refer to capacity. In 1930 and 1954–1955, the Ruhr accounted for 83 per cent and 86 per cent, respectively, of all the German crude steel capacity.

[b] Includes about 500,000 tons outside the Ruhr.

[c] With Siegerland, in the Rhineland, Dortmund-Hörder controls nearly 3.0 million tons.

[d] Stahlwerke Bochum (Michel group).

fourths of it, as Fig. 15, based on Table 35, shows. In 1937 these two groups controlled 35 per cent of Ruhr coal; six groups in the steel industry controlled 54 per cent of Ruhr coal (Table 36).

After World War II the allies sought to reduce the degree of prewar concentrations as shown in Tables 35 and 36.

The deconcentration program was inspired by American notions of competition as an end in itself. Economic expansion and political democracy

Table 36

AMOUNT AND PER CENT OF RUHR COAL CONTROLLED BY THE STEEL INDUSTRY
BEFORE AND AFTER DECONCENTRATION[a]

(*Amount in Thousands of Metric Tons*)

Group	1929[b]		1955	
	Amount	Per Cent	Amount	Per Cent
Private:				
Vereinigte Stahlwerke[c]	35,448	28.7	—	—
Rheinische Stahlwerke			5,198	4.3
Thyssen			12,140	10.0
Dortmund-Hörder			4,640	3.8
Michel group	—	—	1,398	1.2
Mannesmann	3,726	3.0	6,563	5.4
Hoesch	5,982	4.8	6,675	5.5
Klöckner	4,374	3.5	5,238	4.3
Krupp	8,246	6.7	7,386	6.1
Haniel[d]	(9,000)	7.3	10,022	8.3
Ilseder Hütte[e]	1,140	0.9	1,558	1.3
Stumm[f]	3,002	2.4	1,792	1.5
Röchling (Völklingen[f])	1,145	0.9		
Total private	72,063	58.3	62,610	51.7
State-owned steel groups[g]			8,302	6.9
Total integrated with German steel	72,063	58.3	70,912	58.6
Foreign steel groups[h]	2,723	2.2	13,531	11.2
Total integrated with all steel	74,786	60.5	84,443	69.7
Residual production[i]	48,794	39.5	36,663	30.3
TOTAL PRODUCTION	123,580	100.0	121,106	100.0

Sources: William N. Parker, *Fuel Supply and Industrial Strength*, Ph.D. thesis, Harvard University, Cambridge, 1951, Table C4a; and Tables 5-6 and 5-7, Appendix E, in this study.

[a] Post-deconcentration data refer to proprietary control as of early 1959 but to production as of 1955.

[b] Production in 1937 was nearly the same as in 1929 (*L'Economie de la Ruhr*, p. 44); these data therefore reveal the immediate prewar pattern.

[c] Comprises Gelsenkirchener, 28.6 million tons; Concordia, 1.4 million; Rheinische group, 5.4 million. Although the last two were corporately outside Vereinigte Stahlwerke, they were controlled by firms which had merged with it.

[d] The 1929 figure is an estimate comprising one property of Haniel and Gutehoffnungshütte each. The 1955 figure includes Neue Hoffnung, controlled by Oberhausen, and Rheinpreussen. Strictly speaking, only the mines of Gutehoffnungshütte in 1929 and of Oberhausen in 1955 are integrated with steel from a corporate point of view, but all the Haniel properties are nevertheless included because the group as a whole is heavily involved in steel.

[e] Listed separately although the German State now owns 25 per cent of the stock. Ilseder is not a Ruhr steel group.

[f] Saar steel group.

[g] The Prussian State had acquired a large interest in coal mining before the first world war but, except for a short period in the early 1930s, it was not until the late 1930s that these became permanently linked to State-controlled steel operations through a holding company. Only the mines controlled by A. G. für Bergwerks und Hüttenbetriebe are included; the State-owned mines controlled by firms without a direct interest in steel are here excluded.

[h] Excluding German-owned Saar firms, which are included with German groups.

[i] Only a fraction of this is independent, as Table 5-7, Appendix E, shows.

would be encouraged, it was believed, if a sufficient number of viable firms were created and antitrust laws were adopted and enforced.[76]

The final and decisive stages of the deconcentration program were worked out during the negotiations for the ECSC treaty; these two activities were mutually influenced.[77]

The deconcentration program faced some formidable problems: how to distribute the facilities among new firms; how to compensate the owners of the old firms valued at $4 billion; how to keep two or more new firms from falling under the control of the same owners if the owners of the old firms were to be compensated with capital stock in the new ones; how to determine the number of new coal and steel firms that were to be established; how to determine the permissible degree of vertical integration between the coal and steel industries. Although the deconcentration officials had to cut the vertical ties between plants producing coal, coke, pig iron, crude and finished steel, they also had to provide each new firm with the basis for a reasonable degree of economic efficiency.

After protracted negotiations with the Germans, the allied deconcentration authorities created twenty-four individual steel firms and over sixty individual coal-mining firms by the time the ECSC came into force. Only the mining firms previously captive were deconcentrated.[78]

The degree of vertical concentration to be arranged between coal and steel proved a particularly difficult subject of negotiation. The occupying powers had agreed in principle to some vertical concentration as early as 1948 in connection with Public Law No. 75 but the question of degree created difficulties. Long-term contracts between coal and steel firms had been suggested as an alternative to vertical corporate concentration but the Germans rejected the idea. Negotiations among the Germans, the French, the United Kingdom and the United States finally led to the adoption of the so-called "75 per cent compromise." This compromise allowed nine of the steel firms to control no more than 75 per cent of their total coal requirements. Though "necessarily arbitrary," it was the purpose of the "75 per cent compromise" to force the steel companies "to look to the coal market in competition with other steel companies in the single market in order to maintain capacity production and to pro-

---

[76] See Sidney Willner's statement in Friedmann, *op. cit.*, especially p. 176.

[77] *Ibid.*, pp. 180 ff; Goriely, *op. cit.*, pp. 43–45.

[78] This is not the place to describe the long and extremely complicated legal and administrative history of deconcentration under British and then combined United States–United Kingdom responsibility. The British seized the assets of the coal companies in December 1945 and those of the steel firms in August 1946 in General Orders No. 5 and No. 7, respectively, of Public Law 52. Von Oppen, *op. cit.*, p. 209; Herchenröder, *op. cit.*, pp. 12, 337–339; Friedmann, *op. cit.*, p. 156. The texts of the allied decrees, Public Law 75 and Public Law 27, which provided the framework for deconcentration, may be found in von Oppen, *op. cit.*, pp. 335 ff and 490 ff.

vide for expansion."[79] This compromise was embodied in detailed agreements with respect to the assignment of particular coal mining firms to particular steel companies. The captive coal mines were in any case to be organized as individual corporate firms the majority of whose stock would be held by the steel firms. The coal mining firms were to deal with the steel firms at arms length, selling their solid fuels to them at current prices and subject to whatever rules of distribution might be adopted if coal were scarce.

Since the coal mines were to be operated by individual coal mining firms and to be integrated with steel production at the same time, the Konzern reappeared as a device for holding the share capital of the coal and steel companies that were to be tied together. Some steel firms in other cases acquired 50 per cent of the shares in a number of coal mining firms operated by Gelsenkirchener Bergwerks A. G., a new coal operating and holding company.[80]

How were the owners of the old firms compensated and what proprietary participation did they acquire in the new ones?

Public Law 27 provided that the shareholders of the old companies be compensated by a pro rata exchange of shares in the new ones. Single shareholders were each permitted to acquire up to 100 per cent of the shares of any one of the new companies but no more than 5 per cent in any other company. This provision was included to prevent any shareholder from controlling more than one new firm.

Residual shares were subject to sale. These so-called "forced sale" provisions applied particularly to the Krupp assets. A five-year time limit was granted to allow for gradual liquidation. The measures also envisaged a two-year extension if liquidation would threaten to depress stock values.[81]

The antitrust philosophy embodied in the German deconcentration program through the agency of American influence also was incorporated in the ECSC treaty itself,[82] particularly in Articles 65 and 66 with respect to cartels and concentrations.

The French Parliament was led to believe that the German steel and coal industry would continue to be bound by the allied deconcentration measures. For the Germans, on the other hand, Article 66 (paragraph 2) marked the beginning of a new phase. The leaders of the German government made no secret of their belief that Article 66 opened the door to reconcen-

[79] Quoted from Sidney Willner, one of the principal American officials in the allied deconcentration program, in Friedmann, *op. cit.*, p. 183.

[80] *Ibid.*, pp. 158 ff and Willner's rejoinder 182 ff; Reuter, *op. cit.*, pp. 21–22.

[81] Friedmann, *op. cit.*, pp. 160–161.

[82] See the statement by Walter Hallstein, then chief of the German delegation to the ECSC treaty negotiations and now President of the European Economic Community, in *Probleme des Schuman-Plans*, Kieler Vorträge, Kiel, 1951, p. 33.

tration[83] because it required the High Authority when examining a request for permission to combine to "take account of the size of enterprises of the same kind existing in the Community, as far as it finds this jusified to correct the disadvantages resulting from an inequality in the condition of competition."

With the adoption of the ECSC the occupying powers ceased to have responsibility over German concentrations. But the German government assured them that it would enact an anticartel law—the act of 1957 discussed earlier in this chapter—and formally undertook to carry out the forced sale provisions.[84]

THE RECONCENTRATION MOVEMENT
IN GERMANY

The ECSC inherited an extremely unstable situation from the allied deconcentration. From the opening of the common market to April 1958, forty-six new concentrations occurred in German coal and steel; the High Authority approved sixteen of these, closed another group of fourteen cases without adverse action and as of April 1958 was still examining the remaining sixteen cases.[85]

Taking advantage of Article 66 and of the spirit of equality embodied in the Schuman Plan, the German steel and coal industries made no secret of their will to reconcentrate in order to integrate more coal production into the steel industry and to reduce the number of firms in the steel industry.[86] Many a reconcentration was defended by citing the need to balance rolling mills with crude metal producing facilities and to reduce capital costs.

The Steel Industry

The Thyssen group, formerly in Vereinigte Stahlwerke, emerged as the dominant group in the German steel industry. The wife and daughter, heirs of

[83] Chancellor Konrad Adenauer stated as much to the Bundestag; see Ernest Cönen, "Das Verhältnis des Entflechtungsrechts in Deutschland zum Montanunionvertrag," in *Wirtschaft und Wettbewerb*, February 1956, pp. 95–96, especially notes 19 and 20. Hallstein also believed paragraph 2 of Article 66 would allow German firms to reconcentrate; see his statement in *op. cit.*, p. 32. See also Reuter, *op. cit.*, p. 219; Herchenröder, *op. cit.*, p. 49; Goriely, *op. cit.*, pp. 81 ff.

[84] See the protocol (the Paris Protocol) to the instruments which granted West Germany full sovereignty and admission to the Treaty of Western European Union in October 1954. The protocol reaffirmed earlier assurances made in March 1951; see Reuter, *op. cit.*, pp. 21–22; Friedmann, *op. cit.*, pp. 138, 161; von Oppen, *op. cit.*, pp. 549, 628. The protocol became effective in May 1955 when the agreements were fully ratified.

[85] HA, *Sixième rapport général*, Vol. II, p. 106.

[86] See, e.g., the statement by the general director of Phoenix-Rheinrohr with respect to the steel industry's need for more coal, in *Handelsblatt*, July 20, 1956. See also that by the president of the Verein Deutscher Eisenhüttenleute, *Handelsblatt*, October 28, 1957, pp. 1, 4, with respect to the need to concentrate facilities because too many hot strip mills had been developed in Germany. See the *New York Times*, January 26, 1959, p. 5, for an article on the restoration of the prewar structure.

Fritz Thyssen, each control a part of his former assets but have gradually reknit the two branches of the Thyssen complex separated by the allied deconcentration program.

The Krupp group now controls nearly as great a proportion of the Ruhr steel industry as it did in the interwar period. One of the steel plants formerly in the Vereinigte Stahlwerke has fallen under its control. The heir to the Krupp complex has meanwhile refused with the backing of his government to sell his principal steel producing plant on the ground that no buyer can be found to take it at its true value.

The other main groups in the steel industry—Hoesch, Mannesmann, Haniel and Klöckner—have each reknit the parts of their respective complexes pulled apart by the allied deconcentration authorities. Full details of the reconcentration movement are in Appendix D, together with Tables 5-4 and 5-5, Appendix E.

The Coal Industry

Vertical concentration was the key to control in the Ruhr coal industry. The mining firms pulled out of the Vereinigte Stahlwerke proved quite unstable; they either fell under the control of steel firms formerly in Vereinigte Stahlwerke or were placed under the control of the Gelsenkirchener Bergwerks A. G., a holding company created under the allied deconcentration program that also has a number of ties to steel producing firms, for the most part offspring firms of Vereinigte Stahlwerke. The details are in Appendix D, together with Tables 5-6 and 5-7, Appendix E.

RECONCENTRATION OF CONTROL IN THE GERMAN STEEL INDUSTRY

The Ruhr

Six groups controlled 97 per cent of Ruhr, and 80 per cent of German, crude steel capacity in 1930; two of them combined, Krupp and Vereinigte Stahlwerke, controlled 74 per cent of the capacity in the Ruhr. Eight groups controlled 99 per cent of Ruhr, and 85 per cent of German, crude steel production in 1959 (on the basis of production in 1954–1955). Seven groups, producing over one million tons of crude steel each, accounted for 94 per cent of Ruhr, and 81 per cent of German, crude steel output in 1959. (See Table 35 and Table 5-5, Appendix E.)

The groups outside the old Vereinigte Stahlwerke—Mannesmann, Hoesch, Haniel, Klöckner, Krupp—have, except for Krupp, increased their shares of Ruhr crude steel output at the expense of the units formerly in Vereinigte

Stahlwerke. The Krupp group held its own, after having acquired in 1958 the Gusstahlwerk Bochumer Verein, formerly in Vereinigte Stahlwerke.

Dortmund-Hörder, formerly in Vereinigte Stahlwerke, is controlled by Hoogovens, which operates the steel plant at Ijmuiden, Holland, owned by Dutch capital. Hoogovens' interests in Vereinigte Stahlwerke were concentrated in the Dortmund-Hörder firm.[87]

Owing to deconcentration, the number of groups in the Ruhr steel industry has increased and the groups are now more nearly equal in size. Is the industry consequently less concentrated?[88]

An evaluation of the allied deconcentration program depends on the point in time from which one assesses a trend that is still in process. No steel group as yet enjoys the eminence of the old Vereinigte Stahlwerke but prominence has not been eliminated. The Thyssen group, with one quarter of the steel production in the Ruhr, including the Hamborn plant (August Thyssen Hütte), one of the most modern and efficient steel plants in Europe and the only fully continuous wide strip mill in Germany, is able to exercise leadership, and leadership is an important condition for price uniformity. Whether or not the Hamborn plant should be dismantled had in fact been the basic issue of the deconcentration program with respect to steel.[89] It was evident that if the plant were not dismantled it would have to be one of the largest in the industry or else be uneconomic. The plant was not dismantled and the August Thyssen Hütte consequently acquired a dominant position in Ruhr steel. With its daughter firms it controlled about 3.2 million tons of crude steel capacity early in 1958. Early in 1959 the Phoenix-Rheinrohr complex, already interlocked with the August Thyssen Hütte, became, with the High Authority's approval, a daughter firm of the August Thyssen Hütte; the owner of the former, the Fritz Thyssen Vermögensverwaltung, sold its interest in exchange for capital stock in the latter.[90] With Phoenix-Rheinrohr, the Thyssen group had a combined potential of about 5.9 million tons of steel, a group worthy of the geographically dispersed Société Générale-Launoit groups.

The steel groups, furthermore, are not quite independent. Mannesmann and Hoesch respect their individual fields of specialization, tubes and wide strip. As an expression of this community of interest the Mannesmann and Hoesch

[87] The Netherlands Hoogovens group, which controls Dortmund-Hörder, is not related to Handelsmaatschappij, "Montan," a Dutch holding company with an interest in Klöckner Werke but which is beneficially owned by the Klöckner family.

[88] See the suggestion by Bock and Korsch in Friedmann, *op. cit.*, pp. 163–164, that the "outward result" of deconcentration as expressed in "property relations" should be regarded with skepticism. They also point out that the corporate structure of the coal and steel industries appears more complex as a result of deconcentration.

[89] See Sidney Willner's statement about August Thyssen Hütte in *ibid.*, pp. 178–180. For capacity, see *Handelsblatt*, January 6, 1958, p. 1.

[90] *Handelsblatt*, December 10, 1958, p. 9.

groups jointly built and own—65 per cent and 35 per cent, respectively—Grossrohrwerk Mannesmann-Hoesch, which produces tubes and other products. They also coordinate their engineering and motor building operations.[91]

The Thyssen group and Dortmund-Hörder have common interests in Hüttenwerke Siegerland and Gelsenkirchener Bergwerks, the coal operating firm. But for want of further evidence as to whether or not they are rivals, the Thyssen group and Dortmund-Hörder will not be considered a community of interest.

Thyssen and Rheinische Stahlwerke, through Arenberg Bergbau controlled by Rheinische, are jointly developing some coal mining concessions in the northern part of the Ruhr.[92] But neither will this joint venture be considered a community of interest with respect to steel.

If Hoesch and Mannesmann are taken as one group, then seven, rather than eight, groups control 99 per cent of the crude steel in the Ruhr, as follows:[93]

Group	Per Cent of Ruhr Steel
Thyssen	24
Mannesmann-Hoesch	19
Krupp	17
Dortmund-Hörder	15
Klöckner	10
Haniel	9
Rheinische	5
Total	99

It therefore appears that Ruhr steel production was less concentrated in 1959 than in the interwar period but that fewness has not been eliminated.

Other German Areas

The German steel producing areas outside the Ruhr account for only 14 per cent of total German crude steel production. Tables 5-4 and 5-5, Appendix E, show the pattern of ownership in each area.

In Lower Saxony, the most important steel producing area after the Ruhr, there are two firms. The German State owns 100 per cent of Hüttenwerk Salzgitter (formerly part of the Hermann Göring complex) and 25 per cent of Hüttenwerke Ilsede-Peine.

[91] See the statement by the president of Mannesmann in *Financial Times*, February 20, 1957, p. 6; also *Handelsblatt*, February 22-23, 1957, p. 7, and April 5-6, 1957, p. 8; Wolf-Rodé, *Handbuch*, p. 76.

[92] *Handelsblatt*, May 13, 1957, p. 4.

[93] From Table 35.

Three important firms produce crude steel in the Rhineland, south of the Ruhr. The largest of them, Hüttenwerke Siegerland, near Siegen, is controlled by Dortmund-Hörder. Klöckner Werke, the large steel group in the Ruhr, controls 30.5 per cent of Stahlwerke Südwestfalen, also near Siegen. Another firm, Rasselstein-Andernach, is controlled by the Wolff group, which has a large interest in Saar steel through the Neunkircher firm but has no interest in the Ruhr.

Only one firm, Maximilianshütte, at Sulzbach-Rosenberg, controlled by the Flick group, produces crude steel in Bavaria; the Flick group has no other interest in German steel but a substantial interest in Chatillon–Neuves Maisons (Lorraine) and in Hainaut-Sambre (Belgium).

The firms in the areas of Germany outside the Ruhr are thus few in number. Consequently there is very little possibility of substantial competition between firms in each of the German areas outside the Ruhr. The two steel firms in Lower Saxony, both owned by the German State, could compete with Ruhr steel in northern Germany. The few steel firms south of the Ruhr that are not controlled by the Ruhr steel groups could compete with Ruhr steel in southern Germany.

RECONCENTRATION OF CONTROL IN THE GERMAN COAL INDUSTRY

Ruhr Coal

Coal is still a captive industry in spite of the allied deconcentration program. German steel groups as of early 1959 still controlled 59 per cent of the Ruhr coal (measured in terms of production in 1955), about the same percentage as in 1929 (Table 36).

If the individual steel firm, rather than the proprietary group or holding company, were the focus of analysis, then the individual steel producing firms as such would control only 15 per cent of Ruhr coal directly.[94] But this focus would be misleading.

If the so-called "75 per cent compromise" referred to earlier in this chapter had been effective, what proportion of Ruhr coal would the German steel industry then have controlled? Sidney Willner pointed out that the 75 per cent figure was tied to "requirements at capacity production."[95] The permissible amount of coal to be controlled would therefore vary with the volume of steel

[94] See, e.g., the observation in *Glückauf*, July 22, 1957, p. 796, that German steel firms as such control only 11 per cent of the Ruhr coal after deconcentration; this statement was made before reconcentrations on this basis of analysis had raised the figure to 15 per cent by early 1959.

[95] Friedmann, *op. cit.*, p. 183.

production and with estimates of that elusive term "capacity." Since the volume of German steel production increased by nearly 50 per cent from 1952 to 1956, the "75 per cent compromise" would have permitted the German steel industry to control about 17 per cent of Ruhr coal output in 1952 and about 25 per cent in 1956.[96] The German steel groups, private and public, thus controlled more than twice the coal the "75 per cent compromise" would have allowed in relation to steel production in 1956.

Some of the spirit of the "75 per cent compromise" was nevertheless retained inasmuch as the German government and the High Authority persuaded the German steel industry to "give up" some of its coal during the shortage of 1956–1957 and to import some coal from the United States.[97]

Some of the steel groups (other than the Krupp group) that were outside Vereinigte Stahlwerke increased their share of Ruhr coal as a result of deconcentration. The Vereinigte Stahlwerke complex controlled 29 per cent of the Ruhr coal before the second world war. In 1959 the steel groups formerly in Vereinigte Stahlwerke controlled 21 per cent of the Ruhr coal in terms of production in 1955. The other 8 per cent was placed under the control of the Gelsenkirchener Bergwerks A. G. (GBAG), but GBAG itself has fallen more and more under the influence, through proprietary ties and interlocking directorates, of the steel groups, especially of the Thyssen group, formerly in Vereinigte Stahlwerke. The Krupp group's share in Ruhr coal output declined slightly. All the other Ruhr steel groups increased their share, largely at the expense of the Flick group rather than that of Vereinigte Stahlwerke.

There were more groups in Ruhr coal in 1959 than before the war and, more important, there was a greater equality between the groups; but these facts may not be of much practical significance because the sale of Ruhr solid fuels has been concentrated in three common sales agencies, discussed in Chapter 8.

Foreign steel groups increased their share of Ruhr coal from 2 per cent before the war to 11 per cent in 1959 (based on production in 1955).[98] The

[96] Willner in *ibid.*, p. 183, said 17 per cent; Reuter, *op. cit.*, p. 22, said 18 per cent; but Grosser, *op. cit.*, p. 90, said 26.5 per cent.

It is of some interest to note for comparative purposes that 25 per cent of United States coal production was captive, according to Erich W. Zimmerman, *World Resources and Industries*, Harper, New York, 1951, p. 480; *Bituminous Coal Trends*, National Coal Association, Washington, 1956, p. 71, stated that 18 per cent of United States coal production in 1955 was captive. Mines controlled by the United States steel industry alone accounted for 14 per cent of total coal output in the United States and furnished 58 per cent of the coal consumed by the steel industry in 1955; Simon N. Whitney, *Antitrust Policies: American Experience in Twenty Industries*, Twentieth Century Fund, New York, 1958, Vol. I, p. 386.

[97] According to *L'Europe*, May 16, 1957, p. 3, the High Authority persuaded the German steel industry to "give up" 2.3 million tons of Ruhr coal in 1956.

[98] The coal mines controlled by Dortmund-Hörder, owned by foreign capital, are not included in these figures.

acquisition by Sidechar of Harpener Bergbau, a former Flick group firm, and Arbed's purchase of the Lothringen Bergbau in 1957, account for this increase.

All steel groups combined, German and foreign, increased their control of Ruhr coal from 60 per cent in 1929 to 70 per cent in 1959 (based on production in 1955).

Independent coal companies accounted for only 4 per cent of Ruhr coal in 1958. (See Table 5-7, Appendix E.) The remainder was controlled by firms or groups with ties to other industries, including the German State, which controlled 16 per cent of the Ruhr coal in 1959. The German State controlled 26 per cent of the coal mined in all of Germany, including the Saar, after it had reacquired ownership of the Saar mines in 1957.

Aachen and Other Areas

Three foreign groups (mainly foreign steel groups) in 1959 controlled 88 per cent of the coal mined in Aachen in 1955. The Völklingen steel firm in the Saar controlled the rest of it. (See Table 5-7, Appendix E.)

Preussag, a firm owned by the German State, controlled nearly 100 per cent of the coal output in Lower Saxony. This firm, producing electricity and non-ferrous metals as well as coal, was put up for sale to the public in March 1959; eligible purchasers were limited to small investors, savings and loan associations; no single individual could purchase more than five shares (at $25 per share) or purchase shares for the account of third persons.[99] The sale of Preussag will not materially reduce the importance of the State's share, centered in the Ruhr and the Saar, in German coal production.

THE BRITISH STEEL INDUSTRY

Twelve firms controlled merely 60 per cent of British steel capacity in the 1920s though quite a few mergers had occurred after the first world war. The degree of horizontal concentration was then much lower in the United Kingdom than in Germany, where three firms controlled 70 per cent of German, and 82 per cent of Ruhr, steel capacity, and lower than that in the United States, where two companies controlled 55 per cent of the output in the 1920s. Since British steel capacity in the 1920s was about 70 per cent of German capacity (see Fig. 16 and Table 5-8, Appendix E), the size of the average British steel firm was consequently much smaller, too.[100]

---

[99] *Handelsblatt*, January 16, 17, 1959, p. 1, February 4, 1959, p. 1.

[100] See Ingvar Svennilson, *Growth and Stagnation in the European Economy*, ECE, Geneva, 1954, pp. 125–127.

When the British steel industry was reorganized following the introduction of a protective tariff in 1932, the government recommended greater concentration by merger or community-of-interest agreements and measures to that effect were taken.[101] Horizontal concentration increased considerably in the two decades that followed. Nine firms controlled 71 per cent of the crude steel output in 1954. (See Table 37.) The State itself as of 1958 still owned the large

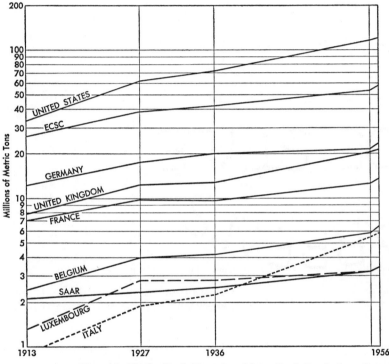

FIG. 16. Crude Steel Capacity, Main Steel Producing Countries, Selected Years, 1913–1956

Source: Table 5-8, Appendix E.

Richard Thomas and Baldwins firm; the latter controlled 9 per cent of the production.

But the degree of horizontal concentration in 1954 was still lower in Britain than on the Continent in spite of the concentration movement that had occurred. Seven steel groups, counting Hoesch and Mannesmann as one, controlled nearly 99 per cent of the output in the Ruhr, whereas the seven largest

[101] *Report of Import Duties Advisory Committee on the Present Position and Future Development of the Iron and Steel Industry*, HMSO, London, July 1937, pp. 43–44.

controlled only 63 per cent in the United Kingdom. The steel industry in Lorraine is virtually under single interpenetrated control. The Société Générale–Launoit groups have a hand in nearly three quarters of the Belgian steel.

British steel production, on the other hand, is more specialized by firm and area than that on the Continent. Scotland, which in 1955 accounted for only 10 per cent of the crude steel produced in the United Kingdom, accounted for

Table 37

UNITED KINGDOM: CONCENTRATION OF CRUDE STEEL PRODUCTION, 1954

	Amount (*Thousands of Metric Tons*)	Per Cent
United Steel Companies	2.5	13.5
Dorman Long & Co.	1.9	10.1
Colvilles	1.8	9.7
Richard Thomas & Baldwins[a]	1.7	9.2
Steel Co. of Wales	1.6	8.7
Stewarts & Lloyds	1.3	6.8
John Summers & Sons	1.0	5.3
South Durham Steel & Iron	0.8	4.3
Consett Iron	0.7	3.9
Total	13.4	71.5
Other companies	5.4	28.5
TOTAL	18.8	100.0

Sources: "The Steel Industry of the United Kingdom," *International Iron and Steel Report*, Washington, U. S. Department of Commerce, January 1956, p. 5; *Financial Times*, January 13, 1956, December 14, 1956, p. 10.

[a] As of 1957, the Iron and Steel Holding and Realization Agency, a government body, still held the assets of this and over 20 other steel firms which had not been resold to the public since denationalization.

25 per cent of the heavy plate and nearly 20 per cent of the tubes and "other heavy rolled products" produced in that country. Colvilles is the main producer in that area.[102] Stewarts & Lloyds dominates in the production of tubes in the United Kingdom.[103] Only three companies in the United Kingdom produce sheet and tinplate on continuous wide strip mills.[104] With 25 per cent of the crude steel output, South Wales accounts for more than half the country's sheet and nearly all its tinplate. Two of the country's continuous wide strip mills are located in that area, where two firms account for the main part of the output.[105]

[102] British Iron and Steel Federation, *Yearbook, 1955*, Vol. I, p. 62; "The British Steel Industry, 1958," special issue of *Steel Review*, 1959, p. 38.

[103] *Financial Times*, August 13, 1957, p. 7.

[104] United Kingdom Iron and Steel Board, *Annual Report, 1955*, HMSO, London, 1956, p. 16.

[105] "The British Steel Industry, 1958," special issue of *Steel Review*, 1959, p. 38.

STATE OWNERSHIP IN THE EUROPEAN COAL INDUSTRY

Nationalization increased considerably in the European coal industry after the second world war, when the French and British mines were nationalized. Only the Saar mines, the major part of the output in the Netherlands, and a small part of German output, were State-owned before the second world war. Nearly all the French output, 26 per cent of the combined German-Saar output and 42 per cent of total output in the ECSC were State-owned in 1955. (See Table 38.) Seventy per cent of the combined output from the ECSC and

Table 38

GOVERNMENT OWNERSHIP OF COAL PRODUCTION
IN SELECTED EUROPEAN COUNTRIES, 1959[a]

Country	Production (Millions of Metric Tons)		Per Cent Government-Owned
	Total	Government-Owned[b]	
ECSC			
Germany	131.8	21.6	16[c]
Saar	17.3	17.3	100
France	55.3	54.3	98
Belgium	30.0	—	—
Netherlands	11.9	7.5	63
Italy	1.1	0.9	94
Total	247.4	104.1	42
United Kingdom	225.1	225.1[d]	100
TOTAL	472.5	329.2	70

Sources: For Germany and the Saar, *Handelsblatt,* March 29-30, 1957, p. 2. This article is accurate except that the percentage for the two areas combined should be 26 rather than 30. For the Netherlands, *Jahrbuch.* The rest is common knowledge.

[a] Ownership as of early 1959, production as of 1955.

[b] In Germany and Italy this refers to production in undertakings in which the government is the determinant shareholder. In the other cases the undertakings are fully nationalized.

[c] Twenty-six per cent for Germany and the Saar combined.

[d] Includes open-pit production, about 5 per cent of the total, operated under contract from the National Coal Board.

the United Kingdom was State-owned. Belgium is the only country in which the State owns no coal mines. Public ownership is, by comparison, very limited in the steel industry in the ECSC. No more than 10 per cent of the steel industry in the ECSC is owned by the States (encompassing the Italian State, which owns more than half the Italian production, and the German State, which controls about 10 per cent of the German output of crude steel).

French and British Coal Mines

The French and British mines were nationalized for fairly similar reasons. Most of the mines in both countries were old, small and inefficient. They had to be concentrated physically in order to be modernized. But several factors—the nature of the private leasehold, lack of private capital, rivalry from petroleum, and the interwar stagnation in demand—discouraged private capital from taking the necessary steps. There was a great deal of political support, dating from the first world war, for nationalization in these two countries. No political group in either the United Kingdom or France has since advocated that the mines be denationalized.

Coal Mines in the Netherlands

State ownership of the major portion of the Dutch mines was caused by circumstances quite different from those described above. When the coal reserves in Limburg and the Campine were discovered early in this century, French and Belgian capital (De Wendel and Société Générale) moved into Limburg. To forestall further penetration, the Netherlands government enacted a law in 1901 that gave the State a monopoly to exploit all deposits that were still unconceded. Production by the State-owned mines began in 1908.[106] The State-owned mines now account for nearly two thirds of the output in Holland.

Coal Mines in Germany

The State of Prussia began to acquire a proprietary interest in the Ruhr coal industry in 1902 in order to protect the publicly owned railroads and the coal-deficient area of southern Germany from the Ruhr coal cartel that had been organized in 1893. It was at first thwarted in its effort to obtain majority control of the Hibernia coal mining firm but it did acquire a minority interest. The State of Prussia finally obtained majority control of Hibernia during the first world war and then caused Hibernia to join the cartel in order to be represented in it.[107] Hibernia is still the backbone of the State's interests in the Ruhr coal industry, where other mining firms are also under State control.

Coal Mines in the Saar

The State of Prussia owned 100 per cent of the Saar mines before the first world war and consequently penetrated the coal sales agency for southern

---

[106] Aszkenazy, *op. cit.*, in *Annales des mines*, May 1957, p. 326; also Lafitte-Laplace, *op. cit.*, pp. 635–636; *Handelsblatt*, October 5, 1956, and April 1, 1957, p. 6.

[107] William N. Parker, *Fuel Supply and Industrial Strength*, unpublished Ph.D. thesis, Harvard University, Cambridge, 1951, pp. 115–120, 126–128; Institut National de la Statistique et des Etudes Economiques, *L'Economie de la Ruhr*, Presses Universitaires de France, Paris, 1947, p. 9.

Germany.[108] All but one mine passed to the French State by the Treaty of Versailles (Article 45) to compensate France for the destruction of the mines in Nord and Pas-de-Calais. This transfer was conditional on the results of the referendum scheduled for 1935. That year, the German State repurchased the mines for 900 million French francs, and agreed to provide France with a fixed volume of Saar coal for a fixed period; this agreement is discussed in Chapter 8.[109] Having repurchased the Saar mines, the German government organized Saargruben A. G., in which it held 100 per cent of the capital.

From 1948 to 1953 the French government controlled the Saar mines completely by means of the operating organization called La Régie des Mines de la Sarre. Under an agreement with the Saar in 1953, France founded the Saarbergwerke to replace La Régie des Mines de la Sarre. The administration of Saarbergwerke was equally divided between Saarlanders and Frenchmen. France recognized the right of the future Saar government to own the mines and promised to support this thesis in the eventual negotiations for a peace treaty with Germany. The Saarbergwerke, as the operating firm, paid a royalty in the meantime to the Saar government, the prospective owner.[110]

The German government rejected the agreements between France and the Saar and claimed to be the legitimate owner of the Saar mines through Saargruben A. G., in which it still had 100 per cent control. After the referendum of 1956, the German State reacquired the Saar mines in 1957 but gave the Saar provincial goverment a 26 per cent share in Saargruben A. G., retaining 74 per cent for itself.[111] This concession to the Saarlanders did not change the substance of administration, which remained centralized in a single corporation, Saargruben A. G.

A Note on Nationalization

Nationalization is still a political issue in those European countries—Belgium and Germany—where the coal mines are privately owned. The economic condition of the mines will have a great deal to do with whether or not public ownership or some other form of public control is introduced. The issue in Belgium feeds on the fact that the mines in the southern part of that country (accounting for two thirds of the Belgian output) are old, small and inefficient, as were the mines in Britain and northern France before they were nationalized.

[108] Lafitte-Laplace, *op. cit.*, p. 141.

[109] André Dubosq, *Le Conflit contemporain des houillères européennes*, Librairie Technique et Economique, Paris, 1936, pp. 27–33; Lafitte-Laplace, *op. cit.*, pp. 12, 141.

[110] See von Oppen, *op. cit.*, pp. 476–482; *Handelsblatt*, March 29-30, 1957, p. 2, April 26-27, 1957, p. 10; *Revue française de l'énergie*, September 1956, pp. 423–424.

[111] *Handelsblatt*, September 4, 1957, p. 5, gives the financial details.

The socialist party in Germany still believes in government control of the Ruhr mines but has weakened on nationalization. The mines came close to nationalization in 1919, when the German parliament, with the socialists in power, passed a socialization act (Kohlenwirtschaftsgesetz of 1919) that also made the regional coal cartels compulsory. Only the latter provision was carried out.[112]

WHAT STIMULATED THE CONCENTRATION MOVEMENT IN THE COMMON MARKET?

Two developments characterized the concentration movement in the common market. First, the German coal and steel industries, after having been deconcentrated by the allied occupation authorities, rejoined the main stream of concentrations after the common market was established. Second, the economic union caused the steel firms or groups in Belgium and France to concentrate further.[113] The coal industry outside the Ruhr did not concentrate any further because it had already been concentrated under public ownership, except in Belgium. There the mines, though privately owned, failed to concentrate though the mines in the southern part of that country were encouraged to concentrate by the High Authority and could have benefited from larger producing units. The concentration movement therefore affected the steel industry mainly.

What stimulated the steel industry to concentrate in the early life of the ECSC? The ECSC treaty sought to make competition an end in itself by eliminating the legal barriers to interstate commerce, by subjecting cartels and new concentrations to administrative scrutiny and by establishing common commercial rules for pricing and sales. In doing so, it made the steel firms uncertain of the conduct of their rivals. The steel firms consequently decided to strengthen their position for defensive or aggressive action. Plants were corporately regrouped; some were even closed; firms under interlocking ownership were combined; steel groups took stronger hold of their daughter companies or acquired an interest in other firms; rival steel firms or groups joined forces by fusing, by exchanging capital shares of the principal or daughter firms or by buying into third companies. The threat of competition, as usual, stimulated combination.

Has Regional Interpenetration of Capital Increased?

The ECSC did not stimulate any further interpenetration of capital across

112 *The World Coal Mining Industry*, ILO, Geneva, 1938, Vol. I, p. 6; Neumann, *op. cit.*, p. 266.
113 HA, *Sixième rapport général*, Vol. I, p. 35.

national frontiers nor did it stimulate any steel firms to branch out into other areas[114] except for the purchase by the Flick group (Germany) of stock in Chatillon-Neuves Maisons (France) and in Hainaut-Sambre (Belgium). But these transactions were based on the fact that the Flick group had acquired French francs from the sale of Harpener Bergbau to the French group Sidechar.

What was the situation with respect to interpenetration before the ECSC was established? No steel firms or groups in ECSC controlled plants in nearly every part of the economic union. This pattern differs from that in the United States, where the U. S. Steel Corporation has plants in nearly every important producing area. The Italian steel industry was not penetrated by steel groups from other parts of the union; neither was the Belgian. Among French producing districts, only Lorraine was penetrated to a small extent—by the Belgian groups Société Générale and Launoit, which control 10 per cent of French and 15 per cent of Lorraine production. Hoogovens' (Holland) control of the Dortmund-Hörder steel firm, issue of Vereinigte Stahlwerke, represented a consolidation of its proprietary interest in the latter before its dissolution. No German steel groups ventured out of Germany after the Treaty of Versailles to produce steel elsewhere in Europe (except in Austria during Hitler's régime).

The steel works in the Saar and Luxembourg—neither country has a large home market or sufficient capital—were largely dominated from the outside, by French steel producers and by Belgian steel groups. The Pont-à-Mousson group penetrated Luxembourg and the Saar after the first world war. The Schneider group had penetrated Luxembourg before that through its investment in Arbed. Arbed itself had a foot in the Saar. These links between the steel producers in Lorraine, the Saar and Luxembourg reflect the fact that all three steel producing areas have overlapping markets. All three producing areas deliver to southern Germany; the Saar furthermore delivers to French markets that are supplied by Lorraine as well. The producers in Belgium and Luxembourg are large world exporters. The proprietary links reflect these marketing patterns.

Most of the interregional capital penetration in the coal industry antedates the second world war or flowed directly out of the war. The only significant purchase by capital of one country of assets in another during the early life of the common market was the purchase by Arbed of the Lothringen coal mines in the Ruhr.

[114] Some cooperation took place, however, between steel firms in different member countries to develop iron ore in Canada, South America and North Africa. *Financial Times*, February 17, 1958, p. 5.

THE HIGH AUTHORITY'S POLICY ON CONCENTRATIONS

What has been the High Authority's policy with respect to concentrations? As of April 1958 it had as yet not stopped any concentration from occurring.[115] There are four aspects to the High Authority's policy on concentrations: whether to consider the firm or the group; whether to focus on the regional market or the common market; whether to make the size of comparable firms determinant; whether to sacrifice efficiency to competition.

The Firm and the Group

The High Authority ignored the group, of whose ramifications it was well aware, as is indicated by the following statement:[116] ". . . the steel firms are often immersed in complex financial ties associating them with banking groups, commercial enterprises or other industries." The Common Market Committee believed that the High Authority could have taken the group into consideration more effectively if the rule of professional secrecy (Article 47) had been modified to allow it to explain its decisions to the public.[117]

Regional Markets

The High Authority treated all producers as if they were effectively in one large market, though this focus is justified only in particular cases because the bulk of the steel and coal is sold within a relatively short radius of the point of production. A concentration seems small when measured—as is the High Authority's practice—in relation to output in the Community as a whole. A glance at the list of approved concentrations thus shows that the largest firms (not to be confused with groups)—Arbed, Dortmund-Hörder, Phoenix-Rheinrohr—each controlled no more than 5 per cent of the Community's production of crude steel.[118] The High Authority used the same procedure for measuring the importance of approved agreements. (See Chapters 6 and 8.)

Size of Comparable Firms

In accordance with paragraph 2 of Article 66 (on concentrations) the High Authority examined each proposed concentration in the steel industry—the industry mainly affected by concentrations—to see if it would exceed the size of the largest firm in the Community. Arbed, with 2.7 million tons of crude

---

[115] HA, *Sixième rapport général*, Vol. II, pp. 106–111, gives the number of cases considered and their disposition.

[116] *Ibid.*, Vol. I, p. 35.

[117] Common Assembly, Document No. 26, May 1957, p. 25.

[118] HA, *Sixième rapport général*, Vol. II, pp. 107–110.

steel in 1955, was the largest steel firm at the time. The Common Market Committee of the Common Assembly thought this procedure was too "mechanical" though it approved of concentrations that reduced the cost of production.[119]

The "common market" for any product consists of many markets. We have already mentioned that steel products are bulky relative to their value and that outbound transport costs consequently restrict the radius within which a steel plant can deliver its output at competitive prices. A small number of large producers therefore account for most of the steel production in any given region. Since all the firms in a given producing district do not produce the same products, the steel producers of a particular product in most regions are furthermore therefore still fewer in number. The same is true of the coal industry, in which the privately owned firms are in any case organized regionally in common sales agencies. (Though some regions have a relatively large number of small nonintegrated steel mills—certain parts of Italy, France and Belgium, for example—the smaller plants combined rarely account for more than a small portion of total output.)

The degree of oligopoly is diluted the greater the distance of the market from the producing district or the greater the deficiency in local supply. The number of rivals a particular steel firm has to contend with increases if it extends its radius to more distant markets or markets supplied by other producing regions. A steel producer in the Ruhr selling to a local consumer normally contends only with the other local producers, but in other markets—the Dutch market, for example—he contends also with producers from other areas. The steel markets in the Netherlands or southern Germany are thus characterized by a relatively small degree of oligopoly, because each of these markets draws supplies from several producing districts. Though steel production in Lorraine is quite monopolized by virtue of the crossties between the steel producing groups in that area, the steel producers there nevertheless sell most of their production outside the area; their degree of control is diluted to the extent that they sell in regions that are supplied by other producing areas. The steel producers in Belgium, the Saar and Luxembourg are in a similar situation. The number of rivals is potentially greatest (in the absence of agreements) in overseas markets, in which nearly all the major world producers participate. Steel producers have consequently reduced potential rivalry in overseas market (or in other markets threatened by competition) by means of formal agreements.

It would therefore appear desirable for the High Authority to analyze concentrations and agreements, whether in the coal or steel industry, by particular

[119] *Op. cit.*, Annexe 1 and p. 24.

markets in the Community, as some members of the Common Assembly have suggested.[120]

Concentrations and Costs

William Fellner has identified three cases of concentration or fewness of sellers:[121]

(1) Large firms create real cost advantages by virtue either of lower costs of production or of better margins where large-scale distribution leads to advantages in marketing.

(2) Though some firms may be too large for efficiency, the owners may still derive a benefit—by virtue of financial power or patent rights—from the ability to control the market or to exclude new entries. Patent rights, however, have never played a role in market domination in the steel industry. Fellner believes that many real cases are hybrids of cases (1) and (2).

(3) A large number of small independent producers, like farmers or coal producers, may coordinate activities for the purpose of stabilizing markets, employment, prices or incomes. Coordination is in most of these instances sponsored or sanctioned by an outside agency—the government or an industry that purchases materials from the small producers—because the number of firms is too large to enable them to coordinate otherwise. The producers and the organizing agency usually strike a compromise if their interests do not coincide.

The Steel Industry. The High Authority believes that most of the concentration that occurred promoted efficiency:[122]

A movement regrouping the steel firms has long been in process in all the member countries in order to form more important and better balanced units. To the extent this end was promoted, this movement, which continued and even increased under the common market, contributed to progress.

The High Authority said that the concentrations it had approved "are those which put a larger number [of firms] in position to compete with each other on equal terms."[123]

The High Authority suggested that steel firms should specialize by means of horizontal concentrations and by mutual agreements copied from British

[120] *Le Monde*, May 18, 1957, p. 2. It is of doubtful relevance to compare the size of American steel firms with the size of those in the ECSC. Though three firms produce more than 50 per cent of the steel in the United States and though the largest American firm produces nearly as much steel as France and Germany combined (as Wehrer, *op. cit.*, pp. 2–5, points out), the large steel groups in the ECSC also enjoy much power in their particular markets, as the data in this chapter indicate.

[121] *Op. cit.*, pp. 44–48.

[122] HA, *Sixième rapport général*, Vol. I, p. 35.

[123] *Ibid.*, pp. 35–37.

experience since 1933. Specialization was promoted in the British steel industry—where firms are more specialized than their counterparts on the Continent—by interlocking stock ownership between firms or by pooling profits.
Since the nonintegrated rolling mills are often at the mercy of integrated
firms, on whom they depend for raw metal and whose costs are generally
lower, the High Authority suggested that the nonintegrated firms should
establish cooperatives to produce raw metal or should finance the installation
of supplementary raw metal producing facilities in the integrated firms in
return for long-term supply contracts.[124]

There is as yet no evidence, however, that concentrations in the ECSC promoted specialization by regions or firms, excepting those effected in the
Centre-Midi by Ateliers et Forges de la Loire.[125]

The High Authority is aware that costs cease to diminish beyond a certain
size. But it said that it would have been unrealistic to fix an arbitrary size limit
because the minimum size for efficiency in conventional plants is rising continuously with technical improvements. But horizontal concentrations should
not, according to the High Authority, lead to the point where certain firms
would be able to exercise "price leadership."

Vertical concentration is justified, according to the High Authority, in order
to reduce progressive taxes on value added and to secure assured sources of
raw materials.[126] The Common Market Committee of the Common Assembly
believed, however, that too much Ruhr coal had fallen under the control of the
steel industry.[127]

The Coal Industry. Since efficient coal mining depends largely, if not mainly,
on the size of the mine, the High Authority believed that mines and preparation plants, too, should be physically concentrated.[128] Physical concentration
programs were already being carried out in the nationalized French mines
before the ECSC was established and the State-owned mines in the Saar and
Holland were already among the largest in Europe. Only the privately owned
mines in Belgium and Germany were therefore available for further proprietary concentration. Since the average mine in Germany was already among
the largest in ECSC, further concentration in Germany would involve physical
concentration between mines in the same firm or further horizontal combinations between firms.

There were still a large number of small firms in southern Belgium that

124 *Ibid.*, pp. 37–38.
125 *Steel Review*, April 1958, p. 24.
126 HA, *Sixième rapport général*, Vol. I, pp. 35–37.
127 Common Assembly, Document No. 26, May 1957, Annexe 1 and p. 24.
128 "Objectifs généraux," *Journal officiel*, May 20, 1957, pp. 207–208.

operated one or more small mines. Many of the firms were owned by one of four financial groups in that country. Nowhere else in the European coal industry would a corporate and physical concentration program make a greater contribution to efficiency. Such concentrations paradoxically enough have not occurred where most needed.[129]

Where coordination, with or without government sanction, fails, nationalization does the job, as in France and Britain. The Ruhr coal mining firms, on the other hand, are organized in publicly authorized common sales syndicates with the help of the Ruhr steel industry (which owns more than half the production) and the German government.[130] In the 1930s the American coal mines also were organized with the help of the government.

Conclusion

Many concentrations place a greater number of operating units under single control without necessarily modernizing them or reducing their costs. It would be useful for the High Authority to try to discriminate between concentrations that promote efficiency and those that promote oligopoly primarily. Efficiency is, however, so closely related to large-scale operations in the coal and steel industries that concentrations can be prevented only by sacrificing some of the cost advantages to the greater long-term advantage of competition. An economically desirable policy would try to keep the cost sacrifice at a minimum, but it may not be realistic, given the nature of modern production, to sacrifice large advantages in cost.[131]

The practical alternative in industries like steel or coal is therefore between different degrees of oligopoly, not between oligopoly and perfect competition.[132]

The prospects for stopping the concentration movement should therefore not be exaggerated. Since the member countries themselves tolerate concentration, it is not surprising that the High Authority apparently has no clearly formulated policy on the limits to concentration and prefers to take each case as it comes. Without support in favor of limiting concentrations from any organized social, economic or political group, the High Authority may not have much choice among possible policies. The European Economic Community treaty, further, places less restraint on the formation of concentrations

---

[129] See Chapter 4.

[130] See Chapter 8. Frederick Haussmann, *The Reorganization of the German Coal Industry and Its International Aspects* (a mimeographed study written after the second world war), pp. 119–121, is, for example, in favor of private ownership but still concedes the need for public supervision of the Ruhr mines on "public utility principles, and internationally with the concept of international commodity agreements."

[131] See Fellner, *op. cit.*, pp. 283–285.

[132] See HA, *Sixième rapport général*, Vol. I, p. 35.

than the ECSC treaty. Since the ECSC is the smaller Community, the High Authority can hardly be expected to isolate itself in a difficult cause.

The Common Market Committee of the Common Assembly believed, however, that the High Authority had not combined all the possibilities offered by the treaty.[133] The High Authority had been too preoccupied with the rule regarding the size of comparable units, in the opinion of the Common Market Committee. The Common Market Committee believed that this rule by itself was not a sufficient basis for policy making. The High Authority, it thought, could use three other possibilities opened by the treaty:

(1) Paragraph 2 of Article 66, which states: "The High Authority may make an authorization subject to any conditions which it considers appropriate for the purposes of this section."

(2) Paragraph 7 of Article 66 gives the High Authority power to control concentrations already in existence.

(3) Article 66 can be interpreted in relation to the goals of the treaty defined in Articles 2, 3, 4 and 5. These articles, the Committee asserted, were not meant to be ignored when Article 66 was up for interpretation.

A more flexible interpretation of the treaty would have enabled the High Authority, in the Committee's opinion, to analyze concentrations in relation to group control in regional markets and to determine when to sacrifice competition to efficiency or efficiency to competition.

Having discussed the degree of concentration, the study will now examine concerted practices in steel and coal, in Chapters 6 and 8, respectively, preparatory to a discussion of market organization and price behavior in the steel industry, Chapter 7, and in the coal industry, Chapters 9 and 10.

[133] Common Assembly, Document No. 26, May 1957.

CHAPTER 6

STEEL:

CONCERTED PRACTICES

Markets may be controlled either by a small number of large firms—concentrations—or by concerted action among independent firms that agree to fix prices, production or sales.

How does the ECSC treaty affect restrictive agreements or cartels?

TREATY PROVISIONS

Article 65, which deals with the subject, forbids "all agreements among enterprises, all decisions of associations of enterprises, and all concerted practices, tending directly or indirectly, to prevent, restrict or distort the normal operation of competition within the common market," in particular if they tend:

"(a) to fix or determine prices;

"(b) to restrict or control production, technical development or investments;

"(c) to allocate markets, products, customers or sources of supply."

These practices are forbidden by the treaty whether or not they are based on formal agreement.[1]

Article 65 applies to already existing cartels. In July 1953, the High Authority requested the enterprises to supply information on agreements in force, to apply for authorization or to terminate illegal practices. The High Authority may obtain the information it requires by special request or by general directives. It is required to publish its decisions and the reasons therefor. Unlike concentrations, agreements are not protected by professional secrecy.

The treaty does not prohibit the enterprises from organizing a cartel to influence other markets than the common market. Agreements that affect ex-

---

[1] Paul Reuter, *La Communauté Européenne du Charbon et de l'Acier*, Librairie Générale de Droit et de Jurisprudence, Paris, 1953, pp. 209–210.

ternal markets and defensive agreements against unfair competitors located in third-party areas are not illegal, provided such agreements do not restrain trade in domestic products.[2]

The High Authority may impose the most severe fines the treaty allows—up to 10 per cent of the annual, or 20 per cent of the daily, turnover of an enterprise or association that violates Article 65 or the decisions of the High Authority.

Article 65, like Article 66, deals with firms rather than with States. Article 65 does not prohibit a State from interfering with the market. The individual firm or legal person is subject to the laws of his State as well as to those of the ECSC. Where the two are contradictory, a national court cannot relieve the firm from obeying the national law. Neither can the firm be punished by and under the ECSC for complying with the national law. Only public authority, the executives of the State and of the Community, can resolve such conflicts by accommodation.[3] Articles 86 to 90 cover such eventualities. These articles rest on Articles 1 to 4, which subject the States, as well as the institutions of the Community, to the same goals. The member States are therefore obligated to comply with the instrument they created. Article 88 authorizes the High Authority to issue a "reasoned decision" to a State to bring it into compliance. The latter may appeal to the Court. Article 88 also authorizes the High Authority to apply sanctions if the Council agrees by two-thirds majority. Article 90 authorizes the Court to arbitrate a dispute in which a State is party.

Concerted Action Under Public Authority

Markets are frequently organized with the assistance of the government or other parties in order to coordinate a large number of small independent producers. Such market organizations may serve a number of mutually dependent purposes that vary with particular circumstances. They generally seek to provide the firm or the employees with a stable minimum revenue by price supports or by spreading production as equally as possible among all producing units. They may try to help the economy as a whole by reducing the costs of production or distribution in that industry, by rationalizing output through a long-term investment program, or by stabilizing production through subsidies or other safeguards. Coal producers are often organized for these purposes. (Nationalization of coal mines, as pointed out already, is another form of organization serving the same ends.)

Concerted action with the help of public authority developed rapidly in the coal industry during the 1930s and even earlier. As an example we need only

[2] *Ibid.*, pp. 211, 269–270.
[3] *Ibid.*, pp. 103–104, 199–200.

to mention the growth of concerted action in the United States coal industry under the National Recovery Act and other legislation that suspended the antitrust laws.[4] Concerted action under government influence proved temporary in the United States but permanent in Europe.

Concerted action under government sponsorship is not necessarily confined to industries like agriculture or mining. Some governments have encouraged concerted activities in the steel industry, especially when the national welfare seemed to justify a long-range investment program to improve efficiency by concentrating production. Concerted action with price stabilization has thus been a matter of settled public policy in the British steel industry since 1932. That industry was theretofore characterized by lack of concentration and by a large number of relatively small, obsolescent plants. The French steel industry was also encouraged to engage in centralized planning for expansion and investments with government supervision under the various Monnet plans after the second world war.

It does not follow that firms organized with the help of the government are necessarily happy with government policy. Agreements sanctioned by a third industry or by government reflect a compromise between the interests of the organized and organizing agency. The government thus may require the organized firms to observe a limit on prices or to provide a specified amount of capacity in the public interest. The firms may believe that they are being forced to sacrifice their own interests or their own conceptions of the public interest.

Article 65 allows the High Authority to resort to the device of concerted action in the public interest. To help improve production or distribution, the High Authority may authorize agreements (and impose provisos as to their duration and influence) for specializing in production or for joint buying or selling. But such agreements may not determine prices, or limit production and sales of a "substantial part of the products in question within the common market," or protect the enterprises from competition within the common market. It has been suggested that this provision allowing the High Authority to authorize agreements serves a function similar to the rule regarding the size of comparable firms in Article 66; that the objective of the treaty is to prevent a few firms from dominating the market rather than to suppress all concerted action. The provision even makes it possible to authorize small enterprises to coordinate activities for the sake of competing on more equal terms with a large concentration.[5]

---

[4] Waldo E. Fisher and Charles M. James, *Minimum Price Fixing in the Bituminous Coal Industry*, Princeton University Press, Princeton, 1955, and Simon N. Whitney, *Antitrust Policies: American Experience in Twenty Industries*, Twentieth Century Fund, New York, 1958, Vol. I, Chap. 7, and Vol. II, Chap. 12.

[5] Reuter, *op. cit.*, pp. 212–213.

The European Economic Community treaty, which sets the practical limits of High Authority policy, also prohibits concerted action that hinders competition in interstate commerce but authorizes concerted action that promotes economic progress in production, distribution or technology provided it does not enable the firms to eliminate competition in a substantial part of the market (Article 85). Administrative measures to carry out these provisions are to be worked out by the Council of Ministers of the EEC by the end of 1960.

The High Authority may authorize concerted action for other purposes besides improving production and distribution. Article 53 allows it to authorize "financial arrangements common to several enterprises."[6]

Article 46 authorizes the High Authority to provide "guidance for the action of all interested parties," by carrying on a "permanent study of the development of the market and price trends"; by drawing up forecasts of production, consumption, exports and imports; by indicating the "general objectives" regarding "modernization, the long-term planning of production and the expansion of productive capacity." In carrying out these responsibilities, the High Authority may consult governments, firms, workers, consumers, dealers and associations of producers, sellers and workers. These parties also may present their views to the High Authority without solicitation.

Article 46 can lead directly to a "system of concerted practices according to the directives of the High Authority" as Paul Reuter observed. He adds:[7]

These measures are without effect unless the interested parties agree; they, therefore, involve the most elaborate form of collaboration between the High Authority and the enterprises. They equally imply agreement among the interested parties and manifestly involve concerted practices; they do not fall under the prohibition of Article 65 because the High Authority is a party to them and even directs them.

The framers of the treaty did not, then, deprive the institutions of the Community of the possibility of providing for concerted action if that appeared to be in the public interest. Indeed, Chapter 8 of this book shows that the High Authority made use of the possibility of concerted action in the coal industry.

The provisions of Article 65 of the ECSC treaty against cartels do not apply during abnormal business conditions. Under Article 58 of the treaty, the free market may be abandoned during periods of low business activity, in order to enable the High Authority, in conjunction with the Council of Ministers, to fix production quotas for the firms, to fine the firms that exceed, and reimburse those that are below, the quotas. Under Article 59, the free market may also be abandoned when supplies are scarce in order to enable the High Authority

[6] Reuter, pp. 237–240, refers to it as "this mysterious article" inserted into that part of the treaty concerned with the finances of the Community.

[7] *Op. cit.*, pp. 225–226.

and the member States to fix distribution quotas. If these articles were invoked, then public authority would probably approve concerted practices or create compulsory associations in order to regulate production, sales and prices.[8] These articles were not used during the transitional period.

The philosophy and objectives of the ECSC cannot therefore be deduced from Article 65 taken by itself. The countervailing possibilities opened by other articles of the treaty are equally significant. The choice of possibilities varies with the climate of opinion, the state of business activity, and the mixture of public and private control prevalent in each national economy as a whole, as well as in the coal and steel industries. Public opinion in Europe is not, furthermore, hostile to anticompetitive practices, as noted in Chapter 5.

THE INTERNATIONAL STEEL CARTEL IN THE INTERWAR YEARS

International and domestic markets were subjected to restrictive agreements by the European steel industry from 1926 to the outbreak of World War II. Domestic market control in some countries and international agreements on some specific products—heavy rails, for example—antedated the first world war.

Three steel producing areas were involved from 1926 to 1939. First, the continental agreement in 1926, known as the Entente Internationale de l'Acier (EIA), encompassed the producers in France, Germany, Luxembourg, Belgium and the Saar, termed "the founder groups," later joined by the steel producers in other continental countries. Second, the British producers and those in the EIA reached an agreement in 1935; it was loosely known as the European Steel Cartel (ESC). Third, the British and EIA producers made an agreement with American producers in 1938. The agreement among all three was loosely called the International Steel Cartel (ISC). Neither the British nor American producers joined the EIA, which was the core of the ISC and represented the continental producers only. The agreements were not enforceable at law but rested merely on consent. Home markets in the United Kingdom and on the Continent were also restricted by agreements among the producers within each country.

Background

Several developments peculiar to the interwar era determined the basis of the cartel movement in steel:

[8] See *ibid.*, pp. 199, 201. W. Friedmann, *Anti-Trust Laws, A Comparative Symposium*, Stevens and Sons, London, 1956, p. 512, says that these articles permit the High Authority to do everything a cartel can do but also require the High Authority to protect the public interest.

(1) Germany controlled the Saar, Luxembourg and the Moselle prior to 1914 and therefore dominated the continental steel industry. German steel output had surpassed that of the United Kingdom in 1893. By 1913 prewar Germany produced nearly 60 per cent of the continental steel, more than twice the amount Britain, and nearly four times the amount France, produced. (See Table 2-2, Appendix E.) Germany and the United Kingdom were the only large European steel exporters before 1914; but their rivalry did not entail any severe or prolonged distress in either country because demand had kept pace with rising capacity from the 1880s to the first world war.

Size relationships changed after the first world war. Though Germany lost steel producing territory, it remained the largest producer, but its lead diminished as capacity in France, Belgium, Luxembourg and Great Britain increased. Total capacity in Germany, France, Belgium, the Saar and Luxembourg combined increased from 25 million tons in 1913 to 36 million tons in 1927, a jump of more than 40 per cent. (See Table 5-8, Appendix E.) But demand failed to keep pace. In 1927 the steel industry in Great Britain—where capacity had grown by more than 50 per cent since 1913—was operating at 75 per cent of capacity. The American steel industry was also down to that rate in 1927. (See Table 17.) The continental steel plants operated at an average of 90 per cent of capacity that year but dropped to 49 per cent in 1932 and 63 per cent in 1934. Their annual average rate of operation in 1932–1938 was 69 per cent; that of the United Kingdom and the United States, 75 per cent and 46 per cent, respectively.

(2) The Treaty of Versailles required Germany to admit a fixed tonnage of steel without duty until January 10, 1925 in order to provide a market for some of its neighbors. When this period came to an end the German tariff was re-established and the German steel industry, which had reorganized the domestic cartel in the meantime, resumed exports and took the initiative in inviting steel producers in neighboring countries to organize an export cartel. In order to regulate trade between Germany and the steel producing regions formerly under German control, the German, French and Luxembourg steel groups concluded several bilateral agreements in 1926 with the following stipulations:[9]

(a) Germany agreed not to export steel or pig iron to France.

[9] For information on these bilateral agreements, see Ingvar Svennilson, *Growth and Stagnation in the European Economy*, ECE, Geneva, 1954, p. 129; Frederic Benham, *The Iron and Steel Industry of Germany, France, Belgium, Luxembourg and the Saar*, London and Cambridge Economic Service, London, October 1934, pp. 5, 7, 46–48; Ervin Hexner, *The International Steel Cartel*, University of North Carolina Press, Chapel Hill, 1943, p. 290; Hans Wolter, *Die französische eisenschaffende Industrie*, Kommissionsverlag Schrobsdorff'sche Buchhandlung, Düsseldorf, 1953, p. 27. These agreements were also made part of the EIA world export agreements and may be consulted in Hexner, *op. cit.*, which carries the text of the merchant bar agreement, one of the key agreements in the interwar steel cartels.

(b) Germany agreed to import from France 3.75 per cent, and from Luxembourg 2.75 per cent, of its total consumption of certain steel products. The German product cartels marketed these imports at internal prices and the exporters in France and Luxembourg paid the German import duty.

(c) Germany agreed to buy 7.895 per cent of its total consumption of pig iron from France and 3.772 per cent from Luxembourg.

(d) Germany agreed to import from the Saar an annual duty-free quota of 1.3 million tons of steel of all types.[10]

(e) France agreed to give the Saar a duty-free import quota of one half million tons annually.

Under these Saar quotas Germany and France combined absorbed about 80 per cent of Saar steel production in the ratio of about three to one, respectively. The steel from the Saar was marketed in each of the two countries by the respective domestic cartel or by the national sales organization of the parent steel group in the country of destination.

The EIA was thus designed to avoid the threat of severe rivalry in the home markets of the steel producers in Germany and the former German territories.[11] All the EIA agreements, as indeed all the agreements constituting the International Steel Cartel, rested on mutual respect of domestic markets. These markets were respected even when the agreements regarding exports to third parties broke down from 1929 to 1933. The agreement between the EIA and the United Kingdom in 1935 regulated exports from EIA members to the United Kingdom.

History

The methods and principles of the EIA changed several times in response to circumstances.

The first agreement in 1926 tried to control overproduction by establishing quarterly crude steel production quotas for each member country.[12] Producers paid a one dollar levy per ton of steel produced. Excess production was fined and underproduction compensated. Quotas and fines were calculated on total national production whether or not all producers were within the cartel; each

---

[10] Svennilson, *op. cit.*, p. 129, puts this figure at 1.5 million tons.

[11] These bilateral and EIA agreements, reached in 1926, coincided with Germany's admission to the League of Nations, the conclusion of the Dawes Plan regarding Germany's external obligations, and the signing of a general commercial treaty between France and Germany—part of the efforts of Briand and Stresemann for *rapprochement*. The steel agreements between the French and German steel producers were conditional on the continuation of the general commercial accord.

[12] The votes of the Saar delegation in the EIA were cast through the German and French groups, two thirds and one third, respectively; the Saar quota was included with the French until 1935 and transferred to the German thereafter. Hexner, *op. cit.*, pp. 74, 290; Federal Trade Commission, *International Steel Cartels*, Washington, 1948, pp. 8, 92.

national group thus was responsible for nonmembers. This very important principle operated throughout the life of the EIA and was later adopted by the British and American groups as well. The first international agreement applied to crude steel rather than individual steel products, except for several products organized independently. The quotas applied without distinction to production for domestic and export sales. The attempt to control both domestic and export markets, the failure to control individual products, and the absence of price and distribution machinery, proved to be the major weaknesses of the first EIA. In attempting to control domestic markets, the EIA became involved in the differences between producers in the same country and between the national steel groups and their own governments.

The German quota in the first EIA agreement soon proved to be too low to enable the German producers to satisfy home demand. Wishing neither to reduce exports nor to import more steel, Germany began to exceed its quota. It requested a higher quota in order to reduce the penalties. In the second quarter of 1927 it received separate export and domestic quotas, with a lower penalty for exceeding the latter.

The EIA began to collapse during the second half of 1929 under growing competition from British exports and falling export markets. The Germans denounced the agreement effective October 1929; the levies and fines ceased but the agreement was extended from month to month until January 1930 in order to save appearances.

International market control broke down from 1929 to the second EIA agreement in June 1933. The steel cartel was not the only one to collapse in the Great Depression.

The United Kingdom, having abandoned free trade, imposed a 10 per cent duty on steel in March 1932 and increased it to 33⅓ per cent two months later. The continental exporters, who had long enjoyed a free market in the United Kingdom, were seriously affected. Severe price competition from steel exporters in Belgium and Luxembourg, whose exports consequently declined proportionately less than those from other countries, interfered with attempts to revive the cartel.

Steel export prices reached their lowest point in 1932, but the prices for rails, wire rod and tube, which had remained under international control, suffered a smaller percentage decline, providing the founder groups with an impressive example of the benefits of international control.

The second EIA agreement was based on the following new principles:

(1) It controlled export markets only and abstained from any control over domestic markets, where the respective national groups were allowed a free hand.

(2) It established subsidiary ententes[13] for individual products. These ententes fixed quotas and prices for their products and otherwise regulated exports by representing the exporters in some cases.[14]

(3) It organized single product ententes in the individual importing countries in which the local producers, if any, and the import merchants were represented.

The second EIA at first established individual ententes for six products: semifinished steel, joists and channels, merchant bars, thick plates, medium plates and universals. Since these did not cover the complete range of products, the second EIA agreement also contained an over-all export quota (in crude steel equivalents) for each member country. The over-all quotas covered more than the six products; the six individual products were therefore subject to dual control. Had all the products been organized in single product ententes, a double system of control would have been unnecessary. As individual ententes were organized for additional products, the over-all quotas became unnecessary and were finally discontinued in July 1936 when fourteen individual ententes had been organized controlling all important steel products but cold-rolled strip and hoop. Four of these ententes—for heavy rails, tubes, wire rods and wire products—operated outside the EIA but cooperated with it.

British and American Participation

The United Kingdom cooperated with the EIA informally from May 1935 to August 1936 when the agreement between the two was formalized. It had taken the British steel producers more than a year to organize their entry into the individual product ententes. Over-all quota control had been discontinued by that time so that British exports were controlled only by the individual export ententes. British participation involved a complex series of controls insofar as the United Kingdom also imported steel. British entry paved the way for the conclusion of penetration agreements between the European Steel Cartel and the local producers, if any, and import merchants in importing countries; penetration agreements in South Africa and Scandinavia were among the most important of these.

---

[13] Single product cartels in French terminology are called *ententes* whereas the over-all policy-making and coordinating organization is the *comptoir*. Hexner, *op. cit.*, pp. 34–35.

[14] The French and German delegations had differed sharply in the negotiations for the first EIA. The German steel group, wishing to fashion the EIA on its own domestic practices, had advocated that it establish export sales ententes for single products and that export sales be treated separately. The French, seriously overexpanded, preferred an over-all quota because they hoped that exports would offset a possible failure in internal demand. The first EIA adopted the French view but the second in 1933 came round to the German view. *Ibid.*, pp. 71, 77–78; U. S. Tariff Commission, *Iron and Steel*, Report No. 128, Washington, 1938, p. 372.

After the EIA and the United Kingdom became permanent associates, they made overtures to secure cooperation from the United States. A tentative understanding was concluded early in 1938; there was some delay, as there had been with the United Kingdom, because the American steel industry was required to organize sufficient control over the exports of individual products to be able to cooperate with the six major product ententes. The United States steel export organization, like the Polish, was distinct from the domestic market.[15]

With the entrance of the United States, the International Steel Cartel controlled virtually the whole world export market and the whole range of steel products.

The ISC did not cover iron ore, pig iron or special and alloy steels. Pig iron was rather competitive during the interwar period in spite of separate agreements between France, Belgium and Luxembourg and also between the Netherlands, Germany and Czechoslovakia. Import duties on pig iron were low and the prices for pig iron fluctuated more than those for steel. Iron ore was not subject to international price agreements. Produced by captive mines or sold on long-term contract, prices varied little over the years and consumers remained faithful to their sources without trying to change for the sake of a price advantage.[16]

Export Market Control Methods

The individual product ententes became the operating units of the export cartel after 1933. Only the ententes for wire rods and for tubes controlled sales in home as well as export markets. The other international ententes were limited to exports. They tried to control individual export transactions but did not always go that far in practice. Where the producers were few in number, each of them generally had more freedom to handle its sales; where there were many, the entente generally handled sales directly.[17] Every large producer-exporter had its own sales agency and its own agents in the importing countries and arranged sales within the conditions set by the entente. The entente reviewed all transactions in any case.

The entente fixed export prices for the base product and for extras. The control office in each entente adjusted price quotations to meet competition from outsiders and adjusted orders in accordance with national export quotas for the product. Independent merchants in the exporting country could not resell for export because home prices generally were higher than world prices.[18]

[15] Hexner, *op. cit.*, p. 112.
[16] *Ibid.*, pp. 7–10.
[17] *Ibid.*, pp. 139–143, 154–157.
[18] *Ibid.*, pp. 164–170; Federal Trade Commission, *op. cit.*, p. 3.

In distributing orders and quotas, the entente did not try to rationalize production or to eliminate crosshauls in transportation; no consistent rule was followed in distributing export quotas but that of the historical reference period. Particular export markets were reserved for particular national groups on historical grounds, whether or not comparative advantage had influenced the pattern of sales. To protect the position of a national group in its reserved export market, other national groups were obliged to quote higher prices in that market.[19]

Prices were quoted c.i.f. rather than f.o.b. in order to eliminate secret price cutting by means of indeterminate transport costs. The ententes and the overseas carriers sometimes agreed on standard freight rates in order to reduce the possibility of secret price cutting.

Prices varied according to the nature of the individual import market, taking account of import duties and the presence of outside competitors, if any.[20] Prices were generally higher in "organized" import markets. The "organized" market was an important technique of control; even the United Kingdom was an "organized" market. In "organized" markets the distributors or import houses, the local steel producers and the local governments cooperated with the entente. The local producers received a recognized share of the market; local distributors were protected from competition by outsiders and received an agreed markup. The entente often dumped in an importing area before inviting the local producers and merchants to establish an "organized" market.

The second EIA provided over-all policy and administrative coordination for the individual product ententes. In spite of the large number of ententes, the system operated effectively because the leading producers played an important role in the national group, in the EIA policy committee, and in the body that coordinated the individual export ententes. The over-all administration and management offices were located in Luxembourg, where Columeta, the export sales agency for Arbed, supplied office space, executive officers and staff.

CONCERTED ACTION IN DOMESTIC MARKETS

The national steel group that controlled the domestic market was the basic unit of organization in the European Steel Cartel. Export market control would have been impossible without it. After the demise of the International Steel Cartel in 1939, the national groups under government supervision

[19] Hexner, *op. cit.*, pp. 244–245.
[20] U. S. Tariff Commission, *op. cit.*, pp. 30–31.

helped to organize production, distribution and prices during the war and early postwar years.

Role of the National Group

The national groups supervised nonmembers as well as members, informed the international policy-making bodies of internal activities and opened their records for audit by the Schweizerische Treuhandgesellschaft, an independent Swiss firm of certified accountants.[21]

The national groups were independent of and not subordinate to the ISC, ESC or EIA. The whole system consisted of coordinate cartels within cartels.[22] The producer-exporter was the smallest unit within the system. The largest producers dominated the national group, represented it in the export ententes and often in the coordinating and policy-making bodies. Each national group was also subdivided into product ententes (the British called the national product ententes "associations"). Except in Poland and the United States, each national product entente was responsible for both exports and home sales. The United States group was formally unable to exercise domestic market control, except during the period of the National Recovery Administration, because of the antitrust legislation and the Webb-Pomerene Act.[23] Each national product entente encompassed the producers of the particular product. Identity of leadership facilitated operation with a minimum of paper work and bureaucracy.[24]

Each major national group provided the chairman for and administered one or more of the export product ententes. The Luxembourg group administered the key merchant bar export entente; the German group administered the ententes for heavy plate and tubes; the Belgian group administered those for semis and wire rods, France for structurals.[25]

The export ententes did not actively influence expansion or investment in the domestic market but tried to restrain plant expansion in importing countries. The national steel groups, on the other hand, generally exercised some control over expansion of domestic facilities and could denounce the international agreements in order to protect themselves against new entries.[26]

The national groups protected the high-cost plant and the nonintegrated producer by assigning quotas and orders and sometimes by making equaliza-

[21] Hexner, *op. cit.*, p. 101.

[22] George W. Stocking and Myron W. Watkins, *Cartels in Action,* Twentieth Century Fund, New York, 1946, p. 191. Federal Trade Commission, *op. cit.*, pp. 11–12.

[23] Federal Trade Commission, *op. cit.*, pp. 32, 95.

[24] *Ibid.*, pp. 3–6, 8–9, 32, 54; U. S. Tariff Commission, *op. cit.*, p. 94.

[25] Hexner, *op. cit.*, pp. 148–149, 157, 160–161, Appendix I.

[26] *Ibid.*, pp. 16, 103.

tion payments that were supported by the industry as a whole through a levy on production. For fear of public criticism and government pressure, the larger producers did not try to drive the smaller ones out of business.[27]

Price discrimination between domestic and export markets was an essential feature of national group policy. The domestic price was generally well above the world price in the interwar period (Table 7-2, Appendix E) and sometimes above the world price plus tariff.[28] The domestic consumer thus subsidized the lower export price during the interwar years. Home steel prices in Belgium-Luxembourg, however, were important exceptions to this rule; home prices in those two countries rarely were higher than export prices because the home market was too small to subsidize exports. These two steel producing countries had to be very aggressive in export markets in order to attain a high volume of output, a factor which had an important influence on the EIA. Home prices in the other countries fluctuated much less than export prices though they tended to move in the same direction. Export prices, on the other hand, were quite flexible and varied between export markets, for price flexibility is not necessarily inconsistent with market control. These points are examined further in Chapter 7.

German Market Control

The German steel industry had reached a high degree of domestic cartelization by 1913. But domestic market controls collapsed from the end of the war to 1925 under the free entry provision of the Versailles Treaty and the currency inflation. Up to 1925, there was much competition in steel, giving the German steel transformers the benefit of low prices they had not theretofore enjoyed. As duty-free imports came to an end, the German steel industry in 1924 organized the Stahlwerksverband A. G., an incorporated association of steel producers, and also established single product ententes. The Stahlwerksverband requested its own government to restore the prewar tariff; the German parliament complied only after the Stahlwerksverband had agreed to provide steel at world prices to the steel transformers for indirect export.[29] The newly organized Vereinigte Stahlwerke took the lead in the Stahlwerksverband in 1926 and Fritz Thyssen, one of the main owners of Vereinigte Stahlwerke, represented the German steel group in the EIA.[30] The Stahlwerksverband, with the assistance of Vereinigte Stahlwerke, which had purchased

---

[27] *Ibid.*, p. 54.

[28] Svennilson, *op. cit.*, p. 267.

[29] Hexner, *op. cit.*, p. 66; U. S. Tariff Commission, *op. cit.*, p. 147; Stocking and Watkins, *op. cit.*, pp. 176–177.

[30] Stocking and Watkins, *op. cit.*, pp. 212–214.

control of several nonmembers, represented 100 per cent of the German steel industry after 1929.[31]

The Stahlwerksverband was one of the most thoroughly organized of the national groups and the strongest in the EIA.[32] It allotted a domestic and an export quota to each producer. Steel in the home market was in most cases marketed by the product entente. The producer's return on each product was determined by the average value per unit of sales (export and home combined) by all national producers combined. This arrangement amounted to a system of interfirm compensation. Producers that sold most of their output in the higher-priced domestic market were unhappy and prevailed on the major exporters to accept a lower average return.

All basing points were in the Ruhr, commonly at Oberhausen, for home sales; but Neunkirchen, in the Saar, was also used as a basing point for the sale of merchant bars to south Germany.[33] Selected merchants obtained exclusive sales rights from the Stahlwerksverband. There were three kinds of merchants (affiliates, independents and importers) divided into four sales regions.

The members of the Stahlwerksverband enlarged capacity or entered into the production of new products only with permission of the organization.[34] The French and British steel producers had similar arrangements with respect to new capacity in their respective countries.

French Market Control

Domestic cartels began to take hold under the influence of the first EIA. The Comptoir Sidérurgique de France (CSF), which had been organized in 1919 and had become merely a study group by 1922, resumed commercial activity in 1926 and assumed responsibility for coordinating the product ententes. The CSF made policy for all the French ententes except wire products and sheets. Each single product entente had a domestic and an export division. CSF was a policy-making body; sales were handled by the product ententes.[35]

Internal organization became increasingly effective with the second EIA in 1933. The introduction of independent arbitrators strengthened the cartels during the 1930s. The arbitrators assigned individual product quotas and also

[31] *Ibid.*, pp. 175–178; Benham, *op. cit.*, p. 25.

[32] Stocking and Watkins, *op. cit.*, pp. 212–215; Hexner, *op. cit.*, pp. 66–69, 124–127; Federal Trade Commission, *op. cit.*, p. 91.

[33] Benham, *op. cit.*, p. 25.

[34] See Hexner, *op. cit.*, pp. 66–69, 123–127, for an excellent description of the Stahlwerksverband.

[35] *Ibid.*, pp. 123–124.

over-all quotas to discourage producers from overproducing on items outside individual product control.

But the steel industry in France was not as effectively organized as in Germany or Luxembourg. The producers of special steel were outside the CFS cartel and, along with the producers of pig iron, were more competitive; occasionally they underpriced ordinary carbon steel.[36] The domestic entente for light sheet broke up from 1935 to 1937. In September 1935 the domestic entente for tinplate and black sheet fell apart. In 1936 a dispute among French producers of wire rod and wire products created difficulties for the international wire rod entente which were not ironed out until May 1939.[37]

The fact that concentration rested on interlocked share ownership, and not on large firms created by corporate mergers, contributed to the difficulty of organizing the industry.[38]

The nonintegrated rolling mills also were partly responsible for the instability of the French national group in the EIA. Outside the CSF, they finally agreed to have the CSF control their intake of semifinished steel, on which they received a price rebate.[39]

It proved difficult to bring the independent merchants into the fold; the price control scheme was precarious without them because they could break the price by reducing their markup or resale price. A 1932 agreement between the CSF and the merchants broke down in 1934. With the encouragement of the Minister of Commerce, the parties reached another agreement in 1936 when the merchants accepted resale price maintenance and the CSF agreed to protect their market by quoting prices above those offered by the merchants to small consumers.[40]

Belgian Market Control

The Belgian steel industry had the weakest internal organization because there were a large number of nonintegrated firms and concentration had taken the form of financial penetration rather than corporate merger. Twenty-three independent rolling mills produced over 10 per cent of the finished steel in 1932. They operated on a high proportion of imported raw materials that placed them beyond the control of the integrated producers in Belgium.[41]

---

[36] Maurice Fontaine, *L'Industrie sidérurgique dans le monde et son évolution économique depuis la seconde guerre mondiale*, Presses Universitaires de France, Paris, 1950, pp. 134–135.

[37] Hexner, *op. cit.*, pp. 123–124, 150–151.

[38] U. S. Tariff Commission, *op. cit.*, p. 375.

[39] Emile Manchotte, *Deux formes de comptoir de vente en commun*, Loos, St.-Dié, 1950, p. 71.

[40] *Ibid.*, pp. 52–55.

[41] Benham, *op. cit.*, pp. 38–39.

With a small domestic market, the Belgian steel producers had little to gain from a high tariff or high domestic prices; they were consequently forced into the more competitive world market for a larger part of their sales. This fact did not contribute to group solidarity.

Lack of a domestic organization in Belgium would have wrecked the negotiations for the second EIA, had not Société Générale, Cofinindus and the Banque de Bruxelles taken a hand. Having increased their degree of proprietary control during the early years of the Great Depression, these financial groups were eager to promote a better organization of the market (as was the Bank of England with respect to British steel) and persuaded the Belgian steel producers to cooperate in creating the second EIA. Indeed, executives of the holding companies and not those of the steel firms represented the Belgian national group in the second EIA from 1933 to 1939.[42]

Under pressure from the holding companies the larger steel producers launched the Comptoir de Vente de la Sidérurgie Belge (Cosibel) a day before the second EIA came into force. Cosibel became the executive agency for the theretofore ineffective Groupement des Hauts-Fourneaux et Aciéries Belges, Société Coopérative. Cosibel sold in domestic and export markets but covered only about 68 per cent of the production (semifinished steel, structurals, merchant bars, heavy and medium plate, black and universal sheets). The other products were marketed by single product ententes outside Cosibel. Cosibel later organized, and became sales agent for, the nonintegrated rolling mills, the weakest link in the chain. The nonintegrated mills obtained a substantial rebate on semifinished products, reported to be 20 per cent or more below official domestic prices.[43]

A month after Cosibel was organized, four large producers—Cockerill, Providence, Angleur-Athus (later absorbed by Cockerill) and Sambre-et-Moselle—accounting for nearly 50 per cent of the crude steel production, organized Ucometal (L'Union Commerciale Belge de Métallurgie) to assist Cosibel. Ucometal studied the market and allotted quotas among the four firms in the group.[44]

The Belgians never established an over-all association, like the Stahlwerksverband or the Comptoir Sidérurgique de France, to represent the whole industry. Some integrated producers even bypassed the national group and directly joined certain export sales ententes of the EIA, from which they obtained individual export quotas.[45]

---

[42] Hexner, *op. cit.*, pp. 87–88.

[43] *Ibid.*, pp. 120–122.

[44] Benham, *op. cit.*, p. 39.

[45] Hexner, *op. cit.*, pp. 155, 157; Federal Trade Commission, *op. cit.*, pp. 25, 30, 38.

In spite, or because, of its relatively weak internal organization, which complicated both its own life and that of the EIA, the Belgian steel industry was the most aggressive, obstructive and successful group in the ISC and obtained the largest export quotas for its size.[46]

Market Control in Luxembourg

Even though it lacked the economic power of the German steel industry, the Luxembourg group, led by Arbed, was a model of cohesion and discipline. After the first world war Arbed, with two thirds of the steel capacity in Luxembourg, established its own sales agency, Columeta, with forty-one worldwide sales offices. Hadir, under the control of the Pont-à-Mousson group, marketed through Davum Exportation, founded in 1928, to handle all the group's exports. Rodange, the other steel producer in Luxembourg, exported through Socobelge, the selling agency for the Belgian parent, Ougrée-Marihaye.[47] Thirty-five per cent of Luxembourg's steel was thus marketed by export sales agencies which also handled the sales for related firms in Belgium, France and the Saar.

The Luxembourg steel group was organized in Le Groupement des Industries Sidérurgiques Luxembourgeoises, Société Coopérative, of which Columeta, representing Arbed, was the executive organ.

After Belgium and Luxembourg formed an economic union, the steel firms in Luxembourg and Belgium—which were largely owned by the same financial groups—soon reached an understanding that allowed Luxembourg to sell 30 per cent of its output in the Belgian market at coordinated prices. This understanding was still observed after World War II.[48]

The Luxembourg group—that is, Arbed through Columeta—supplied the executives for the EIA, and the central administrative staff as well, because it was small, well organized, and free of complicated domestic problems or governmental supervision. Arbed, whose headquarters were in the city of Luxembourg, supplied office space.[49]

The chairman of the board of Arbed was the permanent chairman of the EIA, re-elected annually by common consent. Hector Dieudonné, an Arbed official and the guiding spirit of the world steel cartel, was chairman of the

[46] Hexner, *op. cit.*, pp. 120–122, 294–295.

[47] Benham, *op. cit.*, p. 42; Carlo Hemmer, *L'Economie du Grand-Duché de Luxembourg*, deuxième partie, *La Production secondaire: l'industrie sidérurgique*, Editions Joseph Beffort, Luxembourg, 1953, pp. 106–111, 157.

[48] Hemmer, *op. cit.*, pp. 150–152; Fontaine, *op. cit.*, pp. 174–175; Hexner, *op. cit.*, p. 121; Gerhard Pfeiffer, *Strukturwandlungen und Nachkriegsprobleme der Wirtschaft belgiens*, Kieler Studien, Kiel, 1951, p. 28.

[49] Hexner, *op. cit.*, p. 122.

powerful EIA Comptoir Committee, which coordinated the single product export ententes, and of the EIA Management Committee, which was the executive organ for the top EIA policy committee. Dieudonné also directed the EIA's administrative office, which was staffed with Columeta's personnel.[50]

GOVERNMENT INFLUENCE OVER DOMESTIC MARKETS

Most of the governments in Western Europe have taken an increasing interest in the production and marketing of steel, especially since the Great Depression. This interest tends to promote centralized activities on the part of the industry.

Though the international steel cartel was a private venture, many people thought the first Entente Internationale de l'Acier (EIA) would lay the economic foundations for a peaceful world order. But some groups believed that the EIA and similar agreements should be under public control with consumer representation.[51]

Though the EIA was a major departure from competitive principles, it aroused surprisingly little opposition on those grounds. Neither the League of Nations nor the various world economic conferences expressed any organized opposition.

Socialist groups supported the EIA because they thought it would facilitate government control by promoting concentration. The Belgian government, controlled by the Socialists at that time, favored Belgian membership in the EIA. The German Socialists supported it in the German parliament; only the German Communists and the extreme right-wing parties opposed German membership in the EIA. The French government publicly endorsed the first EIA agreement. Stresemann supported it as the beginning of international economic cooperation and as a token of Franco-German *rapprochement*. The first EIA occupied a place in the so-called Briand-Stresemann era.[52]

The political glory of the EIA had worn off by the time the second agreement was signed. By 1933 it was considered to be no more than an instrument for controlling sales and prices outside the orbit of world political affairs. But

[50] *Ibid.*, pp. 98–99.

[51] *Ibid.*, pp. 217–218.

[52] *Ibid.*, pp. 220–223; Stocking and Watkins, *op. cit.*, pp. 211–212.

Hexner has related the evolution of the ISC to world affairs: The first EIA agreement coincided with Germany's entry into the League of Nations in 1926; the second EIA agreement, with the London Economic Conference in 1933; British association, with the signing of the British-German Naval Treaty in 1935.

the national steel groups still enjoyed support from their respective governments up to the outbreak of the war in 1939.[53]

Each government kept an eye on the activities of its domestic steel producers and intervened at critical moments to induce one section or another of the industry to organize itself. But the ISC itself operated without the cover of an intergovernmental agreement.

The line between public and private control became fainter during the Great Depression. The National Recovery Administration program in the United States was part of this worldwide development. Membership in an industry association became compulsory in Germany under the Nazis. Membership in the British Iron and Steel Federation and in the several product associations was compulsory *de facto* but free *de jure*. The steel groups in Belgium, Luxembourg and France were probably the "freest," but France came close to compulsory cartelization in the mid-1930s. In no country did the steel industry escape direct or indirect public regulation, or the trend to centralized control of prices, production and investments.[54]

As the individual governments increased their influence over domestic steel producers, largely to promote autarkic objectives, it became increasingly difficult for the European Steel Cartel to run its own affairs, especially in the second half of the 1930s, when German rearmament led to an increase in German steel capacity. It managed to survive national economic rivalry by leaving domestic steel problems strictly to the domestic steel groups.[55]

DOMESTIC MARKET CONTROLS ON THE EVE OF THE ECSC

Domestic market regulation by concerted action under government supervision was intensified to serve the war economy after the collapse of the International Steel Cartel in 1939. Such regulation also enabled the countries to cope with the problems of the postwar period—lack of raw materials; scarcity of steel; need to rebuild, expand and modernize steel capacity. National control of domestic prices, of exports and of domestic distribution were therefore quite common after the war. The German steel industry, the largest in Europe, was involved in special controls arising from the occupation, as the preceding chapter has already indicated. In all countries of Western Europe steel prices were controlled at rather low levels, while the limited quantities of steel al-

[53] Hexner, *op. cit.*, pp. 234–237, 240.
[54] *Ibid.*, pp. 30, 55–56, 63, 235.
[55] *Ibid.*, pp. 30, 234–235; cf. Stocking and Watkins, *op. cit.*, pp. 211–215.

lowed for export were sold at soaring world prices. Export market agreements proved unnecessary in such conditions and were not revived until 1953. There was much centralized national planning, with government participation, regarding expansion of capacity; the governments played a considerable role in the provision of loans (including Marshall Plan funds) for approved projects.

Steel supplies in most countries were inadequate until 1949 or 1950. When the Schuman Plan was suggested in 1950 the production of steel on the Continent and in the United Kingdom had reached more normal levels though it was still not equal to that in 1937. (See Table 2-2 Appendix E.) Under the influence of the Korean war steel supplies again became scarce from the latter half of 1950 until the end of 1952, when the ECSC began to operate.

Germany

The allied occupation authorities abolished the cartels immediately after the war but issued directives by which the industry continued to be centrally administered with respect to prices, production, internal distribution and export. The ceiling on domestic steel prices was low but the producers were subsidized until the summer of 1952. The German government thereafter relaxed price control and permitted home prices to rise rather quickly. From the summer of 1952 to January 1953 home prices were fixed by agreement between the steel producers and the steel consuming industries each acting collectively. The German government cancelled price control in January 1953 in anticipation of the opening of the common market for steel.[56]

France

The Comptoir Française des Produits Sidérurgiques (CPS) supplanted the Comptoir Sidérurgique de France (CSF) during the war. It operated by government directive until late 1952, when the government annulled the market control activities that were contrary to the provisions of the ECSC treaty.

The CPS was a centralized administrative agency for the French steel industry and not a sales organization.[57] It had jurisdiction over all carbon steel. The special steels, and hence the Centre-Midi steels, were excluded. There was greater freedom in sales, distribution, and collection of revenue for the producers of wire products, tubes, castings and cold-rolled strip and hoop, though they, too, were members of the CPS and subject to its postaudit. The CPS was responsible for all the output, whether produced by nonmembers or members,

---

[56] HA, *Rapport spécial sur l'établissement du marché commun de l'acier*, May 1953, p. 29; *Exposé sur la situation de la Communauté*, January 1953, pp. 67–68; Fontaine, *op. cit.*, pp. 212–213, 385.

[57] Jacques Ferry and René Chatel, *L'Acier*, collection "*Que sais-je,*" Presses Universitaires de France, Paris, 1957, p. 107.

of the products over which it had jurisdiction. Most producers were members of the CPS. The CPS coordinated the orders placed with steel firms and regulated deliveries in accordance with governmental distribution programs. Certain large clients—notably governmental bodies, railroads, shipyards, the Saar coal mines—dealt with the CPS exclusively. It distributed their orders among the steel plants and consequently controlled and equalized operating rates. A similar device, called the "R" zone, was used by the prewar coal cartels in France. Production programs were drawn up by the Chambre Syndicale de la Sidérurgie Française (CSS).

Maximum steel prices were fixed by the government, but the CPS prepared invoices and collected payment; the steel firms in practice often performed these activities on behalf of the CPS. Government price regulations required the steel industry to put aside funds for amortization, capital investments, housing and other purposes. The CPS collected these funds. It also collected the premium earned on export sales and distributed the proceeds among all the producers.[58]

Belgium-Luxembourg

Domestic steel prices in Belgium were fixed by agreement between the steel producers and Fabrimétal, their main customer, subject to government approval. Domestic prices in Luxembourg were also subject to government approval.

Other Countries

Home steel prices in the Netherlands were subject to government control, if necessary. They were subject in Italy to maximum price control by the government.

Scrap

The French, Italian and German steel producers had national sales cartels for centralized purchase of scrap.[59] The Italian steel industry equalized the cost of domestic and imported scrap. Scrap prices in Belgium and Luxembourg were free and fluctuated considerably.[60]

---

[58] *Avis*, Conseil de la République, No. 64, 1952 (known as Armengaud Report), pp. 24–29; Manchotte, *op. cit.*, pp. 70, 74, 86; Fontaine, *op. cit.*, pp. 155–159; Jean Chardonnet, *Les Grands types de complexes industriels*, Librairie Armand Colin, Paris, 1953, p. 122; HA, *Rapport spécial sur l'établissement du marché commun de l'acier*, May 1953, p. 29.

[59] HA, "Aide-mémoire sur les pratiques contraires au Traité dont l'élimination est commencée ou poursuivi," No. 4903f, n.d., pp. 13–14. Italy, Campsider; Germany, Schrottvermittlungs G.m.b.H.; and France, Union des Consommateurs de Ferailles de France.

[60] HA, *Exposé sur la situation de la Communauté*, January 1953, p. 68.

CONCERTED ACTION SINCE THE COMMON MARKET

Domestic Markets

A glance at some fifteen agreements from 1953 to early 1958 shows that the High Authority authorized agreements covering an extensive portion of coal production but authorized very few agreements in the steel industry.[61] Agreements were authorized in steel to improve distribution and production. The High Authority also authorized concerted action within and between national steel groups in the field of scrap in order to equalize and control the cost of that raw material. (See Chapter 3.)

Though the High Authority has not authorized concerted practices with respect to prices in the steel industry, the steel firms within each country change prices simultaneously. But there is very little simultaneity in price changes in different countries. In each country the steel firms discuss prices among themselves and negotiate collectively with their respective governments through their national trade associations. The steel firms in the small areas like the Saar and Luxembourg follow the price changes made in the major producing areas.

There still is much concerted action, in large part under government influence, among the steel producers in each country—some of it authorized by the High Authority and some, apparently, not requiring its authorization—with respect to investments and expansion. Article 48 of the treaty, furthermore, allows the firms to form voluntary associations and the High Authority to "call upon" them for assistance to help carry out certain ends, particularly those described in Article 46 regarding the study of price and market trends. The High Authority published a list of the organizations it recognized for this purpose in 1956.[62] The steel firms in each country have their own national associations: Chambre Syndicale de la Sidérurgie Française, Associazione Industrie Siderurgiche Italiane (Assider), Groupement des Industries Sidérurgiques Luxembourgeoises, Groupement des Hauts-Fourneaux et Aciéries Belges, Wirtschaftsvereinigung Eisen und Stahl (Germany). These associations

---

[61] HA, *Sixième rapport général*, Vol. II, pp. 92–94. The High Authority, however, authorized several common steel sales organizations in cases of firms under common financial control. It authorized the firms in the Société Générale–Launoit groups (Cockerill–Ougrée, Rodange, Providence and Aciéries et Minières de la Sambre) to sell part of their output in common through Ucosider (*Journal officiel*, March 29, 1956). It had previously authorized Ucometal to sell for the firms in the Société Générale group—John Cockerill, Providence, S. A. Métallurgique de Sambre et Moselle (*Journal officiel*, January 11, 1955). It had also authorized Siderur to sell for the firms in the Launoit group—Ougrée-Marihaye, Rodange, Aciéries et Minières de la Sambre (*Journal officiel*, August 1, 1954). The three selling agencies operated simultaneously.

[62] *Journal officiel*, February 5, 1956, p. 12.

are not necessarily identical with the specialized associations recognized by the High Authority. These national steel associations perform a number of collective functions for the firms and represent them vis-à-vis the government, notably on price, expansion and investment questions. In France the Chambre Syndicale de la Sidérurgie Française has a very important collective role because the French government has had a strong influence on domestic steel prices, expansion and investments. Through the Commissariat Général du Plan, the French government and the steel industry collectively have drawn up four-to-five-year programs (originally termed the Monnet Plans) for expansion, investments and government credits since the end of the war. The margin to be made available for internal financing of investments is determined by the level of steel prices fixed by the French government with or without the agreement of the steel industry.

There is otherwise no evidence to suggest the existence of secret agreements or of anything like the elaborate single product ententes that controlled sales and prices in domestic markets in the interwar period. The relation of "spontaneous" coordination or self-discipline to the behavior of prices is discussed in the next chapter.

The steel producers have significantly made formal agreements that are not directly subject to Article 65, covering tubes, not a treaty product, and exports to third-party countries.

The Tube Agreement

Tubes are an important product. Western Europe accounts for about one fourth of world output, the USSR another fourth and the United States one half. The United Kingdom, Germany, France, Belgium and the Saar are the main producers in Western Europe. The producers in these countries revived the European tube cartel in 1956, effective for five years. It had a distinguished prewar history as the International Tube Convention.[63]

The members of the new agreement are Stewarts & Lloyds in the United Kingdom, the Longwy-Raty group in France and the Saar, Tubes de la Meuse (Société Générale) in Belgium, Phoenix-Rheinrohr and Mannesmann in Germany. The new agreement covered merchant tube (gas, water and steam pipe); oil pipe was not included at the time, probably owing to the absence of the United States. Germany received 42 per cent of the export quota; the United Kingdom, 33 per cent; and France, Belgium and the Saar, a common quota of 25 per cent.[64] The last three areas had one quota because all the

[63] For details on the prewar cartel, see Hexner, *op. cit.*, pp. 159–160; Federal Trade Commission, *op. cit.*, pp. 46, 52–56.

[64] For details on the cartel, see *Handelsblatt*, July 2, 1956, March 29-30, 1957; *Financial Times*, September 4, 1956.

tube production in these three countries is under the interlocked control of the Longwy-Raty group (France) and the Cockerill-Ougrée group (Belgium).

The Agreement on Exports to Third-Party Countries

The steel producers in the ECSC organized an agreement on exports called Entente à l'Exportation des Producteurs de l'Acier, or simply Entente de Bruxelles, in March 1953, two months before the opening of the common market for steel on May 1. It was the first formal agreement since 1939 by the groups that founded the prewar cartel.[65] It was the avowed purpose of the Entente de Bruxelles to fix minimum export prices for all the major products. The Entente de Bruxelles appointed Fiduciare Suisse to oversee sales prices and to report to a committee of five, consisting of a representative from each of the main steel producing countries.[66]

Does the Entente de Bruxelles violate the ECSC treaty or not? Article 65 prohibits agreements that restrain trade and competition in the home market. As in the United States, where export agreements are legal under the Webb-Pomerene Act, the framers of the ECSC had no intention of prohibiting export agreements that have no influence on internal trade. It is up to the High Authority to decide whether or not an agreement on export entails such restraint. If it does not, it is not illegal. Besides the power under Article 65 to nullify such agreements, the High Authority may in any case limit their control over export prices. Article 3(f) stipulates that "equitable limits" be observed on export prices and Article 61 empowers the High Authority to establish maximum prices "if such action can be effectively supervised and appears necessary . . . to pursue in international economic relations the objective defined in Article 3 paragraph (f)."

Pressure from the Scandinavian governments and the prospective GATT conference forced the High Authority to come to a decision late in 1953. The United States government had informed the High Authority and the member countries that it considered the entente illegal. The High Authority apparently shared the American view at first. It is reported to have advised the members of the Entente de Bruxelles to dissolve and considered establishing its own maximum prices in order to undermine the cartel. The members of the entente challenged the legality of the High Authority's request. Forced to seek support from the Council of Ministers, the High Authority in December 1953 requested its advice on the advisability of establishing maximum export prices. It received no encouragement from either the Council or the Consultative

[65] Germany joined in September 1953, when Italy, the Netherlands and Austria also joined. See Henri Rieben, *From the Cartelization of European Heavy Industry to the European Coal and Steel Community*, HA Document 6679/56, Luxembourg, 1956, p. 10.

[66] *L'Europe*, January 9, 1954.

Committee.[67] That month the High Authority affirmed its lack of competence over export cartels that "do not influence competition in the common market" but called attention to its power to fix maximum export prices if necessary.[68]

Can the members of the Entente de Bruxelles exercise market control over more than one fifth the steel they produce without influencing or controlling the rest of it that stays in the common market? This question raises a number of problems treated further in the next chapter.

A NOTE ON THE BRITISH INDUSTRY

The British steel industry, whether under private or public ownership, has been subject to centralized control and planning under government supervision since the British government abandoned free trade in 1932.[69] Competition has been expressly avoided for nearly a generation and horizontal concentration has been encouraged.

Compared with continental producers, the older steel industry in the United Kingdom was obsolete in 1913. Plants were small and production was distributed over many firms. The British steel industry had been forced to expand capacity rapidly during the first world war at high capital costs and not always at well-chosen sites. It was consequently at a disadvantage by comparison with its continental rivals. The physical and corporate structure of the British steel industry did not improve during the 1920s. Production costs and sales prices were high and the return on invested capital low. From 1927 to 1933, nonintegrated plants, using semifinished steel imported at low prices, earned a higher average profit than integrated ones.[70]

In spite of the absence of import duties, domestic steel prices were considerably higher than world prices because some consumers preferred handmill products. This preference permitted small and inefficient plants to operate, but the high level of domestic prices made it possible for the continental pro-

[67] This account is drawn from Rieben, *op. cit.*, pp. 10–11, and also from *Steel Review*, April 1958, p. 25.

[68] *Journal officiel*, December 15, 1953, pp. 202–203.

[69] *Report of the Import Duties Advisory Committee on the Present Position and Future Development of the Iron and Steel Industry*, HMSO, July 1937, gives the history and purposes of governmental and private control from 1932 to 1937, as well as valuable information on the problems of the industry. The industry was nationalized in 1948 and returned to private ownership in 1953. The Iron and Steel Act of 1953 describes the supervisory arrangements since denationalization. The annual and special reports of the Iron and Steel Board, the government supervisory body, contain valuable information; so do "The British Steel Industry, 1958," special issue of *Steel Review*, 1959, and "No Recession in Steel Prices," *The Economist*, August 9, 1958, pp. 471 ff. The chapter on the steel industry in Svennilson, *op. cit.*, contains a provocative analysis of the British steel situation before 1939. *Steel Review*, October 1958, pp. 1–25, also deals with public supervision of the industry.

[70] *Report of the Import Duties Advisory Committee*, p. 11.

ducers to compete with British steel in the British home market.[71] The founder groups did not take the British steel industry seriously enough to come to terms with it when the first EIA agreement was made in 1926.[72] The British steel industry was thus outside the EIA until 1935 though it was a member of several international product ententes, notably heavy rails, tinplate and tubes.

Tariff protection was introduced in 1932. But a report of the Import Duties Advisory Committee, issued October 13, 1932, recognized that protection without reorganization would be insufficient. In the Committee's words:[73]

The central feature of the reorganization which the Committee had in mind was t he creation of machinery which would bring about and maintain coordination of the various sections of the industry and cooperation between the constituent concerns, and facilitate such adjustments in productive capacity and prices as would place the industry on a reasonable profit-earning basis and make possible that technical development and reequipment which was becoming so urgently necessary. Moreover, we envisaged not only such changes as would tend to the maximum efficiency of production and distribution, which we defined as the supply to the using industries of "the right products at the right prices," but also the negotiation with its overseas competitors of agreements which would be mutually satisfactory and also advantageous to our national economy as a whole—agreements which had often been contemplated but had proved impracticable in the absence alike of any body competent to speak for the United Kingdom industry as a whole and to ensure the observance on this side of the terms of any such agreements, and of effective Government support.

The Committee described the British Iron and Steel Federation in the following terms:[74]

In 1933 the industry decided to adapt and improve the existing machinery, consisting of trade associations and the National Federation of Iron and Steel Manufacturers, by grouping the associations into a smaller number of effective instruments for the control of production in the several main divisions of the industry, and by giving to a new central organisation power to support and co-ordinate the activities of the associations and to give effect to the will of the industry in matters of general policy extending beyond the sphere of any one association. Accordingly, the British Iron and Steel Federation was set up in April, 1934, with a constitution . . . giving it the necessary powers to carry out this policy.

On the basis of the principles adopted in the early 1930s, the British steel industry under government supervision engaged in the following concerted activities after denationalization in 1953:

(1) Raw materials—iron ore, scrap and coal—and semifinished steel for

71 Svennilson, *op. cit.*, p. 125.

72 Hexner, *op. cit.*, pp. 73–74, 114.

73 *Report of the Import Duties Advisory Committee*, pp. 12–13.

74 *Ibid.*, pp. 17–18.

further processing are imported by centralized purchase. The price of imported materials is equalized with controlled home prices. The difference is paid by a fund supported by a levy on steel production. All producers therefore contribute to the cost of subsidizing imported materials whether or not they use them, though the scrap subsidy is adjusted to try to discourage steel producers from substituting scrap for pig iron. As world prices for scrap and transport costs for ore declined in 1958, equalization payments were lifted for the first time in two decades.

(2) High-cost steel producers that cannot operate at the maximum price ceiling are subsidized. These payments, too, were tapered off in 1958 when surplus steel capacity developed.

(3) The amount of steel offered on world markets has been controlled.

(4) Imports of steel are determined and controlled by centrally formulated import programs. Home steel prices in Britain have been low; in conjunction with the tariff, they have discouraged imports from occurring outside the import programs. Imports of steel into the United Kingdom are therefore programmed and are not the result of price competition.

(5) Expansion and investments are planned and coordinated by industry and government together. The Iron and Steel Board (responsible to the Board of Trade since 1955) has been responsible for examining and approving specific capital projects since 1953. It works with the British Iron and Steel Federation, which coordinates the rate and balance of expansion on behalf of the industry.[75]

(6) Corporate concentration increased under the influence of this program, as indicated in Chapter 5.

(7) The Iron and Steel Board in consultation with the industry establishes a maximum price for each major product (except castings and forgings). The maximum price takes account of the average cost of labor, materials and other out-of-pocket charges for each major group of products, high-cost plants excluded. The allowance for capital charges (both depreciation and profit) is adjusted to the cost of new plant. The formula encourages expansion by taking account of replacement cost; it especially encourages expansion where capital costs have risen sharply without a major change in production techniques, e.g., in plate production. The policy therefore calls for a low, stable price level that nevertheless provides enough margin to encourage investment by a high proportion of internal financing.

(8) Maximum prices have in practice determined going prices for all products. There were ten "conferences" (formerly associations), one for each major

---

[75] See *The Economist*, November 22, 1958, p. 715, for the details of one specific investment program for a new strip mill in which the decision was made by the Cabinet itself.

group of products, as of 1958, encompassing about 350 firms. The conferences are represented in the British Iron and Steel Federation. In 1957 the Iron and Steel Board requested the conferences to abandon any undertaking that bound their members to accept maximum prices as minimum prices. The board instead allowed the conferences to recommend to their members that maximum prices "should in general be regarded as appropriate selling prices."[76]

The British Iron and Steel Federation has summarized the organization of control in the following terms:[77]

This pyramid of British steel organization, based firmly upon private ownership but linked at its apex, through the independent supervisory board and the Federation itself, with the basic economic coordination and planning of the Government, has been built up since the 'Thirties. It is the result of constant evolution and experiment in developing a pattern of organization that would combine public responsibility with private commercial direction and control. In British industry and in the world of steel, it is unique—and uniquely effective.

Having reversed a process of deterioration that had lasted from the late 1890s to the early 1930s, the British steel industry is now one of the most effective and formidable national steel groups in Western Europe.

[76] *The Economist*, August 9, 1958, p. 472.
[77] "The British Steel Industry, 1958," special issue of *Steel Review*, 1959, p. 47.

CHAPTER 7

STEEL: PRICES

AND COMPETITION

Most steel mills are so large and the number of producers is so few that if any one of them reduces the price, the rest quickly follow suit in order to retain their customers. But small firms operating in the shadow of the giants are sometimes allowed to practice price cutting on the understanding that such behavior on their part constitutes merely a minor nuisance. The initial price cutter gains no advantage if the other firms reduce prices quickly. The steel producers believe that a general price reduction during a recession would simply lead to a loss in total earnings by all the mills because sales would not rise correspondingly. Steel producers collectively and individually are thus reluctant to reduce prices. They count on voluntary self-discipline or on spontaneous coordination backed by individual interest to keep the price level; or they enter into formal agreements to divide the market and maintain prices, especially if formal agreements are acceptable to the public authorities and the population at large. The larger the number of producers in the same market, the more fragile the spontaneous forms of coordination and the greater the tendency for formal agreements to accomplish the same ends.[1]

However strong the forces resisting competition, the peace is an uneasy one whether the arrangements are spontaneous or formal. Each firm assesses the picture differently and tries to obtain a larger share of the market or of profits by enlarging its capacity or reducing its costs. In addition to innovations of this kind, high overhead costs and the high fixed investment induce the mills to try to maintain volume during a recession by secret discounts or price cutting. The lower-cost mills might at such times hope to enforce a new pattern of market shares upon their rivals. Every firm therefore has to plan its own future as though a struggle might occur. A change in the rules of business or

[1] There is an extensive literature on the general principles of spontaneous and formal organization. Only William Fellner, *Competition Among the Few*, Knopf, New York, 1949, and Edward H. Chamberlin, *The Theory of Monopolistic Competition*, Harvard University Press, Cambridge, 6th edition, 1950, are cited here.

the introduction of new rivals—whether by new entries or by the merging of previously separated markets—could also disturb spontaneous or formal methods of coordination.

Price cutting is often concealed in order to gain an initial advantage or to make it difficult for rivals to meet the price. Reductions can be made without changing the official price by secretly varying the charge for extras, by providing a better quality than the official price calls for, by granting better terms of payment to certain customers, or by other forms of discount. A variety of devices helps the producers to attain price coordination: the use of basing points to help the mills to align prices in their own or other producing areas; a standard nomenclature for basic products and extras; a common price list for extras; common rules for varying the standard price, whether by size of order, conditions of payment or other elements; standard freight charges by destination or delivery zones, regardless of the actual means of transport; or price leadership. Obligatory publication of prices also contributes to coordination.

It is difficult to measure the extent of price cutting. A study of the American steel industry covering the years 1939–1942 showed that the average discount from published prices was about 4.8 per cent in the second quarter of 1939, when the industry operated at 51 per cent of capacity, and only .03 per cent in the fourth quarter of 1941, when it operated at 98 per cent of capacity. Secret discounts in the United States, if known, might account for half the slower rate of decline in official steel prices compared with prices for other industrial products during a recession.[2]

Official steel prices are quoted for the base product; charges for extras accounted for about 10 per cent of the delivered value of steel in the ECSC on the eve of the common market.[3] The value of the extras varies with the type of product, being lowest on common products like merchant bars.

In order to close the loophole for price cutting by means of extras, the founders of the interwar continental steel cartel standardized the nomenclature and charges for extras among continental producers before World War II. The British and American producers had been negotiating the extension of this practice to the rest of the international cartel when it dissolved in 1939. On the eve of the common market, the nomenclature and charges for extras were standardized on a national, but not a Community, basis. The producers were, however, negotiating a common set of definitions and charges for the market

[2] Simon N. Whitney, *Antitrust Policies: American Experience in Twenty Industries*, Twentieth Century Fund, New York, 1958, Vol. I, p. 310.

[3] HA, *Rapport spécial sur l'établissement du marché commun de l'acier*, Luxembourg, May 1953, p. 33. An article on "The Effect of 'Extras' in the Measurement of Steel Price," in *Monthly Labor Review*, U. S. Department of Labor, November 1956, emphasizes the danger of using base prices to indicate the price trend in steel.

as a whole. The High Authority encouraged them to adopt a uniform nomenclature in order to enable buyers to compare prices, but frowned on uniform
charges.[4]

Though official prices for base products are on the whole not a reliable
measure of effective prices, particularly during a recession, official prices for
merchant bars and structurals come closer to measuring price behavior in the
industry as a whole than those for any other product because merchant bars
are distributed to a wide range of customers and are less loaded with extras
than most other products. A falling official price for merchant bars often indicates that secret discounts are being given on other products for which the
official price is unchanged.[5] Official prices for merchant bars, as shown in
Table 7-1, Appendix E, are accordingly used in this book to show price relations and trends, but price data for other products are indicated when
necessary.

PROVISIONS OF THE TREATY

The treaty essentially aims to establish equality among buyers and fair competitive practices. Paragraph 1 of Article 60 refers to the general principles
mentioned in Articles 3 and 4. Article 3(c) says that the institutions of the
Community shall "seek" the "lowest possible prices" consistent with amortization and normal returns on invested capital. Article 4(b) prohibits discriminatory practices among producers, buyers or consumers, with respect to
price, delivery terms or transport rates; it also prohibits any measures that
hamper the buyer's ability to choose a supplier.

Price Discrimination

A firm may not injure the competitive system by manipulating prices in
order to reduce the number of firms. Discriminatory practices are defined as
the application by a seller of unequal conditions in comparable transactions.
The seller must under the treaty offer equal terms to comparable customers.
Discrimination according to nationality is expressly forbidden (Article 60,
paragraph 1).

Paragraph 2(a) of Article 60 relies heavily on publication of prices by producing firms to help prevent unfair competition and discrimination; it authorizes the High Authority to prescribe the conditions under which the firms must
publish their prices.

[4] HA, *Rapport spécial sur l'établissement du marché commun de l'acier*, pp. 33–35.

[5] Ervin Hexner, *The International Steel Cartel*, University of North Carolina Press, Chapel
Hill, 1943, pp. 21–22, 180, 182–186, gives much valuable information on the significance of the
price for merchant bars.

Nondiscrimination and price publication involve an "immense revolution," since the member countries themselves have no statutory limits on the freedom of contract in this field; in France, for example, the concept of nondiscrimination is applied only to public services.[6]

Basing Points and Freight Absorption

The mills in the ECSC are free to choose their basing points as long as these are not "abnormal," but they are not required to quote f.o.b. plant. This provision introduces at least one basing point into each producing district. All the mills in the same producing area may therefore align their prices. The provisions of the treaty are thus compatible with a multiple basing point system. If the High Authority finds that a firm has selected an "abnormal basing point," one which enables it to discriminate between buyers or to indulge in unfair competition in another part of the common market, it may address a recommendation to that firm. Such recommendations are binding as to the objective but not the means.

Paragraph 2(b) of Article 60 of the ECSC treaty allows a plant under specific safeguards to absorb freight on sales made at a basing point other than its own. It may therefore penetrate the sales areas served by other producing points. But it may not underprice the other steel mills if it takes advantage of this provision. The treaty authorized freight absorption at the High Authority's discretion, apparently in the belief that it would encourage rivalry and flexibility.[7]

The High Authority may itself limit the amount of freight absorption or eliminate it altogether for the sake of protecting the market against "disturbance." The limitations on price alignment do not prohibit a firm from undercutting its rivals by reducing its own price list and thus taking a lower net return on all its sales, a measure—rare in practice—called uniform price equalization. A plant may not sell above its own price list in order to benefit from higher prices prevailing in another area of the Community.

Since outbound freight costs are an important element in the delivered price of steel, basing points play an important role in pricing practices and have an important bearing on price discrimination. The customer is interested in buying from the nearest plant. Most mills sell part of their production in areas

---

[6] Paul Reuter, *La Communauté Européenne du Charbon et de l'Acier*, Librairie Général de Droit et de Jurisprudence, Paris, 1953, pp. 143–144, 205. Hermann Witte has pointed out that the coal and steel producers experienced difficulty in trying to understand the concept of nondiscrimination in the early years of the ECSC; *Handelsblatt*, December 12, 1956, p. 6.

[7] Freight absorption is authorized in the United States, too. See Fellner, *op. cit.*, p. 307. George W. Stocking, *Basing Point Pricing and Regional Development*, University of North Carolina Press, Chapel Hill, 1954, is recommended for a discussion of basing points in relation to competitive standards of conduct.

that are served by a number of producing districts. Instead of extending its sales area by reducing prices to all customers—uniform price equalization— a mill can, with the help of basing points, tap another sales area without reducing its income on local sales. Market separation is therefore an important element in the ability to maximize average income per unit of sales. When all mills or producing districts are basing points and may absorb freight at other basing points, the practice is called universal freight equalization, distinguished from uniform price equalization. Mills absorb freight in a buyers' market only; the customer otherwise pays the full freight cost. It should also be noted that steel producers in a steel area with a permanent deficit do not necessarily exercise independent initiative in establishing prices for their basing point; they often accept the prices prevailing at a distant basing point instead, and add the freight cost from that point to their own. But long-term considerations discourage the producers in an area with a temporary deficit from raising their prices to the delivered price of the supply coming from other areas for fear of encouraging producers in other areas to encroach on their local outlets.

Freight absorption to meet competition from firms outside the ECSC is allowed under the treaty, but the High Authority may modify this exception in case of abuse, and must be kept informed in any case. This double standard with respect to outsiders also applies to export cartels, which are exempted from the provisions of Article 65.

Subsidies

Subsidies, or "State assistance," are incompatible with the common market (Article 4) and must be abolished according to the terms of the treaty. Article 67, however, authorizes some types of assistance. (See Chapter 13.) Under Article 53, the High Authority has, moreover, authorized "financial mechanisms" common to several firms, as discussed in Chapter 8. Article 62, also, allows the High Authority to authorize interfirm compensation or redistribution of proceeds within and among coal producing districts in order to prevent prices from rising to the cost of marginal production.

The Convention for the Transitional Provisions modified some of the price provisions in the first five years for the sake of easing the transition. The subsidy for Belgian coal, for example, is discussed in Chapter 4. Other subsidies were also allowed in the transitional period. Section 24(a) of the Convention for the Transitional Provisions allowed the High Authority to authorize zonal prices for coal for a limited time.

The governments have continued to provide direct subsidies with or without the consent of the High Authority. The Common Assembly has suggested that the treaty provisions with respect to subsidies be loosened because a rigorous prohibition is not compatible with the problems created in the coal industry by the business cycle.[8]

Violations

The High Authority may fine a producer for violations up to twice the value of an irregular sale, and may double the fine for the second offense (Article 64).

Producers, Merchants and Customers

The price provisions of the treaty fall on the producer. The treaty deals only indirectly, either through the States or through the producers, with the activities of merchants and customers. The High Authority, under Article 63, may require the producers to make their customers and agents comply with the rules. The High Authority may also address recommendations to the States, requesting them to require merchants and customers, particularly public services, to comply with paragraph 1 of Article 60 dealing with discrimination. The High Authority may order a producer to boycott a merchant or customer who violates the law.[9]

Maximum and Minimum Prices

The foregoing price provisions are designed to protect the competitive system itself. Other provisions subject price determination to public control by the Community. The member governments are devoid of unilateral power in this respect. Article 61 provides for price control in a number of cases. Maximum prices may be established to keep prices as low as possible, consistent with "normal returns on invested capital," according to Article 3(c). When a firm enjoys a monopoly in any part of the market, the High Authority may issue a recommendation to prevent it from abusing its power; if the recommendation is ignored, it may fix prices after consulting the government involved (Article 66 paragraph 7).

The High Authority's power to fix minimum prices is more restricted than its authority to fix maximum prices. Minimum prices may be fixed only in potential or actual periods of "manifest crisis"—in case of a business recession and in conjunction with other measures made possible by Article 58. This article provides a number of measures to deal with a recession and authorizes the creation of obligatory cartels.[10]

---

[8] CECA, Assemblée Commune, *Révision du traité instituant la Communauté Européenne du Charbon et de l'Acier*, Luxembourg, n.d., p. 20.

[9] Reuter, *op. cit.*, pp. 113–114, criticizes the treaty for having taken a "detour" to make merchants and customers conform instead of having openly adopted the principle of making the States responsible to the ECSC for their behavior.

[10] See *ibid.*, pp. 199–200, 236.

Export Prices

Article 3(f) obliges the Community to observe "equitable limits" on export prices in order to protect customers in third party countries in a sellers' market. The treaty also authorizes the introduction of minimum export prices in order to protect the producers in the Community in a buyers' market. According to Article 61, the ECSC must in either case act in "accordance with methods adapted to the nature of the export markets . . . if such action can be effectively supervised and appears necessary either because of dangers to the enterprises resulting from the state of the market or to pursue in international economic relations the objective defined in Article 3 paragraph (f)."

Procedures

The High Authority must consult the Council of Ministers and the Consultative Committee before defining the conditions under which prices must be published and before fixing maximum and minimum prices. It must consult the Consultative Committee before establishing intradistrict compensation for coal mining firms and must consult the Council as well before establishing compensation between districts. In establishing maximum and minimum prices, the High Authority must make joint studies with the firms and their associations to determine the facts. A member State may propose to the Council that maximum or minimum prices be established and the Council by unanimous decision may require the High Authority to take such action.

INTERNATIONAL PRICE DISCRIMINATION

Price discrimination may be defined as unequal net mill returns on comparable sales, and the converse. A common form of price discrimination rests on the separation between foreign and domestic markets.[11]

Since there are a greater number of rivals in the foreign than in the domestic market, coordination among rivals is more difficult and is harder to attain by spontaneous methods. Formal export agreements beween national groups of steel producers thus characterize the steel industry over a large part of its history. (See Chapter 6.)

Since domestic markets are more easily controlled, the steel producers in most countries can increase their total revenue by making domestic steel prices less flexible than export prices. This practice coincides with the fact that the domestic market absorbs the major part of their output. Domestic

---

[11] An excellent discussion of the varieties and causes of international price discrimination is to be found in Milton Gilbert, *Export Prices and Export Cartels*, Temporary National Economic Committee Monograph No. 6, Washington, 1940; the factors that determine whether export prices are above or below or equal to domestic ones are discussed in pp. 63–90 therein.

steel prices in Belgium-Luxembourg, on the other hand, tend to be (but are not quite) as flexible as export prices—with a time lag—because the foreign market absorbs most of the steel produced by those two countries.

As a result of the fact that world steel prices are in general more flexible than domestic prices, world steel prices have been lower than domestic prices in the

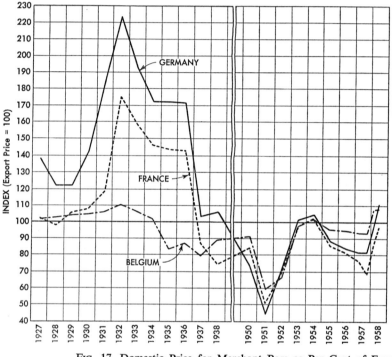

FIG. 17. Domestic Price for Merchant Bars as Per Cent of Export Price, Selected Countries, 1927–1958

Source: Table 7-2, Appendix E.

steel producing countries when business is poor and higher when business is good. (See Fig. 17, based on Table 7-2, Appendix E.) The producers argue that the ability to increase rates of operation by exporting a greater volume at lower prices also helps the domestic consumer because average costs decline with higher rates of operation. Lower average costs, they assert, mean lower domestic prices than would otherwise be necessary or higher profits with which to modernize the industry, both of which benefit the domestic economy.[12]

[12] The *Report of the Import Duties Advisory Committee on the Present Position and Future Development of the Iron and Steel Industry*, HMSO, London, July 1937, p. 53, presented this argument, pointing out that British export prices in the late 1930s barely covered out-of-pocket costs and that home prices provided a profit over and above total costs.

Domestic prices for merchant bars were considerably higher than world prices in most countries in the interwar period, when operating rates were never at capacity except in isolated instances; they were especially high by comparison with world prices in the early 1930s because domestic market control was maintained in spite of the collapse of international steel agreements. The world price for heavy rails was, however, more stable than that for merchant bars during the Great Depression because the international heavy rails cartel survived the depression.[13] German domestic steel prices, which are especially inflexible, were consequently much higher relative to world prices in the interwar years than those in the other countries. The difference between domestic and world prices in the interwar period was smallest in Belgium-Luxembourg. Domestic steel prices in Britain in the early years of the Great Depression were lower than world prices because the British producers were not organized until 1932–1933, when domestic prices began to exceed world prices in that country too. The world price for merchant bars f.o.b. Antwerp dropped 60 per cent from 1929 to 1932 but domestic prices for that product dropped only 20 per cent in Germany in the corresponding period, 30 per cent in France, 55 per cent in Belgium and 42 per cent in the United Kingdom. (See Table 7-1, Appendix E.)

Domestic steel prices were below world prices after World War II as a result of the sellers' market that characterized that period, with the exception of 1953–1954 and 1958, when the differentials narrowed. The price for merchant bars f.o.b. Antwerp rose by 38 per cent from 1954 to 1957 but domestic prices rose by only moderate degrees in Germany and France, and by nearly 25 per cent in Belgium, the United Kingdom and the United States. Similarly, world prices dropped at least 25 per cent from 1957 to mid-1958, though domestic prices remained relatively stable with the exception of those in Belgium-Luxembourg.

Entente de Bruxelles

The producers in the ECSC established a cartel in March 1953 (already described in Chapter 6), two months before the common market for steel began, to better coordinate their behavior in the world steel market as the sellers' market began to show signs of weakening.

The export cartel seems rudimentary by comparison with the second agreement of the Entente Internationale de l'Acier (EIA), effective from 1933 to 1939, but lack of evidence regarding the operations of the Entente de Bruxelles makes it difficult to say exactly how rudimentary it is. It does not seem to have a separate entente to coordinate sales and prices for each main product and

[13] Hexner, *op. cit.*, pp. 29–30.

relies mainly on minimum price control and a uniform basing point at Antwerp. The price at Antwerp applies also for shipment through Dunkerque and Caen in France. Each national group furnishes a representative to the Entente de Bruxelles, implying coordination within each steel producing country. The cartel had only to ride the sellers' market for most of its history from 1953 to 1958, when effective export prices were higher than the official minimum prices it established. Effective export prices tumbled more rapidly than official minimum export prices during the recession of 1958. Official minimum prices fell about 25 per cent in the twelve months ending in mid-1958, but secret price quotations were said to have lowered effective prices by 40 to 50 per cent. French exporters were reported to be undercutting the rest.[14]

There was evidence to indicate that export quotas were in effect part of the time. In July 1957 the Entente de Bruxelles suspended minimum export prices for merchant bars altogether but limited total monthly exports to 83,000 tons; about 70 per cent of this quota was assigned to Belgium-Luxembourg. Minimum prices were restored in August 1957.[15] Export quotas were evidently again apportioned among the national groups during the winter of 1957–1958 but apparently were discontinued thereafter.[16] Fear of the High Authority may have inhibited the members of the entente from openly adopting export quotas at all times. Such quotas would certainly have implied restraint of home markets as well, according to the High Authority.[17]

American and British exporters were not members of the Entente de Bruxelles and there were too many rivals in the market to make that or any other international steel export agreement anything but an unstable arrangement. The Entente de Bruxelles nevertheless had its merits from the point of view of the members. The agreement enabled them to exploit different markets according to circumstances and to keep export prices as high as business conditions permitted. It could not have enabled them to stabilize export prices with the same success as domestic ones. However much stability the members of the Entente de Bruxelles might have wished to create, they had to accommodate themselves to changing situations to avoid being overwhelmed by them.[18]

[14] *Handelsblatt*, August 6, 1958, p. 2, September 19-20, 1958, p. 1. Export merchants contributed to the reduction in export prices by cutting the margins allowed by the producers. The German steel producers consequently reduced the margin in mid–1958 from 5.5 to 3.5 per cent. *Handelsblatt*, August 27, 1958, p. 1. During a buyers' market the members of the Entente de Bruxelles grant a discount for sales to the dollar area, reported to be $10 per ton for merchant bars in 1958. Statistisches Bundesamt, *Preise, Löhne, Wirtschaftsrechnungen*, Teil III, Wiesbaden, summer 1958.

[15] *Bulletin d'information et de documentation*, Banque Nationale de Belgique, Brussels, October 1957, p. 297.

[16] *Handelsblatt*, January 3-4, 1958, p. 1, May 9-10, 1958, p. 1.

[17] *Ibid.*, July 9, 1958, p. 1, July 14, 1958, p. 5, August 6, 1958, p. 2.

[18] Hexner, *op. cit.*, pp. 172–177, 250–251, has called attention to the limits of the steel cartel's price-fixing ability in the interwar period.

Nor is a falling price by itself a symptom of weakness. It accomplishes its purpose if it allows the price cutter to encroach on the rivals' markets in order to keep up his own rate of operation. If official prices are indicative, the British export price for merchant bars declined much less than the Antwerp price, by 7 per cent between March 1957 and July 1958 as compared with 25 per cent for the continental export price, and was considerably higher than the continental export price during the 1958 recession (Table 7-1, Appendix E). The official American export price rose in 1957 and remained stationary thereafter. The members of the Entente de Bruxelles consequently increased their share of the combined exports of the United Kingdom, the United States, Japan and the ECSC countries from 66.3 per cent in the first quarter of 1957 to 69.8 per cent in the corresponding period of 1958, though their exports dropped in volume.[19] They increased their share largely at the expense of exports from the

Table 39

EXPORTS OF STEEL BY SELECTED STEEL EXPORTING AREAS,
AS PER CENT OF TOTAL STEEL EXPORTS, SELECTED YEARS, 1912–1955[a]

| | Annual Average | | | |
Exporting Area	1912–1913	1927–1928	1936–1938	1955
Three main continental[b]	46	55	62	65
United Kingdom	32	28	19	16
United States	22	17	19	19
Total	100	100	100	100

Source: Table 2-3, Appendix E.

[a] Excludes trade between the exporters listed.

[b] Includes Germany, France, Belgium-Luxembourg.

United States, in spite of the fact that they use more manpower per unit of output, because wages are lower and especially because they are more export-minded. The continental steel exporters in fact increased their share of world exports from 1912 through 1955, as indicated by Table 39. The Japanese steel industry, which also practices international price discrimination, is also very competitive in world markets based on lower payroll costs. Its steel export prices have declined relative to those of other countries between 1954 and 1958. Japanese prices for steel plate have helped Japan become a large shipbuilder; and loss of the market for direct steel exports to India, where domestic steel production is expanding, might intensify Japanese competition in durable goods exports.

[19] *The Economist*, July 12, 1958, p. 147. Hexner, *op. cit.*, p. 25, calls attention to the tendency of British and American steel exporters to maintain prices rather than volume during the interwar period.

Structure of Export Prices

The High Authority decided in 1953 that the Entente de Bruxelles does not restrain internal trade and is therefore not illegal (see Chapter 6). But do its export prices conform to the criterion of "equitable limits" in Article 3(f) of the ECSC treaty? Though third-party steel importing countries buy at lower prices than domestic customers in the common market during a recession, they are unhappy when they have to pay higher prices during a sellers' market.

The Scandinavian countries therefore complained to the High Authority and to the General Agreement on Tariffs and Trade (GATT) in 1953. In the winter of 1953–1954 the High Authority decided that prevailing export prices were not unfair to third-party countries inasmuch as they were then in line with, and previously had even been lower than, domestic prices.[20] With subse-

Table 40

EXPORT PRICES FOR SELECTED STEEL PRODUCTS, SELECTED COUNTRIES, MARCH 1957

Product	Export Price Per Metric Ton f.o.b. Port		
	Antwerp[a]	United Kingdom[b]	United States[b]
Merchant bars	$117.41	$121.43	$130.95
Shapes	123.50	156.40	121.25
Wire rod	112.00	...	132.30
Strip	113.00	123.45	113.10
Heavy plate	135.00	161.90	117.05
Sheets	147.65	133.65	134.50

Source: HA, *Cinquième rapport général*, Annexe, Table 26; Table 7-1, Appendix E, this study.

[a] Exports by France, Belgium, Luxembourg, Germany, Netherlands, Saar. Thomas grade for the continental countries (Netherlands excepted).

[b] Open-hearth grade.

quent improvement in business conditions, export prices climbed more rapidly than domestic prices; the High Authority consequently altered its argument later in 1954. It developed the principle at the 1954 session of GATT—where it pledged to maintain reasonable export prices in return for a waiver by GATT of the most-favored-nation clause—that export prices should be compared primarily with world rather than with domestic prices for the purpose of ascertaining whether third-party countries were treated inequitably.[21]

This principle appears to beg the question because the members of the Entente de Bruxelles furnish about two thirds of all the steel exported in the world and therefore establish the world price in certain markets and for certain products. The members of the ECSC also are the largest exporters to all importing markets but Canada and the rest of the Commonwealth. (See

[20] HA, *Troisième rapport général*, April 1955, pp. 32–33.

[21] *Ibid.*, p. 37.

Chapter 2.) The United States is the largest exporter of steel to Canada and the United Kingdom to the rest of the Commonwealth. Owing to the nature of British trade with the Commonwealth, which, exclusive of Canada, absorbs more than 50 per cent of all the steel exported by the United Kingdom, the British had the highest export prices (Table 40) in March 1957—during a sellers' market, the only period that counts for the purpose of determining "equitable limits"—except for merchant bars (for which United States prices were the highest) and sheets (for which the Entente de Bruxelles' prices were the highest). Continental export prices are lowest for bars and wire rod; they are higher than, or equal to, American and British export prices for flat products—strip and sheets. They are higher than the United States, but lower than the United Kingdom, for heavy plate and shapes. The continental exporters specialize in ordinary products, the American and British in flat-rolled products. Each group thus tends to quote the lower price for the product in which it specializes, though the United Kingdom quotes a higher price on heavy plate. Plate and sheet account for only 25 per cent of the exports of Germany, France-Saar and Belgium-Luxembourg combined; they account for 50 per cent of the exports of the United States and United Kingdom combined. Although the two latter countries combined export only half as much steel as do Germany, Belgium-Luxembourg and France-Saar combined, they export as much plate and sheet as the continental exporters.

The continental prices (Table 40), moreover, refer to Thomas steel, the British and American prices to open-hearth steel—Britain and the United States produce virtually no Thomas steel. The two grades of steel are equally acceptable for ordinary products; unless Thomas steel is of ameliorated quality, it is not equally acceptable for other products. Open-hearth steel thus commands a substantial premium over Thomas steel in France, Germany and Belgium-Luxembourg (Table 41). Though continental export prices tend to be lower than British and American export prices for ordinary products, they are much higher where quality counts—especially during a sellers' market.

American and British export prices therefore seem to have only limited bearing on the question of "equitable limits" on export prices during a sellers' market because each of the three major world exporters, the United Kingdom, the United States and the ECSC countries, specializes in different markets and products.

Since all exporting countries practice international price discrimination and since export prices are above domestic price levels when business is good, the only way "equitable limits" could be ascertained would be by comparing the net mill return on domestic and export sales *by the same producer* and not by determining which exporter discriminates the most.

The High Authority in 1958 admonished the steel producers to stabilize export prices, which, it thought, were too variable relative to domestic prices. It argued that it would be in their own interest to do so because high export

Table 41

SCALE OF DOMESTIC STEEL PRICES, BY PRODUCT AND QUALITY, MAIN STEEL PRODUCING COUNTRIES, MARCH 1957[a]

(Price per Metric Ton)

[Belgium, France, Germany, Italy, Luxembourg, Netherlands, United Kingdom, United States]

Merchant Bars		Sections		Wire Rod		Strip		Heavy Plate		Hot-Rolled Sheet	
Country	Price	Country	Price	Country	Price	Country	Price	Country	Price	Country	Price
(1)		(2)		(3)		(4)		(5)		(6)	
					Thomas Steel						
Fr.	$ 89.93	Fr.	$ 91.15	Fr.	$ 93.15	Fr.	$ 99.15	Ger.	$104.00	U. S.	$103.05
Ger.	95.88	Ger.	92.80	Ger.	97.15	U. S.	103.05	Fr.	106.30	Fr.	105.45
U. K.	101.76	U. K.	103.00	U. K.	101.55	Bel.	104.00	U. S.	106.90	U. K.	113.80
Lux.	106.00	Lux.	106.00	Lux.	106.00	U. K.	104.40	U. K.	107.75	Ger.	128.70
Bel.	109.45	U. S.	110.25	Bel.	108.00	Ger.	107.65	Lux.	124.00	Lux.	135.60
U. S.	111.88	Bel.	114.00	U. S.	127.90	Lux.	140.00	Bel.	128.00	Bel.	136.00
					Open-Hearth Steel						
U. K.	$101.76	Ger.	$101.95	U. K.	$101.55	U. S.	$103.05	U. S.	$106.90	U. K.	$116.60
Ger.	104.25	U. K.	103.00	Ger.	106.30	U. K.	104.50	U. K.	107.75	U. S.	125.10
Fr.	110.85	U. S.	110.25	Neth.	118.00	Neth.	119.50	Ger.	117.05	Ger.	139.65
U. S.	111.88	Fr.	112.30	Fr.	121.70	Ger.	120.45	Neth.	127.50	Neth.	143.00
Neth.	128.40	Bel.	136.00	Bel.	123.00	Fr.	121.45	Fr.	128.30	Fr.	147.15
Bel.	132.00	Italy	137.60	U. S.	127.90	Bel.	126.00	Bel.	152.00	Bel.	148.00
Italy	132.00			Italy	136.80	Italy	142.40	Italy	171.20	Italy	172.00

Sources: Col. 1 from Table 7-1, Appendix E; other columns, as well as the data for Luxembourg in col. 1, are from HA, *Cinquième rapport général,* Annexe, Table 25.

[a] Prices, arranged in ascending order, exclude taxes and are f.o.b. plant or basing point. United States prices are f.o.b. Pittsburgh. The United Kingdom and the United States produce negligible quantities of Thomas or Bessemer steel; the Netherlands and Italy produce mainly open-hearth or electric steel. Luxembourg produces no open-hearth steel. In France, Belgium and Germany open-hearth steel accounted for roughly 32 per cent, 11 per cent and 50 per cent, respectively, of total production of crude steel and castings. The United Kingdom and the United States produce mainly open-hearth steel and quote only on open-hearth specifications, but they are also included in the Thomas category because the grades are interchangeable for the common varieties of steel such as merchant bars, shapes, wire rod and in some cases even for strip and flat products where Thomas steel is ameliorated, a practice which is growing rapidly. Nevertheless, in flat-rolled products, where specifications count, open-hearth steel is preferred.

prices encourage importing countries to develop their own steel production and because the metal transforming industries in the ECSC are at a disadvantage when foreign rivals can obtain exported steel at lower prices. It pointed out, furthermore, that a diminishing proportion of total output will go to foreign sales.[22] If the High Authority's forecasts for 1975 materialize, foreign sales, which absorbed 22 per cent of production in 1955, will absorb less than 10 per cent by 1975.

NATIONAL MARKETS ON THE EVE OF THE ECSC [23]

Prior to the establishment of the ECSC the producers relied on formal rather than spontaneous coordination of domestic markets, as described in Chapter 6. Domestic steel prices in Europe were controlled by the respective governments after World War II in order to keep them from running away during the worldwide shortage of steel. Government influence on the decisions of the steel firms therefore increased during that period. The German steel firms in addition were reorganized under allied occupation policies (Chapter 5). Obligatory forms of coordination were therefore predominant.

France

The French steel market was divided into delivery zones; the customer paid the standard freight charge from the basing point—Thionville (in Lorraine) in most cases, though Maubeuge in the northern part of the country was becoming increasingly recognized as a basing point for certain products—whether or not it represented the actual freight. Total billings for freight covered the total industrywide cost of freight. Well-located customers thus helped equalize freight costs for those less well located, while the system of partial basing points equalized locational factors among the steel mills. The principal beneficiaries were the mills in Lorraine since most of the steel produced there is consumed elsewhere; the situation was not unlike that of Pittsburgh in the days of "Pittsburgh plus." The standard freight charges for each delivery zone did, however, reflect the locational advantages of the customer to some extent. The Comptoir des Produits Sidérurgiques, operating with the authority of the government (as discussed in Chapter 6), centralized invoicing and receipts for most carbon steel products in order to eliminate secret discounts and freight absorption, but most mills were otherwise able to deal with their customers directly. The system hardly encouraged innovation and it protected the less efficient producers.[24] The French government, toward the end of 1952, re-

[22] HA, *Sixième rapport général*, Vol. I, pp. 41–43.

[23] See also the section on "Domestic Market Controls on the Eve of the ECSC" in the preceding chapter, pp. 195 ff.

[24] Drawn from *Avis*, Conseil de la République, No. 64, 1952 (cited hereafter as Armengaud Report); see also Emile Manchotte, *Deux formes de comptoir de vente en commun*, Loos, St.-Dié, 1950, pp. 47–55, 70, 74, 86; Reuter, *op. cit.*, pp. 153–155.

voked the authority of the Comptoir des Produits Sidérurgiques over accounts.

Germany

Germany also had a partial basing point system, Oberhausen, in the Ruhr, being the principal point for most products. Steel prices were particularly low in Germany until 1952 (Table 7-1, Appendix E), the government paying a subsidy to keep them down; they were consequently lower than French prices for Thomas steel, whereas the reverse is normally the case. The German government allowed prices to rise in 1952 and abolished formal controls entirely in January 1953.

Other Countries

Italian steel was quoted f.o.b. plant, producers absorbing freight at rival mills. Prices in the Netherlands were quoted f.o.b. Ijmuiden, where the only integrated plant is located. The steel mills in Belgium-Luxembourg sold at standard delivered prices.[25] The steel plants in the United Kingdom also quote standard delivered prices that include the weighted average cost of transport; freight absorption is illegal in the United Kingdom.[26]

PRICE DISCRIMINATION IN DOMESTIC MARKETS

Compulsory Price Publication

The treaty and the rulings of the High Authority make price publication compulsory in order to help enforce the Community's prohibition against price discrimination. Each firm is obliged to publish its prices and other terms five days in advance.[27] The five-day provision makes it harder for a producer to gain an advantage over a rival by a quick change in price. Discounts for quantity and fidelity are allowed if granted to all customers in equivalent circumstances. If a producer grants terms of payment better than those he ordinarily allows, he is expected to add a surcharge.

The mills circumvented compulsory price publication late in 1953 by granting secret discounts during the recession that started that year. It is reported

---

[25] HA, *Rapport special sur l'établissement du marché commun de l'acier*, May 1953, pp. 37–39, and "Aide-memoire sur les pratiques contraires au traité," mimeographed, No. 4603f, p. 8.

[26] *Steel Review*, April 1958, p. 24, and British Iron and Steel Federation, *Yearbooks*.

[27] HA, Decisions 30–53 and 31–53, *Journal officiel*, May 4, 1953.

that actual prices in the second half of 1953 were at times as much as 20 per cent below official published prices.[28]

Early in January 1954, the High Authority issued a series of decisions[29] that permitted the steel firms to deviate by an average of 2.5 per cent by product group from their published prices without revising the published list, provided equal deviations were granted to clients in similar circumstances. (Actual prices at the time deviated by more than 2.5 per cent from published prices.) To facilitate enforcement, the High Authority required each firm to submit periodic data on actual sales prices. New published prices could become effective in one day instead of five days.

The French government challenged these decisions before the Court of Justice as unconstitutional; the Italian government associated itself with the French.

Drawing a distinction between prohibition of price discrimination, which is an end, and price publicity, which is a means, the High Authority argued before the Court:[30]

The rigorous and continuous application of a system of prior price publication for any change, however small, would in effect have prevented free price determination and would have led to producers' agreements incompatible with the Treaty. The rigid system favored by the French Republic would enable the enterprises to dominate the common market, and in addition, would deprive the High Authority of all effective influence over it.

The Avocat Général of the Court, upholding the High Authority's point of view, argued that the treaty should be reconciled with the nature of the steel industry, in which the firms, small in number, can stifle competition by price uniformity and inflexibility.[31]

The Court ruled against the High Authority and upheld the French government on the ground that the treaty made price publication an obligatory means to the prevention of price discrimination and that the concept of nondiscriminatory prices would be devoid of all content in the absence of published prices. Any deviation from published prices or conditions of sale was therefore illegal.[32]

[28] CECA, *Recueil de la jurisprudence de la Cour*, Vol. I, pp. 58, 65; *Europe*, November 9, 1953; Derek Curtis Bok, "The First Three Years of the Schuman Plan." *Princeton Studies in International Finance*, Princeton University Press, Princeton, 1955, p. 37. These departures from the price list do not refer to freight absorption, which was not illegal.

[29] Decisions 1–54, 2–54 and 3–54, *Journal officiel*, January 13, 1954. These decisions were popularly called the "Monnet rebates," after Jean Monnet, then president of the High Authority.

[30] *Journal officiel*, January 11, 1955, p. 550.

[31] *Recueil de la jurisprudence de la Cour*, Vol. I, pp. 35–72.

[32] *Journal officiel*, January 11, 1955, pp. 551–559. The Court decision (No. 1–54) may also be consulted in *Recueil de la jurisprudence de la Cour*, Vol. I.

Since the French, as well as most of the other steel producers, were then deviating considerably from published prices, the French government's intervention against such deviations helped the firms to maintain voluntary discipline for the sake of holding prices.[33] In prescribing sales on the basis of published prices, the Court, going beyond American practice in this respect, has introduced an element that may help curtail rivalry by increasing the area of certainty on which the firms can count. If all rivals were in fact to obey the law and adhere strictly to their published prices, the possibilities for gaining an advantage, which is of the essence, are reduced.[34] Compulsory price publication serves ambivalent purposes. Although its purpose is to curb price discrimination, it may promote coordination as well.

Judicial interpretation in America, which has not made use of the published price concept, has recognized the conflict; the United States Supreme Court has stated that strict enforcement of the Robinson-Patman Act might promote a "price uniformity and rigidity in open conflict with the purpose of other anti-trust legislation."[35] The Robinson-Patman Act (1936) accepted a difference in cost as the basis for a legal difference in price. But problems of definition and of interpretation have discouraged American firms from using differences in cost as a defense. The United States courts have in fact ruled that the plaintiff must prove that a particular price discrimination promotes monopoly.[36] This ruling places the matter in its functional setting, to the extent that price discrimination undermines competition when powerful firms use it to drive their rivals out of business or to bring them to terms. Laws against price discrimination therefore aim to protect the competitive system, usually by protecting smaller firms.

By introducing the notion of "comparable sale," the ECSC treaty likewise (but implicitly) uses cost as the basis for distinguishing between legal and illegal differences in the net mill return. But the concept of price discrimination, apart from the matter of departures from the published price, has not yet received judicial interpretation in the ECSC.

While the improvement in business activity at the beginning of 1955, when the Court annulled the "Monnet rebate," had made the immediate issue academic, the principle at issue was by no means laid to rest. There have been

---

[33] H. Burckhardt, Generaldirecktor, Eschweiler Bergwerksverein, Aachen, declared that the "competitive" and nondiscriminatory price requirements of the treaty have contributed to the stability of coal and steel prices; *Handelsblatt*, November 14, 1956. See also Bok, *op. cit.*, pp. 35–37.

[34] See A. Adelman, "Effective Competition and the Anti-Trust Laws," in *Harvard Law Review*, September 1948, p. 1289; Corwin Edwards, *Maintaining Competition*, McGraw-Hill, New York, 1949, p. 167.

[35] *Automatic Canteen Co. vs. FTC*, 346 U. S. 61, 63 (1953).

[36] *Goodrich Co. vs. FTC*, U. S. D. C., Dist. Col., 1955.

several suggestions, notably from the Netherlands government, to modify the treaty for the sake of greater price flexibility. The Common Assembly has recommended that Paragraph 2 of Article 60 be revised for this purpose, a change that was still pending as of 1959.[37]

Specific Discriminations

The treaty eliminated one important type of discrimination within the common market. The shipment of steel from one member country to another was a foreign sale prior to the ECSC and was consequently subject to the prevailing practice of international price discrimination. Such systematic discrimination by one national group of producers selling in the market of another member country has since been prohibited; the producer must now take the same net mill return as he takes on his published price list, or a lower one if he absorbs freight to align prices.

The High Authority modified the German practice by which transportation charges for delivery in Germany ceased 220 kilometers from the Ruhr basing point. Transportation charges beyond that distance are paid from a fund financed by a charge on all German consumers of steel; the net mill return to the steel mill is therefore not disturbed. The High Authority permitted this practice to continue but ruled that steel producers in Lorraine and in the Saar should also benefit from this equalization scheme on sales in southern Germany, which is over 220 kilometers from the Ruhr.[38] Prices in southern Germany are thus on a zonal basis. The Germans adopted this postwar measure to aid the outlying provinces that had been deprived of their commerce with the Russian zone and to which a large number of unemployed refugees had fled.[39]

DOMESTIC PRICE TRENDS

The High Authority ruled in May 1953 that steel prices should be free from the influence of individual governments, for the first time since World War II. The High Authority itself set no ceiling or floor on price movements. What happened afterwards?

The national steel groups had theretofore established uniform domestic prices based on government price ceilings. In anticipation of, and in response to, the High Authority's ruling, each national steel group apparently aligned

---

[37] *Révision du traité instituant la Communauté Européenne du Charbon et de l'Acier*, p. 23; *Handelsblatt*, December 13–14, 1957, p. 1; *Le Monde*, October 24, 1957, p. 14.

[38] HA, *Sixième rapport général*, Vol. II, pp. 62 ff. This source may be consulted for details on other particular discriminations on which the High Authority took action.

[39] *Ibid.*

its published domestic price with the minimum export prices that they had established in the Entente de Bruxelles. The result was a remarkable twofold phenomenon: (a) For the first (and only) time official domestic prices in 1953–1954 in all the major steel producing member countries were nearly equivalent to official export prices. (See Table 7-2, Appendix E.) (b) Since each national group in the ECSC had apparently aligned prices with the same export price

Table 42

COMPARATIVE INTERNAL PRICES OF MERCHANT BARS,
GERMANY, FRANCE AND BELGIUM, SELECTED YEARS, 1927–1958

Year	Annual Average Price as Per Cent of Price in Germany		
	Germany	France	Belgium
1927	100	74	74
1928	100	80	84
1932	100	78	63
1937	100	84	77
1950	100	114	124
1951	100	113	134
1952	100	98	95
1953	100	97	97
1954	100	98	97
1955	100	96	108
1956	100	97	113
1957			
March	100	94	114
October	100	84	114
1958			
January	100	87	110
February	100	87	110
July	100	87	98

Source: Table 7-1, Appendix E.

scale, domestic prices were also remarkably uniform between the different countries—another phenomenon that had theretofore been rare and that proved to be short-lived. (See Table 42.)

As this event happened to coincide with the beginning of a business recession, and as ingot production in the ECSC in 1953 dropped 5 per cent below that of 1952 (Table 2-2, Appendix E), the producers found they could not hold the published domestic prices. But they gave secret discounts instead of reducing the published prices. The uniformity was therefore apparent rather than real.

After the temporary and misleading signs of Communitywide price uniformity in 1953–1954, domestic steel prices in the several countries of the Community again took on their habitual national characteristics in spite of the common market. Price policies and price changes still emanated from the individual national groups of producers, each acting as a whole in consultation with its government. Price changes were not generalized throughout the Community; while they occurred simultaneously for all the producers in the same country, they occurred at different times from one country to another. Firms in the same country discussed prices among themselves:[40]

Producers appear to have consulted together on the extent and timing of price changes and Governments continued to influence price decisions by informal pressure on producers and by threatening to ignore increases of which they disapproved when adjusting the controlled prices of articles manufactured from steel.

The High Authority expressed its disapproval in 1958 by citing the fact that prices had evolved according to the nationality of the producer, that prices were uniform, and changed simultaneously, within each country. Traditional national ties between producers and customers, and intervention by governments and national producer associations, were responsible for this phenomenon, according to the High Authority.[41]

The governments are interested in stable home prices and income, and in adequate supplies, though their concepts may differ as to the level at which prices should be stabilized. Since steel enters into many other products, the price of steel affects the competitive position of durable goods in export markets. This consideration carries much weight in government policy; it has not been unusual to compensate exporters of metal goods when home steel prices were higher than export prices. The governments expect the steel firms to furnish a reasonable amount of steel to the home market even though home prices may be lower than export prices. Higher export prices compensate the steel firms for stabilizing home prices when business is good; stable home prices, on the other hand, subsidize falling export prices when business is bad. This pattern coincides with government interest in stabilizing income. With or without the ECSC, the steel industry is treated as an integral part of the national economy by the respective member governments.

The European Parliamentary Assembly adopted a resolution in June 1958 inviting the governments to cease interfering with steel prices, which, it said, promoted concerted action among the firms, and the High Authority to make an inquiry into coordinated behavior on national lines.[42] The High Authority

---

[40] *Steel Review*, British Iron and Steel Federation, April 1958, p. 25. See also *Britain and Europe*, Economist Intelligence Service, London, 1957, p. 72.

[41] HA, *Sixième rapport général*, Vol. II, pp. 72–73.

[42] HA, "Communauté Européenne," *Bulletin mensuel d'information*, July-August 1958, p. 2.

launched an inquiry in July 1958 into the causes of price uniformity in the German steel industry with relation to Article 65, which deals with cartels.[43]

HOME PRICES OVER THE COURSE OF THE BUSINESS CYCLE

How did prices react over the course of the business cycle?

Business was very good from mid-1954 to mid-1957 and contracted thereafter. Home steel prices through 1955 tended to stability, and even declined relative to general wholesale prices, in all member countries but Belgium and the Netherlands, as is shown by Table 43, where the data refer to weighted average composite prices.[44]

After 1955 home prices diverged sharply between countries along traditional national patterns. This phenomenon caused the High Authority to criticize the governments, especially the French, for intervening and to recommend that they reconcile national policy differences within the Council of Ministers.[45]

Germany

Home steel prices rose considerably in Germany from 1953 to early 1958, but less than export prices—a case of stabilization of home prices at high levels. Real home prices rose more in Germany than in France or Italy but less than in Belgium and the Netherlands (Table 43). (Italy is a special case discussed later in this chapter.) German prices tend normally to be higher than French prices for most products of the Thomas steel grade and lower for most products of open-hearth grade (Table 41). As Germany is a steel importing country, especially during periods of high business activity, the German steel industry to some extent aligns domestic prices with delivered costs of imported steel of Thomas grade, which grade accounts for only half its output (68 per cent in France and 90 per cent in Belgium). All steel prices rose as wages rose and also, with the government's consent, as a greater degree of internal financing was required when accelerated amortization expired toward the end of 1955.[46] But a countercyclical increase in home steel prices made late in 1957

---

[43] *Usine nouvelle*, July 24, 1958, p. 9. The study was not completed as of this writing. This inquiry caused *Handelsblatt*, July 12, 1958, p. 12, to carry an editorial, entitled "Why Us?," asserting that the behavior of the steel industry in Germany was no different from that in other member countries.

[44] In the *Quatrième rapport général*, April 1956, p. 61, the High Authority commented: "Internal prices in the Community—which have been free since the creation of the common market for steel—still gave proof of great stability in 1955 and the beginning of 1956, in spite of the increasing tension between supply and demand."

[45] HA, *Cinquième rapport général*, April 1957, pp. 108–110.

[46] *Financial Times*, October 2, 1956; *Handelsblatt*, September 28 and October 12, 1956.

—when export prices were falling—aroused the government's displeasure. The latter failed to raise prices at the two steel mills in Lower Saxony which are State-owned and controlled, much to the displeasure of the mills in the

Table 43

AVERAGE REAL WEIGHTED PRICE OF STEEL,
SELECTED STEEL PRODUCING COUNTRIES, SELECTED MONTHS, 1954–1958

(1953 = 100)

Country	July 1954	January 1955	January 1956	January 1957	December 1957	February 1958
Germany						
Steel prices	95	96	100	107	112	112
General wholesale prices	98	100	102	105	106	106
Real price of steel	97	96	98	102	106	106
France						
Steel prices[a]	96	96	98	104	...	122
General wholesale prices	98	98	102	105	119	120
Real price of steel	98	98	96	99	...	102
Belgium						
Steel prices	95	96	111	114	118	116
General wholesale prices	98	100	103	106	106	104
Real price of steel	97	96	108	108	111	112
Italy						
Steel prices	94	97	101	114	110	104
General wholesale prices	100	102	103	104	103	102
Real price of steel	94	95	98	110	107	102
Netherlands						
Steel prices	95	100	107	113	117	116
General wholesale prices	100	102	104	109	107	106
Real price of steel	95	98	103	104	109	109
United Kingdom						
Steel prices	102	99	106	120	131	131
General wholesale prices	101	102	107	110	113	113
Real price of steel	101	97	99	109	116	116
United States						
Steel prices	109	109	116	127	134	134
General wholesale prices	100	100	102	106	108	108
Real price of steel	109	109	114	120	124	124

Sources: Steel prices, referring to average weighted price of all products, are from HA, *Sixième rapport général*, Vol. II, p. 177. The wholesale price index figures are from OEEC, *General Statistics*, and the UN, *Monthly Statistical Bulletin*. The wholesale price figures from 1954 to January 1956, inclusive, are for the quarter in which the month occurs; thereafter they refer to the particular month.

[a] Owing to the devaluation in August 1957, the figures for France are based on local currency.

Ruhr. This event marked an important break in price uniformity, for a short period at least.[47] Phoenix-Rheinrohr indicated in its financial report for 1956–1957 that domestic prices had been raised to offset declining export revenue

[47] *Handelsblatt*, January 3-4, 1958, p. 1, March 5, 1958, p. 1.

and that further increases might be required if export revenue continued to fall.[48] Led by the August Thyssen Hütte, the German steel firms cut operating rates in April 1958 in order to maintain home prices.[49] Production in mid-1958 was about 15 per cent below capacity but actual output was not much lower than that in 1957 because the industry had meanwhile expanded. Published home prices held (Tables 43 and 7-1, Appendix E) except for a decline in the prices of flat products, which had been quite high.[50]

The effect of the recession on the steel industry in the ECSC was much less, and came much later, than in the United States. The output of ingot steel in the ECSC in the first six months of 1958 was still 1 per cent above the corresponding period of 1957. But the output had fallen 7 per cent in Belgium, 3 per cent in Italy and Luxembourg, and had risen 8 per cent in France; German output had remained constant. Steel output in the ECSC for 1958 as a whole was expected to decline only 2 per cent from that of 1957. American mills in early 1958 were at about 60 per cent of capacity; the British mills were also more sharply affected than those in the ECSC.

France

Published domestic prices in France are also stable relative to export prices, but they tend to be stabilized at the lowest levels in the Community. The French government has had difficulties with inflation since the first world war and has consequently encouraged low home prices for steel since then. With a large surplus of steel for export, the low-price policy also coincides with the desire of the French steel industry to discourage foreign rivals from invading the French market. Government price control in France has been quite overt since the "Pinay blockage" in 1952 in spite of the fact that French steel prices are legally free. Under the Pinay blockage, end-product manufacturers must absorb an increase in the cost of domestic raw materials unless they are expressly authorized to raise the price of the end product; they are not required to absorb an increase in the price of imported materials. This regulation blocked the steel industry from raising home prices without government consent and forced it to negotiate every price increase with the government.

Real steel prices rose least in France between 1953 and early 1958—by 2 per cent only compared with 6 per cent in Germany, 12 per cent in Belgium and

---

[48] *Ibid.*, January 10-11, 1958, p. 14. The Netherlands member of the ECSC Council of Ministers, referring to the possibility of concerted action, questioned the economic relation of rising prices and declining demand. *Ibid.*, December 20–21, 1957, p. 2.

[49] According to *ibid.*, March 26, 1958, p. 9, the August Thyssen Hütte announced a 20 per cent cutback in operations effective in April in order to help maintain internal prices. See also *Financial Times*, March 27, 1958, p. 1.

[50] *Usine nouvelle*, July 24, 1958, p. 9.

9 per cent in Holland (Table 43). The French steel industry having complained of limited possibilities for internal financing, the president of the High Authority intervened several times with the French government on its behalf.[51] A price increase in April 1957 followed a reported agreement between the French government and the steel industry, the former promising low interest loans for expansion and the latter promising to hold prices down thereafter. The High Authority requested the French government to comment on the subject.[52]

Since French steel prices had not risen enough to offset the devaluation of the franc in August 1957 and December 1958, the Thomas grade of French steel could in 1958 be delivered nearly everywhere in the Community without freight absorption at prices below those charged by local steel producers.[53] In 1958 French home prices for products of open-hearth grade were also lower than those for comparable products in other parts of the ECSC although open-hearth steel commands a substantial premium in France and French home prices for that quality are normally among the highest in the ECSC (Table 41).

French home steel prices expressed in local currency did not decline in the business recession of 1957–1958 because they were already low and because the recession affected France much less than it did the other countries. France was the only major European steel producing country where home prices were still below export prices in July 1958 (Table 7-2, Appendix E).

Belgium-Luxembourg

Home steel prices in Belgium follow the market nearly as much as do export prices; they are consequently almost as variable. The Belgian domestic market absorbs only about 25 per cent of Belgian steel production and is consequently too small to protect total revenue during a slump. Hence Belgium has had a low steel tariff, too. As a member of Benelux, the Netherlands has had an equally low steel tariff. Dependent largely on exports, the Belgian steel firms are extremely aggressive. This pattern was obvious in the early 1930s, when they reduced export prices by nearly 60 per cent between 1929 and 1931. In that period their total output dropped 30 per cent; output dropped 44 per cent in Germany and 42 per cent in France because the steel firms in these countries were unwilling to meet Belgian competition in world markets at those prices. The domestic price for merchant bars in Belgium in 1932 was about half the domestic price in Germany. When the second EIA was organized in 1933, Belgium-Luxembourg insisted on and obtained a larger ex-

---

[51] *Le Monde*, March 27, April 14-15, 1957; HA, *Cinquième rapport général*, pp. 108–110.
[52] *Ibid.*, pp. 109–110; *Handelsblatt*, April 15, 1957, p. 1.
[53] HA, *Sixième rapport général*, Vol. II, pp. 72–73; *Handelsblatt*, February 2, 1959, p. 1.

port quota in recognition of the larger share this aggressive policy had achieved.[54]

Belgian steel producers are permitted greater freedom in fixing domestic prices than German, French or British producers. The Netherlands government also allows its steel firms, which export a large portion of their production, to be equally free. Real domestic prices in Belgium, and to a lesser degree in the Netherlands, thus increased more than those in other countries in the ECSC between 1953 and 1958. (See Table 43.) Only the American steel producers are as free to follow the market, home steel prices having increased more in the United States between 1953–1958 than anywhere else (Table 43). British home prices also increased more sharply than those in Belgium. But the increase in British prices, discussed later in this chapter, was due to an increase in government price ceilings to provide additional internal financing and not to a free price policy.

Belgian home prices began falling early in 1958, but not as much as export prices (Table 7-1, Appendix E). The former were nearly 8 per cent over the latter in the first half of 1958; they had not been that much above export prices since the early part of the Great Depression. The decrease of 11 per cent in home prices in Belgium was, however, much more than the drop in home prices in any other country, with the exception of Italy, a special situation. Whereas Belgian and American home prices are both free, American steel prices remained quite stable in spite of a severe reduction in operating rates, while Belgian home prices declined. Though they declined, Belgian home prices were still high relative to the French, and at about the German level, in the first half of 1958; they were above the German level for open-hearth grades.

As a result of variations in national price policies, published home prices diverged in different directions at different times (as Table 42 shows), and were less flexible than export prices. The High Authority pointed out that the differences between home prices in various member countries exceeded the cost of transport between them.[55]

The Common Market Committee of the European Parliamentary Assembly called attention in 1958 to the relation between government influence and concerted action on the part of the firms in the following terms:[56]

. . . when the governments put pressure on the industry's representatives to keep prices from exceeding a fixed level, prices are naturally established at this level, uni-

---

[54] Frederic Benham, *The Iron and Steel Industry of Germany, France, Belgium, Luxembourg and the Saar*, London and Cambridge Economic Service, London, October 1934, pp. 13–14, 16.

[55] HA, *Sixième rapport général*, Vol. II, pp. 72–73.

[56] Doc. No. 12, 1958, p. 30.

formly and by agreement. This procedure not only leads to uniform prices but, what is more important, it stimulates the tendency to make agreements; it is unnecessary to add that the procedure discredits the High Authority, which is responsible for prices under the treaty. It is agreed that national economic policies with respect to business activity are equally operative; it is hardly our desire to question this aspect of the matter. We hope this problem receives a satisfactory solution for the ECSC in the light of Article 103 of the Treaty for the European Economic Community, which stipulates that the member States will adjust their policies regarding the state of business activity in the light of the common interest.

A NOTE ON BRITISH PRICES

That which is accomplished informally—and even in contravention of the ECSC treaty—by the national steel groups in the ECSC and by their respective national governments, is accomplished openly by the British steel industry under the supervision of the government's Iron and Steel Board. The goal in either case is price stability at a level that provides for a high rate of self-financing. Coordination within the British steel industry under government supervision rests on the principle that the industry should be responsible to the community "for the extent to which it serves or fails to serve the community's interests."[57]

The methods by which steel prices are controlled in the United Kingdom, both by concerted action among the firms and by the government's price ceilings that take account of the need for internal financing for expansion, have already been described in Chapter 6. The pattern of control has been summarized by *Steel Review* in the following terms:[58]

While the key unit in the industry remains the individual company, it has long been found that the standards of the companies' service to the community, and their own progress, can be greatly helped by co-operative activities through a voluntary central organization. It is, therefore, the task of the Federation and its associated bodies to carry out common services—such as the assembly and dissemination of information and statistics, the buying of imported raw materials, the development of overseas ore-fields and the provision of ore carriers, central research, and the encouragement of training and accident prevention; to provide machinery for solving problems common to all sections of the industry; and to act as the steel companies' spokesman with other industries, with the Iron and Steel Board, with the Government, and with the public. . . .

. . . the Iron and Steel Board ensure the protection of the public interest by their constant scrutiny of the industry (embracing companies and central organization

---

[57] *Steel Review*, October 1958, p. 1. British policy for steel prices is evaluated in P. W. S. Andrews and Elizabeth Brunner, *Capital Development in Steel*, Basil Blackwell, Oxford, 1952, pp. 76–99.

[58] *Steel Review*, October 1958, pp. 2–3.

alike), by their statutory powers at "strategic" points, and by the ultimate power of public intervention if the industry is thought to be failing in its responsibility to the nation. This system takes account both of the historical background and of the special nature of the industry.

These controls have led *The Economist* to point out: "In dealing with the private enterprise steelmakers the Board's influence is now more effective than any the former nationalized Corporation ever had."[59]

Though the European Coal and Steel Community also has broad supervisory powers under its treaty (Article 54 regarding the supervision of investment projects; Article 46 regarding the preparation of long-term market forecasts; Article 61 regarding price control), it has exercised these powers in much less systematic fashion. By declaring steel prices to be free, the High Authority in fact opened the way to a continuation of control by the member governments, which refused to accept the doctrine that the steel industry should be permitted to escape the orbit of national economic policy. Policy has therefore been better matched with practice by the British government than by the High Authority.

Home steel prices in the United Kingdom rose sharply between 1953–1958. Real prices rose by 16 per cent in that period; this increase was steeper than that in any country in the Community but less than that in the United States, where real prices rose 24 per cent (Table 43). Largely dictated by a policy of providing self-financing for the expansion envisaged in the development program for 1954–1962, this sharp increase brought British home prices in 1958 within the range of prices prevailing in the Community, though British prices for flat-rolled products were still lower than those in the Community, in accordance with the traditional difference in price scales between the United Kingdom and United States, on the one hand, and the Community, on the other. British home prices were, however, still lower than prices in the United States, as indicated by the data below on home prices for selected products on March 30, 1958:[60]

	Sections	Wire Rod	Hot-Rolled Light Sheet
Germany	$106.75	$111.55	$146.50
France	105.75	105.20	138.55
Belgium	122.00	117.00	148.00
United Kingdom	105.80	109.50	129.00
United States	116.30	135.60	136.00

[59] Cited in *ibid.*, p. 3.

[60] HA, *Sixième rapport général*, Vol. II, pp. 392–393. The prices refer to open-hearth steel, with comparable extras added.

British home steel prices for ordinary products had therefore by 1958 caught up with those on the Continent after having been lower during most of the postwar period. This change should allay the fear of steel consumers in the Community that British exporters of finished metal goods enjoy an unfair advantage.

Though British crude steel output in 1958 declined 10 per cent from production in 1957 and was 80 per cent of capacity—better than that in the United States but poorer than that in the ECSC—home prices declined only slightly during the recession of 1958 (Table 7-1, Appendix E). The Iron and Steel Board reduced ceiling prices slightly in March 1958 because the cost of scrap and imported iron ore had fallen and not, in fact, because of the drop in demand. The Board's policy reflects changes in cost rather than in demand. This policy caused *The Economist* to say:[61]

. . . the pricing formula used by the Board . . . does not really appear suitable to take account of demand. And the efficient, economic, and at present much more than adequate supply of British steel that the Board is required to promote under competitive conditions is still being sold by producers upon the principle that maximum prices shall be minimum prices, too.

With the disappearance of the export premium, home and export prices for British steel were, however, fairly equivalent in the 1958 recession for the first time since 1954 (Table 7-2, Appendix E).

PRICE ALIGNMENT AND TRADE BETWEEN THE ECSC COUNTRIES

Having covered the behavior of prices within each home market, trade between different parts of the Community is discussed next.

Trade holds the key to the economic goal of an economic union. If sizable countries that produce similar products with different degrees of effort join an economic union, specialization—and consequently trade between them—will be encouraged. This assumes that trade had previously been hampered by tariffs or cartels and that selling prices in each country will reflect the differences in the marginal cost of producing similar products. It also assumes that producers in an economic union will compete.

TRADE BEFORE THE COMMON MARKET

In 1912–1913 Belgium, France and Germany traded only one half million tons of steel a year between them (Table 2-3, Appendix E). At that time Ger-

---

[61] *The Economist*, July 12, 1958, p. 147.

many controlled the production in Luxembourg, the Saar and the Moselle. Trade between them increased after the first world war to over 2 million tons a year in 1927–1928. But this increase was more apparent than real because deliveries from the Saar, Moselle and Luxembourg, which no longer belonged to the German customs union, showed up as exports. As a result of these changes, Germany, which had imported virtually no steel in 1912–1913, became a fairly large importer—1.5 million tons in 1927–1928. France imported very little before or after the war and imports by Belgium-Luxembourg increased from one half million tons in 1912–1913 to almost 800,000 tons in 1927–1928. This trade was subject to the cartel agreements because the members of the EIA respected their domestic markets, as discussed in the preceding chapter. By 1936–1938, trade in steel between France, Germany and Belgium-Luxembourg had declined to less than one half million tons a year, less than the volume in 1912–1913. Germany still absorbed three fourths of this trade, but entirely from producers in Belgium-Luxembourg. It had by that time completely stopped imports from France.

British imports from Germany, France and Belgium-Luxembourg also declined, from 2.7 million tons a year in 1927–1928 to 0.8 million tons in 1936–1938. This reduction followed the agreements between the United Kingdom and the EIA with respect to British and world markets.

RELATION OF TARIFFS TO TRADE RESTRICTIONS

Interwar Years

All the major steel producing countries were protected by tariffs before the first world war, except for the United Kingdom, which went off free trade in 1932. The tariff on merchant bars in 1913, for example, represented about 25 per cent of the domestic price in Germany, 27 per cent in France, 8 per cent in the United States and about 6 per cent in Belgium. Italian rates were very high; the Netherlands had no duty before the first world war.[62] After the first world war, rising steel prices caused the rate of protection to decline where the duties were maintained at the old level, as they were in Germany and Belgium. The tariff on steel was reduced by one half in the 1920s in France owing to the government's deflationary policy; it consequently represented only about 15 per cent of the domestic price for merchant bars. The American duty increased somewhat and the Italian duty increased sharply, after the first world war. Tariffs were raised considerably during the Great Depression, except in

[62] For data on import duties on selected products between 1913–1938, see U. S. Tariff Commission, *Iron and Steel*, Report No. 128, Washington, 1938, p. 439. For the relation of the tariff to domestic prices, Ingvar Svennilson, *Growth and Stagnation in the European Economy*, ECE, Geneva, 1954, p. 267.

Belgium-Luxembourg. The German duty nearly doubled but remained about one fourth of the domestic price for merchant bars. The French duty first increased and then fluctuated during the late 1930s as government views oscillated between a protective and a low-price policy.[63] Duties in the United States were increased and represented about one fourth of the domestic price for merchant bars in 1936–1937. United Kingdom policy went through a revolutionary change in 1932 when tariffs were introduced. After 1936, one scale of duties applied to imports under the agreement with the EIA and a higher scale to imports in excess of a historical base period. Since the United Kingdom imported as well as exported steel, it occupied a special position among the major producers. This position was similar to Germany's in some respects, for Germany also had made arragements with the other members of the EIA regarding the importation of steel.

But the tariff was not among the most essential elements of market control after the European Steel Cartel was organized. Market control was achieved by means of quotas, respect for domestic markets, national group cohesion and product ententes. Domestic prices in the 1930s were consequently substantially higher than world prices plus tariff in all countries except Belgium.[64] Though domestic prices often were higher than the world price plus tariff, the steel exporters made no attempt to invade domestic markets. The producers controlled and limited trade among themselves because they thought that price cutting would otherwise occur. Even Belgium, the most aggressive of the continental exporters in the early 1930s, did not invade the German market during that period.[65] Domestic prices consequently did not reflect the world price plus tariff because domestic producers did not have to meet competition from outsiders.

Some writers believe that the steel cartel would have existed without tariffs. Speaking of the steel cartels of the 1930s, a report of the United States Tariff Commission said: "Such complete power renders governmental trade barriers for steel practically superfluous in most European and some non-European countries." Other writers, however, believe on general grounds that cartels cannot exist without tariffs. The national steel groups found that the tariff gave them additional bargaining power. The German steel firms in 1924–1925, as free entry under the Versailles Treaty came to an end, thus requested tariff protection from their government so that their position vis-à-vis the other steel groups might be strengthened during the negotiations for the EIA. Tariffs

[63] See *Iron and Steel*, p. 376, for a description of French tariff changes in the middle 1930s.

[64] Svennilson, *op. cit.*, p. 267, shows the relation of domestic prices to world prices plus the tariff for selected steel products in several countries.

[65] See *Iron and Steel*, Table III, p. 180; Hexner, *op. cit.*, p. 81.

were raised sharply in Britain in 1935 in order to strengthen the British position in the negotiations which culminated in the European Steel Cartel in 1936; the United Kingdom afterward reduced the tariff.[66]

Tariffs on the Eve of the Common Market

On the eve of the common market, tariffs were more substantial on finished steel than on solid fuels. Steel tariffs varied from an average of about 8 per cent ad valorem in the Benelux countries to between 15 to 25 per cent in France and Italy. German duties had been suspended owing to a dearth of steel for consumption. Steel tariffs in Italy were 10 per cent on pig iron, 15 per cent on semifinished steel and 23 per cent on steel shapes. In Italy the tariffs on imports from member countries were not eliminated with the establishment of the common market but were reduced gradually until they were abolished altogether early in February 1958.[67] Tariffs on ordinary steel traded within the union were abolished in all the other member countries in May 1953.

BASING POINTS

Since all the basing points in the ECSC became part of the common market, each basing point became a potential sales point for the producers at any other basing point, a possibility previously hindered by customs barriers. The High Authority made zonal prices and phantom freight illegal but authorized freight absorption between basing points with the sole exception of sales to the Italian market. Since the Convention for the Transitional Provisions authorized Italy to maintain tariffs until February 1958, the High Authority did not allow the steel producers in other areas to absorb freight on sales in the Italian market prior to that date. Buyers were free to select their suppliers and arrange transportation. Even if the customer agrees to take delivery elsewhere, the invoice must show the price at the basing point separately from all other charges. This regulation is supposed to deprive the seller of the ability to evade price regulations, though enforcement would be difficult when a seller absorbs freight or when delivery is made by private carriers that do not publish their freight rates, viz., truck, maritime or international waterway carriers.[68] The number of basing points increased considerably under the ECSC; there were 41 of them as of 1958, representing all the important producing centers.[69] The

[66] For details see Hexner, *op. cit.*, pp. 67, 88, 245–250; *Iron and Steel*, pp. 374, 408, 410.

[67] See HA, *Sixième rapport général*, Vol. II, p. 23, for the interim duties. Italy suspended the tariffs on pig iron and semifinished steel during part of the transitional period because internal production was inadequate.

[68] See HA, Decisions 30–53 and 31–53, in *Journal officiel*, May 4, 1953; Decisions 1–54 to 3–54, inclusive, as well as the "Communication," in *Journal officiel*, January 13, 1954. The question of the publication of freight rates is treated in Chapter 12.

[69] *Steel Review*, April 1958, p. 22, locates them all on a map.

sellers' market from mid-1954 to mid-1957 encouraged the transition to multiple basing points, as it did in the United States after the second world war, because the producers shifted all freight costs to the buyers' accounts. Only during the recessions of 1953–1954 and of 1958 did the steel producers in the ECSC absorb freight, the extent of which is examined later.[70]

By increasing the number of basing points and allowing freight absorption, the Community increased the number of potential rivals. A market was thus thrown wide open to several national steel groups, each accustomed to cartel practices in its own country and mutual respect for neighboring markets. What happened? This question will be analyzed in relation to the business cycle.

TRADE DURING A SELLERS' MARKET (1954–1957)

Steel firms on a multiple basing point system add full freight costs in a sellers' market—or when operating at capacity—when shipping steel to markets outside their local area. For steel from distant regions the customer in a deficit area then pays a premium over the lowest price at which he can obtain supplies from nearby areas. Under Article 60, the steel firms may not align prices upward; they can take advantage of a higher price level in another sales area than their own only by raising prices at their own basing point.[71] Since national price policies in the ECSC, except for Belgium-Luxembourg, do not permit steel prices to react to the home market in accordance with this rule, the ECSC regulations tend to cause steel producers, after satisfying customers in their own country, to export to third-country rather than to other ECSC markets during an economic boom and to absorb freight on shipments to a basing point in another member country only during a recession.

But trade between France, Germany and Belgium-Luxembourg expanded remarkably during the sellers' market from mid-1954 to mid-1957. (The data are in Table 2-3, Appendix E; this table ends with 1955.)[72] The main producers traded 900,000 tons of steel between each other in 1952, on the eve of

[70] Freight absorption in the United States in 1954, a year of recession, represented about one half to one per cent of the total price of American steel; Whitney, *op. cit.*, Vol. I, p. 280. The transition to f.o.b. mill prices in the American steel industry is described in *ibid.*, pp. 260 ff.

[71] See the statement in *Steel Review*, April 1958, p. 25, that internal steel prices would have been equalized throughout the Community if the treaty had allowed upward as well as downward price alignments. This argument assumes that the governments would have allowed producers to starve domestic markets or to raise prices to Belgian, hence to world, levels.

[72] Though trade between the members of the ECSC in 1956 declined 10 per cent from 1955, it rose again in 1957 to the 1955 level. Annual data for 1952–1957 may be consulted in HA, *Sixième rapport général*, Vol. II, pp. 386–387; these figures are not strictly comparable with those in Table 2-3, Appendix E, which excludes, whereas the High Authority data include, pig iron. Table 2-3, Appendix E, covers exports by Germany, France, Saar, Belgium and Luxembourg to each other and to Italy and the Netherlands but not exports by the last two, small in any case, to the other members of the union.

the common market; this volume was more than twice that in 1936–1938. They exported, in addition, nearly 1.2 million tons to Italy and the Netherlands in 1952. A total of over 2 million tons of steel was thus traded within the ECSC in 1952. Exports by the main steel producers to Italy remained fairly constant, at somewhat more than 300,000 tons a year, between 1952–1955. Those to the Netherlands increased from 825,000 tons in 1952 to 1.3 million tons in 1955. Since the Netherlands is a steel deficit area, and a small producer of specialized products only, the growth of exports to that country was not of major significance to this discussion; German exporters, followed by Belgium-Luxembourg, were the main beneficiaries of the growth of imports by the Netherlands.

More remarkable was the growth in trade between the main producers in the union. From 900,000 tons in 1952, it increased to 2.9 million tons in 1955—more than threefold. Steel exports by the main producers in the ECSC to the rest of the world (exclusive of Italy and the Netherlands) increased only 22 per cent in the same period—from 6.8 million tons to 8.2 million tons. Trade among the main producers in the ECSC accounted for less than 4 per cent of their output in 1952 and for nearly 9 per cent of it in 1955.

This growth will be examined by taking each strand of the steel trade separately, bearing in mind that it was not accompanied by freight absorption or by a displacement of production or operating rates from one area to another. All producers operated at capacity.

Exports to Belgium-Luxembourg

Exports to Belgium-Luxembourg by France-Saar and Germany increased least in volume—from 55,000 tons in 1952 to 165,000 tons in 1955; in both years these imports accounted for about 6 per cent of the total trade between the main producers in the ECSC. Nearly 40 per cent of the steel exported to Belgium-Luxembourg by France-Saar and Germany in 1955 was in crude and semifinished form for further processing within the Belgian steel industry itself and therefore was not the result of commercial rivalry.

Exports to France-Saar

Exports by Germany and Belgium-Luxembourg to France, not a large steel importer, increased from 23,000 tons in 1952 to 570,000 tons in 1955. Nearly 80 per cent of the steel exported in 1955 came from Belgium-Luxembourg, the rest from Germany; France imported virtually no steel from outside the Community. France experienced a shortage of crude and semifinished steel for the integrated and nonintegrated rolling mills and a shortage of strip for the sheet mills. Crude steel, semifinished steel and strip accounted for nearly 60 per cent of the steel exported to France-Saar in 1955. These exports therefore could not have reflected any commercial rivalry among producers of finished steel.

Exports to Germany

Exports to Germany by Belgium-Luxembourg and France-Saar accounted in 1955 for three fourths of the total volume of trade between the main producers in the ECSC and increased from 800,000 tons in 1952 to 2.2 million tons in 1955. Why this large rise in trade?

(1) Since southern Germany takes a substantial amount of steel from the Saar, German imports are in part a statistical phenomenon that depends on whether the Saar is in the German or the French customs union. Thus Germany imported 1.5 million tons of steel a year in 1927–1928 if the Saar were to be considered outside, and 1 million tons if it were to be considered inside, the German customs union. From the second world war to the beginning of 1957 the Saar was outside Germany. But if the Saar is considered part of Germany in the years 1950 to 1955, imports by Germany—from France and Belgium-Luxembourg—are as follows:[73]

	The Saar in France	The Saar in Germany	Deliveries from the Saar
	(Thousands of Metric Tons)		
1950–1951	143	43	100
1952	822	662	160
1953	990	720	270
1954	1,477	963	514
1955	2,206	1,550	656

When the Saar is considered part of Germany, German imports are reduced by roughly 30 per cent. Deliveries from the Saar increased more than fourfold from 1952 to 1955, reflecting the Saar's propinquity to southern Germany but the Saar delivered hardly any steel to the Ruhr. But when the Saar is part of Germany, French "imports" increase because the Saar also exports to France.

(2) Germany has been a steel importing country because its steel production has not kept pace with consumption at peak demand. This situation was true even during the restrictionist interwar era. Steel consumption in Germany increased at an annual rate of 1.39 per cent in 1913–1937; production increased at a rate of only 1.07 per cent. The corresponding rates in 1936–1955 were 2.23 per cent and 1.81 per cent.[74] Germany is the only country in the

---

[73] Data on Saar exports to Germany are from the yearbooks of the *Wirtschaftsvereinigung Eisen- und Stahlindustrie* and British Iron and Steel Federation.

[74] Calculated from data in Tables 2-2 and 7-3, Appendix E. These rates are adjusted for territorial changes.

ECSC where steel consumption grew more rapidly than production between 1936 and 1955. Since the Ruhr is a very favorable site for steel production (see Chapter 3), the wars, rather than a deterioration in relative efficiency, are probably responsible for the fact that production has not kept pace with consumption.

(3) German requirements for finished steel have outstripped the capacity of the rolling mills, and the capacity of the rolling mills has outstripped the capacity of the crude steel producing furnaces in recent years. Ingot steel and semifinished steel thus accounted for nearly one third of the steel exported to Germany in 1955 by Belgium-Luxembourg and France (deliveries from the Saar excluded) and even the Ruhr steel mills imported steel at premium prices for further finishing.[75]

Germany exported 2.5 million tons of steel in 1955 and imported 2.3 million tons; it thus had a small export surplus. German trade, then, is based on its desire to maintain its position in export markets, on the exchange of products, and on the needs of southern Germany.

The growth in the steel trade during the sellers' market cannot thus lead to any simple conclusions regarding the growth of rivalry. It was probably primarily the result of the economic boom. But steel consumers in the Community nevertheless benefited from the fact that price discrimination for sales within the Community had been abolished.

TRADE IN A BUYERS' MARKET

Competition can be tested when producers have surplus capacity. It should be noted that the issue in this context is price competition between producers in different countries; the behavior of producers in the same country has already been discussed above, where it was noted that domestic prices remained fairly stable during the 1958 recession and that countrywide domestic price uniformity continued.[76]

While the steel producers in the Community are no longer protected by tariffs or other customs barriers, several other factors must be kept in mind in determining whether or not changes in the volume of trade are caused by greater specialization owing to differences in efficiency.

(1) When producers absorb freight by aligning prices on a basing point other than their own, they forego the right to establish an independent price in the rivals' market. It would be illegal for them to undersell the rivals under

---

[75] Niederrheinische Hütte A. G., *Geschäftsbericht, 1954–1955*, p. 14.

[76] Price uniformity follows both from perfect competition and from a market dominated by a few firms. But the two situations give different results with respect to equilibrium, output and profits. See Edward H. Chamberlin, ed., *Monopoly and Competition and Their Regulation*, Macmillan & Co., Ltd., London, 1954, p. 256.

Article 60 unless they reduced prices at their own basing point. If their own price scales enable them to undersell their rivals in the latter's markets, a trade-creating development would occur, provided the lower price scale were the result of greater efficiency. Differences in price in an economic union may, however, be due to currency exchange rates. The French steel producers could thus undersell the producers in the other parts of the Community owing to successive devaluations in 1957 and 1958, which the French government allowed the steel producers to offset to a limited extent only. But the French steel industry was not necessarily the most efficient steel industry in the Community. The German steel producers sought relief by requesting their government to raise the compensatory import duty, a measure that would have been of dubious legality. The Council of Ministers early in 1958 approved a recommendation from the High Authority, based on Article 67, asking the French government to impose a temporary 4 per cent tax on its exports of Thomas grade steel to the other members of the ECSC. But the French government was reported to be considering instead a price increase, which had previously been unsuccessfully requested by the French steel producers.[77]

(2) The assignment of prices to different products produced by the same firm is, furthermore, necessarily arbitrary in relation to costs. Producers may sometimes assign prices to different products from a marketing rather than a cost point of view. The international cartel for heavy rails was thus able to maintain export prices during the early 1930s while prices for merchant bars dropped sharply, though the two products are produced at about the same cost.[78] A firm that produces a wide variety of products can reduce the price on one of them in order to squeeze another firm. The High Authority pointed out, for example, that the nonintegrated rolling mills have been squeezed because prices for pig iron and steel billets have been at times too high in relation to those for finished steel.[79]

(3) The cost of transportation can also interfere with the influence of relative efficiency on the exchange of steel products. If transportation costs differ owing to different freight rate policies in the different countries, then differences in the efficiency of production may be offset or aggravated. (See Chapter 12.)

It is therefore not possible to conclude that every increase in exchange between countries is attributable to differences in efficiency.

These considerations are important in an analysis of trade between mem-

---

[77] *Le Monde*, February 27, 1959, p. 14, March 4, 1959, p. 14; *Handelsblatt*, March 18, 1959, p. 1.

[78] Hexner, *op. cit.*, pp. 172–175, 190–193, discusses the relation between cost and revenue for various products.

[79] HA, *Sixième rapport général*, Vol. I, p. 39.

bers of the union during an economic recession. The recession of 1953–1954 was too short and too early in the life of the ECSC to provide a test. Germany, France-Saar and Belgium-Luxembourg traded about 200,000 tons more steel in 1953 than in 1952 (excluding exports from the Saar to Germany). This increase occurred against the business cycle, for 1953 was a poor business year compared with 1952. Germany, still a deficit area in 1953, absorbed part of this 200,000 ton increase; significant, however, was the fact that Germany and France exported more steel to Belgium in 1953 than in 1952, and Belgium-Luxembourg more to France, though Belgium and France are surplus producing areas. This small increase caused a great deal of comment and probably occurred as a result of secret price rebates made in violation of the treaty. The recession was over by mid-1954 and with it the temptation to invade other markets.

The recession of 1958 provided another test. Production and trade in the first half of 1958 are compared in Table 44 with the figures for the corresponding part of 1957. Though exports by the producers in the ECSC to areas outside the union dropped by 18 per cent, or 900,000 tons (their share of the world steel trade increased at the same time, it will be recalled), their production of ingot steel increased slightly. Their situation was therefore much less serious than that of their counterparts in the United Kingdom and the United States. The recession in the ECSC was as a whole not severe enough, though the producers also operated below capacity, to tempt the steel industry into severe cutthroat competition, but it affected the producers in each country differently. Production in Belgium-Luxembourg dropped by nearly 6 per cent between the first half of 1957 and the corresponding part of 1958. Production in Italy dropped by 3 per cent; that in Germany remained constant while that in France increased by 7 per cent and that in the Netherlands by 20 per cent. The index of industrial production was as follows (1953 = 100):[80]

	Germany	France	Belgium	Luxem- bourg	Italy	Nether- lands
March 1957	146	146	131	128	140	135
March 1958	151	161	120	122	141	130
June 1958	154	162	112	122	151	134

Trade among the members of the ECSC increased from 2.3 million tons in the first half of 1957 to 2.6 million tons in the corresponding part of 1958, a net increase of 11 per cent. Exports by France-Saar to the other members of the union declined though France, without absorbing freight, could then deliver

[80] HA, *Bulletin statistique*. The index for France does not include the Saar; data for June 1958 are preliminary.

many steel products below the prices prevailing in other parts of the union.[81] All the other countries increased their exports. Belgium-Luxembourg furnished 43 per cent of the gross increase in trade among the members of the union, indicating that the producers in those two countries made the most aggressive effort to maintain operating rates. Exports by Belgium-Luxembourg to third-country markets declined by 14 per cent. Exports by the Netherlands to the rest of the union accounted for 21 per cent of the gross increase in trade between the ECSC countries; exports by Germany for 26 per cent; exports by Italy for 19 per cent.

Table 44

STEEL EXPORTS AND PRODUCTION, ECSC COUNTRIES, FIRST HALF OF 1957 AND 1958[a]

(*Thousands of Metric Tons*)

			Destination					
Origin	Germany	France-Saar	Belgium-Luxembourg	Italy	Netherlands	ECSC Total	Third Countries Total	Crude Steel Production
Germany								
1957		110	77	52	253	491	1,293	11,868
1958		129	63	55	272	569	901	11,873
France-Saar								
1957	479		39	90	56	664	1,364	8,651
1958	485		26	68	31	610	1,091	9,276
Belgium-Luxembourg								
1957	281	289		50	411	1,031	1,892	5,010
1958	402	477		54	220	1,163	1,630	4,731
Italy								
1957	—	28	1		—	29	248	3,329
1958	1	56	1		—	58	222	3,216
Netherlands								
1957	83	15	19	6		123	110	580
1958	148	10	16	11		185	159	708
Total								
1957	843	442	136	198	720	2,338	4,907	29,438
1958	1,036	722	106	188	523	2,585	4,003	29,804

Source: HA, *Bulletin statistique.*

[a] Data include semifinished and finished steel but not pig iron.

Which countries absorbed the increase in trade? Imports by France-Saar increased the most, followed by imports by Germany; all the other countries reduced their imports from the other members of the union. Exports of steel to France-Saar by other members of the union accounted for 59 per cent of the gross increase in imports from the other members of the union. The economic

[81] HA, *Sixième rapport général*, Vol. II, pp. 72–73.

boom in France had continued until late 1958. French steel production consequently rose in spite of a decline in French steel exports to all destinations. The strong internal demand for steel explains the rise in imports by France and the decline in its exports, though French steel could then be delivered in other parts of the union at the lowest prices. The rise in exports to France therefore did not displace any French production, though the exporters probably absorbed freight in order to sell in the low-priced French market.

Exports to Germany increased owing to pressure from the Luxembourg producers in the south German market and from Dutch producers.[82]

The Italian Market

The existence of rivalry in a recession can be tested in the Italian steel market. With the highest cost and price level in the Community, the Italian steel market was thrown open in February 1958, when the steel mills in Belgium-Luxembourg and in Germany had surplus capacity. The Italian steel market had been allowed to maintain the tariff, and price alignments in that market had been forbidden, up to that date. When the tariff was abolished, Assider, the Italian steel federation, requested the High Authority to limit the right of producers outside Italy to align prices in the Italian market. The High Authority continued to prohibit price alignments until June 15, 1958 and authorized price alignments thereafter for a one-year trial period. It nevertheless requested all non-Italian steel producers that absorbed freight in the Italian market to inform the High Authority of their sales. This provision enabled the High Authority to keep an eye on the Italian market; the provision might have restrained competition, and could have enabled the High Authority to prohibit price alignment if the Italian steel plants had run into difficulties.[83]

What were the facts? Italian prices for open-hearth and electric-furnace grades of steel were the highest in the Community. Nearly all Italian steel is of those grades. Italian prices were higher still in comparison with prices for the Thomas grade produced elsewhere, which is interchangeable with open hearth for many uses. Until January 1957 Italian steel prices had increased as rapidly as Belgian home prices; i.e., they followed the curve of the "free" steel producers in the Community; thereafter they started dropping in anticipation of

[82] The *Financial Times*, March 26, 1958, p. 1, mentioned an agreement reached early in 1958 between the steel producers in France, Belgium, Luxembourg and Germany. If this report is correct, the producers, at the request of the German steel groups, agreed to refrain from further penetration of the market in southern Germany. The German steel group, in return, agreed to limit exports to third-party countries, accepting a quota for rounds and sections for the first quarter of 1958 which was one third of the volume it exported in the corresponding quarter of 1957. These products account for a large portion of exports by Belgium-Luxembourg. See also *Financial Times*, February 5, 1958, p. 7.

[83] HA, Decision No. 6–58, *Journal officiel*, June 11, 1958, pp. 55 ff; HA, *Bulletin mensuel d'information*, May–June 1958, p. 7; *Usine nouvelle*, June 12, 1958, p. 7.

the day when protection would end (see Table 43). Data on comparative prices for comparable products are shown in Table 45.

Home prices were reduced by 6 to 11 per cent between December 1957 and February 1958 as the end of the tariff approached. But Italian home prices in March 1958 were, depending on the product, still from 15 to 35 per cent above home prices in France and Germany (Table 45). Assuming that geographical protection amounts to 10 per cent of the price, producers in France and Germany could have delivered steel in Italy at prices below those published by the Italian mills and without absorbing freight. The Italian steel producers were, however, particularly apprehensive of invasion from Belgium.[84] According to

Table 45
ITALIAN HOME STEEL PRICES COMPARED WITH THOSE IN OTHER COUNTRIES,
MARCH 1957 AND 1958[a]
(Germany = 100)

Country	Sections		Wire Rods		Heavy Plate		Light Sheet	
	1957	1958	1957	1958	1957	1958	1957	1958
Germany	100	100	100	100	100	100	100	100
France	110	99	105	94	109	98	105	95
Belgium	133	114	116	105	129	112	106	101
Italy	135	115	129	113	146	133	123	108

Source: HA, *Sixième rapport général*, Vol. II, pp. 392–393.

[a] Open-hearth steel only. Prices are f.o.b. basing point. Basing points are: Germany, Oberhausen (heavy plate, Essen; light sheet, Siegen); France, Thionville (sheet and plate, Montmédy); Belgium, Seraing; Italy, Novi Ligure (Genoa).

the domestic prices prevailing in March 1958, Belgian producers could not have invaded the Italian market with open-hearth steel unless they absorbed freight on most products. But since Belgian home prices for Thomas steel were lower than those for open-hearth steel by some $10 to $15 per ton, the Belgian producers could have undercut the Italian price scale for open-hearth steel, without absorbing freight, for those customers who could have used Thomas and open-hearth steel interchangeably. In May 1958 the Italian steel producers reduced prices again by 3 to 10 per cent depending on the product, but were still vulnerable owing to the fact that the price scale for Thomas steel in other countries was still appreciably below Italian prices for open-hearth steel. But exports of steel to Italy from other parts of the union declined slightly between the first half of 1957 and the corresponding half of 1958. (See Table 44.)

Costs of production in Italy are much higher than elsewhere, as indicated in Chapter 3, and the average plant is much smaller. Even the two modern tidewater plants and the two "large" private firms, Falck (Milan) and Fiat

[84] *Financial Times*, February 10, 1958, p. 5; *Handelsblatt*, January 31, 1958, p. 4.

(Turin), are relatively small in this industry where size and efficiency go hand in hand.

Besides the sharp difference between the most efficient Italian plants and the average modern plant in the rest of the Community, there is also a large variation in size of plant within Italy itself. At least 65 small firms, grouped mostly around Milan, with secondary clusters in other parts of the country, produced a total of 1 million tons of crude steel in 1954, or 25 per cent of the Italian output. Seventy per cent of these small firms employ under 1,000 men each.

The extremes of size within Italy itself imply large differences in the cost of operation. Though the smaller plants no doubt survive on the basis of a low capitalization and the fact that the price of scrap declines proportionately more than that of steel during a recession, they are no doubt squeezed when home steel prices fall. In the 1958 recession they complained more of rivalry from Finsider, the State-owned firm that controls more than half the Italian steel output, than from producers in other parts of the ECSC.[85]

If the Italian steel industry fails to develop larger plants, the Italian steel market will present some interesting potentials for creation of trade on the basis of international specialization within the Community, provided the implications of the union are permitted to take effect. Will the Italian steel industry continue to be protected by voluntary self-discipline on the part of the neighboring national steel groups, or by an interdiction on price alignment on the part of the High Authority? Italian steel production had expanded remarkably after the second world war by virtue of protectionism, the sellers' market, and the subsidy for imported scrap. But it will become the "Belgian coal problem" of the ECSC steel industry unless the average size of plant in Italy is raised considerably.

Summary

Market penetration, over and above that attained during the sellers' market, was kept within bounds during the 1958 recession. Though trade did not increase by much during the recession of 1958, it would probably have declined had the economic union not existed. It is equally remarkable that trade did not decline and that the steel mills in one part of the Community held on to the foothold they had gained in the sellers' market in other parts of the Community. In comparison with the interwar years, the volume of trade is high indeed. It remains to be seen whether or not the producers would be able to hold on in a more severe recession, whether they would resort to secret price cutting or whether production quotas would be established by the ECSC.

[85] Assemblée Parlementaire Européenne, *Informations mensuelles*, October–November–December 1958, pp. 77 ff.

RANGE OF MARKET CONTROL

Domestic Markets

The Entente de Bruxelles, which has jurisdiction over about 22 per cent of total ECSC production, presupposes the existence of internal market controls. These controls were at the very least nationwide. *Steel Review* reported that there is a "fairly general belief among the well-informed that some kind of marketing arrangement inside the area . . . was, in fact, already in operation," adding that the head of the High Authority's cartel division "said himself that export cartels will only work in a recession, if there is control of the home market too."[86]

American experience with the Webb-Pomerene Act, under which export agreements are exempted from the antitrust legislation, has shown that the domestic market can be separated from the export market only with great difficulty:[87]

[The existence of international price discrimination] is a clear sign that some impediment is restricting competition in the domestic market, even though it is not an illegal impediment. It is the impediment to domestic competition which creates the problem and demands attention, however, and not the signs of the problem in export price policy.

The formal devices of national market control—quotas, single product ententes, centralized sales, delivered pricing—so characteristic of the interwar period, are now absent. But other forms of countrywide coordination, resting on the fewness of producers, are in use. They involve self-discipline and spontaneity mixed with more organized methods of price discussion arising often from government influence. What would otherwise have prevented higher export prices from drawing steel supplies away from domestic customers? Or what would otherwise have prevented domestic steel prices from falling to world prices during a recession?

Interregional Coordination

The steel firms in the ECSC coordinate some activities in their respective home markets and the national steel groups in the ECSC cooperate with each other in the world market, but do the national steel groups in the ECSC also cooperate interregionally within the common market? Will countrywide coordination be supplanted by Communitywide coordination?

[86] *Steel Review*, April 1958, p. 29.

[87] Milton Gilbert, *Export Prices and Export Cartels*, Temporary National Economic Committee Monograph No. 6, Washington, 1940, p. 93. Cf. Theodore J. Kreps, Economic Adviser to the TNEC, who said, *ibid.*, p. ix, that a monopolistic market is invariably inferable only "when the domestic price is high, completely inflexible and completely under control and the foreign price low, highly flexible and uncontrolled . . ."

The evidence with respect to market penetration is inconclusive.[88] Market penetration could have increased further than it did in the 1958 recession. The penetration attained during the economic boom persisted, on the other hand.

Leon Daum, the only one of the nine members of the High Authority drawn from the steel industry, suggested that the steel industry in the ECSC should adopt price leadership as a form of voluntary discipline. He was impressed with the use of price leadership by the American steel industry, which, he pointed out, had maintained published prices in the 1953–1954 recession in spite of a 70 per cent rate of operation.[89] The steel firms in the ECSC have no Communitywide price leader. A Communitywide price leader would help dissolve the national character of the steel industry and, what is more, it would imply a common policy on the part of all the governments or their complete withdrawal from the picture. Communitywide price leadership cannot therefore be adopted without structural changes, though some of the national steel groups have their own national leaders. No steel firm in the ECSC, be it noted, has a mill or subsidiary in all the main steel producing areas, such as has the price leader in the United States steel industry. Daum suggested, however, that four or five firms in the ECSC were large enough to perform the function jointly.

The High Authority disowned Daum's suggestion on the ground that price leadership based on the emergence of such large firms would create "great tension."[90] But the High Authority also disapproved of the existence of national markets based on the influence of national governments and cooperation between producers in the same country.

By what means other than Communitywide price leadership could the transition to a common market be furthered? The High Authority thought that coordination between governments through the Council of Ministers was the right way to break through the pattern of national markets.[91]

Prospects for Competition

On which notion of competition does the ECSC treaty lean: (a) on competition through a large number of producers; (b) on price cutting by market dominating firms; or (c) on nonprice rivalry among large firms or national groups of firms?

[88] The Common Market Committee of the European Parliamentary Assembly, Doc. No. 12, 1958, pp. 30–31, requested the High Authority to make an inquiry into the question of interregional steel agreements in the Community.

[89] Daum's statement was made at an interview reported in *Steel Review*, April 1958, p. 29. See Fellner, *op. cit.*, pp. 120 ff, for a discussion of the economic power relationships between followers and leaders. Whitney, *op. cit.*, Vol. I, p. 304, discusses price leadership in the American steel industry.

[90] HA, *Bulletin mensuel d'information*, April 1958, p. 2, and *Sixième rapport général*, Vol. I, p. 37.

[91] *Ibid.*, pp. 41–42.

(a) Though the treaty (Article 66) frowns on market dominating firms, the market in each steel producing area is dominated by a small number of corporate groups.

(b) The treaty can therefore refer only to competition among market dominating firms or groups of firms. Here the notion of price competition must come to grips with the nature of (to appropriate the title of William Fellner's book) competition among the few. Price cutting is rare in the steel industry. Home prices within each national market in the ECSC have been, as discussed earlier, uniform and fairly stable even during a recession. When price competition does occur among the few, its characteristic posture is that of cutthroat competition often accomplished by secret discounts—a desire by one firm to inflict losses on the other in order to drive it out of business or to form a new pattern of market shares.[92] Such competition is contrary to the treaty, which seeks to maintain the number of producers by prohibiting unfair competition by secret or discriminatory price discounts and by prohibiting producers from underpricing the firms in other markets than their own unless they change their published prices. The High Authority favors freight absorption and a certain amount of price flexibility with changes in the volume of business, but adds that downward price changes should be limited because prices should never drop to the point where investments are discouraged.[93] The Common Market Committee of the European Parliamentary Assembly thought this policy was too vague.[94] The High Authority's recommendation would not, in any case, allow any room for cutthroat competition.

(c) What is the outlook for nonprice competition? Though the economic union brought several national cartels together, or brought together steel firms that coordinated spontaneously on a countrywide basis, will individual steel firms compete or will the national groups compete with each other as units by modernizing their facilities, expanding their capacity and expanding their share of the market through lower costs? This question is the crux of the matter. The common market increased the latent sources of uncertainty and consequently encouraged the producers to combine and modernize facilities. The juxtaposing of nationally coordinated producers within a common market may even have led to a struggle between them for greater shares of the total market and total profits. Such a struggle need not necessarily be expressed through price rivalry. The firm or national group that expands first with the most modern equipment gains an advantage in time as demand expands. Economic union may thus have a greater effect on the volume and distribution

[92] See Fellner's discussion of cutthroat competition in *op. cit.*, pp. 120 ff, pp. 177 ff.
[93] HA, *Sixième rapport général*, Vol. I, pp. 41–43.
[94] Doc. No. 22, 1958, p. 21.

of investments than on the use of existing equipment.[95] As long as the profitableness of each firm rests on its individual share of the market at its own cost curve, individual firms will have an incentive to expand. Interfirm compensation schemes—sharing of markets and profits through common sales organizations, quotas or subsidies—stifle these incentives. The impulsion may also come, additionally or alternatively, from rivalry between national steel groups, stimulated or abetted by the national governments, to maintain or increase national shares.

The tendencies—restriction on the one hand and rivalry leading to expansion on the other—are ambivalent and will in large part be influenced by whether or not producers regard the future optimistically. *The Economist* made this point clear in an article on the prospects for economic union:[96]

There is not going to be perfect competition in a free trade area, of course, whatever the rules. There are some sectors—coal and in some measure transport and other basic services like electricity—where national monopolies mean that the market will inevitably be managed. In the free trade area, as in the common market, the attainment of a common European price pattern might be laid down as a general aim. But there will have to be exceptions to the rule. Our European neighbors may agree that it would be unreasonable to price British coal according to the marginal world price. The double pricing of British coal may go; and the British price may tend to rise towards the continental level. But it is unlikely to reach it.

Outside the recognized managed sectors of the economy, too, competition is bound to be imperfect, as in every modern industrial country. The frontier that divides legitimate technical arrangements between large industrial firms from illegitimate cartels can never be defined precisely. Fortunately, even if competition is far from perfect, not all the advantages of free trade will be lost. The Benelux customs union has no rules of competition and its member countries are a Mecca of cartels. Still, the removal of internal tariffs has brought valuable adjustment in industrial structure. Almost entirely by gentleman's agreement, industries in Belgium and Holland have rationalised, standardised types and shared out the market. And in the European Coal and Steel Community, which has failed signally to stop steel cartels, the pressure of potential competition, if not the real thing, has spurred forward modernisation. The French see the common market in rather the same light; they seek economic regeneration through it, but they do not want plain free trade. They hope to combine the spur of potential competition with managed readaptation and investment in industry.

The risk in the common market, despite Professor Erhard's rules, is that there will be more management than competition. Managed investment is not particularly dangerous in an expanding industry, like steel. But in one which is weak or declining cartels can be vicious.

[95] Tibor Scitovsky, *Economic Theory and Western European Integration*, Allen and Unwin, London, 1958, pp. 19–22, 111, 123.

[96] "Freer Trade in Europe," *The Economist*, October 12, 1957, p. 10.

CHAPTER 8

COAL:

CONCERTED PRACTICES

The European coal industry has been organized since World War I with outside help, usually given by the government, for the sake of enabling the large number of producers to stabilize prices and income over the course of the business cycle. (The treaty provisions regarding concerted actions that interfere with the market have already been discussed in Chapter 7 while the lack of antitrust sentiment in Europe has been mentioned in Chapter 5.) Collective action and control is universal in the European coal industry, and is directly encouraged by governments and the High Authority, which has authorized concerted action subject to its inspection and control, according to rules which are designed to protect the public interest.

THE INTERWAR PERIOD

Each domestic market was organized with varying degrees of success, though the European coal industry failed to reach any comprehensive international agreements during the interwar period.

Background

The coal industry was more overexpanded even than the steel industry after the first world war. In the late 1920s—when business was still fairly good—25 per cent of German, 25 to 33 per cent of British and 50 per cent of Polish capacity was idle. Twenty-seven per cent of American capacity also was idle at that time.[1] The French mines were less overexpanded.[2] The Polish coal in-

---

[1] ILO, *The World Coal-Mining Industry*, Geneva, 1938, Vol. I, pp. 74, 111–112; Temporary National Economic Committee, *Competition and Monopoly in American Industry*, Monograph No. 21, Washington, 1940, p. 24.

[2] André Dubosq, *Le Conflit contemporain des houillères européennes (Perspectives d'entente)*, Librairie Technique et Economique, Paris, 1936, pp. 28–29.

dustry was in the greatest difficulty. Poland had acquired East Upper Silesia from Germany after the first world war. This region had produced 30 million tons of coal before the war and thereafter accounted for 80 per cent of Polish output, which had quadrupled as a result. So large an increase in an essentially agricultural country gave Poland a large export surplus.[3]

Coal producing capacity in the United Kingdom and on the Continent increased between 1913 and the 1920s though coal production in the interwar years never, except for 1929, exceeded that of 1913. Demand failed to keep pace because improvements in the use of coal yielded more energy per unit, because coal importing areas increased their own production, and because the use of water power and petroleum increased.[4]

The decline of overseas demand was particularly sharp. Coal exports from the United Kingdom in the late 1920s were about 75 per cent of the prewar volume and declined to 60 per cent in the 1930s.[5] German exports in the like periods declined to 85 and 80 per cent, respectively, of 1913.[6] The British coal industry was in greater trouble than the German because Poland's entry into the export market had created more difficulties for the former. The United Kingdom and Poland were each large exporters of coal for steam-raising uses to overseas areas, but Germany enjoyed the advantage of supplying metallurgical fuels over interior lines of transport. The United Kingdom and Poland eventually reached an agreement on exports in December 1934 that regulated distribution rather than export prices.[7]

Only six countries—the United Kingdom, Germany, Poland, France, Belgium and the Netherlands—would have had to agree in order to control 90 per cent of the European coal output and nearly all the exports. But their interests proved too contradictory. As a large importer and small exporter France had more to gain from British-German rivalry. The British industry wished to restore the prewar export patterns more favorable to it, though there had been a chronic deterioration in its competitive ability.[8] Resting on a property structure determined by the small leasehold, British coal production was dispersed over many firms. Internal organization in the United Kingdom was consequently weak and prevented it from dictating terms to the

[3] *Statistische Übersicht über die Kohlenwirtschaft im Jahre 1936*, in *Jahresbericht des Reichskohlenverbandes, 1936–37*, p. 22; hereafter cited as *Statistische Übersicht*. For the effect of surplus capacity on export prices, see *The World Coal-Mining Industry*, Vol. I, pp. 195–219.

[4] *The World Coal-Mining Industry*, Vol. I, pp. 104–110.

[5] *Statistische Übersicht*, p. 50.

[6] *Ibid.*, p. 36. Coke is excluded. The comparison would be more favorable to Germany if exports from East Upper Silesia were credited to Germany.

[7] The agreement is summarized in *The World Coal-Mining Industry*, Vol. I, pp. 249–250.

[8] *Coal Mining*, Report of the Technical Advisory Committee, Charles C. Reid, Chairman, HMSO, London, March 1945, p. 29; cited hereafter as Reid Report, one of the best on the problems of the British coal industry in the interwar period.

German coal exporters. Unreconciled to its loss of ground, the United King-dom tried to recapture its former position by currency manipulation, dumping and bilateral agreements. The devaluation of the pound in 1931 gave the British industry a temporary advantage. The Anglo-German negotiations of 1934 for an agreement on coal, which coincided with the negotiations for the steel cartel and the naval agreement, failed because the United Kingdom thought an agreement on coal prices would be sufficient while the Germans wanted to fix export quotas also.[9]

Instead of adjusting capacity to demand, the European coal mines engaged in cutthroat competition and discrimination in order to maintain volume and cover fixed costs. Since labor costs accounted for 55 to 65 per cent of the selling price, competition meant manipulation of wages and working hours. A League of Nations report observed: "It would . . . appear that the competitive lowering of coal prices after 1929 was facilitated to a large degree by the flexi-bility of the wage-cost factor. And certainly part of this competitive lowering of sales prices was made possible by the breakdown of wage rates."[10] In an era of general unemployment, mining labor had few alternative opportunities for employment. To counteract the practice by which each country tried to export unemployment to the other countries, the International Miners Federation and the League of Nations favored an international agreement on coal in the belief that it would help maintain the labor standards gained during the first world war.[11]

The coke export trade proved to be the only field in which a private multi-lateral agreement could be reached. The coke producers of Germany, the United Kingdom, Belgium, the Netherlands and Poland founded the Inter-national Coke Cartel in April 1937 after several years of negotiation. Each country received an export quota and preference in certain markets. Minimum prices were agreed.[12]

Government Influence

As economic conditions declined in the 1930s, the coal problem became in-creasingly political, though the amalgamation of individual properties and im-provement of the conditions of labor had received political attention long before the first world war.[13] The governments controlled production, prices, distribution, wages, working conditions and profits during that war. As living

---

[9] Dubosq, *op. cit.*, pp. 243–244.

[10] *The World Coal-Mining Industry*, Vol. I, p. 217.

[11] Dubosq, *op. cit.*, pp. 185–186, 194–195; *Raw Materials Problems and Policies*, League of Nations, Geneva, 1946, p. 51.

[12] *The World Coal-Mining Industry*, Vol. 1, pp. 248–251; Dubosq, *op. cit.*, pp. 207–208.

[13] *The World Coal-Mining Industry*, Vol. I, pp. 4–5.

standards for miners had improved during the war, the miners later resisted the efforts to reduce them.[14]

Economic nationalism took a turn for the worse in the interwar years as government influence increased. National protective measures in the European coal industry produced some of the outstanding examples of economic nationalism witnessed in the interwar period. The rivalry for export markets in coal was not an example of salutary competition but of dumping, subsidies, discriminatory prices, tie-in sales, currency manipulation, special tax relief, preferential freight rates and domestic market control.[15] The simultaneous pursuit of protection for home production and of dumping on export markets led to a crazy quilt of international countermeasures and discriminations, especially in the 1930s. As in an armaments race, every device stimulated a counterdevice, every alliance a counteralliance. "Private" and "public" measures became hopelessly entangled and the division between them meaningless.

The tariff, exceptional in the 1920s, became the rule in the following decade, but was not the main device for limiting imports. Besides the normal import duty, there were equalization taxes, import license fees, port and river charges. Germany, France, Italy, Belgium and the Netherlands had import quota limitations by 1936.[16] The importing countries extended preferential treatment to selected sources of supply within the framework of preferential bilateral trade agreements. These agreements helped the partners to exchange goods that were surplus to each of them. The United Kingdom made such arrangements with the Scandinavian and Baltic countries in 1933–1934. German coal enjoyed preference in Belgium, the Netherlands and France under agreements that regulated the importation of German coal.[17]

The 1938 League of Nations report saw these "complex systems" of economic supervision and control as "the beginnings of an international mechanism for regulating competition between coal exporting countries."[18] Whatever it was that this was the beginning of, it was certainly the end of the free market mechanism in the coal industry. As the report indicates: ". . . the European coal trade must be viewed as a case of commercial dealing which is far removed from 'perfect competition.'"[19]

In the 1930s the United States also abandoned the free market. The National Recovery Act of 1933 suspended the antitrust laws and provided for minimum prices and wages under government supervision. After the NRA

[14] See *ibid.*, pp. 6–8, 220.
[15] See *ibid.*, pp. 158, 194–200 for details.
[16] *Ibid.*, pp. 158 ff.
[17] *Ibid.*, pp. 188–190, 249–250; Dubosq, *op. cit.*, pp. 102–103, 173–174.
[18] *The World Coal-Mining Industry*, Vol. I, p. 220.
[19] *Ibid.*, p. 190.

had been declared unconstitutional, price control in bituminous coal was continued under the Bituminous Coal Conservation Act of 1935 and later under the Bituminous Coal Act of 1937, but the latter was soon emasculated by an unfavorable Federal Court decision on the minimum price provisions. The anthracite industry was regulated by the laws of the state of Pennsylvania.[20] Overseas exports were, however, of minor significance to the United States coal industry in the prewar period.

AFTER WORLD WAR II

As coal and labor were scarce, the great competitive struggles of the past disappeared after the second world war. Export prices were higher than internal ones—the reverse of the interwar relationship—but the additional revenue on export sales was small in any case, for a smaller proportion of production was exported.

Since the end of the second world war internal coal prices charged by privately as well as publicly owned enterprises have been controlled at low levels in relation to costs and the paucity of coal, first by the individual governments, then by the High Authority and, again, by the governments informally after price controls had been lifted by the High Authority.

Since the second world war all governments in Western Europe have in practice assumed the obligation of stabilizing production, employment and wages and of encouraging modernization and investments, whether the mines are publicly or privately owned. The common sales agency selling for a large number of, or for all, the firms in a given producing district is one of the major devices by which the objectives common to governments and producers are carried out in privately owned areas. In nationalized mining areas concerted action rests on the fact of nationalization itself. The privately owned as well as publicly owned mines are subject to government influence in Europe because the earnings of capital and labor cannot be stabilized unless prices, production and sales by the large number of firms whose costs vary considerably are coordinated. Many firms, furthermore, could not survive when prices are pegged without some form of aid that sometimes goes as far as interfirm compensation.

Several common sales agencies were operating in the non-nationalized portions of the coal industry on the eve of the ECSC. These were in the Ruhr, Aachen, Lower Saxony, Belgium and in the southern German coal market. In France the Association Technique de l'Importation Charbonnière (ATIC) controlled imports of solid fuels. The High Authority's disposition of the sales

[20] *Ibid.*, pp. 239–241.

agency for the Ruhr, which controlled half the production in the ECSC, set a pattern for High Authority policy in the other areas. Three years of protracted negotiations between the High Authority, the Ruhr coal industry and the German government went by before the High Authority established a policy for the sale of Ruhr solid fuels. The High Authority subsequently took action with respect to ATIC and the sales agencies in Belgium and southern Germany.

RUHR SOLID FUELS

The sale of Ruhr solid fuels has been centralized since 1893. The Rheinische Westfälische Kohlen Syndikat (RWKS) was organized that year to stabilize prices. The captive coal mines joined the cartel in 1903 after having obtained important concessions. The RWKS encompassed about 90 per cent of Ruhr solid fuels by 1913 and acquired 100 per cent membership in the first world war, when the State-owned mines joined.[21]

INTERWAR PERIOD

The RWKS emerged stronger than ever from the first world war. In 1919, the German socialists, then in power, passed a socialization bill (Kohlenwirtschaftsgesetz). Expressing the Weimar Republic's wish for economic democracy, the act provided for compulsory membership in the regional coal cartels in order to facilitate public control. It also provided for nationalization but that was not carried out.[22] The RWKS took over the sale of Aachen coal in 1934 and of Saar coal the following year when the latter rejoined Germany. Each of the other coal producing districts—mainly German Silesia, and several minor basins—also had its sales organization before the second world war.

The RWKS—many of the provisions of the Kohlenwirtschaftsgesetz were modeled on it—was an incorporated limited liability company, the stock of which was owned by the coal companies, which had voting rights proportionate to their sales quotas. The RWKS established prices, levies, penalties and quotas for the individual firms. Arrangements between the RWKS and individual firms were made by periodic contracts. Each member had a sales quota and a separate quota for coke and briquettes, adjusted periodically in

[21] William N. Parker, *Fuel Supply and Industrial Strength*, unpublished Ph.D. thesis, Harvard University, Cambridge, 1951, pp. 115–120, 126–128. Frederick Haussmann, *The Reorganization of the German Coal Industry and Its International Aspects* (undated mimeographed study written after the second world war), pp. 27–33, contains an excellent summary of the RWKS.

[22] *The World Coal-Mining Industry*, Vol. I, p. 6; Franz Neumann, *Behemoth*, Oxford, New York, 1942, p. 266. Parker, *op. cit.*, pp. 115–124, describes the structure of public control.

relation to demand. Each member had a consumption quota, in addition to the sales quota, to cover the requirements of the mine, of auxiliary operations and of vertically integrated firms.

Markets in Germany were divided into "uncontested" and "contested" areas. The regional cartel had a sales monopoly in the uncontested area. Contested areas were served by more than one cartel or by imported coal. Among the contested areas were northern Germany, where United Kingdom coal was imported, and southern Germany, where coal was delivered from the Ruhr, Aachen, Bavaria, the Saar and Lorraine.

Prices in uncontested areas were higher than those in contested areas, which also encompassed exports. The RWKS taxed its members in order to cover the lower prices. This tax, called the *Umlage*, equalized unit returns among producers, regardless of the destination of the coal from individual firms. Unit revenue in each firm was therefore determined by the average unit revenue on all the coal distributed in uncontested, contested and export markets. Uncontested markets, contested markets and integrated consumption each absorbed roughly one third the Ruhr coal output.[23]

As the integrated coal mining firms obtained control of the RWKS, they improved their position by obtaining a lower *Umlage* on consumption quotas. High book prices on coking smalls, which represented the major part of the consumption quota, also helped improve their position.[24] The demand for high consumption quotas on the part of integrated firms was a source of sharp conflict between them and the independents.

Official prices in the uncontested areas, approved by the government, were monopoly prices, reflecting the costs of the less efficient producers.[25] Prices in the contested areas took account of the delivered price of coal from other producers. Although average receipts per ton of solid fuels exported by the RWKS declined by more than 50 per cent from 1930 to 1934, the official price in uncontested areas declined by less than 20 per cent. Official prices in uncontested areas must have been about 50 per cent higher than export prices in 1934; the differential at pithead must have been even larger because the export price included freight to the border.[26] The monopoly price in uncontested areas thus subsidized the price in contested markets.

The regional coal producing cartels marketed their coal in contested areas through a common sales agency, referred to as a Kohlenkontor, which also

[23] Robert Lafitte-Laplace, *L'Economie charbonnière de la France*, Marcel Giard, Paris, 1933, pp. 545–551.

[24] See Parker, *op. cit.*, pp. 129–157; Dubosq, *op. cit.*, pp. 132–138; Lafitte-Laplace, *op. cit.*, pp. 545–551; *The World Coal-Mining Industry*, Vol. I, pp. 235–239.

[25] Reid Report, pp. 30–31.

[26] These estimates are calculated from data in *Statistische Übersicht*, 1936, p. 46.

handled imported coal. The Kohlenkontor sold directly to large consumers and to authorized first-hand merchants. The contested areas were therefore not competitive either; they were simply controlled by different ground rules.[27]

One contested area, south Germany, deserves particular attention. The Kohlenkontor in this area handled coal coming from the RWKS, the Saar (incorporated with RWKS in 1935), Lorraine and the Bavarian mines. This Kohlenkontor also controlled inbound transport on the Rhine, an essential and profitable part of the system. The delivered base price in southern Germany for coal from all origins was determined by the RWKS price for that area plus the freight cost, which was based on published rates.[28]

EVE OF THE COMMON MARKET

The RWKS was abolished after the war by the British Military Government.[29] The centralized sale of Ruhr solid fuels was, however, continued by the Deutsche Kohlen Verkauf (DKV), established by the occupation authorities, to which it was responsible.[30] The occupation authorities established the DKV because the acute paucity of solid fuels and the ceiling on prices required centralized control of distribution and exports. The DKV coordinated all coal supplied to the German market by the Ruhr mines, by imports and by the common sales agencies for Aachen and Lower Saxony. It consequently controlled all sources and markets and enjoyed as much influence as the old RWKS, if not more.

The allied occupation officials, particularly those of the United States, considered the DKV temporary pending completion of the deconcentration program. They and the German government, represented by members of the mining industry and the labor unions, later agreed to dissolve the DKV and to establish six sales agencies for Ruhr solid fuels and a coordinating agency called Georg (Gemeinschaftsorganisation). These new organizations were established in February 1953. It was understood at the time that Georg would simply provide central statistical and technical service for the six agencies and would coordinate only when necessary without controlling prices or sales at any time. The sixty-odd mining firms in the Ruhr were to sell through the six sales agencies.

When the common market for coal began in February 1953, the High

---

[27] *The World Coal-Mining Industry*, Vol. I, pp. 235–239.

[28] Lafitte-Laplace, *op. cit.*, pp. 123–137, 141; Dubosq, *op. cit.*, pp. 132–138.

[29] It had abolished all cartels by Article 1 of Ordinance 78, February 12, 1947, and the coal cartel specifically by Order No. 5 of Public Law No. 52; B. Ruhm von Oppen, ed., *Documents on Germany Under Occupation*, Oxford, London, 1955, pp. 203 ff.

[30] By Public Law No. 75, November 10, 1948; von Oppen, *op. cit.*, p. 337.

Authority discovered that the package it had inherited was a completely centralized pricing and sales mechanism through the medium of Georg.[31]

SALE OF RUHR SOLID FUELS

IN THE COMMON MARKET

Article 65, relative to cartels, having become effective in July 1953,[32] the
Ruhr coal sales agencies applied to the High Authority in August for permission to continue.

Sales Agencies for Aachen and Lower Saxony

While its negotiations with the Ruhr mining firms proceeded, the High
Authority in June 1954 authorized the mining firms in Aachen and those in
Lower Saxony to operate common sales agencies in accordance with Section 2
of Article 65, because they produced only 2.3 per cent and 1 per cent, respectively, of the coal in the ECSC and because two of the three firms in each basin
were too small to sell "rationally."[33]

Why Common Sales Agencies in the Ruhr Were Continued

The High Authority decided the fate of the Ruhr coal sales agencies in
February 1956.[34] It allowed the Ruhr to maintain a common sales agency for
export to third countries, the Ruhrkohlenexportgesellschaft, on the ground
that it did not restrain internal commerce.[35] The High Authority established
three sales agencies, instead of six, to handle the sale of Ruhr solid fuels in the
common market. It also established a coordinating agency, Bureau Commun,
and a Commission des Normes to provide common rules of operation.

[31] H. Aszkenazy, "La Reorganisation des comptoirs de charbon de la Ruhr," in *Revue française
de l'énergie*, June 1956, p. 337. The Allied High Commission protested to the German Minister
for Economics in a letter dated March 18, 1953, a copy of which was sent to the High Authority.
Sidney Willner, in W. Friedmann, ed., *Anti-Trust Laws, A Comparative Symposium*, Stevens and
Sons, London, 1956, p. 186, has observed: "In actual operation the central body . . . assumed
the direction over sales policies and continued its old market allocation and price fixing functions,
thus violating the letter and the spirit of the agreed solution."

[32] HA, Decision 37–53, in *Journal officiel*, July 21, 1953, p. 153; see Chapter 6.

[33] These two sales agencies, called Comptoir Aachener Kohlen-Verkauf and Comptoir Nieder-
sächsischer Kohlen-Verkauf, were authorized by HA, Decisions 32–54 and 34–54, respectively, in
Journal officiel, July 6, 1954, pp. 434, 436. These two agencies had been established in 1950. A
fourth mine in Aachen, Gewerkschaft Sophia Jacoba, which traditionally sold through the RWKS,
was subsequently authorized to sell through one of the Ruhr sales agencies called Geitling;
Journal officiel, March 13, 1956, p. 36. This mine withdrew from Geitling in April 1959; HA,
Decision 7–59, in *Journal officiel*, February 11, 1959, p. 192.

[34] HA, Decisions 5–56, 6–56, 7–56 and 8–56, all dated February 15, 1956, are in *Journal
officiel*, March 13, 1956. A minor amendment was made in Decisions 10–57, 11–57 and 12–57, in
Journal officiel, April 16, 1957, pp. 159 ff. See also a decision of the Court with reference to the
definition of the wholesaler in *Journal officiel*, April 16, 1957, pp. 166 ff. These decisions, as well as
those for other coal producers and purchasers, were to expire March 31, 1959. They were later
extended for one year; *Handelsblatt*, December 22, 1958, **p. 2.**

[35] *Journal officiel*, March 13, 1956, p. 31.

The High Authority accepted the centralization of Ruhr coal sales for three reasons:

(1) to enable the firms to provide the required volume and grades of solid fuels at the required time and place;

(2) to enable the firms to equalize production and employment when coal is surplus;

(3) to enable the firms to distribute supplies equitably when coal is scarce.

Thus the High Authority affirmed the proposition that sixty-odd mining firms cannot each sell solid fuels and still satisfy the collective interests of the coal mine operators, of the employees and of the consumers.

The allied authorities had already conceded as much when they created six sales agencies and Georg.[36] They pointed out that all the groups they had consulted—labor unions, the coal industry, the federation of German industry, the railroads, wholesalers and retailers—unanimously favored centralized sales.[37]

The High Authority was in no stronger political position than the allied authorities had been to propose any solution other than centralization. The interests on which it could rely in support of decentralization were few. The groups outside Germany which might have wished to weaken the Ruhr coal cartel favored concerted action in their own coal industries. The Ruhr mining firms made much of the fact that all French coal production was centralized.[38] That there is need of centralized regulation of production, prices and sales in order to mitigate the effects of the business cycle is a proposition that goes nearly unchallenged in Europe.

In spite of the acceptance of centralization by the allied authorities and, later, by the High Authority, both were eager to avoid monopoly and to protect the wholesalers' position. They thus tried to create several independent sales agencies; where the allies had established six, the High Authority created three. Under the High Authority's arrangement each mining firm in the Ruhr is in one of the agencies and each agency encompasses one third the output.

Are the Three Sales Agencies Independent?

While no mining firm is in more than one sales agency, some of the proprietary groups are represented in two, or even in all three, of them. The dis-

---

[36] Allied High Commission, "Report of the Committee on Coal Distribution Problems Relative to the Dissolution of the DKV," October 29, 1951, and Appendix, November 9, 1951.

[37] Ibid., Appendix, p. 1; Aszkenazy, op. cit., pp. 337–338, describes the achievements of the RWKS in stabilizing employment and production.

[38] Friedmann, op. cit., p. 513.

tribution of proprietary interests in Geitling, Präsident, and Mausegatt, as the sales agencies are called, is shown in Table 46. Sixty-six per cent of the produc-

Table 46

DISTRIBUTION OF PROPRIETARY INTERESTS AMONG
RUHR COAL SALES AGENCIES, 1959[a]

(*Amount in Thousands of Metric Tons*)

Group	Geitling Amount	Geitling Per Cent	Präsident Amount	Präsident Per Cent	Mausegatt Amount	Mausegatt Per Cent
Private German steel groups:						
Thyssen	5,201	12.6	—	—	6,939	17.1
Krupp	4,813	11.7	408	1.0	2,165	5.3
Haniel	5,453	13.2	4,569	11.6	—	—
Hoesch	2,931	7.1	3,644	9.3	—	—
Rheinische	—	—	5,198	13.2	—	—
Mannesmann	—	—	6,563	16.7	—	—
Klöckner	—	—	5,238	13.3	—	—
Michel group	—	—	—	—	1,398	3.4
Dortmund–Hörder	—	—	—	—	4,640	11.5
Stumm	1,792	4.3	—	—	—	—
Ilseder[b]	1,558	3.8	—	—	—	—
German State	—	—	2,684	6.8	16,454	40.6
Gelsenkirchener[c]	3,401	8.2	2,628	6.7	2,519	6.2
Stinnes	3,445	8.3	—	—	2,088	5.2
Total	28,594	69.2	30,932	78.8	36,203	89.3
Foreign interests:						
Arbed	2,033	4.9	—	—	—	—
De Wendel	1,562	3.8	2,138	5.4	—	—
Sidechar	7,798	18.9	—	—	—	—
Total	11,393	27.6	2,138	5.4	—	—
Other groups[d]	—	—	4,277	10.9	2,339	5.8
Independents[e]	(1,300)	3.2	1,924	4.9	1,973	4.9
TOTAL[f]	41,287	100.0	39,271	100.0	40,515	100.0

Sources: HA, Decisions 5 to 7–56, inclusive, in *Journal officiel*, March 13, 1956, for the mining firms in each sales comptoir; *Jahrbuch*, for production; Table 5–6, Appendix E, for proprietary control of firms.

[a] Production data as of 1955 but proprietary relationships as of early 1959.

[b] The State has a 25 per cent interest.

[c] Includes only GBAG's 100 per cent owned mines; the mines in which Dortmund-Hörder and August Thyssen Hütte purchased a 51 per cent interest are excluded.

[d] German industrial groups not previously listed; each of them is represented in one agency only.

[e] Each independent is of course represented in one agency only.

[f] The grand total covers 100 per cent of the Ruhr.

tion organized in Geitling, 41 per cent of that organized in Präsident and 85 per cent of that in Mausegatt has proprietary ties to mining firms in one of the other two agencies. In view of the fact that the interests of the proprietary groups spill over into more than one sales organization, the prospects for independence among the three agencies are small.

The High Authority evidently placed the mining firms controlled by the foreign steel groups, and those controlled by the German State, where they might exercise some independence. Thus, foreign steel groups without ties to the other agencies control more than one fourth of the coal represented in Geitling. But there is no evidence to suggest that the foreign groups are taking advantage of the opportunity. Neither is the German State. The State-owned mines, accounting for 41 per cent of the production organized in Mausegatt, could wield a great influence in that sales agency, though they also have a small interest in Präsident. But the State-owned mines refused the opportunity to exercise independence when the Ruhr coal operators raised prices at the end of 1957, to the government's intense displeasure. Ludwig Erhard, the Minister for Economics, threatened to break the common price policy by pulling Hibernia, the State-owned firm, out of the common price list. Hibernia accounts for one fourth the coal organized in Mausegatt and 9 per cent of all the Ruhr output. The common price list for all mining firms in the Ruhr is the cornerstone of control. Erhard did not follow through; had he done so he would have dealt a serious blow to the whole structure of control. Instead he had the Preussag mines in Lower Saxony maintain the old price, but this was merely a gesture because Preussag produces only one fourth as much coal as Hibernia and, located in Lower Saxony rather than the Ruhr, does not compete with Ruhr coal.[39]

The High Authority tried to safeguard the independence of each sales agency by forbidding the officers of one agency to hold office in another and by controlling the transfer of funds and of solid fuels from one sales agency to another.[40]

Wholesalers and Dealers

The RWKS had selected and controlled the merchants and had given them exclusive sales rights. They had been organized in merchants' associations in which the RWKS was represented. The RWKS had granted exclusive rights in foreign markets to one or two large merchants.[41] These devices were important features of market control.

The High Authority has carefully tried to protect the merchant's status and his access to supply. Consumers who consume over 30,000 tons of solid fuels

[39] Details on the incident are from *Handelsblatt*, October 4-5, 1957, p. 2, and October 7, 1957, p. 2.

[40] See, e.g., Articles 2 and 3 of Decision 5–56, *Journal officiel*, March 13, 1956, pp. 36–37.

[41] Aszkenazy, *op. cit.*, p. 338.

annually may deal directly with the sales agencies; those who consume over 50,000 tons may deal with the Bureau Commun, described later. Mining firms may sell directly to local customers who consume less than 12,500 tons annually. A consumer large enough to qualify for direct purchases from the sales agencies may also purchase from a merchant for a limited period if he has been accustomed to using the latter. All other consumers must purchase from first- or second-degree merchants according to size; the first-degree merchant purchases from the Ruhr sales agency, but the second-degree merchant obtains his coal from the first-degree merchant. The first-degree merchant sells at the list prices established by the Ruhr sales agency and deducts a commission agreed between him and the agency; i.e., the latter earns a lower net return on the solid fuels distributed through merchant channels.[42]

To qualify as first-degree merchant, a dealer must have handled a minimum tonnage of Ruhr solid fuels in a historical reference period and must have sold a minimum tonnage in any one of seven sales zones. The zonal provision limits the number of first-degree merchants in any zone and attempts to spread them geographically throughout the common market. Non-German merchants may qualify.

The qualifications set for the merchants were too restrictive and fewer merchants qualified than had been hoped. The High Authority therefore successively reduced the size qualifications by amendment.[43] The number of qualified first-degree merchants in the several sales zones increased slightly or remained fairly stationary from 1956 to the first quarter of 1958.[44]

Freight Charges

The customer who purchases from the sales agency has the right to specify the point at which he takes delivery, i.e., f.o.b. mine, f.o.b. Rhine River port, or f.o.b. seaport. This provision is particularly important because the seller can engage in secret price discrimination by fixing the delivery point. The provision thus protects the consumer against phantom freight charges and allows him to use the most economical means of transport.[45]

Coordination Among the Three Sales Agencies

The Commission des Normes and the Bureau Commun are the coordinating

---

[42] HA, Decision 5–56, *Journal officiel*, Article 3 (8).

[43] HA, *Journal officiel*, March 13, 1956, pp. 279 ff. Articles 7, 8, 9, 10, 11 of HA, Decision 5–56, deal with the merchant trade. The amendments are contained in a series of decisions published in the *Journal officiel* beginning August 10, 1957.

[44] Assemblée Parlementaire Européenne, Commission du Marché Intérieur, Doc. No. 12, 1958, p. 37.

[45] HA, Decision 5–56, *Journal officiel*, March 13, 1956, Article 3 (5) (6) (7).

bodies for the sale of Ruhr solid fuels.[46] The Commission des Normes is a sort of legislative assembly in which the mining firms are represented. It may establish common standards for all the mines with respect to:

(1) The rules that determine the quantity of solid fuels used for Werksselbstverbrauch (mines' consumption, miners' coal, consumption by vertical affiliates) and the quantity sold by the sales agencies to local and other customers. Each sales agency sells about 15 million tons of coal plus 5 to 6 million tons of coke, exclusive of Werksselbstverbrauch and local sales; local sales—small in the aggregate—are made directly by the mines. All three sales agencies combined thus sell 45 million tons of coal—roughly one third the total output of the Ruhr and more than 60 per cent of the coal after coking requirements are deducted—and about 15 million tons of coke, about 40 per cent of the total Ruhr output. The remainder of each class of product goes to Werksselbstverbrauch and to local sales made directly by the mining firms. About one third the solid fuels produced in the Ruhr was used for Werksselbstverbrauch in the interwar period; the proportion increased to one half in the 1950s.

(2) The rules by which mining firms and their corporate affiliates buy solid fuels from one another in order to equalize employment and operating rates during a recession or to give up some of their solid fuels when coal is scarce. These provisions affect the Werksselbstverbrauch. The Commission des Normes established a rule requiring the steel firms that are vertically integrated with the mines to purchase a fixed quantity of coal; the steel firms tried to reduce their obligations as a result of the 1958 recession.

(3) The rules by which orders from other customers will be distributed among mining firms in order to stabilize employment.

(4) The minimum base production tonnage for each mining firm. When there is surplus coal producing capacity, the sales agencies and the Bureau Commun distribute orders in order to enable each firm to come up to the minimum rate of operation. The mining firms that operate above the minimum may be required to pay an indemnity of up to 5 DM per ton of coal to those firms that are below the minimum. This provision and the 5 DM indemnity were applied in the 1958 recession, when sales were running from 10 to 15 per cent below Ruhr mining capacity.[47]

The rules adopted by the Commission des Normes are subject to High Authority approval. The Commission must give the High Authority an annual forecast of the tonnage of coal retained for Werksselbstverbauch and a quarterly report on actual performance.

[46] See HA, Decision 8–56 in *Journal officiel*, March 13, 1956.
[47] *Handelsblatt*, July 30, 1958, p. 1.

Whereas the Commission des Normes provides the rules for coordination, the Bureau Commun is the executive body. It is headed by one representative from each sales agency; the three select a president by unanimous agreement.

The Bureau Commun deals with consumers who consume over 50,000 tons annually and who promise to use the Bureau exclusively for at least a year. But contracts are between the consumer and one of the three sales agencies. The Bureau Commun may manipulate deliveries in order to facilitate vessel loading and to help ship the right quantity of the specific grades and sizes of coal. The Bureau Commun is really a fourth sales agency acting as a balance wheel. The Bureau distributes orders to equalize employment when there is surplus coal producing capacity. When solid fuels are scarce it helps the sales agencies to provide all customers with a fair share.

The Bureau Commun also acts as a financial agency. It administers the subsidy for mines that operate below the minimum base tonnage when coal producing capacity is not fully utilized. It administers payments that equalize the cost of freight absorption among mining firms that sell at delivery points other than f.o.b. mine. When the customer accepts delivery f.o.b. seaport or f.o.b. Duisburg-Ruhrort, a uniform freight charge is applied. The uniform charge must be equal to the average weighted real cost. The mines are compensated or debited for the difference between the actual freight cost and the uniform charge. If the mines absorb freight in order to compete with imported coal, the Bureau may fix the quantities and the charge to be absorbed and may equalize the financial burden among all the mines. When solid fuels were scarce in 1956 and 1957, the High Authority gave the Bureau Commun a delegation of power to apportion supplies. The High Authority could authorize it to establish production quotas when there is a surplus of coal producing capacity.

Public Supervision

The allied authorities had subordinated Georg to a tripartite committee representing the mines, the unions and consumers. They also had envisaged a substantial degree of public supervision by the High Authority and the German government owing to the danger of "monopolistic tendencies" on the part of a "private control selling agency."[48]

The principle of public supervision was later adopted by the High Authority for the sales agencies it authorized. The High Authority has the right to ascertain whether or not the coal mining firms, the selling agencies, the Bureau Commun and the Commission des Normes conform to the terms of the authorization. The High Authority required the mining firms to establish a Consultative Committee of nine producers, nine labor representatives and

[48] Allied High Commission, *op. cit.*, Appendix, November 9, 1951, p. 7.

nine consumers and merchants, and to keep this committee informed of the activities of the Bureau Commun. The High Authority and the German government may also participate in the Consultative Committee.

Conclusion

Are the Ruhr solid fuels sales agencies independent and do they compete with each other?

The High Authority believed that none of the three sales agencies would control a substantial part of the market because it encompasses no more than 13 per cent of the coal output in the Ruhr or 6 per cent of the total output in the ECSC and because, further, it encompasses no more than 11 per cent of the coke output in the Ruhr and 5 per cent of that in the ECSC.[49] The importance of considering these matters from the regional point of view has already been pointed out in Chapter 5. The position of Ruhr coal in regional markets or even in the common market as a whole cannot be measured in percentages alone. Nor is it very realistic to measure the strength of the sales agencies by taking each one separately as though one were completely independent of the others. Though the centralized selling arrangements do not, furthermore, preclude the Ruhr mines as a group from invading the markets of other coal producing districts, the sales agencies refrained during the 1958 recession from challenging the mines in southern Belgium, the most vulnerable of all producing districts, and asked the High Authority to maintain its ban on price alignments between producing districts.[50]

Though the High Authority's authorization does not provide for concerted pricing, the mining firms use a common price list; the common sales agencies are the administrative core for concerted prices. Was the High Authority very realistic to assume that the Ruhr coal industry, in view of its history and wishes, would stop short of concerted pricing after having been authorized to concert on so many other aspects of sales and distribution? The overlapping of proprietary interests points to a reply in the negative. Since the provisions authorized by the High Authority call for an equalized distribution of orders and operating rates between mining firms, as well as for interfirm compensation, when there is surplus producing capacity, why should the mines compete if the results of competition are to be neutralized in a buyers' market? In October 1957 several members of the Common Assembly asked the High Authority whether simultaneous price changes "prove that the facade of Ruhr sales agencies hides a true homogeneous cartel, eluding public control." The

[49] These percentages differ somewhat from those given earlier in this chapter because they are calculated on a somewhat different basis.

[50] *Handelsblatt*, February 3, 1958, p. 9.

High Authority replied that simultaneous price changes do not provide conclusive evidence but that it had started an inquiry.[51]

Fifteen months later, in March 1959, the High Authority ruled that the three sales agencies had concerted on sales and prices. Asserting that the firms should be free to sell independently, the High Authority ruled that the sales agencies would have to be modified or dissolved. But it prolonged their existence, as well as that of the Bureau Commun, the Commission des Normes and the common financial measures, to March 1960 with the possibility of another year's extension for the three sales agencies only. The High Authority was to supervise the three agencies more closely in the meantime. It also ruled that it would meanwhile, together with the operators, labor and the German government, study the measures to be taken to *stabilize employment and earnings* in the Ruhr coal industry. The Ruhr coal operators challenged the decision before the Court.[52]

Does this decision presage the introduction of price competition between the mining firms in the Ruhr. It would be necessary to await the decisions of the High Authority before reaching any conclusions. In view of the High Authority's explicit desire to stabilize employment, the concentration of ownership, the long history of cartelization, and the high degree of nationalization prevailing in other parts of the Community, the High Authority has set itself a hard task indeed if it expects to alter the basic ground rules. The High Authority in any case has thus far authorized a publicly sponsored monopoly in the Ruhr coal industry.[53]

THE FRENCH MARKET

Interwar Period

The French coal problem was simpler than the British, German or Polish.[54] Since France is essentially an importing country, the coal producers there did not depend on overseas outlets and consequently were less overexpanded. The industry was protected by import restrictions and by regional cartels.

At the suggestion of the government, the coal producers in 1931 and 1932 organized the three producing districts, Nord and Pas-de-Calais, Centre-Midi

[51] *Journal officiel*, December 7, 1957, pp. 571 ff.

[52] HA, Decision No. 17–59, *Journal officiel*, March 7, 1959; *Handelsblatt*, March 27-28, 1959, p. 3.

[53] Miriam Camps, *The European Common Market and American Policy*, Center of International Studies, Princeton, November 1956, p. 27, refers to the authorization of the Ruhr sales agency by the High Authority as a "sobering" experience and calls attention to the opposition the High Authority would have encountered had it interpreted the treaty more strictly.

[54] The 1920s are omitted from discussion; that decade was largely dominated by problems connected with the receipt of solid fuels from the Ruhr on reparations and related accounts. Lafitte-Laplace, *op. cit.*, contains a good analysis of the period.

and Lorraine, into separate marketing cartels. Until 1935 the Saar mines were in the cartel for Lorraine. The country was divided into four sales zones and a functional zone of large consumers called the R zone. The northern mines obtained preference in Zone A, which covered the northern market, Paris and Rouen. The eastern mines enjoyed preference in Zone B in eastern France though the northern mines enjoyed preference in supplying coke to the steel plants in this zone; the Centre-Midi mines, in Zone C in southern and central France; all three mining regions had equal status in Zone D. But no zone was exclusively reserved to any producing region. Zone R encompassed the railroads, gas works, etc., which purchased directly from coal producers. Operating rates were equalized between the three mining regions. Each producer received a share of the regional quota. The four sales zones had a common statistical office and an office that adjusted orders so as to coordinate sales with production quotas. The R zone also proved useful in this connection.[55]

The Comptoir de Douai, as the northern coal producers' group was called, exercised leadership over the other French coal producers. It fixed minimum prices for its coal, and hence for all coal in all the French zones.

Since France imported from a quarter to a third of the solid fuels it consumed, import controls were an important means of protecting the French coal producers. To regulate imports into the coastal areas, where briquetting plants predominated, the northern mines in 1928 organized the Comptoir des Charbons Classés et Agglomérés, in which the other regional producers, the import merchants and the briquetting plants joined. This cartel purchased coal for import and sold coal to the briquetting plants.[56] From 1927 to 1939, the Convention des Gailleteries, an agreement among the mining firms in the Ruhr, Netherlands, Belgium and Nord and Pas-de-Calais, regulated the sale and prices of small-sized heating coal in the French market.[57] Beginning in 1933 the northern French coal producers "exchanged views" with the Belgian producers regarding the coal market in northern France for the other types of coal.[58]

With the onset of the Great Depression, the French government adjusted the rate of import regularly. Import license taxes, import duties and turnover taxes were applied selectively to the different sources of imported supplies in accordance with a preferential system. German solid fuels enjoyed preference. The import of coal from South Wales, another important source, varied with the British purchase of French pit props.[59]

[55] *Ibid.*, pp. 722–726.
[56] Dubosq, *op. cit.*, pp. 139–144.
[57] *Ibid.*, p. 171; *The World Coal-Mining Industry*, Vol. I, p. 244.
[58] Lafitte-Laplace, *op. cit.*, p. 720.
[59] Dubosq, *op. cit.*, pp. 170–171.

In 1936, when Léon Blum was Premier, Parliament passed the Coal Industry Act, which gave the government power to fix the price of domestic and imported coal, to subsidize high-cost mines and to conduct an inquiry for the preparation of regional and national marketing controls under closer government supervision.[60]

Since the Common Market

The French coal mines were nationalized after the second world war. The Charbonnages de France was established and given responsibility for the administration of coal production and sales. Commercial and policy-making activities are centralized although mining operations and sales are decentralized in nine regional divisions. According to an official of Charbonnages de France:[61]

The Charbonnages de France enjoys a monopoly, at the least a quasi-monopoly, of French coal production. If the decentralization arising from the existence of nine mining divisions prevents us from calling it a monopoly, Charbonnages de France from the commercial point of view is nevertheless a single sales unit in many respects.

A parallel organization, Association Technique de l'Importation Charbonnière (ATIC), operating by government decree since 1944, monopolizes the import of solid fuels into France—except that imported by the French steel industry for its own use—and thus acts as a shield for the protection of the nationalized mines. Petroleum imports and refining also are regulated by the government to prevent competition in the fuels industries, a policy that has been followed since the interwar period. ATIC has the right to veto any contract for the purchase of non-French solid fuels. French consumers and merchants cannot purchase from other producers or merchants in the common market without mediation by ATIC. Officials of the Ministry of Industry and of Charbonnages de France are on ATIC's Board of Directors. Centralization of imports also has helped the government to equalize the difference between the price of French and imported coal; since the common market this adjustment is made only for solid fuels imported from suppliers outside of the ECSC.[62]

ATIC's role in controlling imports may be appreciated from the fact that when the French government devalued the franc in August 1957, retaining the

[60] *The World Coal-Mining Industry*, Vol. I, pp. 243–246.

[61] Paul Gardent, "Les Houillères françaises et la concurrence sur le marché commun," *Colloque des Facultés de Droit*, Grenoble, June 1955, mimeographed, page 1.

[62] For the French point of view on ATIC's relation to the over-all coal policy in France, see Paul Gardent, "Les Importations de charbon américain et le problème des contrats à long terme," *Revue française de l'énergie*, December 1957, p. 109.

old rate on imports of raw materials, speculative imports of steel rose sharply but coal imports remained constant.[63]

Having disposed of the problem of the Ruhr sales agencies in February 1956, the High Authority then took on the problem of ATIC. ATIC really involved the French government, with whose sanction it operates. The French steel industry has a common purchasing agency for solid fuels called ORCIS, which is represented in ATIC. The government agreed to the High Authority's request that membership in ORCIS be voluntary rather than obligatory. The French government conceded several other points but none involving ATIC's basic operations.[64]

The High Authority brought matters to a head in December 1957 on the strength of Articles 86 and 88, since Article 65 is applicable only to private organizations. The High Authority ruled:

(1) That ATIC's role as sole purchaser in its own name be abolished within one year and that its role as purchaser in the name of other clients be abolished within two years.

(2) That French consumers be given direct access to non-French merchants within two years.

The French government appealed to the Court of Justice in February 1958. The outcome still rested with the Court as of early 1959. The High Authority's decision, if upheld, will not affect ATIC's powers over imports from third-party countries.

The French government has justified ATIC on the ground that France must coordinate its large volume of imports, that the individual buyer is no match for the powerful Ruhr sales agencies, that the Ruhr must be prevented from dumping coal in France during a recession, and that the Ruhr coal producers must be prevented from dominating the French coal importers as they did before the war.[65] The French government insisted that ATIC was simply the counterweight to the sales agencies for Ruhr solid fuels. The French government's defense of ATIC therefore shows little confidence in the High Authority's attempt to regulate the Ruhr sales agencies. The High Authority, on the other hand, felt morally obligated—and the Germans expected it—to reduce ATIC's power once the matter of Georg had been disposed of. Though the French government defended ATIC on the ground that it shielded the Charbonnages de France from the monopoly power exercised by the Ruhr coal industry, the German government had defended the centralized sales agencies

[63] *Handelsblatt*, October 25-26, 1957, p. 1.

[64] The High Authority's *Bulletin mensuel d'information*, July 1956, pp. 33 ff, and January–February 1958, pp. 23 ff, contains a good analysis of the subject, describing the High Authority's efforts to reach a mutual agreement with the French government's concurrence.

[65] *Le Monde*, June 29, 1956, p. 10.

for Ruhr solid fuels on the ground that the Charbonnages de France was a monopoly.

A NOTE ON CENTRALIZED IMPORTS BY LUXEMBOURG

The government of Luxembourg has its own ATIC-type organization, called the Office Commercial Luxembourgeois, which controls the importation of solid fuels for all consumers other than the steel mills, which handle their own imports. The Office Commercial Luxembourgeois imports a small quantity of solid fuels. It had once equalized the delivered price of imported fuels coming from diverse sources in order to sell them to the consumer on a common price list and generally below cost. This subsidy was, and is, financed by a tax on coal for industrial consumption—in practice a tax on steel production. The High Authority and the Court of Justice considered this subsidy to be an indirect tax for revenue equally applicable to all industry, and therefore legal. The High Authority, however, advised the Office Commercial Luxembourgeois that it was illegal to equalize prices—which interferes with competition among suppliers in the Luxembourgeois market—but not illegal to reduce the price of all imported solid fuels by the same percentage.

The High Authority later endeavored to loosen the monopolistic features of the Office Commercial Luxembourgeois by applying measures similar to those it recommended with respect to ATIC.[66] The outcome in both cases still rested with the Court of Justice as of early 1959.

SALE OF COAL PRODUCED IN THE SAAR AND LORRAINE

The Saar and Lorraine supply similar grades of coal to southern Germany and to eastern France.

SAAR MARKETS

The Saar having too small a local market to be able to survive without "exports," and too small an export surplus to dominate any other market, the distribution of Saar coal in France has been organized in relation to the coal supplied by the Lorraine mines. Its distribution in southern Germany has been organized in relation to the coal supplied to that area by the mines in Lorraine, Aachen and the Ruhr.

---

[66] HA, *Bulletin mensuel d'information*, April 1958, p. 15, May 1956, p. 14, November 1956, paragraph 49; HA, *Sixième rapport général*, Vol. II, pp. 99–100; Court of Justice, *Recueil de la jurisprudence*, Vol. II, cases 7–54 through 10–54, inclusive.

Interwar Period

These arrangements have survived successive territorial changes. When the RWKS assumed exclusive control of the distribution of Saar coal in 1935, the delivery of Saar coal to France was regulated by the Naples Agreement of February 1935 between France and Germany; it stipulated, among other things, that Germany would ship to designated consumers in France 2 million tons of Saar coal annually until 1940.

Saar coal was distributed in southern Germany by the Kohlenkontor for that region.[67]

Saar Coal in French Markets

In 1955 the Saar distributed 14.5 million tons of coal and coke as follows (exclusive of coal consumed locally by the mines and cokeries):[68]

Destination	Tons (Millions)	Per Cent
France	4.5	32
Saar	5.2	36
Southern Germany	3.7	24
Austria, Italy, Switzerland	1.1	8
Total	14.5	100

Seventy per cent of the Saar coal distributed in France that year was sold directly by the Saarbergwerke, then under French control, to nationalized industries, such as the French railways, Electricité de France, Gaz de France, and to ORCIS (the centralized purchase organization for the French steel industry). Saarbergwerke also sold directly to the Saar railways and the Saar steel industry. The remaining 30 per cent of the sales in France were handled by two French centralized sales agencies, AREPIC for eastern France and LORSAR for the rest of France.

Coordination of Saar and Lorraine Coal

The transfer of the Saar to Germany, beginning January 1957, would have threatened these arrangements, as well as the coordinated sale of Saar and Lorraine coal in southern Germany, had not the German and French governments regulated the matter in the treaty for the transfer of the Saar.[69] The treaty obliged the French gradually to abandon mining in the Warndt area, astride the Lorraine-Saar frontier. The French government had made large

[67] Dubosq, *op. cit.*, p. 33; Lafitte-Laplace, *op. cit.*, pp. 454-455.

[68] *Glückauf*, December 8, 1956, p. 1503.

[69] Published by the French government as "Sarre-Moselle-Rhin Conventions de janvier 1957," *Journal officiel de la République de France*, No. 57-4S, Paris, January 1957.

postwar investments in the Warndt mines despite protest from the Saar, which accused France of mining coal from the Saar's side of the frontier. The ECSC, unfortunately, did not help allay national rivalry over the possession of coal reserves.

The pertinent provisions of the Saar treaty of 1957 are listed below; the first two items are related to the Warndt question.

(1) The French will draw from the Warndt a total of 20 million tons of coal in 1957–1961 and a total of 46 million tons in 1962–1981.

(2) From 1962 to 1981 the German government will deliver an additional 1.2 million tons of Saar coal annually to Houillères de Lorraine, the regional coal division of Charbonnages de France, at prevailing prices for Saar coal.[70]

(3) The Saar mining organization will, in addition, offer one third of its salable coal annually, at prices prevailing for Saar coal, to an organization named by the French government for distribution in France. This provision, valid for twenty-five years, obligated France to purchase the tonnage offered. The provision adds that if "international authorities" (obviously the High Authority) disturb this commitment, the German government will inform them of the special nature of the case.[71] The French government subsequently requested ATIC to take charge of this tonnage and founded Covesar (Comptoir de Vente des Charbons Sarrois) to distribute the coal.[72]

(4) A private Franco-German enterprise, valid for twenty-five years, will be created to "coordinate" the sale of Saar and Lorraine coal in southern Germany; German and French capital will each have an equal share, and control, in this enterprise. The enterprise's rules for the coordination of sales are subject to approval by the two governments.[73] The two governments subsequently organized Saarlar (Saar-Lothringische Kohlenunion), which will coordinate sales at prices fixed by the mines. It may also buy and sell solid fuels in other parts of the ECSC. The mines in Lorraine and the Saar control 85 per cent of Saarlar's capital.[74]

These arrangements, except for the first item, provide for concerted practices under public authority. The High Authority, demurring, reserved its rights by notifying the two governments of the following points:[75]

(1) The French government may not require anyone to take any portion of the 1.2 million tons against his will (item 2 of the Saar treaty as given above).

(2) Articles 58 and 59 of the ECSC treaty take precedence over any of the

---

[70] *Ibid.*, p. 42.
[71] *Ibid.*, Article 83 of Convention, p. 43, and Annex 28, p. 201.
[72] ATIC, *Exercice 1957*, p. 6.
[73] "Sarre-Moselle-Rhin Conventions de janvier 1957," Article 84, pp. 43–44.
[74] HA, Decision No. 6–59, *Journal officiel*, February 11, 1959, p. 189.
[75] *Journal officiel*, November 23, 1956, pp. 325 ff.

envisaged deliveries. (These articles provide for limitations on production and sales, respectively, as the case may be.)

(3) The agency appointed by the French government to take delivery of one third of the Saar coal (item 3 of the Saar treaty as given above) has no authority to divide the tonnage among French consumers.

(4) With respect to the agency to coordinate the shipment of coal from the Saar and Lorraine to southern Germany (item 4 of the Saar treaty as given above), the High Authority observed:

(a) That the High Authority will examine its legality when it knows the scope of its action, the distribution of capital stock in it, and the proportion of capital stock, if any, to be owned by the coal producers.

(b) That the agency will, in any case, have to file a request for authorization under Article 65 of the ECSC treaty.

(c) That the two governments should not lose sight of the pertinent parts of the ECSC treaty, nor of the fact that the Saar treaty does not relieve them of any of their obligations to the former treaty.

It is too early to determine the full outcome of these reservations made by the High Authority, but it approved Saarlar with reservations early in 1959.[76]

Prior to the Saar treaty of 1957, coal and coke from the Saar and Lorraine were distributed everywhere—but in France and in the Saar—by a monopoly, Union Charbonnière Rhénane, called Unichar. The French owned 65 per cent and the Saarbergwerke 35 per cent of Unichar.[77] Its principal market was in southern Germany; but it also distributed solid fuels in Austria, Italy and Switzerland. Unichar handled about 32 per cent of the Saar's solid fuels available for sale in 1955 and less than 10 per cent of the coal produced in Lorraine.

Unichar was not a sales but a distributing agency; it distributed solid fuels to sales subsidiaries or affiliates and added a 5 per cent service charge to the list price of the mines. It owned capital stock in all its affiliates and granted them exclusive sales rights over the coal which it distributed. Oberrheinische Kohlenunion (OKU) had exclusive sales rights over the solid fuels distributed by Unichar in southern Germany. OKU also monopolized the distribution of solid fuels from the Ruhr and Aachen in southern Germany.

Saarlar replaced Unichar by the terms of the Saar treaty of 1957 (item 4 of the Saar treaty as given above), German and French interests each acquiring 50 per cent control. Saarlar will continue to sell solid fuels from the Saar and Lorraine everywhere but in France and the Saar. (It will not sell to the German railways either.) Sales coordination of solid fuels from the Saar and Lorraine

[76] HA, Decision No. 6–59, *Journal officiel*, February 11, 1959.

[77] *Handelsblatt*, April 18, 1956, lists the French interests in Unichar as follows: ATIC, 17 per cent; Houillères de Lorraine, 10 per cent; Charbonnages de France, 3 per cent; other French interests, 35 per cent.

in the French market will remain substantially unchanged.[78] The German interest in Saarlar's local affiliates will rise to correspond with its 50 per cent interest in Saarlar as compared with 35 per cent in Unichar.[79]

THE SOUTH GERMAN MARKET

Before August 1957

From 1945 to the end of 1952 Kohlenkontor Weyhenmeyer, Mannheim, controlled the distribution of coal in the United States Zone of Germany and the Oberrheinische Kohlenunion (OKU) performed the same function in the French Zone. Kohlenkontor Weyhenmeyer was a branch office of Deutsche Kohlen Verkauf (DKV), which under supervision of the allied authorities controlled all the solid fuels distributed in Germany. In 1945 the United States Military Government had ordered Kohlenkontor Weyhenmeyer to sell only to wholesalers, and hoped that the wholesalers would compete among themselves. But DKV partly circumvented this order by selling directly to the larger consumers in the south German market. In 1952, for example, DKV handled 15 per cent of the solid fuels in the south German market and the wholesalers handled the remainder. The wholesalers, on the rare occasion of a buyers' market, competed by absorbing part of the 3 per cent commission allowed them by Kohlenkontor Weyhenmeyer within the list price.

In the French Zone OKU sold directly to all customers who consumed over 2,400 tons of solid fuels annually; very little was left for the wholesalers. In the British Zone (northern Germany) all customers that consumed 12,500 tons or more of solid fuels annually were reserved to DKV.

All wholesalers in the United States Zone were forced to purchase from Kohlenkontor Weyhenmeyer. All those in the French Zone purchased only from OKU. Both these distribution agencies controlled transport on the upper Rhine to Mannheim and Ludwigshafen, the basing points for coal sold in southern Germany. The wholesalers thus were without means of transporting coal to that area had they wished to circumvent the distribution agencies on which they were dependent.

The prospective dissolution of DKV (which occurred in 1953) spelled the end of Kohlenkontor Weyhenmeyer. With the handwriting on the wall, Kohlenkontor Weyhenmeyer and OKU drew up a fusion agreement in 1950 to control the south German coal market. It was pocket-vetoed by the United

---

[78] See *Glückauf*, December 8, 1956, p. 1504; *Revue française de l'énergie*, September 1956, p. 424.

[79] *Handelsblatt*, April 18, 1956.

States Military Government but supported by the French Military Government, as well as by the German principals. The dormant agreement was executed by its sponsors in 1952 without the approval of the United States Military Government. The new organization, also called OKU, began operations in April 1953. It sold directly to all customers that consumed 30,000 tons or more of solid fuels annually. It sold directly to all wholesalers, who dealt with the smaller consumers. OKU thus handled all the solid fuels consumed in southern Germany and also controlled transport on the upper Rhine and the coal blending facilities at Mannheim.

Unichar owned 3.6 per cent of the capital stock of OKU, the mining firms in the Ruhr and Aachen owned 32 per cent of the stock and several large wholesalers in southern Germany owned about 50 per cent of OKU.[80] But since the mining firms in the Ruhr exercised proprietary control in several large wholesale firms in southern Germany, the coal mining firms as a whole that sold in that market—the Saar, Lorraine, Ruhr and Aachen mines—controlled OKU through direct and indirect ownership ties. These mining firms as a whole furnished two thirds of all the solid fuels consumed in southern Germany. That portion of the two thirds that was transported on the Rhine River—about 7 million tons annually—accounted for about one fifth of all upstream traffic.[81]

In July 1953 the High Authority issued a "recommendation" (which is binding as to objectives but leaves the principal free to select his means) to OKU. It indicated that OKU monopolizes the distribution of solid fuels in southern Germany and divides the clientele between itself and the wholesalers, the latter being able to sell only to customers that consume less than 30,000 tons annually. The High Authority therefore recommended that OKU should take "appropriate measures to eliminate the practices contrary to Article 4 of the Treaty."[82] But this recommendation was simply a holding action that deferred the real solution to the time when Georg should be dissolved—an event that occurred nearly three years later.

After Reorganization by the High Authority (August 1957)[83]

The High Authority as of August 1957 transformed OKU from a common sales agency for the producers into a common purchasing agency for wholesalers. The coal mining firms in the Ruhr and Aachen were required to withdraw from OKU as members and owners. The Saar and Lorraine producers,

[80] *Ibid.*

[81] HA, Decision No. 19–57, *Journal officiel*, August 10, 1957, pp. 352–353.

[82] HA, Recommendation of July 11, 1953, *Journal officiel*, July 21, 1953, p. 154.

[83] HA, Decision No. 19–57, *Journal officiel*, August 10, 1957, pp. 352 ff. The decision, effective August 1, 1957, is summarized in HA, *Bulletin mensuel d'information*, October 1957, p. 11.

as well as Unichar (later Saarlar), were also required to withdraw but were accorded a respite to March 1958. This respite gave them time to establish commercial relations with the wholesalers in the area—relations that the firms in the Ruhr and Aachen had already had for a long time.[84] Designated wholesalers in France were given the opportunity until March 1958 to extend their activities to southern Germany in order to qualify as first-hand wholesalers and purchasers of capital stock in OKU.

Each wholesaler was authorized to own capital shares in OKU in proportion to the volume of solid fuels it purchased through it. The High Authority decision stipulated that wholesalers that are controlled by the Ruhr mining firms or that have proprietary interests in those firms may not capture control of OKU.

The High Authority decision required OKU to become purely a service organization for its members. OKU may not sell solid fuels to consumers, or fix prices or make any agreements limiting the use and availability of Rhine transport. It must purchase for the account of the wholesaler on the latter's instructions as to source and price; at the wholesaler's request, it must try to purchase from any producing district in the ECSC. Where the mining firms in a producing region sell through common sales agencies, OKU must purchase from the latter, not from the former.

OKU was not authorized to monopolize purchases. Consumers that purchase over 30,000 tons of solid fuels annually and first-hand wholesalers may also purchase directly from mining firms or their agents. The wholesalers were not required to join OKU but OKU was obliged to admit any wholesaler who fulfilled the conditions. OKU was thus required to be only a voluntary common purchasing agency.

OKU was authorized to maintain blending facilities, to operate a shipping pool on the Rhine and to maintain stockpiles, in order to coordinate supplies and transports. It was obliged to furnish shipping facilities to nonmembers to the extent available.

The High Authority can review OKU's activities to see that it complies with the authorization. It may if necessary request OKU to help spread orders among the mining firms during a business recession or to help distribute coal fairly when it is scarce.

Southern Germany accounts for about 10 per cent of the solid fuels consumed by the ECSC as a whole. In reorganizing OKU, the High Authority tried to induce the suppliers in that market—the Ruhr, Aachen, the Saar and Lorraine—to compete. This matter is discussed further in Chapter 9.

[84] This respite was prolonged once by the High Authority; a request for a second prolongation was denied. *Journal officiel*, August 4, 1958, p. 286.

THE BELGIAN MARKET

Interwar Period

The efforts of the Belgian coal industry to control markets before the second world war were as turbulent as those of the steel industry. The large number of small independents in the southern coal fields and differences between government and industry created most of the difficulties.

A socialist minister of industry and labor in 1927 proposed that the mines establish a centralized sales agency. This proposal was abandoned under attack from the industry. In April 1929 Société Générale and the Banque de Bruxelles helped found the Comptoir Belge des Charbons Industriels; it lasted until 1934. This agency, in cooperation with another for the Liége mining district, centralized the sale of coal to industry and the exportation and importation of industrial coal; it handled in all about 8 million tons of coal annually on a total production of 26 million tons. Coke was controlled by another agreement. The Comptoir Belge des Charbons Industriels ran into difficulties in 1934 owing to differences between the coal industry and the government. The former was unhappy with the volume of coal imported under the Belgo-German Commercial Treaty and the latter was unhappy with a 5 per cent wage reduction made by the industry. The government introduced a bill early in 1934 calling for government control of production, sales, imports and exports until 1935. The coal industry attacked it as "dirigistic" but appointed a committee to negotiate with the government on the latter's invitation. The government in the meantime reimbursed the employees for the 5 per cent wage cut. Another bill was passed later in 1934; it authorized the government to control the industry by decree. Under this law the producers founded a cooperative called Office National des Charbons in December 1934. The Belgian government simultaneously denounced the commercial treaty with Germany. The Office National des Charbons consisted of eight sections, one for each type of coal. It controlled production, assigned production quotas, regulated prices and foreign trade. It had exclusive control over sales to major public and private consumers and to foreign customers. The cost of the control scheme, under which exports were subsidized also, was covered by a levy of 2 francs per ton of coal produced.[85] An Office Belge des Cokes with similar functions was created in 1937.

Under the Common Market

The High Authority's decision to authorize common sales agencies for the mining firms in the Ruhr set the pattern for the firms in Belgium, one of the few other places where private firms still control most or all of the production.

[85] Dubosq, *op. cit.*, pp. 151–155; *The World Coal-Mining Industry*, Vol. I, pp. 246–247.

In October 1956, several months after the establishment of the three sales agencies in the Ruhr, the High Authority authorized the Belgian coal mines to operate a central sales agency for similar reasons.[86] Comptoir Belge des Charbons (Cobechar), organized in 1934, was authorized to sell coal for the mining firms to certain customers. It was also authorized to fix prices and sales conditions for all sales, including those made by the mining firms themselves. Cobechar also was empowered to fix the rules for delivery terms, for basing points, for discounts and for long-term contracts. Unlike Ruhr firms, the mining firms in Belgium are authorized to concert on prices.

Practically all the mining firms are represented in Cobechar. Each firm has capital shares and voting rights in Cobechar in proportion to its production. Since the Société Générale and the Launoit groups control a large part of the coal industry, the presidency of Cobechar rotates between the two groups from one year to the next.[87]

Cobechar was not authorized to control production but it was authorized to equalize employment and the distribution of orders when there is idle capacity.[88] This stipulation is included as a "restriction" on the powers of Cobechar, and was evidently meant to protect the independent producers.

The large consumers, defined functionally rather than by annual consumption—the independent cokeries, steel plant cokeries, public utilities, public railroads, bunkers, cement, glass and patent fuel plants—are all reserved to Cobechar. Cobechar was to sell to Italian customers until July 1958 unless any of the latter preferred to employ a merchant instead. Cobechar was not authorized to insist on exclusive sales arrangements in the Luxembourg or French coal markets.

The mining firms may sell to all other customers, to firms that own 75 per cent of their capital and to any consumers that have bought from the mines on long-term contracts. The mines may sell directly or through merchants. The High Authority decision does not attempt to protect or define the status of merchant or to divide merchants into zones as it does for the sale of Ruhr coal, although it offers them the general protection of Articles 4(b) and 4(d) of the treaty.[89] If Cobechar fixes the rules for sale to merchants, it must first obtain the High Authority's approval. In Belgium as in the Ruhr, the High

[86] Decision No. 30–56, *Journal officiel*, October 18, 1956, and the amendment thereto, Decision No. 27–57, *Journal officiel*, December 27, 1957.

[87] H. Aszkenazy, "Le Fonctionnement du marché charbonnier en Belgique et en Hollande," *Annales des mines*, May 1957, p. 322.

[88] Article 9 of HA, Decision No. 30–56.

[89] The merchants' markup, fixed by government decree, is added to the list price of the mining firm so that consumers ordinarily prefer to purchase directly from the mine. On sales to the retailer the wholesale merchant may add 3.3 per cent to the mine price. The markup on imports is also fixed by the Belgian government. Aszkenazy, "Le Fonctionement du marché charbonnier en Belgique et en Hollande," p. 324.

Authority decision gives the customer the right to take delivery at mine, inland port or Antwerp and to arrange his own transportation.

The mining firms are authorized to establish uniform freight charges for delivery at Liége, Gand and Antwerp, provided the uniform charge does not exceed the actual average freight charge. The firms may operate a financial scheme to debit and credit the firms for the difference between the uniform charge and the actual freight cost.

Belgium produced an annual average of 29.5 million tons of coal in 1956–1957; 6.5 million tons were consumed by the mines and affiliated concerns, leaving 23 million tons for sale. Cobechar handles about 17 million tons, nearly 60 per cent of the total output or three fourths of the coal available for sale. The mining firms handle the rest. There are more than fifty mining firms. The High Authority decision theoretically provides for a large number of sellers. But sales are more coordinated in practice than appearance indicates, because Cobechar fixes prices and sales conditions for all coal whether sold by it or by the mining firms, because the Société Générale and the Launoit groups dominate Cobechar, and because nearly all the mining firms belong to Cobechar. The coal sold directly by the mining firms is therefore sold by firms that also belong to Cobechar.

OTHER ECSC MARKETS

The Netherlands

The State controls about two thirds of the coal output in the Netherlands. A foreign-owned mining firm controls another 20 per cent. The Dutch coal industry is thus effectively centralized as producer and seller. The Netherlands normally imports nearly two thirds as much as it produces. Germany, Belgium and the United States supply most of the coal imported. Though imports are not centralized, the government supervises the volume of coal imported by the merchants.

Italy

Nearly all the coal consumed by Italy is imported. Italy has no domestic coal industry to protect and therefore has every reason to import freely from the lowest-priced sources. Imports are arranged by the several large consumers and distributors.

CONCLUSIONS

The mining firms in all the mining districts where coal is produced by more than one firm, as in Aachen, Lower Saxony, the Ruhr and Belgium, have been

authorized to sell in common. The High Authority and the individual governments stand behind this policy. The High Authority has also authorized common purchasing arrangements among wholesalers in southern Germany. This
principle will no doubt apply to importers of solid fuels in France as well, provided the French government agrees to eliminate ATIC's exclusive power over
imports and to convert ATIC into a voluntary purchasing agency for the
importers and consumers that wish to employ its know-how.

There appears to be very little likelihood of rivalry between mining firms in
the same producing district for local or distant markets. Will the sales agencies
for different coal fields compete among themselves? Such rivalry is still potentially possible in those markets that are supplied by more than one regional
source and especially in those markets that are accessible to imports from overseas sources, notably from the United States. The markets in southern and
northern Germany, in Italy, and those served through the Low Country ports,
meet these conditions. These prospects are discussed in Chapters 9 and 10, for
which the present chapter serves as background.

CHAPTER 9

COAL:

PRICE REGULATION

The coordination of prices and sales within each coal producing district in the ECSC rests, as shown by Chapter 8, on formal rather than spontaneous methods.

There are a large number of mines in most districts and a large number of firms in most privately operated areas. But production and sales are coordinated, with public sanction, in all mining areas. Coordination is achieved by a common over-all administration in nationalized coal mining areas and by publicly authorized common sales agencies in privately owned districts, as the preceding chapter indicated.[1] Coordination enables the firms to maintain fairly stable prices over the course of the business cycle, to share markets and even revenue—through interfirm compensation—when capacity is not fully utilized. Owing to the large number of firms, prices would otherwise fall sharply during a recession.

Many factors, according to the views prevailing in Europe, stand behind the need for price stability in the coal industry. First, a falling price endangers the miners' standard of living because payroll costs account for 55 to 65 per cent of the sales revenue and also endangers the high-cost mines in an industry where costs of production vary sharply. Second, the smaller coal mining firms (of which there are many) do not have the financial reserves to accumulate stocks, to carry labor, to absorb losses when the demand for coal contracts.

It remains to be seen whether the High Authority will sacrifice price and employment stability for the sake of eliminating concerted practices in the Ruhr coal industry. It included stability of employment and earnings among the ends to be considered in connection with the possible dissolution of the three sales agencies in 1960 or 1961.[2]

---

[1] Formal organization by near compulsory measures was tried in the United States in the 1930s but soon abandoned as a result of judicial rulings; the anthracite producing firms still coordinate production, however, under the supervision of the state of Pennsylvania.

[2] HA, Decision 17–59, *Journal officiel*, March 7, 1959, pp. 279 ff.

Though the private coal operators and public authority, federal as well as national, both stand behind the policy of coordination, their interests are not convergent on all issues. The two differ mainly on price questions; the managers of the nationalized coal mines also differ with their governments on this issue. While operators and governments share the belief in stable prices, the former would like stabilization at levels above those considered by the governments to be consistent with the public interest. Many private coal operators criticize the price policies of the governments—"political prices" they are called by the German operators—but, knowing that common sales agencies cannot operate without government consent, very few of them would challenge the government to the point of endangering the prevailing system of coordination. The private coal operators in Western Europe would not sacrifice coordination for the sake of obtaining price freedom. Whatever the disagreements between operators and governments, between governments themselves, or between the governments and the High Authority, there is general consensus with the proposition that the coal mining industry must be protected by means of coordination from the effects of recession. The extent to which coordination occurs between mining districts also, apart from that between firms in the same district, is discussed later in this chapter.

PRICES ON THE EVE OF THE COMMON MARKET[3]

As a result of postwar measures coping with a severe scarcity of solid fuels, prices were officially controlled by all the member governments prior to the common market.

Germany

Domestic prices were based on the weighted average costs of production in the industry as a whole. The mines in Aachen and in the Ruhr used a common price schedule but the Aachen mines quoted f.o.b. Ruhr for sales on the left bank of the Rhine, which is closer to Aachen than to the Ruhr, in order to earn a higher net mill return on sales to that area. Domestic sales were otherwise quoted f.o.b. mine by the mines in all areas. The mines in Lower Saxony had a price scale slightly higher than that in the Ruhr. By government stipulation, household consumers, maritime transport and deep-sea fishing received

[3] The information on prices on the eve of the common market is drawn from HA, *Les Systèmes de prix dans les principaux pays producteurs de la Communauté*, January 25, 1953 (mimeo.).

a discount of $2.50 per ton. First-hand merchants received a 2 per cent commission from the coal producers.

Export prices were also controlled by the government. Net mill returns on exports were on the average $1.25 per ton higher than those on domestic sales because of systematic international price discrimination. Exports by rail were billed from a common basing point (Wanne-Eickel); those by waterway carried a uniform charge from the mine to the Rhine port of Duisburg-Ruhrort, and those by sea a uniform charge to the maritime port.

The consumer paid the real price for imported coal without subsidy or equalization, the import merchant receiving a contractual commission paid by the customer. General railroad rates applied to the haulage of imported coal; these rates were higher than the special rates for transporting German coal.

The German government fixed zonal prices for coal imported from the Saar and Lorraine for delivery in southern Germany; these prices were based on the delivered price of coal from the Ruhr and Aachen. Since the mines in the Saar and Lorraine absorbed freight to align their prices in southern Germany, the French government reimbursed them for the cost of freight absorption.

Before the establishment of the common market German coal prices were abnormally low in the domestic market—as were steel prices—compared with prices in other countries (Table 47) but receipts were sweetened by higher export prices.

France

The French government also fixed the price level in relation to weighted average production costs in the whole industry. Charbonnages de France determined the average price for each mining district on the basis of the government's price level. The mines in Nord and Pas-de-Calais, which quoted f.o.b. mine, served as the bellwether for prices in the most important markets in France, and those in Lorraine, in coordination with the Saar mines, determined prices to consumers—coking plants excepted—in eastern France. First-hand merchants added a 1 per cent charge to the price.

Imports were centralized by the Association Technique de l'Importation Charbonnière (ATIC) and sold at domestic coal prices. The public treasury paid the difference when imported coal was higher in price and received the credit when it was lower in price.

Belgium

Prices in Belgium were fixed by the government. Deliveries made by waterway incurred a fixed charge of 40 cents per ton. Merchants' markups were also fixed, but varied with the type of consumer. Coal imported from Germany was sold at domestic prices, though the delivered cost was lower; the government used the difference to subsidize the Belgian mines. Most export prices were above those in effect in the domestic market.

Netherlands

The Netherlands government fixed uniform sales prices for domestic and imported coal. Domestic prices included a delivery charge that was uniform for the whole country. The mines were credited with a basic unit revenue fixed by the government in accordance with production costs. Since the gross revenue usually exceeded the basic revenue, the difference was retained by the government and used to subsidize two high-cost mines and high-cost imported coal. Imports were arranged by the merchants at prices approved by the government. Exports—confined almost exclusively to coke—were made at prices above those in effect in the domestic market.

PRICE RULINGS OF THE HIGH AUTHORITY

The common market for coal started in February 1953. The High Authority made a number of decisions in connection with the price provisions of the treaty, already described in Chapter 7.

INTERNATIONAL PRICE DISCRIMINATION

The High Authority, in accordance with Article 60, required the mining firms to publish their prices and terms of sale, to indicate the various surcharges or deductions according to specifications, and to bill the customer f.o.b. mine, itemizing the various additional charges.[4] The High Authority carefully protected the buyer's right to select his own transportation, but authorized the seller to make contracts for delivery at shipping points other than the mine if the customer accepted such terms.

The High Authority tried to protect the independence of the first-hand merchant in order to reduce the monopoly power of the sales agencies; Oberrheinische Kohlenunion was changed from a producers' to a merchants' agency in southern Germany for this purpose. But the role of the first-hand merchant is limited, for he deals primarily—though not exclusively—with small consumers. If supply is scarce, then the first-hand merchant and the consumer are both dependent on governmental protection. In a buyers' market, merchants can compete by reducing their commission; Article 63 (2a)

[4] Decision 4–53, *Journal officiel*, February 12, 1953.

of the treaty requires resale price maintenance, but that provision is weak because the Community has no jurisdiction over merchants and the producers are responsible only for their agents. Some efforts have been made to amend the treaty by giving the ECSC jurisdiction over merchants. In the 1958 recession efforts were made, for example, to compel the first-hand merchants to post their prices and to adhere to them.[5]

Although each mine is a basing point, sales by the common sales agencies in the Ruhr are generally made from a central shipping point, like Duisburg-Ruhrort on the Rhine for waterway transport, or a maritime port. The common sales agency collects coal from a number of mines in order to supply the volume and variety required and equalizes delivery costs to the shipping point among the mines in the district. This practice neutralizes locational differences among the mines in the same producing district.

International price discrimination in the common market was eliminated.[6] The importing member countries, which absorbed about 70 per cent of the solid fuels exported by the producers in the ECSC, reaped the benefit of the ban on international price discrimination. But price discrimination still applies to coal exported to third-party countries. Prices for coal exported to third-party countries are therefore higher than home prices during a boom.[7] But exportation of solid fuels to third areas plays a much smaller role in the coal than in the steel industry; the latter exports more than a fifth of its production to areas outside the Community while the coal industry exports only about 7 per cent of its production.

FREIGHT ABSORPTION

The High Authority in 1953 forbade the coal producers—unlike the steel producers—to absorb freight on sales made at another basing point, for fear the supply of coal in each producing district would be disturbed; this interdiction did not prevent a district from lowering its whole price schedule in order

---

[5] HA, *Sixième rapport général*, Vol. II, pp. 53–54; *Handelsblatt*, October 17-18, 1958, p. 2.

[6] Export prices had been lower than domestic prices in the interwar period, when coal was surplus, and higher after the war, when it was scarce. For a discussion of interwar conditions and prices, see ILO, *The World Coal-Mining Industry*, Geneva, 1938, Vol. I; Robert Lafitte-Laplace, *L'Economie charbonnière de la France*, Marcel Giard, Paris, 1933; André Dubosq, *Le Conflit contemporain des houillères européennes*, Librairie Technique et Economique, Paris, 1936; *Coal Mining*, Report of the Technical Advisory Committee, Charles C. Reid, Chairman, HMSO, London, March 1945 (cited hereafter as Reid Report); for the United States, W. E. Fisher and C. M. James, *Minimum Price Fixing in the Bituminous Coal Industry*, Princeton University Press, Princeton, 1955. For the difference in export and home prices at various times after World War II, see ECE, *Quarterly Bulletin*, Vol. I, No. 3, 1950, p. 19; International Authority for the Ruhr, *Prices of Solid Fuels in Western Germany*, June 10, 1952.

[7] That continental coal exporters still practice international price discrimination on exports to third areas can be seen from the figures on the value of coal imported by the United Kingdom, in *Glückauf*, March 20, 1957, p. 399; see also Gelsenkirchener Bergbau A. G., *Jahresbericht*, 1956, pp. 11–12.

to broaden its sales area. Freight absorption to align prices with those of coal imported from third countries was permitted.[8]

THE END OF STATUTORY PRICE CONTROL?

With the opening of the common market in February 1953, control over prices legally passed from the several governments to the Community. The High Authority decided that maximum price control should be continued under its own auspices on the ground that sales cartels were still operating in the Ruhr and elsewhere and that prices would rise too much if they were set free.[9]

In April 1954, a year later, the High Authority decided to retain maximum price control on the coal produced in Belgium, the Ruhr and Nord and Pas-de-Calais—about 70 per cent of the production in the ECSC—and to release the remainder.[10] Price control for coal from the Ruhr and Nord and Pas-de-Calais was prolonged on the ground that the two districts produced a large proportion of the types that were still scarce and, further, that a common sales organization still monopolized Ruhr coal. The price of Belgian coal was controlled in order to administer the subsidy, paid by the Community under the Convention for the Transitional Provisions, that was designed to bring Belgian prices down to "normal" levels. Belgian prices were accordingly controlled by the High Authority until the transitional period ended in February 1958.

In April 1955 coal prices in Nord and Pas-de-Calais were released, leaving Ruhr and Belgian coal under price ceilings.[11]

In April 1956, the High Authority, having disbanded the old sales agencies for the Ruhr and authorized three agencies in their stead, also freed that district from price control, bringing to an end thirty-five years of statutory price regulation. Prices of solid fuels were therefore free after April 1956 every-

---

[8] HA, Decision 3–53, *Journal officiel*, February 12, 1953, extended in Decision 6–54, *Journal officiel*, March 24, 1954.

Surplus producing districts were allowed to post zonal prices to align their prices in other sales areas (under Paragraph 24 of the CTP) during the transitional period; zonal prices were discontinued in February 1958, when that period ended. The principal zonal prices affected the delivery of Saar and Lorraine coal in southern Germany, of Centre-Midi coal in other parts of France, of Belgian coke and Aachen coal in the rest of the Community. Certain temporary subsidies were authorized to compensate the producers, especially those in the Saar and Lorraine, for absorbing freight under zonal prices. For a list of zonal prices and subsidies in effect during the transitional period, see HA, *Sixième rapport général*, Vol. II, pp. 24–26.

[9] Decision 6–53 stated the general principles and objectives of price control, citing Article 3(c), which calls for the lowest possible price level consistent with costs; Decisions 7–73 through 15–53 and 19–53 through 24–53 fixed maximum prices for each mining district. All these Decisions, dated March 6, 1953, are to be found in *Journal officiel*, March 13, 1953.

[10] Decisions 18–54 through 20–54 for the Ruhr and Nord and Pas-de-Calais, Decision 15–54 for Belgium, all published in *Journal officiel*, March 24, 1954.

[11] Decision 12–55, *Journal officiel*, March 28, 1955, amended by Decision 20–55, *Journal officiel*, May 11, 1955.

where but in Belgium. Controls ended there, too, in February 1958.[12] But the High Authority in 1957 required the sales agencies in the Ruhr and in Belgium to give four weeks', instead of one week's, notice in advance of a price change in order to enable it to investigate the circumstances.[13]

How did the coal producers behave after their prices had ostensibly been freed? Did the facts follow the formulas? In order to answer this question, the next section focuses attention on prices within each country or mining district and the section after that discusses price rivalry, if any, between mining districts—taking each aspect of the matter over the course of a business cycle. There was a short recession beginning in 1953, a sellers' market from mid-1954 to late 1957 and a recession thereafter.

PRICE TRENDS OVER THE COURSE OF THE BUSINESS CYCLE

Though official home prices, having been abnormally low, had risen sharply in 1951–1953 (Table 47), only in the Ruhr and the Netherlands did they weaken slightly in the one-year recession that began in mid-1953. The official maximum price ceilings, in existence throughout the recession, became the prevailing prices.[14] Thanks to the sharp reduction in imports from third-party countries, the industry weathered the 1953 recession without recourse to the secret discounts that then troubled the steel industry, though the French complained that some grades of Belgian coal were sold in northern France below French coal prices.

From mid-1954 to the end of 1956 coal prices tended to resist the economic boom, though payroll costs were rising.[15] The industry absorbed rising costs because domestic prices had already risen considerably in 1951–1952 (Table 47) and had risen again in the Ruhr in 1952–1953, and because efficiency in most areas had increased when declining demand during the 1953 recession permitted more selective mining.

Domestic coal prices (in local currencies in Table 48) began to climb again in 1957 as payroll costs increased more rapidly than efficiency. Nominal coal prices thus rose everywhere in the Community in 1957 and 1958 and more rapidly than the general wholesale price index everywhere but in France (Table 48).

[12] Decision 2–58, *Journal officiel*, February 8, 1958.

[13] Decisions 24–57 through 27–57, *Journal officiel*, December 27, 1957.

[14] See the query of M. Blaisse, member of the Common Assembly, in *Journal officiel*, July 21, 1953, p. 158.

[15] HA, *Informations statistiques*, September-October 1957, p. 379, gives the change in hourly payroll costs from 1953 to 1956.

Table 47

DOMESTIC AND EXPORT PRICES OF COKING SMALLS,
SELECTED COUNTRIES AND YEARS, 1938–1958[a]

(Price per Metric Ton)

			Domestic Price						Export Price	
			France							
Year	Ruhr	Saar	Nord and Pas-de-Calais	Lor-raine	Bel-gium	Nether-lands	United Kingdom	United States	United Kingdom	United States
	(1)	(2)	(3)	(4)	(5)	(6)	(7)	(8)	(9)	(10)
1938	$6.02	$8.20	$4.72	$4.75	...	$5.91	$5.01	...	...	$4.45
1950	7.54	9.80	10.44	9.26	$12.96	9.33	7.74	$5.25	$12.06	8.86
1951	8.29	11.55	12.15	10.30	13.31	10.78	...	5.21	...	9.57
1952	9.92	13.47	14.09	12.72	14.21	13.39	...	5.16	...	9.64
1953	11.91	13.47	14.27	12.59	14.25	13.88	...	5.26	...	9.27
1954	11.67	13.80	14.39	12.90	14.08	13.20	11.42	4.96	14.72	8.98
1955	11.81	13.69	13.88	12.74	13.85	12.95	12.81	4.95	14.88	9.36
1956	12.51	13.94	14.10	13.79	14.16	12.92	14.77	5.55	19.29	10.50
1957										
April	13.39	14.86	14.57	14.00	17.30	14.55	14.97	5.98	22.30	11.35
October	14.01	13.85	13.10	13.57	...	...	15.78	6.13	21.00	10.97
1958										
March	14.01	15.12	13.75	13.69	17.70	15.34	15.78	6.10	18.62	11.20
July	14.01	15.12	13.75	13.69	17.70	15.34	15.78	...	16.55	...

Sources:

Col. 1: *Kohlenwirtschaft* (KWZ); Statistisches Bundesamt, Wiesbaden. Turnover tax excluded by author.

Col. 2: Local taxes excluded; KWZ and *Usine nouvelle*. These prices do not apply for shipments to south Germany and France, where zonal prices were effective during the transitional period.

Col. 3: KWZ; *Usine nouvelle.*

Col. 4: F.o.b. Bening. KWZ; *Usine nouvelle;* zonal prices were effective on sales to south Germany and certain parts of France during the transitional period.

Col. 5: KWZ; *Jahrbuch; Usine nouvelle.* Beginning in November 1957 two prices were quoted, with a range of 40 cents between them, the lower price posted for the lower-cost basins: Campine, Mons, Centre. The price in the table is the higher of the two, that for the southern mines.

Col. 6: Prices posted by Staatsmijnen, the government-owned mines. Turnover tax excluded by author. Prior to April 1953, prices are free destination, thereafter f.o.b. mine for loading by water transport. KWZ; *Jahrbuch; Usine nouvelle.*

Col. 7: F.o.b. Tyne, virtually an f.o.b. mine price. Statistisches Bundesamt, Wiesbaden.

Col. 8: This is a weighted average price for industrial screenings and not strictly comparable with that shown for other countries either as to size or purpose. The price of coking smalls is about $1.00 higher. *Survey of Current Business;* Statistisches Bundesamt, Wiesbaden.

Col. 9: Same as col. 7. In recent years this grade has been exported in limited quantities only.

Col. 10: Statistisches Bundesamt, Wiesbaden, f.o.b. port; this series covers run-of-mine coal for a variety of end uses, in addition to metallurgical ones, and as a weighted average price is not strictly comparable with either col. 8 or the European coking coals, although it has coking properties. European clients purchase U. S. coking, and often other, coals, run of mine, from particular mines for later sorting, crushing and blending in Europe. The prices shown include between 40 per cent and 45 per cent freight to U. S. port.

[a] Unless otherwise indicated, all prices refer to coking smalls under 10 mm. in size. While no grade serves as an ideal indicator, this series has been selected as possibly the best index for price trends and levels, inasmuch as it serves a very specific end use and therefore is fairly homogeneous. Prices are f.o.b. mine unless otherwise indicated. These are base prices, generally for wagon or large load lots, with variations for departures from standard specifications, size of order, type of loading and transportation. Prior to the common market, domestic prices shown for the ECSC producers applied to sales in the respective country only.

Notes continued on next page

The 1958 recession affected the mines in Belgium and Germany severely. The mines in the Community held a total of 22 million tons of producers' stocks as of October 1, 1958, equivalent to five weeks' production; the Belgian mines held 30 per cent of these stocks, equivalent to over two months' production in that country. Producers' stocks in the recession of 1953–1954 had amounted to only three weeks' of the Community's production. Producers'

Table 48

REAL PRICE TRENDS FOR COKING SMALLS, ECSC, 1954–1958

(1953 = 100)

Country	1954	1955	1956	1957 April	1957 October	1958 March
Germany						
Coal prices (Ruhr)	98	99	105	112	118	118
General wholesale prices	98	101	103	105	105	106
Real coal prices	100	98	102	107	112	111
France						
Coal prices (Nord and Pas-de-Calais)	101	97	99	102	110	116
General wholesale prices	98	98	102	104	112	120
Real coal prices	103	99	97	98	98	97
Belgium						
Coal prices (southern mines)	99	97	99	121	...	124
General wholesale prices	99	101	104	107	106	103
Real coal prices	100	96	95	113	...	120
Netherlands						
Coal prices	...	100	100	113	...	119
General wholesale prices	101	102	104	107	107	106
Real coal prices	...	98	96	106	...	112

Sources: Wholesale prices from UN, *Monthly Bulletin of Statistics,* and OEEC, *General Statistics.* Nominal prices from Table 47. Coal prices for the Netherlands adjusted for the change from delivered to f.o.b. mine prices. Coal prices in France exclude discrepancies arising from devaluation.

Notes to Table 47 continued:

Turnover and production taxes are excluded; these are (since 1952): Germany, 4.16 per cent; Saar, 9.11 per cent to 1956, 11.11 per cent thereafter; France, 7.93 per cent to 1956, 9.29 per cent in 1956, 11.11 per cent in 1957; Belgium, 4.50 per cent to 1956, 5 per cent since; Netherlands, 4.16 per cent to 1956, 5.3 per cent since.

Included in the prices shown for the Ruhr and the Netherlands, from 1953 through 1957, are a small degressive High Authority levy to subsidize production in Belgium.

The particular grades are:

Ruhr	Kokskohle I, 19–28 per cent volatile matter (v.m.)
Saar	Gras A, 33–40 per cent v.m.
Nord and Pas-de-Calais	Gras, 22–30 per cent v.m.
Lorraine	Gras B, 35–37 per cent v.m.
Belgium	Gras A, 20–28 per cent v.m.
Netherlands	Vetkolen, 20–25 per cent v.m.
United Kingdom	Durham gas coal I and II, cols. 7 and 9
United States (col. 8)	Industrial screenings (weighted average value at mine)
United States (col. 10)	Run of mine (weighted average value at port)

stocks in the British mines in October 1958 amounted to about three weeks' production.[16] The mines in the Community, as in Britain, by and large maintained production in spite of rising stocks, though recruiting of new manpower ceased; the following figures show production in the first eight months of 1958 as a percentage of production in the corresponding period of 1957:[17]

	Per Cent
Germany	99.4
Saar	99.0
France	100.2
Belgium	95.3
Netherlands	98.7

Though stocks accumulated and competition from petroleum and imported American coal was keen, the mines maintained official home prices but granted temporary discounts on incremental purchases by selected consumers. The Belgian mines later reduced home prices by 3 to 8 per cent, effective January 1, 1959—the only ones that had as of that date reduced the price schedule as a whole.[18] In addition to the normal summer discounts, the Ruhr in April 1959 also reduced prices somewhat on types of coal that represent 5 per cent of the total production.[19]

Official home prices therefore did not decline during the 1958 recession, except in Belgium, where they were brought into line with those in other areas.

TRADE WITHIN THE ECSC OVER THE COURSE OF THE BUSINESS CYCLE

We have thus far discussed prices within each coal producing area. Since the coal produced in each area is either sold or coordinated by a common sales agency—or by several agencies acting as one in the Ruhr[20]—price com-

[16] *Revue française de l'énergie*, September 1958, p. 524; *The Economist*, October 4, 1958, p. 63, and October 11, 1958, p. 130.

[17] HA, *Bulletin statistique*. The miners in southern Belgium lost twelve working days between January and August 1958 but the miners in the Community as a whole lost three and a half days only; *Le Monde*, October 25, 1958, p. 14.

[18] *Revue française de l'énergie*, September 1958, p. 524. All but the Ruhr mines published their discounts; the latter, with the High Authority's permission, refrained on the ground that publication would hinder their efforts to sell more coal outside the ECSC; see the High Authority's reply to Question No. 10, in *Journal officiel*, November 7, 1958, p. 465. *Handelsblatt*, December 22, 1958, p. 2.

[19] *Handelsblatt*, April 2, 1959, p. 1. The Ruhr mines also tried to meet the price of U. S. coal delivered to other parts of the ECSC; *Handelsblatt*, August 5, 1959, p. 3.

[20] HA, Decision 17–59, in *Journal officiel*, March 7, 1959, pp. 279 ff, and *Sixième rapport général*, Vol. I, p. 96. Price decisions seem to be made by the leading firms first and ratified by the sales agencies afterward; in February 1958, for example, the officials of the coal operators' association (Unternehmensverband Ruhrbergbau) promised the German government not to raise prices during the year; the sales agencies ratified this undertaking afterward with some reluctance; see *Handelsblatt*, February 7–8, 1958, p. 2.

petition between firms in the same district is precluded. Have there, however, been any signs of interregional competition since the establishment of the common market?

There are fewer primary sellers in coal than in steel because the regional coal sales agency, whether in privately or publicly owned coal fields, rather than the individual firm sells to large consumers and first-hand merchants everywhere in the Community, whereas the individual steel producing firm sells directly, even though it may coordinate spontaneously.

Importance of the Solid Fuels Trade

The trade in solid fuels between the members of the ECSC has undergone a long-term decline—from 46 million tons a year in 1937–1938 to 35 million tons in 1957—but was still important in the 1950s. (The data on trade are shown in Table 2-6, Appendix E, which covers coal and the coal equivalent of coke.) Except for the Centre-Midi and Lower Saxony, all the coal production in the ECSC occurs near a frontier. Sixteen per cent of the coal produced in the ECSC in 1955 was traded between member countries. Fifteen per cent of the total coal consumed by the ECSC in 1955 originated in other parts of the Community and another 12 per cent in third-party countries. (See Table 13.) All the members of the ECSC import solid fuels and all of them obtain a large proportion of their imports from other members of the Community. The importance of the solid fuels imported cannot be measured in magnitudes alone; imports represent a large proportion of coal supply in some areas, such as northern Germany; they represent a large proportion of specific requirements for a particular industry in other areas, such as the Lorraine steelworks or the Saar coke plants; they represent the total supply in Luxembourg and nearly the total supply of coal in Italy, which, however, produces its own coke.

Trade Within the ECSC During a Sellers' Market

The member countries had relied mainly on centralized purchase, bilateral agreements or currency exchange regulations, rather than on tariffs, to control coal imports before the ECSC was organized; they were not interested in tariff protection because solid fuels were scarce after the second world war. The ECSC treaty eliminated tariffs and other administrative impediments to trade between member countries after February 1, 1953. But the Convention for the Transitional Provisions (Section 27) permitted Italy until February 1958 to retain, but progressively diminish, the tariff on imports of coke; the rate was 13.5 per cent ad valorem before the common market. Considering the dearth of coke in the Community, the Italian producers had little to fear in any case.

The members of the ECSC traded 32.7 million tons of solid fuels a year in 1952–1953. Trade rose to a peak of 38.7 million tons in 1955, and declined to 35.5 million tons in 1957 (Table 2-6, Appendix E).

What caused trade to rise in 1955 and to decline subsequently? Price rivalry between districts had little to do with it in view of the fact that the High Authority, as noted previously, had made freight absorption illegal. The economic recession of early 1954 had caused the coal producers in Belgium and France to accumulate stocks. When demand increased in mid-1954 these producers' stocks were sold; France and Belgium thus enjoyed a marked, but short-lived, increase in exports to the rest of the Community; their exports in 1957 reverted nearly to the 1952–1953 level.

Though the coal trade in the ECSC declined from the 1955 peak, it was still 8 per cent higher in 1957 than the average of 1952–1953 (an increase of 2.8 million tons) whereas coal production in the ECSC had increased by only 4 per cent (an increase of 10 million tons). Was this the result of competition based on regional advantage? Total exports by Germany and the Netherlands accounted for nearly all of the increase in trade between the members of the ECSC between 1952–1953 and 1957. Coke accounted for two thirds of the increase from these two countries, virtually the only ones to export coke of metallurgical grade. More than half the internal trade within the ECSC consists of German solid fuels; half the latter consists of the coal equivalent of coke. Coke production has risen relative to coal production in Germany, because pig iron output, which is based on coke, and gas requirements for the public gas system have grown faster than coal output. In order to fill the requirements for gas, a by-product of the coke oven, Germany produces a surplus of coke. The smaller by-product sizes of coke which cannot be used for pig iron production are also surplus and are used for space heating. Over the last few decades Germany has consequently reduced coal exports to all destinations but has increased coke exports. The steel firms in Lorraine, Luxembourg, Belgium and the Saar, some of which control coal and coke producing companies in Germany and the Netherlands, were therefore the main beneficiaries of the rise in the solid fuels trade between 1952–1953 and 1957. Italy was the main "loser" of German primary coal. Since secondary products are more profitable than primary coal and enjoy a more stable market, Holland, too, has favored the export of coke rather than of primary coal. As this trend will undoubtedly continue, the trade in primary coal between ECSC members is bound to decline. Coke plants without a local source of coal will become increasingly dependent on supplies from America. Because of the limited sources of coke, the trade in this product is unlikely to become competitive; circumstances will, if anything, intensify the movement toward captive sources of coke supply.

The trade in primary coal increased very little between 1952–1953 and 1957 —except for the nonrepetitive rise in 1955—and occurred without price rivalry, the buyer paying the full cost of freight. Imports into the Netherlands from the Ruhr, the low-cost producer, declined while those from Belgium, a high-cost source, increased. Using the price of coking smalls in 1956 as a guide to primary coal prices as a whole, the price difference between coal produced in the Ruhr and that produced in other districts was smaller than the cost of freight between them, indicating that no district could have penetrated the others on the basis of its own prices. The difference in 1956 between the price of coking smalls in the Ruhr and other districts (based on Table 47) was:

	Per Ton
Saar	+$1.43
Nord and Pas-de-Calais	+ 1.59
Lorraine	+ 1.28
Belgium	+ 1.65
Netherlands	+ 0.41

As zonal prices and subsidies tapered off toward the end of the transitional period, exports by Lorraine to southern Germany were lower in 1957 than in previous years. As a result consumers in southern Germany complained of the difficulty of getting coal and of rising costs.

Though consumers in the ECSC paid the full cost of freight during the sellers' market, they benefited from the elimination by the ECSC of international price discrimination and some discriminatory railroad freight rates, as shown in Chapter 12. They probably also benefited when coal was scarce in the coal producing countries from the equal-access provisions of the treaty so far as moral suasion by the High Authority and ordinary prudence on the part of the producers helped to maintain the volume of coal offered to the coal-deficient areas of the Community.

Trade Within the ECSC During the 1958 Recession

With the statutory termination of zonal prices in February 1958, the High Authority faced the problem, aggravated by the then current recession, whether to allow freight absorption. It appointed a study group from among members of the industry to prepare suggestions. All but the Belgian members of the group advised the High Authority against freight absorption on the ground that this would open the door to cutthroat competition because coal is not a standardized product. The Belgians favored freight absorption because of their high price scale.[21] The High Authority nevertheless decided to

[21] *Handelsblatt*, January 20, 1958, p. 1, February 3, 1958, p. 9.

allow a limited degree of potential freight absorption, taking great precautions to deprive the producers or sales agencies of the ability to make independent price decisions in markets outside their own producing areas. Effective April 1, 1958, it allowed any producing district to absorb freight on sales made in other producing districts. But they were not allowed to absorb freight on sales made in small producing districts like northern Saxony or some of the divisions in Centre-Midi, which were thus protected from rivalry.[22] No district could absorb freight on more than 20 per cent of its total sales in the years preceding; it could not absorb freight in certain sales areas on a tonnage in excess of that delivered to that area in the coal year 1956–1957. Secret discounts were discouraged by a number of measures; freight absorption on deliveries made by motor transport were specifically prohibited because the freight rates, being frequently unpublished, are not determinate. Those sellers who absorbed freight were required to keep the High Authority informed. The producers' right to continue to absorb freight in order to align prices with those of coal imported from third-party countries was extended for an unlimited time.

The Charbonnages de France would have preferred a delivered price system, similar to that used in Britain for household coal.[23] A delivered price system deprives the buyer of any ability to select his source and the seller of any incentive to compete. The treaty avoids zonal prices owing to the danger of discrimination by nationality.

Did the 1958 recession stimulate market penetration? Exports of primary coal (excluding coke) by Germany to the rest of the Community—Italy excepted—remained almost stationary in the first half of 1958 compared with the corresponding period of 1957 (Table 49); exports to Italy declined from 1.5 to 0.8 million tons because Italy preferred American coal, then priced lower than German coal. But the Ruhr could have increased its exports to other areas, or even to Italy, by absorbing freight. It could in fact have undersold Belgian producers in Belgian markets *without absorbing freight*, judging by the price for Ruhr coking smalls, which was then lower than Belgian prices by more than the cost of freight between the two areas.[24] The difference between the price of Ruhr coking smalls, which is used as the bellwether for primary

---

[22] Decision 3–58, *Journal officiel*, March 18, 1958. An interim decision had extended zonal prices from February 9 to March 31, 1958; Decision 1–58, *Journal officiel*, February 8, 1958. The principles of Decision 3–58 are explained in HA, *Sixième rapport général*, Vol. II, pp. 26–28.

[23] Paul Gardent, "Les Houillères françaises et la concurrence sur le marché commun," *Colloque des Facultés de Droit*, Grenoble, June 1955, p. 20. The British system for household coal is described by I. M. D. Little, *The Price of Fuel*, Clarendon Press, Oxford, 1953, pp. 47–48. Industrial coals were sold f.o.b. mine in the United Kingdom as of 1952; see Federation of British Industries, *Coal: The Price Structure*, London, 3rd edition, n.d.

[24] HA, *Sixième rapport général*, Vol. II, p. 42.

Table 49

TRADE IN COAL BETWEEN ECSC COUNTRIES AND THIRD-PARTY COUNTRIES, FIRST HALF OF 1957 AND 1958[a]

(Thousands of Metric Tons)

Origin	Destination							Total ECSC	Third-Party Countries	Total Exports	Imports from Third-Party Countries
	Germany	Saar	France	Belgium	Luxembourg	Netherlands	Italy				
Germany											
1957		431	1,698	677	67	905	1,532	5,307	1,314	6,621	7,673
1958		436	1,798	713	67	885	756	4,656	815	5,471	6,531
Saar											
1957	1,710		1,880	0	35	0	67	3,692	304	3,996	0
1958	1,314		2,078	0	33	0	8	3,433	171	3,604	10
France											
1957	224	49		192	29	31	35	561	443	1,004	6,072
1958	213	110		96	31	5	10	467	457	924	3,178
Belgium											
1957	103	0	607		18	876	17	1,623	400	2,023	1,506
1958	32	1	616		6	412	0	1,069	424	1,493	1,079
Netherlands											
1957	73	0	114	169	0		0	356	87	443	2,758
1958	28	0	142	230	0		0	400	85	485	1,997
Italy											
1957	0	0	0	0	0	0	0	0	0	0	4,451
1958	0	0	0	0	0	0	0	0	0	0	3,634
Total											
1957	2,110	480	4,299	1,038	149	1,812	1,651	11,539	2,548	14,087	22,481[b]
1958	1,587	547	4,634	1,039	137	1,302	774	10,025	1,952	11,977	16,429

Sources: HA, *Bulletin statistique*; ECE, *Quarterly Bulletin of Coal Statistics*.

[a] Coke is excluded. [b] Includes 21,000 tons of coal imported by Luxembourg.

coal prices as a whole, and the price of that grade of coal produced in other areas was as follows in March 1958 (based on Table 47):

Saar	+$1.11
Nord and Pas-de-Calais	− 0.26
Lorraine	− 0.32
South Belgium	+ 3.69
Netherlands	+ 1.33

Ruhr coal had almost no range in relation to French coal, a range of less than 50 kilometers by rail and 100 kilometers by inland waterway in relation to Netherlands and Saar coal, but a range of nearly 400 kilometers by inland waterway to southern Belgium;[25] most of the coal shipped from the Ruhr to Belgium goes by waterway. Though the German coal operators could have further penetrated Belgium, they refrained from enlarging their share of the Belgian market during the first half of 1958, though producers' stocks in the Ruhr were high.[26] They did, however, maintain their share.

German coal could enter the Dutch market with little or no freight absorption (the operators in Limburg appear to establish their prices by taking the Ruhr price plus freight) but did not enlarge its share in that market. The German coal operators could have aligned prices in France and the Saar only by absorbing freight. But shipments from Germany to France increased by 5 per cent in the first half of 1958 compared with the corresponding period of 1957 because business was still good in France, which therefore needed additional coal. France was in fact the only country that increased its imports from the rest of the Community. The French coal mines are in any case protected by the Association Technique de l'Importation Charbonnière (ATIC), the government-supervised agency that controls imports of nearly all coal and that the High Authority had not yet been able to modify by early 1957.[27] Imports by all the other countries declined or remained constant (Table 49).

The failure of the Ruhr coal industry to enlarge its markets in the 1958 recession, when freight rates on the Rhine had dropped below those on domestic waterways, indicated a remarkable self-restraint, though it maintained its pressure in the south German market.

[25] These rough measures of the 1958 radii of penetration are derived from data in Paul Wiel, *Untersuchungen zu den westeuropäischen Kohlenwirtschaft*, Rheinisch-Westfälisches Institut für Wirtschaftsforschung, Essen, June 1953, pp. 134–137; the radii of penetration decreased considerably from what Wiel shows them to have been in 1951.

[26] The Ruhr coal operators believed that the Belgian producers, who had sponsored freight absorption, which the Germans had opposed, were ungrateful; cited in *Handelsblatt*, February 3, 1958, p. 9.

[27] Paul Gardent, Director of Economic Studies for Charbonnages de France, pointed out that the French coal mines would be in difficulty without ATIC, by means of which the influence of cyclical changes in home demand is shifted to non-French suppliers; see his article in *Revue française de l'énergie*, December 1957, pp. 109 ff.

The total trade in coal between the members of the ECSC declined by about 12 per cent between the first half of 1957 and the corresponding period of 1958, though exports by Germany remained constant.[28] Exports by the Saar to southern Germany declined. Exports by Lorraine to that market were already quite low at the time because of the disinclination to absorb freight; Lorraine has become a marginal supplier there and has become more oriented to the French market. In spite of the hope that the Oberrheinische Kohlenunion (OKU), the common purchasing agency authorized by the High Authority for the merchants in southern Germany, would play off the producers in the Saar and Lorraine against those in the Ruhr, the last group prevailed in the south German market during the 1958 recession. The Netherlands retained its small share of the market in member countries. Exports by Belgium declined by 40 per cent, as was to be expected, though the Belgian mines absorbed freight —the only mines that had favored this practice—on sales outside Belgium.

It cannot be concluded, therefore, that surplus capacity and large producers' stocks led to commercial rivalry between mining districts. But the decline in trade might have been greater had the countries been free to impose restrictions on imports. The Belgian government indeed resorted to this practice early in 1959 by making all imports—even those from the rest of the ECSC— subject to import license on the ground that it wished to control the entry of non-ECSC coal re-exported by partner countries.

ARE COAL PRICES FREE?

Did coal prices escape from control by the individual governments when the High Authority freed them in the years following the establishment of the common market? A discussion of the pricing methods used in the Community will help answer this question.

Coal prices in Western Europe are based on average rather than marginal costs. The governments believe that prices would be too high if they were based on marginal cost—a level at which prices would be equal to the costs of the least efficient producer at the point where demand and supply are balanced.[29] Since costs vary considerably between mines in the same region, as well as between regions, a considerable number of mines operate close to the borderline of solvency or even at a loss when prices are based on average cost.

[28] The trade in coke declined by 8 per cent, though coke exports from Germany to the rest of the ECSC also held their own. Since Germany dominates 70 to 80 per cent of the trade in coke, there is no question of serious competition in the coke market. Data on the trade in coke are from HA, *Bulletin statistique*.

[29] In the *Cinquième rapport général*, p. 130, the High Authority stated that "the governments have not always refrained from direct action on coal prices. They have kept down the price of coal for the sake of holding down the general price level."

Average cost pricing need not, however, create difficulties in a mining district such as the Campine, where all the mines are modern and fairly efficient.

There is a dearth of information on the dispersion of costs. Average cost figures, given in Chapter 4, are not very helpful for this purpose. Even company data conceal the performance of individual pits when the company operates more than one pit. Yet such data are very important in extractive or agricultural industries owing to great natural differences in yield between different operating units.

NATIONALIZED MINES

British Mines

The late Sir Hubert Houldsworth, former Chairman of the National Coal Board in the United Kingdom, presented some figures on the "worst" 24 million tons of British coal produced in 1951—representing about 12 per cent of the underground output.[30] The average loss varied from $5.65 per ton on the least profitable million, to $1.05 per ton on the twenty-fourth million; a total of over $50 million was lost on the aggregate 24 million tons. Referring to the British coal industry as a whole (exclusive of open-pit mines), Sir Hubert said:

> When the industry as a whole aims to break even, it is obvious that something like one-half of its output will show profits and the other half losses. In fact, in 1951, the industry as a whole made a profit of 2/ a ton (before deducting capital charges or profits tax); 61 per cent of the total tonnage was produced at a profit of a shilling or more; 29 per cent at a loss of a shilling or more; and 10 per cent broke even within a shilling either side. Forty-six out of the 49 areas in the country produced some tonnage at a loss. The marginal cost was 25 per cent over the average.

There is a "gentleman's agreement" between the National Coal Board and the British government not to raise prices without the latter's consent. The British government over a period of eleven years ending in 1957 rejected one increase and reduced the amount of four others.[31] Over the span of its life from 1947 to 1957, the National Coal Board made a small profit, after interest and amortization, in five of the eleven years of operation; it had an aggregate deficit for the period as a whole.[32] Owing to its poor financial position, the

[30] Sir Hubert Houldsworth, "The Pits of Britain," *Manchester Statistical Society*, February 11, 1953.

[31] *The Economist*, June 14, 1958, p. 1015.

[32] National Coal Board, annual issues of *Report and Accounts* and of the *Annual Statistical Statement*.

Average cost pricing in the British coal industry was examined in the Ridley Committee report, entitled *Report of the Committee on National Policy for the Use of Fuel and Power Resources,* Cmd. 8647, 1952; Francis Cassell, "The Pricing Policies of Nationalised Industries," *Lloyd's Bank Review*, October 1956, pp. 1–18; I. M. D. Little, *The Price of Fuel*, Clarendon Press, Oxford, 1953, p. 28.

National Coal Board borrows directly from the public treasury, though the other nationalized industries in the United Kingdom go directly to the capital market with a treasury guarantee.

French Mines

Marginal costs in France are about 20 per cent above the average; costs in the least efficient mines are about 50 per cent above those in the most efficient ones.[33] Charbonnages de France earned a margin (before amortization and financial charges) of considerably less than 20 per cent in 1948–1956, indicating that some mines operated at a loss. The figures below show the margin as a percentage of operating costs.[34]

Year	Per Cent	Year	Per Cent
1948	3	1953	9
1949	10	1954	15
1951	13	1955	12
1952	11	1956	10

Charbonnages de France had an accumulated deficit, after interest and amortization, of 14 billion francs at the beginning of 1952; the deficit rose to 61 billion francs at the end of 1955.[35] The French government extended no outright cash subsidies to the mines in metropolitan France after 1947 but helped with fiscal measures.[36] One of the principal fiscal measures involved a long-term government loan, at 1 per cent interest, made in 1956 in lieu of a capital subscription, to enable Charbonnages de France to reduce its interest obligations, which came to 8 billion francs annually—equivalent to 150 francs (43 cents) per ton produced. The loan was investigated by the High Authority as a possible violation of the treaty provision that forbids measures tending to falsify the cost of production.[37]

The nationalized mines in Britain and France present the paradox of monopoly without profits; operating with statutory autonomy, they are nevertheless effectively supervised by the respective governments. The deficits incurred by both nationalized corporations, it should be emphasized, occurred

[33] Gardent, "Les Houillères françaises et la concurrence sur le marché commun," p. 10.

[34] Calculated from data in *Annales des mines*, July–August 1957, p. 436.

[35] Commission de Vérification des Comptes des Entreprises Publiques, *Cinquième rapport d'ensemble*, p. 5; Sous-Commission sur la Gestion des Entreprises Nationalisées, Assemblée Nationale, No. 4703, March 28, 1957, pp. 64–65. The cumulative deficit for 1946–1955 was equivalent to 120 francs, or 30 cents, per ton produced (at 420 francs to the dollar). The cumulative deficit of the National Coal Board for the first eleven years of its operation came to about the same figure after interest and amortization.

[36] *Revue française de l'énergie*, September 1956, pp. 426–428. The Lorraine mines were, however, subsidized until 1957 to offset the lower net return on sales in southern Germany.

[37] *Le Monde*, June 4, 1957, p. 14. The government also "compensated" the mines for paying higher "social charges" than those in neighboring countries; *Rapport de gestion*, 1955, p. 95.

in a period when coal was usually scarce and could have commanded a much higher price than the controlled prices at which the coal was sold.

THE BELGIAN MINES

Current data on the dispersion of costs in the mines in southern Belgium are not available; the area as a whole, before subsidies, operated at a loss in 1952–1955.[38] Margins in the Campine were, however, substantial because that mining district—with the exception of some types of coal—used the price scale set for the high-cost southern mines. The extent to which earnings, exclusive of other receipts, supported self-financing of investments in the Belgian mines as a whole is not known. Subsidies from the Community and the Belgian government in 1953–1956 were (as indicated in Chapter 4) equal to 58 per cent of gross investments, though part of the subsidy was undoubtedly used for current expenditures. Though data are not available on the distribution of the subsidy between the Campine and southern Belgium, subsidies must have represented most, and self-financing very little, of the funds appropriated to investments in southern Belgium.

THE GERMAN MINES

According to data furnished by a member of the Board of the Unternehmensverband Ruhrbergbau, the cost of the costliest 6 million tons of coal produced in the Ruhr in 1956–1957 was about 15 per cent above the average for the Ruhr as a whole.[39] The difference between average and marginal efficiency was thus substantial in the Ruhr also, because the mines in the southern part of the area, though shallower, are older, smaller and costlier than those to the north; their unit revenue, however, is higher because they produce more anthracite.[40]

The Ruhr coal operators reached an understanding with the government ("Düsseldorf Agreement") in 1955 that rises in coal prices in the ensuing five years would be limited to the prospective increase in labor costs.[41] When the

[38] Wiel, *op. cit.*, pp. 125–126, shows the losses in earlier years.

[39] Calculations based on data reported in *Handelsblatt*, November 11, 1957, p. 4, as follows: If the "worst" 6 million tons added 10 cents to average costs for the Ruhr as a whole (as was alleged), then they added a total of $12.5 million, which was about $2.00 per ton at the margin; $2.00 on an estimated average realization of roughly $12.00 per ton for the Ruhr as a whole gives a difference of 17 per cent between average and marginal efficiency. The average realization per ton on the sale of primary coal—excluding coke, electricity and other by-products but including mine consumption and miners' coal—was calculated from Werner Moritz, *Der Steinkohlenbergbau der Bundesrepublik als Investor*, Vierteljahresheft zur Wirschaftsforschung, 1957, Drittesheft.

[40] Wiel, *op. cit.*, p. 46; according to this source, 87 per cent of the Ruhr production in 1951 fell within a 20 per cent range of the average output per man for the area as a whole.

[41] Moritz, *op. cit.*, p. 319; Institut für Bilanzenanalysen, *Der Ruhrbergbau*, Frankfurt am Main, 1957, p. 7.

High Authority "freed" Ruhr coal prices early in 1956, the operators wished to raise prices by an average of $1.25 per ton; after protracted negotiations with the German government, they reduced the figure to 50 cents per ton because the government assumed the cost of paying a shift premium of 60 cents to contract laborers and 30 cents to other underground workers. These premiums, amounting to about 50 cents per ton produced, were largely financed by the provincial government of North Rhine–Westphalia. Paid to the workers directly and excluded from payroll costs, the shift premiums enabled the coal industry to keep prices down. The High Authority, objecting, suggested that the government could have undertaken a more legal form of remuneration, such as higher social benefits. After negotiations with the High Authority, the German government finally agreed to stop paying the premium as of March 1958; the coal operators paid the shift premium thereafter.[42]

Immediately after the German federal election in September 1957, the coal operators announced a price increase that touched off a sharp controversy with Ludwig Erhard, Minister of Economics. They had evidently decided to gain a lap in the wage-price spiral before the next economic recession, which was then already in sight. Erhard argued that an increase was unjustified because margins were adequate and demand was declining. He threatened to pull Hibernia, the government-owned mine, out of the common sales agency and to have it maintain the old price schedule. He could thereby have wrecked the common sales agencies, for a common price schedule is the cornerstone of coordination.[43] Erhard did not carry out this threat. Instead of disturbing coordination within the Ruhr, the government broke the price coordination between the Ruhr and Lower Saxony, where the government then owned all the mines, by refusing to raise prices in the latter area. But production in Lower Saxony is only 2 per cent of that in the Ruhr.[44]

Erhard was reported to have said that the High Authority should have controlled prices, as well as the three sales agencies, more thoroughly. The High Authority pointed out that Erhard had participated in the negotiations that led to the creation of the sales agencies and, furthermore, that he violated the treaty in fighting the price increase. The High Authority undertook its own investigation, and was reported to have concluded that the price increase was disproportionate to the increase in costs, a view the operators challenged.[45]

[42] *Handelsblatt*, January 24–25, 1958, pp. 1, 3.

[43] Hibernia accounts for 25 per cent of the coal encompassed in Mausegatt, one of the sales agencies, and 9 per cent of the coal produced in the Ruhr.

[44] The government-owned steel plants in Lower Saxony likewise refused to follow a steel price increase that occurred in the Ruhr later in 1957. This break was more serious because crude steel output in Lower Saxony is 15 per cent of that in the Ruhr.

[45] *Handelsblatt*, November 29–30, 1957, pp. 1–2. See also the issues dated October 2, 4, 5, 7, 1957.

In any case, at a meeting of the Common Assembly of the ECSC late in 1957, Erhard declared that the High Authority should take account of the responsibility of the governments for price stability and coordinate its policy with theirs.[46]

Though the coal operators won the battle—the price increase had struck—they came near to losing the war, as shown in the next chapter.

The degree of economic—and monopoly—power represented by the common sales agencies in the privately operated districts inevitably involved some form of government supervision, however informal—the price the operators paid for the benefit of districtwide coordination, common price schedules and price stability.

Though coal prices in the Ruhr are also based on average rather than marginal cost and are also controlled by the government, the margin for self-financing, representing 11 to 13 per cent of turnover in the Ruhr coal mines in 1953–1955, has been greater in Germany than in France or the Saar. The margin was 6 to 10 per cent in the French coal industry, and 4 to 7 per cent in the Saar mines in 1954–1956. These margins suggest that prices in the Ruhr approach full average cost. They covered over 80 per cent of the cost of gross investment for replacement and expansion in the Ruhr, but, varying with the year, only 20 to 46 per cent in France and 40 to 71 per cent in the Saar. But since gross investments per ton produced were high in France, self-financing per ton produced was nearly as high in France as in the Ruhr. Self-financing in the British mines covered 45 per cent of gross investments in 1950–1955, equal to the ratio of self-financing in the French mines in 1955–1956, though the volume of investments per ton produced was higher in the latter. (See Chapter 4.)

In spite of average cost pricing, revenues support a certain amount of expansion in the coal industry in the ECSC—the mines in southern Belgium excepted.

INFLUENCE OF SECONDARY PRODUCTS

The assignment of prices among joint products is necessarily arbitrary. The coal mining industry earns revenue on the sale of secondary products and by-products—some mining areas more than others—as well as from the sale of coal in primary form. The greater the production of secondary products, the more profitable the mining district. A mining district can thus improve its financial position by developing the sale of secondary products. The Ruhr has pushed secondary production further than other mining districts in the ECSC.

[46] *Glückauf*, February 15, 1958, p. 295.

The sale of secondary products provided 55 per cent of the total revenue earned by the German coal mining industry in 1956 compared with 50 per cent in 1953.[47] Nord and Pas-de-Calais and the Dutch mines also earn a large amount of revenue from secondary products. The mines in southern Belgium, on the other hand, have not developed secondary production as much as the grades of coal produced would permit. This backwardness is in part attributable to lack of capital.

For lack of data comparing the total costs of extraction with the revenue earned from the sale of primary coal only (apart from secondary products), the extent to which the sale of secondary products is "subsidizing" the extractive side of the business cannot be measured.

PRICING POLICIES AND THE NEED FOR GREATER AVERAGE EFFICIENCY

The prospects for greater average efficiency in steel production rest on the effect of the economic union on individual steel firms—or proprietary groups —each relying on its own efficiency to make a profit. Individual coal mining firms are less dependent on their individual efficiency and so do not feel the effects of the union the same way. They are, further, too well protected in some cases against imported coal and petroleum to feel the effects of rivalry from without.[48]

Collective support, rather than survival based on individual efficiency, is the logical concomitant of average cost pricing. Inter-mine compensation in some form is inevitable in order to help the firms that are in difficulty under the average pricing formula. The scope of inter-mine and interregional compensation is countrywide in a nationalized mining industry. Current and capital funds can then be distributed to any mine in the country without reference to their financial margins. Nationalization is therefore the administrative counterpart to the policy of average cost pricing.

While nationalization provides the means for inter-mine compensation in France and the United Kingdom, the large mining firm, operating several mines, performs a similar function in the Ruhr. Though efficiency differs considerably between mines in the same firm, average efficiency between the Ruhr firms is fairly uniform. Under the allied deconcentration program each of the newly created large mining firms received a representative mixture of mines; if efficient and inefficient mines had not been equally distributed, some firms

---

[47] Moritz, *op. cit.*, p. 315.

[48] See, e.g., the personal views of Dirk Spierenburg, member of the High Authority, reported in *Le Monde*, September 29, 1958, p. 14.

would have experienced difficulties.[49] The firms began to close some of the inefficient mines as a result of the 1958 recession.

The common sales agency in the privately operated coal field also makes average cost pricing feasible.[50] While some mines are under the umbrella of a large firm, all firms, both large and small, are under the umbrella of the common sales agency. The coordinating agencies in the Ruhr, as authorized by the High Authority, can equalize some costs, can spread working time and can subsidize firms up to $1.25 a ton for short working time—as they did in 1958. The sales agencies also coordinate prices and eliminate price rivalry among member firms. Without these operations, an extractive industry with a large number of firms would find it difficult to maintain prices at average cost. If the common sales agencies in the Ruhr are dissolved, prices might begin to reflect marginal costs in that area, though it remains to be seen what effect the High Authority will give to its desire to loosen the grip of the sales agencies and to stabilize employment and earnings at the same time.[51]

The Ruhr coal industry has come about as close as possible to resolving the problem of maintaining high-cost mines under average-cost pricing within a framework of private ownership. The mines in southern Belgium, by contrast, cannot in present circumstances survive with average-cost pricing because the firms are too small and too uniformly inefficient to support each other. They cannot, on the other hand, adopt a marginal-cost policy without pricing a large proportion of the production out of the market. Public subsidies and obligatory profit sharing have come to the rescue. But concentration under private or public auspices is inevitable if the southern Belgian mining field is to survive.

The High Authority favored the practice of combining efficient and less efficient mines in the same company[52] and supported average-cost pricing. This policy is not inconsistent with Article 3(c) and Article 62, which call for the lowest possible price and which permit the High Authority to authorize interregional compensation, as well as interfirm compensation among firms in the same coal field using a common price schedule. The High Authority indicated that prices should approach full average cost when business is good in order to yield an adequate margin for investment and expansion and should be flexible on the downward side without endangering that margin.[53]

---

[49] The German government supports the policy of mixing efficient and inefficient mines in the same firm; see Erhard's statement reported in *Handelsblatt*, November 29-30, 1957, pp. 1–2.

[50] An article in *Glückauf*, December 21, 1957, p. 1603, pointed out that average cost pricing would be endangered without the common sales agency.

[51] HA, Decision 17–59, *Journal officiel*, March 7, 1959, pp. 279 ff.

[52] HA, *Cinquième rapport général*, p. 321.

[53] See the High Authority's response to Question No. 51, in *Journal officiel*, December 7, 1957; also *Handelsblatt*, February 10, 1958, p. 6.

Since prices in each coal producing district are not equal to the cost of production of the least efficient producer at the point where supply and demand are balanced, the present pricing mechanism cannot perform the function of causing resources to be withdrawn from the less efficient, and to be expanded in the more efficient, areas; it therefore cannot be the means for raising average efficiency in the Community as a whole.[54]

Marginal-cost pricing might promote efficiency if discrete operating units or firms stood on their own feet, but it would not perform its economic function in a nationalized mining industry or in privately operated coal fields where the firms are shielded from the effects of their individual costs of production by common sales agencies and inter-mine, as well as inter-firm, compensation.[55] If, moreover, marginal-cost pricing were used in the privately owned districts, it would still fail to promote its function throughout the Community unless its rationale were also applied to the nationalized coal mines. This policy would indeed imply a radical change in the operation of the nationalized mines; it would in fact require each mine to stand on its own cost record and do away with inter-mine compensation between nationalized mines. The difficulty of marrying different systems of ownership in an economic union thus led James Meade to conclude that all the operating units of the same industry might in such cases have to be placed under centralized supervision by the federal authorities in order to transfer resources from the less to the more efficient units.[56] The burden of raising average efficiency would consequently be shifted to officials—whether private or public—who can make decisions with respect to investments and expansion for a whole coal producing field and who can coordinate investments between different fields in the Community irrespective of prices.

Though I. M. D. Little has advanced a strong case for marginal cost pricing of British coal,[57] that case does not rest on creating competition among the mines—he advocates no change in ownership. It rests on the argument that a price that better reflects costs and discourages wasteful consumption would better distribute resources between gas, electricity and coal producing industries, and would better distribute manufacturing plants spatially. The economic rent that a marginal-cost price would yield should, according to Little,

[54] See James E. Meade, *Problems of Economic Union*, University of Chicago Press, Chicago, 1953, Chap. 1, for a discussion of the relation of pricing to the goals of an economic union.

[55] See the suggestion in *The Economist*, September 13, 1958, p. 831, that the three sales agencies in the Ruhr be replaced by a "large number of competing companies" for the sake of promoting efficiency through competition. But typical industry demands do not betray any inclination to change any fundamental elements of market control; see those of the Ruhr coal industry, for example, in *Glückauf*, December 21, 1957, p. 1604.

[56] *Op. cit.*, pp. 16–21.

[57] Little, *op. cit.*

in part be returned to the Treasury and in part to the workers in the form of a guaranteed income. Little's concept of a marginal-cost price has nothing to do, as he emphasizes, with the point at which demand and supply are balanced because, he says, the production of British coal will be short of demand in the long run. Little suggests in fact that imported petroleum should be taxed whenever it threatens the stability of British coal production and prices. Whatever the merits of Little's case for higher prices, an automatic increase in the average efficiency of the British mines would, under his recommendations, not be one of them; the attainment of greater average efficiency would still depend on administrative decision and not on the price mechanism. Marginal-cost pricing would in this respect involve no fundamental change from average-cost pricing. But marginal-cost concepts—as distinct from marginal-cost prices—are useful in determining the best distribution between alternative sources of energy consistent with desirable policies.

CHAPTER 10

THE ENERGY MARKET

SUPPLY TRENDS

The ECSC member countries are increasingly dependent on imported coal and petroleum and are therefore increasingly affected by developments outside the region. Total consumption of all primary energy combined—coal, petroleum, hydroelectric power, lignite and nuclear power—will increase by nearly 85 per cent between 1955 and 1975 according to the Community's forecasts of gross national product and industrial production as shown in Tables 18 and 19.[1] Per capita energy consumption in 1955 was 2.5 tons (in hard coal equivalents) in the ECSC, half that of the United Kingdom. The ECSC will still be far behind Britain in 1975, though the gap will have narrowed somewhat. Per capita energy consumption in the United States in 1955 was more than three times that in the ECSC and 70 per cent greater than in the United Kingdom. (The figures on comparative per capita consumption are based on the data in Table 50.) Neither the ECSC nor the United Kingdom will by 1975 close more than a small part of the gap between their per capita consumption and that of the United States. The production of energy will grow more rapidly relative to population in the USSR than in the ECSC.[2]

Import requirements for primary energy will rise because Western Europe is poor in domestic reserves of petroleum and natural gas; new discoveries, like the Lacq natural gas field in southwestern France, are not likely to add significantly to the reserve. Hydropower resources, mainly in the Alpine region, are already intensively exploited and limited in potential. The potential for expanding the production of coal is also limited. Indigenous coal production still supplied 60 per cent of the total primary energy consumed by the Community in 1955, other domestic sources 20 per cent, and imported energy another 20 per cent. (Table 19.) But as domestic supplies of energy will fall far behind the aggregate consumption of primary energy in 1955–1975, imports

---

[1] The forecasts, dependent on the projected rates of economic growth, are important for the patterns they reveal; the magnitudes cannot be foretold with exactitude.

[2] François Vinck, "Où vont les industries de base en USSR?" in *Revue française de l'énergie*, July–August 1958, pp. 491–495.

will increase substantially. The home production of hard coal will at most rise by only 16 per cent; the home production of other types of primary energy will more than double but they will still contribute only 20 per cent of the aggregate supply of primary energy in 1975. All home-produced supplies of primary energy, exclusive of nuclear power, will contribute about 60 per cent of aggregate primary energy consumption in 1975, and net imports will contribute 40 per cent of total consumption. The share of consumption furnished by imports will, therefore, double from 1955 to 1975 and will more than triple in

Table 50

COMPARATIVE TRENDS IN CONSUMPTION OF PRIMARY ENERGY, SELECTED AREAS AND YEARS, 1929–1955 AND FORECASTS, 1965–1980

(Energy: Millions of Metric Tons in Hard Coal Equivalents; Index: 1929=100; Rate of Growth: Per Cent)

	ECSC			United Kingdom			United States		
Year	Energy	Index	Annual Growth Rate	Energy	Index	Annual Growth Rate	Energy	Index	Annual Growth Rate
1929	295	100		187	100		803	100	
1937	300	102	0.2	201	107	0.8	759	95	
1950	303	103	0.1	222	119	0.8	1,140	142	1.8
1955	400	137	5.8	252	135	2.6	1,390	173	4.4
1965	565	192	3.5	330[a]	176	2.6			
1975	730	247	2.7	390[a]	209	1.7			
1980							2,800	349	2.8

Sources: 1929–1955 from Table 2-4, Appendix E; forecasts—for the ECSC, from Comité Mixte report p. 103, and Louis Armand, *et al.*, *Un objectif pour Euratom*, Paris, May 1957, p. 55; for the United Kingdom, from OEEC, *Europe's Growing Needs of Energy, How Can They Be Met?* Paris, May 1956, and National Coal Board, *Investing in Coal;* for the United States, from National Planning Association, *Productive Uses of Nuclear Energy, Summary of Findings*, Washington, 1957.

[a] In 1958 the British government was understood to be revising this estimate downward owing to the recession.

volume.[3] With growing imports, the Ruhr's towering position in the ECSC will decline.

The share of net imports to total energy consumption will rise more rapidly from 1955 to 1975 in the ECSC countries that produce coal than in the countries that produce little or no coal; the latter countries have already had to import, whereas the former countries are faced with a new experience.[4] Net imports supplied 2 per cent of total energy consumption in Germany in 1955 and will account for 25 per cent in 1975. Germany will still have the lowest ratio of

[3] Imports contributed only 6 per cent of total energy consumption in the United States in 1955. *Glückauf*, January 19, 1957, p. 90. The forecasts for the ECSC treat supplies obtained from overseas territories like the Sahara as imports.

[4] Louis Armand, *et al.*, *Un objectif pour Euratom*, Paris, May 1957, pp. 68–69.

imports to total consumption but will be one of the largest importers. Net imports will furnish nearly 70 per cent of total energy consumed in Italy and the Netherlands, though the ratio of imports to consumption will rise less than in Germany. The ratio of net imports to total consumption of primary energy will rise in Belgium-Luxembourg from 22 per cent in 1955 to 39 per cent in 1975. It will barely change in France, where it was 39 per cent in 1955.

The members of the Community obtain nearly all their crude oil from politically unstable areas like the Middle East and North Africa, uncertain sources of supply. The ECSC countries have also been disturbed by the foreign exchange implications. Energy imports in 1955 amounted to $1 billion net and

Table 51

HARD COAL CONSUMPTION AS PER CENT OF TOTAL CONSUMPTION OF PRIMARY ENERGY, 1929–1955 AND FORECASTS, 1965–1980[a]

Year	ECSC Member Countries[b]	United Kingdom	United States
1929	83	96	66
1950	72	92	40
1955	65	85	29
1965	57	72	
1975	47	65	
1980			24

Sources: Table 19 and Table 2–4, Appendix E; United Kingdom forecast from *Europe's Growing Needs of Energy, How Can They Be Met?* Paris, May 1956; United States forecast from National Planning Association, *Productive Uses of Nuclear Energy, Summary of Findings*, Washington, 1957, p. 19.

[a] Lignite excluded.   [b] Includes imported coal.

$1.9 billion gross; the latter figure accounted for 10 per cent of the value of all imports by the ECSC countries from third-party areas. The gross value of energy imports may exceed $6 billion (in 1955 dollars) in 1975 unless the development of nuclear energy reduces the need for imports of conventional energy.[5]

As the total consumption of primary energy rises in 1955–1975 more rapidly than indigenous coal production, coal's monopoly of the energy market in Western Europe will come to an end. The coal industry in Europe will go through—and has been going through—the transformation felt much sooner by the American coal industry, as Table 51 shows.

Coal has lost more ground in the United States than in the other areas. Its share in the United States fell from two thirds of the aggregate primary energy

[5] I.e., 289 million tons of imported energy (in hard coal equivalents) at a rough average delivered value of $21–$22 per ton.

consumed in 1929 to 29 per cent in 1955. It might still provide one fourth by 1980. Coal is still plentiful and competitive in the United States, where the government has favored domestic energy resources in recent years. Coal furnished 83 per cent of total primary energy consumption in the ECSC countries in 1929 and two thirds in 1955; it will still supply close to half in 1975 (imported coal included). The United Kingdom has been, and will remain, the most coal intensive of the three areas. Coal still furnished 85 per cent of the aggregate energy there in 1955 and might still furnish two thirds in 1975.

Though the ECSC as a whole was less coal intensive than the United Kingdom in 1955, there were great variations among the countries in the ECSC, as Table 2-4, Appendix E, shows. Italy relies largely on petroleum and water power. (This is also true of Scandinavia.) Belgium and Germany are at the other extreme. These differences will persist even though coal will lose ground in the aggregate.[6]

NUCLEAR ENERGY

The market for interchangeable fuels will expand at a much faster rate than that for energy as a whole. Other sources of energy are not interchangeable with coal in coke production, or with petroleum as a motor fuel or lubricant. But coal, petroleum, nuclear power and other sources of energy are interchangeable as boiler fuel for the production of steam, heat and especially electricity, which account for the major part of the primary energy consumed. Though total consumption of primary energy in the Community will increase by nearly 85 per cent in 1955–1975, the total production of electricity will triple. The production of electricity from interchangeable fuels will, moreover, more than quadruple because the other sources of electricity—water power and blast furnace gas—will fall behind.

Nuclear power holds the promise of reducing the prospective imports of classical energy.[7] How soon and in what magnitudes can nuclear power be developed?

Though nuclear energy can be used for low-temperature heat and for ship propulsion, its most massive application in the next decades will be for electric

[6] *Un objectif pour Euratom*, pp. 68–69, gives the future pattern of consumption by the members of the ECSC.

[7] The data are drawn, unless otherwise indicated, from *Un objectif pour Euratom*, and from a subsequent unpublished study by the High Authority's Comité Mixte that was summarized in *Revue française de l'énergie*, July–August 1958, under the title "Rapport sur la situation des industries nucléaires dans la Communauté," pp. 496–500. See also National Planning Association, *Productive Uses of Nuclear Energy, Summary of Findings*, Washington, 1957; OEEC, *Europe's Growing Needs of Energy, How Can They Be Met?* Paris, May 1956; United States Congress, *Proposed Euratom Agreement*, Joint Committee on Atomic Energy, 85th Cong., 2nd sess., Washington, 1958.

power production. Electric power produced from coal, petroleum, natural gas and nuclear power, which are interchangeable, will increase as follows:

	Total Production	Increase from 1960	Increase as Per Cent of Total Production
	(Billions of K.W.H.)		
1955	90		
1960	141		
1965	208	67	32
1970	302	161	53
1975	410	269	66

Nuclear power could not fill all the additional requirements from 1960 to 1975 because nuclear power plants, whose capital costs are two to three times as great as for conventional plants, must operate at a high rate of capacity—the operating rate is referred to as load factor. The capital cost of a nuclear plant was estimated (as of 1958) at $290 to $405 per kilowatt compared with $125 to $160 per kilowatt for a conventional thermal plant. A nuclear power plant at these capital costs must operate at an 80 per cent load factor in order to keep down the fixed charges per unit of output though the load factor might drop to 70 per cent by 1975 as capital costs decline. There is a great difference between the base load—the amount of electricity needed at all hours of the day—and the amount needed during the peak hours. The average conventional plant therefore operates at a load factor greatly below 80 per cent; the load factor in the ECSC in the late 1950s was 48 per cent. If all the additional electric power requirements from 1960 were to be supplied by nuclear power, nuclear power would by 1975 furnish two thirds of the power from all thermal sources combined. Though the nuclear plants might be able to operate at a 70 per cent load factor if they carried all the base loads, the conventional plants would then be forced into an uneconomic pattern of operation. Nuclear power must therefore be introduced at a rate consistent with the power system as a whole and cannot at present capital costs fill all the additional requirements.

The Six were as of 1958 planning to install from 3.5 to 4 million kilowatts of nuclear capacity by the end of 1965.[8] With the advantage of an early start, the British in 1957 planned to have about 5 million kilowatts in 1965 and to have nuclear power supply one fourth the total electricity by 1967.[9]

[8] Data are from *Revue française de l'énergie*, July–August 1958, pp. 496–500. I. M. D. Little and P. N. Rosenstein-Rodan, *Nuclear Power and Italy's Energy Position*, National Planning Association, Washington, 1957, p. 4, assumed about 0.5 million kilowatts of nuclear capacity in Italy by 1964.

[9] *Financial Times*, December 28, 1957, p. 1. An earlier goal called for 6 million kilowatts.

Estimates of nuclear power in Western Europe beyond 1965 were still quite speculative as of the end of 1958. It was estimated in 1958 that Western Europe as a whole would have an installed capacity of 15 million kilowatts by 1970.[10] The United Kingdom and the ECSC might each have 7 million kilowatts by that time; if so, capacity in the ECSC area will have doubled between 1965–1970. Each area would then save the equivalent of about 20 million tons of coal a year. Forecasts beyond 1970 would be subject to great error.[11]

COST OF ALTERNATIVE SOURCES OF ENERGY

The growing imports of primary energy, the introduction of nuclear power and the rivalry between the different sources of energy for the European coal market present the Six with the necessity of choosing a policy that will reconcile security with costs and enable the Community to guide investments by the light of significant signposts.

LONG-TERM PRICE OF RUHR COAL

The Ruhr is the bellwether for coal prices in the Community because it accounts for half the production, produces a greater variety of the more desirable grades of coal than any other district, delivers more coal to other countries in the Community than any other district, and is more competitive with imported fuels at the Low Country ports or Hamburg than Belgian coal, the only other *major* source of continental coal close to the Low Country ports. If the coal from southern Belgium were considered the bellwether—on the principle that the marginal supplier should determine the price for all coal produced in the Community[12]—then the price level for coal in the Community would be so high that European coal would price itself out of the market unless severe import restrictions were imposed. If such restrictions were imposed at so high a price level, the Belgian mines would not have to reduce costs, average efficiency in the Community would not have to rise and the economic union would indeed have served no desirable economic purpose at all.

[10] By Sir John Cockcroft, Chairman of the British Atomic Energy Authority, at the United Nations Atomic Energy Conference held in Geneva in September 1958.

[11] *Un objectif pour Euratom* called for 15 million kilowatts in the ECSC by the end of 1967 and the addition thereafter of from 4 to 4.5 million kilowatts of nuclear capacity annually. This report, published in May 1957, was lauded for its vision but was soon recognized to be overambitious. With less experience and fewer facilities to construct nuclear equipment than the United Kingdom, the Community could not overtake and triple the British program by 1967.

[12] See the comment, by a spokesman for the Ruhr coal industry, that Belgian costs should determine prices in a true common market; *Glückauf*, December 21, 1957, p. 1602. Average costs in the southern mines were about $17.50 per ton in 1956; marginal costs must have been about $20.00 to $21.00 per ton, about $6.00 per ton above marginal costs in the Ruhr.

The cost of European coal will rise relatively from 1955 through 1975, unless mining wages rise less than those in other industries, because productivity will increase less in coal than in the rest of the economy. Real wages in the German economy as a whole and in German coal mining rose by 35 per cent in 1950–1955; productivity in the former rose by 30 per cent in the same period while productivity in coal mining rose by only 15 per cent.[13] The High Authority expects the over-all output of labor in the area of the Six to rise by 80 per cent between 1955 and 1975 (at a rate of 3.2 per cent annually). If the relative distribution of income among the factors of production remains unchanged, hourly earnings in the economy as a whole are likely to rise by 80 per cent too. Since the status of the coal miner is not likely to deteriorate, his earnings also will increase by 80 per cent, if not more. And since productivity in coal mining, which will grow at a rate of only 1.4 per cent a year, will rise only about 30 per cent between 1955 and 1975, labor costs per ton of coal will rise by about 25 per cent between 1955 and 1975. Assuming no significant change in the ratio of labor costs to total costs of production, real total costs will rise proportionately.[14]

The average price of Ruhr coal on the 25 per cent hypothesis might rise from about $12.00 per ton in 1956 to $15.00 per ton in 1975.[15] Marginal costs in the Ruhr in 1956 were about $2.00 per ton, or 15 per cent, above average cost; assuming that marginal costs in 1975 will still be $2.00 higher per ton than average cost (though the deviation will fall to about 13 per cent), marginal coal will cost $17.00 per ton in 1975. The price of coal in the Ruhr might thus rise to between $15.00 and $17.00 per ton in 1975 (in 1956 dollars), depending on the pricing policy. If the Ruhr sales agencies are effectively dissolved by the High Authority in 1960 or 1961, prices might approach marginal costs.

The northern coast—Hamburg—is the point where imported coal and fuel oil traditionally compete with Ruhr coal; the cost of transporting, handling

---

[13] Hans H. Bischoff, "Produktivität, Löhne, und Preise im Steinkohlenbergbaus," in *Glückauf*, January 5, 1957, pp. 38–45. The data on productivity in Table 4-1, Appendix E, show an increase of only 13 per cent in the German mines.

There is a large literature on the long- and short-run relations among productivity, prices and incomes; some of it is listed in a report of the Joint Economic Committee, *Productivity, Prices and Incomes*, Joint Economic Committee, 85th Cong., 1st sess., Washington, 1957, pp. 10 and 13.

[14] The High Authority estimates that monetary costs will rise about 20 per cent between 1955 and 1975. See HA, *Cinquième rapport général*, p. 281; CECA, Assemblée Commune, Commission des Investissements, *Rapport sur les objectifs généraux*, Exercice 1956–1957, deuxième session extraordinaire, February 1957, p. 38; *Europe's Growing Needs of Energy, How Can They Be Met?* An article in *Revue française de l'énergie*, May 1958, p. 419, estimated that labor costs per ton in the French coal industry would rise about 16 per cent in 1956–1970.

[15] The figure of $12.00 per ton in 1956, derived from Moritz, *op. cit.*, p. 315, refers to average realization on primary coal produced, including miners' coal and mine consumption. It is assumed that average costs were equal to realization and that the more profitable side of the business—electricity, coke, gas and other by-products—provided the margin for depreciation, interest and profits.

and delivering Ruhr coal to the wholesalers' station in the Hamburg area is about $4.00 per ton by rail and $3.00 by canal. The delivered price of Ruhr coal at Hamburg will thus be between $18.00 and $21.00 per ton by 1975.

Imported fuels and Ruhr coal also compete in other parts of the Community, especially in Italy and along delivery routes served by the Rhine River. The delivered price of Ruhr coal shipped by waterway to the industrial area of southern Belgium will be about the same as that at Hamburg. The cost of producing coal in southern Belgium was already about $17.50 to $21.00 per ton in 1956. Average mining efficiency will therefore have to rise more rapidly in southern Belgium than in the rest of the Community if coal from that area is to become competitive.

LONG-TERM COST OF U. S. COAL
IN WESTERN EUROPE

The United Kingdom and Poland exported large quantities of coal in the interwar period but now play a secondary part in the world coal market; the United States supplied no coal to Europe to speak of before the second world war but stepped into the breach afterward. The United States furnished more

Table 52

TRENDS IN COAL PRODUCTION AND IMPORTS, ECSC COUNTRIES, 1947–1958[a]

| | Imports | | Index (*1950 = 100*) | |
| | Total (*Millions of Tons*) | Per Cent from United States | Coal Output | Total Imports |
Year				
1947	27.4	94	75	380
1948	19.5	70	84	271
1949	17.9	49	96	248
1950	7.2	1	100	100
1951	28.9	63	107	401
1952	22.3	73	111	310
1953	13.8	49	110	192
1954	13.9	44	112	192
1955	23.1	69	114	321
1956	38.0	80	115	528
1957	44.0	86	115	611
1958	31.0[b]	84[b]	113	431[b]

Sources: Kohlenwirtschaft; HA, *Bulletin statistique, Momento de statistiques,* and *Cinquième rapport général,* Annexes, p. 46; also Table 2-7, Appendix E, in this study.

[a] Excludes coke and trade between ECSC countries.

[b] Estimated.

than 40 per cent of the coal imported by the Community in all the years but one from 1947 to 1958, 70 per cent or more in all the years but five (Table 52).

Coal imported from the United States by the Community from 1947 to 1957 filled peak requirements and therefore fluctuated violently with the business cycle. European coal producers enjoyed a more stable market and coal pro-

Table 53

TRENDS IN PRICES OF RUHR AND UNITED STATES COAL
AT HAMBURG, IN UNITED STATES COAL AT FRONTIER
AND IN MARITIME FREIGHT RATES, 1951–1958[a]

| | Price per Metric Ton | | | Index | | | |
| | | | | At Hamburg (*March 1951 = 100*) | | U. S. f.o.b. Frontier | Maritime Freight |
Date	Ruhr	U. S.	Average Maritime Freight	Ruhr	U. S.	(*1951 = 100*)	(*1951 = 100*)
	(1)	(2)	(3)	(4)	(5)	(6)	(7)
1951			$12.77			100	100
Mar.	$13.80	$23.93		100	100		
Sept.	13.80	24.97		100	104		
1952			10.14			101	79
Mar.	14.32	24.54		104	103		
Sept.	16.39	18.53		119	77		
1953			5.30			97	41
Mar.	18.20	17.22		132	72		
Sept.	18.20	16.30		132	68		
1954			5.00			94	39
Mar.	18.20	16.31		132	68		
Sept.	17.94	16.20		130	68		
1955			7.26			98	57
Mar.	17.60	17.83		127	75		
Sept.	17.85	19.09		129	80		
1956			7.95			110	62
Mar.	17.85	19.87		129	83		
Sept.	18.37	21.17		133	88		
1957							
Mar.	19.40	22.97	9.34	141	96	118[b]	73
Sept.	19.40	16.00[c]	...	141	67	114[d]	...
1958							
Mar.	20.00	14.35[c]	...	145	60	117	...

Sources: Glückauf, May 11, 1957, pp. 590–593, and November 23, 1957, p. 1494. In col. 2, September 1957 and March 1958 are estimated from HA, *Sixième rapport général*, Vol. II, p. 365. In col. 1, March 1958 is estimated from Table 47.

[a] The prices in col. 1 refer to average value, including turnover tax, f.o.b. mine plus average freight delivered to large consumers at Hamburg of $4.14 per ton. Those in col. 2 refer to average value c.i.f. Hamburg plus unloading, freight and tax charges of $1.35 delivered to large consumer.

Col. 3 refers to the average maritime freight cost of U. S. coal to Germany, not to spot voyage rates, which are much more variable.

Cols. 4, 5 and 7 derived from 1, 2 and 3, respectively.

Col. 6 derived from col. 10 of Table 47.

[b] April 1957.   [c] Based on spot voyage rates.   [d] October 1957.

duction in the ECSC increased slowly but steadily from 1947 to 1957. (See Table 52.) Why was this so? The delivered cost of American coal was so much higher than European coal (which was priced at average cost) during peak periods of demand that coal from the United States was, up to the middle of 1957, considered complementary rather than competitive, although it was lower cost at other times.[16] (Table 53.) European consumers did not—or by virtue of import restrictions could not—purchase American coal in periods of contracting demand when the price was lower; low prices for American coal were considered to be ephemeral due to abnormally depressed freight rates.

But with the passage of time American coal secured a more permanent foothold in the Community because the price of European coal increased relative to the delivered cost of American coal (Table 53) and because the volume of coal imported by the Community from the United States increased with successive peaks of the business cycle.[17] (See Table 52.)

American coal thus continued to flow into the Community during the 1958 recession; about 26 million tons were imported in 1958, compared with 38 million tons in 1957, because the spot price of American coal in 1958 was then considerably lower than the price of European coal (Table 53). Based on spot cargo rates, United States coal in September 1957 was about $3.00, and in March 1958 about $6.00 per ton below the price of Ruhr coal, both delivered at Hamburg. Owing to the fact that international rates on the Rhine River had also fallen drastically with the change in business conditions, United States coal could even penetrate the Ruhr, Strasbourg or southern Germany at prices below those prevailing in Europe. Though the delivered price of American coal purchased on long-term contract was in 1958 still higher than the price of Ruhr coal delivered at Hamburg, the fact that long-term purchases had been made reflected the attempt to create a more stabilized price based on long-term market considerations. Imported coal will in the long run be more competitive with European coal than in the past unless imports are severely restricted by the governments, because the price for European coal has risen—and will contine to rise—relative to that for American coal (Table 53).[18] Efficiency in American bituminous underground mines increased by about 65 per cent between 1913 and the 1950s, whereas efficiency in Ruhr mines increased by

[16] *Glückauf*, November 23, 1957, p. 1495, gives the landed value of United States coal in individual ECSC countries from 1951 to 1956; there is no substantial difference from country to country.

[17] Imports of United States coal in 1947—nearly as high as those in 1956—were influenced by abnormal postwar conditions rather than by the business cycle. Data on imports of United States coal by individual ECSC countries from 1946 to 1958 are to be found in ECE, *Quarterly Bulletin of Coal Statistics*, and are conveniently tabulated in *Glückauf*, November 23, 1957, p. 1492.

[18] In a twenty-year contract for coal deliveries from Gelsenkirchener Bergbau A. G., three Ruhr steel firms pegged the value to the delivered price of United States coal; see *Handelsblatt*, February 12, 1958, p. 8.

only 16 per cent in the same period. (Table 4-2, Appendix E.) Since the gap in efficiency between American and European mines will increase to the latter's disadvantage, American coal will become increasingly competitive. Average prices for American bituminous coal f.o.b. mine rose only 2 per cent from 1949 to 1958; the miners' basic wage rose by 58 per cent in that period, from $14.05 to $22.25 per day.[19]

Two very different elements make up the price of United States coal delivered in Europe: the price of the coal f.o.b. mine and the cost of overseas freight. The former is the more stable of the two elements, as Table 53 shows. The average value of United States coal at Hampton Roads, Virginia (where it is loaded for shipment to Europe), was $10.50 per ton in 1956; this was the price of coal for export to Canada as well as to Europe. European purchasers paid between $11.00 and $12.00 per ton because they bought choice grades of deep-mined coal of coking quality rather than open-pit coal. Since requirements for choice grades will decline as the proportion of coal used for boiler fuel rises, the grade of coal that sold at the average price of $10.50 in 1956 is probably the quality Europeans will buy in the future. The $10.50 price at Hampton Roads included $4.50 per ton freight and handling costs for delivery from the mine—generally in West Virginia—to the port; the price f.o.b. mine was therefore $6.00 per metric ton. The price of United States coal will no doubt continue to be flexible, depending on competitive conditions. It may not rise at all on one hypothesis if the producers obtain long-term contracts and if they find it necessary to compete with imported fuel oil along the northeastern coast of the United States—assuming the United States government does not drastically reduce or tax imported fuel oil. It may likewise remain constant if the American coal producers find it necessary to compete with fuel oil imported into the European market. The American coal producers, on the second hypothesis, may allow prices to rise if the European coal market absorbs the increase. Since costs of production in American coal mines might rise about 15 per cent between 1956 and 1975 if miners' wages should increase more rapidly than mine efficiency, as in Europe,[20] the price might on the second hypothesis increase to $7.00 per ton f.o.b. mine, or to an average of $11.50 per ton at Hampton Roads. The price at Hampton Roads could thus

[19] *New York Times* (domestic edition), April 1, 1959.

[20] Hourly output per man underground in American underground bituminous mines rose about 100 per cent in 1913–1949. According to *Productivity, Prices and Income*, p. 89, hourly output in United States manufacturing rose about 157 per cent in that period. Extending these different rates of increase to 1955–1975 (and assuming coal mine wages are determined by the higher rate of increase), the real monetary cost of United States coal will rise by 15 per cent. The estimate refers to underground coal mines rather than to United States coal mines as a whole; underground mines accounted for only 76 per cent of the total output in 1955, though Europe might start purchasing open-pit coal from the United States. The NPA study, *Productive Uses of Nuclear Energy, Summary of Findings*, p. 15, assumed a 15 to 20 per cent rise in United States fuel costs.

vary from $10.50 per ton assuming no increase and to $11.50 per ton if competitive conditions allowed the coal operators to raise prices.

Since the price of Ruhr coal may in 1975 be about $18.00 to $21.00 per ton delivered to wholesalers' yards or large consumers in the Hamburg area, and since United States coal may be priced at $10.50 to $11.50 per ton at Hampton Roads, United States coal would be competitive at any overseas freight rate between $5.15 to $9.15 per ton, after allowing $1.35 per ton for compensatory import taxes, delivery and handling charges in Germany.[21] This range is well within probability, especially if maritime rates are stabilized, as in the petroleum traffic, by long-term charter contracts. Maritime transport costs may, furthermore, decline. The break-even rate of a Liberty ship was $5.00 per ton of coal in 1956 for the run from Hampton Roads to northern Europe. But the Liberty ship, then obsolete, was being replaced by more economic carriers.

Since fuels of European origin will be scarce in the long run, the American coal industry—barring severe limitations on imports into Europe—will have enough latitude to underprice European coal when demand contracts. But it would invite retaliatory restrictions on the part of European governments if it underpriced European coal over a long period of time.

American coal could be competitive with European coal not only along the northern coast of Europe but in other parts of Europe as well, especially those parts that are accessible by way of the Rhine River.[22] United States coal could in most circumstances therefore compete with Belgian coal in Belgian markets, with French coal, and with Ruhr coal in southern Germany, in the Ruhr itself and in Italy, as well as in northern Germany.

The thesis that European coal is, and always will be, lower cost than imported energy is no longer tenable, especially if marginal rather than average costs of European coal production are taken into consideration.[23]

[21] The $1.35 allowance per ton is based on the German duty in effect before March 1959 when the duty on imports in excess of 5 million tons a year was raised sharply. In 1956 German importers of United States coal signed a number of six-year charter contracts at an $8.00 rate per ton, according to *Glückauf*, March 16, 1957, p. 334.

Un objectif pour Euratom, pp. 64–66, struck an average price of $20.00 for both imported coal and oil. The OEEC study, *Europe's Growing Needs of Energy, How Can They Be Met?* p. 43, also postulated a price of $20.00 for United States coal.

[22] The price of American coal at Rotterdam is about the same as at Hamburg; it is at other points higher than that at Hamburg by the following amounts (1955 differentials): Rouen (France), $0.40 per ton; Dortmund (eastern part of the Ruhr), $0.80; Mons (southern Belgium), $2.00; Nancy (southern Lorraine), $2.70. *Revue française de l'énergie*, November 1956, p. 63.

[23] Articles, in *Revue française de l'énergie*, by J. Moinard, "Le Problème des importations de charbons américains en Europe," November 1956, pp. 57 ff, and by Paul Gardent, "Les Importations de charbon américain et le problème des contrats à long terme," December 1957, pp. 104 ff, indicated that American coal was higher-priced than European coal over the whole of a business cycle. Gardent consequently criticized the High Authority for having recommended that United States coal be purchased on long-term contracts. The ECE's *Economic Survey of Europe in 1951*, Geneva, 1952, pp. 162–163, also concluded that the cost of European coal was so much lower that capital investments for additional coal production in Europe would pay off rapidly. These conclusions ignore the artificial price levels and rising costs.

LONG-TERM PETROLEUM PRICES

Owing to the prospective high price levels for European coal, heavy fuel oil will be able to compete with it and to capture an increasing share of the European energy market, mitigated only by restricted measures by the governments. Petroleum made steady inroads between 1950 and 1955, its part rising from 9 to 14 per cent of the primary energy consumed by the ECSC while that supplied by coal (domestic and imported) declined from 72 to 65 per cent. (See Tables 51 and 2-4 in Appendix E.)

The intensity of the pressure from the oil industry will depend on a number of unpredictable developments. The petroleum industry is controlled by a few dominant companies with worldwide interests in crude production, transportation, refining and marketing. Venezuela and the Persian Gulf are the two main basing points for exports. Though crude oil is produced at lower cost in the Middle East than in the Western Hemisphere, prices at the Persian Gulf have until recently been determined by those in the Caribbean for crude oil and products. But the price for crude oil, though not that for products, from the Middle East has in recent years been reduced in relation to the Caribbean price. Middle Eastern crude therefore competes with Caribbean crude not only on the northeastern coast of the United States but even farther inland, though it does not enjoy an inland market owing to United States import restructions on crude oil, and has been delivered in Europe at a price below the Caribbean price plus freight.

The European refiners obtain their crude oil from the Middle East. But Europe, which is long on the light oils including gasoline and short on the black oils such as heavy fuel oil, still normally draws on the Caribbean for heavy fuel oil, the delivered cost of which normally determines the European, and Middle Eastern, price scale for those products. Prices in the Caribbean, which are oriented to the United States market, reflect the supply relationships between heavy and light oils in that market. But the Western Hemisphere is long on heavy fuel oil and short on gasoline. Though the reverse is true in Western Europe, the refiner in Europe cannot exceed the price for fuel oil set by the Caribbean producers without encouraging the refiners in the Caribbean to encroach on his market in Europe. (Refinery prices are referred to here; this price is rarely commensurate with the final consumers' price, which reflects local taxes and government policy on the part petroleum should play in the total energy market.)

Heavy fuel oil from the Caribbean, which could enter the United States in unlimited quantities prior to April 1959, is competitive with American coal delivered in the northeastern coastal area of the United States, where rivalry for the boiler fuel market is keen. Since American coal and heavy fuel oil also compete for the growing market in northern Europe, price relationships for both products tend to be determined by markets on one side or the other of the North Atlantic.

Will the petroleum producers meet or undercut the price of American coal delivered in Europe? If they meet it, then the Caribbean price would be at a maximum because the cost of maritime freight for United States coal is normally higher per calorific unit than the cost of maritime freight for oil from the Caribbean to, say, Rotterdam.[24] If the petroleum producers undercut the price of American coal in Europe, they will also have to take a lower net return on the sale of heavy fuel oil exported to the United States (assuming a single price structure). The latter policy would yield a larger return only if it enabled the petroleum industry to expand its market in both the United States and Europe. Since both areas have become increasingly restrictive to imports, however, the petroleum producers might follow a less aggressive policy, selecting for the long run a price nearer the upper part of the range.[25] The higher price policy would permit American coal to retain part of the European energy market; the lower one would tend to eliminate it, for the specific need for coal in Europe could be met entirely by local coal producers even if their production fell below the volume attained in the late 1950s. Since American coal delivered in Europe is (as already shown) likely to be quite competitive with European coal along the northern coast, and even inland, the price of heavy fuel oil delivered in Europe would be competitive with European coal in any case.

Relationships between heavy fuel oil prices in Europe and elsewhere have in fact been anything but clear cut. Since European coal prices under government control were low from the end of the second world war to the late 1950s, the oil producers kept down the price of heavy fuel oil in northern Europe, as a result of which it was lower priced than American coal.[26] But as European

[24] The cost of carrying heavy fuel oil, given equal bulk freight rates and distances, is two thirds that of carrying coal per calorific unit because 1 ton of the former equals 1.5 tons of the latter. The distance is about 20 per cent longer from the Caribbean (Venezuela) than from Hampton Roads to Rotterdam but oil tankers are so much more efficient that oil can normally be carried at about half the cost of coal per calorific unit; in 1955, e.g., the maritime transport cost of imported petroleum in the ECSC was half that of coal per calorific unit; Comité Mixte report, p. 35. The greater efficiency of the future large tanker relative to the future coal carrier may give oil an even greater advantage. See Cornelius J. Dwyer, *Nuclear Energy and World Fuel Prices*, National Planning Association, Washington, 1958, pp. 26 ff.

[25] The facts, if not all the conclusions, in these paragraphs on oil prices are drawn from *The Economist*, July 6, 1957, pp. 49–51; *Petroleum Press Service*, January 1958, pp. 7–9; and Dwyer, *op. cit. Europe's Growing Needs of Energy, How Can They Be Met?* p. 46, suggested that world oil prices might remain stable if United States import restrictions are relaxed and might rise otherwise. *Un objectif pour Euratom*, p. 66, and *Productive Uses of Nuclear Energy*, pp. 15 ff, indicated that world oil prices might decline if United States import limitations are relaxed but *Un objectif pour Euratom* suggested that oil prices will not rise in the long run even if United States import restrictions are maintained.

[26] Dwyer, *op. cit.*, pp. 4, 16.

coal prices rose, oil prices rose correspondingly, especially under the influence of the Suez crisis in 1957, when the price of American coal and heavy fuel oil delivered in Europe approached parity. Under the influence of extremely low rates for tankers and coal carriers in the 1958 recession, prices for both American coal and imported heavy fuel oil delivered in Europe fell below the price of European coal and encroached further in those European coal markets where indigenous coal was not then protected—Germany and the non-coal-producing countries. The growth of protectionism on behalf of local coal and oil producers in the United States and Western Europe, as well as political developments in the Middle East, have placed the unified world price structure for petroleum under considerable strain, with a tendency for the petroleum market to break up into hemispheric markets, as well as local or national markets. Cyclical, as well as long-term, factors have contributed to this development. Large oil discoveries in the Sahara and Libya could lead to lower oil prices, though the North African oil has a low fuel content, especially as additional firms are entering production. The lesser dependence on Middle East oil shipped through the Suez Canal might well make world oil prices vulnerable.

COST OF NUCLEAR ELECTRIC POWER

The average cost of electricity from conventional power plants in 1956 was about 9.5 mills per kilowatt-hour in Western Europe and 7 mills per kilowatt-hour in the United States.[27] Prospective conventional power costs in Europe will vary from 9 mills to a maximum of 11 mills per kilowatt-hour, corresponding to a price of $15.00 to $21.00 per ton of coal or oil (in coal equivalents).[28]

The prospective cost of nuclear power could not be firmly estimated as of 1958 because capital costs and technology were still evolving, because many different reactor types and systems were still being considered and because operating experience with large commercial stations was still limited.[29] Estimates developed in 1958 indicated costs on various assumptions, as shown in Table 54. The cost of nuclear power would range from 9.6 to 13.9 mills per

[27] *Un objectif pour Euratom*, pp. 39–40, 83; *The Economist*, December 7, 1957, p. 867. In France e.g., the average cost in 1956 was 8.3 mills (5.5 mills for hydropower and 13.5 for thermal power); see *Revue française de l'énergie*, May 1958, p. 390. The cost of electric power based on fuel oil was 8.2 mills in Italy in 1956 according to Little and Rosenstein-Rodan, *op. cit.*

[28] *Revue française de l'énergie*, July–August 1958, pp. 498 ff; Dwyer, *op. cit.*, p. 18. These future cost estimates for conventional power are based on the normal load factor for such plants. A study by the Comité d'Etude des Producteurs de Charbon d'Europe Occidentale, *L'Application de l'énergie nucléaire*, October 1956, shows average cost of 7.3 mills if conventional plants are operated on the same load factor as nuclear plants, or 80 per cent load factor.

[29] See H. Schult, "Die wirtschaftlichen Aussichten des Atomenergie," *Glückauf*, May 11, 1957, pp. 585 ff.

kilowatt-hour; but nuclear power would be competitive only up to a cost of 11 mills—where the cost of conventional power would correspond to a maximum price of $21.00 per ton of coal or oil in coal equivalents. Only with public financing or private financing on fairly equivalent terms could nuclear power be competitive at 1958 cost estimates. But nuclear power with private financing may become competitive by 1975 as technology improves and capital costs

Table 54

ESTIMATED COST OF CONVENTIONAL POWER AND PROSPECTIVE
NUCLEAR POWER IN WESTERN EUROPE, 1958[a]

Type of Power	Initial Plant Investment per Kw.	Mills[b] per K.W.H.			
		Fixed Charges	Fuel	Operation and Maintenance	Total
Private financing:					
Conventional:					
Coal[c]	$160	3.1	6.8	1.0	10.9
Oil[d]	125	2.5	6.3	1.0	9.8
Nuclear	290	5.5	4.2	2.0	11.7
	348	6.6	4.2	2.0	12.8
	405	7.7	4.2	2.0	13.9
Public financing:					
Coal[c]	160	1.5	6.8	1.0	9.3
Nuclear	328	3.4	4.2	2.0	9.6

Source: Proposed Euratom Agreements, pp. 39 ff. Estimates for nuclear plants are based on 80 per cent load factor.

[a] Private financing is based on a fifteen-year amortization at 6 per cent interest; public financing on a thirty-year amortization at 4.75 per cent interest.

[b] Ten mills is equal to one hundredth of a dollar, or one cent.

[c] Based on a price of $18.50 per ton of coal.

[d] Based on a price of $17.20 per ton of oil in coal equivalents.

decline. Coal may then drop out of use as a source of power if the cost of nuclear power falls below 9 mills per kilowatt-hour, equivalent to a price of $14.50 per ton of coal; oil may start dropping out of use if the cost of nuclear power falls much below 9 mills per kilowatt-hour.[30]

PROTECTION WITHOUT COORDINATION

A free market policy for energy would merge the European energy market with the world market, allowing producers to compete and consumers to choose their sources freely, forcing the production and price of indigenous

[30] Dwyer, *op. cit.,* pp. 18, 21, believes oil will drop out of use when nuclear power falls below 6 mills, corresponding to a price of $4.50 per ton of coal.

coal to fluctuate over the course of the business cycle, and opening the possibility of a decline in the capacity of the European coal industry. The need for coal (exclusive of lignite) in non-interchangeable uses in 1975—primarily for coke production—will amount only to about 175 million tons.[31] The production of indigenous coal could thus decline to a low figure indeed, 70 per cent of what it was in 1955, if coal disappeared from the boiler fuel market.

A free price policy implies a radical change in the present policies of the coal producing countries, where the coal industry is protected from rival sources of supply. The thesis that European coal mines should operate at capacity at all times has been considered axiomatic in Europe since World War II, though the European coal industry carried about 25 per cent reserve capacity throughout the interwar period. But a fluctuating level of operation is now politically and economically unacceptable in Europe; if miners were laid off, they could be replaced only with great difficulty under present conditions of full employment. Moreover, European mines can be maintained in standby condition only at great cost.[32]

The European countries, furthermore, do not—especially since the Suez crisis—accept with equanimity the prospect of a large dependence on imported oil—any more than does the American government, which restricted oil imports for the sake of protecting the domestic production of crude oil and, indirectly, of coal.[33] The desire to protect the domestic supply of energy is in fact responsible for the introduction of nuclear power in Europe before it is fully competitive. The scarcity of dollars caused the European governments, still further, to count the cost of imported energy in terms of foreign exchange; wisely or not, some governments believe the payment of a premium for indigenous fuels is justified by a saving in dollars.

The High Authority in 1957 suggested a long-term policy that tried to reconcile the stability of the domestic coal industry with stable coal imports and to shift the burden of meeting peak requirements to imported petroleum. The High Authority thus hoped to strike a balance between a world and a regional market system. Its recommendations were:[34]

[31] *Glückauf*, April 27, 1957, pp. 519 ff. The High Authority's *Objectifs généraux*, overtly ignoring the problem of relative cost, implicitly assumed that price relationships between the alternative sources of energy in 1955 would remain fairly constant. It consequently established a maximum coal production forecast of 320 million tons in 1975 (compared with our estimate of 285 million tons). But the Investment Committee of the Common Assembly stated that the High Authority should have established the forecast in relation to the price of interchangeable fuels; *Rapport sur les objectifs généraux*, pp. 23–32.

[32] American mines are accustomed to carry 12 to 15 per cent, if not more, reserve capacity because they can be maintained or reopened at less cost than European mines. *Glückauf*, January 19, 1957, pp. 88–89.

[33] See T. Keyser, "Bergbaupolitik in den Vereinigten Staaten als Beispiel einer aktiven Energiepolitik," *Glückauf*, January 19, 1957, pp. 82 ff.

[34] HA, *Cinquième rapport général*, pp. 303–323.

(a) Domestic coal producers should not be expected to meet the low price of American coal when demand contracts or to reduce their output. Internal coal prices should be fairly stable, with only "a moderate play"; this policy should be "coupled with an import policy which provides for continuity of supply and eliminates violent changes in delivered prices."[35] It thus recommended that American coal be purchased on long-term contracts.

(b) A stockpiling program should be developed to help stabilize domestic coal output.

(c) High-cost coal mines should be closed and mines whose costs can be reduced by modernization should be helped financially in the meantime.

(d) The oil industry should bear the burden of meeting peak requirements because it is less labor intensive and petroleum prices should be more rigid over the course of the business cycle to help achieve that end.[36]

What happened to these suggestions during the 1958 recession when the conflict between world and regional principles of market organization became acute?

GOVERNMENT POLICIES

While 26 million tons of American coal were imported in the recession year of 1958, producers' stocks in the Community climbed to 22 million tons in September 1958—five weeks' production, largely concentrated in the Belgian and Ruhr mines. This was the most difficult period yet experienced by the European coal industry since World War II. Demands for protection rose from many quarters as the stability of employment was threatened and as the mines granted temporary discounts on incremental sales. The situation revealed certain fundamental differences in approach between producers and their governments as well as between countries. The German government favored a free energy market in principle but gave way under pressure. The French and Belgian governments, with varying degrees of success, favored a restrictive policy regardless of cost. The Netherlands government supported a free import policy because Rotterdam is one of the main gateways through which imported coal is transshipped to other parts of the economic union and because Dutch coal importers took care not to harm the small but efficient coal industry in Holland. Some political groups in Holland recommended, however, that the privately owned mines, accounting for about one third the output, be nationalized in order to place the whole industry under government

[35] *Ibid.*, p. 319.
[36] See also *Sixième rapport général*, Vol. I, p. 49.

protection and that petroleum prices be controlled for the sake of protecting the coal mines. The Dutch government rejected these suggestions.[37]

Without a domestic coal industry, the Italians have supported a free import policy to obtain coal at the lowest possible price.[38] The importation of Ruhr coal by Italy thus fell by 50 per cent between the first half of 1958 and the corresponding period of 1957 while that of American coal fell by only 20 per cent. (See Table 49.) The coal operators in the Community argued that the importing member countries like Italy benefited from stable internal prices during peak demand periods and should therefore give preference to Community-produced coal during a recession even if the latter were higher priced at such times.[39] Standing in the same relation to coal as to scrap, Italy, during the sellers' market, had suggested without success that the cost of American coal should be equalized when higher than Ruhr coal. France had agreed on condition that imported coal be taxed when below the price of indigenous coal. Germany and the Netherlands had opposed the Italian proposal because they would have had to pay the cost of the compensation scheme.

France

The French mines were completely untouched by rival imports from the United States during the 1958 recession because l'Association Technique de l'Importation Charbonnière (ATIC), which had made scarcely any long-term contracts for United States coal, limited the importation of United States coal to the amount required for specific consumers and needs.[40] (The United Kingdom has a similar policy. The National Coal Board is the purchasing agent for coal imported into Britain and absorbs the difference between the cost of internal and imported coal, which is sold at the same price.) Imports of United States coal into France thus diminished by 50 per cent in the first half of 1958 compared with the corresponding period of 1957, whereas imports by the Community as a whole declined by only 27 per cent. (See Table 49.) ATIC recommended indeed that the Community establish a Communitywide importing agency to coordinate imports with the business cycle.[41]

The coal, gas and electric power industries are nationalized in France and the government has a one third control in Compagnie Française de Petrol.

---

[37] *Handelsblatt*, February 23, 1959, p. 1.

[38] *Revue française de l'énergie*, November 1956, p. 59. All governments levied compensatory import taxes on coal imported from outside, as well as inside, the Community. These taxes were as follows in 1958 (in per cent ad valorem): Germany, 4.16; Netherlands, 5.3; Belgium, 5.0; France and Saar, 11.11; Italy, 7.

[39] *The Economist*, October 11, 1958, p. 130.

[40] *Revue française de l'énergie*, September 1956, pp. 427, 432–433. *Annales des mines*, May 1957, p. 314, divided France's imports into "normal" and "abnormal" sources, calling attention to the policy of purchasing American coal "only in case of physical necessity."

[41] ATIC, *Exercice 1957*, p. 7.

Domestic prices for heavy fuel oil are fixed on the basis of the Caribbean price plus freight by a *commission paritaire*, on which the government and the oil firms are represented; the internal price of heavy fuel oil is thus in practice equalized with that of indigenous coal in order to protect the latter. The French government introduced a tax of 750 francs on imported fuel oil in May 1953 ($2.14 per ton at the 1953 exchange rate) and considered raising the tax again in 1958 and 1959, by which time the price of coal had again over-taken that of imported fuel oil.[42]

The General Report of the Energy Committee of the Commissariat Général du Plan for the Third Modernization Plan stated that the policies of the French government discouraged the best use of energy resources.[43] Particu-larly critical of existing price relationships, it recommended a long-range policy that would better relate prices to true costs. While the report favored more realistic price levels, it opposed a flexible, free competitive price policy on the ground that price competition is not self-perpetuating and leads to corporate concentration and domination by the strong. The report therefore did not recommend that indigenous fuels be subjected to competition from imported energy. It gave preference to the former for the sake of saving dollars.[44]

Belgium

When it comes to coal, the Belgians are as protectionist in principle as the French. Coal still held 85 per cent of the energy market in 1955 in spite of its high cost of production, but the Belgians are less effective than the French in protecting the industry. American coal is imported into Belgium by private merchants. These imports were free during the economic boom of 1955–1957, but were placed under license control in the 1958 recession. License controls were not completely effective because the importers had already purchased American coal on long-term contracts. Belgium thus imported 1 million tons of coal from the United States in the first half of 1958. Import controls by Belgium alone could not, furthermore, fully help the Belgian mines because they need an outlet in other parts of the union. The Belgian government there-fore urged the other governments to reduce their imports of American coal for the benefit of the high-cost Belgian mines. It also recommended that Article 58 be invoked; this article authorizes the use of import quotas by the Community

---

[42] *L'Usine nouvelle*, June 5, 1958, p. 22; *Handelsblatt*, December 14, 1959, p. 1.

[43] Comissariat Général du Plan, Troisième Plan de Modernization et d'Equipement, *Rapport général de la Commission de l'Energie*, Paris, March 1957, pp. 79–84.

[44] The Commission de Vérification des Comptes des Entreprises Publiques, in its *Cinquième rapport d'ensemble*, Paris, 1957, p. 203, also called for a price level in better keeping with the true costs of production.

as a whole and the spreading of production by means of Communitywide production quotas. The other members of the Council of Ministers rejected this suggestion, which came up for discussion a number of times; the French government, in the words of a spokesman, refused to import unemployment. After the miners in southern Belgium struck against the closing of mines, the High Authority, adopting a policy much more protective than that already outlined above from the Fifth General Report, likewise advocated the use of Article 58 as the sole means for attaining a Communitywide solution of the coal crisis.[45] It canvassed the governments to see whether a constitutional majority for the use of Article 58 could be obtained. When action under Article 58 was defeated, the High Authority authorized the Belgian government to subsidize some mines and the government promised to close some of them. The Belgian government, as indicated already, also placed imports from other parts of the Community under control, ostensibly to stop illegal entry of coal from third-party areas. The coal producers in Aachen protested that their deliveries to Belgium were being reduced in violation of the treaty.[46]

Germany

The German government from the early 1950s relied especially on unlimited imports of coal and fuel oil to foster competition.[47] Imported coal was subject to the compensatory import tax of 4.16 per cent but could until February 1959 enter the country in unlimited quantities. Imported heavy fuel oil was not even subject to this tax. Ludwig Erhard, Minister of Economics, had even threatened late in 1957 to waive the compensatory import tax on coal imported from third-party countries because he was displeased by the then recent increase in the price of Ruhr coal; he dropped the matter because the High Authority opposed the exemption as unconstitutional under the treaty.[48] But another measure was introduced to intensify rivalry between German and American coal: the nationalized German railroads in February 1958 extended to coal imported from outside the ECSC the benefit of the lower freight rate that applied to German coal.[49]

The liberal import policy did not create any friction as long as the consumption of total energy expanded much more rapidly than coal production. The

[45] *Handelsblatt*, March 27-28, 1959, p. 2, and April 13, 1959, p. 2.

[46] *Le Monde*, February 24, 1959, p. 16, and February 27, 1959, p. 1; p. 1 of *Handelsblatt*, issues (all in 1959) of February 11, 23 and 25, March 2, 11, 18 and 23; *New York Times* (domestic edition), May 15, 1959, p. 2.

[47] K. Schneider, "La Politique de l'énergie dans l'Allemagne de l'Ouest," *Revue française de l'énergie*, July–August 1958, pp. 481 ff, and September 1958, pp. 534 ff, describes the German policy on energy.

[48] HA, *Sixième rapport général*, Vol. II, pp. 64–65.

[49] *Financial Times*, February 26, 1958, p. 9.

turning point came with the 1958 recession, which not only threw the Ruhr coal mines into difficulty but also served to cast doubt on the ability of the coal industry to market all its product in the long run.

Germany had always imported large quantities of coal for the northern areas; the imported coal came from the United Kingdom before World War II and from the United States afterward. The Ruhr had, however, always preserved a market in the north, which it treated as a "contested" area in the interwar years. As the price of Ruhr coal almost doubled between 1950 and 1957 (Table 47), its vulnerability relative to American coal and imported heavy fuel oil increased. The price of the latter had theretofore been adjusted by the petroleum industry to make it competitive with the price of European coal.[50] The pressure from petroleum increased, especially during the 1958 recession, under the influence of which the price of heavy fuel oil in Germany dropped below world prices. By the end of 1958 the price of residual fuel oil in the coastal regions of Germany was $7.50 per ton lower in coal equivalents than the price of Ruhr coal. The price of American coal delivered at Hamburg at spot cargo rates early in 1958 was also nearly $6.00 per ton lower (Table 53). Though a good deal of the American coal was then brought in on long-term charter contracts made earlier—and therefore at higher costs—new contracts for additional quantities at the lower rates were also made. Germany had imported nearly 16 million tons of United States coal in 1957; the annual rate of import in 1958—when producers' stocks of Ruhr coal were rising—was still 11 million tons a year.[51] Imported coal and fuel oil challenged the Ruhr coal industry not only in northern Germany but also on its home grounds and in southern Germany because interstate freight rates on the Rhine—which fluctuate with the market—were low in 1958.

The German government, at the Chancellor's behest, came to the rescue, on condition that the Ruhr coal operators introduce certain price discounts.[52] In September 1958 the government placed coal imported from third countries under license control; these efforts having proved inadequate, the government in February 1959 subjected imports in excess of 5 million tons a year to an import duty of nearly $5 per ton. The other governments in the ECSC agreed through the Council of Ministers of the ECSC to control any coal imported from third-party countries that might be in transit for Germany.[53] The tax was unpopular in Germany outside the Ruhr. The upper chamber, which repre-

[50] Dwyer, *op. cit.*, pp. 4, 15–16.

[51] HA, *Bulletin statistique.*

[52] International Monetary Fund, *International Financial News Survey*, September 26, 1958, p. 100; *The Economist*, September 13, 1958, p. 831; p. 1 of *Handelsblatt*, issues (all in 1958) of August 11, September 1, and 5-6, November 19.

[53] HA, *Journal officiel*, February 11, 1959, pp. 197 ff.

sents the German states but which has no power to stop the legislative measures of the lower house, rejected the duty.

Germany has a small high-cost domestic production of crude oil, which accounted for one third the 12 million ton intake of the German refineries in 1957; imported refined products in addition amounted to nearly 4 million tons.[54] Imported crude oil was taxed at a rate of $31.20 per metric ton, equivalent to 75 per cent of the price of domestic crude. Germany thus had a highly protected, high-cost price structure for crude petroleum in spite of the interest in competition. But the incidence of this tax fell on the lighter oils, especially gasoline, rather than on heavy fuel oil—interchangeable with coal—because the tax on that portion of the imported crude oil that was converted into heavy fuel oil was waived. Imported heavy fuel oil was also exempt from compensatory import duties. But the waiver of the compensatory import tax on heavy fuel oil was withdrawn late in 1958.[55]

The coal and petroleum industries in 1958 were encouraged by the government to come to an understanding regarding future market shares. The German petroleum industry as of early 1958 had a program to expand refinery intake capacity to 54 million tons of crude oil by 1965. As a result of discussions between the coal operators and the petroleum industry late in 1958, this goal for 1965 was reduced to 40–45 million tons (compared with an actual intake of 12 million tons in 1957).[56]

In February 1959 the Minister of Economics approved the formation of a cartel by the two industries under the German Cartel Act of 1957, Article 8 of which authorizes him to approve "business crisis cartels" in the general interest. Under this cartel, approved for a period of two years, the German petroleum industry agreed that the price of heavy fuel oil would not be permitted to fall below the world price and that new customers would not be accepted in 1959.[57] The petroleum industry thereafter raised prices and posted them in the official journal of the German government in accordance with the requirements of the Cartel Act. The cartel proved ineffective because the merchants outside the agreement undercut the cartel price, causing the members to withdraw. Its failure caused the government in mid-August 1959 to decide to ask the parliament to authorize a compensatory import tax of $7.50 per ton on heavy fuel oil, a proposal that aroused as much discontent as the earlier tax on imported coal. The German Industry Association favors a compulsory coal-oil cartel that would be entrusted with the task of coordinating the two

[54] Schneider, *op. cit.*

[55] *Handelsblatt*, December 3, 1958, p. 1.

[56] *Ibid.*, December 1, 1958, p. 6, December 12-13, 1958, p. 9. *The Economist*, September 13, 1958, p. 831, referred to a "gentleman's agreement."

[57] *Handelsblatt*, December 15, 1958, p. 1, December 22, 1958, p. 1.

industries on the premise that a specific part of the total energy market be reserved to the efficient coal mines. This recommendation recognizes that a tax on fuel oil is insufficient and that producing capacity must be determined on a long-term basis in relation to costs.[58]

The Treaty for the European Economic Community stipulates that the member States, by the end of 1965, should eliminate import duties on petroleum traded between themselves and establish a common import duty on imports from third-party countries. The average of the common duty will be lower than some of the duties in existence in 1957. But the treaty allows the member States to subsidize domestic crude oil production thereafter in order to cover the difference between the cost of domestic and the price of foreign crude oil.[59] If the German government should subsidize domestic crude oil production, would it be able to avoid subsidizing or continuing to protect the Ruhr coal industry as well?

FEDERAL MEASURES

Nearly all the federal measures proposed to protect the coal industry on a Communitywide basis by controlling imports or spreading production were blocked by some of the countries in the Council of Ministers because the governments preferred national measures and failed to agree on coordinate ones.

Article 71 authorizes the governments, under the advice of the High Authority, to give each other mutual assistance for the purpose of restricting the circulation of goods imported and Article 73 authorizes the individual governments to use import licenses to control imports from nonmembers. The High Authority may oversee the use of such controls to keep them from being too restrictive. The Community, through the High Authority, may impose quantitative restrictions on imports into the common market to stop dumping, to avoid unfair competition (provided the Council agrees) and to enforce Article 58 if that is invoked to establish production quotas during a recession.

The High Authority initially shied away from an autarkic policy and rigid import controls, placing greater emphasis on stockpiling and on consultation among the governments with regard to their respective import programs,[60] but later supported the use of Article 58. The President of the High Authority, summarizing the "indirect" measures it had taken in the recession of 1958,

[58] *New York Times* (domestic edition), August 13, 1959, p. 37; *Handelsblatt*, August 5, 1959, pp. 1, 3, August 14–15, 1959, p. 1, September 14, 1959, p. 1.

[59] "Protocole concernant les huiles minérales et certains de leurs dérives," in EEC treaty; Schneider, *op. cit.*

[60] See the statement by Coppé, to the European Parliamentary Assembly, cited by *Le Monde*, June 26, 1958, p. 14; and the meeting of the Council of Ministers reported in *Handelsblatt*, October 17-18, 1958, p. 2.

indicated that it had persuaded the Dutch government to maintain the ratio between coal imported from the rest of the Community and from third-party countries; it had helped persuade the German government to apply the compensatory import tax to imported heavy fuel oil; and it had obtained agreement from all governments to keep each other informed of coal imported from the United States.[61] The High Authority also authorized some firms to postpone payment, free of interest charges, of the levy on production.[62] It unsuccessfully recommended that mine workers be guaranteed 90 per cent of their normal earnings from the proceeds of its own revenue and a special tax.[63] This was not the first guaranteed wage to be recommended. I. M. D. Little, dealing with British coal, had suggested that the additional revenue earned by a price policy based on marginal cost should in part be used to increase the ratio of development to production during recessions and to guarantee employment.[64]

Stockpiling

The only truly federal protective measure adopted by the ECSC provided financial help to the mines that held a large volume of coal in stock. One of the vice presidents of the High Authority having stated that the High Authority preferred stockpiling to unemployment,[65] the High Authority placed a proposal before the Council of Ministers that called for the creation of a stockpiling fund to be financed by a producers' levy of five cents per ton of coal produced. This levy would have raised close to $12 million. The proceeds would have been distributed to the producers to help them carry a limited amount of stocks. The governments of Germany and Luxembourg vetoed this proposal.[66] The High Authority later promulgated a program that was financed by the normal levy on production and approved by the Council of Ministers. The High Authority put up $7 million; the governments that requested aid for their mines were required to match the loans or grants made by the High Authority.[67] If a mining firm received a guarantee from its government, the High Authority agreed to lend $2.00 for a twelve-month period, beginning October 31, 1958, for every ton put into stock in excess of

[61] *Handelsblatt,* December 17, 1958, p. 1.

[62] HA, Decision No. 4–59, *Journal officiel,* January 27, 1959, pp. 108 ff.

[63] *Handelsblatt,* March 13-14, 1959, p. 2; *Le Monde,* February 24, 1959, p. 14, February 28, 1959, p. 14.

[64] I. M. D. Little, *The Price of Fuel,* Clarendon Press, Oxford, 1953, pp. 51–53.

[65] Statement by Coppé before the European Parliamentary Assembly, reported in *Le Monde,* June 26, 1958, p. 14.

[66] HA, *Bulletin mensuel d'information,* May–June 1958, p. 12; *Handelsblatt,* October 17-18, 1958, p. 2.

[67] HA, Decision 27–58, *Journal officiel,* November 14, 1958, pp. 486 ff.

thirty-five days' production. These loans were to be repaid in five years without interest. If a firm applied without a government guarantee, the High Authority agreed to give nonrepayable aid of $1.00 per ton put into stock. Applications for aid had to be submitted through the governments in any case. Aid was conditional on the mining firm's showing, through its government, that it would take steps to modernize operations; uneconomic mines (called Class III mines) were not eligible; mines already receiving other types of aid also were ineligible. The initial scheme was put through largely for the benefit of the Belgian mines; neither the French nor Limburg mines were then in trouble and stocks at the Ruhr mines were then generally below the thirty-five-day level. The High Authority later proposed to raise the fund to $10 million and to broaden eligibility to twenty-five days' production in order to bring the Ruhr mines into the scheme; thirty-nine Ruhr and forty-one Belgian mines, as well as one Dutch mine, would have been eligible.[68] This proposal fell through because the French government wanted eligibility broadened still further for the sake of its mines.[69]

Conclusion

Aside from the stockpiling measures, the major energy producing countries in the ECSC thus protected their own industries by various means, the individual government rather than the Community being the effective unit of control, much to the disillusionment of certain observers.[70]

WHAT PRICE SECURITY?

The trend toward protection on a national basis raises two problems. Will the members of the ECSC be able to create a Communitywide policy? What price will they pay individually or collectively for security?

No one of the three Communities—the ECSC, Euratom or the European Economic Community—has jurisdiction over energy as a whole. The Messina Conference, a meeting of government delegates that fathered the EEC and Euratom, recommended that energy should be coordinated intergovernmentally rather than federally.[71] Since gas and electricity are not transported and distributed like other merchandise, their integration, the Conference stated, depends on investment rather than trade. The Conference report therefore recommended that action be limited to the study of long-term needs and

[68] *Handelsblatt*, December 22, 1958, p. 2.

[69] *Le Monde*, February 7, 1959, p. 16.

[70] See, for example, *ibid.*, March 1-2, 1959, p. 5.

[71] *Rapport des Chefs de Délégation aux Ministres des Affaires Etrangères*, Comité Intergouvernemental Crée par la Conférence de Messine, Brussels, April 1956, pp. 126–129.

of the most productive investments. It suggested that the High Authority prepare such studies in collaboration with the Council of Ministers, particularly studies with respect to projects which the Investment Bank of the EEC might help finance.

The governments, in a formal protocol signed by the High Authority and the Council of Ministers in October 1957, thereafter made the High Authority responsible for these coordinate studies.[72] The Comité Mixte, a group of government representatives chaired by the High Authority, was made the coordinating body; executives of the EEC and Euratom, as well as third countries (if necessary), are represented in the Comité Mixte. The terms of reference are wide; they enable the High Authority to examine comparative costs, taxes, subsidies and security considerations; they enable it to suggest policies and specific measures to carry them out. Although the High Authority is responsible for coordination, the governments, through the Council of Ministers, are still the final judges and executors of any proposals the High Authority may present.

The High Authority described the results of the early studies as follows:[73]

The preliminary studies of the systems and structure of prices and of fiscal regulations affecting the different forms of energy in each of the six countries of the Community revealed an extraordinary disparity between countries with respect to the measures applied to different forms of energy, as well as frequent variations in their application and differences in orientation.

Though the countries in the Community were unable to coordinate in the 1958 recession, they might find it easier to coordinate in the future. As all of them become increasingly have-nots, none of them will have much to give to the others; all of them may then make common cause against the suppliers of energy.[74] The prospects for coordination should in any case not be exaggerated, especially in view of France's growing interest as an oil producer in the Sahara. Should coordination be achieved, it would still be a means rather than an end. The benefits would depend on the policies adopted. The European countries are likely to pay a premium for security. But how much of a premium? Where does a reasonable parity between world and domestic fuel prices slip over into excessive protectionism?[75] Western Europe is already far

[72] In *Journal officiel*, December 7, 1957.

[73] HA, *Bulletin mensuel d'information*, April 1958, p. 6.

[74] See, e.g., the suggestion by Little and Rosenstein-Rodan, *op. cit.*, p. 3, that the Community should present a united front to persuade the United States to import gasoline from, and to export heavy fuel to, Western Europe. Recent discoveries in North Africa of oil with a large gasoline, and a low fuel oil, yield support the argument for this suggestion.

[75] Robert Marjolin, vice president of the Commission of the European Economic Community, believes that parity points should be fixed in advance in order to guide the Community's energy policy. Communauté Européenne, *Bulletin mensuel d'information*, Luxembourg, January 1959, p.3.

behind the United States in the use of mechanical power. Though the influence of prices cannot be separated from the other factors that are responsible for Europe's backwardness, the effect of a higher price structure on the use of mechanical power should not be ignored when security takes precedence over costs.[76] The Community still needs a workable policy that balances the various sources of energy to achieve a reasonable degree of security without unduly sacrificing cost.

The cost of imported fuels is likely to be lower than that of indigenous coal because the coal supply from the United States, the transport of liquified gas (experimental as yet), and the growing availability of oil from North Africa will tend to keep oil prices down. In view of the improvement in Europe's foreign exchange balance, it can possibly afford to put a lower premium on indigenous fuels for the sake of the European economy as a whole, especially as lower costs for energy might enable it to expand the export market for manufactured goods. These considerations imply the adoption of administrative measures to make the price of European coal more competitive with that of imported fuels in the long run, entailing price levels that would limit expansion to the relatively low cost coal mines in order to avoid a structural oversupply of European coal. Indeed, the glut of coal which continued in spite of improving business conditions in 1959, caused the coal producers and governments of France, Belgium and Germany to reduce output goals and to close mines.

[76] Tibor Scitovsky, *Economic Theory and Western European Integration*, Allen and Unwin, London, 1958, pp. 150 ff, calls attention to the possibility that conservatism, as well as the high cost of energy, might be responsible for the lower use of mechanical power in Europe.

CHAPTER 11

EXTERNAL COMMERCIAL
POLICY AND TRADE

The discussion thus far for the main part has covered subjects that the treaty intended to place under the control of the federal authorities. This and the next two chapters cover subjects over which the States retained control but on which they agreed to cooperate in accordance with the treaty.

THE LIMITS OF SUPRANATIONAL POWER

If the Six were one country, one people and one market instead of a collection of countries, then labor and capital would be able to move freely within the area, trade would be regional rather than national, payments would be made in one currency, transport rates would not be influenced by nationality and the federal authorities would control external commercial policies. Though the ECSC is a federal organization in some fields, it is still no more than an international organization in other fields. The free movement of capital and labor, transport rates, taxation (including depreciation allowances), social security payments and benefits, wage standards, monetary and fiscal policies (including currency exchange rates) and commercial policies are still controlled by the States. These matters also influence delivered prices, the cost of production and the standard of living but the ECSC can make no changes in these fields without the agreement of the governments.

Entrepreneurs in the same community expect their rivals to be subject to equal conditions of business, especially the conditions affected by public authority. Workers in the same community expect government regulations affecting earnings, income taxes, social security benefits (including family allocations) and the standard of living to apply to all uniformly. Both capital and labor expect the differences to be regional rather than governmental in a full federation or community. In a full federation the owner of capital and the

337

worker alike would be free to migrate in search of the greatest opportunities. Since the ECSC is not a full federation, these implications are not actual.

Why were some fields excluded from the jurisdiction of the Community and kept under national legislative and administrative control? The six governments would have had to pull the coal and steel industries out of their respective national economies in order to equalize all conditions. Each country would have had to have different wages and direct and indirect taxes for these two industries than for all other industry. But most matters subject to national legislation or administration are indivisible. Currency exchange rates, for example, are influenced by trading possibilities for all goods and services and therefore cannot be adjusted separately for the coal and steel industries (except in a country such as Luxembourg where steel exports furnish the main part of export revenue) though their costs may differ from the average activity for the country as a whole. Consequently the firms in these two industries must live with the prevailing rates of exchange, adjust their prices accordingly or go out of business.

The conditions affecting labor and capital in the coal and steel industries could have been equalized only by common public legislation with respect to all economic activities. This course would have involved a full-fledged and comprehensive political and economic federation. The States were not prepared to go that far. Full equalization was not attempted with respect even to the European Economic Community.

The six governments adopted instead the premise that all conditions need not be equalized at the start.[1] They thought that existing differences in competitive conditions arising from legislation by the States were not serious enough to interfere with the common market for coal and steel. An early report of the High Authority to the Common Assembly stated the matter thus:[2]

False interpretations should be carefully avoided in the field of differences of competitive conditions. Equal fiscal or social charges need not be created in advance in order to encourage and attain the best economic results. On the contrary, trade is based on differences . . . [and] reflects the basic facts, which are the cost of labor and the weight of public charges. . . . The distortions from one country to another are limited. The situation is extremely different when compared with the United Kingdom. Unlike the system in the six countries, the British mines pay practically no payroll taxes and the treasury itself finances social security for miners from indirect taxes, from which coal is exempted, or from profits taxes to which the mines, which sell coal at cost, do not contribute. This legislative difference explains the greater part of the spread between the price of coal in Britain and the Community.

[1] Paul Reuter discusses this matter in *La Communauté Européenne du Charbon et de l'Acier*, Librairie Générale de Droit et de Jurisprudence, Paris, 1953, pp. 276 ff.

[2] *Exposé sur la situation de la Communauté*, January 10, 1953, pp. 85, 91. But see Chapter 13, where lower payroll taxes in the United Kingdom are shown to be offset by higher wages.

It is not a matter of passing judgment on the merits of either system, the one by which social security charges are included in the cost of production, or the one by which they are transferred to the public treasury. One must, however, note that they are incompatible; if the two systems by which costs are so differently influenced were to be included in the same community without prior adjustment, prices would not reflect real costs and production would be artificially raised or reduced in a manner which would be advantageous neither to the country where production fell, nor to the one where it increased.

But national differences, real or imaginary, created pressure from management to equalize the factors affecting the cost of production and pressure from labor to equalize those that affect the standard of living.

Though the ECSC treaty implies that the Community is not incompatible with national control of some important factors affecting costs and living standards, it nevertheless provides for several types of corrective action and for studies to determine the facts:

(1) The States are to take no further action to impair the conditions of competition; this stipulation (Article 67) applies to new measures.

(2) Flagrant distortions, those that are clearly discriminatory, are to be eliminated. This provision applies retroactively as well as to any future discrimination.

(3) Some structural distortions (not specifically discriminatory in intent) are to be gradually eliminated or reduced. The treaty employs the term "harmonization" to describe this objective.[3]

These corrective measures (with certain exceptions which will be noted in the course of discussion) cannot be taken without unanimous agreement by the governments. The Community is thus in the same position as any other international organization with respect to commercial policy and transport rates. But the essential goals pursued by the treaty place the governments under the obligation to coordinate and harmonize the policies over which the States retain individual sovereignty.

The observations presented in this section apply to this and the next two chapters.

COMMERCIAL POLICY UNDER THE TREATY

The ECSC, as Chapter 2 indicates, is not a closed system. An economic union affects the countries outside as well as those within it. The countries outside may lose or acquire supplies or customers within the union or may have to modify their commercial relations with it or with its members.

What does the treaty say?

[3] Sections 2 and 10 of the Convention for the Transitional Provisions.

The member States retain their individual responsibility for commercial relations with third-party countries unless the treaty provides otherwise (Article 71). But an economic union implies coordination between member governments on some policies affecting external affairs. Using the High Authority as its vehicle, the treaty thus attempts to restrain individual sovereignty and to encourage some coordination even if unanimous agreement by the Council of Ministers is still required.

The treaty deals with three kinds of commercial problems in particular:
(1) Protecting the internal market against imports.
(2) National policies with respect to trade.
(3) Coordinating the policies of the individual member States and of the Community as a whole with those of third parties, whether countries or other international organizations.

(1) Import Restrictions

Imports into the Community from the outside may be divided into three types of cases as defined by Article 74: (a) imports which are dumped or are sold by "other practices condemned by the Havana Charter"; (b) imports from producers outside the Community who are able to underprice producers in the Community by virtue of "competitive conditions contrary to the provisions" of the treaty; (c) imports which increase to the point of inflicting or threatening to inflict "serious damage on production" in the Community.

The High Authority in any of these three cases may take any measures and may make any recommendations to the governments to safeguard the common market "in accordance with this Treaty, in particular with the objectives defined in Article 3."

What defensive measures are available under the treaty? In order to impose quantitative restrictions on imports falling under the (b) type of case, the High Authority must obtain the agreement of the Council of Ministers. Such restrictions can be imposed under the (c) type of case only if Article 58 is invoked; this article allows the Community to establish production quotas during a recession. Defensive measures against imports are not, however, limited to quantitative restrictions. Any other measures allowed by the treaty may be taken. Several enterprises, for example, may be authorized to adopt common financial measures to help them meet cutthroat competition from producers outside the Community (Article 53). Or the High Authority under Article 61 may establish minimum prices for products produced within the Community in order to protect their prices from falling excessively in a serious recession.

The powers under Article 74 had not yet been used by early 1959.

(2) Commercial Policy

The treaty deals with export and import policy in a number of places. Though each state retains its sovereignty over commercial policy, the treaty nevertheless gives some policy direction to the member States and some powers and responsibilities to the High Authority. Article 3(a) requires the institutions of the Community to see that "the Common Market is regularly supplied" but also to take "into account the needs of third countries."

A State may negotiate its own commercial treaties but is obliged to submit them to the High Authority before signature (Article 75) because exports may deprive the common market of supplies necessary to it and because imports may disturb home production. The High Authority may call these dangers to the attention of the State. The High Authority must also protect the ability of the Community to alter exports or imports provided for by commercial agreements if Articles 58 and 59 are invoked; these Articles provide, respectively, for production quotas during a recession and distribution controls when supplies are scarce. A commercial agreement made by a State may, further, contain price clauses that might interfere with the High Authority's power to fix minimum or maximum prices in export or home markets. The High Authority may therefore issue a recommendation to a member State to modify a draft agreement or may require the State to insert a clause protecting the High Authority's rights, a power the High Authority has frequently employed.[4] The High Authority would otherwise lose its power to influence the contract subsequently.

The High Authority may under Article 59 recommend the use of internal and export allocations only after consulting the Consultative Committee and the Council of Ministers; the latter can block the proposal only by unanimous vote. If the Council of Ministers initiates the use of allocations, it decides the volume to be exported as well as the contribution from each member State. If allocations are initiated by the High Authority, the High Authority takes account of exports in apportioning supplies to the member States, each of which divides its share between internal use and export, notifying the High Authority of the latter. The State may increase exports over the tonnage notified without incurring a penalty. If the State reduces the volume exported, the High Authority may penalize that State in subsequent periods by a commensurate reduction in the allocation. Under Article 59 the Council of Ministers may also adopt allocations unanimously on its own initiative.

The foregoing provisions appear restrictive but the High Authority's

---

[4] CECA, Assemblée Commune, Sous-Commission de la Politique Commerciale, *Rapport sur la politique commerciale de la CECA et les questions qu'elle soulève*, Doc. No. 1, 1957–1958, p. 19, referred to as the Pleven Report.

powers, as well as the spirit of the treaty, help serve an antiautarkic purpose also. Article 3(f) requires the institutions of the Community "To foster the development of international trade and ensure that equitable limits are observed in prices charged in foreign markets." Article 61(c) authorizes the establishment of maximum export prices to help achieve the objective of Article 3(f). Such prices, however, were not applied in the case that might have called for them, steel exports to third-party countries (discussed in Chapter 7).

Article 73 authorizes each member State to administer the use of export licenses on goods originating in, or of import licenses on goods destined for, its territory. But it empowers the High Authority to supervise their administration and, having consulted the Council of Ministers, to issue a recommendation to a State if license control is too restrictive or if coordination among the States is desirable. In 1959 the Council of Ministers agreed to coordinate for the sake of helping Germany control its restrictions on coal imports from third-party countries.

(3) Coordination

Though the States retain their sovereignty over commercial policy, they are encouraged to coordinate their policies under the treaty because an economic union implies cooperation and a common front. The Council of Ministers is the coordinating vehicle, provided it can reach unanimous agreement. The High Authority presents recommendations to the Council of Ministers to help the States to coordinate their policies. Under instructions from the Council of Ministers, the High Authority represents the States as a collectivity and negotiates with third parties on their behalf.[5]

There are several important provisions for coordination in the field of commercial policy. Article 71 contains a broad stipulation that the member governments "will lend each other the necessary assistance in the execution of measures recognized by the High Authority as being in accordance with the Treaty and with existing international agreements."[6]

Section 15 of the Convention for the Transitional Provisions called for a common external tariff by February 1958 that would be less restrictive than the individual tariffs in effect when the common market opened in 1953. This provision, it should be noted, is antiautarkic. This section also authorizes the

---

[5] For Reuter's comments on the novelty of this last device, see *op. cit.*, pp. 86–87, 116–137, 248–257. The device rests on a temporary grant of power limited to five years (section 14 of the Convention for the Transitional Provisions) but will probably be extended; see Assemblée Commune, *Revision du traité instituant la CECA*, Luxembourg, n.d., p. 26.

[6] The Belgian government invoked this provision without success early in 1958 in order to have the other members of the Community reduce their imports of coal from the United States, a step that would have facilitated the sale of high-priced Belgian coal. See HA, *Sixième rapport général*, Vol. I, p. 94; also Chapters 9 and 10 of this study.

High Authority to decide if a member State may impose a tariff on steel higher than the (less protective) common tariff; in that case it may, up to a period of two years beyond February 1958, authorize the State to restrict the entry into its own territory of steel purchased from third-party countries by other members of the Community. This provision had not been used by early 1959.

A common tariff on imports from outside the Community with free trade inside of it runs up against the most-favored-nation clause in the General Agreement on Tariffs and Trade (GATT) and in other treaties. If a country grants a concession to any one country, the most-favored-nation clause stipulates that it must grant an identical concession to all other countries that enjoy most-favored-nation rights. But the six governments that granted free trade privileges to each other in the ECSC maintained a tariff on imports from third-party countries. This practice required the Six to obtain a waiver from the other most-favored-nation countries. The most important collective waiver was required of GATT, to which most of the countries outside the Soviet bloc belong. Section 20 of the Convention for the Transitional Provisions stipulates that the members of the ECSC will lend each other effective assistance should any country refuse to waive the most-favored-nation clause. Such pressure was fortunately not required, thanks to the successful negotiations in GATT, in which the High Authority represented the Community under instructions from the Council of Ministers.

The adoption of a new steel tariff, and trade relations with the world outside, were the most important fields of commercial activity for the young Community.[7]

IS THE COMMUNITY ANTIECONOMIC?

STEEL

On the eve of the common market for coal and steel, the members of Benelux (Belgium, Netherlands and Luxembourg), itself a customs union, had a common tariff on imports from third-party countries; France-Saar, Germany and Italy each had its own tariffs. There were therefore four tariff levels applying to imports from third-party countries.

The General Agreement on Tariffs and Trade allows the most-favored-nation clause to be waived if a customs union adopts a common tariff no higher or more restrictive than that previously practiced by each of its member

---

[7] Certain transitory matters that created a good deal of activity are omitted from the discussion presented above, e.g.: the control of indirect imports based on the difference between the low Benelux and high French and Italian steel tariffs; the control of indirect exports based on the differences in currency exchange regulations between countries.

countries.[8] In 1953 the ECSC, promising to establish by 1958 a common tariff lower than the average of individual country tariffs existing theretofore, obtained the waiver and the practical, if not legal, status of a contracting party. The waiver was conditional on subsequent performance.[9]

Benelux and the other three members of the ECSC in the meantime maintained their individual tariffs on imports from third-party countries. Benelux had the lowest tariffs. But the Benelux countries quantitatively controlled their imports from third-party countries in order to guard the breach in the economic union for France and Italy, the higher-tariff countries.[10]

The High Authority, acting for the ECSC, in 1956 granted and obtained from GATT several tariff concessions on steel products, mainly to help Austria maintain sales in the Community.[11]

The New Duties

The tariff rates before and after the new tariff of February 1958 are shown in Table 55.

Table 55

IMPORT DUTIES ON SELECTED STEEL PRODUCTS BEFORE
AND AFTER TARIFF OF FEBRUARY 1958

Product	Per Cent Ad Valorem					
	Benelux and Germany		France		Italy	
	Before (B: Benelux; G: Germany)	After	Before	After	Before	After
Bars	3 B / 10 G	5	10	6	22	9
Wire rods	4 B / 12 G	6	12	7	13	10
Strip	6 B / 15 G	8	12	9	23	10
Flat products	3–4 B / 8–22 G	5–6	11–22	6	22–23	9–10
Sections	3–8 B / 10–11 G	5–6	11–22	6	22–23	9–10

Source: Usine nouvelle, December 5, 1957, p. 9.

[8] Article 44 of GATT; see Jacob Viner, *The Customs Union Issue*, Carnegie Endowment for International Peace, New York, 1950, especially Chaps. 2 and 6.

[9] See Reuter, *op. cit.*, pp. 133–134.

[10] Section 15 of the Convention for the Transitional Provisions provided for such controls. Germany, deficient in steel supplies, had waived the tariff before 1953 but had restored it afterward to avoid creating another breach in the union. In the middle of 1956, the Council of Ministers allowed Germany to reduce steel tariffs about 10 per cent on condition that Germany would prevent illegal reshipment to France; this reduction occurred along with a general German tariff reduction. See *Financial Times*, July 26, 1956.

[11] See HA, *Bulletin from the European Community for Coal and Steel*, Washington, June 1956, p. 2, for details on these concessions.

The French rates were originally two to three times, the Italian rates four times, the Benelux rates. France and Italy were later unwilling to accept a common tariff two points above the former Benelux rates.[12] It was reported that the French had urged the Council of Ministers to adopt a common tariff of 12 per cent on the ground that the steel industry in the ECSC required that amount of protection to maintain its margins for self-financing.[13] Although the recommendation for a 12 per cent rate was rejected, France and Italy were allowed to have a somewhat higher rate of protection than the rest. Germany accepted the new Benelux rates. Consequently, there are now three, instead of four, rates; Benelux raised its rates by two points; France lowered its rates to within one point, and Italy to within two to four points, of the Benelux tariff. The ECSC therefore is not strictly speaking a customs union.

Effect of the New Duties on Imports

Are the new steel tariffs less restrictive than the old? Although the average height of the tariff wall is lower, the effect of this change cannot be examined without considering the new position country by country. When an importing country with, say, a 10 per cent tariff joins a customs union, an exporter within the union thenceforth faces no tariff barrier. Even if the importing country reduces the duty to outsiders by one half, the exporter within the union, previously on the same footing as his rival outside, still enjoys a 5 per cent advantage. Italy, France and Germany reduced their rates at least 50 per cent. As a high-cost, high-priced steel producer, Italy is now more vulnerable to competitive imports from third-party countries. It imported about 375,000 to 580,000 tons of steel a year in the 1950s (Table 2-3, Appendix E). But the United Kingdom and the United States furnished no more than 20 per cent of these imports. The other producers within the union, France, Belgium-Luxembourg and Germany, are therefore the major suppliers and enjoy a greater potential advantage than ever in the Italian market.

As a low-price steel producer with favorable production costs, France should not be considered an habitual importer; its imports from the United Kingdom and United States are even less habitual. The lower tariff wall around the French steel market is therefore without practical significance for suppliers outside the Community. Only rival producers in the union can benefit if they decide to absorb freight by selling in the lowest-price area in the union for Thomas steel.

The German case is more complex. The market in southern Germany must

---

[12] Section 15 of the Convention for the Transitional Provisions provided that Benelux would if necessary raise its tariff by a maximum of two points.

[13] *Handelsblatt*, April 24, 1957, p. 2.

be treated separately. This market normally draws on steel from the Saar, Lorraine and Luxembourg as well as the Ruhr. Not very accessible to British and American producers, location rather than the tariff is therefore the main obstacle to imports by southern Germany from producers outside the union. The rest of the German market generally imports only in periods of peak demand when buyers pay a premium. The tariff is no barrier in such cases. The Germans had in fact suspended the duty before 1953, but imported only small quantities of American steel and hardly any British steel in any case. The tariff reduction is therefore of no practical effect. Only producers in other parts of the union can therefore benefit in the German market from the economic union.

The duties on steel were raised by two points around Benelux. This increase is of no practical significance so far as Belgium-Luxembourg are concerned; with a small home market, these two countries imported less steel than any other member of the ECSC even when demand was strong, and they imported mainly from Germany and France even then.

The additional two points of tariff protection around the Netherlands steel market is of much greater significance. This market is the most competitive in the Community.[14] It accounted for more than half the steel imported by the ECSC from the United Kingdom and the United States in 1955 and for nearly one third the steel imported by the ECSC countries combined from other members and from the United Kingdom and the United States (Table 2-3, Appendix E). It always imports, whether business is good or bad. The United Kingdom and the United States furnished between 10 to 20 per cent of all the steel imported by Holland from all the main sources in the early 1950s. It remains to be seen if the United Kingdom and the United States will retain their historic share in face of the two-point increase in the duty or if they will lose to their rivals in the union, who now enjoy a duty-free market.

Qualitatively speaking, one cannot say categorically that the new steel tariffs are less protective.[15]

But even if the new tariffs were more protective, they would not necessarily be antieconomic because the price of steel produced in France, Belgium-Luxembourg and Germany—which supply most of the steel in the Netherlands market—is not higher than that exported by Britain and the United States, though the European countries are less efficient than the United States in the use of manpower. We cannot, therefore, conclude that the Community

---

[14] Thus the Netherlands led the campaign to revise Article 60 (2) in order to allow sellers to quote prices with greater flexibility.

[15] The Austrian government, for example, complained to GATT that the new tariffs were too protective; see *Usine nouvelle*, December 12, 1957, p. 7. On the difficulty of measuring "protection," see Viner, *op. cit.*, pp. 66–68.

diverts steel imports from low- to high-cost sources of supply or that it hinders the best use of world resources.[16]

COAL

Tariffs on coal have been of minor significance in controlling the trade in coal, though the imposition of the temporary tariff introduced by Germany in 1959, as discussed in Chapters 9 and 10, may presage the beginning of a new trend, especially as coal produced in the ECSC gets relatively dearer.

Whereas the Community would not be antieconomic if it were to favor steel producers within the Community against those without, it might be antieconomic if it were to do so in coal or petroleum because the cost of coal production in the Community is rising more rapidly than the cost of American coal or foreign petroleum.

Differences in national interest, together with national differences in the methods of control, as illustrated by the discussion in Chapters 9 and 10, indicate the difficulties of an economic union when commercial policy is left under the jurisdiction of the individual States.

IS THE COMMUNITY AUTARKIC?

The Community is more important as supplier than customer for most third-party countries. Exports of ECSC-type products to third-party countries by members of the Community amounted to nearly $1.5 billion in 1956, accounting for 11 per cent of the value of their combined exports of all goods.[17] There are some mixed cases: Austria buys coal from, and supplies steel to, the Community; Sweden supplies iron ore and buys coke and steel. The United Kingdom and the United States compete with continental producers in overseas steel markets at all times but the United Kingdom, and the United States to a lesser degree, also buy continental steel, especially during high levels of business activity. Besides exchanging steel with the Continent at such times, the United States enjoys an increasing sale of coal and scrap in the ECSC.

STEEL EXPORTS

External customers of the continental steel industry, the largest combined world exporter, need rarely find their supplies jeopardized, but they do have to pay premium prices at high levels of business activity, a fact that troubles

---

[16] See Viner, *op. cit.*, pp. 52 ff, for the trade-diverting dangers of economic union.

[17] CECA, Assemblée Commune, Sous-Commission de la Politique Commerciale, *Rapport sur la politique commerciale de la CECA et les questions qu'elle soulève*, Doc. No. 1, 1957–1958, pp. 13–14.

relations between the ECSC and third-party countries (see Chapters 6 and 7). In view of the fact that steel exports from the ECSC to third-party countries rose sharply when internal supplies were scarce in 1955–1956, the Community was anything but autarkic. Exports of iron ore and scrap by the Community are negligible.

SOLID FUELS EXPORTS

The ECSC, the United Kingdom and Poland were the main factors in the world coal trade before World War II. The members of the ECSC exported an average of 12.5 million tons of solid fuels (in hard coal equivalents) a year in 1937–1938, exclusive of trade with each other; the United Kingdom exported 53 million tons, and Poland 14.5 million tons (of which 6 million tons went to the present non-Soviet countries), to all destinations including the ECSC. These exports came to a total of 80 million tons. Exports from these sources combined had declined to 28 million tons by 1957—one third of those in 1937–1938—not counting Poland's exports to Soviet bloc countries. The United States had supplied most of the difference, with 47 million tons of exports to European destinations in 1957. But while exports by the United Kingdom and Poland (exclusive of Polish exports to the Soviet bloc) declined by 70 per cent, from a total of 59 to 17 million tons, exports by the ECSC to third-party countries declined by only 15 per cent, from 12.5 to 10.6 million tons a year between 1937–1938 to 1957. Exports by the ECSC to external customers declined less than trade between the members of ECSC in the same period, the latter having declined by 23 per cent. Exports by the ECSC to destinations outside still accounted for about 7 per cent of the coal that they produced in 1955.[18]

Why were exports by the ECSC to third-party countries maintained in spite of the scarcity of solid fuels? Germany accounted for about 70 per cent of the solid fuels exported to third-party areas in both 1937–1938 and 1957. But Germany reduced coal exports and increased coke exports during this period. Coal had become scarcer than coke, as pointed out in Chapter 9, but the returns are greater on the sale of coke. The same phenomenon affected exports by the Netherlands, which accounted for 10 to 15 per cent of the solid fuels exported by the ECSC. Some of the coke they export, to Sweden and Austria, is of metallurgical quality; the steel industry in both countries is very dependent on German coke and German imports of the highly sought-after iron ore from Sweden are dependent on the exchange. The coke exported by Germany includes also small sizes, not suitable for metallurgy but highly prized for heating purposes in Scandinavia and Switzerland. While German and Dutch exports of coke to third-party countries nearly offset the decline in coal ex-

[18] Data are from Table 2-6, Appendix E, and ECE, *Quarterly Bulletin of Coal Statistics.*

ports, their exports of coke to the other members of the Community offset less of the decline in coal exports to those destinations. Firms with an investment in coke producing facilities cannot switch from coal to coke imports unless they are prepared to write the investment off and give up the advantages of fully integrated steel production. Part of their requirements for imported coal were thus satisfied by the United States instead of Germany.

France and Belgium furnished more coal (not coke) to third-party countries after World War II than before. In a sellers' market these two marginal suppliers, Belgium with high-cost coal and France with a high-volatile type of steam coal that is not very prized, found it advantageous to export to third-party countries at world prices.

The ECSC's record with respect to solid fuels exports to third countries shows that it was anything but restrictive when coal was scarce. The exporting countries would, moreover, have opposed any attempt by the other members of the ECSC to reduce exports to third-party countries as an interference with normal commercial relations.

COMMERCIAL RELATIONS OF THE ECSC WITH THIRD-PARTY COUNTRIES

Though membership in the ECSC is open to other European countries (Article 98), no other country had joined by 1959. Third-party countries have commercial treaties with the ECSC and maintain accredited delegations to the Community. The governments of Austria, Denmark, Greece, Japan, Norway, Sweden, Switzerland, the United Kingdom and the United States maintain representatives in Luxembourg.[19]

Some governments are especially interested in particular matters: Switzerland, for example, in Rhine traffic and in railroad rates for traffic in transit through that country. Switzerland and the Community ratified an agreement in 1957 for advance consultation when and if the High Authority envisages action under Articles 59 and 61 (allocations and price control, respectively). Another agreement between the two covers traffic in transit through Switzerland. Austria received from the ECSC (in the framework of GATT) some tariff concessions on steel and formally promised the ECSC not to dump or take other measures that might disturb the steel market in the Community.[20]

---

[19] Private and semiofficial observers are also stationed in Luxembourg; most of them are from the coal and steel industries of the member countries; they maintain contact with each other, with officials of the Community and with the delegations from third-party countries.

[20] For details on these agreements, see HA, *Cinquième rapport général*, pp. 60–61, 140. HA, *Bulletin from the European Community for Coal and Steel*, December 1957, contains a good article on the Community's special relations with Switzerland and Austria.

The ECSC's relationships with the United States and the United Kingdom are broader than those just mentioned. The American and British governments are interested in European integration as a whole; their representation is therefore an expression of foreign policy as well as of commerce, especially in America's case. Relationships between the United States and the ECSC are not contractual; they are based on the fact that the United States government staunchly supports European integration. When the ECSC began to operate as an organization in August 1952, the Secretary of State declared:

It is the intention of the United States to give the Coal and Steel Community the strong support that its importance to the political and economic unification of Europe warrants. As appropriate under the Treaty, the United States will now deal with the Community on coal and steel matters.

The United States subsequently announced the appointment of a delegation in terms that adumbrated a pragmatic rather than contractual relationship:[21]

The form of ultimate association between the Community and the United States will be determined on the basis of experience in dealing with matters of common interest and in accordance with the Treaty establishing the European Coal and Steel Community.

In addition to its general interest in European integration, the United States government dealt with the ECSC on particular matters: the $100 million loan granted by the United States government in 1954; exports of scrap by the United States to the Community, which were at times troubled by lack of supply in the United States and by private exclusive purchase contracts made by importers in the Community;[22] and the desire by the United States to ensure free entry for United States coal in the Community, a principle overthrown by the German and other governments in the recession of 1958.

BRITAIN AND THE COMMUNITY

Discussions between Britain and the ECSC concerned the creation of a free trade area, in which the Six and most of the other members of the Organization for European Economic Cooperation would have joined,[23] as well as the mutual interest in coal and steel.

While Britain supported continental unity after World War II, "by small doses of semi-cooperation," it was not prepared to join owing to its Commonwealth ties and the reluctance to cede any of its sovereign powers to federal

---

[21] Both statements cited by Reuter, *op. cit.*, p. 130.

[22] HA, *Sixième rapport général*, Vol. I, p. 90.

[23] The other members of the Organization for European Economic Cooperation are: Austria, Switzerland, Greece, Turkey, the United Kingdom, Portugal and the Scandinavian countries.

institutions.[24] Presented with the problem of joining the Schuman Plan in 1950, it decided to stay out but extended its blessing. The two major political parties in Britain agreed that Britain should stay out of the ECSC. Besides sharing the general view that Britain should favor its ties to the Commonwealth, the Labor Party also thought that the European federalists emphasized free trade to the possible detriment of economic stability and full employment. Shortly after Robert Schuman's proposal was made in May 1950, the Labor Party Executive warned that private industry would try "to pervert the Schuman proposals for their own selfish and monopolistic ends." Pointing to the prewar cartels, it warned that "a coordinated perversion of this type would be far worse than our present uncoordinated competition."[25]

The ECSC treaty alludes to formal arrangements between the United Kingdom and the Community (paragraph 5 of Section 15 of the Convention for the Transitional Provisions). The Benelux countries, it will be recalled, prevented imports of steel into the ECSC from reaching the higher-tariff members of the Community. Section 15 stipulated that these controls be lifted in accordance with the conditions in the agreement to be made with Great Britain (and in any case not later than the end of the transitional period, February 1958). This clause reflected the belief, which proved to be unjustified, on the part of the Community that the United Kingdom might try to invade the common market.

A preliminary association between the two parties was first established as early as 1952. The early contacts were conducted through a joint committee composed of several members of the High Authority (including its president), the head of the United Kingdom delegation to the ECSC, officials of the National Coal Board, the British steel industry and labor unions.

The United Kingdom and the ECSC concluded an Agreement of Association in December 1954.[26] This agreement provides for periodic consultation. But the British are not members of the ECSC under it and have not yielded any sovereignty over coal and steel.

The Six and Britain are in fact competitive, as rivals for overseas steel markets and for supplies of iron ore and scrap, rather than complementary. Each also provides the other with a limited (and intermittent) market for steel but these outlets are not vital to either of them. Britain is now a minor source of coal for the Community, which in 1957 imported less than 10 per cent of its

[24] The quoted phrase is from *Britain in Western Europe*, A Report by a Study Group of the Royal Institute of International Affairs, London, 1956, page x; this study presents the economic, military and political facets of British policy.

[25] Cited in *ibid.*, p. 19.

[26] *Agreement Concerning Relations Between the European Coal and Steel Community and the United Kingdom, London, December 21, 1954*, published by the High Authority, Luxembourg, 1955. The Council of Association established by the agreement publishes an annual report.

foreign coal from the United Kingdom. Exports of coal from the Community to Britain are sporadic. Nor are the two competitors with respect to coal in third markets. The ECSC itself therefore did not have the impact to push Britain into the Community; while the association between them became quite elaborate it was not more than symbolic.

Several permanent, high-level committees were established under the agreement. These committees, meeting regularly, discussed short- and long-term trends of supply and demand, prices, trade, tariffs, cooperation on technical subjects and a number of problems relating to workers' safety, productivity and readaptation. Without any indication as to purpose, the Fifth Annual Report of the High Authority described the discussions on prices between the representatives of the High Authority and the United Kingdom as follows:[27]

. . . Comparative price studies must be made regularly; they require a perfect knowledge of price formation if they are to have any significance. Criteria for comparison of the effective prices of coal and steel have been established.

In coal, the study covers a wide variety of qualities, without being limited to those which are now traded. The coal experts—experts of the National Coal Board and of the principal producers in the Community—have already done important work, having come to agreement on the elements that must be considered in order to compare prices in different basins. They are continuing their studies satisfactorily.

In steel, where the problems are more complex, criteria for price comparison have already been set up and studies are now being made to determine and compare the constituent elements of price, including extras.

Britain and the ECSC as Customers for Steel

The United Kingdom by agreement with the Community reduced its tariffs on steel to an average of 10 per cent in February 1958, when the Community's new duties also became effective. The new British rates, which were theretofore from 15 to 33⅓ per cent, were also extended to other countries under the most-favored-nation clause.[28] The rates adopted in February 1958 represented Britain's first substantial tariff reduction for steel since 1932 when the United Kingdom threw free trade overboard. What effect will these new rates have on British steel imports from the Community?

Britain provided a large market for the continental producers in the 1920s before tariffs were introduced; the producers in the ECSC exported 2.7 million tons of steel a year to Britain in 1927–1928. Exports dropped to 800,000 tons a year in 1936–1938. (See Table 2-3, Appendix E.) The United Kingdom had meanwhile introduced the tariff and the British steel industry had organized

[27] HA, *Cinquième rapport général*, p. 57.

[28] See HA, *Sixième rapport général*, Vol. I, p. 88. The new rates may be found in the United Kingdom's Iron and Steel Board's *Annual Report for 1957*, Appendix V.

itself into a strong national group and had concluded an agreement with the continental steel producers which regulated imports into the United Kingdom and divided the world market.

Since steel consumption grew faster than production in the United Kingdom, as in Germany, from the late 1930s, Britain imported steel to meet peak demands after World War II. The United Kingdom imported 1.2 million tons of steel from the ECSC and the United States in 1952; imports dropped to 260,000 tons in 1954, a recession year, and rose to 1.1 million tons in 1955, 30 per cent of which was furnished by the Community. Ingots and semifinished steel for further processing by the steel mills accounted for over 40 per cent of the total imported by the United Kingdom in 1955 from the ECSC and the United States. Purchases for further processing were made by a subsidiary of the British Iron and Steel Federation, which distributed the steel among the mills at prevailing domestic prices; since British prices were lower than the delivered cost of imported steel, the difference in price was subsidized by a levy on internal steel production.

There is no reason to believe that either of the two steel producing areas, the United Kingdom or the ECSC, enjoys a comparative advantage in the other; though British home prices for flat-rolled products were lower in March 1958 than continental home prices, the British still had an export premium on these products sufficient to price them out of the continental market. The trade in steel between the two areas—the Community also imported 120,000 tons of British steel in 1955 (Table 2-3, Appendix E)—is largely a function of meeting peak demands. This type of trade is precarious, too, for the British steel expansion program for 1954–1962 was based on the premise that the British steel industry would be able to satisfy peak demands by 1962. The program therefore indicated that British steel production in 1954–1962 would increase more rapidly than consumption.[29]

Britain, as well as Germany, suspended the import duty when it required imported steel after World War II. When the new rates became effective in February 1958, the duty on pig iron, crude steel, semifinished steel and bars was in fact suspended until September 1958 and for another six months beyond that date on imports of plate and sheet.[30]

The United Kingdom steel industry is still a well-organized group and the domestic steel market in Britain is still a controlled, noncompetitive market, described in Chapters 3, 5, 6 and 7. The reduction of tariff rates to an average of 10 per cent reflected Britain's confidence in the ability of the steel industry,

[29] United Kingdom, Iron and Steel Board, *Development in the Iron and Steel Industry*, London, 1957.

[30] *The Economist*, April 12, 1958, p. 141; also *Britain and Europe*, Economist Intelligence Unit, London, 1957, p. 73.

after a generation of reorganization and rationalization, to defend its home market on the basis of costs, efficiency and market organization, without the help of a high tariff.

The British home market was not penetrated by steel from the Community during the 1958 recession. Exports from the Community to the United Kingdom declined by 27 per cent in the first half of 1958 compared with the corresponding period of 1957.[31] Though it was argued that British home prices were too low to attract foreign steel,[32] this generalization was true only of certain products at certain times. British home prices for flat-rolled products were lower than continental home prices, and lower even than continental export prices during the 1958 recession. But British home prices for ordinary products —merchant bars, sections, wire rod and semifinished steel—where differences between British open-hearth and continental Thomas grade steel do not matter, were higher than continental export prices in the 1958 recession. (See Table 7-1, Appendix E, and Table 41.)

BRITAIN, THE ECSC AND THIRD-PARTY MARKETS

The formation of a comprehensive economic union by the Six—the European Economic Community—forced Britain to propose a closer association with the Continent than it had theretofore desired. The British view was well expressed by *The Economist*:[33]

> The six-nation treaty of Rome was a historic step towards greater political unity and prosperity in western Europe. But if it goes through by itself it will be almost as much a misfortune as a benefit. For the countries outside the group of six, the three main dangers are plain: tariff and quota discrimination against their exports, political division, and a grave weakening of their working partnership with the Six within OEEC. These last two misfortunes would harm the six countries at least as much as the eleven; for any believer in the European idea—which was supposed to underlie this whole undertaking—the free trade area of seventeen nations is as essential a complement to the common market of six as the tail of a penny to its head.

But Britain preferred a free trade area to joining the European Economic Community. A customs union, involving a common tariff to outsiders, would have required Britain to give up its preferential customs duties for members

[31] Data are from HA, *Bulletin statistique*, and *Sixième rapport général*, Vol. II, pp. 393, 396; *The Economist*, July 12, 1958, p. 147. British home prices for plate and sheet were, however, below continental export prices.

[32] *Britain and Europe*, p. 74, suggests that tariffs were only of nominal importance but that the lower price structure of British steel was the main obstacle to the sale of foreign steel in the British market.

[33] July 19, 1958, p. 186.

of the Commonwealth whereas each of the members of a free trade area may have a different external tariff.[34] Negotiations to form a free trade area encompassing Little Europe and the other members of the OEEC began in 1957. These negotiations broke down late in 1958 because the French government, among other reasons, thought Britain would get much more than she was willing to give.

A European economic bloc comprising the Six and the United Kingdom would have been of great political and economic importance. The United Kingdom and the ECSC combined would have controlled over one quarter of the world's steel output, with a production, as of 1955, 70 per cent as great as that of the United States and 60 per cent greater than the USSR's (Table 10). It would have accounted for three fourths of the steel exported by the ECSC, the United Kingdom and the United States combined (exclusive of the trade among the members of the ECSC and between them and the United Kingdom).

The free trade area would, however, have been more important to the British market for durable goods exports, hence of steel turned into manufactures (so-called indirect steel exports), than for British steel exports *per se*. The United Kingdom exports a large quantity of machinery, engineering, shipbuilding and other investment goods to Europe. So does Germany. British exports of steel and of durable goods to all destinations account for 50 per cent of the value of its total exports; Britain sold 22 per cent of its durable goods exports to OEEC countries in 1956.[35] While only about 4 per cent of British steel production was exported to OEEC countries in the form of steel as such, altogether 9 per cent of its production, comprising direct and indirect steel exports, was exported to these areas. The British steel industry therefore supported the free trade area principally for the sake of the market for durable goods or indirect steel exports.

The negotiations for a free trade area raised some thorny problems with respect to coal and steel. The ECSC treaty contains a stronger antitrust policy and stricter rules against price discrimination than the European Economic Community treaty and, by implication, than the proposed free trade area. Britain preferred the looser rules because those of the ECSC might have required Britain to abolish or modify some fundamental practices.[36]

---

[34] For the United Kingdom's policy on the free trade area, see the British White Paper, *A European Free Trade Area*, HMSO, London, February 1957, Cmd. 72.

[35] "Steel and Western Europe," in *Steel Review*, April 1956, pp. 6–8; also "Steel and the Free Trade Area," in *Steel Review*, October 1957, pp. 1–4.

[36] See Chapters 3, 5, 6 and 7. See "Steel and the Free Trade Area," in *Steel Review*, October 1957, p. 6. *Britain and Europe*, pp. 75–76, stated that the British steel industry was opposed to joining the ECSC "on the grounds that [it] does not work as was intended and that membership would tend to upset the balance of the United Kingdom industry" and assumed that the British steel industry would not be encumbered by Articles 65 and 66 of the ECSC treaty.

But the coal and steel producers in the ECSC, as well as the member governments, insisted that their British counterparts should assume the stricter obligations of the ECSC treaty even if British coal and steel were included in the looser free trade area. This point of view was supported by the High Authority and the Council of Ministers.[37]

The members of the ECSC therefore wished the British government to reach a separate agreement with the Six by which the British coal and steel industries would accept the treaty's rules with respect to prices, subsidies, competition, production quotas and distribution priorities. The British steel industry for its part believed that "special rules should be kept to a minimum."[38]

What effect would the free trade area have had on some of the basic features of the coal and steel common market in the area—such as international price discrimination, stability of home prices and market separation?

Price discrimination or dual pricing would certainly have been forbidden in the free trade area, as in the ECSC. The British believed that this rule would have caused their prices of scrap, coal and steel to rise. They assumed that as the restrictions on exports were eliminated, customers in other parts of the area where higher prices prevailed would have drawn supplies away from Britain,[39] unless British producers raised prices to obtain an equivalent revenue in their home market. The German government and the Ruhr coal operators also believed that the rule against price discrimination would have encouraged its partners in the free trade area to draw coal away from Germany at high levels of business activity and would have discouraged them from purchasing coal during a recession.[40] But these apprehensions did not fully square with the facts. Market separation, resting on paucity of producers, and on nationalization or common sales agencies in the case of coal, might have outlasted the elimination of customs barriers. Markets for coal and steel would have had to be much less administered than they are now, and government influence would have had to wither away, before prices rose by means of a free price mechanism in a truly fused market. It should also be recalled that the distribution of, and prices for, scrap were controlled in the ECSC, as well as in the United Kingdom, when that product was scarce.

Prices might have risen for other reasons, however. The other OEEC countries absorbed 4 per cent of British, and 7 per cent of the Community's, steel production at premium prices in 1955; international price discrimination in

[37] *Journal officiel*, October 11, 1958, p. 423; *Usine nouvelle*, July 31, 1958, p. 7. See also *Le Monde*, February 23–24, 1958, p. 5; *Handelsblatt*, January 31, 1958, p. 1, February 24, 1958, p. 6.

[38] *Steel Review*, April 1958, p. 8.

[39] "Steel and the Free Trade Area," *Steel Review*, October 1957, p. 4. *Britain and Europe*, p. 5, stated that steel prices might rise by $4.20 per ton and added that some British steel firms believed prices might rise between $5.60 and $8.40 per ton.

[40] *Handelsblatt*, February 24, 1958, p. 6.

a sellers' market yields a higher unit revenue on exports than on internal sales. Without the ability to obtain such revenue, the steel producers and governments might have raised prices to all customers in order to maintain average unit revenue.

Steel exports to markets outside the free trade area would still have been important to the ECSC and the United Kingdom. Some British observers[41] believed that in a recession Britain would have been at a disadvantage in those markets vis-à-vis the continental steel producers if the latter continued to co-ordinate export sales through the Entente de Bruxelles or its equivalent. It was therefore suggested that the agreement on the free trade area should prohibit unfair competition in third-party markets or that the British steel industry should coordinate export prices with the Entente de Bruxelles.

The free trade area, like the ECSC, might have stimulated the steel firms to combine, modernize and expand. This trend would have represented a positive contribution to the extent that it raised average efficiency. But the free trade area would have been, as the European Economic Community is, of greater significance for manufactured goods in which national differences in costs of production and protection are greater than in coal and steel.

[41] *Britain and Europe*, pp. 72–73.

CHAPTER 12

TRANSPORT RATE

PROBLEMS

Like customs duties, price discrimination or subsidies, transport rates, often conceived in a national protectionist framework, can also interfere with the efficient use of resources because transport costs represent a large portion of the delivered price of the treaty products.[1] They account for 20 to 25 per cent of the average price of steel products delivered to the consumer in the ECSC, for about 20 to 25 per cent of the delivered price of solid fuels delivered from the Ruhr to Lorraine and for nearly a third of the delivered price of Saar coal in south Germany. These last two cases are close to the upper limit of freight cost by rail haulage. Even in a tight area like the United Kingdom, transport and distribution charges accounted for 37 per cent of the delivered price of household coal in 1958.[2]

Haulage by waterway, particularly international waterway, costs less than carriage by railroad, and maritime haulage costs are lower still. Economic distance, or the cost of transport, therefore counts more than distance itself.

TREATY PROVISIONS

The ECSC treaty does not attempt to equalize the cost of labor or capital but it does attempt to make the cost of transport for similar goods by similar carriers roughly proportional to distance. As with sales prices, the treaty uses the principle of equal rates for comparable transactions (Article 70). If the rates for interstate delivery of the *same* product over the *same* route differ according to the country of origin or destination, they are clearly discriminatory. There are three varieties of discrimination: (a) the rate varies at the origin according to whether the shipment terminates within or outside the country; (b) the rate at the frontier ceases to taper with distance and the country of

[1] HA, *Exposé sur la situation de la Communauté*, January 10, 1953, pp. 74–75.
[2] *The Economist*, June 14, 1958, p. 1015.

entry applies its own rates as though the shipment originated at the frontier; and (c) terminal charges at the frontier exceed the cost of the service rendered. These conditions call for (a) equalization of rates at the origin; (b) through rates that taper off continuously; (c) a modification of terminal charges to avoid duplicate costs for the same service.

Under Section 10 of the Convention for the Transitional Provisions, a Commission of Experts nominated by the governments was established to study these varieties of discrimination and to report to the Council of Ministers. The commission was also requested to prepare proposals to harmonize rates in accordance with Section 10, which reads as follows:

[Examine] the prices and conditions of transport of every kind applied to coal and steel by the different types of transport, in order to harmonize these prices and conditions within the Community as far as may be necessary for proper functioning of the common market, taking into account, among other elements, the real cost of transport.

Harmonization, as distinct from discrimination, refers to differences in basic rate levels.

Under Section 10 of the Convention for the Transitional Provisions, the governments, which retained the power of action over transport, were to remove the discriminations referred to above as follows, by type: (a) by February 1953, when the common market for coal opened; (b) and (c), two years of study (terminating October 1954) were allowed before action was to be taken on these discriminations and harmonization. Action on (b), (c) and on harmonization was to take effect simultaneously as soon as the governments agreed. If the governments could not agree on proposals for harmonization within two and one half years of the creation of the High Authority (by February 1955), they could put the proposals regarding (b) and (c) into effect separately on a date to be fixed by the High Authority.[3]

The treaty also stipulates that "special domestic" rates for the benefit of particular coal or steel firms, i.e., rates which subsidize them, must be discontinued unless authorized by the High Authority (Article 70). Section 10 provides that they be brought to the attention of the High Authority, which was to fix a time limit for their duration.

Transport systems and rate structures are intimately related to public policy. This close relationship goes back to the growth of the railroads, which opened new possibilities for regional and industrial development. The States played

[3] Luxembourg was exempted from Article 70 and Section 10 for an unlimited time, if necessary, because the Luxembourg railway system obtains nearly all its revenue from the movement of steel and raw materials for its production. Luxembourg did not need to make any changes as long as the other governments failed to agree on all the measures provided for by Section 10. The other governments, in any case, could exempt Luxembourg from the stipulations of the treaty after the transitional period.

an important part in financing the railroads, which began as public enterprises in some cases and in Europe wound up as such in all cases.[4] Government development and control of inland waterways, a very important means of transport in Western Europe, anteceded the growth of the railroads. Since carriers often have a monopoly of the means of transport, the State has had to control rates for the consumer's protection. Since transportation and regional development are closely related, the attempt to modify rate structures affects a field in which the State has had a long and well-established tradition of control.

It therefore should not be surprising that the treaty (Article 70) should categorically protect the competence of the State with regard to transport rates. No rates can be changed, except those that amount to subsidies, without the consent of the State and all changes, even changes in subsidy rates, must be carried out through its legislative and administrative machinery; thus no federal institution in the Community has direct jurisdiction over transport. The last paragraph of Article 70 is worth quoting:

> Subject to the provisions of this article, as well as to the other provisions of this Treaty, commercial policy for transport, in particular the fixing and modification of rates and conditions of transport of any type as well as the arrangement of transport prices required to assure the financial equilibrium of the transport enterprises themselves, remains subject to the legislative or administrative provisions of each of the member States; the same is true for the measures of co-ordination or competition among different types of transport or among different routes.

The governments are thus sovereign in transport matters but, in exercising their sovereignty, are nevertheless obliged to respect the treaty. Their obligations with respect to elimination of discriminations and subsidies were much more precise than those with respect to harmonization; the former concerns the relationship of rates in comparable transactions; the latter concerns rate levels.[5]

ACCOMPLISHMENTS WITH REGARD TO DISCRIMINATION

DISCRIMINATION AT THE ORIGIN

The varieties of discrimination referred to in the preceding section as (a), (b) and (c) apply only to railroad rates, which are published. About thirty-two identifiable major cases of discrimination (a) were eliminated early in 1953

[4] For a good account of the early history of the railroads in France, Germany and Belgium, see J. H. Clapham, *The Economic Development of France and Germany*, Cambridge University Press, Cambridge, 4th edition, 1951, *passim*.

[5] Roger Hutter, "Les Problèmes de transport de la Communauté Européenne du Charbon et de l'Acier," *Revue générale des chemins de fer*, October 1954, January and June 1955.

when the common market for coal started.[6] Some of these changes are briefly described below:

(1) The rate for iron ore from Lorraine to the north of France was 25 per cent lower than that for Belgium. The French railroads introduced a uniform rate, 5 per cent higher than the previous domestic rate.

(2) The rates applicable to French steel products exported through Strasbourg were extended to products of Luxembourgian origin; the latter thus obtained a 30 per cent reduction on trainloads of 900 tons.

(3) The Belgian rate for coal and coke of Belgian origin was applied to products originating elsewhere in the Community.

(4) The Belgians created a uniform rate for steel products exported through Antwerp; this involved a 20 per cent increase in the rate for steel of Belgian origin and a 10 per cent reduction on steel originating in France and the Saar.

(5) The German rates for coal of German origin were applied to coal originating elsewhere in the ECSC (even for coal in transit). This change, of interest to the Saar and Lorraine mainly, involved a 20 per cent reduction on non-German coal. German railroad rates were extended to other ECSC products also, as follows: a reduction of about 40 per cent on iron ore entering Germany from Lorraine and Luxembourg; a 25 per cent reduction on manganiferous ore of German origin to the Saar; a reduction of about 35 per cent on steel products originating outside Germany for shipment to the North German ports.

(6) Luxembourg unified the rates for iron ore exports, as a result of which the rate on ore exported to France increased 70 cents per ton.

DISCRIMINATION IN THROUGH RATES AND TERMINAL CHARGES

In the first quarter of 1955, two years after the elimination of discriminations at the origin, the Council of Ministers reached a series of agreements in principle on through rates and terminal charges for railroad haulage.[7]

Though rail rates taper with distance, they ceased to taper at the frontier. Instead, terminal charges were added at each side of the frontier and the rate of the country of entry was applied as though the shipment originated at the frontier. Under the agreements reached in 1955, the terminal charges were re-

---

[6] For a list of the thirty-two cases, see HA, *Second General Report*, pp. 108–119. Several discriminations of this variety developed subsequently and were abolished later; see HA, *Quatrième rapport général*, pp. 156–157.

[7] HA, *Troisième rapport général*, p. 111, and *Quatrième rapport général*, p. 157. The Decisions are to be found in *Journal officiel*, January 31, 1955, p. 607, April 19, 1955, p. 701, April 30, 1956, p. 130. The text of the agreements between the ECSC and Switzerland for tapering transit rates through Switzerland may be found in *Journal officiel*, February 21, 1957, p. 85, and May 29, 1957, p. 223.

duced, and the rates continued to taper beyond the frontier up to, but not beyond, 250 kilometers for solid fuels and iron ore and up to 200 kilometers for other products. It proved impossible for the Council of Ministers to agree to taper rates for an indefinite distance because freight rates taper at a different rate in each country. They *harmonized* the rate at which charges taper within those distances. The national tapering rates continued to apply beyond those distances within upper and lower limits. In order to protect railroad revenue, the principle of tapering rates was also confined within general limits.[8] The new international through rates and frontier terminal charges were introduced gradually over twelve months, beginning May 1, 1955 for solid fuels and iron ore and May 1, 1956 on other products.[9]

RESULTS

The cost of transport on some important railroad routes between countries was substantially modified, as Table 56 shows, by the action taken with respect to discriminations at the origin, through rates and terminal charges. Of what significance are these changes?

Solid Fuels and Iron Ore

All the consumers served by the routes listed in Table 56 (except for item 7) are steel plants that do not have much choice of alternative supplies. These modifications therefore do not promote competition among suppliers of solid fuels or iron ore. They do promote equality in competitive conditions. Financially speaking, however, the steel plants in Lorraine are no better off now because the French government withdrew the subsidy it had paid to offset the discriminatory freight rates on the Gelsenkirchen-Homécourt run (lines 1 and 6 of Table 56).[10] The Lorraine coal mines lost about $2.00 worth of geographic protection per ton as an incidental result of the freight reduction for transporting coal from the Ruhr to Lorraine. On the other hand, the Lorraine steelworks obtained a railroad freight reduction of about $2.60 per ton on the steel they ship to Antwerp for export, owing to a voluntary reduction by the French railroads, whose rates had favored the use of Dunkerque as against Antwerp.[11]

Freight rates had favored the delivery of Ruhr coal in southern Germany.

---

[8] HA, *Troisième rapport général*, p. 115.

[9] HA, *Quatrième rapport général*, p. 159. Terminal frontier charges were completely eliminated for goods entering a country for the purpose of transit. In other cases, the terminal charges for crossing a frontier were reduced by half.

[10] On the eve of the common market discriminatory freight rates added about $.95 per ton to the cost of finished steel in Lorraine, according to data in HA, "Bilan de deux ans de fonctionnement du marché commun pour la sidérurgie française," unpublished mimeographed memorandum, June 4, 1955, pp. 20–21.

[11] *Ibid.*, p. 23.

The reduction, shown as item 7 in Table 56, helped the mines in the Saar (and Lorraine) in that market. Here, again, the French treasury had subsidized the mines in the Saar and Lorraine to enable them to meet the price of Ruhr coal

Table 56

RAIL TRANSPORT COSTS FOR THROUGH SHIPMENT,
SELECTED COMMODITIES AND ROUTES, ECSC, 1953 AND 1957, AND TONNAGE, 1957[a]

	Cost per Metric Ton		Tonnage 1957 (*Thousands*)
Product and Route	Jan. 1, 1953	May 1, 1957	
Coke			
1. Germany to France (Gelsenkirchen-Homécourt)	$6.57	$4.78	3,044
2. Germany to Luxembourg (Gelsenkirchen-Esch)	7.31	5.90	2,142
3. Belgium to France (Zeebrugge-Thionville)	0.69	0.69	424
4. Netherlands to France (Lutterade-Thionville)	5.72	4.02	739
Coking smalls			
5. Germany to Saar (Alsdorf-Saarbrücken)	6.07	4.48	195
6. Germany to France (Gelsenkirchen-Homécourt)	6.62	4.23[b]	737
Coal			
7. Saar to south Germany (Reden Grube–Regensburg)	9.10	6.68	1,654
Iron ore			
8. France to Belgium (Sancy-Ougrée-Marihaye)	2.43	1.81	5,311
9. Germany to Saar (Bingen-Völklingen)	3.45	1.74	52
10. Luxembourg to Germany (Tétange-Duisburg)	3.52	2.72	243
Scrap			
11. France to Italy (Lyon-Turin)	6.14	5.13	231
Semifinished steel			
12. Germany to Belgium (Oberhausen-Seraing)	4.78	3.95	6[c]
13. Germany to Netherlands (Oberhausen-Utrecht)	3.93	3.31	0.0
14. France to south Germany (Thionville-Stuttgart)	8.06	6.63	3[c]
Finished steel			
15. Germany to France (Oberhausen-Paris)	13.38	11.02	6
16. Belgium to France (Flémalle–Fresnoy-le-Gr.)	6.24	4.78	80
17. Luxembourg to Netherlands (Belval-Rotterdam)	8.92	8.22	1
18. Netherlands to France (Beverwijk-Hagondange)	9.48	8.66	0.0

Sources: Costs calculated from data provided by the Transport Division of the High Authority. Data on tonnage are from HA, *Transports des produits du traité,* September 1958.

[a] Shown are the adjustments resulting from elimination of discrimination and the establishment of through rates only. Costs for solid fuels and iron ore are based on complete trainloads of varying tonnage; those for scrap and steel, as well as for coal shipped from the Saar to Germany, are based on individual carloads.
[b] Rate as of May 1, 1956.   [c] Pig iron included.

in south Germany. The French taxpayer thus benefited from the adjustments. The sale of Lorraine coal in south Germany nevertheless declined.

The reduction in the costs of carrying coke from the Ruhr to Luxembourg and of carrying French iron ore to Belgium are also significant (lines 2 and 8 of Table 56).

Steel

The reductions in the freight rates for steel may help to promote rivalry among the steel producers when they have surplus capacity because the new rates mean that freight absorption will cost them less; the volume of traffic in 1957 (Table 56) was, however, small.

SUBSIDY BY TRANSPORT RATES

Article 70 (paragraph 4) prohibits transport rates that subsidize particular coal and steel producing units. This stipulation affected chiefly railroad rates. The treaty provided that subsidy rates were to be terminated gradually by the High Authority in order to avoid serious economic repercussions. They were the only type of discriminatory rates that could be abolished without the consent of the Council of Ministers. The High Authority nevertheless had to request the State rather than the carrier to modify or abolish the rates in question; in case of disagreement, either party could appeal to the Court.

A subsidy rate is lower than the general rate for the same commodity for the sake of reducing inbound or outbound freight costs for particular coal or steel producing plants. But railroads also reduce rates in order to compete with another mode of transport, usually an interior waterway, serving the same customers over the same route. Competitive rates are not illegal in principle, provided they are properly calculated.[12] Special rates, also, are not illegal if they are competitive. The High Authority ruled, furthermore, that special rates are not illegal if they are part of a whole series of measures to help a region.

The High Authority therefore concentrated its attention on those rates that were mainly designed to subsidize particular plants.[13] The High Authority declared certain subsidizing rates illegal in February 1958, when the transitional period expired, and gave the governments two to seven years' time to eliminate them. Before reaching its decisions, the High Authority had invited the governments to adopt a general rate structure that would have given approximately the same economic results as, but that would have replaced, the particular subsidizing rates by taking account of volume and regularity of traffic, turnaround freight and other factors. The French and German governments demurred on the ground that the proposal would entail a serious loss of revenue.[14]

Which subsidy rates were declared illegal by the High Authority?

[12] HA, *Sixième rapport général*, Vol. I, pp. 71–72.

[13] *Ibid.*, p. 73.

[14] *Ibid.*, p. 74; statement by M. Spierenburg, member of the High Authority, cited in *Handelsblatt*, February 19, 1958, p. 4.

France

The High Authority ruled illegal the following special railroad rates: (1) for the haulage of coal to the steel plants in Centre-Midi; (2) for the haulage of coal to Paris from certain fields in the Centre-Midi; (3) for the haulage of iron ore produced in the Pyrenees and the western part of France, and (4) for the haulage of scrap from Paris to a steel plant in the Centre-Midi.[15]

Germany

The High Authority forbade certain rates for the haulage of coal to steel plants outside the Ruhr—plants in the Rhineland, in Bavaria and in the Salzgitter area. The rate between the Ruhr and Lower Saxony (discussed below) is the most important. The High Authority also interdicted certain rates for the carriage of iron and of coal produced outside the Ruhr.

The affected German firms and the German government appealed to the Court of Justice to annul the decisions of the High Authority. The French steel firms affected by the decisions bearing on the haulage of iron ore also appealed.[16]

Salzgitter Rates

The most significant case of alleged subsidy concerns the railroad rate for carrying coal from the Ruhr to the Salzgitter area, which produced nearly 3 million tons of crude steel in 1957, about 13 per cent of the total output of West Germany. The steel plants in this area take about 3 million tons of Ruhr coal annually for coking purposes. The German railroads have granted a special rate for this route, about 50 per cent below the general rate for the transport of coal. Since this rate is competitive with the cost of waterway transport (Rhein-Herne Canal) between the same points, the High Authority decided that this railroad rate is not illegal. But it found that the waterway rate itself violated the treaty because seven tenths of the toll charges are not included. The High Authority therefore ordered these toll charges to be included as of January 1, 1959 and the railroad rate to be raised accordingly. The German government defended the reduction in the toll charges on the ground that the Salzgitter steelworks had lost their normal markets in the Eastern Zone.[17]

Ruhr-Lorraine Railroad Rate

The run from the Ruhr to Lorraine (the main route being Gelsenkirchen-Homécourt) is about 350 kilometers, slightly longer than that from the Ruhr

---

[15] These interdictions and those affecting Germany are described in a number of places, notably in *Journal officiel*, March 3, 1958, and in HA, *Sixième rapport général*, Vol. II, pp. 79–84, 402–404.

[16] *Journal officiel*, April 14 and May 20, 1958.

[17] HA, *Sixième rapport général*, Vol. II, p. 80; *Journal officiel*, March 3, 1958, p. 110.

to Salzgitter, about 280 kilometers. The rate on the former route is based on the general German railroad schedule, which is twice as high per ton-mile as the rate for the route from the Ruhr to Salzgitter. The steel plants in Lorraine, which take about 4 million tons of solid fuels a year from the Ruhr, claim that their assembly costs are thus about 65 cents higher per ton of finished steel—about 0.5 per cent of the average sales value—than they would be if they enjoyed the same rate as the run from the Ruhr to Salzgitter.[18]

The steel firms in Lorraine argue that all the steel plants in Germany that are outside the Ruhr enjoy a lower, special railroad rate because the general (and therefore higher) schedule applies, in effect, only to deliveries within a fifty-mile radius of Gelsenkirchen. They therefore contend that the special rates should also apply to the Gelsenkirchen-Homécourt run, pointing out that Lorraine received the benefit of the lower rate before the first world war when it was in the German customs union, and again when the Germans occupied it during 1940–1945.

In July 1957 the French Prime Minister offered to discuss this matter with his German counterpart and later that year the High Authority requested both governments to negotiate the matter but these efforts came to nought.[19]

The Lorraine steelworks, disappointed by the High Authority decision that ruled the Ruhr-Salzgitter rate to be competitive and therefore legal, appealed to the Court of Justice.[20] The Court had not resolved the issue as of early 1959. But it should be pointed out that the High Authority could only have required the German government to annul the preferential rate. It could not have applied the rate to the Gelsenkirchen-Homécourt run without the consent of the German government, for the harmonization of rates is subject to the agreement of the Council of Ministers.

HARMONIZING RAILROAD RATES

Harmonization of transport rates has been defined as:[21]

. . . the sum total of all measures designed to apply comparable tariffs to consumers in comparable situations. . . . It consists of introducing some degree of uniformity into the relations between the various rates applicable to the same mode of transport in the different countries. . . . It is not concerned with the relationship between the tariffs of different modes of transport, since this belongs to the measures of coordination which are considered by the Treaty to be the exclusive responsibility of governments.

[18] Calculated from data in *Le Monde*, June 21, 1957, p. 14, and July 20, 1957, p. 10.
[19] *Ibid.*, July 20, 1957, p. 10; *Handelsblatt*, December 20–21, 1957, p. 2.
[20] These appeals are in *Journal officiel*, May 20, 1958, pp. 43 ff, and August 4, 1958, p. 290.
[21] HA, *Second Annual Report*, pp. 115–116.

Four principal types of differences between countries would be affected by harmonization of railroad rates: differences between basic rates; differences in the relationship between rates for products in different stages of production; differences based on the size of shipment, ownership of the cars, trainload shipments, empty turnaround, and other factors involving use of facilities; differences in tapering of rates beyond 200 to 250 kilometers.

A limited degree of harmonization was achieved when tapering international through rates were introduced up to 200 to 250 kilometers but these changes did not affect the basic rate structure in each country.

Section 10 of the Convention for the Transitional Provisions, it will be recalled, stipulated that action on harmonization was to be separated from that on through rates if simultaneous agreement on both proved impossible. That separation was made in 1955, the governments having been unable to reach an agreement on harmonization by that date, or indeed thereafter. In March 1957 the High Authority (under Article 46) appointed an independent committee of distinguished economists to prepare general principles, for the commission of experts previously appointed by the governments had failed to agree. It was up to the independent committee to set forth the principles of harmonization from the point of view of the common market in order to help the governments to pursue the matter further.[22]

Why did harmonization prove to be so difficult a problem?

(1) Harmonization would affect such basic matters as market penetration and the location of industry. Established interests therefore have an important stake in the national rate structures. But harmonization is one of the core problems of an economic union, for national transport rate structures may not coincide with the most efficient use of resources; like taxes or customs duties, they can influence costs of production, prices and trade in an uneconomic direction. The High Authority pointed out that harmonization does not mean that rates be made uniform; it means that they be made to reflect the differences inherent in the conditions of transport. The difficulties arise from the diversity of principles in use and from deviations in the use of those principles.[23] Some differences in the costs of production and sales prices arising from differences in basic transport rate structures can be equalized by the currency exchange rates but those that arise from differences in the ratio between rates for products in different stages of production cannot be equalized by the exchange rates. Rates based on the ad valorem principle are lower for products in earlier stages of manufacture; i.e., the rate for coal is lower than that for coke; the rate for semifinished steel is lower than that for finished

[22] See HA, *Cinquième rapport général*, pp. 139, 144.
[23] HA, *Sixième rapport général*, Vol. I, p. 70.

steel. But the relationships vary from country to country and the ad valorem principle is not applied at all for some products in some countries. In Germany, for example, the freight rate for iron ore is 45 per cent of that for coal; in France, the rates for the two products are about equal.[24] In some countries, coke and coal are carried at the same rate; in others, the rate for coke is 40 per cent higher.[25] Rate relationships in some countries encourage processing plants to locate near the market rather than near the raw material (e.g., France, where the rate for raw materials drops more sharply with distance than that for finished goods). The relationship in other countries encourages them to locate near the raw materials (e.g., Germany, where the rates fall sharply with distance for both kinds of products). These differences can be adjusted only by harmonization.

(2) Harmonization proved to be a difficult problem for the further reason that it opened fundamental problems with respect to the relationship of railroad rates to the cost of transport. The last paragraph of Article 70, already quoted above, refers to cost as a criterion for harmonization. But costs are not easily determined and not always applicable. First, if every route and service performed by a carrier had to pay for itself, assuming it were possible to allocate costs, some regions with a light amount of traffic would be condemned economically.

Second, if the rate for a particular service were based on its cost, which is not always a socially desirable principle, there would be a different rate for nearly every case because costs vary with volume and regularity of shipment, with return traffic, and with many other factors. Harmonization might turn out to be an administrative nightmare if costs were strictly applied as the criterion.

Third, the railroads must take account of their ability to hold their traffic against competing modes of transport. The railroads, waterways and maritime routes (exclusive of trucks) carried 400 million tons of ECSC products from one part of the ECSC to another in 1957. Coal accounted for 62 per cent, iron ore for 19 per cent, steel for 13 per cent and scrap for 6 per cent of the 400 million tons.[26] The railroads carried 77 per cent of the total, interior waterways 22 per cent, and maritime carriers 1 per cent. But the railroads carried only 70 per cent of the raw coal owing to the fact that a large proportion of the Ruhr coal is transported by waterway. Though the railroads are still the main carriers, they have lost ground to other carriers in recent years because their rates are higher and because of shifts in the location of industry. They will

[24] HA, *Second Annual Report*, p. 118.
[25] HA, *Sixième rapport général*, Vol. I, p. 70.
[26] HA, *Transports des produits du traité*, September 1958.

probably continue to lose ground, despite their efforts to hold their share against competing carriers, because oil and nuclear power will account for an increasing proportion of energy consumption, because the coal mines will consume a growing portion of their own output for secondary energy production, and because an increasing portion of the steel industry will be located at tidewater.[27]

The railroads are at a further disadvantage because railroad haulage is the costliest form of carriage. The cost of hauling a ton of minerals 250 kilometers varied as follows among the different means of transport in Germany in 1924–1928 (railroads = 100):[28]

Railroads	100
Canal	33
Lower Rhine	14
Maritime	7

Though water transport of bulky material costs less than rail haulage, transport by domestic canals costs more than other water transport during a recession and less during an economic boom, because it is subject to domestic regulation and reserved to domestic carriers while maritime and international waterway rates, not being publicly regulated, fluctuate with the business cycle.

Faced with competition from interior waterway and truck carriers, the railroads are often left with the least remunerative traffic. The railroads therefore have to take account of their ability to compete as well as of costs. Railroad rates in fact reflect a mixture of general and particular principles adjusted to particular regions, industries and even plants. Most rates ignore specific costs, a fact that caused Louis Armand, while general manager of the French railway system, to observe that there are as many discriminations as there are rates.[29]

(3) Harmonization raised a difficult problem for the reason, still further, that rail and water carriers in the territory of the ECSC countries derive a

[27] See the discussion in ECE, *Economic Survey of Europe for 1956*, Geneva, 1957, Chap. 6, pp. 5 ff, on the influence of energy production and steel location on the relative distribution of traffic among various means of transport. The distribution of traffic among the several means of transport was, however, stabilized in France between 1954–1958.

[28] Hanns-Jürgen Kunze, *Die Lagerungsordnung der westeuropäischen Eisen- und Stahlindustrie im Lichte ihrer Kostenstruktur*, Kieler Studien, Kiel, 1954, p. 52. The pattern has not changed substantially since the 1920s. The interwar pattern in the United States was not very dissimilar, according to Paul Reuter, *La Communauté Européenne du Charbon et de l'Acier*, Librairie Générale de Droit et de Jurisprudence, Paris, 1953, p. 152 (railroads = 100):

Railroads	100
Barge	37
Great Lakes	7
Maritime	6–14

[29] Conseil Economique (France), *Communauté Européenne du Charbon et de l'Acier*, Etudes et Travaux No. 2, Presses Universitaires de France, Paris, n.d., p. 78. ECE, *Economic Survey of Europe for 1956*, Geneva, 1957, Chap. 6, pp. 15–16, discusses the problem of rate fixing in relation to cost.

large portion of their revenue from carrying ECSC products. In the first quarter of 1956 these products accounted for 47 per cent by weight of all rail loadings in the ECSC and 40 per cent of all interior waterway loadings.[30] Unlike customs duties, and in some cases even taxes, rate changes for transport cannot be separated from the question of revenue because transport, being an industry, has to cover its expenditures or be subsidized.

The railroads are not in a good financial position. In 1952 through 1954 the French, German, Italian and Belgian railroads had a deficit (on all services) and those in the Netherlands and Luxembourg a very slight surplus.[31] Since ECSC products account for nearly 50 per cent of all the merchandise carried by the railroads, fundamental rate changes for these products would have a serious effect on revenue. The rates for ECSC products cannot be changed without adjusting rates for other classes of merchandise. The problem therefore goes beyond the ECSC.[32] It affects the larger area of economic activity encompassed by the European Economic Community and involves other bulky goods of low unit value, including, in addition to the ECSC products, other metals, building materials, agricultural goods, paper and pulp. The implications of the European Economic Community for the problem of harmonization are discussed later in this chapter.

INTERNATIONAL AND DOMESTIC DIFFERENTIALS

Section 10 of the Convention for the Transitional Provisions invited the governments to coordinate "the different types of transport . . . as far as may be necessary for proper functioning of the common market . . ." Differences in international and domestic rates for haulage by truck, interior waterway and maritime carriers create serious obstacles to the coordination of "the different types of transport." The problems are:

(1) The rates for international shipments within the ECSC by truck, waterway or sea are not subject to public regulation. They are fixed by negotiation or the "market" and embodied in private contracts rather than published rate schedules. But truck, sea or waterway shipments between points in the same country are subject to domestic regulation. The rates for domestic and international commerce on the same route therefore differ without respect to dis-

---

[30] HA, *Cinquième rapport général*, p. 148. In 1954 fuels accounted for 35 per cent of all railroad freight in Belgium, 47 per cent in Germany, 26 per cent in France and 58 per cent in Holland; see ECE, *Economic Survey of Europe for 1956*, Chap. 5, p. 6.

[31] ECE, *Economic Survey of Europe for 1956*, Chap. 5, p. 26.

[32] HA, *Sixième rapport général*, Vol. I, p. 71.

tance or merchandise, and differ in opposite directions over the business cycle, international rates being lower than domestic rates during a recession and higher during a boom. The ECSC treaty does not permit a seller to determine the mode of transport and requires him to sell f.o.b. plant if the buyer wishes to take delivery there. But if a member State of the ECSC requires a buyer to use a domestic carrier for goods shipped by waterway within points in its territory, the ECSC treaty does not relieve him of the obligation to comply with the national regulation even though cheaper carriage may be available on a carrier flying the flag of another State.[33] This rule is not consistent with the treaty stipulations that guarantee equal access and the right to purchase at the cheapest source.

(2) Since the rates in international traffic by water or truck are not subject to regulation and not published, the criteria for determining price discrimination, equal access to supplies and price alignment—the substance of Articles 3, 4 and 60 of the treaty—cannot be applied because the delivered price of two shipments by the same carrier between the same points need not necessarily be the same. What do restrictions against price discrimination or price alignment mean when the facts cannot be determined or if rates are always changing?[34] As with prices, the treaty relies on publication of transport rates, or on direct disclosure to the High Authority, as a means for attaining its purpose. Publication is feasible for public carriers that operate with fixed rates but not for those whose rates are fixed by negotiation between private parties. Both problems—the differences between domestic and international rates, as well as that of publication—would seem to require the same remedy: coordination, stabilization or regulation.

Maritime Traffic

Though maritime traffic accounted for only 1 per cent of the total traffic between different points in the ECSC in 1957, it is significant for the delivery of steel products from Low Country ports or German ports to seaboard points in France or Italy during a recession, and it will grow in importance as more tidewater steel producing capacity is developed. French steel producers deliver steel by rail to coastal points in France; if they ship through Antwerp or Dunkerque they still have to use the railroads to get the steel to those ports. They are consequently worried by possible rivalry from Belgian or German producers that have access to Bordeaux or Rouen by all-water routes. The

---

[33] Reuter, *op. cit.*, pp. 188–189.

[34] See the High Authority's attempted effort to close the loopholes, in its circular "Communication relative aux modes de cotations et aux coûts de transport dans les ventes d'acier," *Journal officiel*, January 13, 1954, pp. 224 ff. The difficulty of collecting data on motor transport is discussed in HA, "Situation actuelle de la statistique routière," *Informations statistiques*, October 1958, pp. 337 ff.

steel plants in Lorraine thus had to absorb freight on shipments to the west coast of France during the 1953–1954 recession.[35] But this disadvantage will be reduced or eliminated when the Moselle Canal is completed.

The High Authority made no effort to have maritime rates published.

Traffic on the Rhine

The Rhine is the most important waterway in the ECSC and contiguous to all the member countries but Luxembourg and Italy. The Act of Mannheim (1868) guaranteed the freedom of international transport on that waterway and prohibited the fixing of international rates by public authority. The rates for interstate shipments on the Rhine thus vary with business conditions and are sometimes lower, sometimes higher, than those for shipment between points on the Rhine in the same country. These disparities are not consistent with the implications of a common market, though some States reimburse the consumer for the disadvantage of using domestic flag carriers.[36] Since the Rhine is a very important waterway for the movement of coal, these differences have a strong influence on the coal market, because rivalry between coal producing districts can be promoted by low international waterway rates during a recession and impeded by high rates during an economic upswing.

The governments in the Council of Ministers ran into difficulties trying to coordinate rates on the Rhine. The French and German governments were favorable to some form of regulation. The Netherlands government was recalcitrant, probably because that country has little interest in the domestic phase of the traffic. The Council of Ministers suspended its efforts pending the outcome of discussions by the European Conference of Transport Ministers. The latter having been unable to reach agreement, the Council of Ministers again took the initiative in 1956, picking up some of the suggestions the conference had developed. The Rhine traffic problem was separated from that of waterways to the west of the Rhine. The Council of Ministers in July 1957 reached an agreement on the former that came into force on May 1, 1958.[37] The High Authority intended to obtain Switzerland's association also, since the latter is a signatory of the Act of Mannheim. The problem of the waterways west of the Rhine was to be resolved later.

The agreement is essentially concerned with coordinating domestic rates with international rates when haulage occurs on the Rhine in both cases. It affirms the right of the shippers to fix rates freely in international haulage

[35] Jean Chardonnet, *Les grands types de complexes industriels*, Librairie Armand Colin, Paris, 1953, p. 174.

[36] HA, *Troisième rapport général*, p. 119. The French operate an equalization fund authorized by the High Authority; HA, *Bulletin mensuel d'information*, May-June 1958, p. 13.

[37] The text is in *Journal officiel*, February 1, 1958, pp. 49 ff.

without public supervision. But the governments affirm their will to coordinate domestic rates with those for international haulage, particularly with long-term contract rates. They hope to achieve such coordination, or to be instrumental in achieving it, in liaison with the High Authority and to the extent made necessary by the ECSC treaty. Each government will devise a procedure for informing the High Authority of the market for shipping and for determining the disparity between rates. If a lack of organization among the carriers, particularly domestic ones, interferes with the application of the agreement, the individual governments will take measures to promote the necessary organization. The agreement itself simply affirms the intentions of the governments; it does not go beyond that. It implies that domestic rates will be raised to the level of international rates during an economic boom and lowered during a recession. Domestic rates were higher than international rates when the agreement became effective but the governments took no action to reduce domestic rates, though secret waterway (and perhaps even railway) discounts may have been granted. It therefore remains to be seen what results will be attained. The agreement does not provide for the publication of international rates though the preamble says the States are resolved to help solve the problem of publishing transport rates.

Under the rule of freedom from public regulation, international rates on the Rhine are in fact influenced by the dominant shippers. The Ruhr coal operators are financially interested in a high percentage of the total carrying capacity and the independent shippers are, in turn, dependent on shipping contracts from the coal producers.[38] The preamble of the agreement of July 1957 says the States are resolved to prevent the carriers from making agreements among themselves that discriminate against wholesalers or consumers and are further resolved to prevent the latter from acquiring a "privileged position." But the 1958 report of the Transport Committee of the European Parliamentary Assembly doubted that the agreement allowed the High Authority to control "cartel practices" on the waterways.[39]

Truck Haulage

Truck haulage of coal in the ECSC is confined to short distances only. But truck haulage has become increasingly important in recent years in carrying scrap and finished steel, the large consumer often operating his own trucks. Truck haulage accounts for about 12 per cent of the total shipment of scrap

---

[38] Assemblée Parlementaire Européenne, Transport Committee, Doc. No. 16, 1958, p. 9. See also *Handelsblatt*, October 19, 1956, p. 8, for some of the shipping pools, including the "Kettwiger Pool" which attempts to control Rhine rates for United States coal transshipped at Low Country ports. This pool was evidently ineffective in the 1958 recession, according to *Handelsblatt*, August 1–2, 1958, p. 3.

[39] Doc. No. 16, 1958, p. 9.

and steel in the ECSC.[40] Truck haulage increases the propensity of steel producers to give secret price rebates that violate the "fair trade" provisions of the treaty. The High Authority forbade coal producers to align their prices on the basis of truck haulage rates altogether.

Profound differences in rate formation and interest made it difficult to reach agreement on the publication of trucking rates for international traffic.[41] As a permanent steel importing country, Holland is the beneficiary of uncoordinated rates. The German steel industry strongly backed publication because Germany is the only country where trucking rates are published under government regulation. In order to hasten action, the German steel industry filed a complaint with the Court of Justice in 1958 charging the High Authority with failure to carry out its responsibility under Article 70 to make the truck carriers publish their rates.

The High Authority issued a decision in February 1959 requiring the governments to take action to cause trucking rates to be revealed by June 30, 1959. Each government was given the choice of publishing the rates directly or ordering the trucking firms to reveal their rates to the public or to the High Authority. The rates did not have to be inflexible—as they are in Germany— but could be maximum and minimum rates. Loads under five tons and up to twenty kilometers were exempted.[42]

Thus, efforts under the treaty to regulate truck, as well as international waterway, rates are leading toward regulation though they have not as yet been fully successful.

SUMMARY OF RESULTS UNDER THE ECSC TREATY

The Community was rather successful in removing discriminations in the narrow sense. But it failed to make substantial progress in the field of harmonization because the ECSC proved to be too limited a basis for action and the power of decision was with the governments rather than with the High Authority. The creation of a partial economic union did not prove to be an invitation to distort other parts of the economy for the sake of unifying two particular sectors.

---

[40] HA, *Sixième rapport général*, Vol. I, pp. 76–77.

[41] The Transport Committee, Assemblée Parlementaire Européenne, Doc. No. 16, 1958, p. 10, refers to an abortive agreement reached in March 1958 and summarized in HA, *Sixième rapport général*, Vol. II, pp. 89–90.

[42] *Handelsblatt,* March 2, 1959, p. 3.

The High Authority stated with disappointment:[43]

The High Authority has come up against great difficulties in the transport field, which is under the competence of the governments, because its power under the Treaty is limited. The limitations of partial integration are particularly clear in this field.

The Transport Committee of the Common Assembly minced no words in accusing the governments of excessive concern for the national interest:[44] ". . . your Committee, to its regret, must once again express its keen disappointment with the meagre progress." Discriminations, it added, were eliminated only in the "narrowest sense" and the international through rates were still imperfect.

". . . the present water and truck transport situation contradicts the fundamental objectives of the treaty," the committee said, and added that without a transport system that offers "comparable rates to comparable consumers," the common market cannot operate properly. Although the States retained their competence, "they should nevertheless have assumed certain obligations in order to make the common market operate properly." Though the "dynamism inherent in the Treaty should have led to an integration and coordination of transport beyond the requirements of the Treaty itself, the conditions necessary to attain this goal have been lacking." The committee concluded with the words:

"In effect, the problems of coordination can be solved only by political decisions in a climate of opinion that cannot be created at present."

The High Authority believes that a comprehensive solution to the transport problems lies beyond the ECSC, because the problems affect the larger area of economic activity covered by the European Economic Committee treaty.[45]

ROLE OF THE EUROPEAN ECONOMIC COMMUNITY TREATY

Will the EEC treaty carry harmonization further than the ECSC treaty?[46] The States retain their sovereignty over transport under the EEC treaty; the Commission (analogous to the High Authority) serves in an advisory capacity in most instances. The preparation of standards on some matters is left en-

[43] HA, *L'Europe en action*, Luxembourg, 1957.

[44] CECA, Assemblée Commune, Commission des Transports, *Rapport intérimaire*, Doc. No. 27, May 1957.

[45] HA, *Sixième rapport général*, Vol. I, p. 71; Assemblée Parlementaire Européenne, Commission des Transports, *Rapport sur les transports dans la CECA*, Doc. No. 16, 1958, pp. 3, 13.

[46] Transport is covered by Articles 74 to 84 of the EEC treaty. According to Article 84, the provisions of the treaty apply to railroads, waterways and road haulage; the Council of Ministers by unanimous vote may later apply the appropriate provisions to maritime and air transport.

tirely to the governments; the treaty provides fairly definite standards on other matters. The latter are in Articles 79, 80 and 81. These articles deal, respectively, with discriminations in the narrow sense, with rates that subsidize particular firms (special rates) and with terminal charges.

Article 79 (not unlike Article 70 of the ECSC treaty) defines a discrimination as a different rate according to destination or origin for the same product "on the same traffic relations" within the union. It provides for suppression of discriminations by December 31, 1965. The Council of Ministers shall by qualified majority establish the rules by the end of 1959 by which this objective is to be accomplished.

Article 80 (like Article 70, paragraph 4, of the ECSC treaty) stipulates that rates that subsidize particular firms are illegal after January 1, 1962 unless authorized by the Commission. The Commission rather than the States are competent in this field. Article 80 contains several escape clauses. First, competitive rates between water, rail and truck carriers are permitted. Second, the Commission must take account of "appropriate regional economic policies, of the needs of underdeveloped regions, as well as of the problems of regions gravely affected by political circumstances . . ."

Article 81 stipulates that terminal charges at the frontier should be reasonable in relation to their cost and that the States will endeavor to reduce charges gradually.

The governments deferred the adoption of definite standards for a common transport policy—the question of harmonization. Article 74 says: "The objectives of the Treaty are to be followed up by the member states with respect to the matter dealt with under the present title in the framework of a common transport policy." This proposition is singularly lacking in substance.

Article 75 states that the Council of Ministers should agree on "common rules" in interstate transport. "Common rules" are also to be worked out for carriers of nonmember States that ship through the transport system of member States. Article 75 authorizes the Council of Ministers to adopt "common rules" regarding "all other useful arrangements."

Articles 77 and 78 seek to protect the carriers' revenue. Article 77 stipulates that subsidies which arise from the need to coordinate the means of transport or to pay for services "inherent in the notion of public service" are compatible with the treaty. Article 78 indicates that any modifications made within the framework of the treaty must keep in mind the "economic situation" of the carriers.

Article 75 provides that the Council of Ministers will decide by unanimity up to December 31, 1965 and by qualified majority thereafter, except that in the latter period unanimous agreement is required whenever a common rule would "gravely affect the standard of living and employment in a region as well as the use of transport equipment, keeping in consideration the necessity of adapting to the economic developments resulting from the creation of the Common Market."

Article 82 exempts Germany from all the transport provisions of the treaty as long as the German government finds it necessary to compensate certain regions for the economic disadvantages caused by the political division of Germany.

The transport provisions of the ECSC and EEC treaties may be compared as follows:

(1) With respect to discrimination proper, which the ECSC has suppressed, the EEC treaty is equally adequate for effective action.

(2) With respect to tapering rates for international through traffic, the ECSC has been moderately effective, while the EEC treaty contains no specific reference or obligation, the problem being among those which may be dealt with later.

(3) With respect to terminal charges the ECSC has been effective, while the EEC treaty provides for later endeavor by the member States.

(4) With respect to rates that protect or subsidize, which the High Authority ordered eliminated in part, the EEC treaty confers the power of decision on the Commission, as the ECSC treaty does on the High Authority, but contains loopholes of indeterminate elasticity.

(5) The ECSC treaty's unequivocal provision for the publication of rates "of all sorts" and for their disclosure to the High Authority (Article 70)—that key device in behalf of nondiscrimination and enforcement so dear to the framers of the ECSC treaty—finds no echo in the EEC treaty.

(6) With respect to harmonization and coordination, which the ECSC member governments made fruitless efforts to accomplish, the EEC treaty is extremely elastic and indefinite. Calling attention to the fact that the EEC treaty postponed the adoption of a common policy by intergovernmental negotiation to a later date, the Transport Committee of the (then) Common Assembly of the ECSC said this postponement involved a twofold risk: It might tend to excuse further inaction in the ECSC; and, in view of the experience in the ECSC, it might make it more difficult to adopt a common policy later.[47] The Committee stated in a later report: "One must keep in mind that in spite of the perspectives opened by the new Treaty, there are neither the directives for, nor the formal obligation to adopt, . . . a [common] policy."[48]

[47] CECA, Assemblée Commune, Commission des Transports, *Rapport intérimaire*, Doc. No. 27, May 1957, p. 9.

[48] Assemblée Parlementaire Européenne, Doc. No. 16, 1958, p. 13.

Unless the governments should come under the spell of a climate of opinion for greater unification under the dynamic of the EEC treaty itself, the stalemate experienced under the ECSC treaty could be prolonged. Since the power of action in any case rests with the same governments under either treaty, it is not likely that the governments will go further under either one of them than they are prepared to go under the other.

A NOTE ON THE MOSELLE CANAL

Transport is a matter of investment as well as of rates. The creation of an economic union may stimulate investments in transport as well as in other industries.[49] This is not the place for a systematic survey of investments in the field of transport, but a note on a very important project, the Moselle Canal, scheduled for completion in 1965–1968, if not later, is pertinent.

The competitive position of the steelworks along the Moselle River (in Lorraine) will be considerably improved by the Moselle Canal. With the aid of thirteen locks, the canal will make the Moselle River navigable by cargo vessels of 1,500 ton capacity between Thionville in Lorraine to Koblentz on the Rhine, a distance of about 170 miles.[50] The steelworks in Lorraine would thus have access to the Low Country ports and to the upper Rhine.

While the steel plants in Lorraine have low production costs, their advantage is diluted by their distance from markets, their access to most of which depends on railroad transport. Attention has already been drawn in Chapter 2 to some of the major difficulties of the steelworks in Lorraine: their landlocked position; the high cost of inbound coal and coke shipments by railroad from the Ruhr, Holland and Belgium (not to speak of the rail shipments from northern France and Centre-Midi); their inability to diversify the supply of solid fuels or iron ore; and the disadvantage of moving steel by rail to Dunkerque, Antwerp or Rotterdam, through which a high percentage of their production is exported.

Projects to canalize the Moselle River go back to the 1800s, when steel production in Lorraine began to expand. But the Ruhr steel firms that controlled

---

[49] Waterway development had lagged in northern France but the French have begun to modernize the waterways in the northern part of the country between Valenciennes and Dunkerque as a result of the ECSC and the EEC. Harbor development has been stimulated by the EEC treaty because the great northern ports of Europe are rivals for the trade to be created by the new Community.

[50] The sources for this discussion of the Moselle Canal are: "Sarre-Moselle-Rhin Conventions de janvier 1957," in *Journal officiel de la République de France*, No. 57-4S, Paris, 1957; *Steel Review*, October 1956, pp. 15–17; *Revue française de l'énergie*, November 1956, p. 47; J. E. Martin, "Location Factors in the Lorraine Iron and Steel Industry," *The Institute of British Geographers, Transactions and Proceedings*, 1957, Publication No. 23. See also Chapter 2.

Lorraine steel before the first world war were not interested in developing transport facilities between that area and the Ruhr. Since the Germans used Lorraine as a source of raw metal for the Ruhr rather than as an exporter of finished steel on world markets, they saw no point in giving Lorraine a water-way connection to the Low Country ports. The Germans instead applied a special low railroad rate for rail shipments between the Ruhr and Lorraine, thus reducing the potential benefit of waterway haulage.

When Lorraine was returned to France by the Treaty of Versailles and became a rival of the Ruhr steel industry, German indifference to the canal turned to hostility. The French government was not at the time very keen to develop ties between Lorraine and Germany either.

With France's appearance as a major world steel exporter after the second world war—the bulk of the exports coming from Lorraine—the French government adopted a more positive policy regarding the canal. The government considered development of the Moselle River a logical outcome of the ECSC; the French Parliament in 1952 made it a unilateral condition for its ratification of the ECSC treaty.

Since the canal was to traverse Germany (80 per cent of it is in German territory) as well as Luxembourg, the consent of the governments of Germany and Luxembourg was required. Consent was obtained in 1956 in a series of negotiations in which Germany reacquired the Saar and agreed to the canali-zation of the Moselle River. French impatience had meantime turned to bitter-ness, the Chambre Syndicale de la Sidérurgie Française announcing early in 1956 that France would withdraw from the ECSC if the Moselle were not canalized.[51]

The canal itself will cost nearly $90 million (at 1955 prices) plus $38 million for 750,000 kilowatts of hydroelectric capacity to be installed and financed by the Germans. The French government will put up two thirds of the funds for the canal and the Germans the rest; Luxembourg will make a token contribu-tion of one half million dollars.

Construction will be supervised by a limited liability corporation under joint Franco-German control which will handle the funds put up and, after corporate adjustments to be agreed later, will manage the canal when com-pleted. Traffic regulations on the canal are to be similar to those in effect on comparable waterways.

The canal will give the Lorraine steel plants a longer economic reach and hence improve their relative position, but it will not give them any advantage not now enjoyed by other sites with access to water transport, like the Ruhr, Belgian or coastal works.

[51] Statement cited in *Le Monde*, March 10, 1956.

The canal will reduce the cost of freight for solid fuels from the Ruhr to Lorraine and will help the steelworks to diversify their sources of coal and iron ore; they will obtain rich ores, which would permit a greater development of open-hearth production, and possibly United States coal. It will also enable the steelworks in Lorraine to strengthen their position as the main area of French steel production and the main source of exports.

Of the three steel producing districts in Lorraine as a whole—Longwy in the northern part, Nancy in the southern part, and the Moselle valley in between —all the benefits will go to the Moselle district, which will probably expand more rapidly than the other two. The plants at Longwy and Nancy are farther from the canal than those in the Moselle valley and would have to reach it by railroad, with the expense of rehandling charges. In order to help the Nancy district, the French government may canalize the Moselle River from Thionville southward to Metz, giving access to Nancy, and it may introduce a special railroad rate to reduce the cost of shipping from Longwy to the canal.

Shortly after the Franco-German agreement was signed, the Denain-Anzin steel group (USINOR) in the north of France announced the construction of a tidewater plant at Dunkerque. The steel group at Nancy (Chatillon-Commentry) has a minority interest in the new plant at Dunkerque, probably to offset its loss of advantage relative to the plants in the Moselle valley.

The Lorraine coal mines will lose some geographical protection relative to Ruhr coal, but this loss is more academic than real in view of the marketing arrangements discussed in Chapter 8.

The steelworks in the Moselle valley expect to save nearly $2.00 per ton of inbound freight for solid fuels from the Ruhr, a saving equivalent to about $1.80 per ton of finished steel (at 1956 rates of production), or 1.5 per cent of the sales value. They also expect to save $3.00 per ton of outbound freight on steel products shipped to Antwerp. The net mill return on exports will thus be greater.

It should be noted that these potential advantages to the Lorraine steel industry rest in large part on the fact that the German government—in return for other concessions, notably receipt of the Saarland—accepted the French government's doctrine that the cost of the canal be borne largely by the public treasury rather than by toll charges, which will be low.

The canal will reduce the cost of shipping Lorraine ore to the Ruhr. The Ruhr is unlikely to increase appreciably its use of Lorraine ore, however, because Lorraine ore will become scarce in the next two decades, because the Ruhr prefers high-grade ore and because government policy calls for the use of German ore.

The canal will, if anything, increase rivalry rather than interdependence in the famous triangle of central Europe, as witnessed by the threat of the Ruhr steel firms to invoke the ECSC treaty against the canal on the ground that, being a public charge, it would provide the Lorraine steel plants with a hidden subsidy.

Some of the other steel producing areas in the ECSC were also unhappy.[52] The Canal will not help the Belgian steel industry or the Saar steel firms unless the Saar River, which meets the Moselle between the cities of Trier and Wasserbillig, is canalized. Although the Moselle bounds Luxembourg on the east, the Luxembourg steel plants are about fifty kilometers westward, closer to the Longwy plants, and will not benefit unless a branch canal is built to Wasserbillig, which would have to be developed as a port. As of the end of 1958 the government of Luxembourg was not planning to construct a branch canal, for the Luxembourg steel plants, which enjoy the same railroad rates as the Belgian steel industry, are not badly placed for rail shipment to Antwerp. But the Luxembourg government was considering the development of a port at Metert (in Luxembourg) to transship iron ore brought by canal from Lorraine.

[52] Several equally unhappy regional groups in France whose commerce depends on the ports of Strasbourg and Dunkerque were appeased by the promise of regional credits from the French government.

CHAPTER 13

SOCIAL POLICIES

WAGES AND COMPETITION

Treaty Provisions

The treaty rests on the proposition that a common market can be reconciled with State sovereignty over transport rates, taxes (direct and indirect, including payroll taxes), wages and social benefits, immigration and mobility of capital. Though many of these factors affect competitive conditions, the status quo was for the most part accepted with the proviso that subsequent distortions be avoided. Paragraph 4 of Section 2 of the Convention for the Transitional Provisions, however, required the High Authority and the governments immediately to examine "existing statutory or administrative measures . . . and contractual social security schemes as far as they are equivalent to administrative measures." It also authorized the High Authority, after consulting the Council of Ministers, to propose measures to the governments to correct or compensate for any distortions that seriously endanger competition.

Article 67 seeks to restrain the States from adopting new measures that impair competitive conditions and requires them to bring new measures to the attention of the High Authority. The High Authority must ascertain if such measures increase the "differences in cost of production otherwise than through variations in productivity." If so, two remedies are envisaged depending on whether the State's action has reduced or increased the difference in costs.

First, if a State causes its enterprises to operate at higher costs, the High Authority may authorize it to grant special assistance to its enterprises. Under Article 68, the High Authority may authorize the State to grant special assistance if a change in payroll taxes causes the firms to operate at a higher cost disadvantage than theretofore. A wage increase, though not necessarily the result of government measures, may also be offset by special assistance. The treaty thus allows compensation for the purpose of maintaining legitimate differences in costs though Article 4 forbids subsidies. It does not, furthermore, interfere with the ability of the State to influence the coal and steel industries by Statewide legislation or even with its ability to influence them for social reasons by special measures adopted without the intention of distorting competition.[1] If a State, for example, granted special retirement or sickness benefits to miners for the dangerous nature of the work and taxed the enterprises to help defray the cost, the measure would not necessarily be illegal.

Second, if a State applies to the coal and steel firms special advantages or burdens not applicable to other industries in its jurisdiction, then the High Authority may address the necessary recommendations to that State. If a governmental measure adversely affects the enterprises in another member State, the High Authority may ask the offending government to take remedial action. The High Authority, with the Council's consent, thus asked the French government in 1959 to tax French steel exported to the rest of the ECSC because the devaluation of the franc had reduced prices abnormally. If a change in payroll taxes enables the firms to improve their competitive position, the High Authority may make recommendations to the offending State under Article 68. Under Article 67, the High Authority must in all instances consult the Consultative Committee and the Council before taking action.

Article 68 restrains the manipulation of wages for purposes of unfair competition but states that the treaty is not, with certain exceptions, to affect current methods of fixing wages and social benefits. The exceptions allow the High Authority to interfere if "abnormally low prices" are the result of "abnormally low" wages compared with those in other industries in the region. In that case it may address the necessary recommendations to the firms in question or consult with the government if the latter is responsible for the low wages. If consultation with the government is unsuccessful, the High Authority may issue a recommendation to the government after consulting the Consultative Committee and the Council of Ministers.

The High Authority may also take action if a wage reduction lowers the standard of living and is at the same time made for the purpose of gaining a competitive advantage. After consulting the Council of Ministers and the Consultative Committee in such cases, the High Authority may address to the enterprise or government concerned a recommendation to have the enterprise compensate the workers.

If an enterprise fails to obey a recommendation from the High Authority under Article 68, the High Authority may impose a daily penalty up to twice "the amount of saving in labor costs illegally effected."

[1] See Paul Reuter, *La Communauté Européenne du Charbon et de l'Acier*, Librairie Générale de Droit et de Jurisprudence, Paris, 1953, pp. 194–195.

Wage reductions are legal under the following conditions of Article 68:

(1) If they are part of over-all measures to attain economic equilibrium.

(2) If they are determined by contractual or governmental sliding scale regulations.

(3) If they are preceded by a reduction in the cost of living.

(4) If they help correct "abnormal increases previously granted under exceptional circumstances which no longer apply."

The treaty calls on the institutions of the ECSC to harmonize "living and working conditions . . . in an upward direction" (Article3[e]) but the High Authority has no direct power to raise living and working conditions, though it may collect information (Article 46[5]). The High Authority described its power and limitations in the field of wages and living standards in the following terms:[2]

The social aim of the Community is to raise living standards in an expanding European economy. Having taken the first step towards economic expansion in creating a Common Market for coal and steel across the six countries where living standards and wages differ, the Community has taken as one of its major objectives the gradual improvement, and, in the Treaty's words, the "equalization in progress" of labourers' conditions of life and work.

Equal social conditions in the different states can only be a long term consequence of a united Europe. The Coal and Steel Community is the first step towards unity. Its executive body, the High Authority, has no powers to fix wages, change social security provisions or modify tax structures. Its aim is more limited: to guarantee for labour the genuine opportunity itself to obtain better conditions of life and work on the Common Market. But the High Authority can prevent a coal or steel firm . . . from paying wages which are abnormally low for the areas in which it is situated; it can stop the lowering of wages as a weapon of competition.

Though the treaty provides the High Authority with more explicit powers to prevent wage cutting than to raise living standards, complex political changes have eliminated wage cutting as a means of price competition. But the High Authority's powers are significant in historical perspective and imply a considerable degree of public control. The Common Assembly has, furthermore, recommended that Article 68 be amended to give the High Authority the power to go beyond competitive conditions for the sake of improving living and working standards.[3]

---

[2] HA, *The Community's Labour Policy*, Luxembourg, April 6, 1955, p. 1 (mimeo.).

[3] CECA, *Revision du traité instituant la Communauté Européenne du Charbon et de l'Acier*, Luxembourg, n.d., p. 24.

NATIONAL DIFFERENCES IN EARNINGS

The High Authority made a number of useful studies in this field.[4] These are used as a basis for the following analysis of differences in earnings between countries, the influence of social security benefits and tax policies on these differences, and whether or not the differences narrowed under the influence of the Community.

The analysis is confined to the coal industry[5] because it is labor intensive and accounts for two out of every three workers in the ECSC. The analysis is further limited to underground workers, the bulk of the labor force in mining.

The data on annual earnings in 1954 are shown in Table 57.

National differences in earnings, when expressed in national currencies at official rates of exchange, do not express the differences in buying power or the standard of living. The studies made by the High Authority consequently measure the differences in real earnings by determining the purchasing power of each currency in each coal mining region for a number of standard articles that comprise the budget of the average mining family in each area. The data in Table 57 show purchasing power, expressed in Belgian francs only. The data are further confined to married workers with no children and with two children; these two categories account for nearly half or more of all married workers in each country.

Only Lorraine, where earnings are above the average for France, shows a significant regional deviation from the national average. Earnings in Lorraine are closer to those in the Saar, in the same coal field, and higher than those in the Nord and Pas-de-Calais because of overtime and cost of living differences and, above all, because the mining conditions require a different pattern of skills.[6]

Married Miners Without Children

Gross earnings are more variable between countries for workers with children than for those without children because Belgium and France, which pay the highest allowance to workers with children, pay no allowance to

---

[4] These studies, made pursuant to Article 46 (5) and to Section 2 (paragraph 4) of the Convention for the Transitional Provisions, are: *Comparaison des revenus réels des travailleurs des industries de la Communauté*, Etudes et Documents, October 1956. This basic study rests on 1954 data. For convenience it is referred to hereafter as *Comparaison*. A preliminary study based on 1953 data was published as "Verbraucher-Geldparitäten," in *Statistische Informationen*, August-September 1955. A follow-up study, giving data through 1956 and 1957, was published as "Evolution des revenus réels des travailleurs dans les mines de houille et dans la sidérurgie de la Communauté," in *Informations statistiques*, May-June 1958. *Evolution des salaires et politique salariale dans les industries de la Communauté*, April 1957 (2 vols.), covers direct earnings only, to the exclusion of other benefits.

[5] Italian coal production is too small to be included here.

[6] *Comparaison*, pp. 63–67.

married workers without children (though France pays an allowance for the first two years of marriage). In Germany and the Netherlands, the employer rather than the State pays the allowance for married workers without children. Net earnings in all countries are smaller than earnings received from the employer because the deductions exceed the family allowance. The Dutch miner

Table 57

AVERAGE NET ANNUAL REAL EARNINGS PER
UNDERGROUND EMPLOYEE, ECSC COAL PRODUCING COUNTRIES, 1954[a]

(Thousands of Belgian Francs)

Country	Direct and in Kind	Family Allowance	Gross Earnings	Less Taxes		Net Earnings
				Social Security	Income	
Married, No Children						
Germany	52.2	1.2	53.4	6.0	3.9	43.6
Saar	56.5	2.9	59.4	6.2	3.6	49.6
France	51.9	0.0	51.9	5.7	0.0	46.2
Belgium	68.4	0.0	68.4	5.2	4.2	58.9
Netherlands	62.1	2.4	64.5	9.2	7.4	47.9
Married, Two Children						
Germany	51.7	2.8	54.5	6.2	1.8	46.6
Saar	55.8	10.7	66.5	6.2	2.6	57.8
France	51.9	16.6	68.5	5.7	0.0	62.7
Belgium	68.3	10.7	79.0	5.2	3.6	70.3
Netherlands	61.2	7.5	68.7	9.2	4.6	54.9

Sources: HA, *Comparaison des revenus réels des travailleurs des industries de la Communauté,* 1956, pp. 30–34, 54, 75.

[a] Covers enrolled underground employees, without adjustment for absences, who live in company lodgings. Values are expressed in Belgian francs at a parity equivalent to the purchasing power of the several currencies for a standard working class budget in each mining area. For the range in earnings, representing the value of each currency paired with each of the other currencies, see source, p. 54. For the difficulty of establishing a single parity, see *ibid.*, pp. 129–142, particularly p. 136 for a tentative single parity.

Married workers without children and with two children account for the following proportions of all families (see source, p. 27):

	No Children	Two Children
Germany	49	16
Saar	22	24
France	39	18
Belgium	36	17
Netherlands	24	22

Lodged and unlodged employees have approximately the same net revenue. *Comparaison,* p. 143. In Germany, 31 per cent of the married workers live in company houses; in the Saar, 15 per cent; in France, 56 per cent; in the Netherlands, 36 per cent. Fourteen per cent of the workers in Belgian mines (married and unmarried) live in such housing. France pays a housing allowance if the family lives in a noncompany house, because the French mining statute guarantees an accommodation. Though the number of shifts worked varies from country to country, the comparability of annual net earnings is not seriously affected. *Ibid.*, pp. 63–64.

pays the highest tax, both on income and for social security; the French miner is liable for social security taxes, which are relatively low, but not for income tax. These differences reflect the influence of national legislation.

Married Miners with Two Children

Although wages received from the employer (direct and in kind) are not determined by size of family, married miners with two children have a much higher take-home pay than those without children because family allowances are greater and income taxes lower. The ratio of take-home pay to direct earnings, however, varies considerably from country to country because social security and income taxes are far from homogeneous. The family allowance in France is six times as great, and that in the Saar and Belgium is nearly four

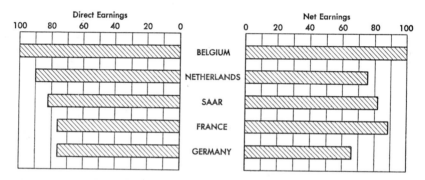

Fig. 18. Indexes of Direct and Annual Net Real Earnings per Underground Employee, Married, with Two Children, ECSC Coal Producing Countries, 1954 (*Belgium = 100*)

Source: Table 57.

times as great, as that in Germany, where it is lowest. Except for Germany, the married worker pays the same amount of social security tax whether or not he has children. But his income taxes decrease sharply with the number of children.

The family allowance exceeds the tax liability in all countries except Germany and the Netherlands. Net earnings are therefore much higher than direct earnings in France and considerably lower in Germany and the Netherlands; they are substantially the same in the Saar and Belgium, where the family allowance does little more than offset the tax liability. The effect of national policy on take-home pay in 1954 is indicated in Fig. 18 (data from Table 57).

The High Authority study nevertheless suggested that net earnings in the coal and steel industries were more homogeneous as between countries than those in other industries. Coal miners are the best paid workers in their respective countries and steelworkers also tend to be at the top of the ladder.[7]

Annual Net Real Earnings, 1953–1956

Were the differences in annual net real earnings between countries narrowed between 1953–1956? The relationships in 1953 and 1956 are shown in Table 58.

Table 58

ECSC COAL MINES: ANNUAL NET REAL EARNINGS, UNDERGROUND WORKERS, MARRIED, WITH TWO CHILDREN, 1953 AND 1956, BY COUNTRY

Country	*Belgium = 100*		*Belgium in 1953 = 100*
	1953	1956	1956
Germany	75	87	93
Saar	99	112	120
France	97	104	111
Belgium	100	100	107
Netherlands	95	104	112

Source: HA, *Informations statistiques*, May-June 1958, p. 142.

Net real earnings in 1953 were highest in Belgium; by 1956, earnings in France and the Netherlands had overtaken, and were slightly higher, than those in Belgium and earnings of underground miners in the Saar were the highest in the ECSC. Belgian miners received next to the lowest pay after having been the highest paid. Though the earnings of the German miner had increased most rapidly between 1953 and 1956, they had still not caught up to what the Belgian miner had earned in 1953 and were still 22 per cent below the highest-paid workers in 1956. The differences were transposed but not eliminated.

But hard and fast conclusions cannot be easily drawn, as the High Authority pointed out:[8]

". . . equalization" evolves continuously and cannot be expected to develop in a straight line or uninterruptedly. Everything indicates on the contrary that it is irregular and proceeds by stages and that it will remain thus as long as the economic

[7] CECA, Assemblée Commune, Commission des Affaires Sociales, *Rapport intérimaire*, Doc. No. 19, 1957–1958, pp. 29–32; *Comparaison*, pp. 146–147.

[8] *Informations statistiques*, May–June 1958, p. 144.

policies of the countries on the road to integration are not coordinated more closely. It should furthermore be added that we have up to the present the experience only of a partial integration of several years' duration to go on—a fact of great significance for the question studied here.

Collective Bargaining

Collective bargaining in the coal and steel industries retained its national character. National differences in the cost of living and supply of labor suggest that common wage scales would be impractical in a partial economic union. It is one of the anomalies of partial economic union that real earnings in the Belgian coal mines, where the marginal product of labor is the lowest in the union, are much higher than those in the Ruhr. Labor organizations, on the other hand, are deeply devoted to the principle of equal pay for equal work regardless of output per man.

Capital and labor were legally free to negotiate and fix wages in all six member countries except the Netherlands, which still retained postwar powers of supervision. Wages were nevertheless still indirectly influenced by government policy in all countries.[9] Harmonization of wages in the coal and steel industries thus affects the over-all labor policy of each of the national governments. It remains to be seen what influence the European Economic Community will have in breaking through national patterns of collective bargaining.[10]

A study group of which William Y. Elliott was chairman suggested that industrywide bargaining across national frontiers would promote a "wage structure which would better reflect differences in labor productivity among firms and industries and create desirable wage incentives for labor."[11] But since management is less able to pass the cost of a wage increase on to the consumer when other firms in the same industry are organized by different unions, collective bargaining on national lines might, depending on circumstances, help stimulate efficiency in an economic union.[12]

The national unions have taken some steps to work together. The national trade unions of the coal and steel workers in the ECSC established a Committee of Twenty-one to safeguard their interests. In January 1958 the trade

[9] CECA, Assemblée Commune, Commission des Affaires Sociales, *Rapport intérimaire*, Doc. No. 19, 1957–1958, *passim*.

[10] Assemblée Parlementaire Européenne, *Informations mensuelles*, March-April 1958, p. 21. The High Authority's study, *L'Evolution des salaires et la politique salariale dans les industries de la Communauté*, 1957, describes the national wage policies.

[11] William Y. Elliott, *The Political Economy of American Foreign Policy*, Holt, New York, 1955, p. 283.

[12] Tibor Scitovsky, *Economic Theory and Western European Integration*, Allen and Unwin, London, 1958, pp. 18–19.

unions in the six countries founded the European Trade Union Committee to serve the common interests of the workers in all three communities.[13]

PAYROLL TAXES AND COMPETITIVE CONDITIONS

Besides paying his employee directly, the employer also makes indirect payments—to the State or to private funds for various kinds of insurance, for retirement, unemployment, sickness, family allowances, etc. Such payments are included in the costs of production though they do not appear in the employee's pay envelope. The employer thus contributes to the "social cost" of maintaining the labor force in accordance with the standards of the community.

Table 59

PERCENTAGE DISTRIBUTION OF CONTRIBUTIONS TO THE COST OF
SOCIAL SECURITY, BY TYPE OF CONTRIBUTOR AND BY COUNTRY, 1955

Country	Public Treasury	Employee	Employer	Other	Total
Germany	15.9	30.3	51.2	2.6	100.0
France	10.7	15.8	68.1	5.4	100.0
Belgium	18.3	24.8	53.7	3.2	100.0
Italy	8.0	7.4	84.6	0.0	100.0
United Kingdom	47.8	19.8	26.6	5.9	100.0

Source: ILO, *Les Salaires et les éléments connexes des coûts de main-d'oeuvre dans l'industrie européenne, 1955*, Geneva, 1957, p. 60. The data cover five social security schemes: family allocations, old age, illness and maternity, unemployment and working accidents.

The employee and the State or the public treasury also contribute to these social security funds. But the proportionate contribution from each of these three sources—employer, employee and public treasury—varies considerably from country to country, as Table 59 indicates. The public treasury supported a relatively small proportion of the total cost of social security in the Community in 1955 but bore nearly half the cost in the United Kingdom. In Germany, France, Belgium and Italy the employer bore more than half the cost, his part rising to 68 per cent in France and 85 per cent in Italy. The employee

[13] HA, *Bulletin from the European Coal and Steel Community*, February 1958, p. 8. See CECA, Assemblée Commune, Commission des Affaires Sociales, *Rapport sur la création, la fonction et la composition d'une ou plusiers, commissions paritaires dans le cadre de la Communauté*, Doc. No. 1, 1956–1957, for an interesting history of the effort to create an international central committee of employers' and employees' representatives within the ECSC to discuss common problems affecting the terms of employment, leading, first, to the formation of a "mixed committee" of national representatives from labor and management in the steel industry and, later (in 1958), of a tripartite committee (labor, management and government) in the coal industry. See CECA, Assemblée Parlementaire Européenne, Commission des Affaires Sociales, Doc. No. 21, 1958, pp. 27–30.

in Belgium and Germany bore a larger proportion of the cost than his counterpart in the other three countries. The employer's contribution is equivalent to a tax on payroll, whether or not the "tax" is based on an administrative obligation, on a collective agreement or on a unilateral decision. Such taxes are indirect; that is, the cost, included in production costs, is transferred to the customer.[14]

What was the effect of differences in national policy, particularly in governmental policy, on the competitive position of the producers in the different countries?

The French government and French business interests assert that French producers are at a disadvantage in a common market because their payroll taxes are higher. They consequently argue either that social charges should be harmonized before a common market is created or that French industry should be protected or exempted from common market provisions until social charges in the different countries are harmonized.[15] But neither the treaty for the ECSC nor that for the European Economic Community made the establishment of the common market conditional on the attainment of harmonization of social charges or exempted France from its provisions, though both treaties accepted the principle that a common market will promote eventual harmony.

The influence of payroll taxes or indirect labor costs on the hourly cost of mining labor in 1956 is estimated in Table 60, in which the French franc was converted at 420 to the dollar (devaluation of August 1957).[16] The countries where direct labor costs were the lowest—the Netherlands, the Saar and France—had the highest payroll taxes; the reverse was the case where direct labor costs were high. Final labor costs—direct payments and payroll taxes combined—were consequently more homogeneous than direct labor costs taken alone; the highest and lowest final costs differed by only 10 per cent whereas the highest and lowest direct costs differed by nearly 12 per cent. Final costs in France, where payroll taxes were the highest, were, however, also the highest—though direct costs were among the lowest—because the French employer in general, under French public policy, supports 68 per cent of the cost of the social security system. Relative final labor costs per man-

---

[14] A study by the Federation of British Industries, *Taxation in the Proposed European Free Trade Area*, London, October 1957, contains a valuable survey of direct and indirect taxes in the various countries.

[15] A typical complaint may be found in Charbonnages de France, *Rapport de gestion, 1953*, pp. 53–54. Another, regarding the European Economic Community, was analyzed in *Le Monde*, April 3, 1958, p. 14.

[16] The data on direct earnings in column 1 of Table 60 differ from those in column 1 of Table 57 because the latter refer to real earnings calculated on the basis of buying power of married underground workers only, the former to average nominal earnings of all workers, underground and surface.

hour in 1953 and 1956 are shown in the last two columns of Table 60. The relative position of the French coal mines with respect to labor costs per man-hour did not appreciably deteriorate during this period.

Was the French coal industry's case that competitive conditions were distorted to their disadvantage sound?

A precise definition of distortion, made by the High Authority, will help to determine whether or not competitive conditions were distorted by payroll tax

Table 60

HOURLY PAYROLL COSTS, ECSC COAL PRODUCING COUNTRIES AND THE UNITED KINGDOM, 1956

Country	Payments to Workers (Direct and in Kind)	Indirect Labor Costs	Indirect Costs as Per Cent of Payments to Workers	Total Costs	Index of Total Costs (*Highest* = 100)	
					1956	1953
Germany	$0.76	$0.21	28	$0.97	92	95
Saar	0.74	0.31	42	1.05	100	100
France	0.73	0.31	41	1.04	99	97
Belgium	0.77	0.18	23	0.95	90	100
Netherlands	0.69	0.29	42	0.98	93	86
United Kingdom	1.04	0.02	2	1.06	a	a

Sources: HA, *Informations statistiques*, September-October 1957, p. 377. France and Saar calculated at 420 francs to the dollar, equivalent to the devaluation of August 1957.

Costs in 1953 were calculated from the index for the change in hourly labor costs between 1953 and 1956 as shown in HA, *Informations statistiques*, September-October 1957, p. 379. Costs in 1953 were then indexed (Belgium and the Saar = 100) but the value of the French franc was held constant at 420 to the dollar.

Data for the United Kingdom are from National Coal Board, *Quarterly and Annual Statistical Statement for 1956*, and refer to average earnings per shift in cash and kind divided by 7½ hours per shift. The weekly payroll tax of 6/2 shillings on men over eighteen is equal to a 2 per cent contribution on weekly earnings. The payroll tax is from Federation of British Industries, *Taxation in the Proposed European Free Trade Area*, London, October 1957, p. 155.

a Confined to the coal industry in the ECSC.

differences. The High Authority pointed out that a distortion rests on the presence of either one of two conditions: (a) Taxes or other charges on one industry are out of line with charges on other industries in the same country. (b) Taxes or charges on an industry in one country place that industry at a disadvantage relative to the same industry in another country.[17] Criterion (a) raises some general issues. The Treaty (Article 4[a]) prohibits "import and export duties, or taxes with an equivalent effect." This prohibition falls on taxes that are protective; it does not interfere with a country's ability to raise

[17] HA, *Sixième rapport général*, Vol. I, p. 21.

revenue by a sales tax on imported goods provided that tax is no higher than the sales tax on goods of domestic origin. Compensatory import taxes are also legal provided they are no greater than taxes that affect internal producers.[18]

According to the High Authority's first criterion for the existence of distortion, it would nevertheless be improper for a State to subject the coal or steel firms in its jurisdiction to a higher or lower revenue tax than the general run of firms. The essence of the principle is that State legislation should apply equally to all comparable entities. The spirit of the legislation is more important than administrative variations in arithmetic; the payroll tax may, for example, vary with the accident rate in particular industries or firms without involving a distortion.

Why does the first of the High Authority's criteria permit, say, payroll taxes to differ between countries but prohibit them from varying between industries in the same country? Equal rates of taxation between countries would of course be more compatible with a common market than unequal ones. But even unequal ones between countries are still compatible with such a market because taxes work their way through the cost structure. The resulting national differences in price structures are adjustable through the currency exchange rates. The country with the high tax would be able to maintain its export volume by adjusting exchange rates. The influence of taxes on prices should therefore be measured in relative rather than absolute terms.

But if taxes differ between industries in the same country, exchange rates, being indivisible, cannot be adjusted between industries unless the industry in question has a very heavy weight in the total value of exports—as steel does in Luxembourg's exports.[19]

Since the French coal industry did not complain of being subject to a discriminatory tax, it was not a victim of the first type of distortion.

The High Authority's second criterion, (b), refers to the sum of advantages and disadvantages affecting a particular industry in all member countries. The sum of all differences may offset the constituent differences. The French coal industry might therefore have a case on this criterion since its total labor costs per man-hour, as a result of high payroll taxes, are high compared with the other countries. But the 5 to 10 per cent difference between total labor costs in France and in the other ECSC countries is not enough to make a strong case.

[18] See the report entitled *Report on the Problems Raised by the Different Turnover Tax Systems Applied Within the Common Market*, prepared by the Committee of Experts (Jan Tinbergen, Chairman) set up under HA Order No. 1–53, dated March 5, 1953. This report, referred to as the Tinbergen Report, deals with the question whether taxation at the place of production or the place of consumption is more compatible with a common market.

[19] See ECE, *Economic Survey of Europe for 1956*, Chap. 4, p. 28; also Tinbergen Report, and Carl S. Shoup, "Taxation Aspects of International Economic Integration," Institut International de Finances Publiques, 9th session, Frankfurt am Main, 1953, p. 92.

The High Authority approached the whole question of distortion with a wary eye, as indicated by the following statement:[20]

The effects of artificial disparities which falsify competition must be eliminated, but not all differences—which would be impossible and ineffective. . . . Isolated distortions may already be offset by other distortions operating in an opposite direction on other elements in production cost. It follows that the establishment of a common market is by no means incompatible with a rather large diversity in fiscal and social legislation, and that the search for harmony might artificially eliminate differences that are economically justified; analysis should on the other hand focus on the few limited problems whose solution will make European integration more effective.

The British coal mines, in spite of the low payroll tax, did not enjoy a competitive advantage with respect to final labor costs per man-hour because total labor costs (Table 60) were as high as those in France. This fact illustrates the rule that where the employer's contribution to social security is low, direct wage payments tend to be high, the final result varying less than the constituent elements. If the British coal mines were to be included in the ECSC or the free trade area, payroll tax differences would therefore not distort competitive conditions.[21]

The ECSC is too limited in the number of industries included to provide a framework for reconciling the differences between countries with respect to social security legislation. Since the European Economic Community provides a larger framework, any further steps in this field depend on the broader economic union. Disparity involves more than a static difference in effective living standards. Rates of economic change are equally important. A population with a rising standard of living and rising opportunities may be better off than a population with a higher standard of living but stagnant opportunities. From this point of view, it may be more desirable for the European Economic Community to devote its energies primarily to achieving a higher standard of living throughout the area than to the very involved task of equalizing current disparities by statutory measures.

MOBILITY OF LABOR

Free trade could of itself equalize the marginal product of labor and capital throughout an economic union, thereby promoting the most efficient use of resources and international specialization. But this result is not likely to occur

---

[20] HA, *Sixième rapport général,* Vol. I, p. 21.

[21] The High Authority's statement, quoted on page 338 of this study, that low payroll taxes in the United Kingdom would create a problem if Britain joined the ECSC is thus not necessarily correct.

on practical grounds unless labor and capital are also free to move.[22] If the common market were interregional rather than international, labor and capital would be free to move from one area to another. The ECSC stopped short of this step because free movement of capital and labor would have raised particularly difficult problems of transition and harmonization. But the ECSC treaty provides ground for intergovernmental cooperation in the field of labor mobility, as does the EEC treaty with respect to the mobility of both labor and capital.

Article 69 of the ECSC treaty deals with labor mobility and with the rights of migrant workers. Paragraph 1 of this article calls on the States to "renounce" any restrictions on employment based on nationality if a worker possesses "recognized qualifications" for a position in the coal or steel industries. This possibility is not extended to unskilled workers. The free movement of unskilled workers "would involve possibilities of emigration under cover of the two industries which can only be envisaged in the framework of a more general economic agreement."[23]

Paragraph 2 of Article 69 called on the States to "work out a common definition of skilled jobs and conditions of qualification" and to prepare the administrative provisions for bringing together the job seeker and the job opening.

The governments ratified an agreement in August 1957 which took effect the month following.[24] Applying only to designated skilled occupations, the agreement potentially covers one sixth of the 1.6 million workers employed by the coal and steel industries in 1956.[25] These skilled workers are entitled to permits allowing them to work in another member country. A very small number of permits was issued the first year.[26] Neither management nor labor in the two industries believed the agreement would yield any substantial results because it applies, in the words of the Social Affairs Committee of the Common Assembly, "only to an élite of specialized and well-paid workers who do not need to emigrate in order to find work."[27] But the High Authority intended to ask the governments to increase the list of skilled occupations eligible for work permits.[28]

The mobility of common labor, and the possibility of training such labor

[22] James E. Meade, *Problems of Economic Union*, University of Chicago Press, Chicago, 1953, pp. 56 ff.

[23] Reuter, *op. cit.*, p. 229.

[24] The text is in *Journal officiel*, August 12, 1957, pp. 367 ff.

[25] HA, *Bulletin from the European Community for Coal and Steel*, June-July 1957, p. 12.

[26] HA, *Sixième rapport général*, Vol. II, p. 198.

[27] Common Assembly, Doc. No. 5, 1957–1958, pp. 12–13. This report criticizes the agreement for administrative weaknesses as well.

[28] HA, *Sixième rapport général*, Vol. I, p. 58.

for more specialized work, is of much more significance than the migration of skilled workers. Italy has a large surplus of common labor available for emigration; the other members of Little Europe need such labor. Here lies the core of the matter.[29] The European coal industry operates with a chronic dearth of labor—except when business activity declines. About 14 million tons of coal were lost in the ECSC in 1955 for lack of men to fill 38,000 openings.[30] Most of the potential supply could have come only from unskilled labor.

The European Economic Community treaty goes beyond that for the ECSC with respect to the mobility of common labor. The EEC treaty (Article 48), affirming the principle of international labor mobility, does not limit mobility to qualified workers because the treaty stipulates that the governments intend to reach an agreement by the end of the transitional period (i.e., after twelve years) permitting common labor to migrate. Substantial further progress in the ECSC must therefore await intergovernmental agreement in the EEC.[31] Under Article 48 the States accept the principle of equal treatment for immigrant labor from other member States. Article 49 stipulates that national legislative or administrative measures that interfere with free movement be eliminated progressively and that national labor ministries collaborate closely. It also contains the proviso that the measures taken to promote labor mobility should not endanger the standard of living and employment in the economic union. Workers will be able to migrate in response only to effective job offers (Article 48[a]). This provision precludes the possibility of a mass migration of workers in search of jobs. It envisages more orderly and limited forms of migration.

Differences in social security legislation (and safety regulations in mining) hinder international migration. The governments agreed in the EEC treaty to reduce these obstacles by subsequent negotiation and agreement. Article 51 of the EEC treaty, tackling the problem of differences in social security legislation, provides that the governments may by unanimous decision adopt social security measures permitting a migrant worker or his beneficiaries: (1) to cumulate all periods of employment and all rights acquired under any of the national systems; (2) to obtain benefit payments from any member State regardless of his place of residence in the Community.

The governments in the ECSC had already initiated a convention in December 1957 (pursuant to paragraph 4 of Article 69 of the ECSC treaty) to harmonize social security regulations; it is called the *Convention Européenne de*

---

[29] Common Assembly, Doc. No. 2, 1956–1957, pp. 22 ff, and Doc. No. 5, 1957–1958, pp. 17 ff.

[30] HA, *Cinquième rapport général*, p. 272.

[31] HA, *Sixième rapport général*, Vol. I, pp. 58–59; Common Assembly, Doc. No. 21, 1958, p. 42.

Securité Social pour les Travailleurs Migrants. It is open to all European States and applicable to all wage workers. It covers all branches of social security (sickness, old age, survivors' benefits, working accidents, occupational illness, unemployment and family allocations). It replaces all existing bilateral or multilateral treaties.[32] The convention takes account of the eventual measures to be taken in this field by the European Economic Community (under Article 51 of its treaty); the EEC Commission subsequently recommended that the governments adopt the convention.[33]

Paragraph 3 of Article 69 of the ECSC treaty stipulates that if there is a dearth of unskilled labor, the States should "adapt their immigration regulations as much as may be necessary." And paragraph 4 of that article, recognizing the influence of wages and working conditions on the ability to recruit foreign labor, calls on the States to prohibit discrimination based on nationality.

The right to migrate is a necessary condition for mobility but it is not sufficient by itself. Migration within the same country is frequently limited by local ties and lack of means. The cost of migrating, the problem of housing and the problem of obtaining a job in advance are among the hindrances to mobility.[34] Since large numbers of common laborers are unlikely to take the initiative or to incur the expense of traveling to another country to look for a job, organized recruiting plays an important role in bringing the foreign worker to the job. The members of the ECSC engaged in international recruiting even before the ECSC was established. They obtained a large number of foreign workers from all sources within and outside the ECSC, mainly for the coal and construction industries, without the benefit of formal legislation regarding the right to migrate.

Twenty-six per cent of all the Italians employed by the steel industry in the ECSC in 1957 worked outside of Italy. Only 78 per cent of the workers employed by the French steel industry were of French origin; only 82 per cent of those employed by the Belgian steel industry were of Belgian origin; and only 85 per cent of those employed by the steel plants in Luxembourg were natives of that country.[35]

Nearly half the workers—74,000, of whom 46,000 were Italian—in the Belgian coal mines in 1957 were foreigners. Foreigners accounted for as much

---

[32] These and the other main provisions are summarized in HA, *Sixième rapport général,* Vol. II, pp. 199–201.

[33] Common Assembly, Doc. No. 21, 1958, p. 15.

[34] For a study of the relocational hindrances in a particular region, see HA, *Auvergne-Aquitaine* Etudes et Documents (Etudes Régionales d'Emploi), Luxembourg, July 1957; also HA, *Obstacles à la mobilité des travailleurs et problèmes sociales de réadaption,* Etudes et Documents.

[35] HA, *Informations statistiques,* May-June 1958, pp. 184–193.

as 60 per cent of the underground labor force at the end of 1955.[36] The mines in Lorraine and in Nord and Pas-de-Calais also employ a large number of foreigners; 20 per cent of the labor force in the French coal mines in 1955 were foreigners.[37]

Italians are recruited through the Italian Ministry of Labor, which circulates requests to regional offices where candidates are received and screened. The approved candidates are then assembled for screening by representatives of the receiving country and thereafter leave immediately for the latter country which pays the expenses from this point forward, the Italian government having paid theretofore. The arrangements for recruiting are usually made by governments, though the enterprise that needs foreign workers sometimes makes its own arrangements with the Italian government.[38]

The arrangements made by the member governments of the ECSC for foreign workers under bilateral or other contractual agreements guarantee equal pay.[39] But foreign workers often find that they do not receive equal treatment. They are generally the first to be laid off in a business recession. Thus, the number of foreign workers in the Belgian mines declined by 6,000 in the recession of 1953–1954, the number of Belgian workers by less than 1,000.[40] This difference is hardly conducive to successful recruiting though it may be a condition for obtaining the consent of local workers to the use of foreign labor. Housing is often inadequate and prevents the foreign worker from bringing his family with him. Factors other than discrimination also hinder international recruiting; training and language problems are not the least of these. Safety on the job is particularly important in recruiting for the mines.[41] The coal mine accident at Marcinelle, Belgium, in August 1956, in which 100 Italians were killed, caused the Italian government to prohibit further recruiting for any destination for nearly two years thereafter.

As a result of the accident at Marcinelle, the six governments organized a conference to study mine safety conditions. By the spring of 1957 the conference and the High Authority had each submitted its recommendations to the Council of Ministers. The High Authority urged the governments to adopt a multilateral mine safety agreement incorporating the recommendations. But the Council, preferring to keep control in the governments, instead established

[36] HA, *Sixième rapport général*, Vol. II, pp. 40, 190; R. Fritz, "Der belgische Bergbau im gemeinsamen Markt der Montanunion," in *Glückauf*, September 15, 1956, p. 1117.

[37] *Revue française de l'énergie*, May 1958, p. 412.

[38] The description of the arrangements given above is based on Common Assembly, Doc. No. 5, 1957–1958, pp. 23 ff.

[39] *Ibid.*, p. 17.

[40] HA, *Sixième rapport général*, Vol. II, p. 40.

[41] This list of problems is not exhaustive; the Common Assembly report Doc. No. 5, 1957–1958, pp. 17 ff, contains a summary of national policies with respect to immigrant labor.

a permanent committee to follow developments and to collect reports from the governments on the safety measures they had taken. The committee consists of twenty-four members, four from each country, plus the chairman, who is a member of the High Authority; each country delegation consists of representatives from the government, workers and employers.[42]

An effective program for re-employing workers who lose their jobs when high-cost plants go under requires money. Section 23 of the ECSC Convention on the Transitional Provisions allows the High Authority to provide financial assistance to workers and enterprises for readaptation. These grants need not be repaid. The government in whose territory the problem occurs must in most cases match the contribution from the High Authority. Such grants may be made for two years beyond the end of the transitional period and may cover purposes other than international migration. As of February 1, 1958 the High Authority had opened credits under Section 23 for $12 million affecting 18,600 workers.[43] It remains to be seen what credits can be put at the disposal of the program to promote labor mobility after Section 23 expires.[44] The High Authority is also empowered to grant nonrepayable assistance under Article 56 but such payments are limited to technological unemployment.

THE HIGH AUTHORITY'S SOCIAL POLICIES

In the course of the transitional period the High Authority, encouraged by the Common Assembly, adopted a bolder posture with respect to social policy than it was first inclined to take. In no field has the Common Assembly, through its Committee on Social Affairs, been more active than in that of social policy. The High Authority believed that it could prevent firms from reducing wages and living standards only if these measures impaired competitive conditions. It believed, further, that improvements in living conditions depend on the dynamic forces released by the Community itself and not on executive policy.[45] The High Authority's concept of limited responsibility was severely criticized by the Committee on Social Affairs when the High Authority issued its report in 1956 on the *Objectifs généraux*.[46] The Committee thought the High Authority had relegated labor to a secondary place, treating it from a very limited and one-sided view as a "factor of production." The High Authority defended the omission of social policy from the 1956 report

[42] See HA, *Sixième rapport général*, Vol. I, p. 56, Vol. II, pp. 262 ff.
[43] *Ibid.*, Vol. II, pp. 201 ff, mentions particular cases.
[44] Common Assembly, Doc. No. 21, 1958, p. 43.
[45] HA, *The Community's Labour Policy*, Luxembourg, April 6, 1955 (mimeo.).
[46] Common Assembly, Doc. No. 11, 1956–1957.

on the *Objectifs généraux* on the ground that Article 46, paragraph 3, was strictly limited to economic matters. This concept, said the Committee on Social Affairs, ignored the spirit of the program for European unity as well as the letter of the ECSC treaty. The Committee said that social policy was an integral and coordinate, not subordinate, factor in the movement for European unity and that labor wanted to be, or thought it was, part of the movement. Labor expected the program for European unity to improve human relations and social services in the factory and to raise living standards by allowing workers to share in the benefits of rising productivity. The Committee on Social Affairs said that if labor were to take second place it would not acquire a sense of direct interest in European unity, the attainment of which would be hindered without the positive support of labor.[47]

The Committee on Social Affairs conceded that the powers given to the High Authority by the ECSC treaty were much weaker with respect to social than economic matters,[48] but thought that the High Authority had interpreted its powers too narrowly. The committee argued that Articles 2 and 3, which voice the ultimate goals of the Community, are as much a part of the treaty as the articles on specific measures.[49] These articles would permit the High Authority, said the committee, to define and promote the social objectives by granting loans only to enterprises that propose to improve human, as well as technical, conditions in the plant and to give labor a share in the benefits of rising productivity.

The High Authority subsequently gave more attention to social problems in its fifth annual report. But it still believed that potential achievements were limited by the ECSC treaty itself and the partial integration it represented because labor policy, being indivisible, must be applied to all workers, not only to coal and steel workers.[50]

The High Authority, taking a more flexible position, nevertheless promised to take advantage of all possibilities to stimulate labor, management and the governments with respect to social policy, and to make intensive studies of industrial hygiene, mine safety, the relation of earnings to productivity and other related subjects. It promised to develop a program to stabilize employment in coal mining by taking measures to finance stockpiling; it also promised to intensify the housing program.

[47] Common Assembly, Doc. No. 2, 1956–1957, p. 11.

[48] *Ibid.*, p. 9.

[49] Common Assembly, Doc. No. 11, 1956–1957, pp. 36 ff. This line of reasoning was also taken by the Common Assembly committee that criticized the High Authority's policy on corporate concentrations.

[50] HA, *Cinquième rapport général*, pp. 233 ff. See also EEC Commission, *Exposé sur la situation sociale dans la Communauté*, September 1958.

The High Authority was later encouraged by the prospects opened by the EEC, for with the latter some of the limitations arising from partial integration were removed. Greater coordination of governmental policies on full employment, labor mobility and social security legislation became possible in the EEC framework. None of the executive divisions of the three Communities—the ECSC, Euratom, the EEC—can now, President Finet of the High Authority of the ECSC pointed out, proceed alone with respect to social affairs, for progress will depend on collaboration.[51]

This chapter concludes the discussion, begun in Chapter 11, dealing with the three main fields—commercial policy, transport rates and social policy—in which the national States have constitutionally retained their sovereignty. The earlier chapters showed that the national States also have continued to exercise power in the fields from which they were supposed to have withdrawn.

The next, and concluding, chapter will isolate some of the factors that are responsible for the persistent influence of the national State.

[51] Common Assembly, Doc. No. 21, 1958, pp. 39–41.

CHAPTER 14

THE ROAD AHEAD

Those who promoted the ECSC expected many things of it though different groups of supporters emphasized different goals—greater average efficiency by means of greater regional specialization and trade; the substitution of federal for national power over many economic activities; greater intergovernmental cooperation with respect to the activities over which the individual States were still sovereign (transport, social affairs, energy, external commercial policy). The proponents also wished to promote Franco-German friendship, to stimulate fusion in other fields of economic activity and to lay the foundations for eventual political federation. Though a simple evaluation would not do justice to an evolving institution as complex as the ECSC, none of the predictions of the dire consequences voiced by some of its opponents—drastic shifts in the location of production, the growth of German hegemony, the development of bureaucratic control by the High Authority—have come true.

GREATER AVERAGE EFFICIENCY

The coal and steel industries were not the most tractable ones with which to start the experiment of freeing trade and prices because freight costs in both industries tend to create separate markets, because of the structure of ownership and the long history of concerted practices, because individual governments exercise strong influence over the two industries, and because the coal industry is so labor intensive.

Steel

Competition through the price mechanism has not been legislated into existence in the steel industry as the means for raising average efficiency through greater regional specialization. Nor is this surprising. Concentration of control and restrictive methods appear to be too ingrained to enable the common market thus far to break through national and international patterns of concentration or to turn back the influence of national producers or of the indi-

403

vidual governments making for coordination among national groups. But the common market disturbed habitual ways, and may have induced a change to more spontaneous methods, of restriction in the steel industry. It therefore promoted a desire on the part of firms or groups of firms to capture a larger share of the market. By inducing the steel firms to strengthen their individual position, the common market hastened the trend to concentration, hence reducing the number of producers. This process was in some cases accompanied by the formation of larger facilities leading to lower costs of production, though some concentrations did not contribute to this end and all of them served other purposes as well. Greater economies of scale through concentration may, however, well be one of the results of the early history of the common market so far as the steel industry is concerned. It still remains to be seen whether that effect will persist. But this process does not seem to have affected the Italian industry, where the average plant is very small.

Practices in the ECSC steel industry are closer in spirit to those in the United Kingdom in spite of formal differences in the rules. Government control of capital investments is accepted practice in the United Kingdom, and is by no means foreign to the steel industry in the ECSC, where most of the individual governments—rather than the High Authority—influence the rate of expansion and self-financing by less organized and less articulate measures. The free price mechanism in steel has been explicitly rejected by the British government; it does not operate in the ECSC either, though it is part of the official dogma of the High Authority, because the individual governments have tacitly rejected it, too. The ECSC thus suffers from a divergence between theory and practice and a fragmentation of authority.

Coal

The ECSC faces a unique problem in the coal industry. That industry is now operated on the principle that mines in the same district be guaranteed a share of the market regardless of differences in cost, that miners' incomes be stabilized and that the industry as a whole be protected from other sources of energy. Though the methods used are not always successful or adequate to the ends they serve, the system is in any case underpinned by the governments with different degrees of determination. Any attempt to introduce a radical change in these concepts of stabilization and control would not only run up against the desire for security, whether on a national or regional basis, but also against the coexistence of public and private systems of ownership—a fact that makes it difficult to subject the whole Community to competitive mechanisms. Improvements in average efficiency through greater regional specialization in coal production therefore depend in present circumstances not on the price mechanism but on administrative decision and coordination. Attainment of the best results for the least amount of capital thus far has depended on exhortations from the High Authority, hoping that each country or mining district will plan its future with the welfare of the Community as a whole in mind.

As the coal producing units in the industry are shielded from internal rivalry, so the industry as a whole is more or less protected, varying with the individual country, from other forms of energy. Here, too, attainment of a federal policy in the general interest—one that will promote the lowest possible cost consistent with security of supply—depends on intergovernmental agreement because no Community has jurisdiction over all the forms of energy, the ECSC being responsible for coal, Euratom for nuclear energy, and petroleum not being intergovernmentally regulated at all. Each individual government, controlling some aspect of all forms of energy and represented in the various Communities, is the least common administrative denominator. Though the six countries have been converging toward more regulation, many of the national interests are divisive rather than common, the major difference being between energy exporting and energy importing countries. In the absence of stronger federal authority, Communitywide coordination therefore raises the problem of intergovernmental accommodation.

THE ECSC AS A SEPARATE COMMUNITY

Is there any reason for the ECSC's being outside the European Economic Community? The fundamental differences between the ECSC and the European Economic Community are: First, trade in coal and steel between member countries was completely freed of customs barriers in 1953, whereas trade, with some exceptions, will not be completely freed in the EEC before 1970–1973. Second, the ECSC treaty provides for more federal authority than the EEC treaty, but this difference will probably disappear in fact because the individual governments are likely to be equally important in both Communities. Third, the ECSC treaty is stricter than the EEC treaty with respect to concentrations and discriminatory prices but the differences regarding concentrations will probably disappear because both Communities live in the same economic and political atmosphere.

The governments might therefore find it worthwhile to consider incorporating the coal and steel industries into the European Economic Community when customs barriers are completely abolished in the latter Community some time after 1970. Cooperation between the two Communities and between the governments is so important that the ECSC's status as the first-born child of the European federal movement does not require it to have a permanently separate existence. If the coal and steel industries require particular rules with respect to basing points, price publication and freight absorption, then those rules could be incorporated in the EEC treaty as well. But Euratom owes its separate existence to the fact that it deals with very special matters, covering not only the development of nuclear power but the control of nuclear materials. Even if it were included in one of the other communities, it would still require a separate administration and separate rules.

In September 1959 the French Minister of Foreign Affairs advised the (French) Parliamentary Committee of Foreign Affairs that the government thought the supranational features of the ECSC should be eliminated by amending the Treaty and that a memorandum to that effect would be sent to the other States in the ECSC. His reasons, somewhat vague, rested on the weaknesses shown by the ECSC in the coal crisis of 1958–1959. But *Handelsblatt* reported that France, with Sahara oil, no longer feared the Ruhr, and therefore no longer needed to sacrifice some of her sovereignty to the ECSC for the sake of curbing the Ruhr. The German coal industry for its part also wished to have the Treaty revised but simply for the sake of eliminating the pricing regulations that deal with publicity, discrimination and freight absorption.[1]

SUPRANATIONAL POWER

Since the ECSC provides for government by federal institutions as well as for an economic union, it raises questions of power as well as of trade. A true federal power would be superordinate to the member governments in the fields from which the latter had agreed to retire, and would have independent political resources with which to buttress its wishes.

But the High Authority operates with the consent of the governments because they have retained power even in those fields in which it was to have been surrendered to the Community. Experience with prices, jurisdiction over which is expressly lodged with the Community, clearly indicates that the individual States are still sovereign. The ECSC thus bears, in the words of one observer, "a closer resemblance to the various intergovernmental bodies than its founders intended."[2] Jean Monnet, the head of the French delegation at the drafting conference for the ECSC treaty in 1950, inspired with courageous idealism, had more or less successfully advanced the thesis that the Community

---

[1] *Handelsblatt*, September 11–12, 1959, p. 1, September 14, p. 1.

[2] Ben T. Moore, *NATO and the Future of Europe*, Harper, New York, 1958, p. 145.

should have supranational power. But the views of the Dutch delegation at the ECSC treaty drafting conference have proved to be more realistic. The Dutch thought that it would not be possible to exclude the governments from the decision-making process because their responsibilities are essentially indivisible.[3] Their thesis was mainly responsible for the powers assigned to the Council of Ministers, which proved to be even more important in fact than in law.

Why is this so? The growth of responsibility for public welfare by the individual governments, the lack of popular representation in the ECSC, and the rudimentary nature of federal loyalties are responsible for the weakness of the federal authority in the ECSC vis-à-vis the individual States.

Weakness of ECSC

Responsibilities of Individual Governments

The individual governments have been increasingly using the powerful instruments of the modern State to stabilize and equalize income, production and employment. Although the modern State has interfered with international integration, it nevertheless has furthered the process of national integration for the sake of reducing risk and equalizing income, often by means of influencing the price mechanism.[4]

Since an economic union will hurt someone in the short run in order to promote the general interest in the long run, it places the individual governments before a dilemma. They must either relax their separate responsibility for stabilization in order to give play to the effects of the union or else go further along the road to federation by transferring their own powers over the public welfare to the federal authorities. The latter course would give the federal authorities control over the all-important monetary and fiscal policies.[5] This course, tantamount to political federation, goes further than the States were originally prepared to go. The process of integration has instead been shifted to intergovernmental negotiation and accommodation. Far from rolling the

[3] Georges Goriely, *Naissance de la Communauté Européenne du Charbon et de l'Acier*, HA, Luxembourg, No. 7889/56f (mimeo.).

[4] These subjects are treated by Gunnar Myrdal, *An International Economy*, Harper, New York, 1956, pp. 3–4; William Y. Elliott, *The Political Economy of American Foreign Policy*, Holt, New York, 1955, p. 246; Walt Rostow, *The Process of Economic Growth*, Norton, New York, 1952, pp. 231, 235, 255.

[5] Tibor Scitovsky, *Economic Theory and Western European Integration*, Allen and Unwin, London, 1958, pp. 17, 97–99, recommended the establishment of a Communitywide "employment policy administered by a supranational employment authority" with power to guide investments in order to stabilize employment and avoid balance of payments difficulties. François Perroux, in an article in *Le Marché commun et ses problèmes*, Sirey, Paris, 1958, advocated the creation of a central monetary and stabilization agency within the framework of the EEC, equivalent to a central bank, for the sake of coordinating the growth of the national product and productivity between countries. The European Parliamentary Assembly in 1959 also recommended, as reported in *Handelsblatt*, January 21, 1959, p. 1, a Communitywide central bank, on the model of the Federal Reserve System, to lay the basis for a common monetary policy.

individual States back, economic union thus has increased rather than reduced the need for intergovernmental negotiation and agreement.

The founders of the ECSC and the EEC tried to reconcile the objective of freer trade in an economic union with the requirements of public responsibility in four ways: first, they continued the competence of the individual State over transport, monetary and fiscal policy, the movement of labor and capital, social security legislation and the treatment of agriculture; second, they provided an escape from the normal provisions of the treaties in case of "crisis"; third, they authorized the federal authorities to influence prices and production in some circumstances; and, fourth, they provided machinery for intergovernmental coordination.[6]

The various Communities were supported by a wide range of political parties that by no means share a common political philosophy regarding the proper mixture of freer trade and public responsibility.

European liberals usually regard unification as an opportunity to dismantle not only the controls whose purpose is economic nationalism, but also most other kinds of governmental intervention in the economic process. Cartel-minded industrialists would like to achieve unification of their industries by extending and formalizing their national and international forms of restrictive "industrial self-government." European socialists think of economic union in terms of supranational socialism and not as a way of creating greater scope for private business enterprise.[7]

These differences have not interfered with the creation of a new international order among the Six but they have weakened the operations of the ECSC.

Owing to the growth of the public power, European unification in the mid-twentieth century is more complex—and more difficult—than American unification in the late eighteenth century. Each of the treaties for the three European Communities is a complex constitutional and law-making document that tries to prescribe for a multitude of specific problems. Jacob Viner has called attention to the problem of reconciling economic union with governmental responsibility in the following words:[8]

There has occurred . . . since 1914, and especially since the 1930's, a new development which makes the removal of trade barriers between countries with important actual or potential economic relations a much more formidable matter than it was in the nineteenth century. This is the growth of governmental intervention in industry, and especially of planned economies, socialist or otherwise. In the nineteenth century, the free market predominated, prices were flexible and unregulated,

[6] See the article by Jacques Rueff in *Le Monde*, February 9–10, 1958, p. 5, and that by Bertil Ohlin in *Le Marché commun et ses problèmes*.

[7] Elliott, *op. cit.*, p. 285.

[8] Jacob Viner, *The Customs Union Issue*, Carnegie Endowment for International Peace, New York, 1950, pp. 136–138.

exchange rates were relatively stable without need of exchange control, and costs were not made rigid by wage regulation, social security programs, cartelization, or extensive collective bargaining. Under these circumstances the removal of a tariff, while it might cause temporary shock, could fairly rapidly be adjusted to, and all that a tariff protected was the given allocation of resources. Now, however, tariffs and other barriers to trade—quotas, import licenses, exchange controls, state import monopolies, etc.—protect not merely the allocation of employed resources but the whole artificial national price and wage structures, the volume of employment, the social security programs, the exchange rate pegs, the monetary and fiscal policies, and so forth. . . . Two neighboring countries contemplating complete customs union today must therefore contemplate also the necessity of harmonizing their general patterns of economic controls, which would involve a much more complete degree of economic unification than would a representative nineteenth-century customs union . . . Whatever may be the strength of the economic case for uniformity for its own sake . . . it is exceedingly difficult politically to negotiate it and to maintain it once negotiated unless it is brought about through a process of substantial political unification.

The difficulties of economic union are allayed by economic expansion and exacerbated by recession. The troubles of the coal industry in the recession of 1958 are a case in point. Intergovernmental differences proved to be an obstacle at that time to the adoption of any effective Communitywide measures. The success of economic union is therefore greatly dependent on continuous economic expansion, which enables the individual governments to relax their responsibilities and to give greater play to the forces generated by freer trade.

Partial unions like the ECSC—even the EEC is partial in the sense that it does not embrace all the public powers exercised by States—are particularly affected by the conflict between the general welfare of individual countries and the effects of economic union in particular industries. As a case in point, the effect of the 1958 devaluation of the French franc upon the price of French steel in the rest of the Community has already been discussed in Chapter 7.[9]

Integration, Representation and Federal Loyalties

Since the European Parliamentary Assembly is appointed by the national parliaments and is not elected by direct suffrage, the High Authority has no direct access to the public or its representatives. Though it is the most "European"-minded of all the institutions, the Assembly cannot legislate. The High Authority has, however, tried to influence the national governments by using the Assembly for moral support.

The High Authority consequently has not had available or been able to create a "public opinion" with the help of which it might have swayed the

[9] Several potential distortions created by partial unions like the ECSC are mentioned by Scitovsky, *op. cit.*, pp. 137 ff, but have not materialized thus far.

groups or governments it has had to influence. The idea of integration is widely but vaguely accepted by the general population, which is not as yet, however, motivated by a hard core of economic interest.

Has the national orientation of specific interest groups been loosened by the ECSC? National legislation and national administrative policies affecting costs, prices and profits are still of major interest to the coal and steel firms. Home prices for steel and coal are still influenced by the national governments and national producer groups. Labor costs are still influenced by national bargaining and national payroll taxes. And taxes on income, as well as amortization allowances, are still governed by the national State. The labor unions are interested in the market for labor, in wage rates and social security legislation. These matters, too, are still within the scope of the national State. Though the firms and the labor unions maintain contact with the institutions of the ECSC, sometimes through newly organized international interest groups, their orientation to the national State is still much more intense and more important than that to the Community. Their political power, furthermore, is still exercised in and through the national State.

Without the ability to summon European loyalties with which to override or balance particular interests, the High Authority has been caught in a crossfire of private as well as governmental interests. The amorphous consumer has scant means of influencing the ECSC. The organized merchants, importers and steel transformers in the Consultative Committee represent industrial rather than general consumer interests. Though some governments represent an importing interest—Italy of coal; the Netherlands of steel; France of coking coal—the governments in the main represent producers' interests, bolstered by producers' associations. The national imperative sometimes overrides the divided interest; the German steel transformers, for example, against their own interest, voted early in 1959 with the German steel producers in the Consultative Committee for a higher price for French steel delivered to other parts of the Community.

Popular support for community is still in its infancy and remains to be deepened and spread. Without direct popular loyalties it will be difficult to carry out the sacrifices entailed by economic union or to submerge national interests in the communitywide interest.

CONCLUSION

Out of its own practical experience, the High Authority said:[10]

Although the industries in a common market constitute a good test of the competitive ability of an economy, experience has shown that governments do not man-

[10] *Sixième rapport général*, Vol. I, p. 15.

age their general economic policy on the basis of the competitive conditions of two of their industries, however important they may be. The effectiveness of the measures [with respect to coal and steel] have been limited. The High Authority firmly believes that economic policies will be more effectively and spontaneously coordinated as integration becomes wider and each country's stake in integration is extended.

The difficulties encountered by a partial economic union devoid of political power, the so-called functional approach, can be resolved only within a union encompassing more activities and more central power. New activities have been added through the European Economic Community and Euratom, but the dosage of federalized central power has been reduced.

Still at the threshold of its existence in 1959, the movement for European federation had taken the first steps to create a new framework for deciding existing problems, a framework that provides greater territorial range for improving the use and yield of resources than any of the constituent countries can provide. But developments are still at the mercy of the individual member States. Further integration will therefore depend on the policies brought forth by the processes of intergovernmental compromise.[11]

It remains to be seen whether or not the addition of two new Communities to the ECSC will provide the push toward a more integral type of federation, whether it will impel governments to take the political decisions to coordinate fiscal and monetary policies and to pave the way for political federation itself. Much will depend on the political currents in the member States, on whether the dominant political groups continue to promote European federation or whether they have reservations about it. The need is for more, not less, integration.

[11] Cf. Ernst B. Haas, *The Uniting of Europe*, Stanford University Press, Stanford, 1958, pp. 451–527. He believes that the six governments in Little Europe have developed a process of compromise "more federal in nature" than that shown by other intergovernmental bodies.

APPENDICES

NOTES AND

ABBREVIATIONS

GENERAL NOTES

TRANSLATIONS BY AUTHOR

Translations from non-English sources, unless otherwise indicated, were made by the author. Such sources are readily identifiable, since titles of non-English sources used are given in the language of the original, though dates and place names may be given in English.

TERMINOLOGY

Coal and solid fuels. All references to coal, unless otherwise indicated, are to "hard coal" in the European terminology, which includes anthracite and bituminous coal combined but excludes brown coal or lignite. The term solid fuels refers to hard coal and its derivatives (coke and, unless otherwise indicated, briquettes and other manufactured products).

Metric tons. All tonnage figures unless otherwise indicated are in metric tons of 2,204.6 pounds as compared with 2,000 pounds for the American short ton and 2,240 pounds for the British long ton.

IRON ORE CONTENT

Unless otherwise indicated, iron ore imported by continental and British steel producers is calculated at an average iron content of 55 per cent. Domestic ores presently mined in these countries have an average iron content of:

	Per Cent
Germany	31–35
France	33
Luxembourg	30
Italy	45
United Kingdom	33

(Data are from ECE, *Quarterly Bulletin of Steel Statistics*, Geneva.)

CONVERSION RATIOS

The conversion ratios used follow; they do not necessarily apply to data taken from other sources.

STEEL

Product	Equivalent in Crude Steel
Semifinished steel (semis)	1.15
Railway material	1.25
Shapes and sections	1.25
Bars and rods	1.25
Strip and hoop	1.25
Wire rod	1.35
Tubes	1.35
Flat products	1.40

METALLURGICAL COKE

	Equivalent in Coal	
	Interwar Years	Post–World War II
Western Germany	1.25	1.33
Saar	1.54	1.32
France	1.29	1.33
Belgium	1.31	1.30
Netherlands	1.35	1.32
United Kingdom	1.47	1.49

(Based on figures showing actual yield as reported in ECE, *Quarterly Bulletin of Coal Statistics*, Geneva.)

ENERGY

Source	Unit	Tons, in Coal Equivalents of 12,500 BTU per Unit
Petroleum products	1 ton	1.50
Lignite	1 ton	0.30
Natural gas	1,000 cubic meters	1.33
Manufactured gas	1,000 cubic meters	0.60
Thermal power	1,000 K.W.H.	0.60*

* Based on average operating results in the ECSC in 1955. Owing to expected improvements in efficiency, a conversion ratio of 0.4 was used for 1975.

ABBREVIATIONS AND BIBLIOGRAPHIC NOTES

Because of the many lengthy and cumbersome titles of publications and organizations cited repeatedly in this study, names of organizations have been abbreviated frequently and short forms have been used for titles of many books and periodicals. A key to these abbreviations and short forms follows. Thereafter is a key to the symbols used in tabular material.

ORGANIZATIONS

ATIC	Association Technique de l'Importation Charbonnière (France)
CECA	Communauté Européenne du Charbon et de l'Acier (European Coal and Steel Community)
DKV	Deutsche Kohlenverkauf (Germany)
ECE	Economic Commission for Europe
ECSC	European Coal and Steel Community
EEC	European Economic Community
EIA	Entente Internationale de l'Acier
ESC	European Steel Cartel
Euratom	European Atomic Energy Community
GATT	General Agreement on Tariffs and Trade
GIS	Groupement de l'Industrie Sidérurgique (France)
HA	High Authority (of the ECSC)
IAR	International Authority for the Ruhr (1949–1953)
ILO	International Labor Office
ISC	International Steel Cartel
NCB	National Coal Board (United Kingdom)
NPA	National Planning Association (Washington)
OEEC	Organization for European Economic Cooperation
OKU	Oberrheinische Kohlenunion (Germany)
RWKS	Rheinische-Westfälisches Kohlen Syndikat (Germany)

BOOKS AND PERIODICALS

Armengaud Report	*Avis*, Conseil de la République, No. 64, 1952, Paris
BID	*Bulletin d'information et de documentation*, published monthly by Banque Nationale de Belgique, Brussels
Chamberlin, *Monopoly*	Edward H. Chamberlin, ed., *Monopoly and Competition and Their Regulation*, Macmillan & Co., Ltd., London, 1954
Chambre Syndicale de la Sidérurgie Française (Paris):	
série verte	Data on monthly steel production
série rose	Irregular reports, each devoted to the steel industry of a particular country
série bleue	Irregular reports, each devoted to the steel trade of a particular country
Comité Mixte report	*Etude sur la structure et les tendances de l'économie énergetique dans les pays de la Communauté*, Comité Mixte, CECA, Luxembourg, no date
Comparaison	HA, *Comparaison des revenus réels des travailleurs des industries de la Communauté*, October 1956
Eisen und Stahl Jahrbuch	Wirtschaftsvereinigung Eisen und Stahl, *Statistisches Jahrbuch*, Verlag Stahleisen, Düsseldorf
FRB	*Bulletin*, published monthly by the Federal Reserve Board, Washington
Import Duties Advisory Committee, *Report*	*Report of the Import Duties Advisory Committee on the Present Position and Future Development of the Iron and Steel Industry*, HMSO, London, July 1937

Inventaire	*Inventaire des productions charbonnières et sidérurgiques dans les départements du Nord et du Pas-de-Calais*, Rapport de la Ire Sous-Commission, Le Comité d'Etudes Régionales Economiques et Sociales, Lille, July 1955
Jahrbuch	*Jahrbuch des deutschen Bergbaus*, published annually by Verlag Glückauf, Essen
Journal officiel	A publication of the ECSC containing official decrees (The publication of the same name published by the French government is cited herein as *Journal officiel de la République Française*.)
Kohlenwirtschaft	*Die Kohlenwirtschaft der Welt in Zahlen*, Verlag Glückauf, Essen, 1955
New York Times	References are to the international edition unless otherwise indicated
"Objectifs généraux"	Published by the High Authority in *Journal officiel*, May 20, 1957
Reid Report	*Coal Mining*, Report of the Technical Advisory Committee, Charles C. Reid, Chairman, HMSO, London, 1945
Statistische Übersicht	*Statistische Übersicht über die Kohlenwirtschaft im Jahre 1936*, in *Jahresbericht des Reichskohlenverbandes, 1936–37*
Statistisches Bundesamt, Düsseldorf	*Die Eisen- und Stahlindustrie*, Statistische Vierteljahresheft (quarterly), Statistisches Bundesamt, Düsseldorf
Statistisches Bundesamt, Wiesbaden	*Die Grosshandelspreise im Ausland*, W. Kohlhammer Verlag, Stuttgart (quarterly)
Tinbergen Report	*Report on the Problems Raised by the Different Turnover Tax Systems Applied Within the Common Market*, prepared by the Committee of Experts (Jan Tinbergen, Chairman) set up under HA Order No. 1–53, dated March 5, 1953
Wolf Report	"Report on Plants Scheduled for Removal as Reparations from the Three Western Zones of Germany," Economic Cooperation Administration, Industrial Advisory Committee, Washington, January 10, 1949
Wolf-Rodé, *Handbuch*	*Handbuch für den Gemeinsamen Markt der Europäischen Montan-Union*, Montan- und Wirtschaftsverlag K. Wolf-Rodé, K. G., Frankfurt am Main, 1955–1956

SYMBOLS USED IN TABULAR MATERIAL

—	Nil; by contrast, 0 is used for a quantity less than .5, and 0.0 for a quantity less than 0.05
. . .	Data not available
( )	Parentheses around a figure indicate that it was estimated by the author

VARIETIES OF

COAL AND STEEL

PROCESSING OF STEEL
AND ITS RAW MATERIALS[1]

Conventional steel plants manufacture iron and steel in three stages: (1) Iron ore is smelted in a blast furnace to produce pig iron. (2) The pig iron is then converted into steel in a steel furnace—open hearth (called Siemens-Martin in Europe), Thomas or electric. (3) The solid steel, called crude or ingot, is then worked, primarily by rolling in the solid state, into basic forms such as blooms, billets, slabs, sheets, plates, bars, wire rod, tube, rails and structural shapes. Some of the steel also is cast in molten form into complicated shapes for more specialized uses.

Iron ore is smelted in order to eliminate impurities and to reduce the ore to metal. Besides iron, the ore contains oxygen and various impurities. In the blast furnace the oxygen is removed by the coke, which also provides heat for the reaction. The coke must be hard and porous in order to permit air to circulate through the blast furnace; efficient heat conversion would otherwise be hindered. Coke accounts for the major part of the coal required for steel production. The remaining impurities in pig iron are eliminated in the steel furnace. The lower the iron content, the greater the amount of ore and coke required. High quality ores may contain as much as 65 per cent iron; the lower limit of iron content is about 30 per cent. To produce one ton of pig iron, from 1.5 to 3.3 tons of ore and 0.9 to 1.2 tons of coke are therefore required, plus about 0.5 tons of limestone. Some ores themselves contain limestone. The blast furnace produces valuable by-product gas, slag for building purposes, and fertilizer if the ore contains phosphorus.

The type of steel furnace used depends on the relative supply and cost of coke, iron ore and scrap. The electric furnace, requiring scrap and consuming large amounts of electricity, is used where scrap is plentiful or where the other raw materials are costly. Since the process can be closely controlled, it yields a high quality of steel and is also used to satisfy a specialized demand, even where other raw materials are available.

---

[1] See American Iron and Steel Institute, "Picture Story of Steel," n.d.; also, for a good brief description, Harold Wien, "Iron and Steel," in Sam H. Schurr and Jacob Marschak, *Economic Aspects of Atomic Power*, Princeton University Press, Princeton, 1950.

The open-hearth and Thomas furnaces were invented in the 1870s and made possible the rapid growth of the steel industry. The Thomas furnace operates with pig iron, the open hearth with a combination of pig iron and scrap. The Thomas furnace is used where pig iron is made from ore that is high in phosphorus, an impurity, and, generally, low in iron content, because it effectively removes this impurity. The Bessemer process, theretofore in use and still used on a small scale, is unable to eliminate phosphorus and therefore limits the kind of ore that can be used. With the Thomas furnace (an adaptation of the Bessemer), the Lorraine ores became usable. The open-hearth furnace gives a higher quality of steel but the Thomas process, improved in recent years with the oxygen blast, can now yield a grade adequate for nearly any specifications of carbon steel. The Thomas furnace, operating at a cycle of about one hour per charge, compared with twelve hours for the open hearth, economizes on heat but consumes a greater amount of coking coal per ton of steel inasmuch as it uses more pig iron.

The supply of scrap comes from two sources: (1) When crude steel is rolled, only 65 to 80 per cent of the steel is recovered in shaping; the more finished the product, the greater the loss. The steel industry thus has its own recurrent supply of scrap, referred to as "generating," "new" or "circulating" scrap. (2) Industrialized countries obtain an additional source from obsolescent equipment (ships, automobiles, railroads, etc.), called "capital" or "old" scrap. Most integrated steel firms produce some open-hearth steel in order to consume their own circulating scrap. Scrap is sometimes also used in the blast furnace to produce pig iron.

Where the ore used for pig iron is of suitable quality and the scrap supply is ample nearly all the steel may be produced in open-hearth furnaces (plus some electric steel), as in the United Kingdom and the United States. The open-hearth process reduces the investment in blast furnace facilities. Other countries balance the Thomas and open-hearth process to obtain the most economical result. Germany has a higher ratio of open hearth to Thomas than the Saar, France and Belgium, while Luxembourg produces only Thomas steel. Italy, where raw materials are scarce, relies largely on the electric process in the north and on Thomas and open-hearth steel at tidewater.

Owing to the large use of heavy raw materials of low unit value, to the large conversion losses and to the large requirements for processing heat, the steel industry must be close to its raw materials or to low-cost transport in order to keep assembly costs down. The successive stages of production, furthermore, must be geographically and technically integrated in order to economize on energy requirements. In an integrated plant, pig iron and crude steel are used without reheating, coke oven and blast furnace gases are used in subsequent melting and heating processes and surplus gas, if any, is sold to the public distribution system or used to produce electricity.

The use of a low-grade ore makes it desirable to locate at the source of ore supply even if the coal must be obtained elsewhere. Generally, only high-grade ore is brought to the coal. In recent years both high-grade ore and coal have been brought increasingly to the scrap, i.e., to the urban and industrial center, where the steel producer can save outbound freight on the finished steel. Location at tidewater—since maritime haulage is the least costly form of transport—also has increased in recent years as domestic raw material supplies have grown scarcer or imported supplies relatively cheaper.

TYPES AND USES OF COAL

Coal is used to produce coke, steam and heat. Although the steel industry takes a large proportion of the coal in industrialized countries, the major part of the coal supply is used for other purposes: space heating alone takes 20 per cent of the coal in many countries; electricity plants also are large consumers. Most consumers require a particular category and size of coal. Although many categories are interchangeable, some grades are not; anthracite, for example, is not readily adaptable for coke or gas production. But many types of coal have been successfully used for purposes conventionally considered unsuitable.[2]

The particular grades suitable for coking are called coking coals; among other characteristics, they have a volatile content of 26 to 32 per cent, though the range can be increased if coals are blended, and they must yield a porous but firm coke low in ash, sulphur and other impurities. Coal is charged into the coke ovens in small sizes—under 10 mm.; these sizes are produced either by sizing and preparation or, if necessary, by crushing.

The larger sizes of coke, over 80 mm., are preferred for blast furnace use, but sizes as small as 60 or even 40 mm. are also used if coke is scarce. The smaller sizes are sold for heating.

Where coking coal is plentiful, as in Germany, it is used for purposes other than coking. Anthracite, which is hard in texture and below 10 per cent in volatile matter, is used mainly for heating; the very small sizes of anthracite are used to produce briquettes (brick-shaped masses of coal dust mixed with pitch, used for fuel). The bituminous coals below 26 per cent volatile are used for steam raising, domestic heating, cement works and bunker fuel. Those above 32 per cent volatile are used for making gas, for locomotive power, reverberatory furnaces, and also for heating if other coal is scarce. The modern electric power plant uses a low-grade, high-ash coal, practically in the form of dust. Hence it is often located near or is operated by the coal mine, and provides an increasingly important outlet for the growing volume of unsalable high-ash coal generated by the use of mechanical cutting and loading equipment underground.

[2] See ILO, *The World Coal-Mining Industry*, Geneva, 1938, Vol. I, pp. 17–24, for a discussion of the interchangeability of types of coal.

THE CONCENTRATION

MOVEMENT IN THE

FRENCH STEEL INDUSTRY

AFTER WORLD WAR II

Six major regroupings occurred in the French steel industry between 1948 and 1956. These regroupings were as follows:[1]

(1) Two large steel enterprises in the north, Denain-Anzin and Forges et Aciéries du Nord et de l'Est, in 1948 merged all their plants, except for their iron ore mines, to create Usinor. With the help of Marshall Plan credits, Usinor in 1950–1951 installed a continuous strip mill and a cold finishing mill of American manufacture. Although the iron ore mines are incorporated separately, they are a captive source of raw material for Usinor. This combination antedates the ECSC.

(2) Sidelor in Lorraine (Pont-à-Mousson group) is the end of a complex series of financial transactions which principally involved two financial groups which merged their facilities in Lorraine toward the end of 1950. The Pont-à-Mousson group contributed the old Rombas plant, most of the facilities of Aciéries de Micheville, and the Briey division of Fonderies de Pont-à-Mousson. It was compensated with a 63 per cent interest in Sidelor. Another group, Forges et Aciéries de la Marine et d'Homécourt, contributed its plants in Lorraine in return for a 35 per cent interest in Sidelor. But Marine et d'Homécourt retained its plants in the Centre-Midi. In 1952 Marine et d'Homécourt absorbed a firm in the Centre-Midi and changed into Forges et Aciéries de la Marine et de Saint-Etienne. Pont-à-Mousson and Marine

---

[1] Data are from Centre de Recherches Economiques et Sociales, *La Concentration financière dans la sidérurgie française*, Paris, April 1956. Albert Wehrer (the Luxembourg member of the High Authority), *Les Fusions et concentrations d'entreprises dans les pays de la CECA*, Luxembourg, November 1955, pp. 12–16, is recommended for collateral substantiation on some points. "Mergers in the ECSC," reprinted from *Monthly Statistical Bulletin*, British Iron and Steel Federation, May 1955, is also recommended. Wolf-Rodé, *Handbuch*, p. 186, gives data on plants, firms and occasionally on stock ownership and can also provide the raw material for an analysis of interlocking directorates. See also Herbert Steiner, *Grössenordnung und horizontale Verflechtung in der Eisen- und Stahlindustrie der Vereinigten Staaten, Grossbritanniens, Frankreichs, Belgiens, Luxembourgs und Deutschlands*, Kieler Studien, Kiel, 1952; Hans Wolter, *Die französische eisenschaffende Industrie*, Schrobsdorff'sche Buchhandlung, Düsseldorf, 1953.

et Saint-Etienne constitute one group. Marine et Saint-Etienne has a minority participation in firms where Pont-à-Mousson has the majority, while Pont-à-Mousson has a minority interest in firms where the other has the majority. Thus Marine et Saint-Etienne has a minority interest in Sidelor and in Hadir (Luxembourg), both of which are controlled by Pont-à-Mousson. The latter has a minority interest in Allevard (a firm in the Alpine region of France that produces special steel) and Anderny-Chévillon (iron ore mine), which are controlled by Marine et Saint-Etienne.

(3) In the course of 1952 and 1953 Marine et Saint-Etienne closed some of its plants in the Centre-Midi and concentrated production in the rest of them. In December 1953 it participated in the formation of Ateliers et Forges de la Loire. This fusion affected the facilities of several firms which produced special steel in Centre-Midi. Marine et Saint-Etienne contributed nearly all its facilities in the Centre-Midi and virtually became a holding company. Aciéries et Forges de Firminy contributed its plants in the Centre-Midi but retained the one at Les Dunes in the north. The firm of Jacob Holtzer was completely absorbed. Besides Ateliers et Forges de la Loire there were still two other major groups in the Centre-Midi, the Schneider group (Le Creusot) and a plant at Montluçon belonging to Chatillon-Commentry. In 1955 the latter joined forces with Ateliers et Forges de la Loire by creating a separate corporation for the Montluçon plant; Chatillon-Commentry retained 60 per cent control of the new corporation. Ateliers et Forges de la Loire acquired 40 per cent of it and compensated Chatillon-Commentry with 8 per cent of the shares of Ateliers et Forges de la Loire. Marine et Saint-Etienne has 44.5 per cent of Ateliers et Forges de la Loire; Firminy has 34 per cent; and the shareholders of the defunct Jacob Holtzer firm have 13.5 per cent. Owing to the ties between Pont-à-Mousson and Marine et Saint-Etienne, Ateliers et Forges de la Loire is herein considered part of that group. Though Sidelor was formed at the end of 1950 it may have been stimulated by the prospect of the ECSC. All the other transactions in the Centre-Midi described in paragraphs 2 and 3 above postdate the ECSC.

(4) Sollac, founded in 1948, is a new enterprise in Lorraine with new facilities financed with new capital. It began to operate in 1953. It essentially replaces the De Wendel group's old facilities in Lorraine, some of which were later absorbed by Lorraine-Escaut (see paragraph 5 below). Designed on the lines of Usinor, Sollac is controlled by the De Wendel group, which has a majority.[2] The Pont-à-Mousson group has 40 per cent; the Usinor group, Lorraine-Escaut and UCPMI also have a small interest. Sollac produces steel for further finishing by the stockholding firms; it does not produce for the open market. The formation of Sollac, which antedates the ECSC, laid the basis for De Wendel's transactions described in paragraph 5 below.

(5) Lorraine-Escaut, founded in January 1953, is one of the major units in the Longwy-Raty group; it comprises a number of plants in northern Lorraine and other

---

[2] De Wendel et Cie holds 45 per cent of the capital. J. J. Carnaud and Gueugnon, both in the De Wendel group, hold additional shares. Wolf-Rodé, *Handbuch*, p. 186.

plants in the north of France and in the Ardennes. Five companies ceded all or part of their facilities to the new firm. The Aciéries de Longwy, one of the five, owns 51 per cent of Lorraine-Escaut's stock; Jean Raty is a large stockholder in Aciéries de Longwy. The De Wendel group contributed facilities through a number of companies and holds in all 49 per cent of the stock, directly or through affiliated companies. In 1954 Lorraine-Escaut reached a long-term agreement with Forges d'Audincourt, producer of sheet for the electrical industry, by which the former became the source of raw metal and the latter closed its crude steel division. Lorraine-Escaut through Louvroil-Montbard-Aulnoye, subsidiary tube producers, owns about 21 per cent of the capital stock of UCPMI, which is herein consequently considered part of the Longwy-Raty group. Lorraine-Escaut was founded after the ECSC began.

(6) In 1955 the Schneider group, through Forges et Ateliers du Creusot, acquired an additional 33.5 per cent interest in Société Métallurgique d'Imphy, which produces quality steel, and concluded a specialization agreement with it.[3] Imphy was reimbursed with a 12 per cent participation in the Schneider firm. This transaction postdates the ECSC.

[3] "Wer sind die Eigentümer?" *Handelsblatt*, August 17, 1956.

THE RECONCENTRATION

MOVEMENT IN

GERMAN COAL AND STEEL

AFTER WORLD WAR II

The German coal and steel industries began to reconcentrate shortly after the ECSC began. The deconcentration pattern inherited by the ECSC from the allied occupation authorities in Germany proved unstable because the Germans understood that the Schuman Plan superseded the deconcentration program and would have opposed any attempt by the High Authority to freeze the corporate structure created under the allies.

The structure of corporate control of German coal and steel production in early 1959 is shown in Tables 5-4 through 5-7, Appendix E. Tables 5-4 and 5-6 show the operating firms (for steel and coal, respectively) approved or created by the allied deconcentration. Most firms retained their corporate identity after reconcentration, which was in most cases accomplished by purchase of stock rather than by merger.[1] The steel firms are classified by major stockholders—firms or groups that own stock—in Table 5-5, Appendix E, in order to show the amount of crude steel each group controls (production as of 1954–1955 but control as of early 1959). Table 5-7, Appendix E, contains the same type of information for coal (based on production in 1955).

THE VEREINIGTE STAHLWERKE COMPLEX

Prewar

Vereinigte Stahlwerke, never very stable during the interwar period, gave birth to some unstable offspring in the deconcentration program.[2]

---

[1] The merger of the Phoenix and Rheinische Röhrenwerke firms into Phoenix-Rheinrohr and the absorption of Essener Bergbau and of Mannesmann Hüttenwerke by Mannesmann A. G. were the major exceptions to this rule.

[2] When Vereinigte Stahlwerke was in financial difficulty in 1933 some of the constituent divisions were separately incorporated to facilitate management and probably also to overcome internal rivalries. See K. H. Herchenröder, *Die Nachfolger der Ruhrkonzerne*, Econ-Verlag, Düsseldorf, 1953, p. 63.

Merged in Vereinigte Stahlwerke in 1926, so far as the steel branch of that firm was concerned, were: the Phoenix group (which brought in tube producing plants); Bochumer Verein für Gusstahlfabrikation; the Thyssen group (August Thyssen Hütte) and Dortmund-Hörder. Some plants that specialized in steel forgings and castings for the engineering industries were brought in by the Rheinstahl group, but this group kept its mine, Arenberg, out of Vereinigte Stahlwerke.

Additional steel plants were brought in after 1926. Hüttenwerke Siegerland, quality sheet producer, was brought in later by Flick. Deutsche Edelstahl, producer of high-grade steel, was absorbed by Vereinigte Stahlwerke in 1936.

Coal mines were brought into Vereinigte Stahlwerke through the Gelsenkirchener Bergwerks A. G.; these supplied solid fuels to the steel division. Vereinigte Stahlwerke also included the Essener Steinkohlenbergwerke, which was not integrated technically with the steel division and later fell under Flick's control.

Deconcentrated Steel Firms from Vereinigte Stahlwerke

The allied deconcentration program essentially tried to restore the *status quo ante*. Each of the constituent parts of the steel division mentioned above was made a separate corporate entity. In addition, the tube producing plants were placed in a new firm called Rheinische Röhrenwerke. The facilities for producing wire rod and other rolled merchant steel were placed in a new firm called Niederrheinische Hütte. The assets that had been brought into Vereinigte Stahlwerke by the Rheinstahl group were assigned to the Rheinische Stahlwerke.[3]

Deconcentrated Coal Mining Firms from Vereinigte Stahlwerke

Vereinigte Stahlwerke also gave birth to nine coal mining firms.[4] The Essener mines also were incorporated separately. The allied authorities authorized the creation of a holding company, Gelsenkirchener Bergwerks A. G. (GBAG) for six of these new firms. GBAG holds 100 per cent of the capital stock in three of them— Rheinelbe, Dortmunder and Bochumer Bergbau (numbers 29, 30 and 31 in Table 5-6, Appendix E). GBAG holds 50 per cent of the stock in the other three—Hansa, Graf Moltke, and Carolinenglück (numbers 1, 18 and 19 in the same table). Steel firms were authorized to hold the remainder of the capital stock in the last three mining firms, as Table 5-6, Appendix E, shows.

POSTWAR RECONCENTRATION IN STEEL

Vereinigte Stahlwerke's offspring firms have proved to be quite mercurial.

The Thyssen Group

The Thyssen group has emerged as the most dynamic and powerful in the German

---

[3] Steel firms numbered 7, 10–17, inclusive, and 19 in Table 5-4, Appendix E, are the offspring of Vereinigte Stahlwerke. Two other offspring do not produce crude steel and therefore are omitted from that table. For a complete list, see Herchenröder, *op. cit.*, p. 81 and chart opposite p. 80.

[4] In Table 5-6, Appendix E, these are numbered 1, 13, 14, 15, 18, 19, 29, 30, 31. Essener is number 10. See also Herchenröder, *op. cit.*, chart opposite p. 64.

steel industry. Fritz Thyssen, the former owner, divided his estate between his wife, Amelie, and his daughter, Countess de Zichy, both of whom now live in Argentina. Their assets in Germany are held, respectively, by the Fritz Thyssen Vermögensverwaltung (FTV) and the Thyssen A. G. für Beteiligungen (TAGB). Combined they held 10.3 per cent in Vereinigte Stahlwerke. According to the allied sales provisions, each was entitled to acquire 100 per cent control of a new firm, no more than 5 per cent of another and to sell the rest. After deconcentration, FTV originally controlled Rheinische Röhrenwerke and had minority interests in Phoenix and in the August Thyssen Hütte. TAGB after deconcentration controlled Deutsche Edelstahl and had minority interests in the Niederrheinische Hütte and in the August Thyssen Hütte. Phoenix and Rheinische Röhrenwerke subsequently merged and FTV obtained over 50 per cent control of the merged firm, Phoenix-Rheinrohr. TAGB sold Deutsche Edelstahl and the Niederrheinische Hütte—in the second of which it had meanwhile obtained majority control—to August Thyssen Hütte. The latter reimbursed TAGB in share capital so that TAGB increased its minority interest in that firm. FTV and TAGB together control August Thyssen Hütte. Late in 1958 FTV sold its interest in Phoenix-Rheinrohr to August Thyssen Hütte in exchange for shares in the latter, which acquired Phoenix-Rheinrohr as a daughter company.[5] The merger was approved by the High Authority.

Some of the other steel branches of the former Vereinigte Stahlwerke also showed a tendency to recombine. Dortmund-Hörder obtained majority control of Hüttenwerke Siegerland, in which August Thyssen Hütte also acquired a 35 per cent minority interest.[6]

Klöckner, Hoesch, Mannesmann, Haniel Groups

In addition to breaking up Vereinigte Stahlwerke, the allied occupation authorities had also separated the several industrial activities conducted by each major *Konzern* or holding company and had established new unit firms for each type of operation. The prewar Hoesch *Konzern* is taken as an example. The Hoesch combine was liquidated; its steel operations were placed in several new firms, of which Westfalenhütte A. G. was the largest; its coal mines were placed in a new firm called Altenessener Bergwerks A. G. The parent company was incorporated as Hoesch Werke A. G. It held 100 per cent of the capital in the new daughter companies. In 1955 Hoesch Werke A. G. simply absorbed the capital stock of Altenessener in exchange for its own.[7]

The allied deconcentration authorities deconcentrated several other combines in parallel fashion, notably the Mannesmann complex and the Klöckner complex. Klöckner Werke A. G. later acquired the share capital of several of its daughter

---

[5] The fusion between the two wings of the Thyssen family was described in *Handelsblatt*, December 10, 1958, p. 9, and March 25, 1959, p. 10.

[6] *Ibid.*, October 14, 1957, p. 5.

[7] Wolf-Rodé, *Handbuch*, pp. 43, 45, 121.

firms in exchange for its own stock. Mannesmann A. G. did the same with respect to some of its daughter firms and then absorbed them completely in 1958.[8]

These transactions represented the first stage of reconcentration. But they can hardly be called "new" concentrations, for the individual daughter firms were under the same control before and after reconcentration. The reconcentration of the Gutehoffnungshütte complex (Haniel family) followed the same pattern. The Hüttenwerk Oberhausen, created by the deconcentration officials to operate the steelworks of the Haniel complex, later acquired majority control of the Bergbau A. G. Neue Hoffnung, which had been set up to operate the Haniel group's coal mines. The Haniel group had, however, never lost control of either of the two new firms.[9]

These transactions often involve an *Organschaftsvertrag* between the daughter and parent firm; it binds the former to transfer its profits to the latter. The remaining "free shareholders," if any, in the daughter firm often obtain a pledge of a guaranteed or minimum dividend.

The Krupp Group

Gusstahlwerke Bochumer Verein, another major offspring of Vereinigte Stahlwerke in the steel sector, fell under the control of the Krupp group late in 1958. After deconcentration, Gusstahlwerke Bochumer Verein had originally been sold to the Swedish group Axel Wenner-Gren. Under the "forced sale" provision, the Krupp group in 1956 had sold a majority bloc of shares in the mining firm Bergbau A. G. Constantin der Grosse to Gusstahlwerke Bochumer Verein. *Handelsblatt* called attention to the "community of interest" between the Krupp and Axel Wenner-Gren groups.[10] Late in 1958 the Krupp group, with the High Authority's approval, purchased 75 per cent of the capital stock of Gusstahlwerke Bochumer Verein.[11]

The forced sale by the Krupp group of Hüttenwerk Rheinhausen fell due in 1959 but the date was extended by the allied governments. The German government about February 1957 had requested the French, United Kingdom and United States governments to modify the forced sale obligations of the Paris Protocol of 1954 on the ground that the capital market could not absorb the sale of these assets without serious damage to the economy.[12] The High Authority ruled that the German

[8] *Ibid.*, pp. 73 ff for Mannesmann and pp. 63 ff for Klöckner. In Klöckner's case, the parent company reacquired control of Bergwerke Königsborn-Werne in 1953–1954. Mannesmann acquired control of the Essener Bergbau by decision of the deconcentration authorities. Essener had belonged to the Flick group before the war. Mannesmann's prewar mining properties were set up as Consolidation Bergbau by the deconcentration officials. Essener later absorbed Consolidation Bergbau by merger. Herchenröder, *op. cit.*, gives the prewar and postwar history of each firm affected by the deconcentration program. See also the report by the German Steel Trustee's Association, which supervised deconcentration for the allies: *Die Neuordnung der Eisen- und Stahlindustrie*, Beck, Berlin, 1954. Details on the 1958 Mannesmann merger may be found in *The Economist*, November 1, 1958, p. 428.

[9] Herchenröder, *op. cit.*, pp. 126 ff; *Handelsblatt*, August 14, 1957, p. 6.

[10] *Handelsblatt*, December 19, 1956, p. 5, and December 28, 1956, p. 1. Krupp also sold one steel firm to his sister.

[11] *Ibid.*, November 10, 1957, p. 5.

[12] *Le Monde*, May 17, 1957, p. 1, May 19-20, 1957, p. 5, February 4, 1959, p. 10; see also *New York Times*, March 22, 1956; *Handelsblatt*, May 22, 1957; *Financial Times*, May 20, 1957, p. 1, May 21, 1957, p. 11.

obligation is outside the jurisdiction of the ECSC because it arises from an inter-governmental agreement and not from Article 66.[13]

POSTWAR RECONCENTRATION IN COAL

The mines that were detached from the prewar steel groups (from Vereinigte Stahlwerke, the Krupp and the Flick groups) have played the main role in subsequent reconcentration. Emscher-Lippe had been detached from the Krupp group and placed in Hibernia, the State-controlled mining firm. In 1957 Hibernia sold 51 per cent of the share capital in Emscher-Lippe to Phoenix-Rheinrohr.[14]

When the prewar Gelsenkirchener Bergwerks complex was separated from Vereinigte Stahlwerke, the steel firm Dortmund-Hörder obtained 50 per cent control of Hansa Bergbau, and another steel firm, Gusstahlwerk Bochumer Verein, obtained 50 per cent control of two other coal-mining firms, Carolinenglück and Graf Moltke. The deconcentration authorities permitted the Gelsenkirchener Bergwerks (GBAG) to own 50 per cent in each of these coal mining firms and to manage them, as well as the three firms in which it had 100 per cent control—Rheinelbe Bergbau, Dortmunder Bergbau and Bochumer Bergbau. In 1958 Dortmund-Hörder and the Thyssen group firms, Phoenix-Rheinrohr and August Thyssen Hütte, each purchased a 51 per cent interest in several different mines owned by Rheinelbe and Dortmunder, two of the three mining firms in which GBAG had obtained 100 per cent control as a result of deconcentration. The transaction stipulated that GBAG may repurchase control after twenty years and must in the meantime furnish the three new steel firm shareholders the equivalent of about 4 million tons of coal annually in the form of coke.[15] GBAG will continue to manage the mines. GBAG is thus increasingly assuming the character of a coal managing firm for some of the former steel units of Vereinigte Stahlwerke.[16]

[13] See *Journal officiel*, June 18, 1958, pp. 61–62.

[14] *Handelsblatt*, May 8, 1957, p. 7.

[15] *Handelsblatt*, February 12, 1958, p. 8. The High Authority, replying to a question from a member of the Common Assembly, stated that the three steel firms had already had a contract with GBAG for the delivery of coal that expired in September 1958 and that the new arrangement therefore simply prolonged deliveries. The High Authority added that it opposed the re-creation of Vereinigte Stahlwerke and that one of the steel firms involved in the transaction had denied such intentions; see *Journal officiel*, April 20, 1958, p. 24. Dortmund-Hörder and the two Thyssen steel firms, it was reported, had previously considered purchasing GBAG on the same type of arrangement by which Sidechar, a group of French steel firms, had purchased majority control of Harpener Bergbau, also in the Ruhr. Purchase of GBAG was, however, reported to have been too costly for them.

[16] Hans-Gunther Sohl was chairman of the board of directors of GBAG and president of August Thyssen Hütte.

TABLES

The tables in this appendix are numbered so that the chapters for which they provide basic data can be readily identified. The first digit in a table number is the number of the chapter to which the table is primarily related. Thus Tables 2-1, 2-2, etc., relate primarily to the discussion in Chapter 2, though references to them may occur in other chapters. There is no Table 1-1 because, there is no appendix table to which the discussion in Chapter 1 relates.

For a list of abbreviations used in source notes to tables, see Appendix A.

Table 2-1

PRODUCTION OF COAL, CRUDE STEEL AND IRON ORE, ECSC, BY REGION, 1955

(Amount in Millions of Metric Tons)

Region	Coal		Crude Steel		Iron Ore	
	Amount	Per Cent	Amount	Per Cent	Amount	Per Cent
West Germany						
North Rhine–Westphalia	121.1	48.9	17.6	33.4	1.3	1.8
Aachen[a]	7.1	2.9	—	—	—	—
Lower Saxony	2.6	1.1	2.3	4.4	6.5	9.2
Other	1.0	0.4	1.4	2.7	3.6	5.1
Total	131.8	53.2	21.3	40.5	11.4	16.2
Belgium						
Campine	10.1	4.1	—	—	—	—
South	19.8	8.0	5.8	11.0	0.0	0.0
Total	30.0	12.2	5.8	11.0	0.1	0.0
France						
Nord and Pas-de-Calais	29.1	11.8	2.8	5.3	—	—
Lorraine	13.2	5.4	8.3	15.8	46.7	66.3
Centre-Midi	12.7	5.2	0.6	1.1	1.1	1.6
Other	0.4	0.2	0.8	1.5	2.5	3.6
Total	55.3	22.5	12.6	24.0	50.3	71.5
Saar	17.3	7.0	3.2	6.1	—	—
Italy	1.1	0.4	5.4	10.3	1.4	2.0
Netherlands	11.9	4.8	1.0	1.9	—	—
Luxembourg	—	—	3.2	6.1	7.2	10.2
TOTAL	247.4	100.0	52.6	100.0	70.4	100.0

Sources: Chambre Syndicale de la Sidérurgie Française; ECE, *Quarterly Bulletin of Steel Statistics* and *Quarterly Bulletin of Coal Statistics;* HA, *Bulletin statistique; Jahrbuch;* Statistisches Bundesamt, Düsseldorf.

[a] Aachen is in North Rhine–Westphalia but is shown separately.

Note: Discrepancies in addition are due to rounding.

Table 2-2

PRODUCTION OF STEEL INGOTS AND CASTINGS,
MAIN EUROPEAN PRODUCERS AND THE UNITED STATES, 1880–1957

(Thousands of Metric Tons)

Year	Germany	Saar	France	Belgium	Luxembourg	Italy
1880	773	—	389	132	—	(3)
1890	2,135	—	683	246	97	(124)
1900	6,461	...	1,565	655	185	135
1910	13,101	...	3,413	1,945	598	732
1913[b]	15,519	2,080	4,687	2,467	1,336	934
1913[c]	12,223	2,080	6,973	2,467	1,336	934
1920	8,538	740	3,050	1,253	585	774
1921	9,997	987	3,102	764	754	700
1922	11,714	1,313	4,534	1,565	1,394	983
1923	6,305	1,064	5,110	2,297	1,198	1,142
1924	9,835	1,485	6,900	2,875	1,887	1,359
1925	12,195	1,582	7,446	2,549	2,084	1,786
1926	12,316	1,737	8,430	3,339	2,244	1,780
1927	16,267	1,895	8,306	3,680	2,471	1,596
1928	10,476	2,073	9,500	3,905	2,567	1,960
1929	16,210	2,209	9,711	4,109	2,702	2,122
1930	11,511	1,935	9,447	3,354	2,270	1,743
1931	8,269	1,538	7,822	3,105	2,035	1,409
1932	5,747	1,463	5,640	2,790	1,956	1,396
1933	7,586	1,676	6,531	2,731	1,845	1,771
1934	11,886	1,950	6,174	2,944	1,932	1,850
1935	14,302	2,117	6,277	3,023	1,837	2,209
1936	16,860	2,315	6,708	3,168	1,981	2,025
1937	17,478	2,339	7,920	3,869	2,510	2,087
1938[c]	20,099	2,557	6,221	2,279	1,437	2,323
1938[d]	17,902	2,557	6,221	2,279	1,437	2,323
1946	2,600	291	4,408	2,297	1,295	1,153
1947	3,100	708	5,733	2,882	1,713	1,691
1948	5,600	1,228	7,236	3,920	2,453	2,125
1949	9,200	1,757	9,152	3,849	2,272	2,055
1950	12,100	1,898	8,652	3,737	2,451	2,362
1951	13,506	2,603	9,835	5,070	3,077	3,063
1952	15,806	2,823	10,867	5,084	3,002	3,535
1953	15,420	2,684	9,997	4,513	2,659	3,500
1954	17,434	2,805	10,627	4,987	2,828	4,207
1955	21,336	3,165	12,592	5,892	3,225	5,395
1956	23,189	3,374	13,399	6,375	3,456	5,908
1957	24,507	3,459	14,096	6,259	3,493	6,768

Sources: 1880–1950 from Ingvar Svennilson, *Growth and Stagnation in the European Economy,* ECE, Geneva, 1954, pp. 260, 262–263; 1951–1957 from ECE, *Quarterly Bulletin of Steel Statistics;* Germany, 1938 post–World War I territory, 1946–1950 from OEEC, *Industrial Statistics, 1900–1955,* Paris, 1955; United States, all years, from *Metal Statistics,* American Metal Market, New York, and American Iron and Steel Institute, *Annual Reports;* world data from *Metal Statistics,*

Table 2-2 (continued)

PRODUCTION OF STEEL INGOTS AND CASTINGS,
MAIN EUROPEAN PRODUCERS AND THE UNITED STATES, 1880–1957

(Thousands of Metric Tons)

Netherlands	Main Continental	United Kingdom	United States	Total World[a]	Year
—	1,297	1,316	1,267	4,247	1880
—	3,285	3,636	4,345	12,475	1890
—	9,001	4,980	10,350	28,271	1900
—	19,789	6,476	26,508	60,270	1910
—	27,073	7,787	31,680	76,300	1913[b]
—	26,013	7,787	31,680	76,300	1913[c]
—	14,940	9,212	42,800	72,429	1920
—	16,304	3,763	20,097	45,200	1921
—	21,503	5,975	36,167	68,800	1922
—	17,116	8,617	45,656	78,300	1923
—	24,341	8,332	38,533	78,500	1924
—	27,642	7,503	46,113	90,339	1925
—	29,846	3,654	49,059	93,400	1926
—	34,215	9,243	45,647	101,800	1927
—	30,481	8,656	52,361	109,900	1928
—	37,063	9,790	57,327	120,800	1929
—	30,260	7,443	41,344	94,575	1930
—	24,178	5,286	26,356	69,493	1931
—	18,992	5,345	13,898	50,690	1932
—	22,140	7,136	23,600	67,817	1933
(10)	26,746	8,992	26,468	81,877	1934
(20)	29,785	10,017	34,633	99,248	1935
32	33,089	11,974	48,524	123,932	1936
49	36,252	13,192	51,370	136,014	1937
52	34,968	10,564	28,799	108,695	1938[c]
52	32,771	10,564	28,799	108,695	1938[d]
137	12,181	12,898	60,409	111,571	1946
196	16,023	12,929	76,999	136,150	1947
334	22,896	15,115	80,397	155,459	1948
428	28,713	15,802	70,726	159,875	1949
490	31,690	16,554	87,830	188,571	1950
554	37,708	15,889	95,416	209,435	1951
685	41,802	16,681	84,503	211,219	1952
860	39,633	17,891	101,230	234,182	1953
928	43,816	18,817	80,099	221,100	1954
973	52,578	20,108	106,152	270,400	1955
1,042	56,743	20,991	104,522	284,000	1956
1,182	59,764	22,056	102,252	293,000	1957

American Metal Market, New York; OEEC, *Industrial Statistics, 1900–1955;* UN, *Monthly Bulletin of Statistics*, New York.

[a] Total world rather than total of countries listed.

[b] Pre–World War I territory. [c] Interwar territory. [d] Post–World War II territory.

Table 2-3

EXPORTS OF STEEL FROM MAIN STEEL PRODUCING COUNTRIES TO ECSC COUNTRIES
AND REST OF THE WORLD, SELECTED YEARS, 1912–1955[a]

(Thousands of Metric Tons)

| | | | | | | Destination | | | | | |
| Origin and Year | Germany | France | Belgium-Luxembourg | Total Cols. 1-3 | Netherlands[b] | Italy[b] | Total ECSC Countries | United Kingdom | United States | Rest of World | Total World |
	(1)	(2)	(3)	(4)	(5)	(6)	(7)	(8)	(9)	(10)	(11)
Germany											
1912–1913		56	240	296	...	...	...	943	14	...	3,892
1927–1928[c]		14	39	53	...	...	...	681	101	...	2,827
1927–1928[d]		(373)	(45)	(418)	...	...	...	(749)	(101)	...	(3,690)
1936–1938		7	26	33	329	92	454	81	51	1,625	2,211
1950–1951		6	23	29	181	61	271	50	304	1,136	1,761
1952		8	26	34	177	57	268	84	198	1,156	1,706
1953		10	88	98	280	64	442	32	126	1,134	1,734
1954		81	81	163	395	81	639	32	118	1,554	2,343
1955		103	68	171	475	57	703	70	53	1,686	2,512
France											
1913	11		208	219	...	...	...	13	1	...	418
1927–1928[d]	1,035		723	1,758	...	...	...	817	69	...	3,889
1927–1928[e]	(548)		(717)	(1,265)	...	...	...	(750)	(69)	...	(2,900)
1936–1938	4		59	63	31	47	141	247	30	872	1,290
1950–1951	123		36	158	78	246	482	128	487	2,244	3,341
1952	244		28	272	47	134	453	104	161	1,845	2,563
1953	484		53	537	96	239	872	145	274	2,147	3,438
1954	830		69	899	79	256	1,234	62	128	2,258	3,682
1955	1,193		98	1,291	70	155	1,516	158	180	3,036	4,890

Belgium-Luxembourg

Period										
1912–1913[e]	6	37	43	...	...	...	371	4	...	1,303
1927–1928[c]	441	66	507	...	...	...	1,156	171	...	4,088
1927–1928[d]	(441)	(66)	(510)	(308)	...	...	1,156	171	...	(4,094)
1936–1938	302	33	335	738	13	656	436	96	1,701	2,889
1950–1951	20	37	58	602	147	943	179	437	2,422	3,981
1952	578	15	593	619	148	1,343	448	371	2,458	4,620
1953	506	64	570	751	144	1,333	311	619	1,951	4,214
1954	647	277	924	785	121	1,796	66	261	2,302	4,425
1955	1,014	466	1,480		100	2,365	110	215	2,730	5,420

Total Germany, France and Belgium-Luxembourg

Period											
1912–1913	17	93	448	558	...	...	...	1,326	18	...	5,613
1927–1928[d]	1,475	80	762	2,317	...	...	...	2,654	341	...	10,804
1927–1928[e]	(992)	(439)	(762)	(2,193)	...	...	...	2,654	341	...	(10,684)
1936–1938	306	40	85	431	668	152	1,251	764	176	4,199	6,390
1950–1951	143	43	59	245	997	454	1,696	357	1,223	5,806	9,082
1952	822	23	54	899	826	339	2,064	636	730	5,460	8,890
1953	990	74	141	1,205	995	447	2,647	487	1,019	5,234	9,387
1954	1,477	358	151	1,986	1,225	458	3,669	160	506	6,115	10,450
1955	2,026	569	167	2,942	1,330	312	4,584	337	448	7,453	12,822

United Kingdom

Period											
1912–1913	66	42	31	140	...	...	...		28	...	2,679
1927–1928	34	20	27	82	...	...	...		14	...	3,068
1936–1938	3	7	11	21	64	2	87		1	1,529	1,617
1950–1951	—	13	3	15	63	15	93		75	1,904	2,072
1952	—	1	5	5	81	12	98		32	1,662	1,792
1953	4	10	16	31	82	59	172		76	1,677	1,925
1954	4	3	6	13	69	33	115		35	1,926	2,076
1955	8	4	8	19	82	18	119		43	2,248	2,410

Table 2-3 (continued) (Thousands of Metric Tons)

					Destination						
Origin and Year	Germany	France	Belgium-Luxembourg	Total Cols. 1–3	Nether-lands[b]	Italy[b]	Total ECSC Countries	United Kingdom	United States	Rest of World	Total World
	(1)	(2)	(3)	(4)	(5)	(6)	(7)	(8)	(9)	(10)	(11)
United States											
1912–1913	5	1	21	26	...	...	...	222		...	2,037
1927–1928	1	5	5	11	...	...	...	45		...	1,838
1936–1938	0	5	3	14	61	7	82	59		1,512	1,653
1950–1951	—	49	24	89	66	63	218	56		2,350	2,624
1952	9	57	26	83	74	90	247	603		2,805	3,655
1953	9	41	22	73	60	75	208	81		2,442	2,731
1954	29	19	14	62	72	79	213	102		2,237	2,552
1955	82	11	45	138	183	44	365	749		2,553	3,667
Total exporters listed											
1912–1913	88	136	500	724	...	...	...	1,549	46	...	10,329
1927–1928[d]	1,511	105	794	2,410	...	...	...	2,699	355	...	15,710
1927–1928[e]	(1,027)	(459)	(789)	(2,286)	...	...	...	2,699	355	...	(15,590)
1936–1938	309	54	98	465	793	161	1,419	824	178	7,239	9,660
1950–1951	143	122	64	349	1,126	532	2,007	413	1,299	10,039	13,758
1952	822	81	85	988	981	441	2,410	1,239	762	9,926	14,337
1953	1,004	129	179	1,309	1,137	581	3,027	568	1,095	9,353	14,043
1954	1,510	381	170	2,061	1,366	570	3,997	262	541	10,278	15,078
1955	2,297	584	219	3,100	1,595	374	5,069	1,086	492	12,252	18,899

Sources: 1912–1950, inclusive, from Ingvar Svennilson, *Growth and Stagnation in the European Economy*, ECE, Geneva, 1954, p. 270, supplemented as follows: exports to the Netherlands and Italy cover 1937–1938 (instead of 1936–1938) and are from *Bulletin du Comité des Forges de France* (série bleue); 1950 data from same sources as 1951–1955, below; exports by and to the United States: 1912–1913 from *Commerce and Navigation of the United States*; 1927–1928 from *Foreign Commerce and Navigation of the United States*; 1937–1938 (1936 excluded) from same source shown for Netherlands and Italy, 1937–1938, above; 1950 from same sources as 1951–1955, below; 1951–1955 from *Yearbooks of British Iron and Steel Federation*; *Eisen und Stahl Jahrbuch*; Statistisches Bundesamt, Düsseldorf; American Iron and Steel Institute, *Annual Reports*; Chambre Syndicale de la Sidérurgie Française (séries verte, bleue et rose); ECE, *Quarterly Bulletin of Coal Statistics.*

[a] Saar included in the French customs union since World War II. See notes *c* and *d* for the interwar period. In 1912–1913 Germany comprised the Saar, Luxembourg and the Moselle.

Tonnages comprise the following shapes: steel ingots, blooms, billets, slabs, bars, structurals, plates, strip, sheet, tinplate, blackplate, wire rod, tubes, rails, sleepers, fishplates, soleplates. Excluded are iron castings and wrought iron products wherever possible; wire products, if reported separately; cast iron pipe. Wherever possible fabricated shapes and sections are excluded. Pig iron and ferroalloys are excluded. These data are shown ton for ton and not in crude steel equivalents (as erroneously indicated in Svennilson, *op. cit.*, p. 333). Where data covers two or more years, the figures show the annual average.

[b] 1936 omitted from data for 1936–1938.   [d] Saar excluded.   [e] Saar excluded.   [e] Luxembourg, then in the German customs union, is excluded.   *Note:* Discrepancies in addition are due to rounding.

Table 2-4

CONSUMPTION OF PRIMARY ENERGY, BY SOURCE, SELECTED COUNTRIES AND YEARS, 1929–1955

Country and Source of Energy	Amount (Millions of Tons of Hard Coal Equivalents)				Percentage Distribution			
	1929	1937	1950	1955	1929	1937	1950	1955
Germany								
Hard coal	88.3	93.1	94.6	124.8	76.3	73.6	73.1	70.0
Brown coal	23.1	26.4	25.8	33.6	19.9	20.9	19.9	18.8
Petroleum	1.5	2.7	3.7	12.3	1.3	2.1	2.9	6.9
Natural gas	—	—	0.1	0.5	0.0	0.0	0.1	0.3
Water power	2.9	4.3	5.2	7.2	2.5	3.4	4.0	4.0
Total	115.8	126.5	129.4	178.4	100.0	100.0	100.0	100.0
France-Saar[a]								
Hard coal	91.2	78.7	69.7	76.8	89.6	82.7	74.8	67.3
Brown coal	1.2	0.9	1.2	1.4	1.2	0.9	1.3	1.2
Petroleum	3.4	7.5	12.3	20.1	3.3	7.9	13.2	17.6
Natural gas	—	—	0.3	0.4	0.0	0.0	0.3	0.4
Water power	6.0	8.1	9.7	15.4	5.9	8.5	10.4	13.5
Total	101.8	95.3	93.2	114.1	100.0	100.0	100.0	100.0
Belgium-Luxembourg								
Hard coal	37.2	33.6	28.7	31.5	98.4	96.8	90.5	85.3
Brown coal	0.1	0.1	0.1	0.2	0.3	0.3	0.3	0.5
Petroleum	0.5	1.0	2.9	5.0	1.3	2.9	9.2	13.6
Natural gas	—	—	0	0.1	0.0	0.0	0.0	0.3
Water power	0	0	0	0.1	0.0	0.0	0.0	0.3
Total	37.8	34.7	31.7	36.9	100.0	100.0	100.0	100.0
Italy								
Hard coal	14.5	13.9	10.0	10.9	57.3	49.5	33.8	23.2
Brown coal	0.3	0.3	0.2	0.2	1.2	1.1	0.7	0.4
Petroleum	1.3	3.4	5.4	12.0	5.1	12.1	18.2	25.5
Natural gas	0	0	0.6	4.3	0.0	0.0	2.0	9.1
Water power	9.2	10.5	13.4	19.6	36.4	37.3	45.3	41.7
Total	25.3	28.1	29.6	47.0	100.0	100.0	100.0	100.0

Table 2-4 (continued)

Country and Source of Energy	Amount (Millions of Tons of Hard Coal Equivalents)				Percentage Distribution			
	1929	1937	1950	1955	1929	1937	1950	1955
Netherlands								
Hard coal	13.3	13.5	16.4	17.4	91.1	87.7	83.3	75.9
Brown coal	0.2	0.1	0.2	0.3	1.4	0.6	1.0	1.3
Petroleum	1.1	1.8	3.1	5.1	7.5	11.7	15.7	22.7
Total	14.6	15.4	19.7	22.8	100.0	100.0	100.0	100.0
ECSC								
Hard coal	244.5	232.9	219.4	260.8	82.8	77.6	72.3	65.4
Brown coal	24.9	27.8	27.5	35.9	8.4	9.3	9.0	9.0
Petroleum	7.8	16.4	27.4	54.5	2.7	5.5	9.0	13.7
Natural gas	0	0	1.0	5.4	0.0	0.0	0.3	1.4
Water power	18.1	22.9	28.3	42.3	6.1	7.6	9.4	10.6
Total	295.3	300.0	303.6	398.9	100.0	100.0	100.0	100.0
United Kingdom								
Hard coal	180.4	189.1	203.4	214.0	96.3	94.2	91.6	85.0
Petroleum	6.6	10.9	17.5	35.5	3.5	5.4	7.9	14.0
Water power	0.4	0.7	1.1	2.5	0.2	0.4	0.5	1.0
Total	187.4	200.7	222.0	252.0	100.0	100.0	100.0	100.0
United States								
All coal	527.0	430.0	451.0	398.0	65.6	56.7	39.6	28.6
Petroleum	173.0	193.0	382.0	570.0	21.5	25.4	33.5	41.1
Natural gas	72.0	104.0	248.0	350.0	9.0	13.7	21.7	25.2
Water power	31.0	32.0	59.0	72.0	3.9	4.2	5.2	5.2
Total	803.0	759.0	1,140.0	1,390.0	100.0	100.0	100.0	100.0

Sources: Kohlenwirtschaft; HA, Momento de statistiques; United Kingdom and United States for 1955 are estimates, drawn from OEEC, Statistiques générales; NPA, Productive Uses of Nuclear Energy, Summary of Findings, Washington, 1957, p. 19; and OEEC, Europe's Growing Needs of Energy, How Can They Be Met? Paris, May 1956.
[a] Though the Saar was in Germany in 1937, it is included with France for comparability.

438

Table 2-5

PRODUCTION OF CRUDE STEEL AND CASTINGS, ECSC AREAS, SELECTED YEARS, 1913–1956

Area	Amount (Millions of Metric Tons)				Percentage Increase 1913–1956	Percentage Distribution			
	1913	1929	1937	1956		1913	1929	1937	1956
Main areas:									
Ruhr	10.112	13.172	14.000	19.076	89	46	43	47	43
Saar	2.080	2.209	2.339	3.375	62	10	7	8	8
Luxembourg	1.336	2.702	2.510	3.455	159	6	9	8	8
Lorraine	4.785[a]	6.659	5.543	8.820	84	22	22	19	20
Nord	1.077[b]	1.698	1.425	2.964	175	5	6	5	7
Belgium	2.467	4.109	3.869	6.375	158	11	13	13	14
Total[c]	21.857	30.549	29.686	44.065	102	100	100	100	100
Other areas[d]	4.156	6.514	6.566	12.666	205	16	18	18	22
Main areas	21.857	30.549	29.686	44.065	102	84	82	82	78
TOTAL ECSC[e]	26.013	37.063	36.252	56.731	118	100	100	100	100

Sources: Table 2-2, preceding; Statistisches Bundesamt, Düsseldorf; Chambre Syndicale de la Sidérurgie Française (série verte); British Iron and Steel Federation; Frederic Benham, *The Iron and Steel Industry of Germany, France, Belgium, Luxembourg and the Saar*, London and Cambridge Economic Service, London, October 1934, pp. 19, 28.

[a] The Moselle area produced 2,286,000 tons; the Meurthe-et-Moselle area, 2,499,000 tons. Latter figure from Reports of French Ministère de l'Intérieur; former from Benham, *op. cit*, p. 28.

[b] Reports of French Ministère de l'Intérieur.

[c] Total of areas listed.

[d] Includes Italy; the Netherlands; the Centre-Midi; west and south-east of France; and, in West Germany, Lower Saxony, the Rhineland and southern Germany.

[e] Post–World War II boundaries.

Table 2-6

Average Annual Exports of Solid Fuels from
Main Coal Producing Countries to ECSC Countries and
Rest of the World, Selected Years, 1927–1955[a]

(*Millions of Metric Tons*)

Origin and Year	Destination				
	Germany	Saar	France	Belgium	Luxembourg
Germany					
1927–1928		0.261	9.942	6.954	
1937–1938		0.235	7.284	4.385	2.560
1950–1951		0.764	6.468	0.344	3.532
1952–1953		0.869	7.040	0.493	3.951
1954–1955		0.902	6.725	1.623	4.052
1955		1.014	7.142	1.267	4.295
1956		0.961	7.347	1.212	4.375
1957		1.051	8.037	1.293	4.231
Saar					
1927–1928	(1.241)		4.292	0.303	
1937–1938	3.584		1.934	0.103	0.025
1950–1951	3.273		5.377	0.001	0.077
1952–1953	3.615		4.807	0.002	0.074
1954–1955	3.932		4.605	0.003	0.068
1955	4.242		4.385	0.002	0.071
1956	3.726		4.567	—	0.071
1957	3.493		4.412	0.001	0.067
France					
1927–1928	0.214	(0.397)		0.984	
1937–1938	0.213	0.129		0.215	—
1950–1951	0.359	0.228		0.011	0.069
1952–1953	0.700	0.197		0.156	0.068
1954–1955	1.000	0.182		0.472	0.063
1955	1.130	0.206		0.611	0.060
1956	0.385	0.160		0.406	0.064
1957	0.563	0.276		0.294	0.056
Belgium					
1927–1928	—	—	3.789		(0.428)
1937–1938	0.112	—	4.281		0.446
1950–1951	0.004	—	0.779		0.235
1952–1953	0.207	—	1.606		0.188
1954–1955	0.495	—	1.790		0.161
1955	0.762	—	1.687		0.161
1956	0.442	—	1.647		0.158
1957	0.214	—	2.017		0.261
Netherlands					
1927–1928	0.655	—	1.504	2.486	
1937–1938	1.245	—	2.058	1.862	—
1950–1951	—	—	0.511	0.004	0.259
1952–1953	0.006	—	0.670	0.105	0.288
1954–1955	0.160	—	1.154	0.513	0.375
1955	0.223	—	1.234	0.457	0.432
1956	0.255	—	1.205	0.429	0.480
1957	0.205	—	1.270	0.529	0.645

440

Table 2-6 (continued)

AVERAGE ANNUAL EXPORTS OF SOLID FUELS FROM
MAIN COAL PRODUCING COUNTRIES TO ECSC COUNTRIES AND
REST OF THE WORLD, SELECTED YEARS, 1927–1955[a]

(Millions of Metric Tons)

		Destination			
Italy	Nether-lands	Total ECSC	Rest of World	Total World	Origin and Year
					Germany
4.771	6.824	28.751	5.718	34.469	1927–1928
6.924	6.450	27.816	8.781	36.597	1937–1938
3.336	2.929	17.373	9.202	26.575	1950–1951
3.264	2.402	18.017	7.939	25.956	1952–1953
3.214	2.904	19.417	8.905	28.322	1954–1955
2.889	2.605	19.212	8.239	27.451	1955
2.944	2.317	19.156	7.161	26.637	1956
2.696	2.168	19.476	6.902	26.378	1957
					Saar
0.584	(0.100)	(6.519)	0.522	7.041	1927–1928
0.557	0.163	6.364	1.035	7.399	1937–1938
0.356	0.009	9.092	0.803	9.895	1950–1951
0.197	0.009	8.705	0.829	9.534	1952–1953
0.209	0.011	8.827	1.531	10.358	1954–1955
0.164	0.018	8.882	1.782	10.664	1955
0.163	0.001	8.528	0.797	9.325	1956
0.093	—	8.066	0.565	8.631	1957
					France
0.682	—	2.277	0.493	2.770	1927–1928
0.101	—	0.658	0.406	1.064	1937–1938
0.385	0.143	1.195	0.963	2.158	1950–1951
0.145	0.046	1.310	0.779	2.089	1952–1953
0.151	0.225	2.090	2.512	4.602	1054–1955
0.142	0.444	2.593	3.590	6.183	1955
0.064	0.043	1.122	1.230	2.352	1956
0.058	0.052	1.299	0.963	2.262	1957
					Belgium
0.030	0.383	4.630	0.067	4.697	1927–1928
0.158	0.489	5.483	0.878	6.361	1937–1938
0.818	0.405	2.254	0.615	2.869	1950–1951
0.702	0.782	3.542	0.966	4.508	1952–1953
0.380	2.505	5.328	2.120	7.448	1954–1955
0.182	2.852	5.644	2.417	8.061	1955
0.099	1.766	4.112	1.553	5.665	1956
0.023	1.484	3.999	1.138	5.137	1957
					Netherlands
...		4.645	0.334	4.979	1927–1928
0.109		5.274	1.526	6.800	1937–1938
—		0.774	0.776	1.550	1950–1951
0.001		1.070	0.851	1.921	1952–1953
0.009		2.211	1.054	3.265	1954–1955
0.007		2.353	1.114	3.467	1955
—		2.369	1.290	3.659	1956
0.004		2.653	1.040	3.693	1957

Table 2-6 (continued)

(Millions of Metric Tons)

Origin and Year	Destination				
	Germany	Saar	France	Belgium	Luxembourg
Total ECSC					
1927–1928	2.109	0.658	19.526	11.154	
1937–1938	5.154	0.452	15.555	6.564	3.031
1950–1951	3.636	0.991	13.135	0.359	4.174
1952–1953	4.533	1.064	14.190	0.757	4.575
1954–1955	5.864	1.083	14.297	2.612	4.723
1955	6.360	1.220	14.471	2.337	5.024
1956	4.808	1.121	14.766	2.047	5.148
1957	4.475	1.327	15.736	2.117	5.260
United Kingdom					
1927–1928	5.019	—	9.311	2.283	
1937–1938	3.743	—	7.631	0.805	—
1950–1951	0.308	—	0.957	0.311	—
1952–1953	0.947	—	0.796	0.382	—
1954–1955	1.300	—	0.976	0.505	—
1955	1.139	—	0.966	0.480	—
1956	0.929	—	0.756	0.607	—
1957	0.620	—	0.797	0.617	—
Main European					
1927–1928	7.128	0.658	28.837	13.436	
1937–1938	8.896	0.453	23.188	7.369	3.031
1950–1951	3.944	0.991	14.092	0.670	4.172
1952–1953	5.526	1.064	14.936	1.139	4.575
1954–1955	6.946	1.083	15.273	3.115	4.723
1955	7.499	1.220	15.437	2.817	5.024
1956	5.737	1.121	15.522	2.654	5.148
1957	5.095	1.327	16.533	2.734	5.260
United States					
1927–1928	—	—	0.173	—	—
1937–1938	—	—	—	—	—
1950–1951	2.767	—	2.587	0.813	—
1952–1953	4.930	—	1.835	0.600	—
1954–1955	4.410	—	0.557	0.638	—
1955	6.998	—	1.031	1.035	—
1956	11.501	—	6.758	1.983	—
1957	15.571	—	7.378	2.167	—
Total, main producers					
1927–1928	7.128	0.658	29.010	13.436	
1937–1938	8.896	0.453	23.188	7.369	3.031
1950–1951	6.711	0.991	16.679	1.483	4.172
1952–1953	10.456	1.064	16.771	1.739	4.575
1954–1955	11.356	1.083	15.830	3.753	4.723
1955	14.497	1.220	16.468	3.852	5.024
1956	17.238	1.121	22.280	4.637	5.148
1957	20.666	1.327	23.911	4.901	5.260

Sources: ECE, *Quarterly Bulletin of Coal Statistics; Kohlenwirtschaft; Energiequellen der Welt; Jahresbericht des Reichskohlenverbandes, 1936/37.*

[a] Includes coal and coke in coal equivalents. Bunkers are included as an export, except for the Netherlands. United States coke exports are excluded because they are negligible. Data on inter-

Table 2-6 (continued)

(*Millions of Metric Tons*)

	Destination				
Italy	Nether-lands	Total ECSC	Rest of World	Total World	Origin and Year
					Total ECSC
6.065	7.306	46.818	7.564	54.382	1927–1928
7.848	7.102	45.706	12.513	58.219	1937–1938
4.894	3.486	30.673	12.374	43.047	1950–1951
4.358	3.238	32.663	11.393	44.056	1952–1953
3.963	5.646	37.917	16.152	54.069	1954–1955
3.384	5.919	38.684	17.142	55.826	1955
3.270	4.127	35.287	12.031	47.638	1956
2.874	3.704	35.493	10.608	46.101	1957
					United Kingdom
6.913	2.413	25.939	45.812	71.751	1927–1928
2.271	1.006	15.456	37.841	53.297	1937–1938
1.105	0.546	3.227	13.158	16.385	1950–1951
1.413	—	4.391	13.202	17.593	1952–1953
1.023	—	4.680	12.633	17.313	1954–1955
0.728	0.809	4.122	12.228	16.350	1955
0.352	0.858	3.502	9.156	12.658	1956
0.159	0.871	3.064	7.984	11.048	1957
					Main European
12.978	9.719	72.756	53.377	126.133	1927–1928
10.119	8.108	61.164	50.353	111.517	1937–1938
5.999	4.032	33.900	25.532	59.432	1950–1951
5.769	4.042	37.049	24.447	61.496	1952–1953
4.983	6.473	42.554	28.631	71.185	1954–1955
4.112	6.728	42.806	29.370	72.176	1955
3.622	4.985	38.789	21.187	60.296	1956
3.033	4.575	38.557	18.592	57.149	1957
					United States
0.158	—	0.331	22.211	22.542	1927–1928
—	—	—	13.899	13.899	1937–1938
2.879	1.766	10.812	31.678	42.490	1950–1951
2.362	1.400	11.127	29.655	40.782	1952–1953
4.739	1.335	11.679	28.765	40.444	1954–1955
5.974	1.482	16.520	33.219	49.739	1955
7.486	4.016	31.744	35.638	67.382	1956
8.772	4.510	38.398	35.154	73.552	1957
					Total, main producers
13.136	9.719	73.087	75.588	148.675	1927–1928
10.119	8.108	61.164	64.252	125.416	1937–1938
8.378	5.799	44.213	57.709	101.922	1950–1951
8.131	5.442	48.178	54.100	102.278	1952–1953
9.723	7.808	54.276	57.352	111.628	1954–1955
10.086	8.210	59.357	62.558	121.915	1955
11.108	9.001	70.533	57.145	127.678	1956
11.805	9.085	76.955	53.746	130.701	1957

war years include exports from former German Silesia. United States exports to the Netherlands are taken from the latter's import data because the U. S. export figures to the Netherlands include a large quantity of coal landed at Rotterdam for reshipment to other countries.

Note: Discrepancies in addition are due to rounding.

Table 2-7

HARD COAL PRODUCTION, SELECTED COUNTRIES, 1880–1957[a]

(Millions of Metric Tons)

Year	Germany[b]	Saar	France	Belgium	Nether-lands	ECSC Countries[c]	United Kingdom	United States	Total World[d]
1880	47.0	0.0	19.4	16.9	0.0	83.3	149.3	64.8	...
1890	70.2	0.0	25.6	20.4	0.1	116.3	184.5	143.1	470.0
1900	99.7	9.6	32.7	23.5	0.3	165.8	228.8	244.6	685.0
1905	109.8	11.4	35.2	21.8	0.5	178.8	239.8	356.2	840.0
1910	139.5	11.6	37.6	23.9	1.3	213.9	268.7	454.9	1,030.0
1913[e]	176.9	13.2	40.1	22.8	1.9	254.9	292.0	517.0	1,201.0
1913[f]	140.8	13.2	43.8	22.8	1.9	222.5	292.0	517.0	1,201.0
1920	131.4	9.4	24.3	22.4	3.9	191.6	233.1	597.0	1,149.0
1921	136.2	9.6	28.2	21.8	3.9	199.8	165.8	459.3	951.0
1922	130.0	11.2	31.1	21.2	4.6	198.3	253.6	432.6	1,023.0
1923	62.3	9.2	37.7	22.9	5.3	137.6	280.4	596.7	1,178.0
1924	118.8	14.0	44.0	23.4	5.9	206.2	271.4	518.5	1,165.0
1925	132.6	13.0	47.1	23.1	6.8	222.8	247.1	527.8	1,166.0
1926	145.3	13.7	51.4	25.3	8.6	244.5	128.3	596.7	1,157.0
1927	153.6	13.6	51.8	27.6	9.3	256.1	255.3	542.3	1,253.0
1928	150.9	13.1	51.4	27.6	10.7	253.8	241.3	522.5	1,225.0
1929	163.4	13.6	53.8	26.9	11.6	269.5	262.0	522.2	1,305.0
1930	142.7	13.2	53.9	27.4	12.2	249.6	247.8	487.0	1,195.0
1931	118.6	11.4	50.0	27.0	12.9	220.1	223.0	400.7	1,047.0
1932	104.8	10.4	46.3	21.4	12.8	196.0	212.1	326.1	927.0
1933	109.9	10.6	46.9	25.3	12.6	205.6	210.4	347.5	970.0
1934	124.9	11.3	47.6	26.4	12.3	222.9	224.3	377.8	1,062.0

444

Year									
1935	134.1	10.6	46.2	26.5	11.9	229.7	225.8	385.1	1,096.0
1936	146.7	11.7	45.2	27.9	12.8	245.1	232.1	447.8	1,199.0
1937	171.1	13.4	44.3	29.9	14.3	274.0	244.3	450.9	1,264.0
1938f	171.8	14.4	46.5	29.6	13.5	277.3	230.6	357.9	1,184.0
1938g	136.9	14.4	46.5	29.6	13.5	242.4	230.6	357.9	1,254.0
1946	53.9	7.9	47.2	22.8	8.3	141.3	193.1	539.3	1,208.0
1947	71.2	10.5	45.2	24.4	10.1	162.8	200.6	624.0	1,360.0
1948	87.0	12.6	43.3	26.7	11.0	181.6	212.8	595.7	1,401.0
1949	103.2	14.3	51.2	27.9	11.7	209.4	218.6	436.0	1,299.0
1950	110.8	15.1	50.8	27.3	12.2	217.2	219.8	508.0	1,418.0
1951	119.8	16.3	53.0	29.7	12.4	232.2	226.5	519.9	1,477.0
1952	124.7	16.2	55.4	30.4	12.5	240.2	230.1	457.7	1,459.0
1953	125.6	16.4	52.6	30.1	12.3	238.0	227.8	436.9	1,450.0
1954	129.0	16.8	54.4	29.2	12.1	242.5	227.9	380.2	1,414.0
1955	131.8	17.3	55.3	30.0	11.9	247.3	225.1	444.4	1,508.0
1956	135.6	17.1	55.1	29.6	11.8	250.2	225.6	480.6	1,560.0
1957	134.3	16.5	56.8	29.1	11.4	249.0	227.2	467.6	1,600.0

Sources: 1880–1950 from Ingvar Svennilson, *Growth and Stagnation in the European Economy*, ECE, Geneva, 1954, pp. 252–253 (estimates for Saar deducted from Germany); Netherlands data from *Kohlenwirtschaft*; Saar prior to 1952 from OEEC, *Industrial Statistics, 1900–1955*, Paris, 1955; 1951 for all countries except United States from *ibid.*; United States for 1952 and subsequent years from ECE, *Quarterly Bulletin of Coal Statistics*, and HA, *Momento de statistiques*; world data to 1947 from OEEC, *op. cit.*; 1948 and thereafter from Statistisches Bundesamt, Düsseldorf.

a Includes bituminous and anthracite.
b Data for Germany exclude the product referred to as pech coal and include the output by "small mines."   c Includes Italy.
d Includes USSR but excludes China.
e Pre–World War I territory.   f Interwar territory.
g Post–World War II territory.

445

Table 2-8

Exports of Steel from Main Steel Producing Areas, by Destination, 1955[a]

Origin	ECSC	United Kingdom	Europe Excluding ECSC and United Kingdom	United States	Canada	British Commonwealth Excluding Canada	Latin America	Africa, Near and Middle East	Far East	USSR	Undistributed	Total
						Amount (Thousands of Metric Tons)						
ECSC[b]		397.4	2,807.5	448.3	83.5	811.6	1,211.9	1,564.1	218.1	45.3	435.3	8,023.0
United Kingdom	119.2		463.3	43.3	99.0	1,308.1	136.7	178.5	21.3	—	40.6	2,410.0
United States	364.7	749.4	142.4		858.6	242.9	606.9	29.8	99.5	—	572.8	3,667.0
Total[c]	483.9	1,146.8	3,413.2	491.6	1,041.1	2,362.6	1,955.5	1,772.4	338.9	45.3	1,048.7	14,100.0
						Percentage Distribution						
ECSC		34.7	82.2	91.2	8.0	34.4	61.9	88.2	64.4	100.0	41.5	56.9
United Kingdom	24.6		13.6	8.8	9.5	55.4	7.0	10.1	6.2	—	3.9	17.1
United States	75.4	65.3	4.2		82.5	10.2	31.1	1.7	29.4	—	54.6	26.0
Total	100.0	100.0	100.0	100.0	100.0	100.0	100.0	100.0	100.0	100.0	100.0	100.0

Sources: British Iron and Steel Federation; American Iron and Steel Institute; *Eisen und Stahl Jahrbuch;* Statistisches Bundesamt, Düsseldorf; Chambre Syndicale de la Sidérurgie Française (série bleue).

[a] Data are from exporters' reports.

[b] Includes exports from Italy and the Netherlands, as well as from the main exporters.

[c] Total of sources listed; about 85 to 90 per cent of world exports are covered.

Table 2-9

IRON ORE: IMPORTS BY ORIGIN, AND HOME PRODUCTION,
SELECTED STEEL PRODUCING COUNTRIES, 1938–1955[a]

(Thousands of Metric Tons)

| | Origin | | | | | | | | | |
| | ECSC | | | | Third Countries | | | | | |
Destination and Year	Total	France	Luxem-bourg	Other	Total	Sweden	Western Hemisphere	Rest of World	Total Imports	Home Production[b]
Germany										
1938	(830.0)	(50.0)	(720.0)	(60.0)	15,170.0	8,992.3	1,258.1	4,919.6	(16,000.0)	9,825.0
1951	659.6	407.7	183.8	68.1	6,711.6	4,578.7	155.9	1,977.0	7,371.2	11,162.0
1952	769.4	368.5	376.8	24.1	8,872.2	5,558.8	393.4	2,920.0	9,641.6	12,921.0
1953	654.4	383.6	249.8	21.0	9,393.7	4,721.4	1,006.4	3,665.9	10,048.1	10,427.0
1954	344.0	237.1	89.6	17.3	8,410.0	4,905.9	1,000.6	2,503.5	8,754.0	9,993.0
1955	790.0	364.0	375.0	51.0	13,524.0	6,297.0	2,021.0	5,206.0	14,314.0	11,381.0
Saar										
1938	(6,000.0)	(5,000.0)	0.0	(1,000.0)	0.0	0.0	0.0	0.0	(6,000.0)	0.0
1951	6,017.3	5,994.2	0.0	23.1	0.0	0.0	0.0	0.0	6,017.3	0.0
1952	6,614.0	6,563.4	22.7	27.9	11.2	4.0	0.0	7.2	6,625.2	0.0
1953	5,989.6	5,702.1	264.8	22.7	41.7	0.9	0.1	40.7	6,031.3	0.0
1954	6,094.0	5,879.6	202.5	11.9	38.2	10.1	0.1	28.0	6,132.2	0.0
1955	7,604.0	7,443.0	149.0	(12.0)	(40.0)	(10.0)	(0.0)	(30.0)	7,644.0	0.0
France										
1938	106.6		106.6	0.0	330.4	102.8	19.4	208.2	437.0	33,176.0
1951	68.8		19.8	49.0	251.5	7.0	0.0	244.5	320.3	35,137.0
1952	54.9		8.4	46.5	382.8	65.6	28.1	289.1	437.7	40,716.0
1953	675.3		615.0	60.3	291.8	91.6	6.9	193.3	967.1	42,443.0
1954	80.7		26.3	54.4	228.6	97.4	29.8	101.4	309.3	43,817.0
1955	(61.0)		(39.0)	(22.0)	(486.0)	170.0	34.0	282.0	547.0	50,326.0
Belgium										
1938	5,646.0	4,787.0	859.0	0.0	325.0	325.0	0.0	0.0	5,971.0	181.0
1951	6,914.0	5,136.0	1,778.0	0.0	1,610.0	1,610.0	0.0	0.0	8,524.0	82.0
1952	7,068.0	4,414.0	2,654.0	0.0	1,572.0	1,572.0	0.0	0.0	8,640.0	138.0
1953	6,819.0	4,956.0	1,863.0	0.0	1,749.0	1,749.0	0.0	0.0	8,568.0	103.0
1954	6,990.0	5,657.0	1,333.0	0.0	2,243.0	2,243.0	0.0	0.0	9,233.0	85.0
1955	8,450.0	(7,150.0)	(1,300.0)	0.0	2,700.0	2,550.0	0.0	150.0	(11,150.0)	106.0

Table 2-9 (continued)

(Thousands of Metric Tons)

| | Origin | | | | | | | | | |
| | ECSC | | | | Third Countries | | | | Total | Home |
Destination and Year	Total	France	Luxembourg	Other	Total	Sweden	Western Hemisphere	Rest of World	Imports	Production[b]
Italy										
1938	2.3	0.4	0.0	1.9	456.4	0.0	0.0	456.4	458.7	1,006.0
1951	7.6	6.7	0.0	0.9	668.7	20.5	0.0	648.2	676.3	577.0
1952	1.4	0.0	0.0	1.4	888.5	42.9	0.0	845.5	889.9	831.0
1953	1.5	0.6	0.0	0.9	885.0	42.4	10.2	832.4	886.5	972.0
1954	0.0	0.0	0.0	0.0	862.1	218.3	55.2	588.6	862.1	1,093.0
1955	3.0	1.0	0.0	2.0	884.0	203.0	69.0	612.0	887.0	1,383.0
Netherlands										
1938	83.1	83.1	0.0	0.0	406.3	167.2	7.3	231.8	489.4	0.0
1951	181.1	180.0	0.0	1.1	822.6	286.0	13.1	523.5	1,003.7	0.0
1952	130.0	129.5	0.0	0.5	1,051.6	292.3	35.7	723.6	1,181.6	0.0
1953	182.2	182.2	0.0	0.0	1,085.1	304.5	67.6	713.0	1,267.3	0.0
1954	165.4	153.4	0.0	12.0	954.1	234.9	36.6	682.6	1,119.5	0.0
1955	130.0	129.0	0.0	1.0	929.0	198.0	92.0	639.0	1,059.0	0.0
Luxembourg										
1938	3,449.0	3,449.0		0.0	0.0	0.0	0.0	0.0	3,449.0	5,141.0
1951	4,192.0	4,192.0		0.0	0.0	0.0	0.0	0.0	4,192.0	5,625.0
1952	4,309.0	4,309.0		0.0	0.0	0.0	0.0	0.0	4,309.0	7,248.0
1953	4,202.0	4,202.0		0.0	0.0	0.0	0.0	0.0	4,202.0	7,168.0
1954	4,717.0	4,717.0		0.0	0.0	0.0	0.0	0.0	4,717.0	5,887.0
1955	(5,100.0)	(5,100.0)		0.0	0.0	0.0	0.0	0.0	(5,100.0)	7,204.0

Total ECSC

1938	16,117.0	13,369.5	1,685.6	1,061.9	16,688.1	9,587.3	1,284.8	5,816.0	32,805.1	49,329.0
1951	18,040.4	15,916.6	1,981.6	142.2	10,064.4	6,502.2	169.0	3,393.2	28,104.8	52,583.0
1952	18,946.7	15,784.4	3,061.9	100.4	12,778.2	7,535.6	457.2	4,785.4	31,724.9	61,854.0
1953	18,524.0	15,426.5	2,992.6	104.9	13,446.3	6,909.8	1,091.2	5,445.3	31,970.3	61,113.0
1954	18,391.1	16,644.1	1,651.4	95.6	12,736.0	7,709.6	1,122.3	3,904.1	31,127.1	60,875.0
1955	22,150.0	20,187.0	1,863.0	(100.0)	18,538.0	9,418.0	2,216.0	6,904.0	40,688.0	70,400.0

United Kingdom

1938	387.6	323.1	0.0	64.5	4,991.7	1,303.6	83.0	3,605.1	5,379.3	12,050.0
1951	432.3	365.5	0.0	66.8	8,843.9	3,526.9	767.8	4,549.2	9,276.2	15,014.0
1952	509.1	445.8	0.0	63.3	9,774.9	3,702.0	733.3	5,339.6	10,284.0	16,493.0
1953	531.4	453.5	0.0	77.9	11,105.7	3,866.7	1,447.7	5,791.3	11,637.1	16,071.0
1954	542.7	457.4	0.0	85.3	11,763.9	4,250.2	1,497.3	6,016.4	12,306.6	15,807.0
1955	700.3	647.4	0.0	52.9	12,401.0	4,144.1	1,967.8	6,289.1	13,101.3	16,435.0

Total ECSC and United Kingdom

1938	16,504.6	13,692.6	1,685.6	1,126.4	21,679.8	10,890.9	1,367.8	9,421.1	38,184.4	61,379.0
1951	18,472.7	16,282.1	1,981.6	209.0	18,908.3	10,029.1	936.8	7,942.4	37,381.0	67,597.0
1952	19,455.8	16,230.2	3,061.9	163.7	22,553.1	11,237.6	1,190.5	10,125.0	42,008.9	78,347.0
1953	19,055.4	15,880.0	2,992.6	182.8	24,552.0	10,776.5	2,538.9	11,236.6	43,607.4	77,184.0
1954	18,933.8	17,101.5	1,651.4	180.9	24,499.9	11,959.8	2,619.6	9,920.5	43,433.7	76,682.0
1955	22,850.3	20,834.4	1,863.0	152.9	30,939.0	13,562.1	4,183.8	13,193.1	53,789.3	86,835.0

Sources: 1938 to 1954, and 1955 for United Kingdom, from Yearbooks of British Iron and Steel Federation; 1955 from HA, *Bulletin statistique*; Statistisches Bundesamt, Düsseldorf; *Eisen und Stahl Jahrbuch*; production data, from ECE, *Quarterly Bulletin of Steel Statistics*, refer to merchantable rather than crude ore. Statistisches Bundesamt, Düsseldorf, in particular is helpful in breaking down the trade figures for Belgium and Luxembourg.

[a] Manganiferous ore and pyrites are excluded, except that the former is included in the Italian data. 1938 trade estimates for the Saar were calculated on the ratio of ore to pig iron, and on the assumption that the Saar obtained all its ore from Luxembourg-Lorraine. The 1938 estimate for Germany was obtained by subtracting the Saar estimate from the actual data for the two combined.

[b] The iron content of home-produced ore is: Germany, 31 to 35 per cent; France, 33 per cent; Belgium, 35 per cent; Italy, 45 per cent; Luxembourg and the United Kingdom, 30 per cent.

Note: Discrepancies in addition are due to rounding.

Table 3-1

PRODUCTION OF PIG IRON, MAIN EUROPEAN PRODUCERS AND THE UNITED STATES, 1880–1957[a]

(Thousands of Metric Tons)

Year	Germany	Saar	France	Belgium	Luxem-bourg	Italy	Nether-lands	Main Continental	United Kingdom	United States	Total World[b]
1880	2,468[c]	...	1,725	690	261	17	...	5,161	7,873	3,896	18,448
1890	4,099[c]	...	1,962	788	559	14	...	7,422	8,031	9,349	27,174
1900	7,550[c]	...	2,714	1,019	971	24	...	12,278	9,103	14,008	40,350
1910	13,111[e]	...	4,038	1,852	1,682	355	...	21,038	10,122	27,736	65,786
1913[d]	15,393	1,371	5,207	2,485	2,548	432	...	27,436	10,424	31,458	78,800
1913[e]	10,916	1,371	9,071	2,485	2,548	432	...	26,823	10,424	31,458	78,800
1920	3,691	644	3,434	1,116	693	109	...	9,687	8,163	37,349	63,846
1921	4,547	896	3,417	876	970	77	...	10,783	2,658	16,871	37,500
1922	9,194	1,157	5,229	1,613	1,679	178	...	19,050	4,981	27,511	55,200
1923	5,028	929	5,432	2,148	1,407	269	...	15,213	7,558	40,848	69,100
1924	7,856	1,345	7,693	2,844	2,157	341	91	22,327	7,436	31,751	67,600
1925	10,089	1,450	8,494	2,542	2,363	536	109	25,583	6,362	37,125	76,889
1926	9,636	1,625	9,432	3,368	2,559	558	143	27,321	2,498	39,821	78,600
1927	13,089	1,771	9,273	3,709	2,732	529	204	31,307	7,410	36,956	86,600
1928	11,804	1,936	9,981	3,857	2,770	555	258	31,161	6,716	38,577	88,300
1929	13,239	2,105	10,364	4,041	2,906	733	254	33,642	7,711	43,081	98,100
1930	9,698	1,912	10,035	3,365	2,473	585	273	28,341	6,291	32,051	80,495
1931	6,061	1,515	8,199	3,198	2,053	552	257	21,835	3,833	18,588	56,074
1932	3,932	1,349	5,537	2,749	1,960	495	236	16,258	3,631	8,846	39,739
1933	5,247	1,592	6,324	2,710	1,888	566	253	18,580	4,202	13,443	49,237
1934	8,716	1,827	6,151	2,952	1,955	573	258	22,432	6,065	16,261	62,881

Year											
1935	10,874	1,972	5,789	3,030	1,872	694	254	24,485	6,527	21,500	74,461
1936	13,090	2,212	6,230	3,161	1,987	806	275	27,761	7,845	31,270	91,730
1937	13,739	2,221	7,914	3,804	2,512	864	312	31,366	8,629	37,342	104,200
1938e	15,635	2,410	6,061	2,426	1,551	929	267	29,279	6,870	19,213	82,721
1938f	15,176	2,410	6,061	2,426	1,551	929	267	28,894	6,870	19,213	82,721
1946	2,100	246	3,444	2,161	1,365	205	187	9,708	7,886	41,312	78,445
1947	2,300	653	4,886	2,817	1,818	384	288	13,146	7,910	53,798	98,581
1948	4,700	1,134	6,559	3,929	2,624	526	442	19,914	9,425	55,367	112,827
1949	7,100	1,582	8,345	3,749	2,372	445	434	24,027	9,651	49,138	115,740
1950	9,500	1,682	7,761	3,695	2,499	573	454	26,164	9,787	59,354	132,769
1951	10,697	2,370	8,750	4,868	3,157	953	524	31,319	9,824	64,604	147,146
1952	12,877	2,550	9,769	4,790	3,076	1,102	539	34,703	10,900	56,371	150,300
1953	11,654	2,382	8,666	4,210	2,722	1,222	593	31,449	11,354	68,802	165,900
1954	12,512	2,497	8,841	4,625	2,801	1,257	610	33,143	12,074	53,229	156,100
1955	16,482	2,879	10,958	5,389	3,085	1,625	670	41,088	12,670	70,555	189,300
1956	17,577	3,031	11,480	5,761	3,316	1,873	662	43,700	13,382	70,452	198,500
1957	18,468	3,168	12,072	5,592	3,372	2,136	701	45,509	14,520	71,976	208,500

451

Sources: 1880–1950 from Ingvar Svennilson, *Growth and Stagnation in the European Economy*, ECE, Geneva, 1954, pp. 257–259; Germany post–World War I and 1938 post–World War II territory from OEEC, *Industrial Statistics, 1900–1955*, Paris, 1955, and ECE, *Quarterly Bulletin of Steel Statistics*, Geneva.; data for United States and total world for all years from *Metal Statistics*, American Metal Market, New York; American Iron and Steel Institute, *Annual Reports*; UN, *Monthly Bulletin of Statistics*, New York; and OEEC, *op. cit.*

a Ferroalloys included.
b Total world rather than total of countries listed.
c Includes the Saar.
d Pre–World War I territory.
e Interwar territory.
f Post–World War II territory.

Table 4-1

HARD COAL OUTPUT PER MAN-SHIFT, UNDERGROUND AND SURFACE WORKERS COMBINED,
SELECTED COUNTRIES AND YEARS, 1913–1956ᵃ (*Metric Tons*)

Year	Germany	Ruhr	Saar	France	Belgium	Netherlands	United Kingdom	United States Bituminousᵇ	United States Anthracite
1913	...	0.943	0.843	0.701	0.538	0.820	1.030	3.270	1.822
1925	...	0.946	0.680	0.563	0.472	0.837	0.910	4.040	1.923
1926	...	1.114	0.692	0.612	0.512	0.991	0.938	4.010	1.896
1927	...	1.132	0.740	0.606	0.513	1.018	1.048	4.060	1.950
1928	...	1.191	0.811	0.642	0.554	1.162	1.080	4.180	1.969
1929	...	1.271	0.836	0.694	0.576	1.247	1.100	4.290	1.968
1930	...	1.352	0.874	0.691	0.575	1.246	1.100	4.470	2.005
1931	...	1.490	0.901	0.720	0.591	1.308	1.098	4.640	...
1932	1.548	1.628	1.034	0.780	0.609	1.445	1.120	4.530	2.304
1933	...	1.677	1.118	0.833	0.663	1.560	1.142	4.173	...
1934	...	1.678	1.147	0.858	0.735	1.689	1.165	3.837	...
1935	...	1.692	0.929	0.871	0.775	1.804	1.190	3.919	2.431
1936	1.643	1.711	0.951	0.860	0.794	1.826	1.200	4.010	2.531
1937	...	1.627	1.054	0.833	0.782	1.774	1.186	...	2.513
1938	1.500	1.547	1.176	0.831	0.753	1.645	1.160	4.173	2.531
1946	0.864	0.877	0.835	0.593	0.563	0.939	1.042	4.926	2.576
1947	0.882	0.893	0.867	0.588	0.584	1.297	1.091	4.981	2.520
1948	0.937	0.954	0.763	...	0.603	1.362	1.124	4.817	2.548
1949	1.032	1.051	0.844	0.702	0.641	1.407	1.179	4.917	2.603
1950	1.063	1.084	0.961	0.770	0.693	1.425	1.211	5.216	2.567
1951	1.102	1.124	1.043	0.843	0.743	1.420	1.229	5.516	2.690
1952	1.114	1.137	1.037	0.892	0.748	1.022	1.212	5.779	2.780
1953	1.104	1.127	1.082	0.927	0.766	0.986	1.239	6.360	2.980
1954	1.126	1.151	1.119	0.988	0.784	0.967	1.250	...	...
1955	1.163	1.185	1.157	1.042	0.825	0.953	1.243	...	...
1956	1.190	(1.200)	1.158	1.078	0.841	0.963	1.250	...	...

Sources: Kohlenwirtschaft; Reid Report; U. S. Department of the Interior, *Minerals Yearbook,* Washington, 1953, Vol. II, p. 170; ECE, *Quarterly Bulletin of Coal Statistics;* Robert Lafitte-Laplace, *L'Economie charbonnière de la France,* Marcel Giard, Paris, 1933, pp. 352–353; ILO, *Productivity in Coal Mines,* Geneva, 1951, p. 26, and 1953 edition, Table A, Appendix I; *Jahrbuch; Glückauf,* July 21, 1956.

ᵃ Auxiliary operations excluded.
ᵇ Underground mines only, which produced 100 per cent of United States coal in 1913 and 77 per cent in 1955.

452

Table 4-2

HARD COAL OUTPUT PER MAN-SHIFT, UNDERGROUND WORKERS ONLY, SELECTED COUNTRIES AND YEARS, 1913–1956[a] (Metric Tons)

Year	Germany			France				Belgium			Netherlands	United Kingdom	United States	
	Ruhr	Aachen	Saar	Total	Nord and Pas-de-Calais	Lorraine	Centre-Midi	Total	Campine	South			Bituminous[b]	Anthracite
	(1a)	(1b)	(2)	(3a)	(3b)	(3c)	(3d)	(4a)	(4b)	(4c)	(5)	(6)	(7a)	(7b)
1913	1.161	0.957	…	0.982	0.998	1.045	0.952	0.731	…	…	1.090	…	3.774	2.422
1925	1.079	0.907	…	0.799	0.783	0.846	0.790	0.698	…	…	1.163	…	4.618	2.359
1926	…	…	…	0.837	0.847	0.856	0.801	…	…	…	…	…	4.600	2.295
1927	1.386	1.045	…	0.833	0.835	0.886	0.815	0.737	…	…	1.415	1.330	4.636	2.341
1928	1.463	1.099	…	0.912	0.898	0.995	0.915	0.796	…	…	1.636	1.380	4.772	2.359
1929	1.558	1.148	…	0.986	0.962	1.116	0.941	0.836	…	…	1.711	1.390	4.917	2.395
1930	1.678	1.198	…	0.982	0.956	1.177	0.935	0.827	…	…	1.690	1.390	5.080	2.386
1931	1.888	1.268	…	1.043	1.002	1.445	1.060	0.853	…	…	1.760	1.400	5.235	2.441
1932	2.093	1.415	…	1.156	…	…	…	0.859	…	…	1.991	1.430	5.262	2.685
1933	2.164	1.535	…	1.236	…	…	…	0.971	…	…	2.197	1.480	4.870	2.560
1934	2.162	1.517	…	1.290	…	…	…	1.076	…	…	2.412	1.500	4.470	2.610
1935	2.183	1.486	1.277	1.333	…	…	…	1.136	…	…	2.633	1.530	4.581	2.758
1936	2.199	1.497	1.306	1.306	…	…	…	1.173	…	…	2.670	1.550	4.663	2.794
1937	2.054	1.452	1.436	1.235	…	…	…	1.139	…	…	2.550	1.530	4.681	2.758
1938	1.970	1.409	1.570	1.229	…	…	…	1.085	…	…	2.368	…	4.881	2.803
1946	1.208	0.987	1.137	0.926	…	…	…	0.816	…	…	1.583	1.403	6.124	2.486
1947	1.215	1.036	1.162	0.953	…	…	…	0.860	…	…	1.639	1.460	5.870	2.468
1948	1.286	1.087	1.196	0.958	…	…	…	0.877	…	…	1.683	1.488	5.879	2.459
1949	1.383	1.162	1.317	1.092	…	…	…	0.930	…	…	1.735	1.561	6.006	…
1950	1.425	1.156	1.498	1.195	…	…	…	1.014	…	…	1.754	1.612	…	…
1951	1.482	1.195	1.617	1.298	1.175	1.969	1.219	1.059	1.315	0.975	1.729	1.632	…	…
1952	1.503	1.194	1.623	1.353	1.228	2.018	1.270	1.051	1.300	0.965	1.609	1.607	…	…
1953	1.486	1.186	1.676	1.416	1.277	2.088	1.343	1.068	1.307	0.986	1.567	1.630	…	…
1954	1.523	1.200	1.744	1.504	1.349	2.214	1.424	1.095	1.352	1.011	1.499	1.614	…	…
1955	1.572	1.279	1.810	1.583	1.426	2.257	1.513	1.148	1.484	1.028	1.486	1.600	…	…
1956	1.591	1.281	1.819	1.645	1.484	2.275	1.590	1.160	1.492	1.034	1.496	1.601	…	…

Sources: Kohlenwirtschaft except as follows: 1955 and 1956 in cols. 2–6, inclusive, from ECE, Quarterly Bulletin of Coal Statistics; 1955–1956 in cols. 1a and 1b, and 1951–1956 in cols. 3b, 3c, 3d, 4b, 4c, from HA, Bulletin statistique.

[a] Hours per underground shift declined considerably during the period covered. In 1913 a regular shift consisted of 9 hours everywhere but the Ruhr, the United Kingdom and the United States, where it was 8.5 hours. In the interwar years, the hours varied from 7.5 to 8; all winding time in some areas, and one winding time in others, was counted as working time; these regulations as well as the length of the shift were unstable during this period owing to the effect of economic rivalry on wages. Since World War II all areas are on a 7.5–7.75-hour shift (but only one winding time is included in the United Kingdom). The United States is on a 7-hour shift portal to portal. The shift was raised to 8 hours in the Ruhr in 1959 to offset the change from a 6- to a 5-day week. Owing to increasing distance between working face and shaft mouth, the decline in hours spent at the working face has been even greater than the decrease in total hours per shift. See ILO, The World Coal-Mining Industry, Geneva, 1938, Vol. II, pp. 216 ff, and Robert Lafitte-Laplace, L'Economie charbonnière de la France, Marcel Giard, Paris, 1933, pp. 54–55, 321–329.

[b] Underground productivity in underground mines only, but open-pit mines, which did not exist in 1913, accounted for 23 per cent of the United States output of bituminous coal in 1955.

Investment figures in this table comprise outlays for coke, briquetting and power facilities. Turnover refers to gross income from sales of primary and secondary products, exclusive of turnover taxes.

Table 4-3

FINANCING OF INVESTMENTS IN THE COAL INDUSTRY, SELECTED COUNTRIES AND YEARS, 1949–1956[a]

Country and Year	Investment as Per Cent of Turnover	Investment per Ton		Self-Financing	
		Total	Available from Earnings	As Per Cent of Investments[b]	As Per Cent of Turnover[c]
	(1)	(2)	(3)	(4)	(5)
Germany[d]					
1949	9.2	$0.77	...	...	...
1950	8.7	0.75	...	...	...
1951	8.7	0.90	...	...	...
1952	11.9	1.41	...	...	...
1953	13.6	1.71	$1.23	78.0	10.6
1954	13.8	1.69	1.47	91.0	12.6
1955	12.1	1.59	1.47	111.0	13.4
1956	9.9	1.44	...	...	...
France					
1953	29.8	4.26	0.87	20.4	6.1
1954	23.3	3.95	1.03	26.1	6.1
1955	21.2	3.41	1.58	46.3	9.8
1956	19.2	3.09	1.32	42.7	8.7
Saar					
1954	10.5	1.23	0.49	39.7	4.2
1955	10.5	1.33	0.95	71.2	7.5
1956	12.0	1.55	0.54	34.7	4.2

b Based on retained earnings as per cent of investments exclusive of debt repayment. According to French accounting procedure, the figures for France would be as follows:

	Col. 4
1953	17.5
1954	23.9
1955	33.1
1956	31.8

c Col. 1 x col. 4.

d Data on amortization since currency reform on June 21, 1950 are available from company reports for a few firms only; they follow:

	Currency Reform Through:	1955 Output of Coal (Millions of Tons)	Per Cent of Investments Self-Financed
Emscher Lippe	1956	1.2	79
Gelsenkirchener	1956	17.8	78
Heinrich Bergbau	1955	1.4	87
Hibernia	1956	10.8	90
Märkische	1955	4.0	75

These firms produced 28 per cent of the Ruhr coal in 1955. Between 75 and 90 per cent of total investments were thus amortized in a period of five to six years.

Combined data for a larger portion of the industry are, to date, available only for 1953–1955. These, shown in cols. 3 to 5, cover 83 per cent of the Ruhr in 1954–1955 and 62 per cent in 1953, whereas the data in cols. 1 and 2 cover all German hard coal production. The firms covered in cols. 3 to 5 show the following results for col. 2:

	Col. 2
1953	$1.68
1954	1.61
1955	1.32

Sources: Germany: Werner Moritz, *Der Steinkohlenbergbau der Bundesrepublik als Investor,* Vierteljahresheft zur Wirtschaftsforschung, 1957, Drittesheft; Institut für Bilanzenanalysen, *Der Ruhrbergbau,* 1957; cols. 1 and 2 refer to total German output, and cols. 3 to 5 to firms producing 83 per cent of Ruhr coal in 1954–1955 and 62 per cent in 1953. France: Annual reports of Charbonnages de France, covering virtually all the French output. Saar: Annual reports of the Saarbergwerke, covering virtually all the Saar output. All together about 82 per cent of ECSC coal production is covered.

a Investments in Germany refer to capital expenditures for fixed assets activated in company balance sheets, exclusive of housing; in France and the Saar they refer to all capital outlays, including housing and working capital but excluding financial charges and debt repayment. Only half the "medium-term" outlays are activated, and housing expenditures are higher than in Germany. See *Glückauf,* March 30, 1957, p. 400. Investments in this table are thus not comparable with those shown in Tables 28 and 30.

Table 5-1

CONCENTRATION OF FRENCH CRUDE STEEL PRODUCTION, BY GROUP AND REGION, 1958[a]

(Amount in Thousands of Metric Tons)

Group	Lorraine Amount	Lorraine Per Cent	North Amount	North Per Cent	Centre-Midi Amount	Centre-Midi Per Cent	West Amount	West Per Cent	Southeast Amount	Southeast Per Cent	Southwest Amount	Southwest Per Cent	Total Amount	Total Per Cent
Denain-Anzin	—	—	1,520	67	—	—	—	—	—	—	—	—	1,520	14
Pont-à-Mousson[b]	1,266	18	—	—	250	47	—	—	100	69	25	36	1,616	15
De Wendel[c]	1,382	19	—	—	—	—	—	—	—	—	—	—	1,382	13
Longwy-Raty[d]	1,532	21	500	22	—	—	—	—	—	—	—	—	2,032	19
Schneider[e]	530	7	—	—	275	52	345	72	—	—	—	—	1,175	11
Chatillon-Commentry[f]	365	5	50	2	—	—	—	—	—	—	—	—	415	4
Société Générale Cofinindus-Brufina	1,100	15	—	—	—	—	—	—	—	—	—	—	1,100	10
Total	6,175	85	2,070	91	525	99	345	72	100	69	25	36	8,687	86
Other	952	15	203	9	8	1	134	28	45	31	45	64	1,940	14
TOTAL	7,127	100	2,273	100	533	100	479	100	145	100	70	100	10,627	100

Sources: Centre de Recherches Economiques et Sociales, La Concentration financière dans la sidérurgie française, Paris, 1956; Wolf-Rodé, Handbuch. Some of the regional production figures were estimated by the author.

[a] Production data are for 1954; concentrations are as of mid-1958.

[b] The firms Marine et Saint-Etienne and Ateliers et Forges de la Loire have been included in the Pont-à-Mousson group because of the financial cross-connections between the two. Marine et Saint-Etienne, which has interests in the southeast, the southwest and the Centre-Midi, controlled over 350,000 tons; the distribution of this tonnage among the three areas is estimated.

[c] The De Wendel group has plants in the Centre-Midi (at Gueugnon) and in the west (at Hennebont and in the Basse-Indre) but the last two produce tin products rather than crude steel; the tinplate originates elsewhere. Gueugnon has a community of interest with Ugine, an important alloy steel producer in the southeast that markets stainless steel under the brand name "Ugine-Gueugnon." See Wolf-Rodé, Handbuch, pp. 198, 206, 218.

[d] The division of the 2,032,000 tons between Lorraine and the north is based on an estimate drawn from ibid., pp. 199–202.

[e] Included is the firm known as Imphy, producing 100,000 tons, which were distributed regionally according to the following estimate: 25,000 tons to the Pamier plant in the southwest, and 75,000 tons to the Centre-Midi, where Le Creusot produced about 200,000 tons.

[f] The Montluçon plant (Centre-Midi), though controlled by Chatillon, is considered part of the Forges de la Loire complex in the Pont-à-Mousson group. Chatillon-Commentry controls a plant in the north at Isbergues to which 50,000 tons were arbitrarily assigned within the 415,000 ton total.

Table 5-2

Key for col. 3:*

L: Launoit group, which comprises:
    B: Brufina;   C: Cofinindus;   BC: Brufina-Cofinindus
SG: Société Générale group, which comprises:
    CO: Cockerill-Ougrée (controlled by SG and L)
S: Schneider family (France)
P-à-M: Pont-à-Mousson group (France)

* For relationships, see Chapter 5, section on "The Steel Industry in Belgium-Luxembourg."

| | Crude Steel Output (1955) | | |
Country and Firm	Amount (*Thousands of Metric Tons*)	Per Cent	Per Cent of Stock Owned by Major Stockholders
	(1)	(2)	(3)
Belgium			
Cockerill-Ougrée[b]	2,000	34	SG, 10.45; BC, 9.12
Aciéries et Minières de la Sambre[c]	300	5	CO, 12; C, 22
Thy-le-Château et Marcinelle[c]	330	6	B, 25
Forges de la Providence[d]	650	11	SG, 30
Hainaut-Sambre[e]	1,050	18	SG; Flick, 20
Total	4,330	74[f]	
France			
French division of Providence[d]	580	4	
S. A. des Hauts-Fourneaux de la Chiers[g]	650	6	CO, 25; C, 20; B, 5
Total	1,230	10	
Luxembourg			
Arbed[h]	1,950	60	SG, 16; B, 4
			S, 25; Barbanson, 15–20
Rodange[i]	405	13	CO, 23; C, 24; B, 12
Hadir[j]	865	27	SG, 15; CO, 8; P-à-M, 48
Total	3,220	100	
Saar			
Saar division of Arbed	740	23	
Total	9,520	18	
Less:[k]			
Hadir	8,655	16	
Arbed and Hadir	5,965	11	
Arbed, Hadir and Hainaut-Sambre	4,915	9	

Sources:

Cols. 1 and 2: company financial reports and Wolf-Rodé, *Handbuch*, pp. 133–162, which provides data on capacity, at that time substantially equivalent to 1955 production.

Col. 3: The main sources, in addition to those given in the notes below, are: *Handelsblatt*, July 22, 1955, p. 14, and February 20, 1957, p. 8; Cockerill-Ougrée, the financial report for 1955, pp. 18–19, lists the firms in which it holds shares; *Holdings et democratie économique*, Federation Générale du Travail de Belgique, Liége, 1956, p. 97; Hans Wolter, *Die französische eisenschaffende*

456

Industrie, Kommissionsverlag Schrobsdorff'sche Buchhandlung, Düsseldorf, 1953, p. 25; Frederic Benham, *The Iron and Steel Industry of Germany, France, Belgium, Luxembourg and the Saar*, London and Cambridge Economic Service, London, October 1934, pp. 40–42; Albert Wehrer, "Les Fusions et concentrations d'entreprises dans les pays de la Communauté Européenne du Charbon et de l'Acier," HA, Luxembourg, November 1955; *Continental Iron and Steel Reports*, May 26, 1956, p. 2; Wolf-Rodé, *Handbuch*, p. 139 re Providence, p. 150 re Brufina's shareholdings as of December 31, 1953, pp. 150–152 re Société Générale's and John Cockerill's shareholdings.

[a] The financial ties are as of the end of 1956; production is for 1955. Data are confined to firms that produce crude steel.

[b] Operates several branch plants in Belgium at Athus, Seraing, Grévignée.

[c] The connection between these two firms, if any, is not clear.

[d] Operates a plant at Marchienne-au-Pont, Belgium, and, across the border, at Rehon and Haumont, France. See *Handelsblatt*, November 26, 1956, p. 6.

[e] This firm comprises a 1955 merger of Usines Métallurgiques du Hainaut and of S. A. Métallurgique de Sambre et Moselle. Société Générale had had a 20 per cent interest in the latter; the size of its interest in the new firm is unknown. The principal stockholders in Hainaut-Sambre, besides Société Générale, are now Banque de Paris et des Pays-Bas and Société de Gestion et de Participations Mercure; the latter represents Flick. SG may not be the dominant stockholder. Flick and Pays-Bas together have a large interest in or control the Société des Aciéries et Tréfileries de Neuves-Maisons-Chatillon, in Lorraine; see *Neue Zürcher Zeitung*, April 11, 1956. Maximilianshütte A. G., a Flick steel concern in Germany, later acquired Mercure's interest in Neuves-Maisons; see *Handelsblatt*, November 2, 1956, p. 1. In December 1954 the High Authority authorized Société Métallurgique de Sambre et Moselle to sell through Ucometal, which also marketed for John Cockerill and Providence; HA, *Journal officiel*, January 11, 1955, p. 541.

[f] The other 26 per cent of production comprises Forges de Clabecq, 480,000 tons; Espérance-Longdoz, 500,000 tons; and another half million tons distributed among smaller firms. Data are not available to indicate whether these plants are independent or not; *Holdings et democratie économique*, pp. 181–184, assigns Espérance-Longdoz to the Coppée group. Wehrer, *op. cit.*, p. 10, says SG and L control 80 per cent.

[g] Operates in both Belgium and France but its principal crude steel facilities are at Longwy (France), where about 90 per cent of the capacity is located. Data on the distribution of stock in this firm are from Wolter, *op. cit.*, p. 25; *Holdings et democratie économique*, p. 172; *Handelsblatt*, July 22, 1955, p. 14; Herbert Steiner, *Grössenordnung und horizontale Verflechtung in der Eisen- und Stahlindustrie der Vereinigten Staaten, Grossbritanniens, Frankreichs, Belgiens, Luxemburgs und Deutschlands*, Kieler Studien, Kiel, 1952, pp. 89, 110.

[h] Arbed falls under the control of several groups. See the data in *Handelsblatt*, March 22-23, 1957, p. 10; Centre de Recherches Economiques et Sociales, *La Concentration financière dans la sidérurgie française*, Paris, April 1956, p. 6. *Handelsblatt*, October 28, 1955, p. 8, is probably inaccurate in assigning one third the share capital to the Launoit group; see Arbed's financial reports for its own stockholdings in other firms.

[i] See Carlo Hemmer, *L'Economie du Grand-Duché de Luxembourg, 2ème partie*, J. Beffort, Luxembourg, 1953, pp. 113–114; Benham, *op. cit.*, pp. 40–42; Rodange's financial statement for 1955.

[j] Pont-à-Mousson is the principal stockholder. See *La Concentration financière dans la sidérurgie française*, pp. 21, 25; Benham, *op. cit.*, p. 40; Steiner, *op. cit.*, p. 58; Hemmer, *op. cit.*, pp. 111–112; Hadir's financial statement for 1955.

[k] Size of the SG and L group after subtracting firms in which other major groups also have an important share interest.

Table 5-3

ITALY: CONTROL OF CRUDE STEEL PRODUCTION, BY FIRM, REGION AND PROCESS, 1954[a]

Firm	Tidewater				Inland			Total			
	Thomas	Siemens-Martin	Electric	Total	Siemens-Martin	Electric	Total	Thomas	Siemens-Martin	Electric	Total
	(1)	(2)	(3)	(4)	(5)	(6)	(7)	(8)	(9)	(10)	(11)
				Percentage Distribution							
Italian State (IRI and Finsider)[b]											
Ilva	100	(61)	(16)	(63)	(3)	(4)	(4)	100	(30)	(6)	26
Terni	—	(35)	—	—	—	(9)	(5)	—	—	(8)	3
Cornigliano	—	—	—	(23)	(13)	—	—	—	(16)	—	9
Dalmine	—	—	—	—	—	(10)	(12)	—	—	(9)	7
Other	—	—	(62)	(8)	(6)	(18)	(12)	—	(11)	(22)	10
Total	100	(96)	(78)	(94)	(22)	(41)	(33)	100	(57)	(45)	55
Fiat[c]	—	—	—	—	(21)	(12)	(16)	—	(11)	(10)	10
Falck[d]	—	—	—	—	(17)	(15)	(16)	—	(9)	(13)	10
Total listed	100	(96)	(78)	(94)	(60)	(68)	(65)	100	(77)	(69)	76
Other enterprises[e]	—	(4)	(22)	(6)	(40)	(32)	(35)	—	(23)	(31)	24
TOTAL ITALY	100	100	100	100	100	100	100	100	100	100	100
				Amount (Thousands of Metric Tons)							
TOTAL PRODUCTION[f]	317	1,033	216	1,566	1,175	1,466	2,641	317	2,208	1,682	4,207

Sources: Annual financial reports of individual companies; company data in Wolf-Rodé, *Handbuch*, pp. 249–284; *Neue Zürcher Zeitung*, April 17, 1956; *Steel Review*, British Iron and Steel Federation, London, January 1957, pp. 53–55; *Yearbooks* of British Iron and Steel Federation. Table 9 explains the classification by regions. See also sources in notes below.

[a] Cols. 1–7 are approximate, cols. 8–10 fairly exact, and col. 11 is based on actual total production by each enterprise.

[b] Included here are enterprises in which IRI and Finsider combined control 50 per cent or more of the capital stock. They control over 77 per cent of Ilva; nearly 100 per cent of Cornigliano; 51 per cent of Terni, Dalmine and Breda Siderurgica; 50 per cent of ATUB; 100 per cent of Nazionale Cogne and of SIAC. The last four companies are included in "other" under Italian State. Several companies, notably Ilva, operate more than one plant.

[c] Annual company reports and Wolf-Rodé, *Handbuch*, p. 262.

[d] Estimated from annual company reports and Wolf-Rodé, *Handbuch*, p. 251.

[e] Derived by subtraction.

Sources on financial control: *Neue Zürcher Zeitung*, April 17, 1956, November 8, 1956; Wolf-Rodé, *Handbuch*, pp. 258–259; Maurice Fontaine, *L'Industrie sidérurgique dans le monde et son évolution économique depuis la Seconde Guerre Mondiale*, Presses Universitaires de France, Paris, 1950, pp. 292, 295; *Handelsblatt*, "Wer sind die Eigentümer?" July 13, 1956; Hans-Joachim Otto, *Strukturwandlungen und Nachkriegsprobleme der Wirtschaft italiens*, Kieler Studien, Kiel, 1951, p. 38; *Financial Times*, June 22, 1956; *Neue Zürcher Zeitung*, April 17, 1956, indicates that IRI and Finsider control 50.5 per cent of Italian steel; these figures exclude Nazionale Cogne and Breda Siderurgica, which produce 4 per cent.

[f] British Iron and Steel Federation, *Yearbooks*.

Table 5-4

GERMANY: CONTROLLING GROUPS IN STEEL PRODUCING FIRMS, 1959[a]

Area and Firm	Parent Firm or Group and Percentage Control		Source of Data (Key in Source Note)
Ruhr			
1. Hüttenwerk Oberhausen A. G.	Haniel family	70.0	(A) 36–37, 50
2. Westfalenhütte A. G.	Hoesch Werke A. G.[b]	100.0	(A) 43, 121
3. Hüttenwerk Rheinhausen A. G.[c]	(Krupp) Hütten- u. Berg-werke Rheinhausen A. G.	100.0	(D) Mar. 22, 1956; (A) 52
4. Hahnsche Werke A. G.	Mannesmann A. G.[b]	45.0	(C) Sept. 4, 1956; (A) 75
5. Mannesmann Hüttenwerke	Mannesmann A. G.	100.0	(A) 79; (B) Je. 20, 1956
6. Stahlwerke Bochum A. G.	Gewerkschaft Michel	100.0	(B) Je. 26, 1957, p. 7
7. Dortmund-Hörder Hüttenunion	Hoogovens, Ijmuiden	40.8	(B) Apr. 18, 1956 (WSE)
8. Georgsmarienwerke A. G.	Klöckner Werke A. G.	100.0	(A) 62–63
9. Hüttenwerk Haspe A. G.	Klöckner Werke A. G.	100.0	(A) 62–63
10. Gusstahlwerk, Oberkassel	Rheinische Stahlwerke	100.0	(B) Nov. 16, 1956 (WSE)
11. Gusstahlwerk, Witten	Rheinische Stahlwerke	30.0	(B) Nov. 16, 1956 (WSE)
12. Ruhrstahl A. G., Witten	Rheinische Stahlwerke	95.4	(B) Dec. 3, 1956 (WSE)
13. Phoenix-Rheinrohr	Fritz Thyssens Vermögens-verwaltung (FTV)	53.0	(B) Apr. 10, 1957, p. 7
14. August Thyssen Hütte A. G.[d]	FTV	12.0	(B) Apr. 10, 1957, p. 7
	Thyssen A. G. für Beteili-gungen (TAGB)	41.0	(B) Apr. 10, 1957, p. 7
15. Niederrheinische Hütte A. G.	A. Thyssen Hütte	96.0	(B) Mar. 27, 1957, p. 7; Apr. 17, 1957, p. 6
16. Deutsche Edelstahlwerke A. G.	A. Thyssen Hütte	61.0	(B) Mar. 26, 1958, p. 10
17. Gusstahlwerk Bochumer Verein	H. u. B. Rheinhausen (Krupp)	75.0	(B) Jan. 7, 1959, p. 7
Rhineland			
18. Stahl- u. Walzwerke Rasselstein-Andernach	Eisen- u. Hüttenbetriebe A. G. (Wolff)	75.0	(A) 105; (B) Jy. 6, 1956
	A. Thyssen Hütte	25.0	(B) Mar. 26, 1958, p. 10

Continued on next page

Table 5-4 (continued)

Area and Firm	Parent Firm or Group and Percentage Control		Source of Data (Key in Source Note)
19. Hüttenwerk Siegerland[e]	A. Thyssen Hütte Dortmund-Hörder	34.4 majority	(B) Mar. 26, 1958, p. 10 (B) Oct. 14, 1957, p. 5
20. Stahlwerke Südwestfalen A. G.	Klöckner Werke A. G.	30.5	(E) 188
Bavaria			
21. Maximilianshütte A. G.	Merkur (Flick)	74.0	(A) 22
Lower Saxony			
22. Hüttenwerk Salzgitter	A. G. für Berg- u. Hütten- betriebe (German State)	100.0	(A) 3, 54
23. Hüttenwerk Ilsede-Peine	Ilseder Hütte A. G., in which German State has 25.1% interest thru VIAG[f]	100.0	(B) Sept. 14, 1956; Je. 6, 1956 (WSE)
Bremen			
24. Klöckner Hütte Bremen A. G.	Klöckner Werke A. G.	99.8	(B) Je. 6, 1956 (WSE); (A) 62–63

Sources:

(A) Wolf-Rodé, *Handbuch.*

(B) *Handelsblatt* (WSE refers to a series called "Wer sind die Eigentümer?").

(C) *Financial Times.*

(D) *New York Times* (international edition).

(E) K. H. Herchenröder, *Die Nachfolger der Ruhrkonzerne,* Econ-Verlag, Düsseldorf, 1953.

(F) *Neue Zürcher Zeitung.*

(G) Robert Lafitte-Laplace, *L'Economie charbonnière de la France,* Marcel Giard, Paris, 1933.

[a] Ninety-eight per cent of crude steel production covered. Firms numbered 7, 10, 11, 12, 13, 14, 15, 16, 17 and 19 are offspring of the former Vereinigte Stahlwerke. See also the article entitled "The Dynasties of the New Ruhr" in *Financial Times,* February 14, 1956.

[b] Stock ownership in the parent firm is putatively scattered.

[c] Subject to sale by the parent firm (Krupp group) by 1959 by terms of agreement between the German government and the former occupying powers. The German government in 1957 requested the latter to modify this agreement.

[d] FTV and TAGB controlled 53 per cent, but this degree of control was subject to reduction if August Thyssen Hütte issued new share capital.

[e] August Thyssen Hütte, which sells 40 per cent of its output of hot-rolled strip to Hüttenwerk Siegerland, announced in May 1957 that it had purchased an interest in that firm in order to protect its sales outlet.

[f] VIAG stands for Vereinigte Industrie-Unternehmungen A. G., a 100 per cent State-owned holding company.

Table 5-5

GERMANY: CONCENTRATION OF CONTROL IN CRUDE
STEEL PRODUCTION, BY GROUP AND REGION, 1959[a]

	Crude Steel Production		
	Amount *(Thousands of Metric Tons)*	Per Cent:	
Area, Group and Firm		Of Region	Of Germany
Ruhr			
Thyssen group:			
Phoenix-Rheinrohr	2,220	13.3	11.4
August Thyssen Hütte	1,280	7.7	6.6
Niederrheinische Hütte	360	2.1	1.8
Deutsche Edelstahl	225	1.3	1.2
Total	4,085	24.4	21.0
Dortmund-Hörder (Hoogovens)	2,529	15.1	12.9
Mannesmann group	1,768	10.5	9.0
Krupp group[b]	2,801	16.7	14.4
Klöckner group	1,610	9.6	8.2
Hoesch group	1,512	9.0	7.7
Haniel group	1,484	8.8	7.6
Rheinische Stahlwerke[c]	801	4.8	4.1
Michel (Stahlwerke Bochum)	(180)	1.1	0.9
Total	16,770	100.0	85.8
Rhineland			
Rasselstein-Andernach (Wolff)	196	23.5	1.0
Dortmund-Hörder through Hüttenwerk Siegerland[d]	354	42.5	1.8[d]
Klöckner through Stahlwerke Südwestfalen	282	34.0	1.4
Total	832	100.0	4.2
Bavaria			
Maximilianshütte (Flick group)[e]	575	100.0	3.0
Lower Saxony			
Salzgitter (German State)	569	42.3	3.0
Ilsede-Peine (German State)	778	57.7	4.0
Total	1,349	100.0	7.0
TOTAL	19,526		100.0

Sources: Table 5-4, preceding; production data from company financial reports for fiscal year ending September 30, 1955; those for Mannesmann, Michel group, Krupp group and Ilsede-Peine refer to calendar 1955.

[a] Covers practically 100 per cent of German production in 1954–1955. But concentration of control is as of early 1959.

[b] Hüttenwerk Rheinhausen in the Krupp group was still subject to sale as of early 1959 but the German government had requested modification of the forced sale provision. The High Authority in late 1958 approved the purchase by the Krupp group of Gusstahlwerk Bochumer Verein.

[c] Provisional grouping.

[d] Dortmund-Hörder thus accounts for 14.7 per cent of German crude steel output.

[e] Maximilianshütte has an interest in Chatillon-Neuves-Maisons in Lorraine and through its owner, the Flick group Merkur, it is linked to Hainaut-Sambre in Belgium. *Handelsblatt*, November 2, 1956, p. 2.

461

Table 5-6

GERMANY: CONTROLLING GROUPS IN COAL PRODUCING FIRMS, 1959[a]

Coal Producing Firm by Vertical Affiliation	Parent Firm or Group and Percentage Control		Source of Data (Key in Source Note to Table 5-4)
GERMAN GROUPS			
German steel			
1. Hansa Bergbau	Dortmund-Hörder		
	(Hoogovens)	50.0	(A) 14
	GBAG	50.0	(A) 14
2. Rheinpreussen	Haniel family	100.0	(E) 141; (B) Feb. 8/9, 1957, p. 10
3. Neue Hoffnung	Hüttenwerk Oberhausen[b]	99.5	(B) May 1, 1957, p. 7, Aug. 14, 1957, p. 6
4. Altenessener	Hoesch Werke A. G.	majority	(C) Jy. 2, 1956, p. 4; (A) 43
5. Hoesch Bergbau	Hoesch Werke A. G.	100.0	(C) Jy. 2, 1956, p. 4
6. Klöckner B. Königsborn	Klöckner Werke A. G.	57.0	(B) Nov. 19, 1956; (A) 62–63
7. Klöckner B. Victor Ickern	Klöckner Werke A. G.	100.0	(A) 62–63
8. Essen Rossenray	H. u. B. Rheinhausen A. G.		
	(Krupp)	100.0	(A) 52; (B) Je. 3, 1956
9. Hannover Hannibal	H. u. B. Rheinhausen A. G.		
	(Krupp)	majority	(D) Mar. 22, 1956; (B) Jy. 7, 1956
10. Essener	Mannesmann A. G.	76.4	(B) Je. 20, 1956; (A) 74
11. Niederrheinische	Gewerkschaft Michel	86.4	(B) May 14, 1956 (WSE)
12. Arenberg	Rheinische Stahlwerke	100.0	(B) Apr. 17, 1957, p. 6
13. Friedrich Thyssen Bergbau	Phoenix Rheinrohr	50.0	(A) 48; (B) Sept. 3, 1956 (WSE)
	Hamborner Bergbau	50.0	(E) 66
14. Hamborner Bergbau[c]	Heirs of Hans and Julius Thyssen	50.0+	(E) 114; (B) Jy. 25, 27, 1956
15. Erin Bergbau	GBAG	34.0	(F) Sept. 15, 1956; (B) Dec. 31, 1956, p. 8
	A. Thyssen Hütte	51.0	(B) Mar. 26, 1958, p. 10
16. Walsum	Familie Thyssen-Bornemisza	100.0	(B) Mar. 8/9, 1957, p. 10,
	Transferred in 1958 to:		Mar. 18, 1957, p. 7
	Familienstiftung Kaszony,	60.0	Jan. 26, 1959, p. 7 (WSE)
	Bank voor Handelen		
	Scheepvaart, Rotterdam	40.0	
17. Constantin der Grosse	Gusstahlwerk Bochumer Verein (Krupp)	75.0	(B) Jan. 22, 1958, p. 8
18. Graf Moltke	G. Bochumer Verein (Krupp)	50.0	(B) Je. 13, 1956
	GBAG	50.0	(B) Je. 13, 1956
19. Carolinenglück	GBAG	50.0	(B) Je. 13, 1956
	G. Bochumer Verein (Krupp)	50.0	(B) Je. 13, 1956
20. Ewald-König Ludwig	A. G. f. Berg- u. Hüttenbetriebe[d]	85.7	(A) 3; (B) Jy. 18, 1956, p. 8
21. Märkische[e]	A. G. f. Berg- u. Hüttenbetriebe[d]	55.0	(A) 3; (B) Jy. 18, 1956, p. 8, May 22, 1957, p. 6
22. Friedrich der Grosse	Ilseder Hütte[f]	100.0	(F) Aug. 18, 1956; (B) Sept. 14, 1956
23. Minister Achenbach	Gebrüder Stumm	...	(Possibly controlled by Stumm group)
24. Emscher-Lippe	Phoenix Rheinrohr[g]	51.0	(B) May 8, 1957, p. 7
25. Zeche Pluto and Holland of Rheinelbe Bergbau[h]	A. Thyssen Hütte	51.0	(B) Feb. 12, 1958, p. 8
26. Zeche Nordstern of Rheinelbe Bergbau[h]	Phoenix Rheinrohr	51.0	(B) Feb. 12, 1958, p. 8
27. Zeche Germania of Dortmunder Bergbau[h]	Dortmund-Hörder	51.0	(B) Feb. 12, 1958, p. 8
28. Carl Alexander (Aachen)	Völklingen (Saar)	majority	ATIC, *Exercice 1957*, p. 6

Table 5-6 (continued)

Coal Producing Firm by Vertical Affiliation	Parent Firm or Group and Percentage Control		Source of Data (Key in Source Note to Table 5-4)
German non-steel groups[i]			
29. Rheinelbe	GBAG	100.0[h]	(B) Feb. 4, 1957, p. 11
30. Dortmunder	GBAG	100.0[h]	(B) Feb. 4, 1957, p. 11
31. Bochumer Bergbau	GBAG	100.0	(B) Feb. 4, 1957, p. 11
32. Steinkohlen-Bergwerke Mathias Stinnes	Mathias Stinnes G.m.b.H.	majority	(B) Aug. 15, 1956, p. 8
33. Diergardt-Mevissen	SB Mathias Stinnes	100.0	(B) Sept. 26, 28, 1956
34. Mülheimer	SB Mathias Stinnes	100.0	(B) Sept. 26, 28, 1956
35. Victoria Mathias	SB Mathias Stinnes	...	(Possibly controlled by Stinnes)
36. Hibernia	VEBA	100.0	(B) Mar. 29/30, 1957, p. 2
37. Graf Bismarck	Deutsche Erdöl	majority	Deutsche Erdöl, *Geschäfts-bericht 1955*, pp. 12–13
38. Auguste Victoria Gewerkschaft	Badische Anilin	...	(Possibly controlled by Badische Anilin)
39. Preussag (Lower Saxony)	VEBA	100.0	(B) Jy. 20, 1956
40. Concordia Bergbau	Schering A. G. Berlin	55.0	(B) Jy. 4, 1956
41. Dahlbusch	Deutsche Libbey Owens	majority	(B) Je. 29, 1956
FOREIGN GROUPS			
French steel			
42. Heinrich Robert	De Wendel et Cie	large majority	(G) 636; De Wendel et Cie, *Exercice 1955*, p. 12
43. Friedrich Heinrich	De Wendel et Cie	large majority	(B) Nov. 30, 1956, p. 8; De Wendel et Cie, *Exercice 1955*, p. 12
44. Harpener Bergbau	Sidechar	75.0	(B) Dec. 23, 1957, p. 8
45. Carolus Magnus (Aachen)	Pont-à-Mousson	majority	(G) 634–636; *Jahrbuch*, 1956, p. 309
Netherlands industry			
46. Sophia Jacoba, Aachen	...	...	
Arbed Luxembourg steel			
47. Lothringen	Arbed	majority	(B) Apr. 5/6, 1957, p. 9
48. Eschweiler Bergwerksverein (Aachen)	Arbed	95.6	(B) Oct. 28, 1955, p. 8

Sources: Same as Table 5-4, preceding.

[a] All the mining firms are in the Ruhr except where otherwise indicated. About 97 per cent of German coal production is covered. The mines formerly in Vereinigte Stahlwerke are numbered 1, 10, 13, 14, 15, 18, 19, 29, 30 and 31. Those numbered 25, 26 and 27 were also in Vereinigte Stahlwerke; they are now part of GBAG without separate incorporation. Essener was not incorporated in Vereinigte Stahlwerke but was under common ownership. Later in 1959, Rheinpreussen (Number 2) was sold to Deutsche Erdöl, in which the Haniel family acquired a minority interest.

[b] Haniel group.

[c] Hamborner Bergbau and August Thyssen Hütte have each 50 per cent control of Kraftwerk Hamborn, a power station.

[d] One hundred per cent owned by the German State.

[e] Without Viktoria Lünen, now in Harpener Bergbau. Viktoria Lünen produced 1.3 million tons of coal in 1956; *Handelsblatt*, May 22, 1957, p. 6, June 21–22, 1957, p. 7. In 1957 the group Ignaz Petschek obtained a 45 per cent interest in Märkische Bergwerke from A. G. für Berg- und Hüttenbetriebe.

[f] Ilseder Hütte is 25 per cent owned by the German State.

[g] Hibernia owned 100 per cent of Emscher Lippe prior to 1957 and sold 51 per cent to Phoenix Rheinrohr that year; *Handelsblatt*, May 8, 1957, p. 7.

[h] GBAG owns the remainder of the capital stock in these mines and operates them. The firms that have majority control have a twenty-year contract for solid fuels supplies from these three properties. Rheinelbe Bergbau operates mines numbered 25 and 26; Dortmunder Bergbau operates mine numbered 27. GBAG otherwise owns 100 per cent of Rheinelbe and Dortmunder, which operate other mines in addition to those numbered 25, 26 and 27.

[i] The mining firms in this class for the most part belong to groups whose main activity is in chemicals (Badische Anilin), petroleum (Deutsche Erdöl), manufacturing (Schering A. G. and Deutsche Libbey Owens), or electricity (VEBA, a 100 per cent State-owned firm called Vereinigte Elektrizitäts- und Bergwerks A. G.).

Table 5-7

(*Amount in Thousands of Metric Tons*)

Parent Firm or Group	Ruhr Amount	Ruhr Per Cent	Aachen Amount	Aachen Per Cent	Lower Saxony Amount	Lower Saxony Per Cent	Total Amount	Total Per Cent
GERMAN GROUPS								
German steel groups:								
Ruhr								
Haniel	10,022	8.3	—	—	—	—	10,022	7.7
Hoesch	6,675	5.5	—	—	—	—	6,675	5.1
Krupp	7,386	6.1	—	—	—	—	7,386	5.7
Mannesmann	6,563	5.4	—	—	—	—	6,563	5.0
Michel group	1,398	1.2	—	—	—	—	1,398	1.1
Dortmund-Hörder	4,640	3.8	—	—	—	—	4,640	3.6
Klöckner	5,238	4.3	—	—	—	—	5,238	4.0
Rheinische	5,198	4.3	—	—	—	—	5,198	4.0
Thyssen group[b]	12,140	10.0	—	—	—	—	12,140	9.3
Total	59,260	48.9	—	—	—	—	59,260	45.3
Non-Ruhr								
A. G. für Berg- und Hüttenbetriebe (Salzgitter, owned by German State)	8,302	6.9	—	—	—	—	8,302	6.4
Ilseder-Hütte (Lower Saxony)	1,558	1.3	—	—	—	—	1,558	1.2
Total	9,860	8.1	—	—	—	—	9,860	7.5
Stumm (Saar)	1,792	1.5	—	—	—	—	1,792	1.4
Völklingen (Saar)	—	—	850	12.4	—	—	850	0.6
Total German steel groups	70,912	58.6	850	12.4	—	—	71,762	54.9
German non-steel groups:								
Gelsenkirchener (GBAG)[c]	8,548	7.1	—	—	—	—	8,548	6.5
Stinnes	5,533	4.6	—	—	—	—	5,533	4.2
German State (other than State-owned steel firms)	10,836	8.9	—	—	2,477	96.7	13,313	10.2
Other German industry[d]	6,616	5.5	—	—	—	—	6,616	5.1
Total	31,533	26.0	—	—	2,477	96.7	34,010	26.0
Total German groups	102,445	84.6	850	12.4	2,477	96.7	105,772	80.9

Sources: Table 5-6, preceding. The data on production are from *Jahrbuch*.

[a] Production data, covering 100 per cent of the output in the regions indicated, are as of 1955 but concentration of control is as of early 1959.

[b] Includes Walsum (production, 2.0 million tons), which, if not integrated with steel or controlled by any branch of the Thyssen family, is in any case integrated with a public utility under the control of the Thyssen group; *Handelsblatt*, May 13, 1957, p. 4. Also included are Zeche Pluto and Holland (1.9 million tons) and Zeche Nordstern (1.3 million tons) of Rheinelbe Bergbau, which mines were purchased by ATH and Phoenix Rheinrohr, respectively, in 1958, by obtaining from GBAG a 51 per cent interest; *Handelsblatt*, February 12, 1958, p. 8.

[c] Only the mines in which GBAG has 100 per cent control are included. The ones in which steel firms have a control of 50 per cent or more are assigned to the respective steel producing groups. In 1955 all the mines

Table 5-7 (continued)

(*Amount in Thousands of Metric Tons*)

Parent Firm or Group	Ruhr Amount	Per Cent	Aachen Amount	Per Cent	Lower Saxony Amount	Per Cent	Total Amount	Per Cent
NON-GERMAN GROUPS								
French steel								
Pont-à-Mousson	—	—	615	8.3	—	—	615	0.5
De Wendel	3,700	3.1	—	—	—	—	3,700	2.8
Sidechar (Harpener Bergbau)	7,798	6.4	—	—	—	—	7,798	6.0
Total	11,498	9.5	615	8.3	—	—	12,113	9.3
Arbed (Luxembourg steel)	2,033	1.7	4,546	64.4	—	—	6,579	5.0
Total foreign steel	13,531	11.2	5,161	72.7	—	—	18,692	14.3
Netherlands (non-steel)	—	—	1,051	14.9	—	—	1,051	0.8
Total non-German groups	13,531	11.2	6,212	87.6	—	—	19,743	15.1
Total all groups listed	115,976	95.8	7,062	100.0	2,477	96.7	125,515	96.0
Other mines	5,130	4.2	—	—	83	3.3	5,213	4.0
GRAND TOTAL	121,106	100.0	7,062	100.0	2,560	100.0	130,728	100.0
RECAPITULATION								
Integrated with steel, total	84,443	69.7	—	—	—	—	90,454	69.2
German	70,912	58.6	850	12.4	—	—	71,762	54.9
Foreign	13,531	11.2	5,161	12.7	—	—	18,692	14.3
Other German groups[e]	31,533	26.0	—	—	2,477	96.7	34,010	26.0
Other foreign groups	—	—	1,051	14.9	—	—	1,051	0.8
German State[f]	19,138	15.8	—	—	2,477	96.7	21,615	16.5
Total non-independents[g]	115,976	95.8	7,062	100.0	2,477	96.7	125,515	96.0
Total independents	5,130	4.2	—	—	83	3.3	5,213	4.0

Sources: (continued)

in which GBAG had an interest, majority or minority, produced a total of 19 million tons of coal, 16 per cent of the Ruhr's total output.

[d] Included are Concordia, Graf Bismarck, Auguste Victoria, and Dahlbusch, mining properties.

[e] Included are the mining properties belonging to the groups Stinnes, VEBA, Deutsche Erdöl, Badische Anilin and those that are 100 per cent owned by GBAG.

[f] Included are Hibernia and the mines of A. G. für Berg- und Hüttenbetriebe (Märkische and Ewald–König Ludwig) in the Ruhr and Preussag in Lower Saxony. The mine controlled by Ilseder Hütte is excluded although the State has a 25 per cent interest in the latter.

[g] Comprises the mines integrated with steel and with other industries, foreign and domestic.

Table 5-8

CRUDE STEEL CAPACITY, MAIN STEEL PRODUCING COUNTRIES,
SELECTED YEARS, 1913–1956[a]

(*Millions of Metric Tons*)

Country	1913[b]	1927	1936	1955	1956
ECSC					
Germany	12.2	17.3	20.0	21.3	23.2
Saar	2.1	2.3	2.5	3.2	3.4
France	7.0	9.9	9.8	12.5	13.4
Belgium	2.4	4.0	4.1	5.8	6.4
Luxembourg	1.3	2.8	2.8	3.2	3.4
Italy	0.9[c]	(1.9)	(2.2)	5.4	5.9
Netherlands	—	—	0.0	1.0	1.0
Total	25.9	38.2	41.4	52.4	56.7
United Kingdom	7.8	12.2	12.8	20.1	21.0
United States	31.8	61.0	70.9	114.1	116.5
TOTAL	65.5	111.4	125.1	186.7	194.2

Sources: United States data from *Metal Statistics,* American Metal Market, New York, and American Iron and Steel Institute reports. Other data as follows: 1913 and 1927 from Ingvar Svennilson, *Growth and Stagnation in the European Economy,* ECE, Geneva, 1954, p. 125. 1936 data are estimates based principally on Frederic Benham, *The Iron and Steel Industry of Germany, France, Belgium, Luxembourg and the Saar,* London and Cambridge Economic Service, London, October 1934, p. 15, for Germany; and on Hans Wolter, *Die französische eisenschaffende Industrie,* Kommissionsverlag Schrobsdorff'sche Buchhandlung, Düsseldorf, 1953, pp. 10–11, for France. Capacity between 1927 and 1936 was assumed to have remained constant except where data to the contrary were available. The Groupement de l'Industrie Sidérurgique report for 1955 mentioned a capacity of 10.5 million tons for France in 1938. 1936 data for the United Kingdom are from Import Duties Advisory Committee, *Report,* HMSO, London, July 1937, pp. 15, 92–93. 1955–1956 data are actual production since the industry, except for the United States, was then operating at practical capacity.

[a] Includes ingots and castings. Data for 1913 refer to interwar territory wherever boundaries were changed after World War I. Data for 1936 refer to post–World War II territory wherever boundaries were changed after that war. The present Russian zone, excluded from the figure for 1936, produced about 1.4 million tons of crude steel that year.

[b] Data for 1913 refer to production, which was then tantamount to capacity.

[c] 1914.

Table 7-1

DOMESTIC AND EXPORT PRICES OF MERCHANT BARS,
MAIN STEEL PRODUCING COUNTRIES, 1900–1958[a]

(*Average Price per Metric Ton*)

Year	Domestic					Export		
	Germany	France	Belgium	United Kingdom	United States	United Kingdom	F.o.b. Antwerp	United States
	(1)	(2)	(3)	(4)	(5)	(6)	(7)	(8)
1900	$42.36	...	...	$48.72	$35.05	...	...	...
1901	26.08	...	...	34.45	31.53	...	...	...
1902	26.48	...	...	31.96	34.83	...	...	...
1903	25.51	...	...	30.93	34.39	...	...	...
1904	25.96	...	...	29.97	29.32	...	...	...
1905	26.36	$33.30	$31.66	29.53	32.63	...	...	...
1906	31.37	39.10	37.26	33.32	33.29	...	$29.67	...
1907	32.83	44.53	40.67	35.24	35.28	...	32.78	...
1908	25.12	37.87	31.96	31.67	32.85	...	24.33	...
1909	24.30	29.25	24.46	30.40	29.32	...	23.01	...
1910	26.65	30.66	26.21	31.36	31.75	...	24.10	...
1911	25.08	31.48	25.39	31.91	27.78	...	22.57	...
1912	28.39	33.57	29.47	36.56	28.44	...	27.09	...
1913	25.79	33.74	28.22	38.68	34.17	...	24.49	...
1925	31.50	25.77	28.33	43.02	44.53	...	...	...
1926	31.80	26.80	{ 25.19 / 21.35[b] }	39.46	44.09	$34.94	24.76	...
1927	31.84	23.49	23.48	39.57	40.57	36.11	22.99	...
1928	33.28	26.79	28.00	37.19	41.23	34.88	27.33	...
1929	33.57	29.14	28.70	38.05	42.33	38.70	27.57	...
1930	33.07	25.07	24.32	37.80	37.70	37.88	23.18	...
1931	30.14	19.40	17.39	{ 33.74 / 24.62[b] }	35.94	{ 34.83 / 26.44[b] }	16.39	...
1932	26.12	20.48	12.89	22.95	34.61	21.37	11.70	...
1933	33.57	27.56	18.51	28.17	36.16	27.48	17.41	...
1934	43.32	36.79	25.63	38.75	39.90	36.79	25.20	...
1935	44.29	36.96	21.54	39.68	39.90	36.19	25.80	...
1936	44.33	37.09	22.58	45.00	42.55	39.18	25.95	...
1937	44.22	37.14	34.01	52.55	52.91	52.01	42.85	...
1938	44.18	31.10	37.18	57.66	51.81	54.25	41.68	...
1950	51.95	59.25	64.16	60.08	76.50	68.48	70.26	$88.40
1951	62.24	70.40	83.41	66.23	81.57	97.37	139.27	93.48
1952	87.61	85.88	83.49	84.12	85.55	136.16	124.54	95.90
1953	91.68	88.56	88.78	87.56	89.51	111.54	90.86	102.29
1954	88.50	86.45	85.89	87.80	93.03	90.65	84.75	105.38
1955	89.43	86.11	96.30	88.86	98.55	105.34	100.84	109.79
1956	91.74	88.62	104.08	95.39	106.26	119.25	109.62	124.56
1957	96.29	90.03	108.00	108.06	115.74		117.41	135.17
March	95.88	89.93	109.45	101.76	111.88	121.43	117.41	130.95
October	95.88	80.74	109.45	116.48	119.71	...	117.41	139.33

Continued on next page

Table 7-1 (continued)

(Average Price per Metric Ton)

Year	Domestic					Export		
	Ger-many	France	Belgium	United Kingdom	United States	United Kingdom	F.o.b. Antwerp	United States
	(1)	(2)	(3)	(4)	(5)	(6)	(7)	(8)
1958								
January	99.36	86.69	109.45	116.48	119.71	...	117.41	139.33
February	99.36	86.69	109.45	116.48	119.71	...	102.00	139.33
April	99.36	86.69	97.00	...	119.71	...	93.00	139.33
July	99.36	86.69	97.00	116.00	119.71	112.96	90.00	139.33

Sources: 1900–1938, inclusive, from Ingvar Svennilson, *Growth and Stagnation in the European Economy,* ECE, Geneva, 1954, p. 266 and notes thereto on p. 332. Data for subsequent years as follows:

Col. 1: *Stabstahl,* f.o.b. Oberhausen, Statistisches Bundesamt, Wiesbaden and Düsseldorf; 4 per cent turnover tax excluded. Adjusted for average 5 per cent rebate granted by industry from July 23, 1953 to January 31, 1954. Includes equalization levy for freight absorption on deliveries to West Berlin and to south Germany, which averaged 0.25 DM per ton from November 1, 1950 to June 30, 1952 and 0.50 DM thereafter.

Col. 2: *Ronds à beton, toutes nuances, sans réception,* f.o.b. Thionville; *Usine nouvelle;* Statistisches Bundesamt, Wiesbaden and Düsseldorf. Interwar data not strictly comparable with those after 1950 because the former, from Svennilson, *op. cit.,* refer to minimum rather than prevailing prices for the quality called *doux.*

Col. 3: *Barres marchandes,* f.o.b. Seraing or Charleroi, from *Bulletin d'information et de documentation* (BID), Banque Nationale de Belgique, and *Usine nouvelle.* Prior to May 20, 1953, prices were quoted free destination and included, from 1950, an average of $2.80 freight, which is included in the prices shown.

Col. 4: Angles, tees and channels, open-hearth quality; prices are free destination, and include an average of 15 shillings ($2.16) freight as from 1950. Chambre Syndicale de la Sidérurgie Française (série verte); *Yearbooks* of British Iron and Steel Federation; *Iron and Coal Trade Review,* London, first issue of month.

Col. 5: Hot-rolled bars, open-hearth quality, f.o.b. Pittsburgh. *Metal Statistics; Yearbooks* of British Iron and Steel Federation; Statistisches Bundesamt, Wiesbaden.

Col. 6: *Metal Bulletin,* London; prices refer to angles, open-hearth quality, f.o.b. port.

Col. 7: *Acier marchand,* in BID, cited above, or *ronds à beton,* 20–30 mm., in *Usine nouvelle.* Alternative delivery at Caen or Dunkerque at same prices. Prices for Switzerland, quoted f.o.b. Basle, vary; prices f.o.b. Antwerp quoted in hard currencies, Belgian francs or dollars. During buyers' market North American clients enjoy a $2.00 discount. After May 1953 the Brussels Export Convention set the price, which is minimum. Actual prices are above the minimum in a sellers' market and tend to fall more quickly than the minimum price in a buyers' market.

Col. 8: See col. 5; price is f.o.b. port.

ᵃ Prices are for Thomas quality and exclude turnover, transmission and production taxes except where otherwise indicated. These are base prices excluding extras; base prices vary according to size of order. For national variations with respect to size of order, local taxes, open-hearth and Thomas qualities, and average freight charges where prices are free destination, see Vol. II of the *Annual Statistical Yearbooks* of the British Iron and Steel Federation.

Except in Germany, domestic prices are not adjusted for the 2.5 per cent "Monnet rebate" effective from February to about September 1954.

Exchange rates are from FRB, certified noon buying rates for cable transfers at New York.

ᵇ After devaluation.

Table 7-2
DOMESTIC PRICE FOR MERCHANT BARS AS PER CENT OF EXPORT PRICE, SELECTED COUNTRIES, 1906–1958

Year	Germany	France	Belgium	United Kingdom	United States
1906	105.7	131.8	125.6	...	...
1907	100.2	135.9	141.1	...	...
1908	103.2	155.6	131.4	...	...
1909	105.6	127.1	106.3	...	...
1910	110.6	127.2	108.8	...	...
1911	111.1	139.5	112.5	...	...
1912	104.8	123.9	108.8	...	...
1913	105.3	145.9	115.2	...	...
1926	128.4	108.2	{ 101.7 / 86.2[a] }	112.9	...
1927	138.5	102.2	102.1	109.6	...
1928	121.8	98.0	102.5	106.6	...
1929	121.8	105.7	104.1	98.3	...
1930	142.7	108.2	104.9	99.8	...
1931	183.9	118.4	106.1	{ 96.9 / 93.1[a] }	...
1932	223.3	175.0	110.2	107.4	...
1933	192.8	158.3	106.3	102.5	...
1934	171.9	146.0	101.7	105.3	...
1935	171.7	143.3	83.5	109.6	...
1936	170.8	142.9	87.0	114.9	...
1937	103.2	86.7	79.4	101.0	...
1938	106.0	74.6	89.2	106.3	...
1950	73.9	84.3	91.3	111.7	86.5
1951	44.7	50.6	59.9	83.8	72.6
1952	70.3	69.0	67.0	62.8	87.1
1953	100.9	97.5	97.7	80.3	87.5
1954	104.4	102.0	101.3	102.6	88.3
1955	88.7	85.4	95.5	93.5	89.8
1956	83.7	80.8	94.9	89.1	85.3
1957					
March	81.7	76.6	93.2	92.1	85.4
October	81.7	68.8	93.2	...	85.9
1958					
February	97.4	85.0	107.3	...	85.9
July	110.4	96.3	107.7	102.7	85.9

Source: Table 7-1, preceding.   [a] After devaluation.

469

Table 7-3

APPARENT CONSUMPTION OF STEEL, SELECTED COUNTRIES, 1913–1955[a]

(Millions of Metric Tons of Crude Steel Equivalents)

Year	Germany (1)	Saar (2)	France (3)	Belgium-Luxembourg (4)	Italy (5)	Netherlands (6)	Total ECSC (7)	United Kingdom (8)	United States (9)
1913[b]	(11.860)	(0.200)	5.230	1.620	1.350	1.020	21.280	(7.250)	...
1913[c]	(11.750)	(0.150)	4.750	1.440	1.150	(0.960)	20.200	(6.270)	28.100
1925	(10.200)	(0.200)	(5.450)	1.280	2.430	0.860	20.420	6.470	...
1926	(8.925)	(0.175)	(6.680)	1.760	2.130	0.990	20.660	4.100	...
1927	(14.485)	(0.225)	(4.910)	1.160	1.870	1.120	23.770	8.930	...
1928	(11.870)	(0.250)	(6.750)	1.670	2.250	1.340	24.130	7.350	...
1929	(14.095)	(0.325)	(8.190)	1.840	2.430	1.360	28.240	8.310	...
1930	(8.800)	(0.300)	(7.800)	1.420	2.050	1.130	21.500	7.130	...
1931	5.900	0.300	(6.050)	1.020	1.590	1.030	15.890	6.070	25.830
1932	4.660	0.290	(4.720)	0.840	1.550	0.770	12.830	4.920	13.760
1933	6.940	0.360	(5.480)	0.840	1.890	(0.830)	16.340	6.030	23.180
1934	11.070	0.410	(4.970)	0.910	2.020	(0.910)	20.290	8.050	25.540
1935	13.550	0.400	4.490	1.060	2.450	(0.850)	22.800	8.790	33.830
1936	15.750	0.450	5.250	1.450	2.100	1.050	26.050	11.010	47.480
1937	17.490	(0.500)	6.140	1.750	2.270	1.460	29.610	12.000	48.770
1938	19.500	(0.500)	4.730	1.040	2.450	1.090	29.310	9.730	27.250
1947	...	...	5.700	1.940	1.830	1.090	10.560	11.730	71.720
1948	5.290	0.340	7.760	2.320	2.300	1.530	19.540	13.690	77.130
1949	8.710	0.530	8.440	1.720	2.240	1.450	23.090	14.590	67.460
1950	10.147	0.530	6.490	2.020	2.940	1.710	23.837	13.950	85.951
1951	11.011	0.770	7.970	2.252	3.514	1.841	27.358	13.933	94.346
1952	14.640	0.950	10.300	2.396	3.994	1.800	34.080	16.006	81.337
1953	14.601	0.790	8.340	2.224	4.109	2.045	32.109	16.302	99.640
1954	16.522	0.850	9.040	2.611	4.826	2.210	36.059	16.430	77.683
1955	21.482	(0.975)	10.000	2.511	5.660	2.535	43.163	18.856	102.164

Sources:

COL. 1: 1913–1930 from Ingvar Svennilson, *Growth and Stagnation in the European Economy*, ECE, Geneva, 1954, pp. 276–277, less estimated tonnage for Saar; 1931–1949 from OEEC, *Industrial Statistics, 1900–1955*, Paris, 1955; 1950–1955 calculated from data in Statistisches Bundesamt, Düsseldorf.

COL. 2: OEEC, *op. cit.*

COL. 3: 1913–1938 from Svennilson, *op. cit.*; 1947–1954 from OEEC, *op. cit.*

COLS. 4, 5, 6, 8: 1913–1950 from Svennilson, *op. cit.*, 1951–1954 from Statistisches Bundesamt, Düsseldorf.

COL. 9: 1950–1954 from Statistisches Bundesamt, Düsseldorf; other years from OEEC, *op. cit.*

[a] Production plus imports minus exports in crude steel equivalents. Not corrected for stock changes.

[b] Steel and wrought iron.

[c] Steel only.

INDEX

A

AREPIC (Fr.), 272
ATIC (Association Technique de l'Importation Charbonnière, Fr.), 255–56, 269–70, 273, 281, 285, 298, 298n., 327
ATUB (Italy), 458n.
A. G. der Dillinger Hüttenwerke (Ger.), 142–43, 144; and Neunkircher, 143; and Otto Wolff, 134; and Pont-à-Mousson, 134, 142, 143; and Stumm, 134
A. G. für Berg- und Hüttenbetriebe (Ger.), 153, 462; and German State, 460, 462–63, 464, 465n.
AKV, see Aachener Kohlen-Verkauf
Aachen area (Ger.): coal capital expenditure, 104, 115; coal labor costs, 97, 98; coal mining conditions, 99; coal production, 21, 22, 101–02, 111, 431, 464; coal productivity, 101–02, 111, 453; markets, 29
Aachener Kohlen-Verkauf G.m.b.H. (AKV) (Ger.), 259n.
Abbreviations, 416–18
Aciéries de Longwy S.A., Société des (Fr.): and Lorraine-Escaut, 424
Aciéries de Micheville (Fr.): and Pont-à-Mousson, 422
Aciéries et Forges de Firminy, S.A. des (Fr.): and Ateliers et Forges de la Loire, 423
Aciéries et Minières de la Sambre S.A. (Belg.), 137; and Cockerill-Ougrée, 456; and Cofinindus, 456; and Launoit, 137, 198n.; and Siderur, 198n.; and Société Générale & Launoit, 138, 198n.; and Ucosider, 198n.
Aciéries et Tréfileries de Neuves-Maisons-Chatillon, see Société des Aciéries et Tréfileries de Neuves-Maisons-Chatillon
Aciéries Réunies de Burbach-Eich-Dudelange, see Arbed
Act of Mannheim (1868), 373
Adelman, A., 222n.
Adenauer, Konrad, 156n.

Agreement of Association (ECSC, U.K., 1954), 351
Aims of ECSC, 3, 13
Alex Wenner-Gren group (Sweden): and Krupp, 428
Allevard, Société des Hauts-Fourneaux et Forges d' (Fr.), see Société des Hauts-Fourneaux et Forges d'Allevard
Altenessener Bergwerks-A.G. (Ger.): and Hoesch, 427, 462
Alti Forni e Acciaierie d'Italia, see ILVA
Anderny-Chevillon, see Société des Mines d'Anderny-Chevillon
Andrews, P. W. S., 49n., 65n., 231n.
Angleur-Athus (Belg.), 192; and John Cockerill and Ucometal, 192
Antitrust legislation in Europe, 126–29
Antitrust philosophy of ECSC, 129
Arbed (Aciéries Réunies de Burbach-Eich-Dudelange S.A., Lux.), 140, 141, 141n., 143, 144, 162, 170–71, 193, 261, 463, 465; and Barbanson, 140, 456; and Brufina, 456; and Schneider, 134, 136, 140, 169, 456; and Société Générale, 136, 140, 456; and Société Générale & Launoit, 134, 138
Areas of production within ECSC, 20–58 passim
Arenberg Bergbau-G.m.b.H. (Ger.): and Rheinische Stahlwerke, 159, 462
Armand, Louis, 75n., 101, 112n., 310n., 370
Assemblée Parlementaire Européenne, see European Parliamentary Assembly and Common Assembly
Assider (Associazione Industrie Siderurgiche Italiane), 198, 244
Association Technique de l'Importation Charbonnière, see ATIC
Associazione Industrie Siderurgiche Italiane, see Assider
Aszkenazy, H., 135, 142n., 166n., 259n., 260n., 262n., 279n.
Ateliers et Forges de la Loire (Fr.), see Compagnie des Ateliers et Forges de la Loire
Audincourt et Dépendances S.A., Compagnie des Forges d' (Fr.): and Lorraine-Escaut, 424
August Thyssen-Hütte A.G. (Ger.), 158, 228, 228n., 429, 459, 460, 462, 464n.; and FTV and TAGB, 427, 459; and Thyssen group, 461; and Vereinigte Stahlwerke, 426, 426n.
Auguste Victoria, see Gewerkschaft Auguste Victoria
Austria, 27, 47, 272

471